THE ROUGH GUIDE TO

Moscow

There are more than two hundred Rough Guide titles
covering destinations from Alaska to Zimbabwe
and subjects from Acoustic Guitar to Travel Health

Forthcoming travel guides include

Devon & Cornwall • Malta • Tenerife
Thai Beaches and Islands • US Rockies • Vancouver

Forthcoming reference guides include

Cuban Music • 100 Essential Latin CDs • Personal Computers
Pregnancy & Birth • Trumpet & Trombone

Rough Guides Online

www.roughguides.com

Rough Guide Credits

Text Editor:	Olivia Eccleshall
Series Editor:	Mark Ellingham
Editorial:	Martin Dunford, Jonathan Buckley, Jo Mead, Kate Berens, Amanda Tomlin, Ann-Marie Shaw, Paul Gray, Helena Smith, Judith Bamber, Orla Duane, Ruth Blackmore, Geoff Howard, Claire Saunders, Gavin Thomas, Alexander Mark Rogers, Polly Thomas, Joe Staines, Andrew Tomičić, Richard Lim, Duncan Clark, Peter Buckley, Sam Thorne, Lucy Ratcliffe, Clifton Wilkinson, David Glen (UK); Andrew Rosenberg, Mary Beth Maioli, Stephen Timblin, Yuki Takagaki (US)
Online:	Kelly Cross, Anja Mutić-Blessing, Jennifer Gold, Audra Epstein, Suzanne Welles (US)
Production:	Susanne Hillen, Andy Hilliard, Link Hall, Helen Ostick, Julia Bovis, Michelle Draycott, Katie Pringle, Robert Evers, Mike Hancock, Zoë Nobes
Cartography:	Melissa Baker, Maxine Repath, Ed Wright, Katie Lloyd-Jones
Picture Research:	Louise Boulton, Sharon Martins
Finance:	John Fisher, Gary Singh, Edward Downey, Mark Hall, Tim Bill
Marketing & Publicity:	Richard Trillo, Niki Smith, David Wearn, Chloë Roberts, Birgit Hartmann, Claire Southern (UK); Simon Carloss, David Wechsler, Kathleen Rushforth (US)
Administration:	Tania Hummel, Demelza Dallow, Julie Sanderson

Acknowledgements

The author would like to thank all those in Russia for their help and hospitality: Lena Ifkina, Neil McGowan, Robert and Olga Farish, and Alexandra Lanskaya. In England, thanks to Olivia Eccleshall at the Rough Guides for her skilful and patient editing, Amy Brown and Narrell Leffman for Basics research, Maxine Repath and The Map Studio, Romsey, Hants, for maps, Katie Pringle for typesetting and Anne Hegerty for proofreading; and to Irina Gaylard at CIS Travel Services, and Olga Scott at Scott's Tours.

This third edition published May 2001 by Rough Guides Ltd, 62–70 Shorts Gardens, London WC2H 9AH.

Distributed by the Penguin Group:
Penguin Books Ltd, 27 Wrights Lane, London W8 5TZ.
Penguin Putnam, Inc., 375 Hudson Street, New York, NY 10014, USA.
Penguin Books Australia Ltd, 487 Maroondah Highway, PO Box 257, Ringwood, Victoria 3134, Australia.
Penguin Books Canada Ltd, 10 Alcorn Avenue, Toronto, Ontario M4V 1E4, Canada.
Penguin Books (NZ) Ltd, 182–190 Wairau Road, Auckland 10, New Zealand.
Printed in England by Clays Ltd, St Ives PLC.
Typography and original design by Jonathan Dear and The Crowd Roars.
Illustrations throughout by Edward Briant.

496pp. Includes index

A catalogue record for this book is available from the British Library.

ISBN 1-85828-700-6

THE ROUGH GUIDE TO

Moscow

Written and researched by
Dan Richardson

With additional research and contributions by
Alexei Pechenin, Neil McGowan and Lera Kuteeva

Help us update

We've gone to a lot of trouble to ensure that this third edition of *The Rough Guide to Moscow* is accurate and up to date. However, things inevitably change, and if you feel we've got it wrong or left something out, we'd like to know: any suggestions, comments or corrections would be much appreciated. We'll credit all contributions and send a copy of the next edition – or any other Rough Guide if you prefer – for the best correspondence.

Please mark letters "Rough Guide to Moscow" and send to:
Rough Guides, 62–70 Shorts Gardens, London WC2H 9AH or
Rough Guides, 4th Floor, 345 Hudson St, New York, NY 10014.

Email should be sent to:
mail@roughguides.co.uk

Online updates about Rough Guide titles can be found on our Web site at *www.roughguides.com*

The Author

Dan Richardson was born in England in 1958. Before joining Rough Guides in 1984, he worked as a sailor on the Red Sea and lived in Peru. Since then he has travelled extensively in Russia and Eastern Europe, and is also the author of *The Rough Guide to St Petersburg* and co-author of *The Rough Guide to Romania*. While in St Petersburg in 1992 he met his future wife, Anna; they have a daughter, Sonia.

Readers' letters

Many thanks to all the readers of the previous edition who took the trouble to write with updates, criticisms and suggestions for this book: Heidi Berry; Rosa M. Bettess; Carol Clark; Sophie Cotgrove; Chris Ferguson; Laura Howlett; Andy Johnstone; Marek Krzyzanowski; Dr C.M. Leyland; Marc Mills; Chris Mogelin; Sandra L. Molyneaux; Suzy Price; Almut Schlepper; Kim Skerten; Doug & Cynthia Strong; Mrs J.J.R. Turnbull; Sue Wheeler.

Apologies to anyone whose name has been omitted or misspelt.

Rough Guides

Travel Guides • Phrasebooks • Music and Reference Guides

We set out to do something different when the first Rough Guide was published in 1982. Mark Ellingham, just out of University, was travelling in Greece. He brought along the popular guides of the day, but found they were all lacking in some way. They were either strong on ruins and museums but went on for pages without mentioning a beach or taverna. Or they were so conscious of the need to save money that they lost sight of Greece's cultural and historical significance. Also, none of the books told him anything about Greece's contemporary life – its politics, its culture, its people, and how they lived.

So with no job in prospect, Mark decided to write his own guidebook, one which aimed to provide practical information that was second to none, detailing the best beaches and the hottest clubs and restaurants, while also giving hard-hitting accounts of every sight, both famous and obscure, and providing up-to-the-minute information on contemporary culture. It was a guide that encouraged independent travellers to find the best of Greece, and was a great success, getting shortlisted for the Thomas Cook travel guide award, and encouraging Mark, along with three friends, to expand the series.

The Rough Guide list grew rapidly and the letters flooded in, indicating a much broader readership than had been anticipated, but one which uniformly appreciated the Rough Guides' mix of practical detail and humour, irreverence and enthusiasm. Things haven't changed. The same four friends who began the series are still the caretakers of the Rough Guide mission today: to provide the most reliable, up-to-date and entertaining information to independent-minded travellers of all ages, on all budgets.

We now publish 150 titles and have offices in London and New York. The travel guides are written and researched by a dedicated team of more than 100 authors, based in Britain, Europe, the USA and Australia. We have also created a unique series of phrasebooks to accompany the travel series, along with the acclaimed series of music guides, and a best-selling pocket guide to the Internet and World Wide Web. We also publish comprehensive travel information on our Web site: *www.roughguides.com*

Contents

List of maps

MAP SYMBOLS

Railway	Telephone
Road	Metro station
Path	Riverboat station
Road with steps	Gate
River	Fountain
Wall	Forest
Chapter division boundary	Building
Gorge	Church
Airport	Cemetery
Synagogue	Park

Introduction

Moscow is all things to all people. In Siberia, they call it "the West", with a note of scorn for the bureaucrats and politicians who promulgate and posture in the capital. For Westerners, the city may look European, but its unruly spirit seems closer to Central Asia. To Muscovites, however, Moscow is both a "Mother City" and a "big village" (*bolshaya derevnya*), a tumultuous community with an underlying collective instinct that shows itself in times of trouble. Nowhere else reflects the contradictions and ambiguities of the Russian people as Moscow does – nor the stresses of a country undergoing meltdown and renewal.

The city is huge, surreal and apocalyptic. After a few weeks here, the bizarre becomes normal, and you realize that life is – as Russians say – *bespredel* (without limits). Traditionally, Moscow has been a place for strangers to throw themselves into debauchery, leaving poorer and wiser. Its puritan stance in Soviet times was seldom heartfelt, and with the fall of Communism it has reverted to the lusty, violent ways that foreigners have noted with amazement over the centuries, and Gilyarovsky chronicled in his book, *Moscow and the Muscovites*.

As the home of one in fifteen Russians, Moscow exemplifies the best and worst of Russia. Its beauty and ugliness are inseparable, its sentimentality the obverse of a brutality rooted in centuries of despotism and fear of anarchy. Private and cultural life are as passionate as business and politics are cynical. The irony and resilience honed by decades of propaganda and shortages now help Muscovites to cope with the "Wild Capitalism" that intoxicates the city. Yet, for all its assertiveness, Moscow's essence is moody and elusive, and uncovering it is like opening an endless series of *Matryoshka* dolls, or peeling an onion down to its core.

Both images are apposite, for Moscow's concentric geography mirrors its historical development. At its heart is the Kremlin, whose foundation by Prince Dolgoruky in 1147 marked the birth of the city. Surrounding this are rings corresponding to the feudal settlements of medieval times, rebuilt along more European lines after the great fire of 1812, and ruthlessly modernized in accordance with Stalin's

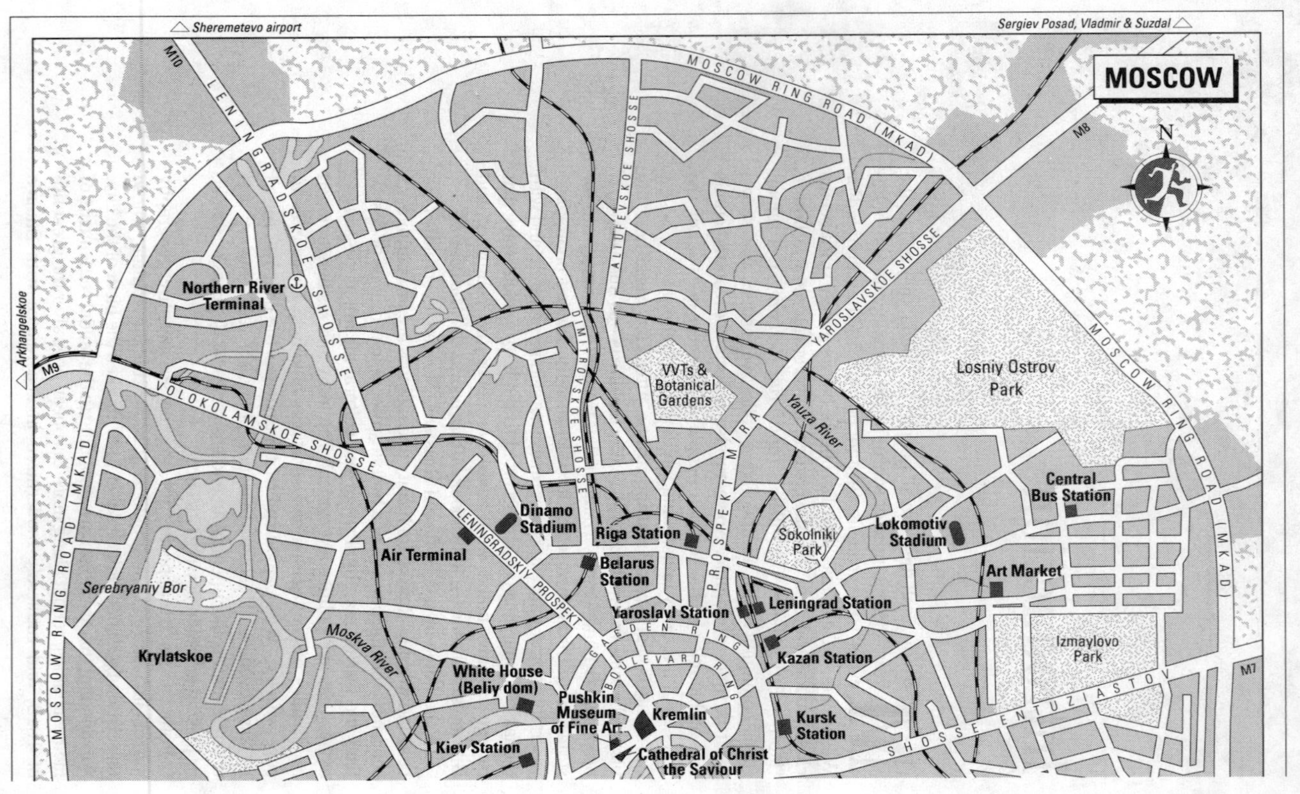
MOSCOW
N
Sergiev Posad, Vladmir & Suzdal
Sheremetevo airport
Arkhangelskoe
MOSCOW RING ROAD (MKAD)
M7
M8
M9
M10
Losniy Ostrov Park
Central Bus Station
Art Market
Izmaylovo Park
Lokomotiv Stadium
YAROSLAVSKOE SHOSSE
SHOSSE ENTUZIASTOV
Yauza River
Sokolniki Park
Leningrad Station
Kazan Station
Kursk Station
PROSPEKT MIRA
VVTs & Botanical Gardens
ALTUFEVSKOE SHOSSE
Riga Station
Belarus Station
Yaroslavl Station
SADOVOE RING
BOULEVARD RING
Kremlin
Cathedral of Christ the Saviour
DIMITROVSKOE SHOSSE
Dinamo Stadium
Pushkin Museum of Fine Art
White House (Beliy dom)
Kiev Station
LENINGRADSKIY PROSPEKT
Air Terminal
Moskva River
LENINGRADSKOE SHOSSE
VOLOKOLAMSKOE SHOSSE
Northern River Terminal
Serebryaniy Bor
Krylatskoe

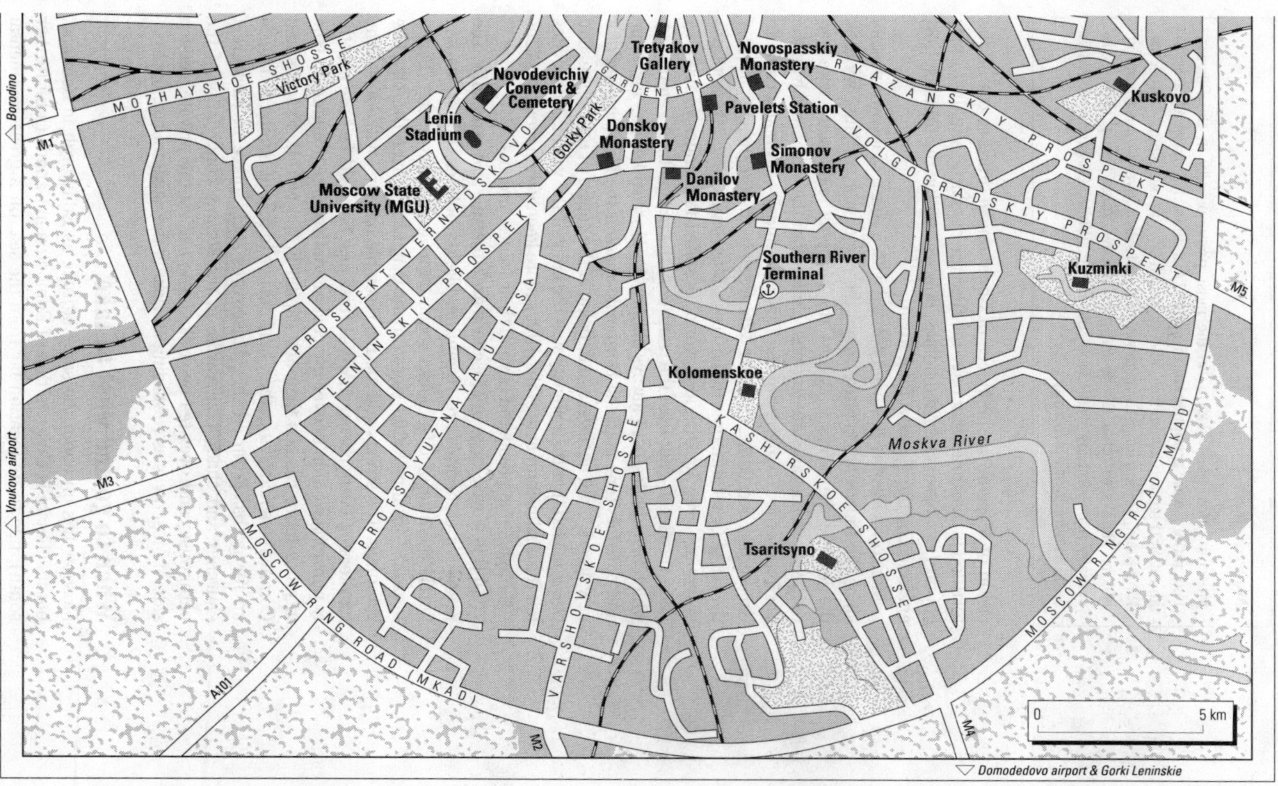
Kuskovo
Kuzminki
RYAZANSKIY PROSPEKT
VOLGOGRADSKIY PROSPEKT
MOSCOW RING ROAD (MKAD)
Novospasskiy Monastery
Pavelets Station
Simonov Monastery
Southern River Terminal
Tretyakov Gallery
Danilov Monastery
GARDEN RING
Donskoy Monastery
Kolomenskoe
KASHIRSKOE SHOSSE
Moskva River
Tsaritsyno
VARSHAVSKOE SHOSSE
Novodevichiy Convent & Cemetery
Gorky Park
Lenin Stadium
Moscow State University (MGU)
PROSPEKT VERNADSKOVO
LENINSKIY PROSPEKT
PROFSOYUZNAYA ULITSA
Victory Park
MOZHAYSKOE SHOSSE
MOSCOW RING ROAD (MKAD)
M1
M2
M3
M4
M5
A101
0
5 km
Borodino
Vnukovo airport
Domodedovo airport & Gorki Leninskie

Moscow facts

Moscow (*Moskva* – Москва) is the most populous city in the Russian Federation, with a population of some 14 million. It covers an area of about 880 square kilometres, encompassed by the oval-shaped Moscow Ring Road, 109km long, through which the Moskva River wends for about 80km. Thanks to other rivers and the Moscow–Volga Canal, the city is actually accessible by water from the Baltic, White, Caspian and Black seas, hundreds of miles away.

vision of Moscow as the Mecca of Communism. Further out lie the fortified monasteries that once guarded the outskirts, and the former country estates of tsars and nobles, now well within the urban sprawl encircled by the Moscow Ring Road.

Moscow's identity has been imbued with a sense of its own destiny since the fourteenth century, when the principality of Muscovy took the lead in the struggle against the Mongols and Tatars who had reduced the Kievan state to ruins. Under Ivan the Great and Ivan the Terrible – the "Gatherers of the Russian Lands" – its realm came to encompass everything from the White Sea to the Caspian, while after the fall of Constantinople to the Turks, Moscow assumed Byzantium's suzerainty over the Orthodox world. Despite the changes wrought by Peter the Great – not least the transfer of the capital to St Petersburg, which Slavophiles have always abhorred – Moscow kept its mystique and bided its time until the Bolsheviks made it the fountainhead of a new creed. Long accustomed to being at the centre of an empire, and being misled that their society was the envy of the world, Muscovites felt the disillusionments of the 1990s more keenly than most Russians – though some prospered beyond their wildest dreams.

All this is writ large in Moscow's **architecture** and **streetlife**. The Kremlin's cathedrals are Byzantine, like its politics. Ministries and hotels the size of city blocks reach their apotheosis in the "Seven Sisters" – Stalin-Gothic skyscrapers that brood over the city like vampires. The streets and metros resemble bazaars, with kiosks and hawkers on every corner. BMWs cruise past *babushki* whose monthly pensions wouldn't cover the cost of admission to a nightclub (the city has more casinos than any capital in the world). Fascists and Communists march together, bankers live in fear of bombs and life is up for grabs. From all this, Muscovites seek solace in backstreet churches and shady courtyards; in the steamy conviviality of the bathhouse; and over tea or vodka. Discovering the private, hidden side of Moscow is as rewarding as visiting the usual tourist sights.

When to go and what to take

Moscow lies on about the same latitude as Edinburgh in Scotland, but its climate is closer to that of Edmonton in Canada (a bit further south), due to its location far from the sea, on a great continental land mass. Summers are hot, and winters cold by Western European standards – although the dry, often sunny weather makes them tolerable, if not always pleasurable.

As most foreigners have an exaggerated fear of the cold in Russia, the most popular time to go is **summer**, lasting from the beginning of June to mid-September. Days and nights are warm and sultry, with heat waves likely during August, when Muscovites leave in droves for their dachas in the countryside. Culturally, things are rather slack during this period, with the Bolshoy Ballet away from June until early September and many other theatres closed for the duration. Conversely, politics often hot up in August, sometimes boiling over a month or so later. By mid-September, **autumn** is under way, with cloudy skies and falling temperatures, but you can still look forward to a week or two of *Babe leto* ("Granny's Summer"), when Moscow is an Impressionist's vision of autumnal hues, in the final glow of warmth.

Subzero temperatures and snow can set in up to two months before **winter** officially begins in December. Blanketed in fresh snow, Moscow is magically hushed and cleansed, and Muscovites revel in the crispness of the air. Days are often gloriously sunny, and the temperature only a few degrees below zero, so skiing and sledging are popular pursuits. The secular New Year and Orthodox Christmas in early January are occasions for shopping and merrymaking, much as in the West – so if you have friends here, it's a great time to come. At some point, however, a cold snap will send the temperature down to -20°C or lower, while traffic and thaws turn the snow into mounds and lakes of black ice or brown slush, which linger on until late March.

By this time, everyone is longing for **spring**, whose arrival is unpredictable, with trees starting to bud weeks before the slush disappears in mid-April. Mid- to late spring is perhaps the best time for festivals, with the Orthodox Easter celebrations followed by the "Moscow Stars" festival, May Day, and the Victory Day celebrations on May 9. On the downside, however, cold snaps can happen at any time until the end of the month, and thundery showers may occur well into the summer.

It's wise to give some thought as to **what to take** – and worth packing that bit more to stave off problems later. Expect occasional showers almost any time of the year, and bring a waterproof jacket or compact umbrella. Mosquitoes can also be a pest in summer, so some form of barrier/treatment cream is advisable. For travel in winter (or late autumn or early spring), take as many layers as you can pack. Gloves, a hat and scarf, and thick socks are mandatory;

Average daily temperatures and rainfall in Moscow

	Jan	Feb	Mar	Apr	May	Jun	Jul	Aug	Sep	Oct	Nov	Dec
Max °C	-7	-5	0	8	15	20	21	20	15	9	2	-3
Min °C	-13	-12	-8	0	6	11	13	13	9	4	-2	-8
mm	35	30	31	36	45	50	72	78	64	76	46	40

thermal underwear saves you from cold legs; and a pair of boots with non-slip soles are recommended for the snow and ice. Indoors, you'll have nothing to worry about, as most apartment buildings and hotels are well (if not over-) heated.

A note on the calendar

In 1700, Peter the Great forced the Russians to adopt the Julian calendar which was then in use in Western Europe, in place of the old system dictated by the Orthodox church. Ironically, Western Europe changed to the **Gregorian calendar** not long afterwards, but this time the Russians refused to follow suit. The Julian calendar was less accurate and by the twentieth century lagged behind the Gregorian by almost two weeks. The Soviet regime introduced the Gregorian calendar in February 1918 – January 31 ran straight on to February 14. This explains why the Soviets always celebrated the Great October Revolution on November 7. In this book we have kept the old-style calendar before February 1918, and the new style only after it was introduced.

Changes in the new Russia

The speed of change in Russian society inevitably means that certain sections of this book are going to be out of date by the time you read them. Laws and regulations frequently change without warning, especially concerning visas and currency exchange; restaurants, clubs and services come and go; and there is always the possibility of radical decrees from the Kremlin. Yet, despite universally gloomy news reports about Russia, Muscovites are resilient and the city is big enough to absorb a lot of trouble – so don't be deterred by run-of-the-mill reports of Mafia killings, horrendous accidents, and so on.

Cyrillic script, street names and abbreviations

Throughout the text, we've transliterated the names of all the streets and squares, and translated those of the sights, which means that no Cyrillic appears in the main text. To help you find your way around the city, however, we've included a list of the main streets, squares and museums in the original Cyrillic at the end of chapters 2 to 9, 18 and 19. For details of the transliteration system we've used from the Cyrillic to the Latin alphabet, see p.450.

Many streets have officially reverted to their former (mostly pre-Revolutionary) titles, though some people still use the old Soviet names. In the following chapters, streets are referred to by their "correct" name at the time of writing, and few further changes are likely, but don't be surprised at the occasional difference between the names given in this book and those on the ground. The main abbreviations used throughout are: ul. (for *ulitsa*, street); nab. (for *naberezhnaya*, embankment); pr. (for *prospekt*, avenue); per. (for *pereulok*, lane); and pl. (for *ploshchad*, square). Other terms include *most* (bridge), *bulvar* (boulevard), *shosse* (highway), *alleya* (alley) and *sad* (garden).

Part 1

The Basics

Getting there from Britain

By far the most convenient way to reach Moscow is by plane. Scheduled flights from London take just three hours (compared to over 48 hours by train), and there are direct services every day on Aeroflot, Transaero and British Airways. If you have more time to devote to the journey itself, then trains or buses become a more attractive proposition, since you can travel via Berlin, Prague or the Baltic States – though travelling independently won't necessarily save you any money and your visa arrangements will be more complicated (see p.23).

By plane

British Airways (BA) and the Russian airlines Aeroflot and Transaero operate about thirty **direct scheduled flights** a week from London to Moscow. Transaero flies from Heathrow every day except Tuesday and Thursday, and at £247 return throughout the year is usually the cheapest option. It's a night flight that arrives at 5am, at Moscow's older Sheremetevo-1 airport. Both Aeroflot and BA fly from Heathrow into Sheremetevo-2; Aeroflot at least once a day and BA twice daily. Aeroflot's prices are generally lower than BA's, but both vary widely throughout the year and their Web sites are of little help in determining which offers what.

Rather than getting bogged down with Aeroflot or BA, you can check out the **specialist travel agencies**, who usually get the best discounts going on all routings to Moscow. Aside from Transaero, whose own price is rock bottom, you can fly Aeroflot to Moscow through Airborn Travel from £254, IMS Travel from £258, or Scott's Tours from £268. Discounts on BA are rarer, but Major Travel can do Gatwick to Moscow from £321. It's also worth checking with the youth/student specialists Campus Usit Travel or STA (see box overleaf for addresses) and looking at sites on the **Internet** such as *www.atab.co.uk, www.cheapflights.com* and *www.lastminute.com.*

Other discounts are based on **indirect flights** to Moscow via a European "hub" city and national airline, such as Lufthansa via Frankfurt, KLM UK via Amsterdam, Air France via Paris, Austrian Airlines or Lauda Air via Vienna, CSA via Prague, SAS via Stockholm, Sabena via Brussels and Finnair via Helsinki. Some also offer connections from cities other than London: Lufthansa flies from Birmingham and Manchester; Sabena from Manchester, Newcastle, Glasgow and Edinburgh; SAS and Finnair from Manchester; and KLM UK from most airports. For example, Farnley Travel offers Heathrow to Moscow on CSA from £250, or Manchester to Moscow on Austrian Airlines from £300, Airborn Travel does Moscow on CSA from £274, and Interchange Austrian Airlines from London from £281, or a **one-way ticket** to Moscow for £182.

It's also worth investigating **low-cost airlines** such as Buzz, easyJet and Ryanair, which frequently offer amazingly cheap fares to European cities where onward flights to Moscow are available from other carriers. Although these offers are subject to restrictions and entail research into onward flights – which you'll probably have to book on the spot abroad – they can be especially economical for those who wish to fly from regional airports, who might otherwise have to travel via London. At the time of writing, Ryanair does cheap returns from Glasgow to Frankfurt (£32) or Paris (£32), and London to Stockholm (£28) or Frankfurt (£29), while rival airlines offer one-way tickets: easyJet from Edinburgh (£22) or Liverpool (£17) to Amsterdam, and Gatwick to Geneva (£87); Buzz from Stansted to Berlin (£29), Frankfurt (£29), Vienna (£39) or Helsinki (£39).

Airlines

Aeroflot ☎020/7355 2233, *reservations@aeroflot.co.uk*

Air Baltic ☎01293/596684 or 020/7393 1207.

Air France ☎0845/0845 111; *www.airfrance.co.uk*

Austrian Airlines ☎020/7434 7300; *www.aua.com*

British Airways ☎0345/222111; *www.british-airways.com*

Buzz ☎0870/2407070; *www.buzzaway.com*

CSA ☎020/7255 1898; *www.csa.cz*

easyJet ☎0870/6000000; *www.easyjet.com*

Estonian Air ☎020/7333 0196; *www.estonian-air.ee*

Finnair London ☎020/7408 1222; Manchester Airport ☎0161/499 0294; *www.finnair.com*

KLM UK ☎08705/074 074; *www.klmuk.com*

Lauda Air ☎0845/8340 230; *www.laudaair.co.uk*

Lufthansa ☎0345/737747; *www.lufthansa.co.uk*

Malév ☎020/7439 0577; *www.malev.hu*

Ryanair ☎0870/1569569; *www.ryanair.com*

SAS London ☎020/7734 4020; Manchester Airport ☎0161/499 1441; Aberdeen Airport ☎01224/770220; national number ☎0845/607 2772; *www.sas.se*

Transaero ☎020/7436 6767; *www.transaero.ru*

Discount ticket agents

Airborn Travel, 50a Fenchurch St, London EC3M 3JY; ☎020/7929 3616; *www.airborn.co.uk*

Benz Travel, 83 Mortimer St, London W1R 7PV ☎020/7462 0000; *www.benztravel.co.uk*

Major Travel 28–34 Fortress Rd, London NW5 2HB ☎020/7393 1087; *www.majortravel.co.uk*

North South Travel, Moulsham Mill Centre, Parkway, Chelmsford, Essex CM2 7PX ☎01245/608291. Contributes profits to projects in the developing world.

STA Travel, 86 Old Brompton Rd, London SW7 3LH; 117 Euston Rd, London NW1 2SX; 38 Store St, London WC1E 7BZ ☎020/7361 6161; 25 Queens Rd, Bristol BS8 1QE ☎0117/929 4399; 38 Sidney St, Cambridge CB2 3HX ☎01223/366966; 75 Deansgate, Manchester M3 2BW ☎0161/834 0668; 88 Vicar Lane, Leeds LS1 7JH ☎0113/244 9212; 78 Bold St, Liverpool L1 4HR ☎0151/707 1123; 9 St Mary's Place, Newcastle-upon-Tyne NE1 7PG ☎0191/233 2111; 36 George St, Oxford OX1

If you have more time, it might be worth considering **flying to Berlin or Helsinki** and continuing the rest of the way by bus or train. From Berlin there are onward coaches to Moscow and the Baltic States (see "By coach" on p.8), while from Helsinki there's a daily train to Moscow which takes fifteen hours and costs £50 one-way, £100 return – for details see *www.vr.fi/heo/itaane.htm*. Alternatively, if you'd like to visit Estonia before travelling on to Moscow, Estonian Air flies from Gatwick to **Tallinn** every day except Saturday, for £265 return throughout the year.

Package tours

Given the price of flights and hotels in Moscow, there's a strong incentive to look for a **package tour** – an easy way of cutting the cost and trouble of organizing a trip. There are all kinds, from city breaks to Trans-Siberian tours and luxury cruises. Unless otherwise stated, all prices below are for a single person, twin share; where two prices are given, these refer to low- and high-season rates.

The former Soviet travel agency **Intourist** offers a range of packages that include flights, hotels and escorted visits. You can spend three nights in Moscow in a three-star (£299–489) or deluxe (£665–799) hotel, or enjoy a luxury break featuring a visit to the Bolshoy (£715–799). Their Moscow/St Petersburg package features three nights in each city in deluxe hotels (£1099–1349), while their eight-day coach tour of Moscow and the "Golden Ring" towns of Vladimir, Suzdal, Pereslavl Zalesskiy and Sergiev Posad utilizes three-star hotels (£879–899). By comparison, Interchange does three nights in Moscow for £405–529, while Norvista's week-long Moscow/St Petersburg package costs £906. Neither features any guided tours.

2OJ ☎01865/792800; 30 Upper Kirkgate St, Aberdeen ☎0122/465 8222; and branches on university campuses in Birmingham, Canterbury, Cardiff, Coventry, Durham, Glasgow, Loughborough, Nottingham, Warwick and Sheffield; *www.futurenet.co.uk/STA/Guide/Europe/GetThere.html*
Worldwide specialists in low-cost flights and tours for students and under-26s.

Trailfinders, 1 Threadneedle St, London EC2R 8JX (all destinations ☎020/7628 7628); 42–50 Earls Court Rd, London W8 6FT (long-haul flights ☎020/7938 3366); 194 Kensington High St, London, W8 7RG (long-haul flights ☎020/7938 3939); 215 Kensington High St, London W6 6BD (transatlantic and European ☎020/7937 5400); 58 Deansgate, Manchester M3 2FF (☎0161/839 6969); 254–284 Sauchiehall St, Glasgow G2 3EH (☎0141/353 2224); 22–24 The Priory Queensway, Birmingham B4 6BS (☎0121/236 1234); 48 Corn St, Bristol BS1 1HQ (☎0117/929 9000); *www.trailfinders.co.uk*
One of the best-informed and most efficient agents for independent travellers; they produce a very useful quarterly magazine worth perusing for round-the-world routes (for a free copy ☎020/7938 3366); all branches open daily until 6pm, Thurs until 7pm.

Travel Bug, 597 Cheetham Hill Rd, Manchester M8 5EJ ☎0161/721 4000; 125a Gloucester Road, London SW7 4SF ☎020/7835 2000.
Large range of discounted tickets.

Travel Cuts, 295a Regent St, London W1R 7YA ☎020/7255 1944; *www.travelcuts.co.uk*
British branch of Canada's main youth and student travel specialist.

Usit Campus, national call centre ☎0870/240 1010; 52 Grosvenor Gardens, London SW1W 0AG; 541 Bristol Rd, Selly Oak, Birmingham B29 6AU ☎0121/414 1848; 61 Ditchling Rd, Brighton BN1 4SD ☎01273/570 226; 37–39 Queen's Rd, Clifton, Bristol BS8 1QE ☎0117/929 2494; 5 Emmanuel St, Cambridge CB1 1NE ☎01223/324283; 53 Forest Rd, Edinburgh EH1 2QP ☎0131/225 6111, telesales 668 3303; 122 George St, Glasgow G1 1RF ☎0141/553 1818; 166 Deansgate, Manchester M3 3FE ☎0161/833 2046, telesales 273 1721; 105–106 St Aldates, Oxford OX1 1DO ☎01865/242 067; *www.usitcampus.co.uk*
Student/youth travel specialists, with 51 branches, including in YHA shops and on university campuses all over Britain.

Usit Council, 28a Poland St, London W1V 3DB ☎020/7287 3337 or 437 7767. Flights and student discounts (part of Usit Campus).

Other operators' packages cover accommodation, transfers and the services of a guide but not flights, since it's assumed that clients are travelling to Russia under their own steam – though flights and visas can be arranged if needed. The Russia Experience, for example, does an eight-day twin-centre deal starting in St Petersburg and ending in Moscow with an overnight train journey between the two, using hotels (£500) or half-board in a Russian home (£360), or a tri-centre package including Novgorod as well (£465), that's also based on half-board homestay accommodation.

If you decide to do things **independently**, homestay or hostel accommodation in Moscow can be arranged through local firms or hostels via email or fax (see Chapter 10, "Accommodation"), but it's vital that they can handle visa support and registration (see p.25), and that you allow enough time for the process of obtaining a Russian visa. You'll also need to factor in the cost of getting to Russia when calculating the cost of doing things independently, which may well work out as no cheaper – or even dearer – than a package holiday.

From May to September, a luxuriously laid-back option is to **cruise** from St Petersburg to Moscow via the magical Kizhi Island and the historic Volga towns of Yaroslavl, Kostroma and Uglich. All the packages on offer include return flights and last eleven or twelve days. Intourist's cruise (£989–£1035) includes the monastic island of Valaam on its itinerary, unlike the otherwise similar Voyages Jules Verne (£995-1085), Norvista and Noble Caledonia cruises. Intourist also does a twenty-day cruise from Moscow down to Volgograd – better known as Stalingrad – and back (£1789).

The other main area of tourism is **Trans-Siberian railway** packages and "soft adventure"

Specialist travel agents and tour operators

Bridge the World, 45 Chalk Farm Rd, London NW1 8AJ ☎020/7911 0900; *www.bridgetheworld*
RTW flight specialist that offers Trans-Siberian packages in partnership with The Russia Experience.

CIS Travel Services, 5 Hobart Place, London SW1W 0HU ☎020/7393 1212, *cistravel@chapman-freeborn.co.uk*
Sales agents for Air Baltic, Transaero, Aeroflot and other CIS airlines.

Eastern European Travel Ltd, 138 Drake St, Rochdale, Lancashire OL16 1PS ☎01706/868 765, *eetravel@breathe.co.uk*
Weekly coaches from London and Manchester to Moscow, Minsk and Kiev.

Farnley Travel, 4 Royal Opera Arcade, Haymarket, London SW1Y 4UY ☎020/7930 7679.
Discounts on Russian and Baltic flights.

Findhorn EcoTravels, The Park, Forres, Morayshire, IV36 0TZ ☎01309/690995, *ecoliza@rmplc.co.uk*
Affiliated to the Ecologia Trust, a charity running youth exchanges and a summer language school at the Kitezh children's community, Kaluga. Can arrange visa support, flights, homestay and hostel accommodation in Moscow and St Petersburg.

IMS Travel, 9 Mandeville Place, London W1U 3AU ☎020/7224 4678, *info@imstravel.co.uk*
General Sales Agent for Aeroflot.

Inntel-Moscow Travel Co. Ltd, Orchard House, 167–169 High St Kensington, London W8 6SH ☎020/7937 7207; *www.russiatravel.com*
Visa support, flights and hotel bookings within the CIS.

Interchange, Interchange House, 27 Stafford Rd, Croydon CR0 4NG ☎020/8681 3612, *interchange@interchange.uk.com*
Tailored short breaks, flights, hotel and homestay bookings; tours to Georgia and Armenia.

Intourist, 219 Marsh Wall, London E14 9PD ☎020/7538 8600; Suite 2F, Central buildings, 211 Deansgate, Manchester M3 3NW ☎0161/834 0230; *www.intourist.com*
Moscow or St Petersburg city breaks, a Moscow/Golden Ring tour, cruises from St Petersburg to Moscow and from Moscow to Volgograd; Trans-Siberian packages; independent travel (no homestays).

Noble Caledonia Ltd, 11 Charles St, London W1X 8LE ☎020/7409 0376.
Upmarket all-inclusive St Petersburg–Moscow cruises.

Norvista, 227 Regent St, London W1R 8PD ☎020/7409 7334, *reservations@norvista.co.uk*
Scandinavian and Baltic specialists, acting as ferry agents and rail agents for the region, and also offering a Moscow/St Petersburg cruise and twin centre packages.

Progressive Tours, 12 Porchester Place, London W2 2BS ☎020/7262 1676, *101533.513@compuserve.com*
Flights, accommodation and services.

Scott's Tours, 141 Whitfield St, London W1T 5EV ☎020/7383 5353, *sales@scottstours.co.uk*
Specialists in discount flights to the CIS, visa support, accommodation and other services.

The Russia Experience, Research House, Fraser Rd, Perivale, Middx UB6 7AQ ☎020/8566 8846, *info@trans-siberian.co.uk*
Trans-Siberian specialists in individual and small group travel, from B&B in Moscow and St Petersburg to exploring Tuva, Mongolia and China. Over summer, they also operate the Beetroot Bus between Moscow and St Petersburg (see p.41).

The Russia House Ltd, 50 Southwark St London SE1 1RU ☎020/7450 3262, *russiahouse@btinternet.com*; *www.therussiahouse.ltd*
Visa support, hotel bookings and other services, mainly for business travellers.

Voyages Jules Verne, 21 Dorset Square, London NW1 6QG ☎020/7616 1000; *www.vjv.co.uk*
Does a luxurious river cruise, and a Pullman train ride from Moscow to Beijing.

spin-offs in Siberia or Mongolia. Although most tourists heading eastwards on the Trans-Sib are bound for Beijing rather than the Russian Pacific port of Vladivostok, the attractions en route are identical until the lines diverge at Ulan Ude. Intourist's sixteen-day Moscow–Beijing trip includes visits to Irkutsk, Lake Baikal, the Great Wall and the Ming Tombs, plus return flights from Britain (£1379–1499), while The Russia Experience offers numerous land-only trips starting in Moscow or St Petersburg and ending up in China, Mongolia or Vladivostok, from a basic fifteen-day trip to Beijing that includes cycling by Lake Baikal and staying in a felt tent on the Mongolian steppes (£860), to a mega-trip (£1570) featuring jeep trekking in the Karakorum Desert, with the possibility of forays into Tuva or Buryatia to witness Buddhist and shamanistic traditions, or the Altay Mountains to go whitewater rafting, as add-on extras. Alternatively, you can travel from Moscow to Beijing in a luxurious 1920s Pullman train with Voyages Jules Verne, whose package (£2795) includes flights.

By train

Travelling by train **from London to Moscow** takes two days and two nights, and costs easily as much as flying there, so the only incentive to travel by rail is the chance to stop and savour the countries en route.

A regular second-class **return ticket** from London (through Rail Europe or Usit Campus branches; *not* their telesales – you must go in person) will currently set you back £283 if you travel via the Channel Tunnel or about £263 using a ferry. This includes a sleeper supplement for the outward journey but not for the return trip, which must be paid in Moscow.

A more flexible option is the **InterRail pass**, available in under-26 and over-26 versions, both covering 28 European countries (including Turkey and Morocco) grouped together in zones. The one-zone pass is valid for 22 days and costs £129 for under-26s, £179 for those 26 and over. The two-zone, three-zone and all-zone passes are all valid for a month: two zones costs £169 for under-26s, £235 for 26s and over; three zones is £195/£269; and the all-zone pass costs £219/£309. Alas, none of them are valid in Russia, Belarus, Ukraine or the Baltic States. InterRail passes are available from major train stations or travel agents; to qualify for one you must have been resident in one of the participating countries for at least six months. The pass must be purchased at least fourteen days in advance; there's a £5 discount for online bookings and £3 charge for credit card bookings.

Routes

There are no direct train services from London to Moscow, but there are through trains from Brussels four or five days a week that enable you to connect with a Moscow train at Cologne. To make the connection, you can take Eurostar via the Channel Tunnel or the overnight Ramsgate–Ostend ferry leaving Victoria the night before, to catch the train leaving Brussels at 4.25pm, that arrives at Cologne just half an hour before the departure of the train to Moscow, which includes a **Russian carriage** visibly shabbier than the German and Polish ones. It's a good idea to bring **food and drink** for the whole journey, since there's nothing available in the wagon except hot water from the samovar, and the odd can of beer. The route will take you **through Poland and Belarus**, with a stringent **customs check** at Brest on the Polish–Belarus border, where trains are jacked up in order to change their wheel-bogies to fit the Russian tracks, whose

Train information

InterRail *www.inter-rail.co.uk*

Rail Europe, 179 Piccadilly W1J 9BA ☎0990/848848.
Agents for Eurostar and SNCF (French railways).

European Rail Ltd, Tavistock House North, Tavistock Sq, London WC1H 9HR ☎020/7387 04444.
Agents for Eurostar and European railways.

Eurostar, Eurostar House, Waterloo Station, London SE1 8SE ☎0990/186186; *www.eurostar.com*

Eurotunnel, Customer Service Centre, jct #12 off M20, PO Box 300, Folkestone, Kent CT19 4DQ ☎0990/353535; reservations *callcentre@eurotunnel.com*

Transit visa requirements for overland travel

The following list covers requirements for nationals of Britain, Ireland, the USA, Canada, Australia and New Zealand. Nationals of other countries should consult the relevant embassy (see list below).

BELARUS *All foreigners need visas.*
UK 6 Kensington Court, London W8 5DL ☎ 020/7937 3288 or 020/7938 3677; *http://belemb.port5.com;* double-entry transit visa £20 (5–10 working days).
USA 1619 New Hampshire Ave NW, Washington DC 20009 ☎ 202/986-1606; *www.belarusembassy.org*; transit visa $50 (5 days).
Canada 130 Albert St, Suite 600, Ottawa, ON K1R 5G4 ☎ 613/233-9994; *www.belarusembassy.org*; tourist and transit visas are combined: single-entry Cdn$35, double-entry $62. No embassy in **Australia** or **New Zealand**.

ESTONIA *Visa required by Canadians. For Australians/New Zealanders, no visas required for stays up to 90 days.*
UK 16 Hyde Park Gate, London SW7 5DG ☎ 020/7589 3428, *Embassy.London@estonia.gov.uk*
USA 2131 Massachusetts Ave NW, Washington, DC 20008 ☎ 202/588-0101.
Canada 958 Broadview Ave, Toronto, ON M4K 2RG ☎ 416/461-0764; *www.estemb.org*; tourist visas only: single-entry Cdn$21, double-entry Cdn$42.
Australia/New Zealand 86 Louisa Rd, Birchgrove, NSW 2141 ☎ 02/9810 7468.

LATVIA *Canadians, Australians and New Zealanders require visas.*
UK 45 Nottingham Pl, London W1M 3FE ☎ 020/7312 0040.
USA 4325 17th St NW, Washington, DC 20011 ☎ 202/726-8213.
Canada 280 Albert St, Suite 300, Ottawa, ON K1P 5G8 ☎ 613/238-6868; tourist visa: single-entry Cdn$20, double-entry Cdn$30; transit visa: single-entry Cdn$10, double-entry Cdn$20.
Australia/New Zealand 32 Parnell St, Strathfield, NSW 2135 ☎ 02/9744 598; single-entry tourist/transit visa A$40/NZ$50.

LITHUANIA *No visa required.*
UK 84 Gloucester Place, London W1H 3HN ☎ 0171/486 6401.
USA 2622 16th St NW, Washington, DC 20009 ☎ 202/234-5860; *www.ltembassyus.org*
Canada 235 Yorkland Blvd, Ste 502, Willowdale, ON M2J 4Y8 ☎ 416/538-2992.
Australia/New Zealand 86 Louisa Road, Birchgrove, NSW 2141 ☎ 02/9810 7468.

wide gauge was designed to make it difficult for invaders to use the network.

See "Transit Visa Requirements for Overland Travel" above regarding transit **visas** for Belarus and Poland. You will also need to obtain a Russia tourist visa in advance (see p.23).

By coach

Though it's not the most obvious approach, you can reach Moscow directly or with stopovers in Berlin, Vilnius or Riga, using a network of **international coaches**. While the various Baltic Eurolines' Web sites aren't in English yet, enquiries by email should be understood and answered in that language, so it's feasible to make advance bookings. The coaches have toilets, air conditioning, refreshments and videos, so the journey isn't as uncomfortable as it could be.

Between May and October a **direct service to Moscow** departs on Tuesdays from London (Green Line terminal, Victoria), Leicester (Forest East service station, M1 junctions 21–22) and Manchester (Chorlton St coach station), travelling via Berlin and Minsk (Belarus) to arrive in Moscow about 11pm on Thursday. The fare is £110 one way/£160 return from London; £130/£180 from Manchester or Leicester; a six-month open ticket costs £20 extra. For details contact Eastern European Travel Ltd, which can arrange a Belarus transit visa for UK residents (but not others).

For those with more time to spend on the journey, another possibility is to take a low-cost flight to **Berlin** (see "Flights") and then travel on **to Moscow via Latvia**. There's a Eurolines Estonia coach from Berlin's central bus station (Sat, Sun & Tues; also Fri in summer) that arrives in Riga 22

POLAND *No visa required for British, Irish or US citizens.*
UK 73 Cavendish St, London W1M 8LS ☎020/7580 0476 or 0900/1600 0358 (premium line); 4 Palmerston Rd, Sheffield S1D 2TE ☎0114/276 6513.
Ireland 5 Ailesbury Rd, Dublin 4 ☎01/283 0855.
USA 2640 16th St NW, Washington, DC 20009 ☎202/234-3800; *www.polishworld.com/polemb*; 12400 Wilshire Blvd, Suite 555, Los Angeles, CA 90025 ☎310/442-8500; *www.pan.net/konsulat* lists other US consulates.
Canada 443 Daly Ave, Ottawa, ON K1N 6H3 ☎613/789-0468; *www.polonianet.com/pol/ambasada*; tourist visa: single-entry Cdn$89, multiple-entry Cdn$207; transit visa: single Cdn$33, multiple Cdn$96.
Australia 7 Turrana St, Yarralumla, Canberra, ACT 2600 ☎06/6273 1208; single-entry tourist visa A$85, multiple-entry A$155, student discount single-entry A$68 and multiple-entry A$121.
New Zealand 17 Upland Rd, Kelburn, Wellington ☎04/475 9453; single-entry tourist visa NZ$85, multiple-entry NZ$155, student discount single-entry NZ$68 and multiple-entry NZ$121.

UKRAINE *All foreigners require visas.*
UK Ground Floor, 78 Kensington Park Rd, London W11 2Pl ☎020/7243 8923 or 0900/188 7749 (premium line).
USA 3350 M St NW, Washington, DC 20007 ☎202/333-0606; *www.ukremb.com*; 240 E 49th St, New York, NY 10017 ☎212/371-5690; 10 E Huron St, Chicago, IL 60611 ☎312/642-4388; *www.ukrchicago.com*; single-entry transit visa $15, plus $45 application fee.
Canada 310 Somerset St W, Ottawa, ON K2P 0J9 ☎613/230-2961; visa information 230-8015; Consular division 331 Metcalfe St, Ottawa, ON K2P 1S3 ☎613/230-8015; Consulate General of Ukraine 2120 Bloor St W Toronto, ON M6S 1M8 ☎416/763-3114; information for both online at *www.infouks.com/ukremb*; single-entry tourist visa Cdn$65, double-entry Cdn$105; single-entry transit visa Cdn$50, double-entry Cdn$155; student visa Cdn$35.
Australia and New Zealand 4 Bellview Rd, Bellview Hill, NSW 2023 ☎02/9388 9177, 3/902 Mount Alexander Road, Essendon, VIC 3040 ☎03/9326 0135.
Single-entry tourist or transit visa A/NZ$75, multiple-entry A/NZ$240.

hours later (£43/$61 one-way; £79/$113 return), which can also be boarded in Cologne (Fri summer only; 33hr; £52/$74; £95/$135), Munich (Sat; 32hr; £52/$74; £95/$135) or Hamburg (Sun & Tues; 26hr; £49/$69; £90/$128). From **Riga**, a Eurolines Latvia coach (Mon & Thurs) travels overnight to Moscow (tickets from Baltijas Autobusv Linijas in the central bus station), or there are **trains**, reaching Moscow in sixteen and a half hours (£55/$77 one-way).

Another approach is **via Lithuania**, with a choice of connections to Vilnius. Eurolines Lithuania runs a bus from London (Tues & Fri) that gives you ten hours in Paris before boarding their service to Vilnius, which arrives two days later. As the bus from **Vilnius** to Moscow only runs on Monday, you could have two days or the best part of a week to spare in Lithuania – or leave at any time on one of the two daily **trains** to Moscow (17hr or 24hr), instead of taking the coach (18hr).

Although **Estonia** is too far from Moscow to make a viable approach, its own Eurolines routes to Tallinn offer the possibility of reaching St Petersburg with yet another operator, Eurolines Russia.

Each of these journeys entails obtaining certain **visas** before you leave; see "Visa Requirements for Overland Travel" for details.

By car

It doesn't make a lot of sense to travel from Britain to Moscow **by car**, especially since Western vehicles are so vulnerable to unwelcome attention inside Russia, but if you're intent on doing so, it's just about possible to make the journey in under three days. However, since this allows little time for stopping and sleeping, it is

Coach operators

Eastern European Travel Ltd ☎01706/868 765, *eetravel@breathe.co.uk*; weekly coaches from London and Manchester to Moscow, Minsk and Kiev.

Eurolines Estonia *mreis@online.ee*; coaches from Germany to Latvia and Estonia.

Eurolines Latvia *agency@eurolines.lv*; twice-weekly service from Riga to Moscow.

Eurolines Lithuania *info@eurolines.lt*; connections from London to Moscow via Paris, Warsaw and Vilnius.

Intercars Russia Ukrainskiy bul. 13 ☎095/243 56 33, fax 095/243 71 63; Moscow agents for Eastern European Travel Ltd.

sensible to spread the journey out over a longer period and take in a few places en route.

The most convenient way of taking your car to the Continent is to drive down to the Channel Tunnel, load your car onto the train shuttle, and be whisked under the Channel in 35 minutes. The Channel Tunnel entrance is off the M20 at Junction 11A, just outside Folkestone. For daytime summer trips, advance bookings are a good idea, but at other times you can just arrive and wait to board. Cheaper cross-Channel options are the conventional ferry or hovercraft links between Dover and Calais or Boulogne, Folkestone and Boulogne, and Ramsgate and Dunkerque or Ostend. Ferry prices vary according to the season and, for motorists, the size of car. There's lots of competition between operators, so it's always worth checking out what offers are currently available (see "Ferry information" below).

Once across the Channel, the most direct route is through Germany, Poland and Belarus, broadly sticking to the following itinerary: Ostend–Berlin–Warsaw–Brest–Minsk–Smolensk–Moscow.

See "Visa Requirements for Overland Travel" regarding transit **visas** for Belarus and Poland. You will also need to obtain a Russia tourist visa in advance (see p.23). Driving licence and insurance requirements in Russia are covered on p.38.

Ferry information

Hoverspeed ☎0990/240241 or 0990/595522, *info@hoverspeed.co.uk*; *www.hoverspeed.co.uk* Dover to Calais and Boulogne; Folkestone to Boulogne.

P&O North Sea Ferries ☎01482/377177; *www.ponss.com* Hull to Zeebrugge and Rotterdam.

P&O European Ferries ☎0870/2424999; *www.poef.com* Dover to Calais; Portsmouth to Cherbourg and Le Havre.

DFDS Seaways ☎0990/333000 or 0191/296 0101; *www.dfdsseaways.co.uk* Harwich to Esbjerg; Newcastle to Gothenburg.

Sea France ☎0990/711711; *www.seafrance.co.uk* Dover to Calais.

Stena ☎0990/707070; *www.stena.co.uk* Dover to Calais; Newhaven to Dieppe; Harwich to Hoek van Holland.

Getting there from Ireland

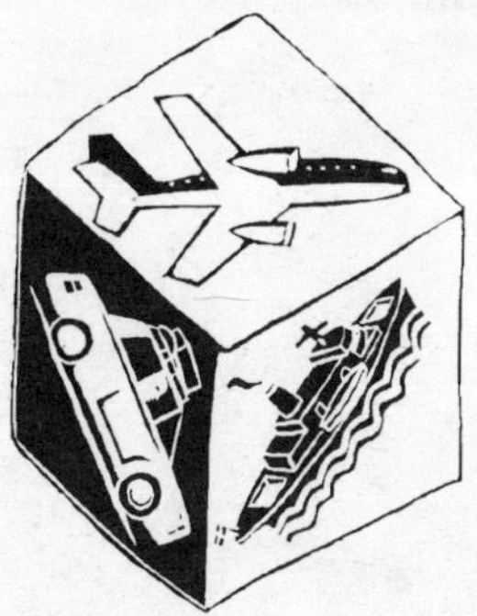

Aeroflot flies direct to Moscow from Dublin every Sunday, and from Shannon, County Clare, on Wednesday and Sunday; flights take about three and a half hours. Return fares start at IR£260 for an APEX return bookable fourteen days in advance for a stay of six days (including a Saturday night) to a month, with unchangeable outward and return dates. Indirect flights on other airlines, with a stopover at their "hub" airport, are generally dearer than Aeroflot, unless there happen to be any special offers or the flight ends up being discounted for the youth/student market by firms such as USITNow. For example, you can fly from Dublin to Moscow via Vienna on Austrian Airlines for IR£379, or Belfast International to Moscow via Zurich on Swissair (IR£315).

It's worth checking also to see if you're better off flying to London in the first instance and pick-

AIRLINES, TRAIN TICKETS, AGENTS AND OPERATORS

AIRLINES

Aer Lingus Dublin airport ☎01/844 4777; Belfast ☎0645/737747; Cork ☎021/327155; Limerick ☎061/474239; *www.aerlingus.ie*

Aeroflot Dublin ☎01/844 6166; Shannon airport ☎061/472 299; *www.aeroflot.com*

British Airways Republic c/o Aer Lingus (reservations ☎0141/222 2345); Northern Ireland ☎0345/222111; *www.british-airways.com*

British Midland Dublin ☎01/283 8833; Belfast ☎0345/554554; *www.iflybritishmidland.com*

Lauda Air *www.laudaair.com*

Lufthansa ☎01/844 5544

Ryanair ☎01/609 7800; *www.ryanair.com*

Sabena ☎01/844 5440

SAS ☎01/844 5440

TRAIN TICKETS

Continental Rail Desk ☎01/836 6222

Northern Ireland Railways ☎028/9023 0621

Both sell InterRail passes and through tickets to Moscow.

TRAVEL AGENTS AND TOUR OPERATORS

Joe Walsh Tours, 8 Lower Baggot St, Dublin 2 ☎01/676 3053; 69 Upper O'Connell St, Dublin 1 ☎01/872 2555; 117 St Patrick St, Cork ☎021/277 111. General budget fares agent.

Thomas Cook, 118 Grafton St, Dublin 2 ☎01/677 0469; 11 Donegall Place, Belfast ☎028/9055 4555. Package holiday and flight agent, with occasional discount offers.

Trailfinders, 4–5 Dawson Street, Dublin 2 ☎01/677 7888.

USIT Now, O'Connell Bridge, 19 Aston Quay, Dublin 2 ☎01/602 1777 or 677 8117; 10–11 Market Parade, Patrick St, Cork ☎021/270900; Victoria Place, Eyre Square, Galway ☎091/565177; Central Buildings, O'Connell St, Limerick ☎061/415064; 36–37 Georges St, Waterford ☎051/72601; Fountain Centre, Belfast BT1 6ET ☎028/9032 4073; 33 Ferryquay St, Derry ☎01504/371888. Ireland's main student and youth travel specialists.

ing up a connecting flight or package from there. There are numerous daily flights **from Dublin or Shannon to London**, operated by Ryanair, Aer Lingus and British Midland. Ryanair have IR£29 midweek returns to Luton or Stansted, but you will have to pay on top of that to travel across London to Heathrow or Gatwick (expect to pay between £15 and £40). **From Belfast**, there are BA and British Midland flights to Heathrow, but you may well be better off flying easyJet to Amsterdam (IR£32 one-way) for an onward connection on KLM.

Getting there from the USA and Canada

It's relatively easy to fly direct to Moscow from the US or Canada. Aeroflot flies direct from a number of cities and generally offers the best value, while other European carriers with daily flights to their hub city usually offer onward connections to Moscow (see box overleaf for a list of airlines and flight frequencies). Alternatively, you could fly direct to a European city and then proceed overland by train or bus. The nearest (and cheapest) jumping-off point for Moscow is the Latvian capital Riga. See "Getting there from Britain", p.8, for a rundown of the trans-European options. Low season generally runs from November to March plus the first two weeks of September, with shoulder season in April and May, and high season from June to August.

Shopping for tickets

Barring special offers, the cheapest of the airlines' published fares is usually an **Apex** (Advance Purchase Excursion) ticket, although this will carry certain restrictions: you will, most likely, have to book – and pay – 21 days before departure, spend at least seven days abroad and limit your stay to from one to three months. Moreover, you will probably get penalized if you change your schedule, and get only a percentage refund, if any, should you cancel. So make sure to check all the restrictions carefully before buying a ticket.

You can normally cut costs further by going through a **specialist flight agent** – either a **consolidator**, who buys up blocks of tickets from the airlines and sells them at a discount, or a discount agent, who in addition to dealing with discounted flights may also offer special student and youth fares and a range of other travel-related services such as travel insurance, rail passes, car rentals, tours and the like. Bear in mind, though, that penalties for changing your plans can be stiff. Remember too that these companies make their money by dealing in bulk – don't expect them to answer lots of questions. Some agents specialize in **charter flights**, which may be cheaper than anything available on a scheduled flight, but again departure dates are fixed and withdrawal penalties high (check the refund policy). If you travel a lot, **discount travel clubs** are another option – the annual membership fee may be worth it for benefits such as cut-price air tickets and car rental.

Don't automatically assume that tickets purchased through a travel specialist will be cheapest – once you get a quote, check with the airlines and you may turn up an even better deal. Be advised also that the pool of travel companies is swimming with sharks – exercise caution and never deal with a company that demands cash up front or refuses to accept payment by credit card.

All ticket prices quoted below are round-trip, exclusive of taxes and subject to availability and change. Where applicable, fares are for midweek travel. Weekend flights cost around $50–70 extra.

Flights from the USA

Fares differ according to the seasons: low (Nov–March, except Christmas/New Year), shoulder (April–May, mid-Sept to Oct), and high (June to mid-September & Christmas/New Year). **Aeroflot** fares start from $500 from New York in

Airlines

Aeroflot US ☎888/340-6400; Canada ☎514/288-2125; *www.aeroflot.com*

Commonwealth Express, US agents for Aeroflot ☎1-800/995-5555; Canada ☎514/288-2125. Although you can call Aeroflot directly and make reservations, travellers flying from the US will probably find it easier dealing with Commonwealth Express. Aeroflot flies daily from New York; two times a week from Miami and Seattle; three times a week from Chicago, Washington DC, Anchorage, San Francisco and Montréal.

Air Canada ☎1-800/776-3000; *www.aircanada.ca*
Daily flights from all their gateways to Paris, London or Frankfurt, with onward connections to Moscow on another carrier.

Air France US ☎1-800/237-2747; Canada ☎1-800/667-2747; *www.airfrance.com*
Daily flights from New York, Washington DC, Miami, Chicago, Houston, Los Angeles, San Francisco, Toronto and Montréal via Paris. Some routes involve an overnight stopover in Paris.

British Airways US ☎1-800/247-9297; Canada ☎1-800/668-1059; *www.britishairways*
Daily flights to London from many cities in the US and Canada; an overnight stopover may be required before flying on to Moscow.

Czech Airlines US ☎1-800/223-2365 or 212/765-6022; Canada ☎416/363-3174 (Toronto), ☎514/844-6376 (Montréal); *www.czechairlines.com*
Daily flights from New York in summer, less frequently the rest of the year; also from Toronto and Montréal. The return flight to New York and some Canadian flights involve an overnight stay in Prague.

Delta Airlines US ☎1-800/241-4141; Canada ☎1-800/221-1212; *www.delta.com*
Daily direct flights from New York.

Finnair US ☎1-800/950-5000; Canada ☎1-800/461-8651; *www.finnair.com*
Daily from New York via Helsinki.

Lufthansa US ☎1-800/645-3880; Canada ☎1-800/563-5954; *www.lufthansa.com*
Daily flights from all their US gateways and from Toronto, Vancouver and Calgary via Frankfurt.

Northwest/KLM ☎1-800/447-4747; *www.nwa.com* or *www.klm.com*
Daily flights from their US and Canadian gateway cities via Amsterdam.

SAS ☎1-800/221-2350
Daily flights from Seattle, Chicago and New York via Copenhagen or Stockholm.

low season, $575 in shoulder season and $790 in high season. From Miami and Washington DC prices start around $570 (low), $590 (shoulder) and $800 (high). Fares from Chicago for the different seasons are around $600/$720/$850 respectively and from San Francisco and Seattle, $700/$750/$1000.

European carriers can usually offer more flexibility, although they tend to be pricier than Aeroflot and fly via their home bases. Unless there's a special deal on offer, you can expect to pay around $560 (low season)/$780 (shoulder)/$880 (high) from New York; $660/$850/$1030 from Chicago; and $810/$970/$1110 from LA.

Before running out to book with a major airline, however, check with a reputable **discount travel agent**, like STA, Council Travel, Nouvelles Frontières, or others listed in the box opposite. These firms have special deals on **non-direct flights** with the major carriers, some of which are just for students or younger travellers, while others have no age restrictions. For example, at the time of writing, you could track down high season non-student return fares from New York for about $770 and from LA for a ridiculously low $860.

Flights from Canada

Depending on the carrier, you can fly directly from **Montréal to Moscow**, or from a wider range of gateway cities to a European airport, and then on to Moscow with the same airline.

Aeroflot flies direct once a week from Montréal to Moscow, with fares ranging from CDN$1200 to CDN$1450, depending on the time of year. Other European carriers offer a wider choice of gateway cities and flights, with daily

Discount agents, consolidators and travel clubs

Council Travel, Head Office, 205 E 42nd St, New York, NY 10017 ☎1-800/226-8624, 1-888/COUNCIL or 212/822-2700; other offices: 530 Bush St, Suite 700, San Francisco, CA 94108 ☎415/421-3473; 931 Westwood Blvd, Westwood, CA 90024 ☎310/208 3551; 1138 13th St, Boulder, CO 80302 ☎303/447-8101; 3301 M St NW, 2nd Floor, Washington, DC 20007 ☎202/337-6464; 1160 N. State St, Chicago, IL 60610 ☎312/951-0585; 273 Newbury St, Boston, MA 02116 ☎617/266-1926; *www.counciltravel.com*
Nationwide US organization. Mostly, but by no means exclusively, specializes in student travel.

New Frontiers/Nouvelles Frontières, 12 E 33rd St, New York, NY 10016 ☎1-800/366-6387 or 212/779-0600; 1001 Sherbrook East, Suite 720, Montréal, PQ H2L 1L3 ☎514/526-8444; *www.newfrontiers.com*
French discount travel firm. Other branches in LA, San Francisco and Quebec City.

STA Travel, 10 Downing St, New York, NY 10014 ☎1-800/777-0112; 212/627-3111; 7202 Melrose Ave, Los Angeles, CA 90046 ☎213/934-8722; 36 Geary St, San Francisco, CA 94108 ☎415/391-8407; 297 Newbury St, Boston, MA 02115 ☎617/266-6014; 429 S Dearborn St, Chicago, IL 60605 ☎312/786 9050; 1905 Walnut St, Philadelphia, PA 19103 ☎215/382-2928; 317 14th Ave SE, Minneapolis, MN 55414 ☎612/615-1800; *www.statravel.com*
Worldwide specialists in independent travel.

Travac, 989 6th Ave, New York NY 10018 ☎1-800/872-8800; *www.travac.com*
Consolidator and charter broker, with another office in Orlando.

Travel Avenue, 10 S Riverside, Suite 1404, Chicago, IL 60606 ☎1-800/333-3335; *www.travelavenue.com*
Discount travel company.

Travel Cuts, 187 College St, Toronto, ON M5T 1P7 ☎1-800/667-2887; 888/238-2887 from US; 180 MacEwan Student Centre, University of Calgary, Calgary, AB T2N 1N4 ☎403/282-7687; 12304 Jasper Av, Edmonton, AB T5N 3K5 ☎403/488-8487; 1613 Rue St Denis, Montréal, PQ H2X 3K3 ☎514/843-8511; 555 W 8th Ave, Vancouver, BC V5Z 1C6 ☎888/FLY CUTS or 604/822-6890; University Centre, University of Manitoba, Winnipeg, MB R3T 2N2 ☎204/269-9530; *www.travelcuts.com*
Canadian student travel organization.

Unitravel, 11737 Administration Drive, St Louis, MO 63146 ☎1-800/325-2222; *www.unitravel.com*
Consolidator.

connections to Moscow from their hub airport. Their Apex fares from Montréal and Toronto start at around CDN$1200 (low season) rising to CDN$1540 (high season), with fares from Vancouver ranging from CDN$1520 (low) to CDN$1920 (high). It's also worth checking with the student/youth travel agency Travel Cuts for their latest flight deals. For instance, at the time of writing, you could pick up a non-student, high-season return fare from the East Coast for just CDN$1320.

Package tours

With the situation in Russia still very changeable, **travel agencies specializing in Russia**, such as Pioneer Tours and Travel, are excellent sources of up-to-date advice, as well as being the best way to find out about any available cheap flight deals. See the box on p.16 for addresses and examples of the packages on offer; unless otherwise stated, all prices quoted exclude taxes and are subject to change. Where applicable, return flights are from New York and accommodation is based on one person sharing a double or twin room.

Travelling by train

If you're interested in seeing more of Europe en route to Moscow, travelling by train from Britain or the Continent may appeal. However, although you can use **Eurail** passes for unlimited travel in sixteen countries, they are **not valid** in Russia, Belarus, Poland, Ukraine or the Baltic States, so it's only worth getting one if you plan to travel fairly extensively around Europe by train, in addition to visiting Moscow.

The **Eurail Youthpass** (for under-26s) costs US$388 for 15 consecutive days, US$499 for 21 consecutive days; $623 for one month or

Specialist tour operators

Abercrombie & Kent ☎1-800/323-7308; *www.abercrombieandkent.com*
Offers a 9-day deluxe tour of Moscow and St Petersburg from $6975 (flight included).

Adventure Center ☎1-800/227-8747; *www.adventurecenter.com*
US division of the UK-based Overland Travel, dealing mostly in active holidays. From June to August their 15-day "Treasures of the Tsars" tour features Tallinn, Moscow, Suzdal, Yaroslavl, St Petersburg and Finland ($1455).

Cruise Marketing International ☎1-800/578 4472, *sales@cruiserussia.com*; *www.cruiserussia.com*
Luxurious fly/cruise packages featuring Moscow and St Petersburg.

Delta Dream Vacations Eastern Europe ☎1-800/872-7786 or 221-2216; *www.generaltours.com*
Individual city stays as well as a 6-day Moscow/St Petersburg escorted tour with an overnight train journey between the two cities, $1129–1899 (flight included, price fluctuates according to season).

Elderhostel ☎1-877/426-8056; *www.elderhostel.org*
Specialists in educational and activity programs, cruises and homestays for senior travellers, offering a two-week "Treasures of Russian Art and Literature" tour focused on Moscow and St Petersburg (from $3347).

Host Families Association (HOFA) ☎202/333-9343; *www.webcenter.re/~hofa*
US contact for St Petersburg-based firm offering private rooms and various services in Moscow and other cities in the former Soviet Union.

IBV Bed and Breakfast Systems ☎301/942-3770, fax 933-0024.
Arranges B&B in Russian homes (US$75 single, $85 double) and visa support.

International Market Place Tours ☎1-800/641-3456; *www.imp-world-tours*
Nine-day journey between Moscow and St Petersburg from $2049 (flight included).

International Gay Travel Association ☎1-800/448-*8550; www.iglta.com*
Trade group with lists of gay-owned or gay-friendly travel agents, accommodation and other travel businesses.

Intourist USA ☎1-800/556-5305 (US & Canada), *info@tourist-usa.com*
Individual and group tours, special interest and educational tours, plus language training tours. The Wonders of Russian Art and Culture tours include 6 days in Moscow ($685, $1349, or

$882 for two months; if you're 26 or over you'll have to buy a first-class pass, available in fifteen-day ($554), 21-day ($718), one-month ($890), two-month ($1260) or three-month ($1558) forms.

You stand a better chance of getting your money's worth out of a **Eurail Flexipass**, which is good for a certain number of travel days in a two-month period. This also comes in under-26/26-and-over versions: ten days costs

Rail contacts in North America

USA

CIT Tours, 9501 W Devon Ave, Suite 502, Rosemont, IL 60018 ☎1-800/CIT-RAIL; *www.cit-tours.com*

DER Tours/GermanRail, 9501 W Devon Ave, Suite 400, Rosemont, IL 60018 ☎1-800/421-2929; *www.dertravel.com*

Rail Europe, 226 Westchester Ave, White Plains, NY 10604 ☎1-800/4EURAIL in US; ☎1-800/361-RAIL in Canada; *www.raileurope.com*

ScanTours, 1535 6th St, Suite 205, Santa Monica, CA 90401 ☎1-800/223-7226; *www.scantours.com*

Canada

Nouvelles Frontières, 1001 Sherbrook East, Suite 720, Montréal, PQ H2L 1L3 ☎514/526-8444; *www.newfrontiers.com*

DER Travel, 904 East Mall, Etobicoke, ON M9B 6K2 ☎416/695-1209; *www.dertravel.com*

$1429, depending on level of accommodation) or 6 days in St Petersburg ($679 or $1079, depending on level of accommodation), airfare not included.

Intours Corporation Canada ☎1-800/268-1785 or 416/766-4720, *intour@pathcom.com*; *www.intourist.ru*
Canadian offshoot of Intourist, with tours featuring Moscow, the Golden Ring, St Petersburg, Siberia and the Russian Far East. Five days in Moscow from CDN$499 (land only). Their Web site belongs to Intourist in Russia, and is years out of date.

Mir Corporation ☎1-800/424-7289; *www.mircorp.com*
Seattle-based company offering a huge range of small group tours on diverse themes such as Siberian shamanism or the Gulag Archipelago, besides more mainstream St Petersburg and Moscow packages, including homestays.

Pioneer Tours and Travel ☎1-800/369-1322 or 617/547-1127; *www.pioneerrussia.com*
Specializes in customized individual tours, special interest and educational tours to suit a wide range of budgets, plus homestays ($37.50 per night including half-board) and trips on the Trans-Siberian Railway (approx. $4000, land and air).

Russia House ☎202/986-6010, fax 667-4244; *www.russiahouse.org*; in Moscow: 44 Bolshaya Nikitskaya ul. ☎095/290 34 59, fax 095/291 15 95, *aum@clcp.ru*
Arranges visas, registration, tickets and accommodation, mainly for business travellers.

Russian National Tourist Office ☎1-877/221-7120 or 212/575-3431; *www.russia-travel.com*

Russian Travel Bureau ☎1-800/847-1800; *www.russiantravelbureau.com*
Packages, customized tours, authorized visa processing. Eight days in Moscow & St Petersburg from $899 (land and air).

Russian Travel Service ☎ & fax 603/585-6534.
Arranges visas, B&B ($30–45 per night depending on location of flat) and other tourist services in Moscow.

Russiatours, Inc ☎1-800/633-1008, *info@exeterinternational.com*; *www.exeterinternational.com*
Offers four deluxe tours focused on St Petersburg, including a 15-day tour led by the historian Suzanne Massie, that includes a rare chance to visit the Terem Palace in the Kremlin ($8600); a 10-day itinerary with 3 days in Moscow and 1 day in Helsinki (from $4250) and a 13-day cruise featuring Uglich, Kostroma and Kizhi Island ($3500).

$458/$654, fifteen days $599/$862. If you're travelling with at least one other person, you might also want to consider the **Eurail Saverpass**. This costs $470 for fifteen consecutive days, $610 for 21, $756 for a month, $1072 for two months, or $1324 for three. Finally there's also a **Flexi Saverpass** at $556 for ten days, or $732 for fifteen.

Getting there from Australia and New Zealand

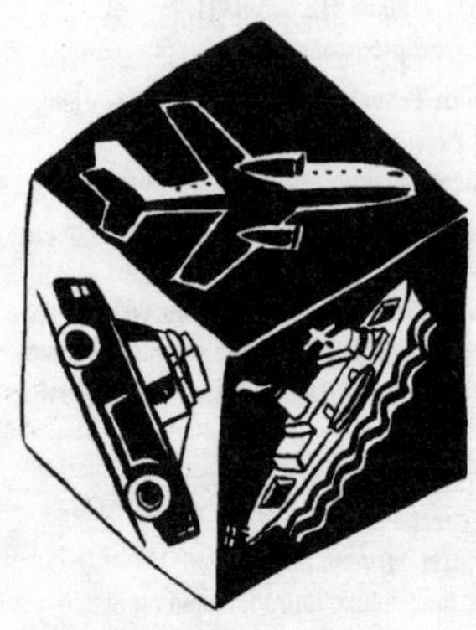

There are no direct flights from Australia or New Zealand to Moscow; all involve either a transfer or stopover in the airline's Asian hub city. If you have plenty of time and an adventurous spirit there are several plane-train combinations that will get you to Moscow and beyond, such as the Trans-Siberian and Eurail networks. For extended trips, a round-the-world (RTW) ticket can work out very good value – especially from New Zealand, where airlines offer fewer bonuses to fly with them. As travelling time can exceed twenty hours, you may want to take advantage of a stopover and good night's sleep en route.

Fares are seasonally adjusted and vary slightly depending on the airline, with high season mid-May to August (the European summer) and December to mid-January, shoulder seasons March to mid-May and September, and low season the rest of the year. Tickets purchased direct from the airlines tend to be expensive; travel agents generally offer much better deals, and have the latest information on limited special offers and stopovers. The best discounts are offered by companies such as Flight Centres, STA and Trailfinders (see box on p.21); these can also help with visas, travel insurance and tours. You might also want to have a look on the Internet: *www.travel.com.au* offers discounted fares online, as does *www.sydneytravel.com*.

Flights

From Australia Aeroflot team up with Qantas to offer flights three times a week via Singapore – from A$1699 in the low season and A$2099 in the high season. Other good deals are with Egypt Air going via Singapore and a stopover in Cairo also for around $1699–2299, Japan Airlines (JAL) to Tokyo, with a flight on to Moscow next day (which includes a night's accommodation) and Korean Airlines, via either a transfer or stopover in Seoul, both for A$1799–2499. For a slightly more comfortable, but more expensive flight, Qantas code-share with a number of European carriers such as KLM via Amsterdam, Alitalia via Rome, and Lufthansa via Frankfurt, to provide a reliable connecting service from major Australian cities for around A$1899–2499, while British Airways have a daily service from Sydney to London with onward connections to Moscow for A$2099–2899. Alternatively, for around A$2099–2699, Qantas-SAS and Qantas-Finnair can take you to Stockholm and Helsinki respectively, where you can get a connecting flight or alternative transport to Moscow. From Perth the best deal to Moscow is with Air India via Delhi/Bombay (from A$1699, plus A$599 for Sydney–Perth return).

There are no direct flights **from New Zealand** to Moscow, although JAL offers a good connecting service from Auckland (with overnight accommodation in Tokyo included in the price) for around NZ$2099–2599. The alternatives use combinations of airlines across Asia or the US to Europe, and then on to Russia. For example, Qantas/Air New Zealand flies from Auckland to Singapore/Bangkok or Los Angeles, and thence to Moscow either with KLM via Amsterdam, Alitalia via Rome or Lufthansa via Frankfurt. For roughly the same price Qantas along with SAS and Finnair have several flights a week to Stockholm and Helsinki respectively, where you can either get a connecting flight or travel overland to Moscow, all for around NZ$2399–2899.

If you want to take in Moscow as part of a world trip another option is a **round-the-world ticket**. Of the ever-increasing choices available Qantas-Air France's is the cheapest, allowing three stopovers in each direction from A$1699/NZ$2099, while the most flexible are offered by airline alliances such as One World and Star Alliance, enabling you to take in destinations in the USA and Canada, Europe, Asia as well as South America and South Africa; prices are mileage-based from A$2500/NZ$2700, for a max of 29,000 miles up to A$3500/NZ$3700 for 39,000 miles.

Alternatively, Cathay Pacific fly several times a week to Hong Kong and Beijing – where you can connect with the Trans-Siberian network – from around A$1299.

Specialist agents and operators

The Adventure Specialists, 69 Liverpool St, Sydney ☎ 02/9261 2927.
Agents for Sundowners Trans-Siberian and Trans-Kazakhstan "Silk Route" rail journeys.

Croydon Travel, 34 Main St, Croydon, Victoria ☎ 03/9725 8555.
Homestays from A$1000/NZ$1300 for 7 nights with English-speaking families plus hotel accommodation and river cruises

Eastern European Travel Bureau-Russian Travel Centre, 5/75 King St, Sydney ☎ 02/9262 1144, *eetb@ozimail.com.au*
Branches in Melbourne, Brisbane and Perth. All rail travel including Trans-Siberian from Beijing to St Petersburg via Mongolia, Lake Baikal and Moscow, cruises between Moscow and St Petersburg and homestays (A$95 per night). Can also provide visa support for B&B clients.

Gateway Travel, 48 The Boulevard, Strathfield, Sydney ☎ 02/9745 3333; *www.russian-gateway.com.au*
Russian specialists whose land-only packages include 8 days in Moscow and St Petersburg in hotels ($1599) or B&B ($675); a 12-day Volga cruise ($1840); and 3 days in Vladimir and Suzdal ($510).

Moonsky Star Ltd, Chung King Mansion, E-block 4th floor flat 6, Nathan Rd 36-44, Kowloon, Hong Kong ☎ 852/2723 1376, *MonkeyHK@compuserve.com*
Hong Kong-based tour firm offering numerous Trans-Siberian and Moscow/St Petersburg itineraries, starting from Hong Kong or Beijing.

Passport Travel Services, Suite 11a, 401 St Kilda Rd, Melbourne, ☎ 03/9867 3888 or 1800 337 031; *www.travelcentre.com.au*
Rail trips from Beijing to Moscow/St Petersburg via Manchuria ($658) or Mongolia ($685), with extensions including a bike tour of Lake Baikal from June to mid-Sept ($282). Also 7 nights homestay in Moscow/St Petersburg ($339), and day excursions from Moscow to Suzdal ($128) and the Trinity Monastery ($124).

Russia and Beyond, 191 Clarence St, Sydney ☎ 02/9299 5799 or 1800/637 756; *www.russiabeyond.com.au*
Specialists in trips to western Russia and the Baltic States. Packages such as their 11-day "Waterways of the Tzars" includes two nights aboard in St Petersburg, six nights cruising along the Volga and two nights aboard in Moscow (from A$1700).

Silke's Travel, 263 Oxford St, Darlinghurst, Sydney ☎ 1800/807 860 or 02/9380 5835, *info@silkes.com.au*; *www.silkes.com.au*
Specially tailored holidays for gay and lesbian travellers.

Sundowners Adventure Travel, Suite 15, 600 Lonsdale St, Melbourne ☎ 03/9600 1934 & 1800/337 089; *www.sundowners.com.au*
Rail itineraries from Shanghai to Moscow via Mongolia (A$5130), and Beijing (A$3870) or Vladivostok (A$ 2930) to St Petersburg via Lake Baikal, plus add-ons such as 14 days' trekking in the High Pamirs (A$2190).

Topdeck Travel, 65 Grenfell St, Adelaide ☎ 08/8232 7222; *www.topdecktravel.com.au*
Three-night city stays in Moscow (from $360), also escorted coach and river tours from St Petersburg to Moscow and vice versa (from $1850).

Airlines

Aeroflot Australia ☎ 02/9262 2233; *www.aeroflot.com*
Three times a week to Moscow from Singapore: teams up with Qantas from Australian and New Zealand cities.

Air India Australia ☎ 02/9299 2022; New Zealand ☎ 09/303 1301; *www.airindia.com*
Twice-weekly flight to Moscow via Bombay or Delhi from Perth.

Air New Zealand Australia ☎ 13 2476; New Zealand ☎ 0800 737 000 or 09/357 3000; *www.airnz.com*
Several flights a week from Sydney, Melbourne, Brisbane and Auckland to Frankfurt via Los Angeles: an onward connection with another airline is required.

British Airways Australia ☎ 02/8904 8800; New Zealand ☎ 09/356 8690; *www.british-airways.com*
Daily flights from Sydney, Melbourne, Brisbane and Perth to London via Singapore and from Auckland via LA, with onward connections to Moscow.

Cathay Pacific Australia ☎ 13 1747 or 02/9931 5500; New Zealand ☎ 09/379 0861; *www.cathaypacific.com*
Several flights a week to Hong Kong and Beijing from major Australian and New Zealand cities: where you can connect with the Trans-Siberian network.

EgyptAir Australia ☎ 02/9232 6677; *www.egyptair.com*
Twice-weekly flights to Moscow from Sydney via a transfer in Cairo.

Finnair Australia ☎ 02/9244 2299; New Zealand ☎ 09/308 3365; *www.finnair.com*
Four flights weekly from Sydney via Bangkok/Tokyo to Helsinki and twice-weekly from Auckland via Singapore to Helsinki with onward connections to Moscow.

Garuda Australia ☎ 1300/365 330; New Zealand ☎ 09/366 1862 or 1800/128 510.
Several flights weekly from major Australian and New Zealand cities to Frankfurt via Denpasar/Jakarta.

Japan Airlines Australia ☎ 02/9272 1111; New Zealand ☎ 09/379 9906; *www.japanair.com*
Several flights a week to Moscow from Brisbane and Sydney, and several flights a week from Cairns and Auckland, all with either a transfer or an overnight stop in Tokyo or Osaka. Code-share with Air New Zealand.

KLM Australia ☎ 1300 303 747; New Zealand ☎ 09/ 309 1782; *www.klm.com*
Several flights a week from Sydney to Amsterdam via Singapore, with onward connections to Moscow.

Korean Air Australia ☎ 02/9262 6000; New Zealand ☎ 09/307 3687; *www.koreanair.com*
Several flights a week to Moscow from Sydney and Brisbane with overnight stop in Seoul.

Qantas Australia ☎ 13/13 13; New Zealand ☎ 09/357 8900 or 0800/808 767; *www.qantas.com.au*
Daily flights from major cities to London and Frankfurt via Singapore/Bangkok: an onward connection with another airline is required. Also flies daily to Hong Kong and twice-weekly

Package tours

Package tours available in Australia do not usually include flights, as it's assumed that you'll be making your own way there – though most specialist agents listed in the box above will also be able to arrange them if required. The main reason to take a tour is to avoid the hassle of booking train tickets between Moscow, St Petersburg and/or Beijing, and finding somewhere to stay there. All the prices given are for a single person, at twin share rates.

The most popular tours link **Beijing, Moscow and St Petersburg** with a journey on the **Trans-Siberian**. Eastern European Travel Bureau's includes stopovers at Ulan Bator and Lake Baikal, five nights in Moscow and the same in St Petersburg (from A$2099). Sundowners Adventure Travel packages range from an eleven-day tour between Vladivostok and Moscow (A$700) to an extensive all-inclusive 39-day journey from Vietnam through China, Mongolia and Russia (A$9850). Two shorter tours focusing on **Moscow and St Petersburg** are Eastern European Travel Bureau's eight-day tour (A$895) and Russia and Beyond's eight-day "Grand Russia" package (A$1280), including a visit to the Moscow Circus.

to Beijing, where you can connect with the Trans-Siberian network. Teams up with several airlines to provide a through service to Moscow from major cities.

SAS Scandinavian Airlines Australia ☎ 02/9299 9800 & 1800/251 157; New Zealand agent: Air New Zealand ☎ 0800 737 000 or 09/357 3000; *www.flysas.com*
Several flights weekly from Sydney and Auckland to Stockholm via Bangkok, with onward connections to Moscow.

Discount Flight Agents

Anywhere Travel, 345 Anzac Parade, Kingsford, Sydney ☎ 02/9663 0411; *anywhere@ozemail.com.au*

Budget Travel, 16 Fort St, Auckland, plus branches around the city ☎ 09/366 0061 or 0800/808 040.

Destinations Unlimited, 220 Queen St, Auckland ☎ 09/373 4033.

Flight Centre Australia: 82 Elizabeth St, Sydney, plus branches nationwide ☎ 02/9235 3522, nearest branch ☎ 13 1600. New Zealand: 350 Queen St, Auckland ☎ 09/358 4310, plus branches nationwide; *www.flightcentre.com.au*

Northern Gateway, 22 Cavenagh St, Darwin ☎ 08/8941 1394), *oztravel@norgate.com.au*

STA Travel, Australia: 855 George St, Sydney; 256 Flinders St, Melbourne; other offices in state capitals and major universities (nearest branch ☎ 13 1776, fastfare telesales ☎ 1300/360 960). New Zealand: 10 High St, Auckland ☎ 09/309 0458, fastfare telesales ☎ 09/366 6673, plus branches in Wellington, Christchurch, Dunedin, Palmerston North, Hamilton and at major universities, *traveller@statravel.com.au*; *www.statravel.com.au*

Student Uni Travel, 92 Pitt St, Sydney ☎ 02/9232 8444, *sydney@backpackers.net* Branches in Brisbane, Cairns, Darwin, Melbourne and Perth.

Thomas Cook, Australia: 175 Pitt St, Sydney ☎ 02/9231 2877; 257 Collins St, Melbourne ☎ 03/9282 0222, plus branches in other state capitals (local branch ☎ 13 1771, Thomas Cook Direct telesales ☎ 1800/801 002); New Zealand: 191 Queen St, Auckland; ☎ 09/379 3920; *www.thomascook.com.au.*

Trailfinders, 8 Spring St, Sydney ☎ 02/9247 7666; 91 Elizabeth St, Brisbane ☎ 07/3229 0887; Hides Corner, Shield St, Cairns ☎ 07/4041 1199.

Travel.com.au, 76–80 Clarence St, Sydney ☎ 02/9249 5444 or 1800/000 447, *consultant@travel.com.au*; *www.travel.com.au*

USIT Beyond, cnr Shortland St and Jean Batten Place, Auckland ☎ 09/379 4224 or 0800/788 336. Branches in Christchurch, Dunedin, Palmerston North, Hamilton and Wellington; *www.usitbeyond.co.nz*

From May to September, both these operators also offer eleven-day **Volga cruises** (A$1700), with two nights in Moscow and three in St Petersburg. All these deals are fully inclusive (except for flights and sightseeing tours).

If you just want accommodation, you can arrange **Bed and Breakfast** in Moscow with the Eastern European Travel Bureau (A$95 a night), or hotel rooms through Russia and Beyond (two nights from A$280 twin share). There are also short city-stays with Gateway Travel (four nights from A$295 twin share) and Sundowners Adventure (from A$392 twin share).

Lastly, it's worth knowing that you can also arrange a Trans-Siberian itinerary terminating in St Petersburg through the **Hong Kong** specialist travel agency Moonsky Tours Ltd, which also maintains an office in Beijing during the summer.

Travelling by train

If you're planning to visit Moscow as an extension to a European trip it may be worth looking into a variety of **rail passes** which need to be bought in your home country before you leave. The **Eurail Youthpass** (for under-26s) costs A$733/NZ$915 for fifteen consecutive days,

Rail contacts

CIT, 263 Clarence St, Sydney 2000 ☎ 02/9267 1255, plus offices in Melbourne, Brisbane, Adelaide and Perth.

Rail Plus, Australia ☎ 1300/555 003 or 03/9642 8644, *info@railplus.com.au*; New Zealand ☎ 09/303 2484.

A$942/NZ$1175 for 21 days, A$1176/NZ$1470 for one month, A$1665/NZ$2080 for two months and A$2055/NZ$2570 for three months; if you're 26 or over you'll have to buy a first-class pass, available in fifteen-day (A$1046/NZ$1307), 21-day (A$1355/NZ$1695), one-month (A$1680/NZ$2100), two-month (A$2378/NZ$2970) and three-month (A$2940/NZ$3675) increments.

The **Eurail Flexipass** is good for a certain number of travel days in a two-month period and also comes in youth or first-class versions: ten days cost A$865/1234 or NZ$1080/1542, fifteen days A$1131/1627 or NZ$1415/2033. A scaled-down version of the Flexipass, the **Europass**, allows travel in France, Germany, Italy, Spain and Switzerland for (youth/first class) A$440/$657 or NZ$550/821 for five days in two months, on up to A$968/1374 or NZ$1210/1717 for fifteen days in two months; there's also the option of adding adjacent "associate" countries (Austria, Hungary, Benelux, Portugal and Greece) for around A$85/NZ$110 per country.

Note that none of these passes are valid for travel inside Russia.

Red tape and visas

Bureaucracy has been the bane of visitors to Russia since the Middle Ages, and despite the collapse of the USSR, little has changed in this respect. All foreign nationals visiting Russia require a full passport and a visa, which must be obtained in advance from a Russian embassy or consulate abroad. Each embassy sets its own visa prices according to the speed of delivery (see below). The cheapest method is to apply by post a month in advance. If you foresee having to register yourself or extend your visa in Moscow, check that the agency has a bona fide address there.

Since visa regulations may change, and the following account applies only to British, Irish, US, Canadian, Australian and New Zealand citizens, it's advisable to check how things stand before applying for a visa. Your own passport must be valid for at least three months beyond your expected date of departure from Russia.

Visas

There are several types of visa available, so it's important to know which one you want. The most common is a straight **tourist visa**, valid for a precise number of days up to a maximum of 28 days. To get this, you must have proof of pre-booked accommodation in Russia for the duration of your visit, in the form of a voucher from a foreign or Russian tourist company accredited to the MID (Russian Ministry of Foreign Affairs). If you're going on any kind of package tour, all the formalities can be sorted out for you by the tour firm (though they may charge extra for this). If you're travelling independently, the *G&R Hostel Asia* or the *Travellers Guest House* in Moscow (see p.319) can usually arrange visa support for their guests, if you fax or email them the relevant details.

A **business visa** is more flexible in that it is valid for up to sixty days (occasionally longer), and doesn't require that you pre-book accommodation. You don't actually have to be involved in any business in order to get one; you simply need to provide the embassy/consulate with a stamped letter of invitation (or fax) from an organization accredited to the MID. This can be arranged by firms like Scott's Tours in Britain (see p.6) or Russia House in America (p.17). The cost may depend on whether or not you also book a tour and/or accommodation with them. There are also firms in Moscow that can provide visa support at exorbitant rates, depending on the time period: US$60 (in twelve days) to $185 (two working days) is fairly standard.

If you don't have a business visa, and wish to stay with Russian friends, you'll need a **private individual visa**, which is the most difficult kind to obtain. This requires a personal invitation (*izveshchenie*) from your Russian host, cleared through OVIR (see overleaf) and guaranteeing to look after you for the duration of your stay. You must supply the original document (not a fax or photocopy), and the whole process can take up to three or four months to complete.

If you are only planning to pass through Russia en route to another country, you must apply for a **transit visa**, valid for a 24-hour stopover in one city (usually Moscow). Although the authorities claim to issue them at Sheremetevo-2 airport, the cost exceeds $150, and it's by no means a sure thing that they'll grant you one. Travellers without a visa are confined in the so-called *Transit Hotel* – a lock-up for illegal aliens – until their flight leaves Moscow. It pays, therefore, to get one from a Russian consulate beforehand; you'll need to show a ticket for your onward journey from Russia.

With all these visas, what you get is a document to slip into your passport. With the single-entry visas, one half (the entry visa) is collected on arrival, the other half (the exit visa) on departure. Multiple-entry visas are stamped, as is your passport, on arrival and departure. **Lost visas** must be reported to the main OVIR office in Moscow, which should eventually issue you with a replacement.

Note that if you intend to leave Russia and enter any other republics of the former Soviet Union, you need not only a separate visa for each independent state, but also a multiple-entry visa to get back into Russia. Foreigners wishing to stay in Russia for longer than three months must obtain a **doctor's letter** certifying that they are not HIV-positive, and bring it with them to Russia (the original, *not* a photocopy).

How to apply for a visa

Although all applications require that you submit your passport, three photos (signed on the back), the fee (cash or money order only, no cheques) and a prepaid SAE envelope (for postal applications), the finer points differ from country to country.

In Britain, the Edinburgh consulate is more helpful than the London one, so better for applications by post (or in person, if you live in Scotland). Application forms can be downloaded from *www.russialink.couk.com/embassy* or faxed on request. Applying for a tourist, business or transit visa, it's acceptable to enclose a fax or photocopy of your accommodation voucher, invitation or ticket for onward travel. The visa fee is directly related to the speed of processing your application: £30 for six or more working days; £50 for three working days; £70 for two days; £80 for one day; and £120 for one hour.

In the US, you can download the application form from *www.ruscon.com*, which specifies the

Russian embassies and consulates abroad

Australia
Embassy: 78 Canberra Ave, Griffith, Canberra, ACT 2603 ☎02/6295 9474.
Consulate: 7–9 Fullerton St, Woollahra, NSW 2000 ☎02/9326 1866.
Web site: *www.rusconsul@computeraction.com.au*

Britain
Consulates: 5 Kensington Palace Gardens, London W8 4QS ☎020/7229 8027, fax 020/7229 3215; 58 Melville St, Edinburgh EH3 7HF ☎0131/225 7098; *www.russialink.couk.com/embassy*

Canada
Embassy: 52 Range Rd, Ottawa, ON K1N 8J5 ☎613/236-7720 or 613/236-6215; *www.russianembassy.net*
Consulate: 3655 Ave du Musée, Montréal, PQ H3G 2E1 ☎514/842-5343 or 843-5901, *consulat@supernet*; *www.intranet.ca/~rusemb*

Ireland
Embassy: 186 Orwell Rd, Rathgar, Dublin ☎01/492 3492.

New Zealand
Embassy: 57 Messines Rd, Karori, Wellington ☎04/476 6742.

USA
Consulates: 2641 Tunlaw Rd NW, Washington, DC 20007 ☎202/939-8907, fax 202/483-7579; 9 East 91st St, New York, NY 10128 ☎212/348-0926, fax 212/831-9162; 2790 Green St, San Francisco, CA 94123 ☎415/928-6878, fax 415/929-0306; 2323 Westin Bldg, 2001 6th Ave, Seattle, WA 981121 ☎206/728-1910, fax 206/728-1871; *www.ruscon.com*

Foreign embassies in Moscow

Note: Details for embassies refer to the consular section.

Australia
Kropotkinskiy per. 13 ☎956 60 70 (☎956 72 00 after hours).
Mon–Fri 9am–1pm & 2–4.30pm. Metro Park Kultury.

Britain
Smolenskaya nab. 10 ☎956 72 00 (24hr), *britembppas@glas.apc.org*; *www.britemb.msk.ru*
Mon–Fri 9am–1pm & 2–4.30pm. Metro Smolenskaya.

consulate to which residents of each US state need to apply, and the firms that must deliver the application if you're not doing so in person (regular postal or messenger service deliveries are not accepted). You must supply the *original* voucher, invitation or tickets to support your application for a tourist, business or transit visa (not faxes or photocopies), and payment must be in the form of a bank or postal order, not cash. Again, fees are related to the speed of issue: $70 for two weeks, $80 for one week, $110 for three working days, $150 for the next day, and $300 on the same day.

In Canada, the consular Web site doesn't provide downloadable application forms, you're not required to deliver your application by a specified agency, and you should enclose a photocopy of the information pages of your passport rather than the passport itself. Fees likewise reflect the speed of issue: two weeks CDN$75, one week CDN$135, three days CDN$165.

In Australia and New Zealand the Web site *www.visatorussia.com* provides a downloadable tourist application form which can be forwarded to the nearest consulate along with a photocopy of the information pages of your passport and proof of return or onward travel.

Registration and OVIR

By law, all foreigners are supposed to register within three days of arrival at **OVIR**, the Visa and Foreign Citizens' Registration Department, and obtain a stamp on their exit visa to that effect. In practice, registration isn't as bad as it sounds, since anyone coming on a tour or staying at a hotel will have this done for them automatically, so it only applies to those staying in some kind

Canada
Starokonyushenniy per. 23 ☎956 66 66.
Mon–Fri 8.30am–5pm. Metro Kropotkinskaya.

Ireland
Grokholskiy per. 5 ☎937 59 00.
Mon–Fri 9.30am–12.30pm. Metro Prospekt Mira.

New Zealand
Povarskaya ul. 44 ☎956 26 42 or 956 35 79; *www.nzembassy.msk.ru*
Mon–Fri 10am–noon & 2–4pm. Metro Barrikadnaya.

United States
Novinskiy bulvar 19/23 ☎728 50 00 (after hours 728 59 90).
Mon–Thurs 9–12.30am & 3–4pm. Metro Barrikadnaya/Krasnopresnenskaya.

Visa services in Moscow

Unless otherwise stated, all prices are for a single-entry visa, and "days" means working days.

Andrews Consulting, Novaya pl. 10, 5th floor ☎258 51 98, *moscow@andrews-consulting.ru*; *www.andrews-consulting.ru*; Metro Kitay-Gorod.
The most reliable agency for arranging visas, extensions and other related services for business travellers. For rates see their Web site.

Astrotour-XXI, Komsomolskaya pl. 3/9 ☎975 38 24 or 975 33 24, *aztour@glasnet.ru*; Metro Komsomolskaya.
Provides tourist visa support ($35) in one day, single-entry business visa support in 4 days ($80 for one month/$110 for three months), 8 days ($70/$110) or 15 days ($60/$90); also for double- and multi-entry business visas. Registration $10; free for guests at the *Nasledie Hostel*.

IRO Travel, Komsomolskiy pr. 13 ☎234 65 53, fax 234 65 56, *iro@iro.lz.space.ru*; Metro Park Kultury.
Tourist visa support in 15 days ($40); business visa support in 15 ($50) or 4 ($70) days. Visa, MC.

Travellers Guest House, Bolshaya Pereyaslavskaya ul. 50, 10th floor ☎971 40 59, fax 280 76 86, *tgh@glasnet.ru*; Metro Prospekt Mira.
Provides tourist visa support for its guests within 2 days ($20), and free registration.

TourService International, Tverskaya ul. 10, office #323 ☎788 05 15, fax 292 35 56, *Alexpopov@cybrex.ru*; Metro Okhotniy Ryad/Teatralnaya.
Visas and other tourist services for the CIS; free registration for clients.

of "unofficial" accommodation. Then, the problem is that OVIR insists that whoever supplied or sponsored your visa becomes involved in your registration. If you got a visa through a firm abroad, with no office in Moscow, one solution is to check into a hotel for a few days (or bribe a receptionist to stamp your exit visa and date it for the period needed). Visitors who do *not* get a registration stamp may be fined $200 upon leaving Russia.

OVIR is also responsible for issuing visa extensions, residence permits, and passports for Russian citizens. Their **head office** in Moscow – called UVIR – is at ul. Pokrovka 42 (Mon, Tues, Thurs & Fri 10am–1pm & 3–6pm; ☎200 84 27; Metro Kurskaya). Its bureaucrats are notoriously rude and lazy, guaranteeing hours of tedium and annoyance for anyone who comes into contact with them. Bring along a Russian friend to help out if possible.

The process of obtaining a **visa extension** depends on which kind of visa you have. If you're here on a personal invitation, the extension must be arranged through the local OVIR office in whichever part of Moscow you're staying – a full list of the forty-odd offices can be found in *Moscow Traveller's Yellow Pages* (see p.43). You'll need to write a letter explaining your need for an extension, and present another letter from your host, guaranteeing that they will look after you. Tourist or business visas can only be extended by the head UVIR office on Mondays or Thursdays, and the process must be initiated by the tourist firm or company that sponsored your original application, which can charge you as much as they like for the favour. All visa extensions are deemed to start from the day of application, rather than the expiry date of the original visa. It is impossible to extend visas that have already expired, though you can obtain an exit-only visa, and then apply for a whole new visa once outside the country.

Nor can you change a single-entry visa into a multi-entry one within Russia; you have to leave the country and apply for an entirely new visa. Business travellers in a hurry usually go through **Andrews Consulting** (see the box on p.25), which has an arrangement with the Russian Consulate in Vilnius, whereby foreigners travel to Lithuania to submit their application on Friday, and collect the visa on Monday before returning to Russia. Needless to say, it isn't cheap.

Customs and export

Border controls have relaxed considerably since Soviet times. Bags are no longer searched for "subversive" literature, but simply passed through an X-ray machine. However, you should declare all foreign currency that you bring into the country, plus any laptops or mobile phones, and you will be asked to do the same when you leave (see p.47 for details).

Export controls are more of a problem, as the rules change so frequently that even customs officials aren't sure how things stand. The main restriction is on exporting antiques and contemporary art, though it's unclear where they draw the line between artwork and ordinary souvenirs (which aren't liable to controls). However, you can be fairly sure of encountering problems if you try to take out icons, antique samovars or anything of that ilk. You can export 250 grams of black caviar and any amount of red, and there are no limits on alcohol or cigarettes – though the last two are subject to allowances set by other countries.

Permission to export **contemporary art and antiques** (anything pre-1960, in effect) must be applied for at the Cultural Assessment Committee, ul. Neglinnaya 8 (Mon & Tues 10am–2pm; ☎921 32 58) – which charges a valuation fee of $4 for one item or $6 for any number of items – but you would be well advised to ask the seller to do the paperwork for you. If the export is approved, you can be liable for tax of up to 100 percent of the object's value. **Pre-1960 books** and dictionaries of any vintage must be approved by the Russian State Library's Committee on the Export of Publications Abroad, which requires details of the edition, publisher, print run, number of pages, and the price paid for the book.

Insurance

On production of a passport, most foreign nationals can technically get free emergency medical care in public hospitals, with a nominal charge for certain medicines. However, if you don't want to go to a Russian hospital, then the only option is a private clinic charging US rates, which means that it's vital to take out some sort of travel insurance policy, preferably one that covers you for medical evacuation, before you leave home. Without insurance, an accident such as breaking a leg could cost you up to $10,000.

A typical travel insurance policy usually provides cover for the loss of baggage, tickets and – up to a certain limit – cash or cheques, as well as cancellation or curtailment of your journey. Most of them exclude so-called dangerous sports unless an extra premium is paid. Read the small print and benefits tables of prospective policies carefully; coverage can vary wildly for roughly similar premiums. Many policies can be chopped and changed to exclude coverage you don't need – for example, sickness and accident benefits can often be excluded or included at will. If you do take medical coverage, ascertain whether benefits will be paid as treatment proceeds or only after return home, and whether there is a 24-hour medical emergency number. When securing baggage cover, make sure that the per-article limit – typically under £500 – will cover your most valuable possession. If you need to make a claim, you should keep receipts for medicines and medical treatment, and in the event you have anything stolen, you must obtain an official statement from the police.

Before you purchase any insurance, however, check what you have already. Bank and credit cards (particularly American Express) often have certain levels of medical or other insurance included, especially if you use them to pay for your trip. Some all-risks home insurance policies may cover your possessions against loss or theft when overseas, and many private medical schemes such as BUPA or PPP include cover when abroad, including baggage loss, cancellation or curtailment and cash replacement as well as sickness or accident. In Canada, provincial health plans usually provide partial cover for medical mishaps overseas, while holders of official student/teacher/youth cards in Canada and the US are entitled to meagre accident coverage and hospital in-patient benefits. Students will often find that their student health coverage extends during the vacations and for one term beyond the date of last enrollment.

Disabled travellers

In the past, very little attention has been paid to the needs of the disabled anywhere in Russia. Attitudes are slowly changing, but there is a long way to go, and the chronic shortage of funds for almost everything does not help matters.

Contacts for disabled travellers

UK and Ireland

Disability Action Group, 2 Arnedale Ave, Belfast BT7 3JH ☎028/9049 1011. Voluntary organization for people with disabilities, including services for holidaymakers.

Holiday Care, 2nd floor, Imperial Building, Victoria Rd, Horley, Surrey RH6 7PZ ☎01293/774535, fax 784647, Minicom 776943; *www.freespace.virgin.net/hol-care*. Provides free lists of accessible accommodation abroad.

RADAR (Royal Association for Disability and Rehabilitation), 12 City Forum, 250 City Rd, London EC1V 8AF ☎020/7250 3222, Minicom 7250 4119. A good source of advice on holidays and travel abroad, with an annual *Getting There* guide (£5 inc p&p.) and a useful Web site: *www.radar.org.uk*

Tripscope, Brentford Community Resource Centre, Alexandra House, Brentford High Street, Brentford, Middlesex TW8 0NE ☎08457/585 641, *tripscope@cableinet.co.uk*; *www.justmobility.co.uk/tripscope*
Free advice on UK and international transport for those with a mobility problem.

US and Canada

Directions Unlimited, 720 N Bedford Rd, Bedford Hills, NY 10507 ☎1-800/533-5343. Tour operator specializing in custom tours for people with disabilities.

Jewish Rehabilitation Hospital, 3205 Place Alton Goldbloom, Chomedy Laval, PQ H7V 1R2 ☎514/688 9550 ext 226.
Guidebooks and travel information.

Mobility International USA, PO Box 10767, Eugene, OR 97440, Voice and TDD ☎541/343-1284; *www.miusa.org*
Information and referral services, access guides, tours and exchange programmes. Annual membership $35 (includes quarterly newsletter).

Society for the Advancement of Travel for the Handicapped (SATH), 347 5th Ave, New York, NY 10016 ☎212/447-7284; *www.sath.org*
Non-profit-making travel industry referral service that passes queries on to its members as appropriate.

Travel Information Service ☎215/456-9600
Telephone-only information and referral service for disabled travellers.

Twin Peaks Press, Box 129, Vancouver, WA 98666 ☎360/694-2462 or 1-800/637-2256; *www.disabilitybookshop.virtualave.net*
Publisher of the *Directory of Travel Agencies for the Disabled* ($19.95), listing more than 370 agencies worldwide, and *Wheelchair Vagabond* ($19.95), loaded with personal tips.

Wheels Up ☎1-888/389-4335; *www.wheelsup.com*
Provides discount air fares, tours and cruises for disabled travellers, and publishes a free monthly newsletter.

Australia and New Zealand

ACROD (Australian Council for Rehabilitation of the Disabled) Box 60, Curtin ACT 2605 ☎02 6282 4333; 24 Cabarita Road, Cabarita NSW 2137 ☎02 9743 2699.
Provides lists of travel agencies and tour operators for people with disabilities.

Disabled Persons Assembly, 173–175 Victoria St, Wellington ☎04/801 9100.
Resource centre with lists of travel agencies and tour operators for people with disabilities.

Wheelchair access to most of the top international **hotels** is possible with some assistance, but only the *Metropol, Marriott-Grand* and *Radisson Slavjanskaya* are fully wheelchair-accessible. **Transport** is a big problem, since buses, trams and trolleybuses are impossible to get on with a wheelchair, and the metro and suburban train systems only slightly better. Though major **sights** like Red Square, the Kremlin, the Tretyakov Gallery and the Novodevichiy Convent are wheelchair-accessible, churches and museums often require you to negotiate steps.

Planning a holiday

There are **organized tours and holidays** specifically for people with disabilities – the contacts in the box will be able to put you in touch with any specialists for trips to a certain country. If you want to be more independent, it's important to become an authority on where you must be self-reliant and where you may expect help, especially regarding transport and accommodation. It is also vital to be honest – with travel agencies, insurance companies and travel companions. Know your limitations and make sure others know them. If you do not use a wheelchair all the time but your walking capabilities are limited, remember that you are likely to need to cover greater distances while travelling (often over rougher terrain and in hotter temperatures) than you are used to. If you use a wheelchair, have it serviced before you go and carry a repair kit.

Read your travel **insurance** small print carefully to make sure that people with a pre-existing medical condition are not excluded. And use your travel agent to make your journey simpler: airline or bus companies can cope better if they are expecting you, with a wheelchair provided at airports and staff primed to help. A **medical certificate** of your fitness to travel, provided by your doctor, is also extremely useful; some airlines or insurance companies may insist on it. Make sure that you have extra supplies of drugs – carried with you if you fly – and a prescription including the generic name in case of emergency. Carry spares of any clothing or equipment that might be hard to find; if there's an association representing people with your disability, contact them early in the planning process.

Points of arrival

Most visitors arrive by air and enter the city by the Leningrad highway, passing a monument in the form of giant anti-tank obstacles that marks the nearest that the Nazis got in 1941. If you're not being met at the airport, finding a bus or haggling for a taxi will be your first taste of the uncertainties of life in Moscow. Arriving by train at one of the city's main-line stations, you'll be pitched straight into streetlife at its rawest, and the Moscow metro. Few people arrive by bus or boat.

Airports

Moscow's main **international airport**, **Sheremetevo-2**, is 28km northwest of the city centre. Built for the 1980 Olympics, it is still inadequate as it was then – with too few passport control kiosks and baggage carousels, causing awful bottlenecks. The concourse contains a hard currency duty-free shop, car rental and hotel reservation desks, an exchange bureau and an ATM.

If you know that you'll be **arriving late** or with a lot of baggage, it's worth arranging to be met at the airport. Most top hotels offer this service for $35–60. The **taxis** outside the arrivals terminal have formed a cartel, charging $95 for a ride into the centre. However, by walking past them down the slope towards the *Transit Hotel*, you'll find unlicensed *chastniki*, willing to take $40–50 after a little haggling. Another possibility are the **shuttle buses** run by certain airlines or top hotels, which are intended for their own passengers or guests, but which you might be able to board if you're smartly dressed, as they don't usually check one's identity; you'll have to have a fair idea where your hotel is in relation to the central, big hotels (see below under "Leaving Moscow"), then hang around after disembarking until the bus driver leaves before you head off for your own hotel.

The alternative is to get into town by **public transport**, which involves a two-stage journey by minibus and metro, costing the ruble equivalent of $1. Due to Mafia intimidation, vehicles leave from a slip road 200m from the arrivals terminal, and stop running at 11pm. The most convenient are Avtolayn **minibuses**, running every 15–20 minutes to the Air Terminal on Leningradskiy prospekt, 600–700m from Dinamo or Aeroport metro; or Rechnoy Vokzal and Planernaya, right next to metro stations of the same name. Due to the one- or two-hourly interval between services, and the fact that they stop running at 6pm, you're less likely to use the **express buses** to Rechnoy Vokzal (#551), Planernaya (#517), and the Air Terminal (via Sheremetevo-1), or the non-express service to Planernaya (#817). Whereas it's an easy ride into the centre by **metro** from Rechnoy Vokzal or Planernaya, the Air Terminal is sufficiently far from a metro station yet near to the Garden Ring to make taking a taxi an affordable option.

If you're flying on Transaero (or from St Petersburg) you'll arrive at the older **Sheremetevo-1** airport, across the runway, which is likewise connected by irregular express buses to Rechnoy Vokzal and the Air Terminal (until 6pm), and by a free **Transaero bus** to Voikovskaya metro station. Moscow's three **other airports** handle flights from Central Asia, Siberia or southern Russia, and have fewer facilities. Bykovo, to the west of the city, is linked by suburban train to Kazan Station, while Domodedovo and Vnukovo, south of Moscow, are connected by bus #405 to Domodedovskaya metro, and by bus #611 to Yugo-Zapadnaya metro, thirty minutes' ride from the centre. All three stations are also connected to the **Air Terminal** by express buses, running every one or two hours until 6pm. **Taxi fares** are comparable to (or higher than) those from Sheremetevo-2.

Leaving Moscow

When **leaving Moscow**, allow plenty of time to get to the airport. The options are as outlined

Airport enquiries

Sheremetevo-2 ☎ 578 91 01; *www.sheremeteyevo-airport.ru*

Sheremetevo-1 ☎ 578 23 72

Bykovo ☎ 558 47 38

Domodedovo ☎ 155 09 22

Vnukovo ☎ 245 00 15

Airline offices in Moscow

Unless stated otherwise, airline offices at Sheremetevo-2 airport work until the last flight has landed or departed.

Aeroflot, ul. Koroviy val 7 ☎158 80 19 (Mon–Sat 9am–7.30pm, Sun 9am–4pm); Frunzenskaya nab. 4 ☎723 82 62 (same hours); Sheremetevo-2 ☎956 46 66 (24hr).

Alitalia, ul. Usacheva 33/3 ☎258 36 01 (Mon–Fri 10am–4pm); Sheremetevo-2 ☎578 82 46 (daily 1–5.30pm).

Air France, ul. Koroviy val 7 ☎937 38 39 (Mon–Fri 9am–6pm); Sheremetevo-2 ☎578 31 56 (Mon–Fri 6am–7pm).

Austrian Airlines, *Zolotoe Koltso Hotel*, ul. Smolenskaya 5 ☎995 09 95 (Mon–Fri 9am–6pm); Sheremetevo-2, office #629 ☎578 29 32 (daily 10.30am–6.30pm).

Balkan, Sadovaya-Chernogryaznaya ul. 13 korpus 3 ☎937 59 54 (Mon–Fri 9am–6pm); Sheremetevo-2, office #643 ☎578 27 12.

British Airways, *Tverskaya Hotel*, 1ya Tverskaya Yamskaya ul. 34 ☎956 46 76 (Mon–Fri 9.30am–6.30pm, Sat 10am–2pm); Sheremetevo-2 ☎578 29 23.

CSA, 2ya Tverskaya-Yamskaya ul. 31/35 ☎978 17 45 (Mon–Fri 10am–1pm & 2–5pm); Sheremetevo-2, office #634 ☎578 82 20.

Continental Airlines, Neglinnaya ul. 15 ☎925 12 91 (Mon–Fri 9am–5pm).

Delta, Gogolevskiy bul. 11 ☎937 90 90 (Mon–Fri 9am–5.30pm, Sat 9am–1pm); Sheremetevo-2 ☎578 27 38.

Finnair, Kropotkinskiy per. 7 ☎933 00 56 (Mon–Fri 9am–5pm); Sheremetevo-2, office #612 ☎578 76 67 (Mon 6am–4pm, Tues 9am–4pm, Wed 10am–6pm, Thurs 9am–11pm, Fri 9am–6pm, Sat 9am–4pm, Sun 9pm–midnight).

KLM, ul. Usacheva 33/2 str. 6 ☎258 36 00 (Mon–Fri 11am–5pm); Sheremetevo-2, office #616 ☎578 35 95 (Tues, Wed & Fri 11am–10pm).

Korean Air, *Palace Hotel*, 1ya Tverskaya-Yamskaya ul. 19 ☎956 16 66 (Mon–Fri 9am–12.30pm & 1.30–5.30pm).

Lufthansa, *Renaissance Penta Hotel*, Olimpiyskiy pr. 18/1 ☎737 64 00 (Mon–Fri 9am–6pm); Sheremetevo-2, office #639 ☎737 64 15 (daily 10am–8pm).

Malév, Povarskaya ul. 21 ☎202 84 16 (Mon–Fri 9am–5pm); Sheremetevo-2 ☎578 27 10.

SAS, ul. Kuznetskiy most 3 ☎925 47 47 (Mon–Fri 9am–5.30pm); Sheremetevo-2 ☎578 27 27.

Swissair, Gogolevskiy bul. 11 ☎937 77 67 (Mon–Fri 8.30am–6pm, Sat 9am–1pm); Sheremetevo-2 ☎578 81 43.

Transaero ☎241 76 76 (24hr); *Moskva Hotel*, ul. Okhotniy ryad 2 (daily 9am–9pm); Nikolskaya ul. 11/13 str. 2 (daily 10am–7pm); Air Terminal, Leningradskiy pr. 37 (daily 9am–6.30pm); 2y Smolenskiy per. 3/4 (daily 9am–8pm); Sheremetevo-1 (24hr).

Other airlines are listed in the Moscow Traveller's Yellow Pages.

above, though it's worth noting that the trip to the airport by taxi (see box on p.37) or pre-arranged transfer often costs less than the journey in. By public transport, the best starting points are the bus depots near **Rechnoy Vokzal** and **Planernaya** metro stations, whence there are frequent minibuses to Sheremetevo-2. Services operate far less often from the **Air Terminal** (*Aerovokzal*) on Leningradskiy prospekt (behind two sea-green tower blocks midway between Dinamo and Aeroport metro stations), while the express buses from all these depots are too unreliable to depend on. By minibus, the journey from Rechnoy Vokzal or Planernaya takes about 25 minutes; from the Air Terminal, about an hour. Passengers on Swissair and Delta flights may also use a **shuttle bus** leaving from the *Baltschug Kempinski*, *Renaissance* and *Marriott* hotels, seats on which should be reserved the day before (☎722 60 43; $16).

The **departures** terminal at Sheremetevo-2 is even gloomier than arrivals – especially at night – and you should guard your baggage. Check-in opens ninety minutes before take-off for Western airlines and two hours before Aeroflot flights. The customs officer will expect to see your original currency declaration (see p.47) and a duplicate form detailing what you're taking out of the country (forms are available in the hall). Your baggage will be X-rayed before you can pass through to the check-in desk. Another official will then check your passport and remove your exit visa before you're allowed into the departure lounge, with its bar and duty-free shop, both of which only accept hard currency.

Train stations

Most of Moscow's eight main-line **train stations** are on the Circle line of the metro, and relatively central. Don't hang around, as they're full of beggars, thieves and drunks, and have nothing useful aside from left-luggage facilities and exchange bureaux.

Arriving by train **from London, Berlin or Warsaw**, you'll end up at **Belarus Station** (*Belorusskiy vokzal*), about 1km northwest of the Garden Ring, which is served by Belorusskaya metro. Most trains **from the Baltic States** arrive at **Riga Station** (*Rizhskiy vokzal*), 2km north of the Garden Ring (Rizhskaya metro), while services **from Prague, Budapest or Kiev** terminate at **Kiev Station** (*Kievskiy vokzal*), south of the Moskva River (Kievskaya metro).

Trans-Siberian trains **from China or Mongolia** pull into **Yaroslav Station** (*Yaroslavskiy vokzal*) on Komsomolskaya ploshchad, while services **from St Petersburg** and some trains from Finland and Estonia arrive at the neighbouring **Leningrad Station** (*Leningradskiy vokzal*), and trains **from Central Asia** and western Siberia terminate at **Kazan Station** (*Kazanskiy vokzal*), across the square. All three stations are linked to Komsomolskaya metro.

Trains **from Crimea and the Caucasus** arrive at **Kursk Station** (*Kurskiy vokzal*), on the southeastern arc of the Garden Ring (Kurskaya metro), while services **from central southern Russia** wind up at **Pavelets Station** (*Paveletskiy vokzal*), further round the Ring to the south of the river (Paveletskaya metro).

Bus terminals

Passengers arriving on Eastern European Travel's coach from England disembark at the Intercars Russia office on Ukrainskiy bulvar, near Kievskaya metro, which is far more central than the so-called **Central Bus Station** (*Tsentralniy Avtovokzal*) used by Baltic Eurolines and Russian intercity buses, which is actually in the northeastern suburbs near Shchelkovskaya metro (15 minutes' ride from Kurskaya metro, on the Circle line). It's not that bad a place to arrive, however.

River terminals

Passengers arriving by boat **from St Petersburg or Nizhniy Novgorod** dock at one of Moscow's river terminals, miles from the centre. The **Northern River Terminal** (*Severniy rechnoy vokzal*) is ten minutes' walk from Rechnoy Vokzal metro on the Zamoskvoretskaya line, while the **Southern River Terminal** (*Yuzhniy rechnoy vokzal*) lies a similar distance from Kolomenskaya metro, at the other end of the same line. In both cases, the route to the metro station is signposted at the terminal.

City transport

Although central Moscow is best explored on foot, the city is so big that you're bound to rely on its famous metro system to get around. As almost everywhere that you're likely to want to visit is within fifteen minutes' walk of a metro stop, there's little need to take buses, trolleybuses, trams or minibuses. Unless you speak good Russian and know the score, taxis may try to overcharge. In fine weather, a riverboat cruise makes a great sightseeing tour.

The old centre within the Boulevard and Garden Rings is best explored by **walking**, starting from a convenient metro station. Off the Stalinist squares and avenues that were imposed in the 1930s and 1950s, you find a mellower Moscow of courtyards and lanes in every hue of crumbling brick and stucco, with gaunt trees that burst into greenery as the slush of winter recedes. Moscow is a city of hidden charms, and whenever you least expect it localities are enlivened by a fairytale church, or some glimpse into a private world.

Less metaphysically, there are several minor **hazards** to bear in mind. Traffic is unpredictable and totally ignores zebra crossings, while the surface underfoot can't be taken for granted, either. Watch out for potholes, crevices, open storm drains and protuberant bits of metal. In winter, everything is covered with snow or ice, causing hundreds of Muscovites to slip and break their legs every week. With the spring thaw, beware of roofs shedding their layers of snow; where roof-clearing is in progress, the pavement below is "marked" as a danger zone by a plank laid across two benches, or something similar.

Organized **walking tours** of Moscow are covered on p.43.

Tickets and passes

Tickets (*talony*) for **buses, trams and trolleybuses** are available individually from the driver or conductor or in batches of ten from *Proezdnye bilety Mosgortrans* kiosks in or around metro stations, which are usable on any vehicle. You must use a separate *talon* each time you board, punching it in one of the gadgets mounted inside the vehicle. In rush hour, when it may be difficult to reach one, fellow passengers will oblige. Roaming plain-clothes inspectors will issue on-the-spot fines to anyone caught without a ticket.

Unless you're going to be in Moscow for a long time and make regular use of particular services, it's not worth buying a one- or three-month **pass** for any combination of the above vehicles, though you might get a one-month *yediniy bilet*, valid for up to 70 journeys on buses, trolleybuses, trams and the metro, simply to avoid buying *talony* or metro tickets all the time. The *yediniy bilet* goes on sale in metro stations and kiosks towards the end of the calendar month, for a few days only.

A different system applies on the **metro**, where you can buy a **ticket** (*prisnoy bilet*) valid for 1, 2, 5, 10, 20 or 60 journeys within a 30-day period, or a one-month *prisnoy bilet* valid for up to 70 journeys. Alternatively, you can buy a **transport card** (*transportnaya karta*) valid for an unlimited number of journeys within a one-month (*na mesats*) or three-month (*tri mesyatsa*) period or an entire year (*na god*), starting from the date of issue. With all of these, you feed the ticket or card into the lower slot of the turnstile, wait for the light to switch from red to green, and retrieve it from the upper slot. If you're using a *yediniy bilet*, you flash it as you walk past the guardian at the end of the row of turnstiles.

Although the **price** of tickets and passes is liable to increase in line with inflation, public transport is still affordable for the locals and amazingly good value for tourists. At the time of writing, a *talon* cost the equivalent of 5 pence/7 cents, a one-month *prisnoy bilet* £4/$5.70, a monthly *yediniy bilet* £8/$11, and a one-year *transportnaya karta* £53/$75. A single metro ride costs the equivalent of 1 pence/a cent and a half.

The metro

The Moscow **metro** was one of the proudest achievements of the Soviet era – its efficiency and splendour once seemed a foretaste of the Communist utopia that supposedly lay ahead. Inaugurated in 1935, the system had four lines by the time of Stalin's death and has since grown into a huge network of 11 lines and 160-odd stations, of which four lines are still being extended. In 1994, its Soviet title, "The Moscow Metro in the name of Lenin", was quietly replaced by the plain "Moscow Metro" (*Moskovskiy Metropolitan*).

As everyone knows, the **decor** in many of the stations is palatial, with marble, mosaics, stained-glass, life-sized statues, elaborate stucco and bronze fittings. With practice, you can distinguish the styles associated with each phase of construction, from the Neoclassical prewar stations to the High Stalinist opulence of the Circle line, or the lavatorial utility of 1970s stations. See the box overleaf for more about **sightseeing** on the metro, which is one of Moscow's major tourist attractions.

Notwithstanding a few escalators being out of action, the metro works remarkably well. Trains run daily from 5.30am; the entrances and underground walkways linking interchange stations close at 1am, and services stop about half an hour afterwards, though on festivals and holidays they may run until later. There are trains every 1–2 minutes during the day and every 7 minutes at night.

Stations are marked with a large "M" and have separate doors for incoming and outgoing passengers. Many have two or three **exits**, located 500–700m apart at street level, which can be disorienting if you pick the wrong one. Though each exit is signposted with the appropriate street names (and even bus routes) at platform level, this is of no help if you can't read Cyrillic. Where directions in the text advise that you use the exit near the front (or rear) of the train, it's assumed that you're travelling out from the centre.

It's a peculiarity of Russian metros that where two or three lines meet, the **interchange stations** often have different names. In a quirk of its own, the Moscow metro also has two sets of stations called "Arbatskaya" and "Smolenskaya", on different lines (the Filyovskaya and Arbatsko-Povarskaya).

Though carriages now feature bilingual maps of individual lines, other **signs** and **maps** are in Russian only, so you'll have to learn to recognize the Cyrillic form of the words for "entrance" (*vkhód*), "exit" (*výkhod*) and "passage to another line" (*perekhód*). If the station names seem incomprehensible, concentrate on recognizing the first three letters only (our colour metro map at the back of this book shows both the English and Cyrillic versions).

Since the platforms carry few signs indicating which station you're in, it's advisable to pay attention to Tannoy **announcements** in the carriages (in Russian only). As the train pulls into each station, you'll hear its name, immediately followed by the words *Sléduyushchaya stántsiya* – and then the name of the next station. Most importantly, be sure to heed the words *Ostorózhno, dvéry zakryváyutsa* – "Caution, doors closing" – they slam shut with great force.

Due to Moscow's swampy subsoil – and the prospect of war – many of the lines were built extremely deep underground, with vertiginous **escalators** that almost nobody walks up, although the left-hand side is designated for that purpose. Interchange stations are often on several levels, with intermediary passages and transit halls where beggars and vendors have staked out their patch. Muggings are rare, but obvious foreigners may be targeted by pickpockets, so try to be inconspicuous and avoid speaking unless necessary.

Generally, however, the main problem is being jostled by **crowds** – during rush hour, you can well believe that nine million people travel on the metro each day. Beware of trolleys that can bruise your ankles. The problem is worst on the **Circle line**, which connects seven main-line stations; their respective metros are choked by passengers in transit with vast amounts of luggage.

Buses, trams, trolleybuses and minibuses

In theory, Moscow has a fully integrated network of buses, trams and trolleybuses, covering almost every part of the city. The reality is an overstretched and dilapidated system that battles on

A sightseer's guide to the Moscow metro

When sightseeing on the metro, try to avoid rush hour and forgo photography or blatant gawping. Stations are apt to be less crowded during August, when many Muscovites leave the city. Bear in mind that some stations have two or even three levels, whose decor varies with their vintage; get the wrong level and you'll miss the real attraction.

Our alphabetical list of **top ten stations** includes all the obvious classics. Many can be seen by riding the Circle line in a clockwise direction, between Park Kultury and Komsomolskaya stations.

Arbatskaya (Filyovskaya & Arbatsko-Pokrovskaya lines). The platforms on the Arbatsko-Pokrovskaya line, opened in 1953, share a vestibule whose arches rise from red marble seat-plinths to vaults dripping with ceramic flowers and hanging bronze lamps. At the top of the escalator to street level is an arched wall that originally bore a mural of Stalin smoking a pipe, which periodically emerges from coats of whitewash.

Belorusskaya (Circle & Zamoskvaretskaya lines). The lower Circle line station, opened in 1952, has a stuccoed, coffered hall with a tessellated floor in a Belarus rug pattern, and mosaic panels of flower-bedecked citizens in national dress enjoying a peaceful life won by the sacrifices of the muscular partisan figures in the transit hall between the two levels.

Kievskaya (Filyovskaya, Arbatsko-Pokrovskaya & Circle lines). Its Circle line station was completed shortly after Belorusskaya, and likewise has an ethnic slant. Mosaic vignettes from the history of Russo-Ukrainian amity, in stucco frames imitating lace, unfold under the benign gaze of Lenin. The Arbatskovo-Pokrovskaya line station features variations on the same.

Komsomolskaya (Sokolnicheskaya & Circle lines). Dedicated to the Communist Youth activists whose work on the first line in 1935 is depicted on majolica panels in the rose marble columned hall on the upper level. A ceiling awash with gold-encrusted mosaics ennobles the Circle line station, opened in 1952. The mosaic of the parade in Red Square was retouched as the Soviet leadership changed, with Beria and Stalin being effaced in the mid-1950s, and Khrushchev in 1964.

Kropotkinskaya (Sokolnicheskaya line). Built in 1935, when metro stations were classical in their perfection, Kropotkinskaya has an open-plan platform of dazzling simplicity, its vault upheld by a row of lotus-bud columns. Sadly, however, there is no sign of its namesake, the Anarchist Prince Kropotkin.

Mayakovskaya (Zamoskvaretskaya line). Part of the second line, completed in 1938; its magnificent design – by Alexei Dushkin – won the Grand Prix at the World Fair that year. The station is spacious, rhythmic and stylish, with ribbed steel, red and black marble columns, lit by 36 oval cupolas decorated with mosaic panels on the theme of sports and aviation. Stalin spoke here during the dark days of 1941 (see p.175).

Novokuznetskaya (Zamoskvaretskaya line). Built and opened during wartime, this station's pale marble hall (designed by Vladimir Gelfreykh and Igor Rozhin) is decorated with a bas-relief frieze of military heroes, and mosaic ceiling panels showing athletic youths garlanded in flowers. The artist responsible, Frolov, died during the siege of Leningrad; his designs were airlifted out of the city as a vital contribution to the war effort. Less heroically, the marble benches came from the dynamited Cathedral of Christ the Saviour.

Park Kultury (Sokolnicheskaya & Circle lines). Originally the end station of the Sokolnicheskaya line, its barrel-vaulted main hall (by Rozhin) is clad in marble to head-height, with niches displaying bas-relief medallions portraying workers skating, dancing, playing chess and reading poetry (by Sergei Ryabushkin).

Ploshchad Revolyutsii (Arbatsko-Pokrovskaya line). Opened as part of the third line, which employed the most renowned Soviet architects of the late 1930s. Dushkin designed the red marble central hall, flanked by 36 life-sized crouching bronze statues personifying the defence of Soviet power and its achievements (by Matvei Manizer), interspersed with Art Nouveau sheaves of corn and circular lamps.

Taganskaya (Circle & Tagansko-Krasnopresnenskaya lines). Its Circle line station is themed on the Great Patriotic War, with marble archways bearing pale blue and white ceramic cameos of partisans, pilots, tank drivers and munitions workers, in tulip-shaped frames.

somehow, but is hardly user-friendly. Aside from the clapped-out vehicles, the **overcrowding** on some routes is such that you may find it physically impossible to get on board. Many visitors are also discouraged by the pushing and shoving, but Russians rarely take this personally, and once inside the vehicle will cheerfully help each other to punch tickets or buy them from the driver. Should anyone ask if you are getting off at the next stop – *Vy vykhodite?* – it means that they are, and need to squeeze past.

The other big problem is that **routes** are often altered due to roadworks, so even the most recent transport maps can't be relied on. As a rule, buses and trolleybuses are supposed to operate from 6am to 1am, and trams from 5.30am to 1.30am, although cutbacks may see these hours reduced on some lines after 9pm. The most useful route for sightseeing is bus #б, which circles the Garden Ring. Trams mostly take roundabout routes, and don't run in the centre at all.

Stops are relatively few and far between, so getting off at the wrong one can mean a lengthy walk. Bus stops are marked with an "A" (for *avtobus*); trolleybus stops with what resembles a squared-off "m", but is in fact a handwritten Cyrillic "t" (for *trolleybus*). Both are usually attached to walls, and therefore somewhat inconspicuous, whereas the signs for tram stops (bearing a "T" for *tramvay*) are suspended from the overhead cables above the road.

In addition to the services outlined above, Moscow is also covered by a network of **minibuses**, which Russians call *marshrutnoe taksi* (*marshrutki* for short). Operated by various firms and painted in different liveries, they mostly leave from metro or main-line stations and serve outlying residential areas, making them of little use to tourists. They can be flagged down at any point along their route but don't take standing passengers. You pay the driver the flat fare posted on the window, which is higher than the regular bus fare.

Taxis and hitching

Officially registered taxis are run by many different companies. They are usually Volgas or Fords, painted grey or bright yellow with a chequered logo on the doors. If the domed light on the roof is on, the taxi is unoccupied. At the time of writing, taxis no longer use meters, and one simply pays the going rate per kilometre, or five minutes' travel (a higher rate applies to journeys beyond the Moscow Ring Road, or MKAD). Though obviously open to abuse, this laissez-faire system is kept within bounds by strong competition from ordinary vehicles acting as taxis (see below), except at airports and hotels, where the "taxi mafia" has a stranglehold and drivers have agreed on fixed rates for certain journeys.

Besides official taxis, there are unmarked **private taxis** that have a near monopoly at the airport and certain big hotels. They too are unmetered and charge whatever they think they can get away with, especially if you're a foreigner – avoid them if at all possible.

Most Russians ignore both types of taxi and favour **hitching rides in private vehicles**, which enables ordinary drivers to earn extra money as *chastniki* (moonlighters). It's especially common after the public transport system closes down; you'll see people flagging down anything that moves. You simply state your destination and what you're willing to pay ("*Mozhno -- za -- rubley?*"); the driver may haggle a bit, but there's so much competition that it's a buyer's market. As a rule of thumb, one pays about 30¢ per five minutes' journey time, with a minimum fare of 60¢; rates double after the metro has stopped run-

Taxi companies (24-hour)

With the exception of Sheremetevo airport, all charges relate to destinations within the Moscow Ring Road (MKAD).

Central Moscow Taxi Bureau ☎927 00 00
Flat rate of $0.25 per kilometre; $0.75 call-out charge; to Sheremetevo-2 $11.

Moscow Taxi ☎238 10 01
Flat rate of $0.60 per kilometre; no call-out charge; to Sheremetevo-2 $13.

Krasnaya Gorka ☎381 27 46
Hourly rate of $7/$11 by day/night. $13 to Sheremetevo-2 airport.

Taxi Blues ☎128 94 77
Hourly rate of $5/$8 by day/night. $16 to Sheremetevo-2 by day or night.

ning. Foreigners may be asked for more, but can usually get the same price by remaining firm – though if travelling with Russian friends, it's best not to speak until the deal is concluded.

As the above system is unregulated, it's as well to observe some **precautions**. Don't get into a vehicle which has more than one person in it, and never accept lifts from anyone who approaches you – particularly outside restaurants and nightclubs. Instances of drunken foreigners being robbed in the back of private cars are not uncommon, and women travelling alone would be best advised to give the whole business a miss.

Driving and car rental

Newcomers to Moscow are strongly advised not to try **driving** there. The combination of anarchic drivers, fascist traffic cops and numerous one-way systems is guaranteed to cause problems for anyone who doesn't know the city well. **Traffic** is heavy and local motorists act like rally drivers, swerving at high speed to avoid potholes and tramlines, with a reckless disregard for pedestrians and other cars. Another alarming peculiarity is the habit of overtaking in any lane. Bear in mind also that many drivers are likely to have purchased their licence rather than passed a test.

Should you decide to risk driving anyway, you are required to carry all the following **documents**: your home driving licence and an international driving permit (available from motoring organizations) with a Russian-language insert; an insurance certificate from your home insurer, and one from a Russian insurance company such as Ingosstrakh (Pyatnitskaya ul. 12 ☎233 20 70) or ASTROVAZ (ul. Ostozhenka 13/12 ☎290 43 80); your passport and visa; the vehicle registration certificate; and a customs document stating that you'll take the car back home when you leave (unless, of course, you rented it in Moscow).

If you don't have an international permit and you're staying there a while, it's possible to get a **Russian driving licence** (foreigners who become legal residents must do this if they plan to drive) by taking your valid home licence plus two photos to the GIBDD's Foreigners' Department (see below). Besides a road test, you will probably have to pass a written test and a simulation using model cars. Good luck..

Various car rental agencies offer Western models, with or without a driver. Hiring a **driver** deserves serious consideration; it could spare you a lot of anxiety, and may not cost more than self-drive rental if you only need the car for a few hours. The per-day rates given below refer to a 24-hour period. Most rental agencies prefer payment by credit card and require the full range of documentation for self-drive rental. Some addresses are given in the box below.

Rules of the road – and the GIBDD

Despite drivers' cavalier attitude to the *kírpich* (the red-slashed sign meaning "no entry") and an utter disregard for keeping in lane, other **rules of the road** are generally observed. Traffic coming from the right has right of way – something that's particularly important to remember at roundabouts – while left turns are (theoretically) only allowed in areas indicated by a broken centre line in the road and an overhead sign. If you are turning into a side street, pedestrians have right of way crossing the road. **Trams** have right of way at all times, and you are not allowed to overtake them when passengers are getting on and off, unless there is a safety island.

Unless otherwise specified, **speed limits** are 60km (37 miles) per hour in the city and 80km (50 miles) per hour on highways. It is illegal to

Car repairs and parts

ABC Opel, Aviamotornaya ul. 65/7 ☎373 44 85.

Avtodom, ul. Zorge 17 ☎943 30 33. Land Rover repairs and BMW parts.

BMW-Mercedes Service, 2y Selskokhozyaystvenniy proezd 6 ☎181 13 74.

Forto, Mytnaya ul. 11 ☎236 02 51. Ford, Chrysler and GM repairs.

Interavto, Bulatnikovskaya ul. 2a ☎385 24 54. Repairs and parts for Russian cars.

Mitsubishi Service, 2y Magistralniy tupik 5a ☎241 74 35.

Renault-Kuntsevo, Gorbunova ul. 14 ☎933 40 33.

Rosartson, 2ya Baumanskaya ul. 9/23, korpus 18 ☎265 70 94. Audi, Seat, VW repairs.

Car rental agencies

Budget, Sheremetevo-2 ☎578 73 44; *Sheraton Palace Hotel* ☎931 97 00 ext 117.
Only rents cars with drivers, starting at $30 per hour for a Ford Escort.

Europcar, Leningradskiy pr. 64, MADI Bldg. Office #306A ☎155 01 70, *europcar@madi.ru; www.europcar.com*
Also at Sheremetevo-1 and -2.
Self-drive Zhiguli $40 per day; Volvo $100 per day; Mercedes $90 per day.

Intourist, Mokhovaya ul. 13 ☎292 12 78.
Volga with driver for $15 per hour (plus one hour booking charge).

Intourist Hotel, Tverskaya ul. 3/5 ☎937 27 75, fax 956 83 76.
Cars with drivers for $7–10 per hour.

Hertz, Sheremetevo-2 ☎578 56 46; ul. Chernyakovskovo 4 ☎937 32 74, *hertz.mos@co.ru*
Self-drive rates $50–200 per day, or $170–300 with driver.

Karlet ☎165 52 10 (24hr) or 165 91 47.
Self-drive rates per hour: Zhiguli $5, Volga $6, foreign cars $7–17. Discounts for day or long-term rental. Delivery is charged as an extra hour.

Rolf, Shubinskiy per. 2/3 ☎241 53 93.
Mitsubishi cars for $60–120 per day, or $18 per hour with driver.

drive after having consumed any alcohol; the rule is stringently enforced, with heavy fines for offenders. Safety belt use is mandatory (though many Russians only drape the belt across their lap), and crash helmets are obligatory for motorcyclists.

Rules are enforced by the **GIBDD**, or traffic police (see p.62), whose uniformed officers are empowered to stop vehicles and impose on-the-spot **fines** for real or imaginary violations. The GIBDD regards cars driven by foreigners as a prime source of income, so unless your Russian is fluent it's better not to argue, but simply concentrate on negotiating a lower fine. Officers may try to extract hard currency, but will probably settle for rubles in the end. On no account ignore a **summons** to pull over (indicated by a wave of a baton), as Moscow's GIBDD have been known to shoot at motorists "trying to escape".

Although cars involved in **accidents** are legally obliged to wait until the GIBDD arrive, where minor damage has occurred drivers may agree to settle in cash on the spot, and scram before the cops appear. Unless you get a *správka* from the police or GIBDD, you'll lose the right to claim insurance. Russian insurers won't pay compensation if you are found to be driving under the influence of alcohol. An average of ninety **car thefts** a day occur in Moscow; if your car is stolen, report it to the GIBDD's **Foreigners' Department** (Stariy Tolmachevskiy pereulok 8, str. 1 ☎200 93 57; Mon–Wed 9am–2pm & 3–7pm, Fri 9am–2pm & 3–4pm), which is also responsible for the issuing of Russian driving licences to foreigners.

Fuel and breakdowns

Petrol (*benzín*) is easy to come by, but the decent stuff – 95 octane (3-star) or 98 octane (4-star) – is as expensive as in Western Europe. If you're driving a Russian car it's safe to use 93 or 92 octane, but 76 invites trouble (and will ruin Western cars). One of the few filling stations where you can be sure of getting **lead-free petrol** and high-octane fuel suitable for cars fitted with catalytic converters is Nefto Agip at Leningradskoe shosse 63, on the way to Sheremetevo, which accepts credit cards. Poor-quality diesel is widely available.

If you **break down**, 24-hour emergency help is available from firms like Spas Stolitsa (☎259 80 08), Alfa-Rinako (☎936 25 55) and Angel-NSA (☎747 00 22 or 747 00 20). Though many Western dealers now have branches in Moscow, **parts** and labour both cost more than you'd pay back home. However, low-priced Lada spares are universally available, and the charge for repairs is fairly modest. See the box opposite for addresses.

Out from Moscow

The main reason for travelling **out from Moscow** is to visit outlying sights such as the Trinity Monastery of St Sergei or the Abramtsevo artists'

Riverboat cruises

In fine weather, **riverboat cruises** are an enjoyable way to see Moscow while getting some sun and fresh air. The Moskva River is navigable from the last week in April until the end of September or later (weather permitting). Sightseeing boats depart every 20–30 minutes (daily noon–8pm) **from the Novospasskiy Bridge** (10min from Proletarskaya metro), calling at piers near the Kremlin, Gorky Park and the Novodevichiy Convent, before terminating near Kiev Station (1hr 45min). Tickets cost about $5; you can get off at any point, but you can't use the same ticket to board a subsequent boat – you'll have to buy another ticket (if there are seats available).

colony (described in Chapter 18), or Vladimir and Suzdal (see Chapter 19). Some are accessible by suburban train (*prigorodniy poezda*, or *elektrichka*) from one of Moscow's main-line stations. Most of the stations have a separate ticket office (*prigorodniy kassa*) for suburban trains, which may depart from an annexe to the main building. To make it easier to buy tickets and check timetables, get someone to write out the name of your destination in Cyrillic. Fares are extremely cheap, as foreigners pay the same price as Russians do – unlike on long-distance and international trains. A few sites that are not accessible by train can be reached by suburban bus (*prigorodniy marshruty*) from an outlying depot near the end of a metro line. Fares are also low, but the bus is likely to be standing room only for much of the way. Specific routes are detailed in Chapters 18 and 19.

To St Petersburg by train or bus

Many tourists plan to travel onward **to St Petersburg by train**. Of the fifteen trains leaving Moscow's Leningrad Station, the fastest are daytime services – the ER-200 (Tues & Fri; 5hr) and the Aurora (daily; 6hr), which have comfortable seating and provide a fine view of the countryside en route. However, most people prefer to travel overnight (8–9hr) on the Krasnaya Strela, Express, Nikolaevskiy Express or Afanasiy Nikitin (all daily), which arrive in St Petersburg at a reasonable hour in the morning. Though unjustly notorious for **robberies**, the risk is slight providing you secure the door handle with the plastic device provided, or insert a wedge into the flip-lock in the upper left corner of the door. Shortly after leaving Moscow the sleeping-car attendant will come around dispensing sheets (for a surcharge), and offering tea to passengers in first class.

While the journey itself is easy, **buying tickets** is another matter. Aside from being unsure which outlet currently handles bookings for their destination, foreigners are also subject to ever-changing rules, and charged twice as much for tickets as the natives are. While you can't do much about the latter aside from qualify for a student discount, the hassle of getting a ticket can be minimized by booking through Intourist or other travel agencies.

If you're determined to handle things yourself, the best place is generally the Central Railway

Ticket agencies

Central Railway Agency
Maliy Kharitonovskiy per. 6
Turgenevskaya/Chistye Prudy metro. Daily 8am–1pm & 2–7pm.
Information on domestic (☎262 25 66) and international (☎262 06 04) trains. For bookings on either, ☎262 96 05.

Intourtrans
ul. Petrovka 15/13 Chekhovskaya or Teatralnaya metro.
Air (☎928 87 17 or 929 87 75; Mon–Fri 9am–7pm & Sat 10am–6pm) and rail (☎929 87 56 or 929 87 57; Mon–Fri 9am–6pm) tickets within the CIS (including the Baltic States).

Mostransagentstvo
Myasnitskaya ul. 24/7 str. 1
Turgenevskaya/Chistye Prudy metro. Mon–Fri 9am–6pm.
☎927 00 07 for information on air and rail tickets within the Russian Federation.

Agency, followed by the Intourtrans or Mostransagentsvo agencies (see box opposite for addresses). Alternatively, you can buy a ticket from the station from which the train departs, up to one month ahead. For Warsaw, visit the office at Leningradskiy pr. 1, just past Belarus Station (daily 8am–1pm & 2–8pm); for Mongolia or China, Krasnoprudnaya ul. 1, next to Yaroslav Station (daily 8am–8pm). All these offices also sell **same-day tickets**. Always bring your **passport** along when buying tickets.

Public buses from Moscow to St Petersburg are elusive, uncomfortable and take forever; travellers who fancy seeing something of the towns and scenery in between should instead avail themselves of the **Beetroot Bus**, a summertime service operated by The Russia Experience (see box below).

The Beetroot Bus

The **Beetroot Bus** is an agreeable compromise between packaged and independent travel, which enables foreigners to see more of Russia without all the hassles that this would otherwise entail. From July to September, it runs once a week between Moscow and St Petersburg, visiting or staying overnight at Sergiev Posad, Kostroma, Novgorod and other places of interest. The trip includes guided tours of monasteries and museums, and experiences such as a *banya* beside the River Volga. Passengers can join the tour in either Moscow or St Petersburg at a few days' notice. There's a full 15-day tour ($750) starting and finishing in Moscow, or an 8-day "half" tour ($395) beginning in either city and ending in the other one. The price includes accommodation en route and two or three nights' at either end, but not meals.

Full **details** appear on *www.beetroot.org*. For **bookings** contact The Russia Experience in London (see p.6) or Moscow (☎453 43 68, fax 456 66 06), *info@trans-siberian.co.uk*
The bus **departs** from the *Travellers Guesthouse* in Moscow (p.319) and the *St Petersburg International Hostel*.

Information, maps and addresses

The implosion of the old state tourist monopoly, Intourist, has resulted in a fragmentation of tourist services in Russia and abroad, which is good news in some respects, but hasn't made it any easier to ask questions on the spot. However, you can now obtain a mass of publications that supply much of the information tourists might need, and there are some useful Web sites, too.

Information and tours

Despite the Mayor's rhetoric about making Moscow more tourist-friendly, there is still no centralized **tourist information centre** where you can walk in and get a map, or an answer to any question. **Intourist** offices and service bureaux at Sheremetevo-1 (☎578 91 34) and -2 (☎578 44 75) airports, and in the *Intourist* (Tverskaya ul. 3–5; ☎956 84 02), *Moskva* and other hotels, can make hotel, plane, car and concert bookings, and maybe supply a brochure or two, but that's about all you can expect, while service desks at

Useful Web sites

http:/gorussia.about.com Russia for visitors. News, hotels, links and chat rooms.

www.all-hotels.ru All hotels in Russia. Up-to-date hotel information and reservations.

www.exile.ru The determinedly non-PC *eXile* newspaper (see p.55) online.

www.gay.ru Gay and lesbian travel advice and links.

www.glas.apc.org Ecological, educational and aid projects and connections.

www.glasweb.ru Info on visas, hotels and transport, aimed at business travellers.

www.infoservices.com Online *Traveller's Yellow Pages* for Moscow, St Petersburg and Novgorod.

www.kremlinkam.com Static views of the Kremlin and Red Square, with a weather report.

www.kremlin.museum.ru The official Web site of the Kremlin Museum.

www.mbtg.net A–Z of Moscow services, plus maps, weather, photos and historical images.

www.moscow-guide.ru Official tourist site of the Moscow city government; rather outdated.

www.moscowkremlin.ru Static virtual tour of the Kremlin buildings.

www.museum.ru Museums of Russia. Links to numerous Russian museums.

www.museum.ru/gmii/ The Pushkin Museum of Fine Arts online.

www.russiajournal.com The *Russia Journal* (see p.55) online.

www.themoscowtimes.com Online version of the *Moscow Times* (see p.55).

www.online.ru Russia-On-Line, the leading Internet Service Provider in the CIS.

www.spartak.home.ml.org The official homepage of Russia's most popular soccer team.

www.soccer.ru/dinamo/ Unofficial Web site for Dinamo fans.

the *Metropol* or *National* may be more helpful but charge heavily for their booking services. Staff at the *Travellers Guesthouse* can also advise guests. For addresses, see the Accommodation chapter (pp.319–328).

Some **publications** are useful. If you're planning to stay several months it's worth investing in the pocket-sized *Moscow Traveller's Yellow Pages*, listing all kinds of businesses and services, with lots of maps and advice on diverse aspects of life. It is regularly updated and sold at leading hotels and Sheremetevo-2 airport, while a Russian version, *Luchsee v Moskve* ("Best in Moscow"), is more widely available. There's also an online version of the previous edition in English, but it's so out of date you'd do better using the *Moscow Business Telephone Guide* (*www.mbtg.net*) for data searches.

For reviews of restaurants, clubs, concerts and exhibitions, check out the free **English-language papers** the *Moscow Times*, the *eXile* and the *Russia Journal* (see p.55) – to be found in hotels, restaurants, bars and shops frequented by Westerners. The *Times* features arts and club listings on Fridays and Saturdays, while the *eXile* and *Russia Journal* review clubs and restaurants in each issue. You may also run across the monthly colour magazine *Where Moscow*, whose reviews are biased towards their advertisers, but can also be useful. And for those who can understand Russian, there is the weekly listings magazine *Vash Dosug*, a kind of pocket-sized version of *Time Out*, sold all over the place.

For those with access to the **Internet**, there are Web sites belonging to tourist agencies, museums and hotels, plus online editions of the *Moscow Times*, the *Russia Journal* and the *eXile*. Frustratingly, however, many are way **out of date** or otherwise dubious. For example, there are two official city tourist sites: *www.moscow.city.com*, untouched since it was set up for Moscow's 850th birthday in 1998, and *www.moscow-guide.ru*, last modified in 1999; while the sites of Russia's National Tourist Office (*www.interknowledge.com/russia/*) and their US branch (*www.russia-travel.com)* are equally antiquated – and even Intourist in Moscow (*www.intourist.ru*) can't be bothered to keep their site up to scratch.

Last but not least, **Russian friends** or acquaintances are often generous with their help and time, and know their city well. News of good places to eat, shop or have fun was traditionally spread by word of mouth rather than the media, and old habits die hard, despite there being less need for a grapevine nowadays.

Guided tours

If you don't speak Russian and you find Moscow a bit daunting, **guided tours** can make things a lot easier. As in Soviet times, Intourist runs daily sightseeing tours of the city ($10), the Kremlin and the Armoury Museum ($20) or the State Diamond Fund ($29) every day except Thursday – all museum tickets are included in the prices. Their tours are well run but rather impersonal, with large groups and prosaic commentary.

A wider, more offbeat programme is offered by **Patriarshy Dom Tours** (Vspolniy per. 6, School #1239; Mon–Fri 9am–6pm, Sat 11am–5pm; ☎ & fax 795 09 27, *alanskaya@co.ru*; *http://Russiatravel-pdtours.netfilms.com/*), which does themed walking tours of Moscow; visits to the KGB Museum, monasteries and literary shrines; cookery lessons, lectures and other activities. You'll find leaflets detailing their schedule in Starlite Diners, American Express, the *Aerostar* and *Slavjanskaya* hotels, Anglia and Shakespeare & Co. Phone to verify the departure point and register, a couple of days ahead. Tours cost $10–16 per person, excluding admission tickets.

Patriarshy Dom also runs **out-of-town excursions** ($20–30) to the Trinity Monastery of St Sergei, Tchaikovsky's home and other places covered in Chapter 18 of this book – plus longer day-trips to the "Golden Ring" towns of Vladimir and Suzdal ($55; covered in Chapter 19). Weekly day-trips to the Trinity Monastery ($40) and Vladimir/Suzdal ($60) are also organized by Intourist over the summer.

If you can understand Russian, there's a large choice of **Russian-language tours** available from the **Moscow City Bureau for Excursions**, at ul. Rozhdestvenka 5, behind *Detskiy Mir* (daily 10am–2pm & 3–6pm; ☎921 72 04). You can sign up for a whiz around the Kremlin or Moscow at their outdoor stand near the Historical Museum on Red Square; ask their office on Rozhdestvenka about literary, historical and architectural walking tours, or excursions to Vladimir and Suzdal.

Maps

The **maps** in this book should be fine for most purposes, but it's worthwhile investing in a

MAP OUTLETS

UK and Ireland

Blackwell's Map and Travel Shop, 53 Broad St, Oxford OX1 3BQ ☎01865/792792; *www.bookshop.blackwell.co.uk*

Daunt Books, 83 Marylebone High St, London W1M 3DE ☎020/7224 2295; 193 Haverstock Hill, NW3 4QL ☎020/7794 4006.

Easons Bookshop, 40 O'Connell St, Dublin 1 ☎01/873 3811; *www.eason.ie*

Heffers Map and Travel, 3rd Floor, in Heffers Stationery Department, 19 Sidney St, Cambridge CB2 3HL ☎1223/568467; *www.heffers.co.uk*

James Thin Melven's Bookshop, 29 Union St, Inverness IV1 1QA ☎01463/233500; *www.jthin.co.uk*

John Smith and Sons, 57–61 St Vincent St, Glasgow G2 5TB ☎0141/221 7472, *malcolm.heroine@jthin.co.uk*; *www.johnsmith.co.uk*

National Map Centre, 22–24 Caxton St, London SW1H 0QU ☎020/7222 2466; *www.mapsworld.com*

Newcastle Map Centre, 55 Grey St, Newcastle upon Tyne NE1 6EF ☎0191/261 5622, *nmc@enterprise.net*; *www.newtraveller.com*

Stanfords, 12–14 Long Acre, London WC2E 9LP ☎020/7836 1321; maps can be ordered on this number or via email: *sales@stanfords.co.uk*. Other branches within Campus Travel at 52 Grosvenor Gardens, London SW1W 0AG ☎020/7730 1314; British Airways at 156 Regent St, London W1R 5TA ☎020/7434 4744; and 29 Corn Street, Bristol BS1 1HT ☎0117/929 9966.

The Map Shop, 30a Belvoir St, Leicester LE1 6QH ☎0116/2471400.

The Travel Bookshop, 13–15 Blenheim Crescent, London W11 2EE ☎020/7229 5260; *www.thetravelbookshop.co.uk*

Waterstone's, 91 Deansgate, Manchester M3 2BW ☎0161/837 3000, *enquiries@waterstones-manchester-deansgate.co.uk*; *waterstones.co.uk*; plus branches across Britain and at Queens Bldg, 8 Royal Ave, Belfast BT1 1DA ☎028/9024 7355.

US

Book Passage, 51 Tamal Vista Blvd, Corte Madera, CA 94925 ☎415/927-0960; ☎1-800/999-7909; *www.bookpassage.com*

The Complete Traveler Bookstore, 3207 Fillmore St, San Francisco, CA 92123 415/923-1511.

The Complete Traveller Bookstore, 199 Madison Ave, New York, NY 10016 ☎212/685-9007.

Elliott Bay Book Company, 101 S Main St, Seattle, WA 98104 ☎1-800/962-5311; 206/624-6600; *www.elliottbaybooks.com*

detailed street plan of Moscow if you're staying outside the centre, or for a long time. The most commonly found in the West are two identically entitled fold-out plans called the *Moscow City Map*. Both are 1:20,000 scale and cover the entire city; a metro plan, blow-up maps of the Kremlin and the VVTs are likewise a feature of both. You may also run across the older *New Moscow City Map and Guide*, which comes in fold-out or laminated wall chart form (published by Russian Information Services, Inc., Montpelier, VT).

In Moscow, some or all of these maps are available at Sheremetevo-2 airport, the *Travellers Guesthouse* (p.319) and English-language bookshops (p.372), while a variety of **locally produced maps** are sold from newspaper and souvenir kiosks all over town. If you can read Cyrillic, the handiest is the pocket-sized *Atlas Moskva*, which has the advantage of not revealing anyone consulting it as a foreigner. You can buy one in almost any metro station. Alternatively, there's the fold-out 1:45,000 *Karta Moskva*, that's annually updated and shows overground **transport routes** (which don't feature in the *Atlas*) – although it's seldom that you'll need to use any other form of transport than the metro, for which our colour map should be more than adequate;

Forsyth Travel Library, 226 Westchester Ave, White Plains, NY 10604 ☎1-800/367-7984; *www.forsyth.com*

Map Link Inc., 30 S La Patera Lane, Unit 5, Santa Barbara, CA 93117 ☎805/692-6777; *www.maplink.com.*

The Map Store Inc., 1636 I St NW, Washington, DC 20006 ☎1-800/544-2659 or 202/628-2608.

Phileas Fogg's Books & Maps, #87 Stanford Shopping Center, Palo Alto, CA 94304 ☎1-800/533-FOGG.

Rand McNally, 444 N Michigan Ave, Chicago, IL 60611 ☎312/321-1751; 150 E 52nd St, New York, NY 10022 ☎212/758-7488; 595 Market St, San Francisco, CA 94105 ☎415/777-3131. *More than 20 stores across the US; call ☎1-800/333-0136 ext 2111 or check www.randmcnally.com for other locations, or for direct mail maps.*

Sierra Club Bookstore, 6014 College Ave, Oakland, CA 94618 ☎510/658-7470; *www.sierraclubbookstore.com*

Travel Books & Language Center, 4437 Wisconsin Ave, Washington, DC 20016 ☎1-800/220-2665.

Canada

Open Air Books and Maps, 25 Toronto St, Toronto, ON M5C 2R1 ☎416/363-0719.

Ulysses Travel Bookshop, 4176 St-Denis, Montréal PQ H2W 2M5 ☎514/843-9447; *www.ulyssesguides.com*

World Wide Books and Maps, 1247 Granville St, Vancouver BC V6Z 1G3 ☎604/687-3320.

Australia

Mapland, 372 Little Bourke St, Melbourne ☎03/9670 4383.

Perth Map Centre, 1/884 Hay St, Perth ☎08/9322 5733.

The Map Shop, 6 Peel St, Adelaide ☎08/8231 2033.

Travel Bookshop, Shop 3, 175 Liverpool St, Sydney ☎02/9261 8200.

Walkers Bookshop, 96 Lake Street, Cairns ☎07/4051 2410.

Worldwide Maps and Guides, 187 George St, Brisbane ☎07/3221 4330.

New Zealand

Specialty Maps, 46 Albert St, Auckland ☎09/307 2217.

Mapworld, 173 Gloucester St, Christchurch ☎03/374 5399, fax 03/374 5633, *maps@mapworld.co.nz*; *www.mapworld.co.nz*

there are also maps posted in stations and carriages.

Addresses

The street name is always written before the number in **addresses**. When addressing letters, Russians start with the country, followed by a six-digit postal code, then the street, house and apartment number, and finally the addressee's name; the sender's details are usually written at the bottom of the envelope. The number of the house, block or complex may be preceded by *dom*, abbreviated to *d.* Two numbers separated by an oblique dash (for example, 16/21) usually indicates a corner, the second number being the address on the smaller side street. However, buildings encompassing more than one number are also written like this (for example, 4/6); you can tell when this is the case as the numbers will be close to each other and both even or both odd. Blocks sharing the same number are identified as *stroenie* or *str*, *korpus* or *k.* indicates a building within a complex; *podezd* (abbreviated to *pod.*) an entrance number, *etazh* (*et.*) the floor and *kvartira* (*kv.*) the apartment.

Floors are numbered in the American or continental fashion: the ground floor is known as the first floor (*1-y etazh*) – a usage followed in this book to avoid confusion. In residential buildings, the lift may be located on a landing up the stairs from the entrance, and the outer door may be locked by a device that requires you to punch in a code. **Door codes** usually have three digits; you have to push all three buttons simultaneously to make it work. In some flats they're connected to an entry-phone.

The main **abbreviations** used in Moscow (and in this book) are: *ul.* (for *ulitsa*, street); *nab.* (for *naberezhnaya*, embankment); *pr.* (for *prospekt*, avenue); *per.* (for *pereulok*, lane); and *pl.* (for *ploshchad*, square). Other **terms** include *most* (bridge), *bulvar* (boulevard), *shosse* (highway), *alleya* (alley), *tupik* (cul-de-sac) and *sad* (garden).

Virtually all **street names** in central Moscow have reverted to their pre-Revolutionary form, though you may still hear some Soviet names used in everyday speech. It's indicative of the difference between the two cities that Moscow's street signs are in Cyrillic only, whereas St Petersburg has bilingual ones. One final oddity is that some names are preceded by an **ordinal number**, for example: 2-y Kadashevskiy per. 1-ya or 1-y (pronounced *pérvaya* or *pérviy*) mean "1st"; 2-ya or 2-y (*vtóraya* or *vtóriy*) "2nd", and so on. This usually applies to a series of parallel lanes or side streets.

Cyrillic address terms

alleya	аллея	pereulok	переулок
bulvar	бульвар	ploshchad	площадь
dom	дом	prospekt	проспект
etazh	этаж	sad	сад
kvartira	квартира	shosse	шоссе
most	мост	tupik	тупик
naberezhnaya	набережная	ulitsa	улица

Street names are listed in Cyrillic and English at the end of each chapter in the Guide.

Costs, money and banks

Successive booms and slumps during the 1990s have shown the folly of trying to predict the future of Russia's economy, but one feature that's likely to remain is the infuriating two-tier price system used by museums, hotels and theatres, and on some long-distance trains and internal flights, whereby foreigners are charged anything from two to ten times what locals pay. In other spheres they pay the same and competition prevails, so it's worth shopping around for all consumer goods and services.

For the sake of convenience and security, you should bring a mixture of US dollars or Deutschmarks in cash, American Express travellers' cheques, and a widely accepted debit or credit card, which should be carried in a moneybelt worn under your clothing.

The following will give you a general idea about how much you are likely to spend during a visit but for more detail you'll need to refer to the relevant listings chapters of the book, such as "Accommodation" and "Eating and drinking".

Package tourists with prepaid accommodation including full- or half-board really only need money for tickets to museums and palaces, buying gifts and grabbing the odd snack or drink. Unless you go overboard in expensive places, £25/$40 a day should suffice. Independent travellers will of course have to add accommodation costs and food on top of this figure, and for those on a tight budget, staying in a hostel is inevitable.

Staying in a fancy hotel and frequenting only upmarket restaurants and bars, you'll soon realize why businesspeople rate Moscow the most expensive city in the world after Tokyo, so the sky's the limit, really. Alternatively, if you stay with a family and do what the Russians do, you could spend £40/$64 a day or less on the whole works – lodging, food and drink – and by renting a flat you could cut this down to £20/$35.

Currency

Since the **ruble** was revalued in 1998, the denominations in circulation are coins of 5, 10 and 50 kopeks (100 kopeks equals one ruble) and 1, 2 and 5 rubles; and notes of 5, 10, 50, 100 and 500 rubles. In the unlikely event of you being palmed off with "old" rubles (recognizable by their strings of noughts), these are supposedly exchangeable in banks until the end of 2002, but have already vanished from circulation and are no longer legal tender.

Given that anything might happen to the ruble during the lifetime of this edition, **all prices in this book** are quoted in US dollars at the rate of exchange at the time of writing – but you will be expected to pay in rubles at the current rate, unless the transaction is with a private individual such as a landlord, who may well prefer to receive hard currency. To find out the exchange rate set by the Central Bank, check at any bank or in the financial section of the *Moscow Times* or *Russia Journal*.

Although almost everywhere specifies prices in rubles, a few restaurants, bars and hotels quote them in so-called **"standard units"** (*uslovnye yedenitsy*, abbreviated to УЕ in Cyrillic), which basically means dollars, converted into rubles. So far as restaurants go, this is often an indication that the establishment is way overpriced, and best avoided by visitors.

Currency declaration

Despite talk of abolishing the system, visitors arriving in Russia should still assume that they'll have to fill in a **currency declaration** form stating exactly how much money they are carrying, and listing valuables such as gold jewellery, video cameras, laptop computers and mobile phones (the latter under the heading "high-frequency radio-electronic devices and means of communication"). Upon leaving Russia, you're obliged to fill in a duplicate form and show both forms to customs – although since it is now okay to take out up to $500 without any declaration, it isn't necessarily a major problem if you lose the original form.

Changing money

As the **black market** is now a thing of the past and the exchange rate (*kurs*) is determined by market forces, there's no reason to change money anywhere other than in an official bank or a **currency exchange bureau** (*obmen valuty*). These are to be found all over town, including inside shops and restaurants (they usually stay open the same hours as the establishment). Most **banks** set fairly similar rates, but it's worth seeking out the best one if you're changing a lot of money at once, or currencies that aren't in much demand on Moscow's money markets. The various rates are listed in the financial sections of the *Moscow Times* and *Russia Journal*. Commission should be negligible. You'll need your **passport** for any exchange of currency.

Though basically straightforward, there are a few snags to **changing money**. Most exchange offices only handle US dollars or Deutschmarks, so other currencies must be exchanged in a regular bank. Due to widespread counterfeiting, dollars are only accepted if they're in good condition, and printed since 1990 in the case of $50 and $100 bills. Likewise, be on your guard against receiving any unusable notes in return. The only time you should ever **change unofficially** is with friends, having first checked the rate in a bank and making sure that you're both happy with the deal.

Surplus rubles can be converted back into hard currency at most banks, for which you'll need your passport and currency declaration. Better, though, to spend your rubles before you go, or give them to beggars.

Travellers' cheques, credit cards and ATMs

Despite very few banks or exchange bureaux accepting them, it's wise to carry some of your funds in **American Express travellers' cheques**, which if lost or stolen can be replaced by their Moscow office on the Garden Ring, ten minutes' walk from Mayakovskaya metro (Sadovaya-Kudrinskaya ul. 21a; ☎755 90 00; *www.americanexpress.com;* Mon–Fri 9am–7pm, Sat 10am–2pm). If you can't get through during office hours, call their 24-hour international refund **hot line** for Amex traveller's cheques (☎8 10 44/1273 571600) or credit cards (☎8 10 44/1273 696933). Replacing either will take up to a week. Amex will give you dollars for your travellers' cheques or as an advance on your credit card, but you'll have to exchange these for rubles at a bureau de change (there's one inside the Amex office but it gives a poor rate). Other brands of traveller's cheques can't be replaced in Moscow.

Credit cards have more utility in Moscow than anywhere else in Russia, but you should never take it for granted that you can pay by card and always check that your particular card is taken. Visa, Mastercard and Cirrus are the most widely accepted. You will usually need to show your passport or some other form of identification. Always make sure that the transaction is properly recorded and keep the receipt. Visa and Eurocheque cardholders will find it relatively easy to get **cash advances** (in rubles); even small bureaux de change tend to offer this service (you'll need your passport). Mastercard and other major credit cards are generally accepted only at the larger banks. The commission fee varies from bank to bank; Visa advances from AlfaBank are commission-free.

With a valid credit or debit card you can also make cash withdrawals from **ATM**s (*bankomaty* in Russian). Of the several hundred in Moscow, most are in banks or stores and only accessible during working hours, but you're rarely that far from a **24-hour** ATM in the city centre. To gain access to some, you need to swipe or insert your card in a slot by the door. All MostBank ATMs accept Visa, Eurocard, Mastercard, American Express, Union Card, Cirrus and Plus; AlfaBank takes Visa, MC, Union Card, Maestro and Cirrus. Visa cardholders can find a complete list of ATMs that accept them on the Web site *www.visa.com*. Nowadays, few ATMs pay out in **dollars** as well as rubles (unlike a few years ago), but you can still get this service from Rosbank at Tverskaya ulitsa 15 (near the Night Flight club) and in the *Slavjanskaya Hotel*, or AlfaBank on the corner of ulitsa Kuznetskiy most and ulitsa Neglinnaya, or in the *Grand Hotel* on Tverskaya ulitsa (all 24hr).

A **warning** is in order, however. Banks' securi-

Essential terms in Cyrillic	
ATM (bank machine)	Банкомат
currency exchange	обмен валюты
convertible currency	СКВ
standard units	УЕ
buying rate	покупка
selling rate	продажа
exchange rate	курс

ty systems have been penetrated and clients' accounts cleaned out as recently as 1999, so it would be prudent to use a debit or credit card with a relatively low limit, and keep the receipts for every withdrawal that you make. Russian experts in bank fraud recommend that one eschews ATMs in favour of cash advances from a bank teller – but then again, the last sting on 250 Visa and Europay users was thought to have been an inside job at Sberbank. Also beware of deactivated ATMs, belonging to banks that went under during the crash of 1998.

Transferring money to Russia from abroad is quite feasible, as most British and American banks now have an agreement with one of the Russian banks. One of the easiest methods is to use Western Union, who will transfer money in your name to specific banks in Moscow (for a full list, ☎119 82 50 or see *www.westernunion.com*). With all transfers you should check beforehand exactly how much it will cost you, as both the Russian and British or American bank will levy a fee.

Health

Because of previous health scares, visitors to Moscow and other cities in western Russia are advised to get booster shots for diphtheria, polio and tetanus, but there's no need to be inoculated against typhoid and hepatitis A unless you're planning to visit remote rural areas. Though there's no danger of malaria, mosquitoes can be fierce during the summer, so a good repellent or a mosquito net is advisable. The most likely hazard for a visitor, however, is an upset stomach, caused by the food or water. To play safe, wash fresh fruit and vegetables in boiled water; treat dairy products with caution in the summer; and watch out for bootleg liquor (see p.336).

Specific problems: pollution, dirt and stress

Moscow's **water** supply is obtained from four reservoirs outside the city rather than the polluted Moskva River, but even so, few Muscovites will drink tap water unless it has been boiled first. It is regarded with particular suspicion in the spring, when the melting snow cover is believed to cause manure and other pollutants to enter the reservoirs. To play safe, use only bottled water for drinking and cleaning your teeth, or tap water that has been boiled for fifteen minutes and then allowed to stand overnight. Bottled water is widely available in kiosks and supermarkets.

While the authorities maintain that the concentrations of heavy metals, nitrates, phenol, ammonia and other chemicals in the water supply are well below the limits set by the World Health Organization, **air pollution** is acknowledged as a serious problem. In many areas of Moscow, the level is thirty to fifty times above WHO limits – or even higher. Though brief exposure shouldn't do you any harm, visitors may feel inexplicably tired after a day or two, while long-term residents can suffer from apathy and skin complaints as a result.

The commonest visitor's ailment is **diarrhoea**, caused by spoilt food or poor hygiene. While restaurants and cafés are generally safe, street food should be regarded with more caution. While on the streets, moreover, it's hard to escape from **dirt**, as practically every surface is covered with dust, mud or grime, according to the season. Always wash your hands before eating or preparing food, and don't use the reusable towels in restaurants or public toilets.

Anyone staying in Moscow for several months or longer should beware of **other, subtler malaises**. As winter lasts up to six months, you can easily get run-down owing to a lack of vitamins, and depressed by the darkness and ice. According to a survey of Moscow's expat community, the chief problems are alcoholism, nervous breakdowns and sexually transmitted diseases. A lot of this stems from the stress of living in an exhilarating, brutal and bewildering city, where foreigners can take little for granted. If you're going to be here a while, pace yourself and adapt to the rhythms of Russian life. Because Moscow is, as Russians say, "without limits", you must determine your own in order to stay sane here. **Aids**, especially, is a real danger, with HIV spreading fast among prostitutes and their clients.

Pharmacies, doctors and hospitals

For minor complaints, it's easiest to go to a high-street **pharmacy** (*aptéka*), which will stock a good selection of imported drugs; most are open daily from 8am to 9pm and identifiable by the green cross sign. It goes without saying, however, that if you are on any prescribed medication, you should bring enough supplies for your stay. This is particularly true for diabetics, who should ensure that they have enough needles.

The standard of **doctors** varies enormously, so seek recommendations from friends or acquaintances before consulting one. Some specialists are highly skilled diagnosticians, who charge far less for a private consultation than you'd pay in the West. If your condition is serious, public **hospitals** will provide free emergency treatment to foreigners on production of a passport (but may charge for medication). However, standards of hygiene and care are low by Western standards and horror stories abound. Long-term expats advise, "Get an interpreter first and then a doctor."

Aside from routine shortages of anaesthetics and drugs, nurses are usually indifferent to their

Ambulances

Public ambulances (☎03) leave much to be desired. There are more reliable fee-paying services attached to the American Medical Center, the Athens Medical Center and Mediclub Moscow (see below).

Contact lenses and sundries

Optika, Frunzenskaya nab. 54 ☎242 30 69. Mon–Fri 10am–7pm, Sat 11am–5pm.

Optikor, Nikoloyamskiy per. 3a, korpus 2 ☎911 96 16. Mon–Fri 10am–5pm, Sat 10am–3pm.

Videoekologiya, Tverskaya ul. 12, block 7, entrance 11 ☎209 48 69. Mon–Fri 10am–1pm & 2–5pm, Sat 10am–4pm.

Medical and dental care

Adventist Health Centre, pr. 60-Letiya Oktyabrya 21a ☎126 79 06. Dentistry. Mon–Thurs 10am–7pm, Fri 9am–1pm, Sun 10am–5pm.

American Medical Center (AMC), Grokholskiy per. 1 ☎956 33 66 (24hr). Almost Western-style medical and dental care at very high prices; OK if you're insured. Consultants work 8am–8pm.

Athens Medical Center, Michurinskiy pr. 6 ☎147 93 22 or 143 23 87. Private clinic with a 24-hour emergency service and a well-equipped ambulance. Mon–Fri 9am–5pm.

Delta Consulting Group, pr. Mira 69, 3rd floor ☎ 937 64 88 or 937 64 50. 24-hour medical evacuation service.

Dental Invest, ul. Kuznetskiy most 9/10 ☎923 53 22. Mon–Fri 8.30am–9pm, Sat 9am–5pm.

European Medical Centre, Konyushkovskaya ul. 34 ☎254 06 60 (24hr). French joint-venture similar to the AMC, plus a pharmacy. Dentists ☎254 53 11. Mon–Fri 9am–6pm, Sat 9am–1pm.

Intermed, ul. Durova 26, k. 1, 5 ☎971 28 36. Eastern medicine and dentistry with Chinese specialists. Mon–Fri 8.30am–7.30pm.

Medical-Biological Centre "Pasteur", Bolshaya Cheremushkinskaya ul. 28 ☎124 87 44. Testing for urino-genital and other bacteriological problems. Mon–Fri 9am–2pm & 3–7pm, Sat 10am–6pm. Also has veterinary service ☎124 71 28.

Mediclub Moscow, Michurinskiy pr. 56 ☎931 50 18. Canadian joint-venture with family doctor, testing facilities, pharmacy and ambulance (24hr).

US Dental Care, ul. Shabolovka 8, k. 3 ☎931 99 09. Mon–Sat 8am–8pm.

Pharmacies

Besides the following, there are pharmacies in Mediclub Moscow, the American and European Medical Centres (see above).

Domashnaya Meditsina, ul. Tverskaya 12, str. 8 ☎209 38 53. Mon–Fri 9am–8pm, Sat 10am–2pm & 2.45–6pm.

Doktor-N, Sadovaya-Kudrinskaya ul. 8/12 ☎208 25 81. Daily 8am–8pm. Homeopathic pharmacy.

Eczacibasi, ul. Maroseyka 2/15 ☎928 91 89. Mon–Fri 8.30am–8pm, Sat & Sun 10–6pm.

International Pharmacy, Gruzinskiy per. 3, korpus 2 ☎254 49 46. Mon–Fri 10am–8pm, Sat 10am–6pm.

Stariy Arbat, ul. Arbat 25 ☎921 71 01. Mon–Fri 8am–8pm, Sat & Sun 10am–8pm.

patients unless bribed to care for them properly. Anyone found to be **HIV-positive** or carrying an **infectious disease** like hepatitis risks being confined in a locked isolation ward and treated like a subhuman. If you suspect such a condition and need to see a doctor, leave Russia at once.

Consequently, foreigners tend to rely on **private clinics** with imported drugs and equipment, which charge American rates – a powerful reason to take out insurance. There are now so many in Moscow that foreign embassies no longer feel obliged to let tourists in need consult their staff doctors.

Post, phones and the media

Telecommunications and the media are among the strongest sectors of the Russian economy and crucial to Moscow's business world, so international communications have never been better. However, some things still suck and unpredictability still rules, so don't assume that things will go smoothly. The media, especially, has its disappointments for visitors – especially TV – and unless you can read Russian, local English-language papers will be your chief source of information.

Post

The Russian **postal system** is notoriously inefficient and old-fashioned. Incoming international mail takes up to three weeks to arrive and anything of value will surely be stolen, while the outbound service is even less reliable. As a result, most Russians entrust letters with someone travelling to the West, for safer postage there, or employ an international courier firm or mail service (see below).

Assuming you decide to risk the postal system, all district post offices have **poste restante** (*do vostrébovaniya*) sections. If not, you can receive mail sent via the British or US offices of Global Post (PO Box 426, 37 Store St, London WC1E 7BS; 666 Fifth Ave, Suite 426, New York NY 10103) or mail services in Moscow such as PX Post (see below), or to American Express at Sadovaya-Kudrinskaya ul. 21, 103001, which holds mail for their clients for up to two months. Write "c/o [the firm]" after the addressee's name.

So far as post offices go, the most centrally located poste restante facilities are in the **Central Telegraph Office** (*tsentrálniy telegráf*) at Tverskaya ul. 7, 103009 (Mon–Fri 8am–2pm & 3–9pm, Sat 8am–2pm & 3–7pm, Sun 9am–2pm & 3–7pm; ☎924 90 04, fax 292 65 11), or the **Intourist Hotel post office** (Mon–Fri 9am–1pm & 2–5pm, Sat 9am–1pm & 2–4pm) just down the road at Tverskaya ul. 3/5, rather than the **Main Post Office** (*glávniy póchtamt*) at Myasnitskaya ul. 26/2, 101000 (daily 8am–8pm; ☎924 66 00), near Chistye Prudy metro. The **International Post Office** at Varshavskoe shosse 37 (daily 8.30am–7pm; ☎114 46 45) is even further out, so seldom used by visitors.

Parcels must be taken to the Main or International post office unwrapped; there they'll be inspected and wrapped for you, whereupon you can send them from any post office, or by courier (see below). If you only want stamps, it's easier to go to the postal counters in hotels like the *Intourist* or *Moskva*, rather than queue in a post office, though there's a mark-up on the price.

For more reliable international post, there are **mail services**. If you don't mind delivery in three or four days, the cheapest option (£3/$5) for letters under 500g is EMS Garantpost at any post office – though they don't like parcels. Otherwise compare rates at Global Post (Leninskiy pr. 45, office #427 ☎135 11 72) and PX Post (ul. Zorge 10, korpus 125 ☎956 22 30, *sales@pxpost.com*; *www.pxpost.com*), where regular customers can get discounts by opening a mailbox account. Pricier **courier firms** include DHL (*Slavjanskaya Hotel* ☎941 84 17; AlphaGraphics in the Okhotniy ryad mall), Federal Express (Aviatsionniy per. 8/17 ☎234 34 00 free pick-up, *euromaster@fedex.com*; *www.fedex.com*), Pony Express (MGU "Vysokie energii" Bldg. room #407 ☎930 20 80, *sales@ponyexpress.ru*; *www.ponyexpress.ru*) or TNT (ul. Arbat 46 ☎241 62 32; ul. Svobody 31 ☎797 27 28, *tnt@tnt.com*; *www.tnt.com*).

Signs			
Communications centre	Переговорный пункт	International telephone	Международный телефон
Fax	Факс	Internet	Интернет
Email	Электронная почта	Local telephone	Таксофон *or* телефон
Intercity telephone	Междугородный телефон	Post office	Почта
		Poste restante	До Востребования

Phones

Public phones taking phonecards have largely superseded the old-style payphones that used *zhetony* (tokens). The most common type is the blue MTTS phone, found in metro stations and other public places, which can be used for local, intercity or international calls; press the black-flagged button for instructions in English. Metro stations and some kiosks sell MTTS phonecards; a 60-unit card costs the equivalent of £1.50/$3. In hotels, you may also find other phones taking specific phonecards sold on the spot for a hefty mark-up, which are best avoided unless there's no alternative.

Nowadays it's possible to call just about any country direct. To **make a direct international call** dial 8, wait for the tone to change and then dial 10, followed by the country code number and area code (omitting any initial zero). Calls placed through the international operator (☎8-190) cost twice as much as those dialled direct and may take a couple of hours to come through. To call anywhere in Russia, or most of the former Soviet republics (except the Baltic States), dial 8 followed by the city code (including the initial zero).

If you're lucky enough to have access to a private phone, local calls are still virtually free for domestic subscribers, and the rates for intercity and international calls are as low as you'll get. If you don't have access to a private phone, you can go to a communications centre (*peregovórniy punkt*) – there's one in every district. The main ones are the **Central Telegraph Office** (see "Post") and the **House of Communications** (*Dom Svyázi*) at ul. Noviy Arbat 22, both of which are open 24 hours. Each has card-phones that can be used for direct-dialling abroad; cards are sold on the spot. Alternatively, you can prepay from the international calls desk and wait for your name and booth number to be announced over the Tannoy. The latter method is cheaper, costing about the same as from a private phone.

You can also economize using **international discount phonecards** issued by Dentel (sold at AlfaBank branches), Kontakt or Tario.net (both from PC or mobile phone stockists) – although they can only be used with push-button (not dial) phones. First you ring the firm's number, then switch the phone from pulse to tone, tap in your PIN number, and finally the number that you want to call. This is cheaper than using the Comstar phones in the lobbies of major hotels, which take prepaid cards (sold on the spot) or Amex, Visa or JCB **credit cards** – although Comstar rates are still a lot less than calling through a hotel switchboard or business centre, which may cost up to $25 a minute. The final option (mainly useful for calling the USA) is the so-called **country direct service**, whereby you call a toll-free number in Moscow and get connected to a US operator who can place collect calls (for which you don't need a card – the recipient is billed) or chargecard calls to the USA, and occasionally other countries. Companies offering this service are AT&T (☎755 55 55), Sprint (☎155 61 33 or 155 40 50) and MCI (☎8 10 800 497 72 22).

Mobile phones are widely used in Moscow, but anyone bringing a mobile to Russia should check with their phone company that it will work there, and be certain to list it on their customs declaration (see p.47). Since roaming **tariffs** are extremely high, visitors who intend to use a mobile extensively, or over several months, will save money by renting a phone from one of the many local dealers. Tariffs appear on the Web sites of GSM (*www.nwgsm.com)* and Delta Telecom (*www.deltatelecom.com*).

Under the current **banding system**, the cheapest times to call are between 10pm and 8am on weekdays, and any time on Saturday and

Direct dialling codes

To Moscow		From Moscow	
From Britain	☎00 7 095	Australia	☎8 (pause) 10 61
From Ireland	☎00 7 095	Ireland	☎8 (pause) 10 353
From the US & Canada	☎011 7 095	New Zealand	☎8 (pause) 10 64
From Australia & New Zealand	☎0011 7 095	UK	☎8 (pause) 10 44
		US & Canada	☎8 (pause) 10 1

Sunday; this applies equally to calls made from public phones, hotels, communications centres and mobiles. However, between 10 and 11pm it's hard to get a connection as the lines are so busy.

Always bear in mind the **time difference** when calling Russia from the West (3 hours ahead of GMT, 8 hours ahead of EST). Lines are at their busiest during UK or US office hours, but you'll have fewer problems getting through at, say, 7am in the UK – which is 10am in Moscow. Conversely, should you phone Moscow after 3pm UK time, everyone will have already left the office (it's acceptable to call people at home up to 11pm, local time).

Fax, email and the Internet

Given the inadequacy of the postal system, a lot of international communications are carried out by fax or email, and the Internet is rapidly expanding as a business and communications tool.

You can send a **fax** (*faks*) from almost any local post office or communications centre; international rates are $1–1.50 per page. Be sure to write the number exactly as it should be dialled (codes and all). It should be sent within a few hours, but confirmation is only supplied to customers who rent a mailbox at the branch.

Email (*elektronnaya pochta*) is generally faster, cheaper and more reliable in that you send it yourself. You can send emails from the Central Telegraph Office, the Main Post Office, district communication centres, business centres or Internet cafés. Rates vary, with business centres and hotels usually charging the highest rates. As with the **Internet**, the main problem is that most public facilities have PCs with tool bars and instructions in Russian, so unless you know the language or the system well they can be awkward to use – business centres and a very few Internet cafés are the exception.

If you bring your own PC to Russia and need to **get connected** to the Internet, you'll require an (American) Bell lead for your modem that can connect directly to a five-pinned Russian telephone plug, or a UK/Russian adaptor. Since AOL and Compuserve closed down their Russian gateways the field has been dominated by homegrown ISPs like Golden Telecom (Krasnokazarmennaya ul. 12a ☎787 10 00, *info@goldentelecom.ru*; *www.goldentelecom.ru*), Matrix (Leningradskiy pr. 53 ☎967 81 52, *support@matrix*; *www.matrix.ru*) or Russia-On-Line (Krasnokazarmennaya ul. 12a ☎258 41 61, *info@online.ru*; *www.online.ru*). Clients must open an account and choose between prepaying or buying Internet scratch-cards from a computer retailer, valid for a set number of hours' use. With these, you call up the ISP, give your account number and then the PIN number on the scratch-card, every time you go online. If you bring a computer into the country, make sure you write it in your customs declaration and avoid putting it through any X-ray machines (insist on a hand examination). When using a computer in Russia be wary of the fluctuations in the electricity current.

Business centres and Internet cafés

If you can afford their prices, **business centres** offer all communication links, photocopying and use of computers and printers, with English-speaking staff. They include the Americom Business Center in the *Radisson Slavjanskaya Hotel*, Berezhovskaya nab. 2 (☎941 84 27); Business Service in the *Savoy Hotel*, ul. Rozhdvestvenka 3 (☎929 75 71); the Metropol Business Center in the *Metropol Hotel*, Teatralniy proezd 1/4 (☎927 60 90); and Sovincenter in the *Mezhdunarodnaya Hotel*, Krasnopresnenskaya nab. 12 (☎253 28 84). However for printing and document processing, it's cheaper to use AlphaGraphics in the Okhotniy ryad mall on

Cyrillic script and the Internet

One difficulty with accessing Web sites and receiving emails from Russia is that there are two different systems for representing Cyrillic letters. One is the so-called **WIN encoding** (officially CP-1251), the other is the **KOI-8** system, favoured by Russians among themselves. PCs with Windows 98 or later have everything needed to handle either system, providing you activate your machine by following the simple instructions on Paul Gorodyansky's free site *http://ourworld.compuserve.com/homepages/PaulGor/*. This enables Outlook Express users to set up both their browser and email for Cyrillic, and Hotmail and Yahoo! users to read and write emails in Cyrillic. For those with Macs or PCs with Windows 95 or earlier, you need to install Cyrillic fonts from *http://funet.fi/pub/culture/russian/comp/fonts/fonts.html* or *http://babel.uoregon.edu/yamada/fonts/russian.html*, by changing the default font in your email programme. For Web page access, PC users with Windows 98 and Internet Explorer version 5.0 or later should follow Gorodyansky's instructions. With other browsers – including Netscape or any Mac software – you need to replace the existing default font by KOI-8 or WIN Cyrillic. If you receive a document composed of question marks you've been sent it in an unreadable "ornamental" Cyrillic font, and need to ask for it to be re-sent in Arial, Courier or some other standard font.

Manezhnaya ploshchad (which also has a DHL pick-up point), the Tverskoy Passazh at Tverskaya ul. 18, and other locations.

Though **Internet cafés** are mushrooming, the only places that have PCs with English text are Chevignon in the *Baza-14* store at Stoleshnikov per. 14 (daily 2–6pm; *base14@gin.global-one.ru*), which charges $4 per hour (30min free for any purchase at the bar), and the *Travellers Guesthouse* (see p.319), which charges $6.50. If you can handle Russian tool bars, rates fall to $3 an hour at such central venues as Club Kutuzovskiy Most (ul. Kutuzovskiy most 12 ☎924 21 40; *www.iclub.ru;* daily 10am–10pm), Ostrov Formoza, in the restaurant of the same name off Tverskaya ulitsa (Bolshoy Trehsyvatitelskiy per. 2, *café@formoza.ru*), or Nirvana (ul. Rozhdestvenka 29 ☎208 43 21; *www.nirvana.ru;* daily 10am–8am) – the last being the largest of Moscow's Internet cafés, with a restaurant attached. Magnit (ul. Tverskaya Zastava 3; *www.magnit.ru*; daily 24hr) and Tarantul (shosse Entuziastov 4a ☎278 91 53; *www.tarantulclub.narod.ru*; daily 24hr) are more games-oriented (although you can nevertheless send email there), while hourly rates at Nice (Dom Torgovliy, ul. 1905 goda, *info@nice.ru*; *www.nice.ru*; daily 24hr) are as low as $2 an hour at night.

The media

Much of Russia's **media** is controlled by the same oligarchs that own the country's banks and industries, whose battles are fought by their media proxies with blatant disregard for journalistic ethics. The main players are Boris Berezovsky, who controls ORT, TV6, TV Centre, *Kommersant* and *Nezavisimaya Gazeta*; Vladimir Gusinsky, whose MediaMOST group owns *Sevodnya*, *Igoti* and NTV; Uneximbank's Vladimir Potanin, who owns *Komsomolskaya Pravda*, *Izvestiya* and *Russkiy Telegraf*; and Mikhail Khodorkovsky of Bank Menatep, whose publications include the *Moscow Times* and the Russian *Cosmopolitan* and *Playboy*. Recently, both Gusinsky and Berezovsky have come under fire from the Kremlin, and the struggle for control of the media is one of the hottest issues in Russian politics.

Newspapers

If you can understand the language, the **Russian press** holds some surprises for those who remember it from olden days. *Izvestiya*, once the organ of the Soviet government and later pro-Yeltsin, has seen the breakaway *Novie Izvestiya* – Russia's first colour daily – take its best journalists and most of its readers away, despite financial backing from the oil giant LUKoil; *Pravda*, the old Party daily, has also split, with the original, still Communist paper suing the new, Greek-owned *Pravda-5* for the right to the name; and the erstwhile Young Communists' daily *Komsomolskaya Pravda* has become a popular tabloid backed by Uneximbank, Gazprom and Mayor Luzhkov. The elite themselves peruse

Kommersant, the most sober and insightful paper since *Nezavisimaya Gazeta*'s reputation for integrity succumbed to Berezovsky's patronage – while Russia's angry dispossessed buy *Sovetskaya Rossiya* or *Zavtra*, both unashamedly far right, xenophobic hate-sheets. However, Moscow's best-selling daily is a **local paper**, *Moskovskiy Komsomolets*, that specializes in crime, sex and showbiz scandals. Since one of its journalists was murdered after exposing corruption in the Army high command, the paper has shied away from serious investigative journalism.

While **foreign newspapers** aren't widely available in Moscow, you can be sure of finding them in major hotels at heavily marked-up prices, and often up to a week old. If you're staying a while and desperate to have foreign papers delivered, contact IPS (ul. 2ya Brestskaya 43 ☎250 42 72, *post@online.ru*).

Many tourists prefer the **local English-language press**, which is better distributed, free and up to date, if nothing else. The *Moscow Times* is a hardy perennial that appears every day except Monday and carries listings of what's on in its Friday and Saturday editions. Written for the expat business community, it combines local news with press agency reports and prim editorials. Similar but duller are the weekly English/German *Moscow Kurier* and the *Russia Journal*, whose LifeStyle supplement is a cross between the reviews in the *Times* and the racy listings in the *eXile* – an "alternative" paper published every other Wednesday, that flaunts its commitment to partying, whoring and drugs. Though sure to offend some, its view of Russia is a welcome affront to the bland consensus peddled by the others. All these papers are available free of charge at Western watering holes and eateries like the *American Bar & Grill*, *Starlite Diner* and *DeliFrance* (see Chapter 11 for addresses) – and you can also find the *Moscow Times* (*www.themoscowtimes.com*), the *Russia Journal* (*www.russiajournal.com*) and the *eXile* (*www.exile.ru*) **online**.

TV and radio

Russia's three main national **television** stations are at war over more than just ratings, as the Kremlin and media magnates Berezovsky and Gusinsky vie for the power to mould public opinion. **ORT** (Channel 1) is the nation's favourite for its soaps, game shows and classic Soviet films. Its support for Yeltsin and Putin swung their elections, making Berezovsky the kingmaker of Russian politics; but now he's at loggerheads with Putin, under the same pressure that was previously applied to Gusinsky (who spent three days in Moscow's infamous Butyurka prison) after his **NTV** (Channel 4) angered the Kremlin with its reportage of the war in Chechnya and the *Kursk* disaster. It also screens slick thrillers, drama and documentaries, putting it streets ahead of the wholly state-owned **RTR** (Channel 2), whose mixture of soaps, tedious state events and servile news gives it the lowest rating of the three. In any case, many viewers prefer the light entertainment stations **TVC** (Channel 3) and **TV6** (Channel 6), or switch over to **Kultura** (Channel 5) for more highbrow offerings. Additionally, there are half-a-dozen domestic **cable** stations that can only be received with special aerials in some parts of the city – including a Russian version of MTV and two film channels – plus such foreign imports as Sky, Eurosport, Pro7, BBC World and Discovery.

It's not exactly thrilling stuff: the big hits are soaps like *Santa Barbara* and game shows such as *Sto k Odnomu*. Though all six terrestrial channels regularly show **foreign movies** they are always dubbed into Russian, which can prove rather a barrier if you haven't seen the film before. A weekend TV guide appears in the Saturday edition of the *Moscow Times*.

As far as **radio** goes, most cafés and bars tune into Russkoe Radio (105.7 FM) for Russian teeny pop; Serebryaniy Dozhd (100.1 FM) for international chart music; Hit-FM (107.4 FM) for pop and rock; Radio Rox (103.0 FM) for rock; Radio Maximum (103.7 FM) for indie and electronic music; or Stanitsiya 2000 for techno. Other faves are Nostalgie (100.5 FM), playing French and other romantic music, and Retro (72.92 SW), devoted to Soviet songs from the 1930s to the 1980s. Should you have a short-wave radio, it is also possible to pick up the BBC World Service and Voice of America.

Opening hours, holidays and festivals

Shops in Moscow are generally open Monday to Saturday from 9am to 6 or 7pm, though some large stores stay open later than this and some neighbourhood shops stay open 24 hours. Most shops close for an hour or two for lunch between 1pm and 4pm. Sunday opening is erratic, with an increasing number of food shops, bars and restaurants choosing to open. As for the street kiosks in every neighbourhood, many stay open every day until 10pm, and some until the small hours.

Opening hours for **museums and galleries** tend to be from 10 or 11am to 5 or 6pm. They are closed one day a week, but there are no hard and fast rules as to what day that might be. In addition, one day in the month will be set aside as a *sanitarniy den* or "cleaning day". Full opening hours are detailed in the text. Note that some museums oblige visitors to take a guided **tour** and others have it as an option. You should assume it will be in Russian unless you take the trouble to arrange an English-speaking guide by phoning ahead, and even then it may depend on the museum's staffing roster. Some museums require visitors to put on *tapochki* (felt overshoes) to protect their parquet floors.

Almost all of the **churches** that were converted into museums or factories during Soviet times have now reverted to their original purpose, and are open for (and between) services. The morning liturgy (*liturgia*) – which commemorates the Last Supper – begins at 8 or 9am; there may also be an evening service (*vechernaya sluzhba*) at 5 or 6pm; both usually take about one and a half hours. Additional services may occur on saints' days (*Prestolniy prazdnik*), accompanied by processions. Orthodox believers cross themselves with three fingers (first the head, then the stomach, followed by the right shoulder and then the left). Visitors must dress modestly; women should wear headscarves, and men remove their hats in church.

The times of religious services in non-Orthodox Christian, Muslim and Jewish places of worship appear in the Thursday edition of the *Moscow Times*.

Public holidays

The list of **official public holidays** (*prazdnik*) combines some associated with the former Soviet regime with others of post- or pre-Soviet vintage. While traditional religious holidays such as Christmas and Easter have made a comeback, Good Friday is still a working day, much to the Church's annoyance. As Easter is a moveable feast according to the Orthodox calendar, it may

Public holidays

January 1 New Year's Day

January 6/7 Orthodox Christmas

February 23 Defenders of the Motherland Day

March 8 International Women's Day

May 1 and 2 International Labour Day/Spring Festival

May 9 Victory Day

June 12 Russian Day

November 7 Day of Reconciliation and Accord (formerly the anniversary of the October Revolution)

coincide with public holidays in May, giving rise to an extended holiday period of three to four days. It's also worth noting that if public holidays fall at the weekend a weekday will often be given off in lieu.

Festivals

Moscow's **festive calendar** is a fickle one. Years of profligate expenditure – such as the city's 850th anniversary celebrations in 1997 and the World Youth Games in 1998 – are followed by a drought as funding dries up; it all depends on Mayor Luzhkov and Kremlin politics. The absence of any central co-ordinating body or tourist office also means that it's nearly impossible to find out what's going to happen in advance; a contact address is usually the best you can hope for.

Bearing that in mind, it's best to start with the English-language press (see p.55), and keep a lookout for posters or banners advertising concerts and other events. It's also worth knowing about several historic sites that organize their own festivities, which get less publicity than they deserve. **Kolomenskoe** hosts a dozen events throughout the year (see p.262), while **Kuskovo** (p.285) and **Ostankino** (p.308) hold summer concerts and performances.

The main public spectacles are **City Day** on a Sunday in September, which sees a parade of floats down Tverskaya ulitsa followed by fireworks and perhaps a pop concert, and the **Russian Winter Festival** (Jan 1–5), when Red Square is transformed by amazing ice sculptures. Music festivals are varied but unpredictable, the most reliable being the international festival of **Orthodox church music** (late Jan/early Feb), and the **December Evenings** of classical music at the Pushkin Museum and other venues. Besides the main international **jazz** festival in spring or autumn (contact Vladimir Kaushansky ☎941 22 86, *mcla@cea.ru*), there are mini-festivals in the Hermitage Garden in late August (Mikhail Green ☎236 33 63, *mgreen@home.relline.ru*) and the Jazz Art Club (see p.356). The festival of **contemporary music** (mid-May to mid-June) brings together all kinds of avant-garde musicians, while Russia's top rock bands and DJs appear at the **Maxidrome** (last Sat in May) and **Maxidance** (no set date) festivals, sponsored by Radio Maximum. Last but not least, there's the **Tchaikovsky Competition**, the world's stiffest test of classical musicianship, held at the Conservatory every four years in June (next scheduled for 2002).

Moscow's international **film** festival is now an annual event (late June or Aug) that strives to attract foreign stars and directors as well as Russian ones; the main venue is the Pushkin cinema on Pushkinskaya ploshchad. For **drama** lovers, there's the Golden Mask festival honouring the previous year's best drama, opera, dance and puppetry productions in Russia (last week in Feb & first week in March), and the Chekhov International Theatre Festival, where troupes from different countries perform their interpretations of the master's works (every three years from April to June; next scheduled for 2001).

Although parades are now seldom held on Red Square, die-hard Communists still celebrate **May Day** by laying flowers at Lenin's Mausoleum, while the National Bolshevik Party rallies on Oktyabrskaya ploshchad on the **anniversary of the October Revolution** (Nov 7) – now euphemistically entitled the Day of Reconciliation and Accord. **Victory Day** (May 9), commemorating the surrender of the Nazis in 1945, is fervently marked by the older generation, with gatherings of bemedalled veterans in Victory Park and firework displays around the city. In 1995, the anniversary of the birth of the Red Army was resurrected as a holiday called **Defenders of the Motherland** Day (Feb 23), marked by wreath-laying ceremonies at the Tomb of the Unknown Soldier (near the Kremlin) and other war memorials.

During spring, the run-up to the Orthodox Easter overshadows the **Day of Slav Culture** (May 24), which isn't a holiday but is nonetheless marked by a procession of priests bearing icons from the Kremlin to the Cyril and Methodius statue on the edge of the Kitay-gorod. **Easter** (*Paskha*) is the highlight of the Orthodox calendar, with services and processions where celebrants exchange the salutation "Christ has risen" – "Verily, He has risen". Whereas Easter is a moveable feast whose date changes each year, the **Orthodox Christmas** (*Rózhdestvo*) service always starts at midnight on January 6 and goes on until dawn the following day. The choir, the liturgy, the candles and the incense combine to produce a hypnotic sense of togetherness, which Russians call *sobornost*. Despite their emotional charge and Byzantine splendour, Orthodox services are come-and-go as you please, allowing non-believers to attend without embarrassment, though women should cover their heads and avoid wearing trousers. At midnight, worshippers circle the church holding candles – an unforgettable sight.

Less obviously, there are also the religious festivals of other faiths. The synagogue on Bolshoy Spasoglinishchevskiy pereulok comes alive at Rosh Hashana, Yom Kippur, Hannuka and other **Jewish festivals**, while the mosque near the Olympic Sports Complex is the focus for **Ramadan** celebrations among the city's Muslim community.

Except among the expat community, the Western Christmas is passed over in the rush to prepare for **New Year** (*Noviy God*). Generally, this remains a family occasion until midnight, when a frenzied round of house-calling commences, people getting ever drunker and continuing until dawn. People also gather on Red Square to pop bottles of champagne as the Saviour clocktower tolls the New Year and fireworks explode overhead. In residential areas, people dressed as *Dyed Moroz* (Grandfather Frost, the Russian equivalent of Father Christmas) and his female sidekick, *Snegurochka* (Snow Maiden), do the rounds wishing neighbours Happy New Year (*s Novim Godom!*). To enjoy it all over again, many Russians also celebrate the Orthodox New Year or **Old New Year** on the night of January 13–14 – though this isn't an official holiday.

Lastly, there are a few **expatriate celebrations** worth noting, namely the **Independence Day** and **Bastille Day** festivities at Kuskovo, held on the Saturday and Sunday nearest to July 4 and July 14, respectively; plus wild **Halloween parties** at Westernized watering holes like *Moosehead* and *Churchill* (see the "Eating and drinking" and "Nightlife" chapters), as advertised in the *Moscow Times* and the *eXile*.

Popular culture: sport, music and the arts

The ending of censorship and the economic crises of the 1990s brought mixed blessings to sport, music and the arts, all of which enjoyed considerable state backing under the Soviet system. Many of the best artists, musicians and sporting figures have been lured to the West by the prospect of large earnings, leaving big gaps in the domestic scene, while imported films and sounds have reduced the demand for native offerings. On the other hand, players, directors and artists enjoy new possibilities for developing their careers and reaching a wider audience.

Sport

There were very few **sports** at which the former Soviet Union didn't excel, such was the money poured into the system, and the rewards of foreign travel available to successful athletes. In Moscow, however, there are only a couple of sports that command a mass popular following: soccer and ice hockey.

Soccer

Moscow has been at the forefront of Soviet and Russian **soccer** ever since the sport became popular in the 1920s, and the city's Dinamo team was founded as long ago as 1887. Despite the humiliation of seeing the long-despised St Petersburg club Zenit win the cup in 1999, Moscow fans remain confident in the ultimate supremacy of their home teams, Dinamo, Spartak, Lokomotiv and TsKA – although TsKA has yet to recover from a devastating bust-up in 1997. The football season runs from early March to early November, with a break in June if the national team have other commitments. There are two tournaments, running concurrently: the Russian Championship, starting in spring and ending in the autumn, and the Russian Cup, starting in the summer and ending the following summer. To find out more, see p.379 or visit the Russian Football Union's official Web site (*www.rfs.ru*); a schedule of matches for the year ahead can be found on *www.russianfootball.com*.

Ice hockey

Ice hockey is Russia's second most popular sport and Moscow is a major venue on the national and international circuit. Somewhat confusingly, the names of its major hockey clubs are the same as the city's soccer teams: Spartak, Dinamo and TsKA (which, like the football club, has also split into two rival teams and done disastrously ever since). The Spartak Cup in August is a pre-season tournament featuring the Russian All-Stars, top players from various teams in the National League, whose official season starts in September and culminates in the annual World Championships the following summer, when the Russians do their best to defeat Sweden, Canada and the US, usually playing abroad.

Music

Russia is one of the great musical nations of Europe, and Russians are justifiably proud of their **classical music** tradition. Tchaikovsky, Rimsky-Korsakov, Mussorgsky, Glinka, Stravinsky and Shostakovich are just some of the more famous figures closely associated with Moscow, and their music can still be heard regularly in concert halls across the city. Perhaps even more famous is the city's **Bolshoy ballet** (see p.359). Venues and festivals are detailed in Chapter 13, "The Arts".

One hears **folk music** in the city's metro subways throughout the year, as once-state-sponsored folk groups now busk for a living. The accordion and the balalaika are the mainstays of Russian folk music, but you'll see brass ensembles and manic fiddlers too. Travesties of folk songs and romances are often performed in restaurant floorshows, but a few of the ensembles are worth listening to. More rewarding are the so-called **bards** or singer-songwriters, who continue the satirical and bittersweet traditions of the great Soviet bards Alexander Gallach, Bulat Okudzhava and Vladimir Vysotsky. Contemporary exponents of the genre can be heard at the web site: *http//:Bard-cafe.komkon.org* or the Gnezdo Glukhanya in Moscow (see p.357).

Popular music

In a curious exception to their brilliance in other fields, Russian **pop** music is usually regarded by foreigners as dire – and that's too polite a word to describe the depths of bad taste plumbed by the giants of the scene, Alla Pugachova and Filipp Kirkorov. Alla gained national fame in the early 1980s and resembles a hybrid of Janis Joplin and Liberace, while Filipp is a six-foot-four, bug-eyed Adonis who sings and dresses like Elton John. They first met when he was an adoring schoolboy fan; their wedding in 1994 was like a coronation. Otherwise, the airwaves are dominated by girl and boy bands doing ultra bland Europop, with the Pulp-like exception of Mummi Troll from Vladivostok and the multi-instrumental Chiz, whose fusion of Celtic, Russian and Soviet **Roots** music and imagery fits the prevailing mood of retro-patriotism. **Rap** and **Hip-Hop** are also popular with young Muscovites; Delphin and Bogdan Titomir are the best-known artists.

Theatre and cinema

Moscow is the undisputed centre of Russian **theatre** (*teatr*), with over 150 playhouses ranging from the famous Moscow Art Theatre (MkhAT) where Chekhov and Stanislavsky made their names, to such cutting-edge companies as the Satirikon Theatre and the Theatre of Young Spectators (MTYuZ). Directors to look out for include Konstantin Raykin and Valery Fokin at the Satirikon, Vladimir Mirzoev at the Stanislavsky Drama Theatre, and Pyotr Fomenko at the Fomenko Studio. The Debut Centre is a showcase for up-and-coming new talent. For more details, see Chapter 13, "The Arts".

Since 80 percent of Russia's wealth is concentrated in Moscow, the capital's dominance over Russian **cinema** (*kino*) is even more pronounced. Unfortunately, the main beneficiary of all the dosh and political patronage is Nikita Mikhalkov, the Kremlin's favourite director, who is able to blow millions on dozy epics like *The Barber of Siberia* (in which his cameo role as Alexander III was about the only riveting moment) while other directors struggle to raise funds. However, the St Petersburg director Andrei Balabanov has made his name with box-office hits *Brother* and *Brother 2* – tales of sibling love and contract killing – and two critically acclaimed Grand Guignol dramas, *Of Beasts and Men* and Kafka's *The Castle*.

Security, police and the Mafia

It's a reflection of the new Russia that tourists no longer worry about hidden microphones or KGB agents, but muggers and mobsters. The Western media portray Moscow as a gangster-ridden city with shootings on every corner – an exaggeration of the situation when it was at its worst in the early 1990s, which ignores any improvements since then. However, visitors should certainly observe the usual precautions such as not flashing money or cameras around, or going off with strangers. Try to blend in wherever possible; the less you look like a tourist, the smaller the risk of being targeted by petty criminals.

Personal **security** in Moscow is generally in inverse proportion to personal wealth. The main targets of crime (both Mafia-related and petty) are rich Russian businessmen, next to whom tourists are considered small fry. While local financiers are in danger of assassination, the average citizen – or visitor – is no more likely to be a victim of crime than in any other large European city.

The police

The Ministry of the Interior (MVD) has several forces to maintain law and order, all of them armed. Foremost are the regular police, or **Militia** (*Militsiya*), which drives around in Ladas or imported patrol cars; they wear grey parkas or leather blouses, with a field cap or fur hat, depending on the season. Militiamen are much in evidence around metro stations, markets and on the streets, where they often conduct spot checks of people's identity papers.

The other main branch of the Militia is the **GIBDD**, or traffic police – still universally known by their former title, the **GAI**. This notoriously corrupt force is only a potential problem if you're driving or happen to be involved in an accident (see p.39). They wear Militia uniforms or grey jump suits emblazoned with an armband, badge or large white letters reading ГИБДД or ДПС (for *Dorozhno Patrulnaya Sluzhba* – Highway Patrol Service).

Under normal circumstances the paramilitary **OMON** are only seen guarding important state buildings or patrolling demonstrations and football matches, but they may be deployed in force during political crises or to lend muscle to Militia crackdowns on Mafia gangs. Dressed in green or grey camouflage and toting Kalashnikovs or pump-action shotguns, they look fearsome but are unlikely to bother tourists unless they get caught up in a raid of some kind. Should you be so unlucky, don't resist in any way – even verbally. The same goes for operations involving **RUOP**, the smaller Regional Force Against Organized Crime, whose teams wear civilian clothes or paramilitary uniform (like the OMON's, only the patch on the back reads РУОП instead of ОМОН.

Aside from having your passport scrutinized by a plainclothes agent at Sheremetevo airport, you shouldn't have any contact with the once-feared KGB in its post-Soviet incarnation as the **Federal Security Service (FSB)** unless you get involved in environmental activism or high-tech acquisitions. While it remains to be seen if the FSB will become more intrusive now that one of its own chiefs has become president, for the time being, its self-publicized coups of counter-espionage are so remote from everyday life that Russians are happy to ignore it. Visitors are free to do likewise, or saunter past the Lubyanka out of curiosity (taking photos is not advised).

You're far more likely to encounter **private security guards**, in banks, stores, clubs or restaurants. Many are ex-KGB or OMON goons who can be brusque with customers at the door, especially if there's a house policy of excluding people who don't fit the bill.

The Mafia

Throughout the former USSR, the term **Mafia** is loosely applied to all kinds of rackets and crimes, whether they involve a handful of perpetrators or gangs with hundreds of members in different cities. The catch-all usage reflects the fact that so many of them originated in the nexus between black marketeering and political power in Soviet times, when the vastness of the USSR and the vagaries of central planning fostered widespread corruption during the Era of Stagnation (see p.436). With the transition to capitalism the whole economy came up for grabs, as ex-Party bureaucrats acquired vast assets through privatization and black marketeers became merchant bankers. Legitimate entrepreneurs and foreign investors were forced to pay protection money to one gang or another, while in turn leading Mafiosi found their own protectors among the political elite, police and judiciary – resulting in everyone being covered by what Russians call a *krysha* (roof).

Given its manifold links with business and politics, organized crime seems set to remain a feature of society, but its manifestations may change as "first generation" Mafiosi seek a quieter life and Russia's financial and political power blocs mature. In Moscow, the frequency of shoot-outs (*razborki*) and car-bombs has considerably declined in the last few years, as the territories of rival gangs are by now well established.

Personal security

Unless you spend a lot of time in nightclubs frequented by low-grade mobsters, the only hazard you're likely to encounter is **petty crime**, such as thefts from cars and hotel rooms. Sensible precautions include making photocopies of your passport and visa, and noting down travellers' cheque and credit card numbers. If you have a car, don't leave anything in view when you park it. Vehicles without an alarm are regularly stolen and luggage and valuables make a tempting target, particularly from easily recognizable foreign and rental cars.

Though there's less risk of being **mugged** in Moscow than in, say, Miami, it's equally dangerous to resist, given the availability of firearms. Most crimes of this type are faced only by drunken tourists who follow prostitutes back to strange rooms or into a taxi late at night. You're far more likely to be at risk from **pickpockets** – particularly groups of street kids or gypsies, whose tactic is to rush in from all sides and pick your pockets while you're too shocked to resist – relying on their youth to inhibit any resistance, or escape prosecution if they're caught. Don't take pity on the gypsy children or give in to hassle from groups of women – they often simply note where you keep your money and somebody else gets you further down the street.

In the unlikely event of your stay coinciding with some kind of **civil unrest**, it's obviously best to avoid focal points like the White House or the Kremlin, and demonstrations anywhere. Tune into foreign radio or TV for news; the Russian stations will be censored. Real trouble should be localized in a few areas, with life continuing as normal elsewhere.

By law, you're supposed to carry some form of **identification** at all times, and the Militia can stop you in the street and demand it – dark-skinned people are especially likely to be stopped. Although the Militia should be satisfied with a cursory passport check, any irregularities in your visa – such as the lack of a registration stamp – might entail a trip to the police station or an on-the-spot "fine".

If you are unlucky enough to have something stolen, you will need to go to the police to report it, not least because your insurance company will require a police report. It's unlikely that there'll be anyone who speaks English, and even less likely that your belongings will be retrieved, but at the very least you should get a statement detailing what you've lost for your insurance claim. Try the phrase *Menya obokrali* – "I've been robbed". There are Militia departments in most metro stations and large hotels. If in serious trouble, phone Petrovka 38 – Moscow's equivalent of Scotland Yard – on their **24-hour hot line** (☎200 89 24 or 200 97 45); the operator will hopefully put you on to an English-speaking officer. The regular police **emergency number** is ☎02.

Women's Moscow

The "emancipation" of women under Communism always had a lot more to do with increasing the available workforce than with promoting equality or encouraging women to pursue their own goals. Although equal wages, maternity benefits and subsidized crèches were all prescribed by law, their provision fell far short of the ideal, saddling women with a double burden of child-care and full-time work. As a result, "feminism" is something of a dirty word in Russia, and self-proclaimed feminists will get short shrift from both sexes here.

As a visitor to Moscow, you will find that Russian men veer between extreme gallantry and crude chauvinism. Sexual harassment is marginally less of a problem than in Western Europe – and nowhere near as bad as in Mediterranean countries – but without the familiar linguistic and cultural signs, it's easy to misinterpret situations. Attitudes in Moscow are much more liberal than in the countryside, where women travelling alone can still expect to encounter stares and comments. Single women should nonetheless avoid going to certain nightclubs and bars, where their presence may be misconstrued by the local pimps and prostitutes. Although you'll see plenty of Russian women flagging down cars as potential taxis, unaccompanied foreign women would be ill-advised to do likewise.

Should the worst occur, support is available from a **24-hour English Crisis Line**: call the paging operator (☎ 564 82 82), give the code word "Crisis" and leave your phone number – someone will call you back soon.

Directory

BRING In summer bring a waterproof jacket or compact umbrella for occasional showers. In winter, late autumn and early spring, gloves, a hat or scarf that covers your face, and thick socks are essential. Thermal underwear goes a long way to keeping your legs warm, and a pair of boots with non-slip soles is recommended for the snow and ice. A pocket torch for dark stairwells also comes in handy.

CHILDREN Although children (*détey*) and babies are doted on by Russians, public facilities for younger children are thin on the ground. Most supermarkets stock baby food, but you may wish to bring a small supply with you to tide you over. Disposable nappies are readily available in many stores. Note that breast-feeding in public is totally unacceptable. Children up to the age of seven ride free on all public transport. For a list of places in Moscow that might appeal to children, see p.373.

CIGARETTES Nearly all Western brands are available, though many of the packets sold from kiosks are made under licence (or counterfeited) in Russia or Turkey, with a higher tar content than their foreign counterparts. Traditional Soviet brands like Belomor and TU-144 are truly revolting. Belomor are what are called *papirosi*, with an inch of tobacco at the end of a long cardboard tube, which is twisted to make a crude filter. The brand name Belomor celebrates the White Sea Canal – built by slave labour – a map of which decorates the packet. It is normal to be approached by strangers asking for a light (*Mózhno pokurit?*) or a cigarette. While museums, cinemas and public transport are no-smoking (*ne kurit*) zones, Russians puff away everywhere else, and see nothing wrong with it.

COMPUTERS If bringing a portable computer into the country, write it on your customs declaration. When using a computer in Russia, be wary of the fluctuations in the electricity current. The scores of computer dealers in Moscow will only honour guarantees on machines purchased in Russia. You can buy all kinds of software, both pirated and legit.

CONTRACEPTIVES Turkish-made condoms (*prezervativiy*) are available in most pharmacies and many booze shops, but are generally untrustworthy, so either bring your own or buy known brands in upmarket shops.

DRUGS Grass (*travka*) and hash (*plastilin*) are commonplace on the club scene, where acid, mushrooms and Ecstasy also do the rounds; smack and coke are sold on the streets of Yugo-Zapadnaya. Although Russian law distinguishes between possession and the intent to sell, the quantitative limits are set so low that almost any amount could be interpreted as for sale, rendering offenders liable to years in prison, or possibly even the death penalty. Obviously, the safest policy is to avoid drugs entirely.

ELECTRICITY A standard Continental 220 volts AC; most European appliances should work as long as you have an adapter for European-style two-pin round plugs. North Americans will need this plus a transformer.

FILM AND PHOTOS Hundreds of kiosks around Moscow sell imported colour film, and many offer one-hour developing. When leaving the country by air, put films in your pocket, as Russian film-safe X-rays do not always live up to their name.

GAY AND LESBIAN LIFE This is emerging from the closet after decades of repression, but Russian society remains extremely homophobic. Although it is no longer a criminal offence and there are some self-declared gay singers and artists, generally people are unlikely to be open about their sexuality. Besides such contacts as the Moscow Information Centre, PO Box 44, 105318 (email *kremln@dol.ru*) and the lesbian organization Rozovaya Svecha, PO Box 123424, Antilenko AA (☎095/490 27 58, *koryk@mail.ru*), there is a useful Web site (*www.gay.ru*) with lots of facts and advice in English. See the "Nightlife" chapter for a rundown of gay and lesbian clubs in Moscow.

LANGUAGE COURSES The Moscow Linguistic Centre (ul. Presnenskiy val 17 ☎737 01 93, *mlc@mail.infotel.ru*; *www.worldwide.edu/russia/mlc*) is a good place to study Russian, and can provide visa support and homestay accommodation if needed. Tutition can also be arranged by Patriarshy Dom Tours in Moscow (see p.43), or agencies abroad. In **Britain**, try RLE (53–56 Great Sutton St, London E1V 0DE ☎020/7608 3794, *101367.1025@compuserve.com*), or the South Manchester College (Wythenshawe Park Centre, Moor Rd, Manchester M23 9BQ ☎0161/957 1500). In **America**, most universities offer some kind of course in Russian. Two of the most reputable short-term programmes are: The Russian School (Middlebury College, Middlebury, VT 05753-6131 ☎802/443-5000), offering a 9-week summer programme; and The Rassiac Foundation (105 Wentworth Hall, Dartmouth College, Hanover, NH 03755 ☎603/646-1110, fax 603/646-2240), offering a 10-day intensive summer programme. For more suggestions contact the American Council of Teachers in Russian (ACTR/ACCELS, ☎202/833-7522). The Web site for schools offering Russian language courses in North America is *www.russnet.org*. In **Australia**, tuition in Moscow can be arranged by The Eastern European Travel Bureau-Russian Travel Centre (75 King St, Sydney, NSW 2000 ☎02/9262 1144).

LAUNDRIES Russians do their laundry at home, in the bathtub if necessary; public launderettes are nonexistent, and private cleaners unreliable and/or expensive. If you don't want to do your own laundry, you can pay $4 to have it washed at the *Travellers Guesthouse* (ul. Bolshaya Pereyaslavskaya 50), or slightly more to have it collected and returned two days later by BFT-Diana, aka "Zolushka" (daily 9am–5pm; ☎336 25 33). A costlier option is the same-day service from Aist in the *Gamma-Delta Hotel* (daily 8am–10pm; ☎166 75 17).

LEFT LUGGAGE Most train stations have lockers and/or a 24-hour left-luggage office, but you would be tempting fate to use them.

LOST PROPERTY For similar reasons, anything you might lose is unlikely to end up at the lost property depots (*Stol Nakhodok*) handling documents (3y Kolobovskiy per. 8 ☎200 99 57; Mon–Thurs 9am–2pm, Fri 9am–2pm & 3–5.30pm) or other items lost on the metro (at Sportivnaya metro ☎222 20 85; Mon–Thurs 9am–noon & 1–6pm, Fri 9am–4pm). Only Russian is spoken.

MARRIAGE AGENCIES The foreign-language press is full of advertisements by agencies offering Russian brides for foreign males. Questions of morality and taste aside, a lot of them are purely aimed at extracting money from hapless foreign males, and even where "genuine", many of the women are planning to divorce their spouses as soon as they obtain a foreign residency permit or passport. For a real relationship find somebody yourself, guys.

PATRONYMICS AND FIRST NAMES Besides their first name and surname, every Russian has a patronymic derived from their father's name, such as Konstantinovich (son of Konstantin), or Ivanova (daughter of Ivan), which follows the first name as a polite form of address. While many older Russians abide by its use and find Western informality rather crass, the patronymic is falling out of use in society at large. Once genuine intimacy has been established Russians love to use affectionate diminutives like Sasha or Shura (for Alexander), Anya or Anichka (for Anna) and may try to make one out of your name.

PROSTITUTION Prostitution is not illegal under Russian law, and is rife in Moscow's hotels, nightclubs, and some areas of the city. Business is fairly blatant and usually in hard currency; the risks are the same as anywhere else in the world. In nightclubs, foreign men may not realize that talking to or dancing with a woman can create expectations that a deal will follow; three dances constitutes an unwritten contract, so pimps may demand money if they baulk at going any further. Less obviously, it also causes problems for Russian women *not* involved in prostitution, who fear to enter such places alone lest they be mistaken for freelance prostitutes and get beaten up by the mob. If you arrange to meet with a Russian woman, respect any doubts she might express about the venue, and rendezvous outside so you can go in together.

RACISM It is a sad fact that racism in Russia is a casual and common phenomenon. Mostly directed against other ethnic groups of the old Soviet Union, such as Chechens, Gypsies, Azerbajanis and Central Asians, it also extends to Africans, Arabs, Vietnamese and Jews (the last being an old enmity, exploited by tsars and Communists alike). Anyone dark-skinned can expect to be stopped by the police on a regular basis.

SUPERSTITIONS Russians consider it bad luck to kiss or shake hands across a threshold, or return home to pick up something that's been forgotten. Before departing on a long journey, they gather all their luggage by the door and sit on it for a minute or two, to bring themselves luck for the journey. When buying flowers for your hostess, make certain that there's an odd number of blooms; even-numbered bouquets are for funerals. It's also considered unlucky to whistle indoors or in a cemetery, or to put your handbag on the floor.

TAPOCHKI Visiting a Russian home, you'll be invited to slip off your shoes and ease into *tapochki* (slippers), thus preventing dirt from being tracked into the flat, and drawing you into the cosy ambience of domestic life. Their institutional equivalent (such as museum visitors are obliged to wear) are felt overshoes with tapes to tie around the ankles.

TAMPONS All pharmacies and supermarkets stock Ukrainian-made Tampax and imported brands.

TIME Moscow time is generally three hours ahead of Britain and eight hours ahead of EST, with the clocks going forward one hour on the last Saturday in March, and back again on the last Saturday of October.

TIPPING In taxis, the fare will be agreed in advance and there's no need to tip. In restaurants it's considered proper to leave an extra ten percent or so, but it's seldom compulsory, so check that it hasn't already been included. It's also done to give a small tip to the cloakroom attendant if he helps you on with your coat.

TOILETS Public toilets (*tualét* or *WC*) mostly take the form of Portaloo cabins superintended by a *babushka*. Toilets in restaurants or hotels are preferable; the cleanest and most accessible are in *McDonald's*, at various locations in the centre of Moscow.

Part 2

The City

Chapter 1

Introducing the City

Discounting a couple of satellite towns beyond the outer ring road, Moscow covers an area of about 900 square kilometres, which makes mastering the public transport system (or at least the metro) a top priority. Yet, despite Moscow's size and the inhuman scale of many of its buildings and avenues, the general layout is easily grasped – a series of concentric circles and radial lines, emanating from the Kremlin – and the centre is compact enough to explore on foot.

Red Square and the Kremlin are the historic nucleus of the city (Chapter 2), a magnificent stage for political drama, signifying a great sweep of history that includes Ivan the Terrible, Peter the Great, Stalin and Gorbachev. Here you'll find Lenin's Mausoleum and St Basil's Cathedral, the famous GUM department store, and the Kremlin itself, whose splendid cathedrals and Armoury Museum head the list of attractions.

Immediately to the east of Red Square lies the **Kitay-gorod** (Chapter 3), traditionally the commercial district, and originally fortified like the Kremlin. Stretches of the ramparts remain behind the *Metropol* and *Rossiya* hotels, and the medieval churches of Zaryade and the shops along Nikolskaya ulitsa may tempt you further into the quarter, where you'll find the former headquarters of the Communist Party.

The Kremlin and the Kitay-gorod are surrounded by two quarters defined by ring boulevards built over the original ramparts of medieval times, when Moscow's residential areas were divided into the "White Town" or **Beliy Gorod** (Chapter 4), and the humbler "Earth Town" or **Zemlyanoy Gorod** (Chapter 5). Today, both are an inviting maze where every style of architecture is represented. Situated within the Boulevard Ring that encloses the Beliy Gorod are such landmarks as the Bolshoy Theatre and the Lubyanka headquarters of the secret police, while the Zemlyanoy Gorod that extends to the Garden Ring is enlivened by the trendy Old and New Arbat streets, with three Stalin-era skyscrapers dominating the Ring itself.

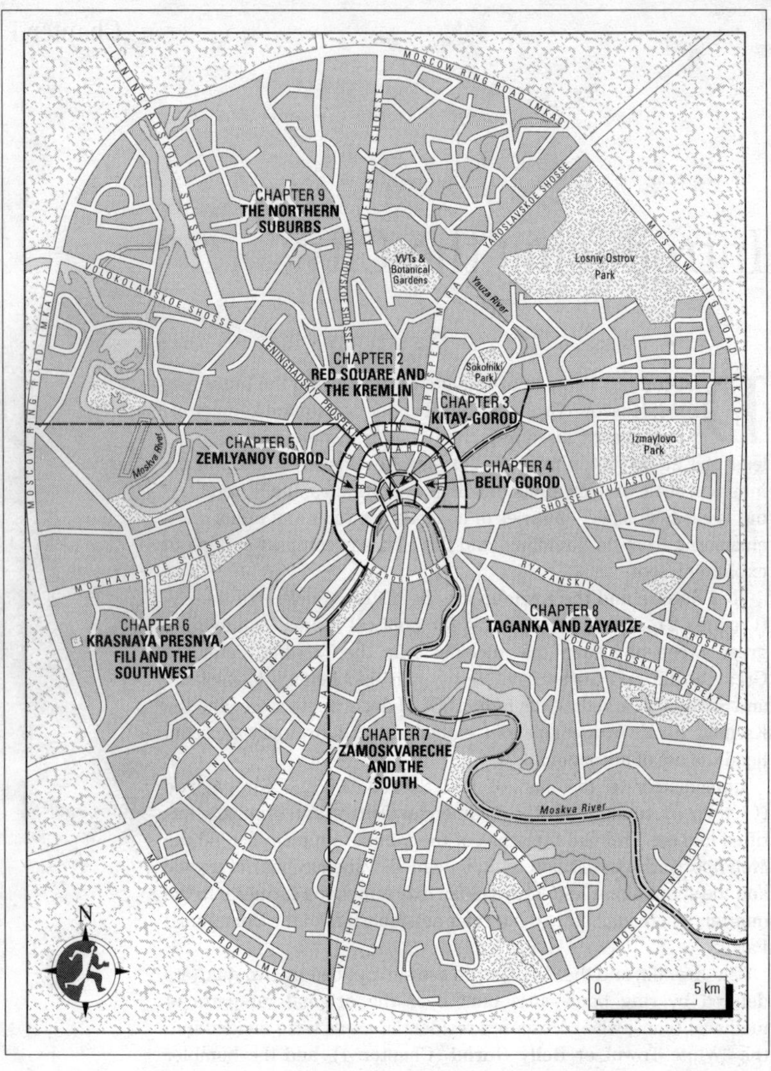

Beyond this historic core Moscow is too sprawling to explore on foot: you'll need to rely on the metro, which is why our division of the city is based mostly on transport connections and ease of access. **Krasnaya Presnya, Fili and the southwest** (Chapter 6) describes a swathe which includes the former Russian Parliament building (known as the White House); Tolstoy's house and the Novodevichiy Convent further south across the Moskva River;

Transliteration

The problem with transliterating Russian from the Cyrillic alphabet into the Roman alphabet is that there is no agreed way to do it. In addition to the German, French and American systems, there are several English systems. In this book we've used the Revised English System, with a few minor modifications to help pronunciation and readability. All proper names appear as they are best known, not as they would be transliterated (for example Tchaikovsky not Chaykovskiy).

Place-names (streets and squares, metro stations, museums and landmarks) are listed in Cyrillic and English at the end of each chapter.

Victory Park, out beyond Fili; and Moscow State University, in the Sparrow Hills.

Across the river from the Kremlin, **Zamoskvareche and the south** (Chapter 7) are the home of the Tretyakov Gallery of Russian art and the well-known Gorky Park, and also of the Donskoy and Danilov monasteries that once stood guard against the Tatars, and the romantic ex-royal estates of Kolomenskoe and Tsaritsyno.

Taganka and Zayauze (Chapter 8), to the east of the centre, likewise harbour fortified monasteries – the Andronikov, Novospasskiy, and Simonov – and erstwhile noble estates (Kuskovo and Kuzminki), but the main lure for tourists is the Izmaylovo Art Market, near Izmaylovo Park. Other attractions include the Pet Market and the Old Believers' Commune, and a trail of Baroque churches culminating in the stupendous Stalin-Gothic Kotelnicheskaya Apartments.

The **Northern Suburbs** (Chapter 9) cover a vast area with a sprinkling of sights. Foremost is the VVTs, a huge Stalinist exhibition park with amazing statues and pavilions, in the vicinity of the Ostankino Palace, Moscow's Botanical Gardens and TV Tower. Closer to the centre are a clutch of museums and the Durov Animal Theatre, while further east lies the verdant Sokolniki Park. In the opposite direction, stadiums and a racetrack flank Leningradskiy prospekt as it runs out towards Sheremetevo Airport, north of the lakeside summer resort of Serebryaniy Bor.

Out of the city (Chapters 17, 18 and 19) there is scope for day excursions to such diverse places as the Trinity Monastery of St Sergei, the Abramtsevo artists' colony, Tchaikovsky's house in Klin, Lenin's country retreat at Gorki Leninskie, and the battlefield of Borodino; with more time an overnight trip to Vladimir and Suzdal is worthwhile – two historically linked towns that today present opposing faces. Many of these destinations can be visited on tours, sparing you the trouble of getting there by public transport.

Practicalities

Transport details – bus, trolleybus and tram routes, as well as metro stations – are given throughout the following chapters, but for a full rundown of how to use the network you should turn to p.34. Also, a colour plan of the metro is included at the back of the book. Most visitors arrange **accommodation** in advance, but if you need to find somewhere to stay, or want to know about a place beforehand, all the options are covered on pp.319–328. The last decade has seen the emergence of scores of new and increasingly affordable **restaurants, cafés and bars**; to choose among them, consult the listings of places to eat and drink on pp.329–350. The "Listings" section also gives details of nightlife and cultural events, activities for children, sports and shopping.

Chapter 2

Red Square and the Kremlin

Every visitor to Moscow is irresistibly drawn to **RED SQUARE AND THE KREMLIN**, the historic and spiritual heart of the city, so loaded with associations and drama that they seem to embody all of Russia's triumphs and tragedies. Exalted by the poet Mayakovsky as the centre of the world, the vast square has a slight curvature that seems to follow that of the earth's surface. On one side, the Lenin Mausoleum squats beneath the ramparts and towers of the Kremlin, confronted by the long facade of GUM, while St Basil's Cathedral erupts in a profusion of onion domes and spires at the far end. For sheer theatricality, Red Square is only surpassed by the Kremlin itself, whose fortifications, palaces and cathedrals are an amalgam of European and Asiatic splendour, redolent of the Italian Renaissance and the court of Genghis Khan alike. While the treasures of its Armoury Palace and other museums are a must for visitors, it's the frisson of proximity to power and the sense that history is being made here that sets the Kremlin apart from other palatial citadels the world over.

This chapter begins with Red Square, as you can and should visit it at any time of the day or night, without worrying about **opening times and admission tickets**. The Kremlin is different, insofar as it's only open at set times, and each cathedral or museum requires a ticket. Moreover, the visitors' entrance is around the far side, in the Alexander Gardens, rather than on Red Square as you might expect. Otherwise, access is simple, with three metro stations (Ploshchad Revolyutsii, Okhotniy Ryad and Teatralnaya) within a few minutes' walk of Red Square, and two others (Aleksandrovskiy Sad and Biblioteka Imeni Lenina) equally near the entrance to the Kremlin.

Starting from Okhotniy Ryad or Teatralnaya metro, you'll probably approach Red Square via a long pedestrian underpass running beneath Manezhnaya ploshchad, which brings you out near the *Moskva Hotel*, within sight of the Resurrection Gate. The faded no-smoking signs affixed to buildings date from Soviet times, when

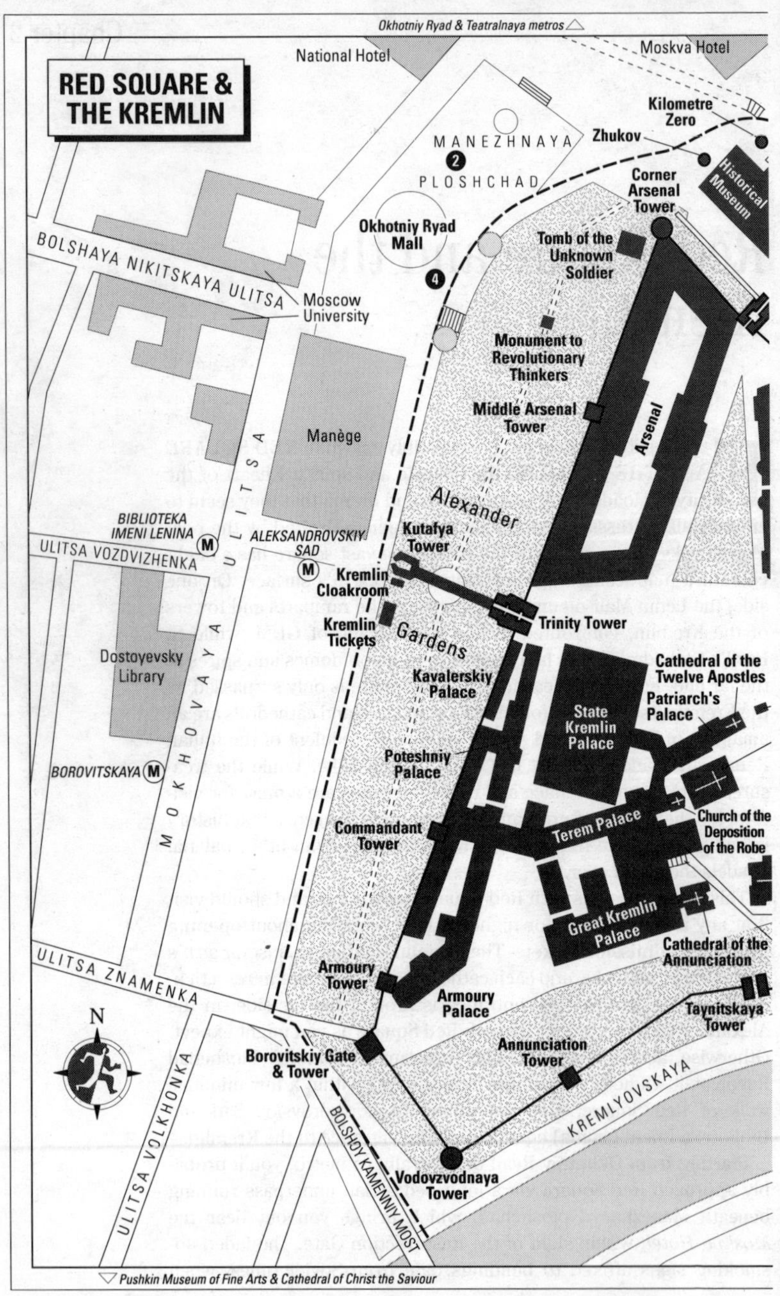

RED SQUARE & THE KREMLIN
Okhotniy Ryad & Teatralnaya metros
National Hotel
Moskva Hotel
Kilometre Zero
Zhukov
MANEZHNAYA
PLOSHCHAD
Historical Museum
Corner Arsenal Tower
Okhotniy Ryad Mall
Tomb of the Unknown Soldier
BOLSHAYA NIKITSKAYA ULITSA
Moscow University
Monument to Revolutionary Thinkers
Middle Arsenal Tower
Arsenal
Manège
Alexander
Gardens
BIBLIOTEKA IMENI LENINA
ALEKSANDROVSKIY SAD
ULITSA VOZDVIZHENKA
Kutafya Tower
Kremlin Cloakroom
Kremlin Tickets
Trinity Tower
Dostoyevsky Library
Kavalerskiy Palace
Cathedral of the Twelve Apostles
Patriarch's Palace
State Kremlin Palace
Poteshniy Palace
BOROVITSKAYA
MOKHOVAYA ULITSA
Terem Palace
Church of the Deposition of the Robe
Commandant Tower
Great Kremlin Palace
Cathedral of the Annunciation
ULITSA ZNAMENKA
Armoury Tower
Armoury Palace
Taynitskaya Tower
N
Annunciation Tower
Borovitskiy Gate & Tower
KREMLYOVSKAYA
ULITSA VOLKHONKA
BOLSHOY KAMENNIY MOST
Vodovzvodnaya Tower
Pushkin Museum of Fine Arts & Cathedral of Christ the Saviour

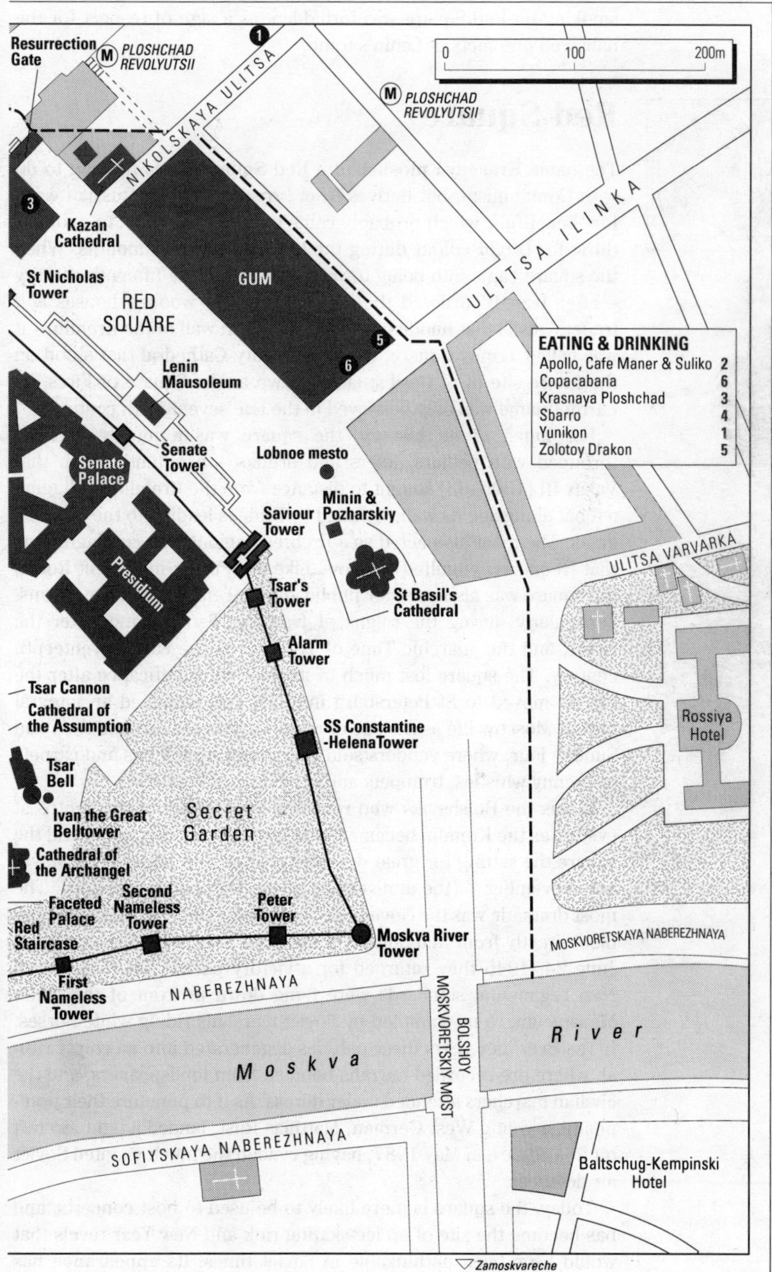
Resurrection Gate
PLOSHCHAD REVOLYUTSII
NIKOLSKAYA ULITSA
0
100
200m
PLOSHCHAD REVOLYUTSII
ULITSA ILINKA
Kazan Cathedral
St Nicholas Tower
RED SQUARE
GUM
EATING & DRINKING
Apollo, Cafe Maner & Suliko 2
Copacabana 6
Krasnaya Ploshchad 3
Sbarro 4
Yunikon 1
Zolotoy Drakon 5
Lenin Mausoleum
Senate Tower
Lobnoe mesto
Senate Palace
Minin & Pozharskiy
Saviour Tower
ULITSA VARVARKA
Presidium
Tsar's Tower
St Basil's Cathedral
Alarm Tower
Tsar Cannon
Cathedral of the Assumption
SS Constantine -HelenaTower
Rossiya Hotel
Tsar Bell
Ivan the Great Belltower
Secret Garden
Cathedral of the Archangel
Faceted Palace
Second Nameless Tower
Peter Tower
Red Staircase
Moskva River Tower
MOSKVORETSKAYA NABEREZHNAYA
First Nameless Tower
NABEREZHNAYA
BOLSHOY MOSKVORETSKIY MOST
River
Moskva
SOFIYSKAYA NABEREZHNAYA
Baltschug-Kempinski Hotel
Zamoskvareche

smoking on Red Square was forbidden, as a sign of respect for the hallowed precincts of Lenin's tomb.

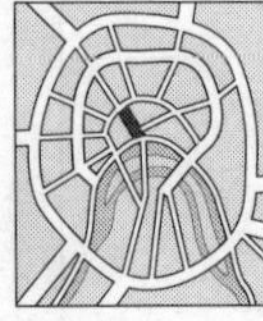

Red Square

The name **Krasnaya ploshchad – Red Square** – has nothing to do with Communism, but derives from *krasniy*, the old Russian word for "beautiful", which probably came to mean "red" due to people's thirst for bright colour during the long, drab winter months. When the square came into being towards the end of the fifteenth century – after Ivan III ordered the clearance of the wooden houses and traders' stalls that huddled below the eastern wall of the Kremlin – it was called Trinity Square, after the Trinity Cathedral that stood on the future site of St Basil's; later known as the Square of Fires, its current name was only bestowed in the late seventeenth century.

For much of its **history**, the square was a muddy expanse thronged with pedlars, idlers and drunks – a potential mob that Vasily III (1505–33) sought to distance from the Kremlin by digging a moat alongside its wall, spanned by bridges leading to the citadel's gates. The moat also acted as a firebreak against the conflagrations that frequently engulfed Moscow. Like the Forum in ancient Rome, the square was also used for public announcements and executions, particularly during the reigns of Ivan the Terrible and Peter the Great, and the anarchic Time of Troubles in the early seventeenth century. The square lost much of its political significance after the capital moved to St Petersburg in 1712, but remained an integral part of Moscow life as the site of religious processions and the Palm Sunday Fair, where vendors sold everything from icons and carpets to "penny whistles, trumpets and chenille monkeys".

It was the Bolsheviks who returned Red Square to the centre of events, as the Kremlin became the seat of power once again, and the square the setting for great **demonstrations and parades** on May 1 and November 7 (the anniversary of the October Revolution). The most dramatic was the November 7 parade in 1941, when tanks rumbled directly from Red Square to the front line, only miles away; on June 24, 1945 they returned for a victory parade where captured Nazi regimental standards were flung down in front of the Lenin Mausoleum, to be trampled by Soviet marshals riding white horses. In the Brezhnev years these parades degenerated into an empty ritual, where pre-recorded hurrahs boomed from loudspeakers, and the civilian marchers attended under duress. As if to puncture their pomposity, a young West German, Matthias Rust, landed a light aircraft on Red Square in May 1987, having evaded the much vaunted Soviet air defences.

Today, the square is more likely to be used to host concerts, and has become the site of an ice-skating rink and New Year revels that would have been unthinkable in Soviet times. Its **appearance** has also changed, since Mayor Luzhkov ordered the re-creation of the Kazan Cathedral and the Resurrection Gate that were demolished in the 1930s, and affixed gilded Tsarist eagles atop the Historical Museum. His wish to restore Red Square to its pre-Revolutionary state would have been much harder to achieve had several "visionary" projects been realized in Soviet times, when the architect Leonidov wanted to erect a fifty-storey building in the shape of a giant factory chimney, the Futurist Tatlin dreamed of raising his 425-metre-high Monument to the Third International, and Stalin contemplated the demolition of St Basil's. More recently, President Putin has dreamed of leaving his own mark on Red Square, in the form of a $300 million "Kremlin Centre" just behind St Basil's, incorporating a luxury hotel, a diamond and precious metals auction centre, and deluxe boutiques – but hopefully it will never happen.

See the Glossary on p.455 for an explanation of the various styles and features of Russian architecture.

The Resurrection Gate and the Kazan Cathedral

Most people approach Red Square from the north, via one of the cobbled streets that slope uphill beside the Historical Museum, for a thrilling first glimpse of Lenin's Mausoleum alongside the Kremlin wall, and St Basil's Cathedral looming at the far end of the square. The view of St Basil's is framed by the **Resurrection Gate** (*Voskresenskie vorota*), a 1990s replica of a sixteenth-century gateway that was pulled down in 1931 as part of Stalin's campaign to rid Moscow of its holy relics and churches, and make Red Square more accessible for tanks and marchers. While its twin towers with their green spires topped by Tsarist eagles could be described as something from a fairytale, the external **chapel** (daily 8am–8pm), with its portal flanked by gilded reliefs of saints Peter and Paul, is simply kitsch. The chapel of the original gateway held a revered icon, the Iberian Virgin, to which every visitor to Moscow paid their respects before entering Red Square. Today, Russian tourists have their photo taken standing on a brass relief set into the ground in front of the gate, marking **Kilometre Zero**, whence all distances from Moscow are measured. Nearby, facing Manezhnaya ploshchad, a stiffly poised equestrian **statue of Marshal Zhukov** tramples a Nazi battle-standard under his horse's hooves, as occurred at the Victory Parade on Red Square in 1945. Zhukov was the most successful commander of World War II, who fell from grace under Khrushchev, but never lost his place in the pantheon of Soviet heroes. Erected in 1996, the monument is by Vyacheslav Klykov, the creator of a controversial statue of Nicholas II that he hoped would stand outside the Kremlin, but which ended up in a village outside Moscow, where it was blown up by neo-Bolsheviks the same year.

As you pass through the gate, the entrance to the Historical Museum (see overleaf) is on your right, while the turquoise-coloured building on your left once contained a prison known as "the Pit", where the eighteenth-century writer Alexander Radishchev awaited exile for his critique of Catherine the Great's autocracy. However, your eyes will inevitably be drawn instead to the diminutive Kazan Cathedral, on the corner of Nikolskaya ulitsa.

The original **Kazan Cathedral** (*Kazanskiy sobor*) was built in 1636 to commemorate Tsar Mikhail Romanov's victory over the Poles, and dedicated to the Virgin of Kazan, whose icon was carried into battle by Prince Pozharsky during the Time of Troubles. It's said that during the darkest days of 1941, Metropolitan Ilya of Liban had a vision that by parading the icon around Moscow, Leningrad and Stalingrad, the Nazi invaders would be repelled, and informed the Church hierarchy. The icon was duly sent on tour on the orders of Stalin, despite the fact that it was he who had ordered the Kazan Cathedral destroyed in the 1930s and replaced by a public toilet. Its later reconstruction owed much to the architect Pyotr Baranovsky, who secretly made plans of the building even as it was being pulled down, and later risked his life to save St Basil's from a similar fate (see p.86). The modern-day Kazan Cathedral sports a strawberry-and-cream coloured exterior replete with the ornate window frames (*nalichniki*) and ogee-shaped gables (*kokoshniki*) characteristic of early Muscovite church architecture, crowned by a cluster of green and gold domes. Opened in 1993 on the feast day of the Icon of Kazan (November 4), the cathedral is unpatined by age, but already warm in spirit. Though sightseers are welcome (daily 8am–7pm), they should forgo taking photographs inside.

The Historical Museum

The Historical Museum is open 11am–7pm; closed Tues & the first Mon of each month; $5. Guided tour in English by arrangement: ☎292 37 31; $9 (group rate); www.shm.ru.

Though you'll probably want to wander around Red Square first, the **Historical Museum** (*Istoricheskiy muzey*) is definitely worth a visit at some point. Established by order of Alexander III, and opened in 1894, the museum occupies a liver-red building cluttered with pinnacles, chevrons and saw-toothed cornices, whose interior is lavishly decorated with murals and carvings harking back to medieval Russia. Closed for more than a decade, just ten of its forty rooms are currently occupied by permanent exhibits – though major temporary exhibitions are regularly held in other rooms. The ticket office is inside the entrance to the right, and the cloakroom downstairs to the left, further in. Multilingual videos in the lobby give a general idea of the museum's contents, but all captions are in Russian only. To reach the exhibition on the second floor, you ascend the stairs of a grand hall that used to be the ceremonial entrance from Red Square. Its ceiling features a pictorial family tree of Russian monarchs from Vladimir and Olga of Kiev (shown watering the roots of the tree) to Alexander III, the whole of which was whitewashed over in the 1930s.

The first two rooms are notable for a pair of mammoth tusks, a replica of a grave containing the remains of a boy and girl, and scenes of Paleolithic life by Viktor Vasnetsov. Room 3 boasts a 5000-

year-old oak **longboat** that was unearthed beside the River Volga, while Room 4 opens with a haunting wooden idol from the Gorbunkovskiy peat bogs, and concludes with nephrite axe heads and gold-inlaid silver spearheads, used for ritual purposes. Also notice the Bronze Age **stele** with a sun face, from the Altay Mountains of southern Siberia.

Room 5, covering the Iron Age, has many wonderful exhibits, such as the **Kazbekskiy Hoard** of deer and bird figurines. The first millennium BC was the heyday of the **Scythians**, warlike nomads whose veneration for horses was expressed in **gold bridle ornaments** shaped like horses' heads or dragons – a style that influenced other nomadic cultures. From the Altay come **funerary masks** of diverse ethnic groups, a leather coat decorated with painted fur and wooden studs, and two stelae carved with deer, such as are erected on the Mongolian steppes to this day.

The hybrid nature of steppe culture is further evinced by the **Turmanskiy Sarcophagus**, shaped like a Greek temple with Chinese-style decorations on its "roof"; and glassware that bespeaks contact between the Scythians and Sarmatians and the Hellenized and Roman trading cities on the Black Sea coast (Room 6). Whereas the Finno-Ugrians, Mordovians and Khazars left tumuli containing bronze and amber **jewellery** during the Age of Migrations, the earliest Slavs left nothing more sophisticated than hand-moulded pots, attesting to their isolation from other cultural influences (Room 7).

In the ninth century AD these disparate peoples gave rise to the **Kievan Rus**, or Old Russian state, ruled by Scandinavian warriors known as the Varangians, who used the Volga and Dniepr as trade routes from northern Europe to Byzantium. Room 8 displays artefacts from this period and the conversion of the Kievan Rus to Christianity by Prince Vladimir in 988. On the walls hang two huge canvases depicting *The Night of Sacrifice* of infants to the pagan gods, and the *Funeral of the Great Rus*, a Varangian ruler surrounded by human and animal sacrifices.

Room 8 allows access to an exhibition entitled **Relics of the Russian State**, mustering a splendid array of portraits of the Romanov Tsars, court dress and uniforms, photos of Moscow before the Revolution, the thrones of Alexander III and Tsar Alexei, and the silver death-mask of Peter the Great made by Caro Rastrelli, the father of the renowned St Petersburg architect. **Temporary exhibitions** are mounted in other rooms, and the museum has a small **cinema** where Russian and foreign historical films are screened at 1pm.

GUM

Almost the entire eastern side of Red Square is taken up by **GUM** (pronounced "Goom": the initials stand for "State Department Store"), whose ornate Neo-Russian facade – drawing on motifs from the medieval churches of Borisoglebsk and Rostov Veliky – conceals

GUM is open Mon–Sat 9am–9pm, Sun 11am–8pm.

an elegantly utilitarian interior, employing the same steel-frame and glass construction techniques as the great train stations of London and Paris. Executed by Alexander Pomerantsev in 1890–93, this three-storey, modern arcade replaced the old hall of the Upper Trading Rows that burned down in 1825, and whose 1200 shops shared a common roof "so awkwardly constructed, that in the strongest sunshine people stumble in darkness, and after the slightest shower wade through mud".

Nationalized and renamed GUM after the 1917 Revolution, it continued to function as a shop until bureaucrats overseeing the First Five-Year Plan took over the building. In 1932 it was used for the lying-in-state of Stalin's wife, Nadezhda, after her suicide; Stalin stayed there for days, silently noting who came to pay their respects. Here, too, the giant photographic portraits of Communist leaders that emblazoned Red Square were assembled, having been developed in swimming pools. Not until 1952 was GUM reopened as a great emporium famed throughout the world. Less well known was "Section 100", a special clothing store for the Party elite, tucked away on the top floor. With the advent of perestroika, GUM received an infusion of investments from Western firms keen to get a prestigious foothold on the Russian market, and a face-lift in time to celebrate the store's centenary in 1993.

GUM is laid out in three parallel arcades or "lines" (designated *1-ya liniya*, *2-ya liniya*, *3-ya liniya*), crossed by a transverse arcade with a central fountain, overlooked by galleries. Glass canopy roofs flood the whole complex with light, or give a startling view of the stars on winter nights. The first and second floors have been entirely colonized by foreign stores like Estée Lauder and Body Shop, but a few old, Soviet-style shops survive on the third floor.

Lenin's Mausoleum

The Mausoleum is open Tues–Thurs, Sat & Sun 10am–1pm; free. Bags and cameras are not allowed inside; you can leave them at the cloakroom by the Kutafya Tower in the Alexander Gardens.

For nearly seventy years, the Soviet state venerated its founder by acts of homage at the **Lenin Mausoleum** (*Mavzoley V.I. Lenina*) – an image associated with Soviet Communism the world over. In post-Communist Russia, the Mausoleum tends to be regarded as either an awkward reminder or a cherished relic of the old days: hence the uncertainty surrounding the fate of Lenin's corpse and the future of the Mausoleum, whose inviolability was one of the last taboos of glasnost to go. Indeed, not until October 1993 – in the first flush of victory over the White House – did Yeltsin feel bold enough to strip the Mausoleum of its guard of honour and pledge the removal of Lenin's body "within months". However, the parliamentary elections backfired, returning a majority of Communist and ultra-nationalist Deputies, so the whole idea was quietly dropped.

Although Yeltsin subsequently raised the issue again, he never put it to the test. When the removal of Lenin's body was last mooted in 1997, neo-Bolsheviks vowed to blow up the monument to Peter the

Great (see p.232) in retaliation, and planted explosives around its base to prove that it was no idle threat. Since then, even the Partriarch of the Orthodox Church has opposed the idea; and with Putin now in power, Lenin's position seems as assured as it was under Soviet rule.

The Mausoleum

When Lenin died on January 21, 1924, his widow Krupskaya pleaded: "Do not let your sorrow for Ilyich find expression in outward veneration of his personality. Do not raise monuments to him, or palaces to his name, do not organize pompous ceremonies in his memory." Nonetheless, a crude wooden mausoleum was hastily erected on Red Square for mourners to pay their respects, and the Party leadership decided to preserve his body for posterity. The embalming was carried out by Professors Vorobyov and Zbarskiy, and by August 1924 the body was fit to be viewed in a newly built wooden mausoleum, which was replaced by a permanent stone one in 1930, once it became clear that the embalming process had been successful.

Designed by Alexei Shchusev, the **Mausoleum** itself is basically a step-pyramid of cubes, a form revered by Russian avant-gardists. Faced with red granite and black labradorite, it bears the simple inscription *Lenin* above its bronze doors, which were flanked by a **guard of honour** (changed every hour, as the Saviour Tower clock chimed) until Yeltsin removed it in 1993. After Stalin's death in 1953 he too was displayed in what became the Lenin-Stalin Mausoleum, but in 1961 it reverted to its old title after Stalin's body was spirited away and reburied by the Kremlin wall. For decades, the Politburo reviewed **anniversary parades** from its podium (with a supply of machine guns stashed behind them in the event of trouble), and diplomats noted who stood nearest the General Secretary as an indication of their influence. The septuagenarian Chernenko contracted fatal pneumonia from standing there on a chilly day*, and the swan song of such events occurred when Gorbachev was booed during the October Revolution parade in 1989, and on May Day the following year.

In the days when **visiting Lenin's tomb** was *de rigueur* for visitors to Moscow, the queue stretched right around the corner of the Kremlin into the Alexander Gardens, and guards made visitors line up in pairs, remove their hats and their hands from their pockets, and refrain from talking except in whispers – a regime that has slightly relaxed today, when you're unlikely to have to wait in line for more than ten minutes. Before joining the queue, visitors must stash their bags and cameras in the cloakroom beneath the Kutayfa Tower in the Alexander Gardens. Descending into the bowels of the

---

*The deaths of three successive leaders between 1982 and 1985 gave rise to the joke about a loyal citizen hurrying to Red Square to watch Chernenko's funeral. When asked if he had a pass, he replied, "No, I have a season ticket."

Mausoleum, past motionless sentries and doors that emit the crackle of walkie-talkies, you enter the funerary chamber, faced in grey and black labradorite inset with carmine zigzags. Softly spotlit in a crystal casket, wearing a polka-dot tie and a dark suit-cum-shroud, Lenin looks shrunken and waxy, his beard wispy and his fingers discoloured. The chamber's layout ensures that it's impossible to linger, so that visitors emerge blinking into the daylight less than a minute later.

During the latter years of glasnost, it was revealed that Lenin's body was dabbed with embalming fluid twice a week and received a full bath and a new suit every eighteen months, under the supervision of one Dr Debov (who denies rumours that the body was long ago replaced by a wax model). Until 1991, this was done in a laboratory two floors below the funerary chamber, beneath another sub-level containing a bar-buffet for VIPs and a gymnasium where the guards exercised when off duty – but since the amenities were mothballed, body-maintenance has occurred at the **Lenin Laboratory** on ulitsa Krasina across town. Its most recent client was Kim Il Sung of North Korea, for which the establishment reputedly received $1 million. With an eye on Russia's new rich, the laboratory offers to embalm anyone for $300,000 – sarcophagus not included.

The Kremlin wall and its towers

The Kremlin wall behind the Mausoleum constitutes a kind of Soviet pantheon, containing the remains of up to 400 bodies. Visitors leaving the Mausoleum pass a mass grave of Bolsheviks who perished during the battle for Moscow in 1917, to reach an array of luminaries whose ashes are interred in the Kremlin wall. These include the American journalist John Reed; Lenin's wife Krupskaya, and his lover Inessa Armand; the writer Maxim Gorky; various foreign Communist leaders; and the world's first cosmonaut, Yuri Gagarin. Beyond lies a select group of Soviet leaders, distinguished by idealized busts on plinths. The first to be encountered is Chernenko's (looking smarter than he ever did in real life), followed by an avuncular Andropov, a pompous Brezhnev and a benign-looking Stalin (whose tomb is marked by lilies, as well as red roses). Conspicuously absent from this roll call of leaders is Khrushchev, who died in obscurity and was buried in the Novodevichiy Cemetery (see p.223).

The **Kremlin wall** is 19m high and 6.5m thick, topped with swallow-tailed crenellations and defended by eight towers mostly built by Italian architects in the 1490s. The distinctive jade-green spires were added in the seventeenth century, and the ruby-red stars (which revolve in the wind) in 1937. At the northern end is the round **Corner Arsenal Tower**, which takes its name from the adjacent Kremlin Arsenal. Further along is the triple-tiered **St Nicholas Tower**, built by Pietro Antonio Solari. The tower's massive red star (3.75m wide and 1.5 tons in weight) gives it a total height of 70.4m.

Beyond the **Senate Tower**, named after the green-domed building visible behind Lenin's Mausoleum, looms the Gothic-spired **Saviour Tower**. In Tsarist times, an icon of the Saviour was installed above its gate, and everyone who entered doffed their hats; when Napoleon rode in without doing so his horse shied and his hat fell off, confirming the Russians' belief in its miraculous powers. On Lenin's orders, the chimes of the tower's clock were adjusted to play the *Internationale*; they have now been altered to play the new Russian national anthem – which is the same as the old Soviet one from 1943, but with different words. It was from the Saviour Gate that soldiers formerly goose-stepped to the Mausoleum to change the guard at what was known as Sentry Post No.1.

The small **Tsar's Tower**, erected in 1680, gets its name from an earlier wooden tower whence the young Ivan the Terrible used to hurl dogs to their deaths and watch executions on Red Square. Also opposite St Basil's is the **Alarm Tower**, whose bell warned of fires; Catherine the Great had the bell's tongue removed as a "punishment" after it was rung to summon a dangerous mob during the Plague Riot of 1771. In medieval times, the chunky **SS Constantine-Helena Tower** served as the Kremlin's torture chamber; the screams of victims were audible on Red Square. The circular **Moskva River Tower**, built by Marco Ruffo in 1487, protects the southeastern corner of the Kremlin wall, which was usually the first part of the fortress to be attacked by the Tatars.

St Basil's Cathedral

St Basil's is open Mon & Wed–Sun 11am–6pm, in winter till 4pm; closed the first Mon of each month; $3. The ticket office closes 1hr earlier, and for 30min at lunchtime.

No description can do justice to the inimitable and magnificent **St Basil's Cathedral** (*sobor Vasiliya Blazhennovo*), silhouetted against the skyline where Red Square slopes down towards the Moskva River. Foreigners have always seen it as a cryptic clue to the mysterious Russian soul. The French diplomat the Marquis de Custine thought its colours combined "the scales of a golden fish, the enamelled skin of a serpent, the changeful hues of the lizard, the glossy rose and azure of the pigeon's neck", and questioned whether "the men who go to worship God in this box of confectionery work" could be Christians.

St Basil's was commissioned by Ivan the Terrible to celebrate his capture of the Tatar stronghold of Kazan in 1552, on the feast day of the Intercession of the Virgin. Officially named the Cathedral of the Intercession of the Virgin by the Moat (after the moat that then ran beside the Kremlin), its popular title commemorates a "holy fool", St Basil the Blessed (1468–1552), who came to Ivan's notice in 1547 when he foretold the fire that swept Moscow that year, and was later buried in the Trinity Cathedral which then stood on this site. St Basil's was built in 1555–60, most likely by Postnik Yakovlev (nicknamed "Barma" – the Mumbler) who, legend has it, was afterwards blinded on the Tsar's orders so that he could never create anything to rival the cathedral (in fact he went on to build another cathedral in Vladimir).

Napoleon was so taken by St Basil's that he planned to dismantle it and reassemble it in Paris, while Stalin resented that it prevented his soldiers from leaving Red Square en masse, and considered demolishing the cathedral. Its survival was due to the architect Baranovsky, whose threat to cut his own throat on the cathedral steps in protest changed Stalin's mind, though he was punished by five years in prison. Today, St Basil's requires another Baranovsky; action is needed to prevent the cathedral slipping down the hill towards the river, yet the government dallies over committing funds to underpin the building, and would rather contemplate absurd new follies that would ruin Red Square if ever they were realized.

Despite its apparent disorder, there is an underlying **symmetry** to the cathedral, which has eight domed chapels (four large and octagonal, the others smaller and squarish) symbolizing the eight assaults on Kazan, clustered around a central, lofty tent-roofed spire, whose cupola was compared by the poet Lermontov to "the cut-glass stopper of an antique carafe". In 1588 Tsar Fyodor added a ninth chapel on the northeastern side, to accommodate the remains of St Basil; its small yellow-and-green cupola is studded with orange pyramids. Rather than using the main arcaded staircase, visitors enter the cathedral through an inconspicuous door near the ticket kiosk. Sadly, the interior is far plainer than the facade, with restorers' scaffolding making the small chapels even more claustrophobic. The floral designs covering the walls and vaults (painted in the seventeenth century), and the fact that the floor tiles have been so worn down that the grouting forms ridges underfoot, are the most notable features.

In the garden out in front stands an impressive bronze **statue of Minin and Pozharsky**, who rallied Russia during the Time of Troubles. They made a curious team, as Dmitry Pozharsky was a prince, while Kuzma Minin was a butcher from Nizhniy Novgorod, whose citizens funded the volunteer army that drove out the invading Poles in 1612, after Minin took their womenfolk hostage. Erected in 1818 by public subscription, the statue was Moscow's first monumental sculpture, and originally stood in the middle of Red Square, until Stalin had it moved as an impediment to parades.

The Lobnoe mesto

En route to St Basil's, you'll see the circular stone platform known as the **Lobnoe mesto**, whose name (derived from *lob*, meaning "forehead") is usually translated as the "place of executions" or the "place of proclamations", since it served for both. It was here that, early in his reign, Ivan the Terrible begged for the people's forgiveness after Moscow was razed by a fire that the Patriarch pronounced to be God's punishment for his misdeeds. In 1570, however, Ivan staged a

The Streltsy

In medieval times, Red Square and the suburbs across the river teemed with thousands of **Streltsy**, the shaggy pikemen and musketeers who guarded the Kremlin and were Russia's first professional soldiers. Garbed in caftans, fur-trimmed hats and yellow boots, their banners emblazoned with images of God smiting their foes, they made a fearsome host whenever they assembled at the tsar's bidding – or in revolt. In 1682, when Peter was ten years old, they butchered several of his relatives on the Red Staircase in the Kremlin – an experience that crystallized his hatred for Old Muscovy and its ragtag army. It was to beat them that Peter later formed his own "toy" regiments drilled in European tactics by foreign officers, which routed the Streltsy when they revolted again in 1698. A famous painting by Surikov (in the Tretyakov Gallery) depicts the tsar gazing pitilessly over the wives and children of the condemned, in the shadow of St Basil's.

festival of torture on the square, where two hundred victims perished in a man-sized frying pan or on ropes stretched taut enough to saw bodies in half; on another occasion, he amused himself by letting loose wild bears into the crowd. In 1605, the False Dmitry proclaimed his accession here; after his downfall, his mutilated corpse was burned to ashes and fired from a cannon in the direction of Poland, from the same spot. Most famously, in 1698 Peter the Great carried out the mass execution of the mutinous Streltsy regiments on scaffolds erected nearby – personally wielding the axe on a score of necks (see box above).

Confusingly, there were two False Dmitrys during the Time of Troubles: for more about them see p.422.

The Alexander Gardens

To visit the Kremlin or merely view it from another angle (or to deposit your bags before going to the Mausoleum), leave Red Square to the northwest and turn left around the corner into the **Alexander Gardens** (*Aleksandrovskiy sad*). The gardens were laid out in 1819–22, after the Neglina River that ran alongside the western wall of the Kremlin was channelled into an underground pipe. Just inside the gates is the **Tomb of the Unknown Soldier**, whose eternal flame was kindled from the Field of Mars in Leningrad when the memorial was unveiled in 1967. Beneath a granite plinth topped by a giant helmet and furled banner lie the remains of a nameless soldier disinterred from the mass grave of those who died halting the Nazi advance at Kilometre 41 on the Leningrad highway; the inscription reads: "Your name is unknown, your feat immortal." The tomb is flanked by a **guard of honour**, changed every hour on the hour. Nearby is a line of porphyry blocks containing earth from the "Hero Cities" of Leningrad, Kiev, Volgograd, Sevastapol, Minsk, Smolensk, Odessa, Novorossisk, Tula, Murmansk, Kerch and the Brest Fortress. Newly-weds and VIPs often come here to lay flowers beside the monument, and it is carpeted with floral tributes on Victory Day (May 9).

The Alexander Gardens are open day and night, except when closed at short notice for visits by VIPs.

By contrast, the opposite side of the gardens features an array of **statues** based on Russian fairytales such as the Prince and the Frog and the Fox and the Stork, spotlit amid mosaic-encrusted basins and balustraded walkways linked to the shopping mall beneath Manezhnaya ploshchad; a token of Luzhkov's desire to transform Moscow's image from that of a drab metropolis into a prosperous fun city.

Previously, the only note of levity was a whimsical arched **Grotto** near the **Middle Arsenal Tower**, and it was more typical of the Soviet Union that an obelisk erected to mark the 300th anniversary of the Romanov dynasty should be converted on Lenin's orders into a **Monument to Revolutionary Thinkers**, inscribed with the names of Bakunin, Marx, Engels, Hume and other personages. In Bulgakov's famous novel, *The Master and Margarita*, it was on one of the nearby benches that the grieving heroine Margarita met the Devil's sidekick, Azazello, and accepted an invitation to Satan's Ball, which led to the release of her beloved from a mental asylum.

Midway along the ramparts, a brick ramp with swallow-tailed crenellations descends to the white **Kutafya Tower**, the last survivor of several outlying bastions that once protected the bridges leading to the Kremlin, whose decorative parapet was added in the seventeenth century. The bridge leads up to the eighty-metre-high **Trinity Tower**, the tallest of the Kremlin towers, whose gateway admits visitors to the citadel (see below). Further south, the **Commandant's Tower** and the **Armoury Tower** abut the Kremlin's Armoury Palace, while another rampway leads up to the multi-tiered **Borovitskiy Tower**, whose name derives from the pine-grove (*bor*) covered hillock on which the citadel was founded. In winter, when the steep hillside is covered with snow, kids zoom down on sledges and shoot across the path of unsuspecting tour groups heading for the Borovitskiy Gate.

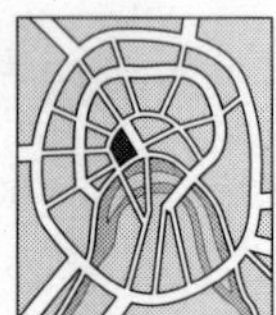

The Kremlin

This curious conglomeration of palaces, towers, churches, monasteries, chapels, barracks, arsenals and bastions . . . this complex functions as fortress, sanctuary, seraglio, harem, necropolis and prison, this violent contrast of the crudest materialism and the most lofty spirituality – are they not the whole history of Russia, the whole epic of the Russian nation, the whole inward drama of the Russian soul?

Maurice Paléologue, *An Ambassador's Memoirs*

Brooding and glittering in the heart of Moscow, the **Kremlin** thrills and tantalizes whenever you see its towers stabbing the skyline, or its cathedrals and palaces arrayed above the Moskva River. Its name* is synonymous with Russia's government, and in modern times assumed connotations of a Mecca for believers, and the seat of the Antichrist for foes of Communism. Hostile foreign perceptions long predate the Soviet era, for as far back as 1839 the Marquis de Custine fulminated: "To inhabit a place like the Kremlin is not to reside, it is to protect oneself. Oppression creates revolt, revolt obliges precautions, precautions increase dangers, and this long series of actions and reactions engenders a monster." Unsurprisingly, Russians generally feel more respectful than paranoid, being inclined to agree with Lermontov, who rhapsodized: "What can compare to the Kremlin which, having ringed itself with crenellated walls and adorned itself with the golden domes of cathedrals, sits on a high hill like the crown of sovereignty on the brow of an awesome ruler?"

A brief history

According to **legend**, a band of boyars (nobles) hunting in the forest saw a giant two-headed bird swoop down on a boar and deposit its corpse on a hilltop overlooking two rivers. That night, they dreamt of a city of tent-roofed spires and golden domes, where people shuffled in chains towards a huge gallows – and waking next morning, they resolved to build upon the site. More prosaically, the **founding of the Kremlin** is attributed to Prince **Yuri Dolgoruky**, who erected a wooden fort above the confluence of the Moskva and Neglina rivers in about 1147 – although the site may have been inhabited as long ago as 500 BC. Crammed with wooden houses, churches and stables, Dolgoruky's Kremlin was razed to the ground by the Mongols in 1238 but, like the city that had grown up around it, soon arose from the ashes, bigger and stronger than before.

Between 1326 and 1339 the Kremlin was surrounded by oaken walls and the first stone cathedral appeared in its midst; some forty years later the original fortifications were replaced by stone walls, whose colour earned Moscow the sobriquet "the White City". Despite being sacked by the Tatars in 1382, its development proved unstoppable. During the reign of Grand Duke **Ivan III** (1462–1505) – dubbed "the Great" – the realm of Muscovy quadrupled in size and threw off the Tatar yoke, becoming pre-eminent among the Russian states. To confirm Moscow's stature Ivan embarked on an ambitious building programme, using craftsmen from Pskov, Tver and Novgorod, supervised by Italian architects, who arrived in 1472.

It was the Italians who built most of the cathedrals and fortifications that exist today, which were subsequently embellished by Ivan III's grandson Ivan IV (1553–84) – better known as **Ivan the**

---

*In Russia, *kreml* means fortress, and every medieval town had one. The origin of the word is obscure: some think it derives from the Greek *kremn* or *krimnos*, meaning a steep hill above a ravine; others from a Slav term for thick coniferous woods in a swampy place.

Terrible (Ivan Grozny) – who first assumed the title of "Tsar", and made the Kremlin notorious for murders and orgies. The demise of his son Fyodor I brought the Rurik dynasty to an end, and the wily **Boris Godunov** to power in 1598. His unpopularity with the nobility encouraged a pretender, claiming to be the youngest son of Ivan the Terrible, to invade Russia from Poland and proclaim himself tsar following Godunov's death in 1605. This so-called **False Dmitry** soon alienated his supporters and was murdered by a mob; the ensuing **Time of Troubles** saw Russia ravaged by famine, civil wars and invasions. After the Kremlin was recaptured from the Poles by Minin and Pozharskiy in 1612, the nobility elected **Mikhail Romanov** as tsar, inaugurating the dynasty that would rule Russia until 1917.

Under Mikhail and his successors, Alexei and Fyodor II, the Kremlin was rebuilt and order restored; the Terem and Patriarch's Palaces date from this era. The next tsar, **Peter the Great** (1682–1725), changed everything by spurning Moscow and the Kremlin for the new city that he founded by the Gulf of Finland, and by enforcing reforms that struck at everything held dear by traditionalists. Henceforth, the tsars and the government dwelt in St Petersburg, only visiting the Kremlin for coronations, weddings and major religious celebrations. Although **Catherine the Great** added the Senate building and commissioned a vast new palace that was never built, the Kremlin was otherwise neglected until the French invasion of 1812, when the great fire that destroyed Moscow and forced **Napoleon** to withdraw necessitated major repairs to the parts of the Kremlin that he had spitefully blown up.

During the reign of the arch-conservative **Nicholas I** (1825–55), the Russo-Byzantine-style Armoury and Great Kremlin Palaces were constructed, and the Terem Palace was refurbished in a re-creation of early Romanov times. However, St Petersburg remained the capital and the focus of events until after the fall of the Romanov dynasty and the overthrow of the Provisional Government by the **Bolsheviks**, whose Moscow contingent took the Kremlin by storm on November 3, 1917.

In March 1918, **Lenin** moved the seat of government back to Moscow and into the Kremlin, as if anticipating how a party founded in the spirit of internationalism would later, under the rule of **Stalin** (1929–53), identify itself with Ivan the Terrible and other "great Russian patriots". Like "Genghis Khan with a telephone", Stalin habitually worked at night, obliging his ministers and their staffs to do likewise, giving rise to the pasty "Kremlin complexion". As purges decimated the Party, fear and secrecy pervaded the Kremlin, which remained closed to outsiders until 1955. Yet, despite the murderous decisions taken here, it saw little actual blood spilt, the most dramatic moment being the arrest of Lavrenty Beria, the dreaded chief of the secret police, following Stalin's demise.

Under later Soviet leaders, the Kremlin retained an aura of power and mystery, but gradually lost its terrible associations. In the aftermath of the break-up of the Soviet Union it seemed that the occupants of the Kremlin wielded less power than at any time in its colourful history, but autocratic mastery and subterfuge have definitely made a comeback since then.

Visiting the Kremlin

In general, **visiting the Kremlin** is surprisingly easy. The complex is open to the public from 10am to 5pm every day except Thursday, but may be closed without notice for state occasions or during political crises. Two significant exceptions to this rule are the **Armoury Palace**, which can only be entered at set times on Kremlin open days, and the **State Diamond Fund**, which only admits tour groups (see p.112) – these usually enter through the Borovitskiy Gate at the far end of the western wall, rather than via the Kutafya and Trinity gates, as other visitors do.

Assuming you're not with a group, the procedure is to deposit your bag at the cloakroom (open till 6pm) tucked away at the base of the Kutafya Tower's southern side, and buy **tickets** at one of the kiosks nearby. All the buildings in the Kremlin are covered by a single ticket ($7, students/children $4; half-price after 4pm), except for the Armoury Palace, which requires a separate ticket ($7, students/children $5) – besides which, you'll need a **photo permit** ($3) for each if you want to take pictures. **Video cameras** are not allowed within the Kremlin.

There's no need to sign up for a tour unless you want to. The **tours** run by folks touting their services through megaphones on Red Square simply whisk you around the outside of the cathedrals, with a commentary in Russian. More expensive ones by Intourist take you into the buildings, escorted by an English-speaking guide, but don't necessarily provide any more enlightenment than a decent guidebook. Alternatively, you can engage a **personal guide** from the hopefuls that wait near the Kutafya Tower. Rates are negotiable and the quality is variable; accredited guides should wear a badge issued by Intourist. If you're seriously interested in icons or history, the English-speaking consultants on duty inside the Assumption and Annunciation cathedrals can answer most questions for free.

You can check out the official Web site of the Kremlin Museum at www.kremlin.museum.ru/ and a guide to the Kremlin's monuments at www.online.ru/sp/cominf/kremlin/kremlin.html

Visitors' **movements** within the Kremlin are strictly controlled, with white lines and whistle-tooting policemen marking the limits beyond which you can't stroll (or even cross the road) – the descriptions in this book are structured to take account of these restrictions. While it's possible to see almost everything in one visit, a couple of visits are better if you have the time: one to see the inside and outside of the cathedrals, and another for touring the Armoury Palace. Visitors with a ticket for the latter may enter the Kremlin through the Borovitskiy Gate rather than the regular entrance by the Kutafya Tower.

Those with the energy should also try viewing the Kremlin from **different vantage points**. The view from across the Moskva River is the finest in Moscow, with a glorious panorama of palaces and cathedrals arrayed above the wall that stretches from the Vodovzvodnaya (Water-Drawing) Tower to the Moskva River Tower below Red Square. From high up on the Bolshoy Kamenniy bridge, you can even glimpse the Terem Palace, which is inaccessible to visitors. Lastly, you might consider walking right around the outside of the Kremlin walls, which total 2,235 metres in length.

Restricted zones and the State Kremlin Palace

Roughly two-thirds of the Kremlin is off-limits to tourists, namely the trio of buildings in the northern half of the citadel – the Arsenal, the Senate Palace and the Presidium – and most of the wooded Secret Garden sloping down towards the river. Entering via the Trinity Gate, the "government zone" lies to your left, where cannons captured during the Napoleonic Wars are ranged alongside the **Arsenal**. Commissioned by Peter the Great, but virtually redundant by the time it was completed in 1736, this occupies the site of the medieval boyars' quarter, where the higher nobility resided until the fifteenth century.

Opposite the Arsenal stands the imposing **Senate Palace**, erected in 1776–87 by Matvei Kazakov, whose Neoclassical design was cleverly adapted to the awkward triangular site. The edifice was commissioned by Catherine the Great for meetings of the Moscow branch of the Senate, an advisory body established in 1711; since 1991 it has been the official **residence of Russia's president**. From Red Square you can see the green cupola of its grand hall, formerly used for meetings of the USSR Council of Ministers and the awarding of Lenin Prizes. During the late 1990s, the modernization of the Senate's interior gave Yeltsin an excuse to get rid of Lenin's quarters, which had been preserved as a hallowed shrine; and revealed a secret passage beneath Stalin's former study, that may have enabled the secret police chief, Beria, to eavesdrop on his boss. The staggering cost of the modernization was equalled by its tackiness, the inner courtyard being turned into a winter garden of artificial trees made from green and yellow glass. And that was only the start of what became known as the Mabetex scandal (see box opposite).

To the southeast is another Neoclassical structure, built in 1934 as a school for "Red Commanders", which subsequently housed the Presidium of the Supreme Soviet and now contains government offices; for want of a new title, it is still referred to as the **Presidium**. In June 1953, it was here that Beria was arrested at gunpoint during a meeting. Some allege that he was shot on the premises, and the body smuggled out in a carpet for fear that his bodyguards would take revenge on the other ministers. Previously, in Tsarist times, the site was occupied by the Monastery of Miracles and the Convent of the Ascension, which many royal daughters were forced to enter as nuns, owing to a lack of suitably Orthodox foreign rulers whom they could marry. By the nineteenth century, the convent had become so disreputable that one visitor described it as a "complete bagnio", where "the favours of any particular nun may be had for the asking".

To the right of the Trinity Gate a narrow lane runs parallel to the Kremlin wall; also out of bounds, this contains the former **Kavalerskiy Building** where Lenin and Krupskaya lived after they first moved into the Kremlin, before moving into a modest suite of rooms in the Senate Palace. Across the way is the seventeenth-cen-

The Mabetex scandal

The **Mabetex scandal** gets its name from the Swiss firm that won contracts to "refurbish" two of the Kremlin palaces in the late 1990s. As a former builder, President Yeltsin's experience in such matters was matched by his desire to stamp a new aesthetic on the Kremlin – one that looked back to the future, and revelled in the panoply of power. "Go to St Petersburg. Go to the Winter Palace, to Tsarskoe Selo, to Pavlovsk, to the Yusupov House. Look at everything there. Look at what Russian culture is, what great power is, and then report back to me," he instructed **Pavel Borodin**, the Kremlin's property and financial chief, whose association with Mabetex went back to his days as mayor of Yakutsk.

An audit later revealed that renovation of the Senate Palace cost at least $457 million, or $13,125 a square metre. The cost of the Great Kremlin Palace remains a secret, but is thought to also run into hundreds of millions. In 1999 Mabetex's boss admitted guaranteeing credit cards for Yeltsin's family, but denied helping Borodin divert funds from the state budget and oil privatization proceeds into Swiss banks, on behalf of "The Family".

The Family were Yeltsin's inner circle – his daughter Tatyana, who crafted his image; his wife Naina; their other daughter Yelena and her husband; and Borodin – aided by Boris Berezovsky, the "kingmaker" of Russian politics, who had his own agenda.

Russia's prosecutor general, **Yuri Skuratov**, asked Swiss prosecutors to help, who responded by freezing millions of dollars in assets, including accounts in Borodin's name. Although Skuratov was sacked after he was shown on state TV in bed with teenage prostitutes – in what was widely assumed to be a set-up by the KGB's successor, the FSB – the Swiss investigators carried on regardless.

To avoid their nemesis, The Family engineered Putin's succession using Berezovsky's media empire. Putin's first decree was to grant Yeltsin and his family lifelong immunity from prosecution or seizure of assets. He then dismissed Borodin and Tatyana from their Kremlin posts, probably forewarned that the Swiss were about to issue an international warrant for Borodin's arrest. While the cover-up may well succeed, any major disclosures could be awkward for Putin, who was head of the FSB at the time of Skuratov's downfall, and Borodin's deputy at the Kremlin when the Mabetex contracts were signed. No wonder, then, that the Kremlin was outraged by Borodin's arrest in the US, whilst attending George W. Bush's inauguration.

tury **Poteshniy Palace**, where Stalin had his private apartments, and his wife Nadezhda shot herself in 1932. The yellow palace is recognizable by its protruding bay window; its name derives from the word for "amusements" (*potekhi*), as Tsar Alexei had a theatre here.

Further east stands the **State Kremlin Palace** (previously the Palace of Congresses), a 120-metre-long glass and concrete box sunk 15m into the ground so as not to dwarf the other buildings in the Kremlin. Built in 1959–61 to host Party congresses, the stage of its 6000-seat auditorium was formerly adorned by a giant bas-relief of Lenin's head, and the foyer still flaunts the crests of the Soviet Republics. Performances by the Bolshoy and Kremlin Ballet Company are held here; for details, see p.360.

The Patriarch's Palace and Cathedral of the Twelve Apostles

As far as tourists are concerned, the accessible part of the Kremlin begins around the corner from the State Kremlin Palace, where the **Patriarch's Palace** (*Patriarshie palaty*) and the **Cathedral of the Twelve Apostles** (*sobor Dvenadtsati Apostolov*) come into view. The two form one structure, with an arched, covered balcony inset with polychrome tiles, and gilt frills on the three rounded gables and the balcony roof, surmounted by five small domes. Though the palace was begun in 1640, it is chiefly associated with **Patriarch Nikon**, who split the Russian Orthodox Church by his reforms during the years that he held the post (1652–58). While Nikon desired to restore the Church to the purity of its Byzantine origins, many Russians saw him as a heretic bent on imposing foreign ways. He also tried to assert the primacy of the Church over the state, thus angering Tsar Alexei, who refused to reinstate Nikon as Patriarch after he resigned in a fit of pique.

Today, the palace is a **Museum of Seventeenth-century Life and Applied Art**, displaying ecclesiastical regalia, period furniture and domestic utensils – an English-language guide tape can be rented inside. The palace's highlight is the vaulted **Cross Chamber** (*Krestovnaya palata*), measuring 19 by 13 metres, which was the first hall of such size to be built in Russia without a central supporting column. Its inauguration occasioned a day-long feast where guests placed their empty **goblets** on their heads between toasts, while monks chanted the Life of the Saints. Among the goblets in case 3 is one without a base which can't stand up, and which was given to guests who arrived late, to drain in one go. Decades later, the chamber was used for the preparation of *miro*, or holy oil, which explains the huge stove.

Other **exhibits** worth noting include a box for wine bottles made in the shape of an evangelistary, and a wine ladle with a capacity of 100 litres, belonging to Peter the Great's "Drunken Synod", whose riotous parties mocked Church rituals. The exhibition concludes in the former Cathedral of the Twelve Apostles, which was built above the archway leading to Sobornaya ploshchad, as it was deemed sacrilegious to site an altar above rooms used for everyday life. The cathedral's Baroque iconostasis was moved here from the now-demolished Convent of the Ascension; on the wall to the left hangs the *Passion of the Apostles*, depicting a dozen martyrdoms in detail. Also notice the small window high up on the west wall, through which Nikon could observe services from his private chapel on the floor above. Like all the windows in the palace, this is glazed with mica instead of glass, imparting a frosty hue to views of the outside world.

The Cross Chamber occasionally hosts **concerts** of choral or instrumental music by top Russian soloists; for details ☎202 66 49.

The Tsar Bell and Cannon

Before passing through the archway into Sobornaya ploshchad, you can make a brief detour to find two of the Kremlin's most famous sights. The **Tsar Cannon** (*Tsar-pushka*) is one of the largest cannons ever made; its bronze barrel (bearing a relief of Ivan the Terrible's son, Fyodor) is 5.34m long, weighs 40 tons and has a calibre of 890mm. Cast by Andrei Chokhov in 1586, it was intended to defend the Saviour Gate, but has never been fired in battle (though it was used to fire the ashes of the False Dmitry back towards Poland). Its enormous chassis, decorated with a lion and a snake fighting on either side, and a snarling lion's head beneath the barrel, was cast in 1835, like the cannonballs piled in front (which are purely ornamental, as the cannon was originally meant to fire stone case-shot).

Further along, behind the Ivan the Great Belltower, looms the earthbound **Tsar Bell** (*Tsar-kolokol*), the largest in the world, weighing 200 tons (almost fifteen times as much as London's Big Ben) and measuring 6.14m in height and 6.6m in diameter. Its bronze surface is emblazoned with portraits of Tsar Alexei and Empress Anna, who decreed the creation of the original and existing versions of the bell. The first, 130-ton version was cast in 1655, during Alexei's reign, but nineteen years elapsed before anyone could work out how to hoist it into the belfry, whence it fell to the ground and shattered in the fire of 1701. Thirty years later, Anna ordered the fragments to be used for a much larger bell, which lay in its casting pit for over a century, having cracked in 1737, when fire once again swept the Kremlin and water was poured on the red-hot bell. Finally, in 1836, the Tsar Bell was excavated and installed in its present location, accompanied by a chunk that broke off, itself weighing 11 tons.

The nineteenth-century dissident Pyotr Chaadaev mused that, "in Moscow every foreigner is taken to look at the great cannon and the great bell – the cannon which cannot be fired and the bell which fell down before it was rung. It is an amazing town in which the objects of interest are distinguished by their absurdity, or perhaps that great bell without a tongue is a hieroglyph symbolic of this huge, dumb land."

Sobornaya ploshchad and the Ivan the Great Belltower

Beyond the Patriarch's Palace lies the historic heart of the Kremlin, surrounded by a superb array of buildings that gives the square its name. **Sobornaya ploshchad** (Cathedral Square) was first laid out in the early fourteenth century, making it the oldest square in Moscow, although the buildings that you see today were erected later. Throughout Tsarist times the square was used for Imperial coronations and weddings, and before the capital was transferred to St Petersburg it was also the setting for court life and political dramas. Every morning the boyars and gentry converged here in carriages or sledges to assemble in order of rank; the *ploshchadniki* or "people of the square" being inferior to the *komnatniki* or "people of the apartments", who enjoyed access to the Tsar's palace. At other times commoners were free to gather on the square – providing they prostrated themselves whenever the Tsar appeared.

Soaring above the square, the magnificent white **Ivan the Great Belltower** (*Kolokolnya Ivana Velikovo*) provides a focal point for the entire Kremlin, being the tallest structure within its walls. The main belltower was erected in 1505–08 by the Italian architect **Marco Bono** (known in Russia as Bon Fryzain), whose octagonal tower was increased to its present height of 81m during the reign of Boris Godunov, as proclaimed by the inscription in gold letters beneath its gilded onion dome. It remained the tallest structure in Russia until 1707, and dominated Moscow's skyline for long after that. Adjacent is the four-storey belfry (*Zvonitsa*) added in 1532–43 by the architect Petrok Maliy, and which also has a gilded dome. The 64-ton Resurrection Bell, dating from the nineteenth century, is the largest of its 21 bells. On the ground floor of this section is a hall used for **temporary exhibitions**, for which an extra ticket ($5; sold on the spot) is required. The final, tent-roofed part of the building – known as the Filaret Annexe, after the Patriarch who commissioned it in 1624 – was badly damaged in 1812, when the French attempted (but failed) to blow up the entire belltower.

The Cathedral of the Assumption

Across the square from the Ivan the Great Belltower stands the oldest and most important of the Kremlin churches, whose massive walls and gilded helmet-shaped domes have the stern serenity of a warrior monk. The **Cathedral of the Assumption** (*Uspenskiy sobor*) has symbolized Moscow's claim to be the protector of Russian Orthodoxy ever since the seat of the Church was transferred here

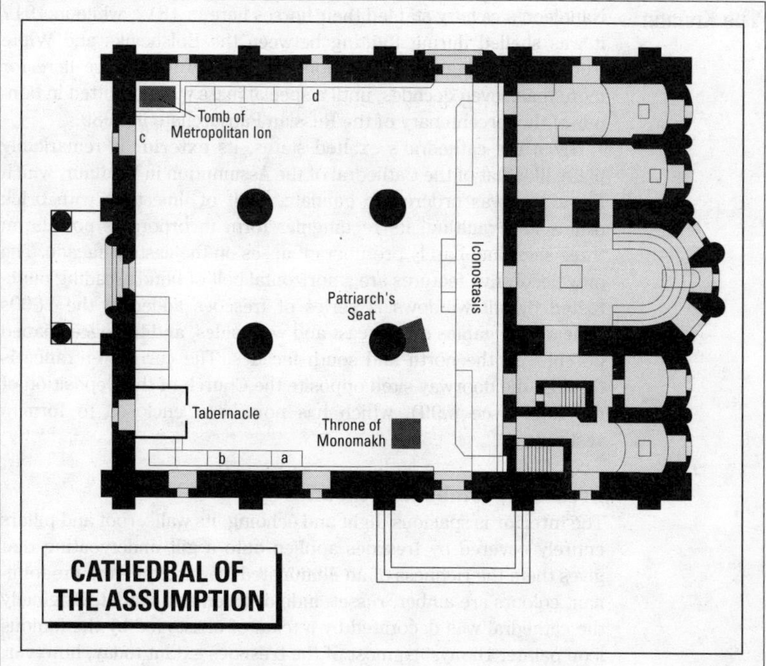

from Vladimir in 1326, together with a revered icon that was installed in a small cathedral erected by Ivan I.

By the 1470s this cathedral had become so decrepit that Ivan III ordered a replacement worthy of Moscow's stature; unfortunately the first effort by native builders collapsed before completion, so Ivan hired the Bolognese architect **Alberti Fioravanti** – dubbed "Aristotle" – who arrived in 1475, bringing engineering techniques a century ahead of any in Russia. Having visited the ancient cities of Vladimir, Suzdal and Novgorod to study Russian architectural traditions, he took only four years to finish the cathedral, which so harmonized with native forms that Patriarch Nikon would later recommend it as a model for Russian architects. Fioravanti's reward was to be thrown in prison after he begged permission to return to Italy; he died there in 1486.

The cathedral's subsequent **history** reflects its role as Russia's premier church, used throughout Tsarist times for coronations and solemn acts of state. Here, Ivan III tore up the charter that bound Russia's princes to pay tribute to the Tatar Khans; divine intercession was invoked during calamities; Te Deums were sung to celebrate victories; and the Patriarchs of the Orthodox Church were inaugurated and buried. In times of woe, the cathedral also suffered:

Napoleon's cavalry stabled their horses here in 1812, while in 1917 it was shelled during fighting between the Bolsheviks and White troops. Following the Revolution, no services took place here for more than seven decades, until a special mass was permitted in honour of the tercentenary of the Russian Patriarchate in 1989.

Given the cathedral's exalted status, its **exterior** is remarkably plain, like that of the Cathedral of the Assumption in Vladimir, which Fioravanti was ordered to emulate. Built of limestone with brick drums and vaulting, its rectangular form incorporates portals on three sides and barely protuberant apses on the eastern facade. The only decorative features are a horizontal belt of blind arcading punctuated by slit windows, a series of frescoes added in the 1660s beneath the gables on the east and west sides, and the ogee-shaped porches on the north and south facades. The current entrance is through the doorway sited opposite the Church of the Deposition of the Robe (see p.99), which has now been enclosed to form a vestibule.

Frescoes, tombs and thrones

The **interior** is spacious, light and echoing, its walls, roof and pillars entirely covered by frescoes applied onto a gilt undercoating that gives them the richness of an illuminated manuscript – the predominant colours are amber, russet, indigo, green and scarlet. Originally the cathedral was decorated by a team of artists led by the famous icon painter Dionysius; most of the **frescoes** extant today, however, date from the cathedral's first restoration in the 1640s, and were restored in Soviet times. As is usual in Orthodox churches, the west wall bears a huge Apocalypse, with Christ flanked by the saintly host floating above a pair of scales. Notice the infernal serpent writhing in coils of iron, prodded by angels (below), and sinners being scourged and fed into the maw of Satan (bottom right). The upper three tiers on the north and south walls depict the life of the Virgin, while the pillars are adorned with five rows of paintings portraying saints and martyrs (which decrease in height towards the roof, so as to accentuate the loftiness of the cathedral).

Around the walls are the **tombs of the Metropolitans* and Patriarchs**, encased in metal caskets resembling caterers' hotboxes, with the conspicuous exceptions of a bronze Tabernacle containing the remains of Patriarch Hermogenes, who perished in prison for opposing the Polish occupation in 1612 and was later canonized; and the tomb of Metropolitan Ion in the northwest corner, surmounted by a gold and silver arch. Aside from Patriarch Nikon, who lies in the New Jerusalem Monastery, the only absentees are Tikhon and Alexei I, two Patriarchs of Soviet times.

---

*The title reflected the Russian Orthodox Church's nominal subordination to the Patriarchate of Constantinople until 1589, when it finally became fully autonomous, with its own Patriarch.

When not officiating during services, the head of the Church sat in the stone **Patriarch's Seat**, built into one of the cathedral's pillars. Nearby stands the **Throne of Monomakh**, covered by an elaborate tent-roofed canopy crowned with a double-headed eagle, made for Ivan the Terrible in 1551. The throne's name derives from its carvings, depicting the campaigns of Grand Prince Vladimir, who supposedly received the famous Crown of Monomakh from the Byzantine Emperor Constantine IX – a legend that Ivan used to support Moscow's claim to be the "Third Rome" and the heir to Byzantium.

The Crown of Monomakh can be seen in the Armoury Palace.

Icons

The cathedral's lofty **iconostasis** dates from 1652, but its bottom row incorporates several older icons. On the far left is the enthronement of the Virgin known as *All Creatures Rejoice in Thee*, followed by a cutaway section revealing fragments of the cathedral's original frescoes, both of which were painted by Dionysius. A tent-roofed box to the left of the central Royal Door contains an early sixteenth-century copy of the revered *Our Lady of Vladimir*, while to the right of the southern door is a blue-cloaked St George the Victorious, painted in Novgorod during the twelfth century. Between the two pillars nearest the iconostasis hangs the 46-branch **Harvest Chandelier**, presented to the cathedral by Cossacks after they recaptured much of the 5330 kilos of silver that had been looted from the premises by the French army in 1812.

Around the walls hang **other icons** of historic interest. Dionysius is supposed to have painted *The Life of Metropolitan Peter* [**a**], which honours the prelate who engineered the transfer of the Metropolitanate from Vladimir to Moscow; the foundation of the original Cathedral of the Assumption is depicted near its bottom left corner. Nearby hangs *The Apostles Peter and Paul*, painted by an unknown Greek master of the fourteenth or fifteenth century [**b**]. By the west wall, an early fifteenth-century Crucifixion is followed by another copy of *Our Lady of Vladimir* [**c**] which, like the copy in the iconostasis, was venerated almost as much as the original (now held by the Tretyakov Gallery), believed to have been painted by St Luke and to have saved Moscow from the army of Timerlane. The aptly named *Saviour with the Severe Eye*, painted in the 1340s, hangs nearby, while along the north wall are *St Nikolai and his Life*, by the school of Novgorod, and several icons from the Solovetskiy Monastery in the White Sea [**d**].

The Church of the Deposition of the Robe

Almost hidden behind the Cathedral of the Assumption, the lowly white **Church of the Deposition of the Robe** (*tserkov Rizpolozheniya*) was built by craftsmen from Pskov in 1484–86, on the foundations of an older church erected to celebrate the prevention of a Tatar attack on Moscow some thirty years earlier. Its name refers to the festival of the deposition of the robe or veil of the Virgin Mary in Constantinople, which was believed to have saved the city from capture on several occasions; the miraculous relic was paraded around the city walls in times of danger, as was an icon of the same name in Moscow during medieval times.

Externally, the church is notable for the slender pilasters and intricate friezes that decorate its apses, and the ogee-shaped portal on its south side, reached by an open stairway. Nowadays visitors enter by a covered stairway facing the Cathedral of the Assumption, which leads up to an **exhibition of wooden figures**, which believers once imbued with almost as much holiness as icons. The effigies of Nikita Muchenik (wearing armour and hefting a flail) and Patriarch Nikola (carrying a model of a cathedral) are particularly striking.

Inside the chapel there's hardly room to swing a censer, but it's worth lingering over the **frescoes**, which were painted in 1644 by Sidor Osipov and Ivan Borisov, and restored in the 1950s. Above the door as you come in are Mary and Joseph in the wilderness and the *Adoration of the Magi*; on the other walls, the uppermost tiers depict scenes from the apocryphal life of the Virgin, while the bottom two rows illustrate the 25 stanzas of the *Hymn to the Virgin*. Christ, the Virgin and the prophets cover the ceiling, while the pillars bear portraits of Prince Vladimir, Alexander Nevsky and other heroes of Russian Christianity.

The Cathedral of the Archangel

The last of the great churches to be erected on Sobornaya ploshchad, the **Cathedral of the Archangel** (*Arkhangelskiy sobor*) was built in 1505–08 as the burial place for the rulers of Muscovy, who claimed the Archangel Michael as their celestial guardian. Unlike the vernacular Cathedral of the Assumption, its debt to the Italian Renaissance is obvious, for the architect **Alevisio Novi** incorporated such features as Corinthian capitals and the Venetian-style shell scallops that form the gables. Another characteristic is its asymmetrical layout, with the east and west walls being divided into three sections, and the north and south walls into five. To compensate for this, the western pair of domes is larger than the eastern pair; both sets are clad in silvery iron, in contrast to the gilded central dome. The cathedral's plan was further complicated by the addition of chapels to the apses during the sixteenth century; buttresses along the south wall were added after it cracked in 1773; and an annexe or *palatka* was attached to the southwest corner in 1826.

You enter the cathedral through its west **portal**, whose archway is framed by carvings of plants and a faded fresco depicting Christ and the saints (above), and the mass baptism of the Russians during the reign of Prince Vladimir (at the bottom, on either side).

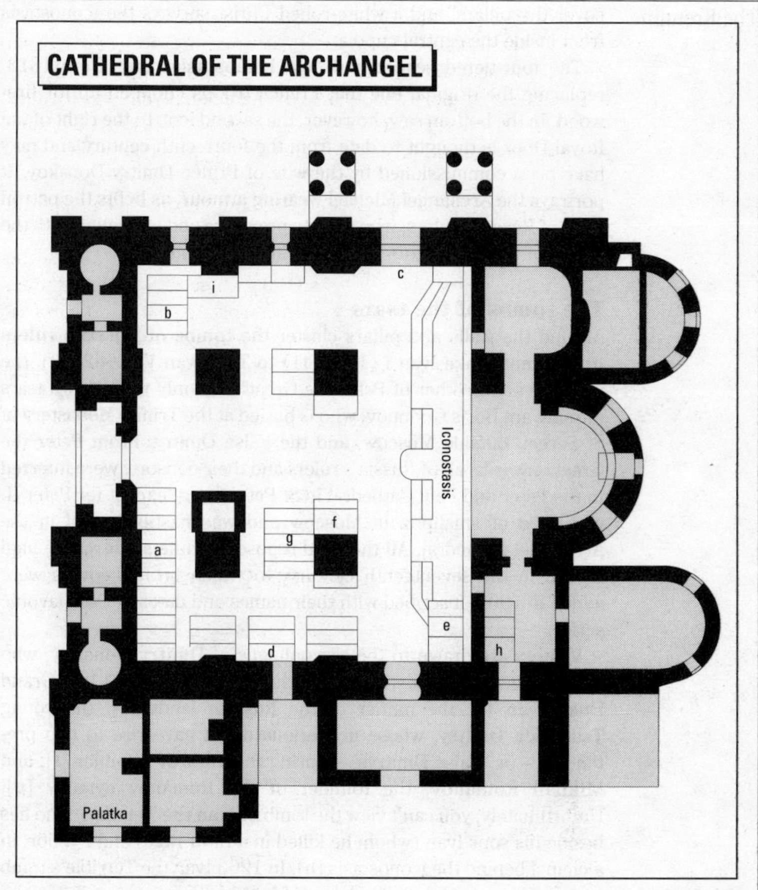

The frescoes and iconostasis

Four heavy square pillars take up much of the dimly lit interior, which is covered in frescoes executed (1652–66) by a team of artists under Simon Ushakov and Stepan Rezanets, which replaced the originals by Dionysius. Ochre, pale blue, red, white and dark brown predominate, with *The Apocalypse* in its usual position on the west wall. Notice the angels summoning the dead from their graves [**a**], and Satan sitting on a fiery beast whose mouth emits a serpent that drags sinners down into Hell [**b**]. *The Adoration of the Magi* and *The Annunciation* are depicted on the third and fourth tiers of the north wall [**c**], while the south wall portrays the deeds of the Archangel Michael. Stylized portraits of early Russian rulers, martyrs and saints cover the pillars, and a white-robed Christ surveys the iconostasis from inside the central cupola.

The four-tiered scarlet and gold **iconostasis** dates from 1813, replacing the original one that French troops chopped up for firewood. In the bottom row, however, the second icon to the right of the Royal Door is thought to date from the fourteenth century and may have been commissioned by the wife of Prince Dmitry Donskoy. It portrays the Archangel Michael wearing armour, as befits the patron saint of Russia's rulers, who used to pray here and commune with the spirits of their ancestors before setting off to war.

The tombs of the tsars

Around the walls and pillars cluster the **tombs of Russia's rulers** from Grand Duke Ivan I (1328–41) to Tsar Ivan V (1682–96), the moronic half-brother of Peter the Great. The only well-known tsars missing are Boris Godunov, who is buried at the Trinity Monastery of St Sergei, outside Moscow, and the False Dmitry. From Peter the Great onwards, all of Russia's rulers and their consorts were interred in the Peter and Paul Cathedral in St Petersburg, except for Peter II, who died of smallpox in Moscow and was hastily buried in the Archangel Cathedral. All the dead repose in white stone sarcophagi carved in the seventeenth century, to which bronze covers were added in 1903, inscribed with their names and dates in Old Slavonic script.

Visitors are drawn to the sarcophagus of **Dmitry Donskoy**, who inflicted the first major defeat on the Mongols in 1380 [**d**]; Grand Duke **Ivan III**, the unifier of the Russian lands [**e**]; the young **Tsarevich Dmitry**, whose mysterious death gave rise to two pretenders – or "False Dmitrys" – during the Time of Troubles [**f**]; and **Mikhail Romanov**, the founder of the Romanov dynasty [**g**]. Unfortunately, you can't view the tomb of **Ivan the Terrible**, who lies beside his sons Ivan (whom he killed in a fit of rage) and Fyodor, in a chapel behind the iconostasis [**h**]. In 1963 Ivan the Terrible's tomb was exhumed and a model of his head was created by the anthropologist Gerasimov, an expert at reconstructing the features of unidentified corpses from their skulls, who makes a pseudonymous appearance in Martin Cruz Smith's novel *Gorky Park*.

One final tomb, overlooked by Russian guides and guidebooks, is that of **Vasily Shuysky**, whose brief reign (1606–10) is regarded as somewhat inglorious – hence the tomb's lowly position by the north wall (**i**).

The Faceted, Terem and Great Kremlin palaces

Sadly, the fabulous Imperial palaces within the Kremlin are generally inaccessible to visitors except for **occasional special tours** of the Great Kremlin Palace, run by Patriarshy Dom Tours (see p.43), which cost $500, split between however many people comprise the group. Therefore, the following brief accounts merely provide some historical context; a better idea of their interiors can be gained from illustrated books like *Moscow Revealed* (see p.445).

The white **Faceted Palace** (*Granovitaya palata*) that juts out between the cathedrals of the Assumption and the Annunciation is so called for its diamond-patterned facade. Built for Ivan III in 1487–91 by Marco Ruffo and Pietro Antonio Solario, its outstanding feature is the large chamber that forms its upper storey, whose vaults are supported by a single massive pillar. Painted and gilded, this traditionally served as a banqueting hall and audience chamber. Ivan the Terrible's feasts lasted six hours or more, and began with grilled swan in saffron sauce; he regarded it as a compliment when guests collapsed from too much alcohol.

In medieval times, the tsars descended from the hall to Sobornaya ploshchad by the **Red Staircase** (*Krasnaya lesnitsa*), whence several relatives of the ten-year-old Peter the Great were thrown down onto the pikes of the Streltsy during the revolt of 1682. Wantonly demolished in the 1930s, the staircase was rebuilt in 1994, complete with Tsarist eagles above its arches and lions on the balustrade. It isn't red, however; as with Red Square, its name originally meant "beautiful".

Directly behind the Church of the Deposition of the Robe you can see the eleven gilded onion domes of the **Terem Palace** (*Teremnoy dvorets*), the oldest building in the Kremlin, which served as the Imperial residence until Peter the Great moved the capital to St Petersburg in 1712. The palace incorporates two medieval churches built one on top of the other and two levels of service quarters, above which is the royal suite created for Mikhail Romanov in 1635–36 – *terem* means "tower-chamber". All the rooms were connected by a corridor used for the *smotriny*, the selection of the tsar's bride from eligible virgins, ostensibly asleep on eiderdowns – Ivan the Terrible indulged in this rite at least seven times. In 1837, the long-disused palace was refurbished in a recreation of the seventeenth-century style, with elaborately tiled stoves, gilded stucco and painted vaultings.

The aptly named **Great Kremlin Palace** (*Bolshoy Kremlevskiy dvorets*) stretches for 125m along the crest of the Kremlin hill. Commissioned in 1837 by Nicholas I, who preferred Moscow to St Petersburg and admired ancient Russia, its yellow-and-white facade employs old Russo-Byzantine motifs according to the rules of Classical harmony. Under Yeltsin, the palace's reception halls received a makeover that appalled art historians – including two replica thrones and several foyers and galleries that never existed before – but visitors are invariably staggered by their splendour.

The Cathedral of the Annunciation

To the south of the Faceted Palace glints the golden-domed **Cathedral of the Annunciation** (*Blagoveshchenskiy sobor*), which

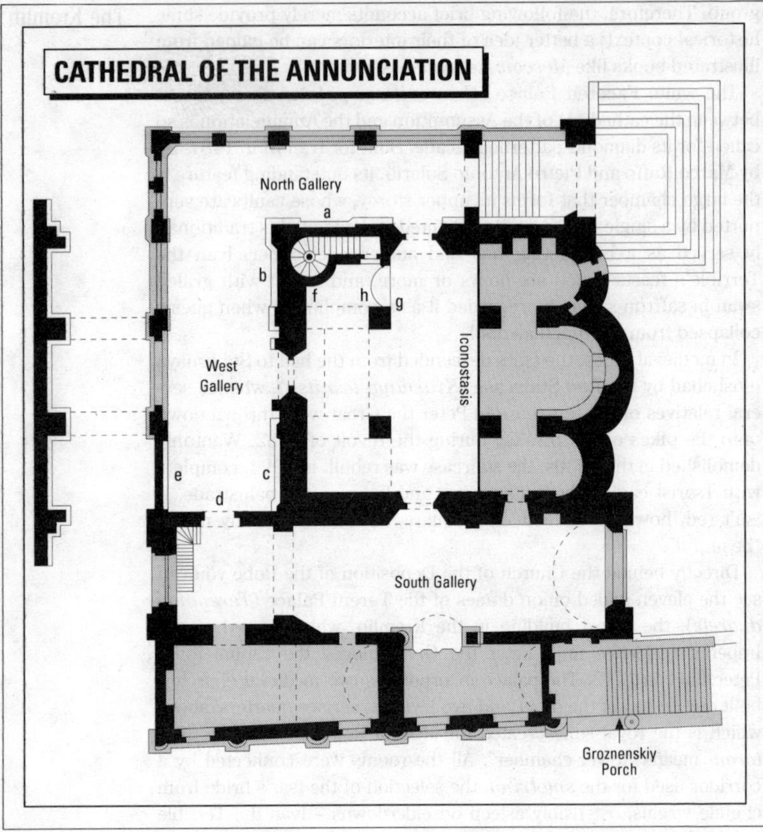

served as the private church of the grand dukes and tsars. It stands on the site of a church built by Dmitry Donskoy's son, Vasily I, the foundations and undercroft of which were incorporated into the existing structure, erected in 1448–49 by master stonemasons from Pskov at the behest of Ivan III. The cathedral was badly damaged in the conflagration that swept Moscow in 1547, shortly after the coronation of Ivan the Terrible, and it was restored in 1562–64. The tsar had the cathedral's gallery enclosed, a domed chapel added to each corner, and two false domes erected, bringing the total to nine. The domes, roof and tops of the apses were then sheathed in gold (supposedly looted from Novgorod, after Ivan sacked the city), giving rise to the cathedral's nickname, "gold-topped" (*Zlatoverkhniy*). Its tiers of gables and *kokoshniki* reflect the influence of early Moscow architecture, while the intricately carved frieze below the domes is a typical feature of Pskov churches.

Visitors enter via the steps at the northeast corner; the other, covered, porch was added in 1572, after Ivan the Terrible married for the fourth time, contrary to the rules of the Orthodox faith, which allow only three marriages. The Church Council dared not refuse him a special dispensation, but salved its conscience by stipulating that the tsar henceforth attend services via a separate entrance, and observe them from behind a grille. You can follow in his footsteps by climbing the steps of the **Groznenskiy Porch** (whose name derives from the sobriquet *Grozny*, meaning "Awesome" or "Terrible") alongside the road leading to the Armoury Palace.

The galleries

The royal chapel is enclosed by three **galleries**, two of which are richly decorated with frescoes painted in the 1560s. An elaborate but faded *Tree of Jesse*, symbolizing the continuity between the Old and New Testaments, covers the ceiling and merges into portraits of Muscovite princes and Greek philosophers on the vaults and pilasters. Just beyond the magnificent blue-and-gold portal carved with floral tracery, you'll see *Jonah and the Whale*, with two anatomically preposterous fish, one swallowing Jonah and the other disgorging him [**a**]. In the west gallery, another gilded portal is flanked by the hymn to the Virgin known as *In Thee Rejoiceth* [**b**] and *The Trinity* [**c**], around the corner from which the *Feats of the Monastic Recluses* [**d**] shows their fasts and flagellations, and a brightly coloured *Annunciation* [**e**] was added in the nineteenth century. The third gallery, decorated at the same time, now exhibits diverse icons and ecclesiastical objects, including two crosses carved with miniature biblical scenes, which are best viewed after the royal chapel.

The chapel and its iconostasis

Lofty and narrow, with much of the space occupied by the pillars supporting a gallery from which the female members of the royal family would have observed services, the interior seems far more "Russian" than the other cathedrals within the Kremlin. Its floor of irregularly shaped, brown jaspar flagstones enhances the impression of warmth and intimacy created by the soft-toned murals and lustrous iconostasis. The restored **frescoes** were originally painted in 1508 by a fraternity of icon-painters from the Iosifo-Volotskiy Monastery, headed by the monk Feodosius, son of the Dionysius who created the original murals in the Cathedral of the Archangel.

The *Last Judgement* in the northwest corner is populated by mythical creatures and huddled sinners, covetously regarded by Satan [**f**], while on the overhead gallery you can discern toppling buildings and beasts attacking men in *The Apocalypse* [**g**]. Portraits of Russian princes, including Dmitry Donskoy and Vasily I, adorn the nearby pillar [**h**]; the other one features the Byzantine emperors and their families. Scenes from the lives of Christ and the Virgin cover the north and south walls, while angels, patriarchs and prophets cluster around Christ Pantokrator in the central dome.

The **iconostasis** – which dates from 1405 and survived the fire of 1547 – is regarded as the finest in Russia, containing as it does the work of three masters: Theophanes the Greek, Andrei Rublev and Prokhor of Gorodets. In the bottom row to the right of the Royal Door are *Christ Enthroned* and the *Ustyug Annunciation* (whose central panel is a copy of the twelfth-century original now in the Tretyakov Gallery). To the left of the Royal Door are icons of the *Hodegetria Virgin* and *Our Lady of Tikhvin* (far left), both dating from the sixteenth century. Theophanes created most of the icons in the third, Deesis Row, where Christ is flanked by John the Baptist and the Virgin, next to whom is an Archangel Michael attributed to Rublev, who collaborated with Prokhor on the Festival Row, above. This is surmounted by a row devoted to the prophets, topped by ogee-shaped finials containing small images of the patriarchs.

The Armoury Palace

Situated between the Great Kremlin Palace and the Borovitskiy Gate, the **Armoury Palace** (*Oruzheynaya palata*) conceals a staggering array of treasures behind its Russo-Byzantine facade. Here are displayed the tsars' coronation robes, carriages, jewellery, dinner services and armour – made by the finest craftsmen with an utter disregard for cost or restraint – whose splendour and curiosity value outweigh the trouble and expense involved in seeing them.

As an institution, the Kremlin Armoury probably dates back to the fourteenth century, if not earlier, though the first recorded mention was in 1508. Initially, its purpose was utilitarian – one foreigner described it as being "so big and so richly stocked that twenty thousand cavalry men could be armed with its weapons" – but it soon became a storehouse for state treasures and, in 1806, a semi-public museum. The existing building was completed in 1851 in the same style as the Great Kremlin Palace, by Nicholas I's favourite architect, Konstantin Ton.

Visiting the Armoury

Unless you sign up for an Intourist tour, **visiting the Armoury** requires a little planning. Admission is limited to four times a day (10am, noon, 2.30 & 4.30pm), and you can only remain inside for a single session of one hour and 45 minutes' duration. It's advisable to buy a ticket before you enter the Kremlin and start queuing outside the Armoury entrance at least fifteen minutes early, otherwise you'll waste time waiting to buy a ticket in the foyer (which has an ATM for Visa cards that pays out in rubles).

Beyond the cloakroom is an information desk, followed by stalls selling books and souvenirs, where you can rent a **guide-tape** ($4), buy a **guidebook** to the Armoury ($8) or even a CD-ROM tour of the Kremlin. Stairs at the far end lead to a small foyer with two doors, one leading to the Armoury Museum, the other to the State Diamond Fund (see p.112), whence you ascend to a larger foyer with two staircases, the left-hand one leading to the lower floor of the Armoury, the other to the upper floor.

The lower floor

Although guided tours often start on the floor above, it's the **lower floor** that holds the most appeal, as it displays the fabulous costumes, thrones, crowns and carriages of Russia's rulers, from medieval times onwards. Besides their sheer sumptuousness, one is struck by the abrupt stylistic change from Russo-Byzantine forms to the fashion of Western European courts, introduced by Peter the Great in the early eighteenth century. Though each section has an explanatory note in English, the actual exhibits are labelled in Russian only, but the keyed plan below should help you to figure out what's what.

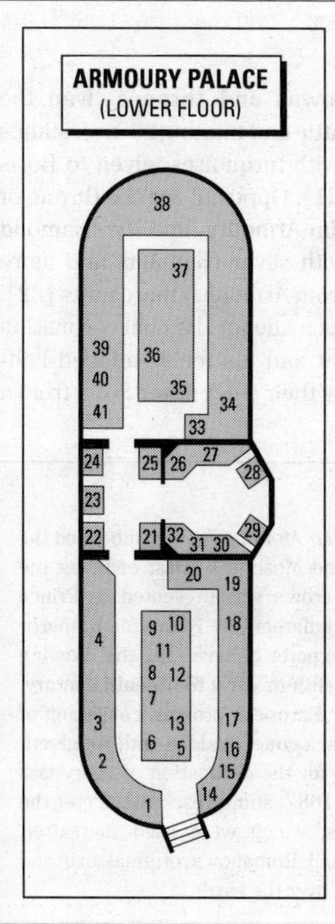

Court dress and vestments

The first room is largely devoted to **court dress**. In the left-hand case are a black velvet caftan worn by Peter the Great whilst working in the shipyards of Amsterdam, and his thigh-boots and cane [**1**]; a falconry outfit with a Tsarist eagle on its breast [**2**]; typical long-sleeved, old-style caftans [**3**]; the gold brocade robes and jewellery worn by Peter at his coronation, and the house-caftans that he relaxed in [**4**]. The central display is fronted by an archaic gold caftan and sable hat worn by Nicholas II at a costume ball in 1903 [**5**], with Peter the Great's Dutch-style frock coat nearby. Beyond the cerise coronation dress of Catherine I [**6**] are the frock coat and stockings of Peter II; the gold-embroidered coronation dresses of empresses Anna [**7**] and Elizabeth [**8**]; and the wasp-waisted wedding dress of the future Catherine the Great

[9]. Finest of all are Catherine's coronation dress [**10**] and the ermine-trimmed cape [**11**] of Nicholas II's wife Alexandra. The coronation dresses of Alexandra Fyodorovna [**12**] and Maria Alexandrova [**13**] are in the French Empire style of the 1820–50s.

Along the right wall are **ecclesiastical vestments and fabrics**, the oldest of which is the pale blue and silver satin *sakkos* (ceremonial robe) of Metropolitan Peter, made in 1322 [**14**]. Metropolitan Photius had two sakkos [**15**]: the Maliy, decorated with Crucifixions, saints and royal portraits; and the Bolshoy, with similar designs outlined in pearls (a symbol of good luck in old Russia). Past a *sakkos* given by Ivan the Terrible to Metropolitan Dionysius [**16**] are the pearl-embroidered Venetian velvet robes, mantle, cuffs and crowns of Patriarch Nikon [**17**] – the mantle alone weighs 24 kilos. Imported European fabrics began to be used from the seventeenth century onwards, as evinced by the cloth-of-gold pearl-hemmed cape given by Mikhail Romanov to the Novospasskiy Monastery [**18**]; Patriarch Adrian's Italian robe, embroidered with Tsarist eagles [**19**]; and an Italian velvet cape criss-crossed with pearl tracery and emblazoned with a diamond and emerald cross, given by Catherine the Great to Metropolitan Platon [**20**].

Crowns and thrones

The corridor beyond showcases **crowns and thrones**. Ivan the Terrible's ivory throne, carved with battle and hunting scenes, stands beside a low golden throne studded with turquoises, given to Boris Godunov by Shah Abbas I of Persia [**21**]. Opposite are the throne of Mikhail Romanov, made in the Kremlin Armoury, and the Diamond Throne of his son Alexei, adorned with silver elephants and more than eight hundred diamonds, a gift from Armenian merchants [**22**]. The huge silver double throne [**23**] was made for the dual coronation in 1682 of the young Peter the Great and his feeble-minded half-brother Ivan V, who were prompted by their elder sister Sofia from a

The Crown of Monomakh

The Cap or **Crown of Monomakh** (*Shapka Monomakha*) symbolized the tsars' claim to heritage of Byzantium and Moscow's boast of being the "Third Rome". Legend has it that the crown was presented to Prince Vladimir of Kiev (1053–1125) by his grandfather, the Byzantine Emperor Constantine IX Monomachus, though experts believe that the existing crown actually dates from the late thirteenth or early fourteenth century. In any event, it visibly differs from other European crowns, consisting of eight gold-filigree triangles joined to form a cone, studded with rough-cut gems and trimmed with sable. It served for the coronation of every tsar from the end of the fifteenth century to 1682; some years later Peter the Great introduced Western-style crowns, which were used thereafter. However, his successors retained Mikhail Romanov's original orb and sceptre, symbolizing the tsar's dominion over the earth.

secret nook behind the throne (now exposed). The hefty Empress Elizabeth sat on a wide Empire-style "armchair" throne, while the runty Tsar Paul had a smaller one with a foot-tuffet [24].

Best of all are the **crowns and imperial regalia** in the last case [25]. On the top shelf are the famous Crown of Monomakh (see box); the eighteenth-century European-style Silver Crown that belonged to Empress Anna, encrusted with 2500 diamonds; and a cruder "second" Crown of Monomakh that was made for the joint coronation of Peter and Ivan V. On the lower shelf can be seen the latter's Siberian Crown, trimmed in silver sable; the gold-leafed Kazan Crown of Ivan the Terrible, made to celebrate the capture of that city from the Tatars in 1552; and Mikhail Romanov's emerald-topped Dress Crown and enamelled orb and sceptre.

Saddlery and coaches

The adjacent octagonal room displays **equestrian regalia**, including Ivan the Terrible's saddle, covered in dark red velvet, turquoises and gold embroidery [26]. Beyond the saddles of Prince Pozharsky and Boris Godunov (the latter embossed with lions' heads) is a saddle decorated with gems, given by the Persian Shah to Mikhail Romanov in 1635 [27]. The stuffed horse in ceremonial attire was one of a hundred such horses that used to precede the Imperial coach during processions. Catherine the Great received jewelled harnesses and saddles from sultans Abdul Hamid [28] and Selim III [29], as did Alexei and Mikhail Romanov from earlier Turkish rulers [30], and tsars Fyodor and Boris Godunov from the monarchs of Persia [31] and Poland [32]. Also notice the splendid saddle from Gdansk, embroidered with hunting scenes in silver wire.

The oldest of the **carriages and coaches** in the end room is an English carriage presented to Boris Godunov by James I, decorated with hunting scenes on the sides [33]. Nearby stand an early seventeenth-century Russian coach with mica windows [34] and tiny summer and winter coaches made for the son and niece of Peter the Great, which had dwarves for coachmen and were drawn by ponies [35]. The French coach with paintings of cherubs by Boucher [36] was given to Empress Elizabeth by the Hetman of the Ukraine; she also owned a winter coach whose sleds were carved with dolphins [37], a fleet of travel coaches [38] and a coronation coach that was a present from Frederick II of Prussia [39]. By comparison, Catherine the Great's collection seems modest, consisting of two carriages for travel and state occasions [40], and a summer coach that was a gift from her favourite, Orlov [41].

The upper floor

From the same lobby, a grand staircase with brass balustrades ascends to the **upper floor**, whose landing is decorated with paintings of parades and processions outside the Kremlin, with the Soviet crest incongruously inset above a massive doorway. The rooms that follow are crammed with treasures and armour, which soon overwhelm visitors, and eventually pall. As on the lower floor, each case has an explanatory note in English, although individual pieces are labelled in Russian only.

Russian gold and silver

The first room contains the **Russian gold and silver** collection ranging from the twelfth to the sixteenth centuries, plus a few rare items from the Age of Migrations, such as a silver-gilt jug decorated with figures of the nine Muses [1]. Though many medieval treasures disappeared during the Mongol invasion, two buried troves of jewelled pectorals and necklaces were found at Ryazan and Tula in the nineteenth century [2]. Bibles and icons often used to be encased in gold covers like the foliage-engraved *okhlad* for *Our Lady of Vladimir* [3], while holy relics were kept in cathedral-shaped receptacles such as the Great Sion [4]. The sixteenth century was the golden age of Russian jewellery [5]. Notice the Evangelistry studded with gems as big as grapes, which Ivan the Terrible gave to the Cathedral of the Annunciation, and the pearl-rimmed crucifix that he bestowed upon the Solovetskiy Monastery [6]. The life-sized gold tomb covers [7] from the shrines of Tsarevich Dmitry and St Cyril, the founder of the Belozersk Monastery, are unique specimens of this form of art.

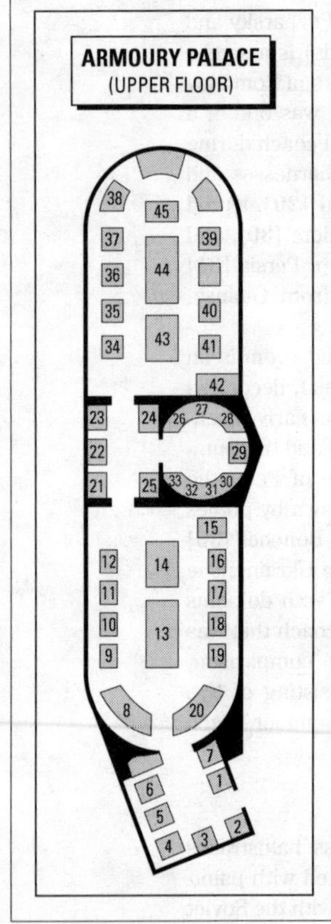

The dark green hall beyond exhibits more of the same, from the seventeenth century onwards. Near a squinting *Our Lady of the Don* with a pearl choker is a gold cover for an icon of The Trinity, featuring three face-shaped ovals suspended in mid-frame [8]. At court, mead was drunk from a scoop-shaped *kovsh*, while guests toasted each other with a shared friendship cup, or *bratina* [9]. Moscow craftsmen specialized in the technique of niello, whereby etched grooves were filled with a powder that turned a soft black after firing, highlighting the designs that appeared on the surface [10]. At Solvychedosk, they excelled at enamelling, with tiny birds a favourite motif [11], whereas the Volga towns went in for minutely detailed silverwork [12]. The Kremlin workshops produced the enamelled chalice given by Boyarina Morozova to the Monastery of Miracles, and the gold goblet presented by Tsar Alexei to the Monastery of the Ascension [13].

The early eighteenth-century inlay and enamel work on display [**14**] is less striking, as is the collection of French Empire-style stuff [**15, 16 & 18**], snuffboxes and Evangelisteries [**17**].

However, don't miss the **Fabergé Eggs** that were exchanged as Easter gifts by the tsar and tsaritsa every year from 1884 until the fall of the Romanov dynasty [**19**]. Among the fourteen examples owned by the Armoury are the *Clock Egg*, with its bouquet of diamond lilies; the *Shtandart* and *Azov* eggs, containing models of the Imperial yacht and the cruiser *Azov*; and the *Kremlin Egg*, which played the anthem *God Save the Tsar*. Even more ingenious was the *Grand Siberian Railway Egg*, produced to mark the completion of the line to Vladivostok, which held a tiny replica of the Trans-Siberian Express, that ran for 20 metres when its clockwork locomotive was wound up. The *Dandelion* and *Pansies* are so artfully carved from crystal that they resemble jars full of water; the latter bears portraits of the tsar's children on its stamens, revealed by squeezing the stem.

A sauce boat surmounted by a beetle and a Style Moderne cup, jug and sugar bowl are the highlights of the twentieth-century display case [**20**].

Weapons and armour

Among the **foreign weapons and armour** in the next room are arquebuses and plate armour from Germany [**21**]; a complete set for a horse and rider, presented to Tsar Fyodor by King Stephen Bathory of Poland [**22**]; and a miniature suit of armour made for Tsarevich Alexei in 1634 [**23**]. Across the way are jewelled maces and Egyptian sabres, rifles inlaid with ivory and mother-of-pearl, gilded helmets and arm-guards studded with turquoises and carnelians – all hailing from various parts of the Ottoman Empire [**24**]. Also notice the spiked helmets with sinister face-masks, and the gem-encrusted dagger presented by the Shah of Persia to Mikhail Romanov, in the showcase of Persian arms and armour [**25**].

The adjacent circular chamber – decorated by a frieze of royal portraits – displays **Russian weapons and armour**. To the left are the spiked helmets and chain mail armour of Boris Godunov and Prince Shuyskiy, and a teardrop-shaped helmet made for Ivan Ivanovich, the three-year-old son of Ivan the Terrible [**26**]. The *saadak* (weapons case) and quiver of Mikhail Romanov are made of gold and encrusted with jewels [**27**], while his gold-chased helmet appears beyond the mail-and-plate armour of his son, Alexei [**28**]. Russian cavalrymen customarily wore a mixture of Russian-made and Turkish or Persian armour, as on the life-sized model [**29**]. Beyond various products of the Kremlin Armoury [**30**] are a host of drums, trumpets and officer's throat guards, captured from the Swedes during the Northern War [**31**]. Brilliants glitter on the hilt and scabbard of Alexander I's sword, made in Tula [**32**], and a display of the Chivalric Orders of the Tsarist Empire concludes the exhibition [**33**].

European gold and silver

The final hall is stuffed with **European gold and silver**, much of it presented as ambassadorial gifts. The Dutch gave Count Stroganov ewers, tankards and a leaf-shaped wall candelabra [34], while Tsar Alexei received a silver banqueting set from the Poles, which included a bird-figure that poured water on guests' hands [35]. In 1644, the Danes lavished similar gifts in the hope of marrying their Crown Prince to Tsarevna Irina, and the Hanseatic League sent huge goblets with gryphons on the lids [36]. Nuremburg goldsmiths devised receptacles moulded to fit pineapples [37] and a drinking vessel in the form of a cockerel [38], while Hamburg specialized in "smoking hills" that wafted aromatic fumes across the table [39]. From France came gold *toilette* sets for the Stroganovs and Trubetskoys [40], the *Tête-à-Tête* tea service [41], and the *Olympic* dessert service that Napoleon gave to Alexander I to commemorate the Treaty of Tilsit [42]. Among the Armoury's peerless collection of English Tudor silver are two leopard-shaped flagons and a pair of jugs with dragon spouts [43]. Finally, don't miss the triple-layer Swedish table fountain [44], nor the caseful of *objets* fashioned from shells, bone and other unusual materials [45].

The State Diamond Fund

The Armoury Palace also houses the **State Diamond Fund** (*Almazniy Fond*), a separate section under the auspices of the Ministry of Finance, which contains the most valuable gems in Russia. Access is strictly limited to groups, with a twenty-minute **guided tour** at 11.15am, and sometimes in the afternoon, too. **Tickets** are usually only available from Intourist for the equivalent of $30, and must be booked a day or two in advance.

Streets and squares

Krasnaya ploshchad	Красная площадь
Sobornaya ploshchad	Соборная площадь

Metro stations

Aleksandrovskiy Sad	Александровский сад
Biblioteka Imeni Lenina	библиотека имени Ленина
Borovitskaya	боровицкая
Okhotniy Ryad	Охотный ряд
Ploshchad Revolyutsii	Площадь Революции
Teatralnaya	Театральная

Museums

Armoury Palace	Оружейная палата
Historical Museum	Исторический музей
Kremlin	Кремль
Lenin Mausoleum	мавзолей В.И. Ленина

The exhibition features such treasures as the diamond-encrusted **Coronation Crown** of Catherine the Great, and the 190-carat **Orlov Diamond** that she was given by Count Grigory Orlov, in an attempt to revive their relationship; she never wore it, but had it set into the **Imperial Sceptre**. Another notable gem is the 89-carat **Shah Diamond**, presented to Nicholas I by the Shah of Persia as compensation for the murder of the Russian diplomat and playwright Griboedov by a mob in Teheran. Besides this, there are dozens of jewelled necklaces and earrings, the world's largest sapphire (258.8 carats), and a gold nugget weighing 36 kilos. You may also see some **Fabergé Eggs**, besides the ones on display in the Armoury Palace Museum.

Chapter 3

The Kitay-gorod

To the east of Red Square lies the old quarter of **KITAY-GOROD**, whose eclectic mix of churches and palaces, banks, workshops and offices reflects its 800-year-old history. Although Kitay-gorod means "China Town" in modern Russian, there is no evidence that Chinese merchants ever resided here, and most scholars believe that the name derives from *kita*, an old word meaning "wattle", after the palisades that reinforced the earthen wall erected around this early Kremlin suburb. In the fifteenth century nobles began to settle here in preference to the Kremlin, displacing the original population of artisans and traders, but the nobility later moved further out to escape the risk of fires and plagues, leaving the quarter to rich merchants. Finally, the merchants too relocated to more salubrious areas, and the Kitay-gorod became what it still is today, predominantly commercial, with new banks and emporiums replacing the older shops and dwellings.

Aside from the busy **streetlife** on thoroughfares like Nikolskaya ulitsa, the main attractions are the quarter's churches, particularly the **Church of the Trinity**; while the interior of the **Palace of the Romanov Boyars** and the **English Court** in the Zaryade area should also not be missed. The **Archeological Museum** and two sections of the **fortified walls** that once ran for 2.6km around the Kitay-gorod attest to its ancient history, while the former Lenin Museum and Communist Party headquarters are reminders of the not so distant Soviet era.

Being just off Red Square, **ploshchad Revolyutsii** is a good place to start, with access from Ploshchad Revolyutsii or Okhotniy Ryad metro stations; or you can approach the quarter from its periphery instead, starting from the Kitay-gorod or Lubyanka stations. As the Kitay-gorod is small and contained, you can walk around the whole quarter in an hour.

Around ploshchad Revolyutsii

Proximity to Red Square makes **ploshchad Revolyutsii** (Revolution Square) a meeting-place for Communist and far-right agitators, who

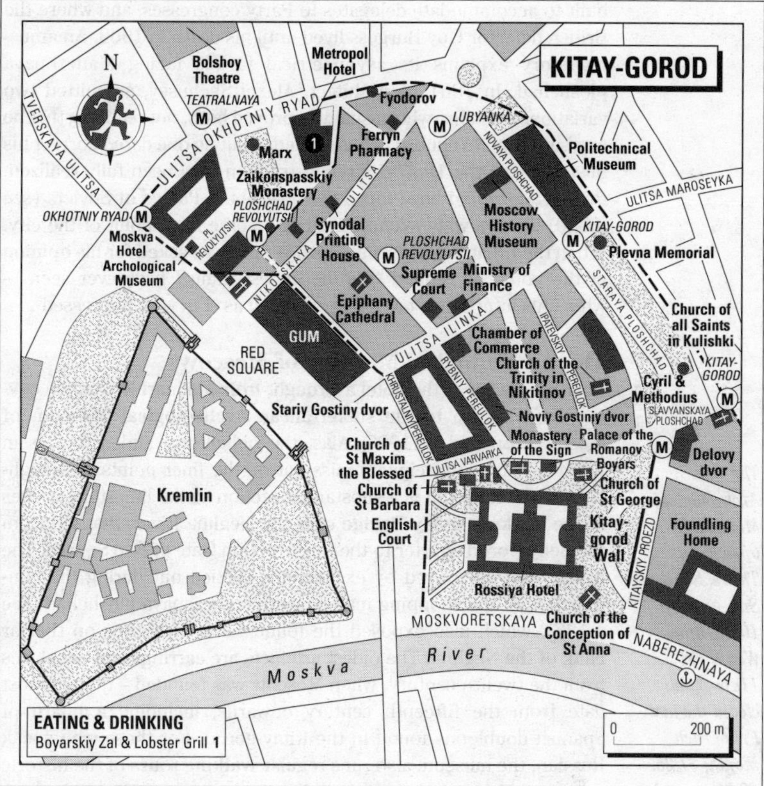

hawk Soviet memorabilia and anti-Semitic tracts outside the former Lenin Museum, a striking red-brick, Neo-Russian edifice that originally housed the pre-Revolutionary City Duma, or municipal council. Its 22 halls once contained the world's largest collection of Leninalia, including Lenin's Rolls-Royce Silver Ghost and a replica of his study in the Kremlin. After the 1991 putsch, the museum lost its state funding and was forced to shed 150 staff, but struggled on until 1993, when Luzhkov decreed its eviction to make way for the new City Duma. In fact, the building ended up being the site-headquarters of the contractors constructing the mall beneath Manezhnaya ploshchad, and its future use has yet to be decided. The flight of steps alongside leads through a passage to Nikolskaya ulitsa (see p.117).

At present, the ploshchad is a rather dreary expanse, but there are plans to landscape it in conjunction with the re-greening of Teatralnaya ploshchad, the larger square beyond the metro pavilion. Meanwhile, nothing softens the dour mass of the **Moskva Hotel**, built to accommodate delegates to Party congresses, and where the British defector Guy Burgess lived until his death in 1963. An amusing story explains its asymmetrical facade facing Manezhnaya ploshchad. In 1931 its architect, Alexei Shchusev, submitted two variations to Stalin, who casually approved both, not realizing that he was supposed to choose between them – but no one dared correct his mistake. Had the 1935 city reconstruction plan been fully realized, this facade would have faced the never-built Palace of Soviets (see p.150) down a wide avenue, intended as the focal point of the city. When the US architect Frank Lloyd Wright was asked for his opinion of the hotel, he replied "It's the ugliest thing I have ever seen" – which his interpreter tactfully translated as "I'm very impressed".

The Archeological Museum of Moscow

The Archeological Museum is open Tues, Thurs, Sat & Sun 10am–6pm, Wed & Fri 11am–7pm; closed the last Fri of each month; $1.25, $0.75 at weekends.

Near the corner of the hotel a wrought-iron and marble pavilion covers the entrance to the subterranean **Archeological Museum of Moscow**, opened in 1997. Alas, the obligatory guided tour is in Russian only, so foreigners miss out on the finer points. The highlight of the museum is a substantial section of the limestone arches of the **Voskresenskiy Bridge** over the Neglina River, that led from the Beliy Gorod quarter to the Resurrection Gate of Red Square. The bridge was uncovered by excavations carried out during the construction of the shopping mall beneath Manezhnaya ploshchad (see p.127), which also exposed the foundations of houses on the far bank of the Neglina. The oldest artefacts are earrings and necklaces from the twelfth century, when Moscow was founded – though most date from the fifteenth century onwards, including a hoard of Spanish doubloons found in the Kitay-gorod. For those who speak Russian, the museum also runs regular **walking tours** of the historic centre of Moscow, for groups of up to twenty people ($28 group rate, plus the price of admission to the museum itself).

Teatralnaya ploshchad, the medieval walls and the Metropol

Teatralnaya ploshchad (Theatre Square), on the far side of the hotel, is the next part of downtown Moscow set to be transformed now that Manezhnaya ploshchad has been finished, so you'll have to see what the outcome is. There's certainly room for improvement, as the square was cut in half by ulitsa Okhotniy ryad in the 1930s, leaving the Bolshoy and other theatres isolated from the greenery that did them justice. At present, the park behind the hotel is a stamping ground for prostitutes, and still harbours a **statue of Karl Marx** looming out of a granite menhir. The testimonials on either side read: "His name will endure through the ages, and so will his work" (Engels); "Marxist doctrine is omnipotent because it is true" (Lenin).

As a foretaste of what's to come, the end of the square is now dramatized by a replica of the **medieval walls** of Kitay-gorod, complete with swallow-tailed crenellations and a tent-roofed tower, added to a genuine portion that jinks off behind the **Metropol Hotel** due to a bend in the now-buried Neglina River. While the Proofreading House and belltower of the Zaikonspasskiy Monastery above the ramparts are accessible by a stairway, you're more likely to be drawn to the hotel. A Style Moderne masterpiece built (1899–1903) by the Odessa-born British architect William Walcott, its north wall features a huge ceramic panel, *The Princess of Dreams*, designed by the Symbolist artist Vrubel in his characteristic palette of indigo, violet and bottle green. Notice the wrought-iron gateway, and the two plaques beside the main entrance, attesting to the hotel's role as the "Second House of Soviets", where the Central Executive of the Soviets of Workers' and Peasants' Deputies met in 1918–19. Famous guests include Tolstoy, Chaliapin, George Bernard Shaw, JFK and Michael Jackson.

As an alternative route back into the Kitay-gorod you can continue uphill past the Metropol and cut in through the tent-roofed **ornamental gateway** that fronts Tretyakovskiy proezd. This passage is named after the merchant Sergei Tretyakov, who knocked it through the wall in 1871, for quicker access to the banks along Kuznetskiy most. Just uphill from the gateway is an appealing statue of Ivan Fyodorov, Russia's first printer (see below).

Nikolskaya ulitsa

Running off from Red Square either side of GUM are the two main thoroughfares of the Kitay-gorod, Nikolskaya ulitsa and ulitsa Ilinka. Named after the St Nicholas Gate of the Kremlin, facing the Red Square end of the street, **Nikolskaya ulitsa** bustles with shoppers emerging from GUM or the passage leading from ploshchad Revolyutsii. As its shop fronts are gradually restored to their pre-Revolutionary elegance, it's easy to imagine Nikolskaya ulitsa becoming a swanky pedestrian precinct – though it still has a long way to go.

On the left-hand side, the iron gateway of no. 9 leads into a courtyard harbouring the remains of the **Zaikonspasskiy Monastery**. Founded in 1600, the monastery supported itself by selling icons on the street outside – hence its name, "Behind the Icon of the Saviour". In 1687, its seminary was converted into Russia's first institution of higher education, the Slavo-Greco-Latin Academy. Now being restored, the monastery's cathedral has a red-and-white octagonal belltower crowned by a gilded finial, linked to the adjacent monks' quarters by an overhead arcade.

It's indicative of how many monasteries there were in Moscow that just up the road and around the corner, past the *Stariy Gorod* kiosk-row, is the Monastery of the Epiphany. Its hulking **Epiphany Cathedral** (*Bogoyavlenskiy sobor*) is decorated with crested *nalichniki* and an intricate cornice, while the crimson-and-white belltower is inset with mosaic portraits of saints, and topped by a gilded dome. Although the cathedral was constructed in the 1690s, the monastery itself was founded by Prince Daniil in the thirteenth century, making it the second oldest in Moscow. Here the restoration process is advanced due to gift-shop funds, and so services are held in the cathedral.

Returning to Nikolskaya ulitsa, you'll catch sight of the **Synodal Printing House**, a picturesque sky-blue structure with Gothic pinnacles and lacy stucco-work, erected on the site of the sixteenth-century Royal Print Yard (*Pechatniy dvor*), where Ivan Fyodorov produced Russia's first printed book, *The Apostle*. Ivan the Terrible took a keen interest, visiting nearly every day until it was completed in 1564, whereupon superstitious Muscovites incensed by this "Satan's work" stormed the press, forcing Fyodorov to flee for his life. In 1703, however, Russia's first newspaper, *Vedomosti*, was produced here without any mishap. The heraldic lion and unicorn of the old print yard appear over the existing building's central arch. In the courtyard out back lurks the original Proofreading House, tiled blue and red, which can be reached by entering the door on the left and turning right down some stairs – although you may need to persuade them to let you in.

Of equal significance to Moscow's cultural life was the Slavyanskiy Bazaar, at no. 17, which was famous for hosting an eighteen-hour discussion between Konstantin Stanislavsky and Vladimir Nemirovich-Danchenko, that led to the foundation of the Moscow Art Theatre (see p.132) – the restaurant obligingly stayed open till they had finished, at two o'clock in the morning! Unfortunately it burned down in 1994, and rebuilding work has only recently begun.

Nikolskaya ulitsa's commercial life concludes with the century-old **Ferryn Pharmacy** at no. 21 (Mon–Fri 8am–8pm, Sat 10am–6pm), which is worth a look for its Empire-style facade and the gilded and pillared room upstairs. Since the demolition in the 1930s of the medieval gate-tower at the end of the street, there's been an uninterrupted view of the secret police headquarters on the far side of Lubyanskaya ploshchad (p.155). Assuming you don't cross the square for a closer look, a right turn will take you in the direction of the Politechnical and Moscow History museums, described on p.124.

Ulitsa Ilinka

The parallel **ulitsa Ilinka** used to be the financial centre of the Kitay-gorod, and is gradually reverting to type. Its name derives from the former Church of St Elijah (*tserkov Ili*) – which worshippers are now restoring – across the road from the oval-shaped **Stariy Gostiniy dvor** that occupies the entire block between Khrustalniy (Crystal) and Ribniy (Fish) pereulok. The Russian equivalent of an oriental caravanserai for visiting merchants and their wares, it was designed in the 1790s by Catherine the Great's court architect, Quarenghi, who embellished its facade with colonnades of Corinthian pilasters. After much neglect its interior is now being totally refurbished, while the exterior has been painted a fetching pale blue-grey with a cream trim.

On the other corner of Ribniy pereulok stands the former Stock Exchange that now serves as Moscow's **Chamber of Commerce**. Painted tangerine and white, its Ionic pillars and bas-relief gryphons confront a small square flanked by buildings of equal probity. Across the way stand the **Supreme Court** – housed in another Neo-Russian pile – and the former **Ryabushinskiy Bank**, a pale green edifice with glazed brick facings, designed by the Style Moderne architect Fyodor Shekhtel. Pavel Ryabushinsky, Chairman of the Stock Exchange, also commissioned Shekhtel to build him a house that is one of the glories of Moscow (p.175). Take a brief look down Ribniy pereulok, where the Noviy Gostiniy dvor bears a kitsch bas-relief of a merchant's ship sailing into the sunset.

Continuing along Ilinka, you'll pass a striking pair of buildings: to the right, a pistachio facade upheld by writhing atlantes and caryatids, facing the austere grey tiers of the **Ministry of Finance**, across the road. Further on, gates bar access to the side streets leading to the complex previously occupied by the Communist Party's Central Committee – beyond which Ilinka emerges on to Novaya and Staraya squares (see the final section of this chapter).

Zaryade

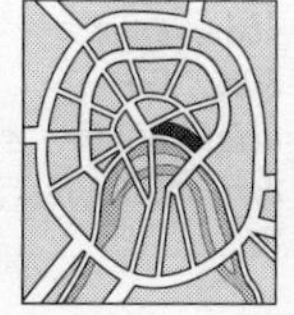

The most interesting part of the Kitay-gorod is the area known as **Zaryade**, situated due east of St Basil's. From the twelfth century onwards, the swampy slope above the Moskva River was settled by craftsmen and artisans, whose homes lay behind the rows (*za ryade*) of stalls that covered what is now Red Square. Though nobles and foreign merchants displaced them during the fifteenth and sixteenth centuries, the quarter gradually reverted to being the heart of popular Moscow, crammed with booths and huts, and smelling of "perfumed Russian leather, spiritous liquors, sour beer, cabbages, and grease of Cossacks' boots", and undrained cesspits that rendered it prone to epidemics. In *War and Peace*, Tolstoy wrote of peasants lying unconscious in the mud, and drunken soldiers staggering after prostitutes.

Today, Zaryade's main sights lie along or just off **ulitsa Varvarka** (St Barbara Street), which is the oldest street in Moscow, dating back to the fourteenth century. During Soviet times it was called ulitsa Razina, after the leader of the 1670 peasant revolt, Stenka Razin, who was led along it to his execution on Red Square. Seen from Red Square, Varvarka's vista of onion domes and gilded crosses is marred only by the towering **Rossiya Hotel**, a 1960s eyesore covering nearly ten acres, whose architects originally intended to demolish the

Zaryade

churches and medieval residences lining the street's south side. The appeal of the churches owes less to their interiors than to the totality of their variegated facades, which appear taller on the hotel-facing side, being built against a steep bank.

First comes the compact salmon-pink-and-white **Church of St Barbara** (*tserkov Varvary*), built in 1796–1804, on the site of an earlier church by Alevisio Novi, the architect of the Archangel Cathedral in the Kremlin. Having suffered decades of neglect under the stewardship of the All-Russia Society for the Protection of Monuments of History and Culture, it has now been returned to the Orthodox Church, but remains closed for repairs.

The English Court

The English Court is open June–Aug Tues, Thurs, Sat & Sun 11am–6pm, Wed & Fri 11am–6.45pm; Sept–May Tues–Thurs, Sat & Sun 10am–6pm; $0.50. For details of concerts ☎298 39 61.

At the bottom of the slope beyond the Church of St Barbara stands a chunky white building with a steep wooden roof and narrow windows of varying sizes, identified by a plaque on the wall facing the hotel as the **English Court** (*Angliskoe podvore*). As the exhibition inside relates, trade between England and Russia began in 1553 with the arrival of Richard Chancellor's merchant ship in Murmansk and the foundation of the Muscovy Company, which was granted duty-free privileges by Ivan the Terrible and given the house as a kind of embassy. While the first two envoys were warmly received, the third incurred Ivan's wrath by prevaricating over his demand to marry Queen Elizabeth I, and was confined under house arrest until Ivan's anger had abated. In return for English muskets, gunpowder and broadcloth, the Company exported furs, honey, caviar and mica, until it was expelled from Russia in 1649 by Tsar Alexei, who was outraged by the English Parliament's execution of Charles I.

The collection of old prints and coins is less interesting than the house itself, whose narrow staircases and extremely low doorways are typical of early Muscovite architecture. Its vaulted Official Hall has a huge fireplace-cum-stove made of bricks incised with zoomorphic designs, and was once used for banquets; it now hosts monthly **concerts** of medieval music. The final section of the exhibition tells how the house was saved from demolition in the 1960s by the architect Baranovsky, who recognized its medieval origins beneath what was by then an apartment block. It was restored to coincide with the state visit of Queen Elizabeth II in 1994.

The nearby **Church of St Maxim the Blessed** (*tserkov Maksima Blazhennovo*) is a simple Novgorod-style church with a yellow belltower, erected by merchants from Novgorod in 1690–99, as a repository for the mortal remains of the fifteenth-century "holy fool", St Maxim, venerated for his mortification and self-denial. Behind St Maxim's rises another, pointed belltower, belonging to the **Monastery of the Sign** (*Znamenskiy monastyr*), established on the Romanov family estate in 1634, following the death of the tsar's mother. The monastery's red-brick Cathedral, beyond the overpass leading to the hotel, is decorated with intricate *nalichniki* and *kokoshniki*, surmounted by four onion domes covered in green-and-red shingles, and a central, gilded dome. Like most of the churches on Zaryade, it was founded on oak piles that became harder than stone when wet. During Soviet times it was converted into a concert hall, but religious services are now once again held in the lower level of the church.

Zaryade

The Palace of the Romanov Boyars

Ulitsa Varvarka's most interesting building is the rambling **Palace of the Romanov Boyars** (*Muzey Palaty v Zaryade*), entered from the bottom of the embankment. Built in the sixteenth century by Nikita Romanov (Ivan the Terrible's brother-in-law), it once formed the nucleus of a vast complex of seven thousand households stretching down to the river, made almost entirely of wood, with the exception of the palace.

The Palace is open Mon & Thurs–Sun 10am–5pm; Wed 10am-6pm; closed the first Mon of each month; $ 3.

The Romanov family's menfolk used the first floor, built of stone, whose rooms are low and vaulted, with mica windows, tiled stoves and gilded, embossed leather "wallpaper", in contrast to the spacious, airy women's quarters upstairs, panelled in blonde wood. Here, married couples slept on benches against the walls, while unmarried daughters spent the daytime weaving in the adjacent *svetlitsa* or "light room", with its latticed windows overlooking the street. The residence was abandoned after Mikhail Romanov was elected tsar in 1613, and the whole family and their retainers moved into the Kremlin. In 1859, it was restored on the orders of Nicholas I as a tribute to his ancestors, and opened as a public museum.

Beyond the palace rises the sky-blue belltower of the **Church of St George** (*tserkov Georgiya na Pskovskoy Gorke*), whose sea-green onion domes spangled with gold stars and sprouting intricate crosses add a final touch of colour to the street. Although dedicated to the patron saint of Moscow, it was erected by merchants from Pskov in 1657, the belfry being a nineteenth-century addition. From here you can cross the road and walk up Ipatevskiy pereulok to find the wonderful Church of the Trinity, or head downhill towards Slavyanskaya ploshchad.

The Church of the Trinity on Nikitinov

By following Ipatevskiy pereulok uphill and turning right, you'll come upon the **Church of the Trinity on Nikitinov** pereulok (*tserkov Troitsy v Nikitinkakh*), whose exuberant colours and asymmetrical form are all the more striking for being hemmed in by the anonymous premises of the Moscow Regional Council and the former Central Committee of the Communist Party. The church defies its confinement with an explosion of decorative features: white ogee-shaped *nalichniki* and *kokoshniki*, columns and cor-

To enquire whether the Church of the Trinity is open ☎298 34 51.

Zaryade

nices contrasting with crimson walls, green roofs and domes. Its height and dynamism are accentuated by a tent-roofed stairway climbing above a deep arcaded undercroft, and an open pyramid-spired belfry that would have soared above the wooden houses of the medieval Kitay-gorod.

Erected in 1635–53 by the wealthy merchant Grigory Nikitinov, who stashed his valuables in its basement, the church was squatted by numerous families after the Revolution, before being turned into a museum in 1967 (it is still classified as a museum rather than a church). Owing to long-overdue repairs at the time of writing, you probably won't be able to enter the church and see its beautiful **frescoes** by Simon Ushakov and other icon painters from the Kremlin Armoury. The nave's right-hand wall depicts the Passion, while Christ calms the Disciples in a storm-tossed boat on the opposite wall. Best of all is the side chapel of St Nikita the Martyr, where members of Nikitinov's family are portrayed alongside various martyrdoms and a green seraph.

Due to the proximity of many government institutions, Nikitinov pereulok is patrolled by **plainclothes security agents**, who may demand that you produce some ID, and object to anyone taking photographs.

Down towards the river

Downhill from the Church of St George and around the corner to the right, another remnant of the **Kitay-gorod wall** runs alongside Kitayskiy proezd. Though its swallow-tailed crenellations resemble those of the Kremlin, the Kitay-gorod walls were constructed a century later, when Russian fortifications became lower and thicker owing to the advent of cannons in siege warfare, and they were originally wide enough for a carriage to drive along the top. The pedestrian subway exposes some fragments of the **Varvarka Gate** that once straddled this exit under the protection of a supposedly miraculous icon of the Virgin. During the plague of 1771, this was taken down and repeatedly kissed in frenzied services that spread contagion; when Archbishop Amvrosy realized this and tried to replace the icon above the gate, he was pursued by a mob to the Donskoy Monastery and torn to bits.

Visible through the trees across the road from the ramparts is the vast classical edifice of the **Foundling Home** (*Vospitalniy dom*), established by Catherine the Great to discourage infanticide and teach orphans trades useful to the state. Over 13,000 children resided here; but in 1812 as the French army approached, although the older ones were evacuated, the toddlers and babies were left behind in the care of a general (and, amazingly, survived). It now houses the Dzerzhinsky Artillery Academy and the grounds are off-limits.

Beside the embankment below the *Rossiya Hotel* stands the small white **Church of the Conception of St Anna** (*tserkov Zachatiya*

Anny), where Salomonia Saburova, Grand Duke Vasily III's barren wife, often prayed for a child. In 1526 she was confined to a convent (see p.409) so that he could marry Yelena Glinskaya, who gave birth to the future Ivan the Terrible four years later.

Zaryade

From Slavyanskaya ploshchad to the Lubyanka

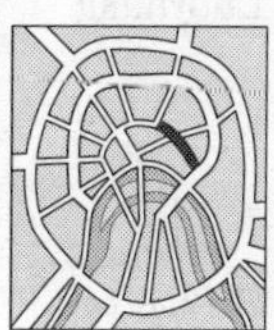

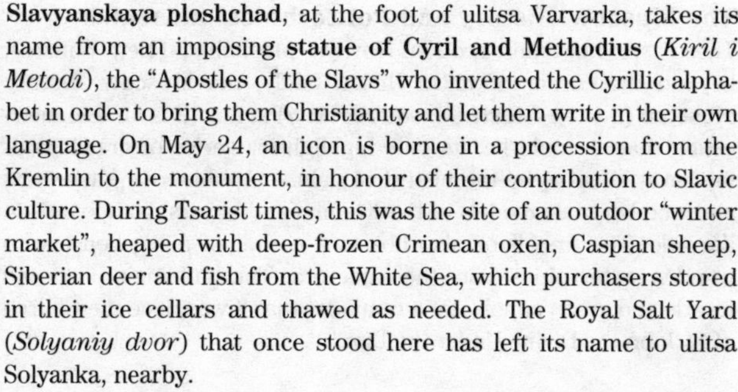

Slavyanskaya ploshchad, at the foot of ulitsa Varvarka, takes its name from an imposing **statue of Cyril and Methodius** (*Kiril i Metodi*), the "Apostles of the Slavs" who invented the Cyrillic alphabet in order to bring them Christianity and let them write in their own language. On May 24, an icon is borne in a procession from the Kremlin to the monument, in honour of their contribution to Slavic culture. During Tsarist times, this was the site of an outdoor "winter market", heaped with deep-frozen Crimean oxen, Caspian sheep, Siberian deer and fish from the White Sea, which purchasers stored in their ice cellars and thawed as needed. The Royal Salt Yard (*Solyaniy dvor*) that once stood here has left its name to ulitsa Solyanka, nearby.

With the Kitay-gorod's transformation into a modern financial centre early this century, the market was superseded by the **Delovy dvor** (Business House), on the corner of Kitayskiy proezd. During the "heroic phase" of Socialist construction during the 1930s, it housed the Commissariat for Heavy Industry, whose boss, Sergei Ordzhonikidze, also had a hand in building the first line of the metro system. Almost next door is the small but striking blood-red, gold-domed **Church of All Saints in Kulishki** (*tserkov Vsekh Svyatykh na Kulishkakh*), erected by Ivan III to replace a wooden church built in a forest clearing (*kulishki*) by Prince Dmitry Donskoy, whose army passed by en route to the battle of Kulikovo on the River Don (1380), where the Russians defeated the Mongols for the first time.

Behind the statue of Cyril and Methodius, the steep slope called **Staraya ploshchad** (Old Square) falls away from an embankment crowned by a row of office blocks dating from the beginning of the century. On the corner stands the former premises of the Moscow Insurance Company, an early design by Shekhtel, distinguished by its sea-green tiles and sinuous balconies. In Soviet times, this became the headquarters of the Moscow Regional Party organization, while the adjacent building (no. 4) housed the **Central Committee of the Communist Party**, the nexus of power in the Soviet Union. The day after the failure of the 1991 putsch, its nervous *apparatchiki* frantically shredded compromising documents, afraid to burn them lest the smoke cause the angry crowd outside to storm the building. Now flying the Russian tricolour, the buildings harbour the Prime Minister's office and regional government.

From Slavyanskaya ploshchad to the Lubyanka

At the top end of the wooded Ilinskiy Gardens that run down the middle of the hill stands the bell-shaped **Plevna Memorial**, honouring the Russian Grenadiers who died in the 1878 siege of Plevna, which liberated Bulgaria from the Turkish yoke. Financed by battle veterans, it was designed by Vladimir Sherwood, the architect of the Historical Museum on Red Square. The gardens are named after the former Ilinskiy Gate, which was demolished in the 1930s, like the other gates in the Kitay-gorod wall.

The Moscow History and Politechnical museums

The Moscow History Museum is open Tues, Thurs, Sat & Sun 10am–5pm, Wed & Fri 11am–6pm; closed the last Fri of each month; $0.50. More of Vasnetsov's scenes can be seen at his former apartment on Furmanniy pereulok (p.195).

These two museums are on **Novaya ploshchad** (New Square), beyond the corner of ulitsa Ilinka. Sadly, the **Moscow History Museum** (*muzey Istorii Goroda Moskvy*) at no. 12 is far less interesting than it could be, its only highlights a series of drawings of medieval Moscow by the historical painter Apollinarius Vasnetsov, and wooden scale models of the Kremlin and boyars' compounds in Zaryade. The first floor also boasts a corner of a log house with wooden water pipes from the same era. The building's porticoed facade and green cupola are a reminder that it was once the Church of St John the Divine Under the Elm.

Streets and squares

Ipatevskiy pereulok	Ипатьевский переулок
Kitayskiy proezd	Китайский проезд
Nikitinov pereulok	Никитинов переулок
Nikolskaya ulitsa	Никольская улица
Novaya ploshchad	Новая площадь
ploshchad Revolyutsii	площадь Революции
Slavyanskaya ploshchad	Славянская площадь
Staraya ploshchad	Старая площадь
Teatralnaya ploshchad	Театральная площадь
Tretyakovskiy proezd	Третьяковский проезд
ulitsa Ilinka	улица Ильинка
ulitsa Varvarka	улица Варварка

Metro stations

Kitay-Gorod	Китай-Город
Lubyanka	Лубянка
Okhotniy Ryad	Охотный ряд
Ploshchad Revolyutsii	Площадь Революции

Museums

Archeological Museum of Moscow	музей Археологии Москвы
English Court	Английское подворн
Palace of the Romanov Boyars	музей Палаты в Зарядье
Moscow History Museum	музей Истории Города Москвы
Politechnical Museum	Политехнический музей

Across the road at Novaya ploshchad 3–4 stands the **Politechnical Museum** (*Politekhnicheskiy muzey*; Tues–Sun 10am–5pm; closed the last Thurs of each month; $0.30), a long, mustard-coloured edifice in the Neo-Russian style. Founded in the 1870s to promote science and technology, the museum hosted experiments in telepathy in the 1960s that were subsequently conducted in secret under the auspices of the KGB. It has an endearingly old-fashioned character, with archaic instruments and models rather than VDUs or audio-guides. The first floor covers everything from the development of lamps and typewriters to mining and the petroleum industry, while the floor above deals with space travel, antique music boxes, clocks and computers. Among the classics of Soviet design are a TV set the size of a fridge with a screen so small it required a magnifying glass; and a hilarious ghettoblaster from the 1980s.

Before entering via the main door opposite the Moscow History Museum, you must buy a ticket inside entrance 9, on the side facing the Lubyanka. While there, don't overlook the **monument to the victims of the Gulag** protruding from the ground: a boulder from the Solovetskiy Isles, whose ancient monastery became one of the earliest Soviet concentration camps.

From Slavyanskaya ploshchad to the Lubyanka

Chapter 4

The Beliy Gorod

The **BELIY GOROD**, or "White Town", is the historic name of the residential district that encircled the Kremlin and the Kitay-gorod – derived from the white stone ramparts erected around it at the end of the sixteenth century. It remains a useful designation for the area within the horseshoe-shaped **Boulevard Ring** (*Bulvarnoe koltso*), laid out on the rampart sites after the great fire of 1812. Despite widening and modernization, many of the boulevards are still divided by long parks with wrought-iron lampposts and fences, redolent of nineteenth-century Moscow, and many squares bear the names of the original gate-towers. Fortunately, the Futurist El Lissitskiy's vision of buildings suspended above the Ring on giant legs (trumpeted as "architecture for world revolution", to "raise human consciousness") was never implemented.

Much of the cultural life and other pleasures of Moscow are found in the Beliy Gorod, from the **Bolshoy Theatre**, the **Pushkin Museum of Fine Arts** and the **Conservatory**, to restaurants, nightlife, and piquant juxtapositions of old and new Russia – which often turn out to be much the same. The rebuilding of the **Cathedral of Christ the Saviour**, decades after Stalin destroyed the original, is only the tip of the iceberg when it comes to reinventing the past, as brash new banks pose as pre-Revolutionary financial houses, and casinos and nightclubs call themselves *Chekhov* and *Stanislavsky*. The discordances are echoed by the architecture: Stalinist behemoths with Italianate loggias stitched across a patchwork of Neoclassical and Style Moderne backstreets, studded with **medieval monasteries**. A visit to the **Sandunovskiy Baths** or the "KGB Museum" attached to the infamous **Lubyanka** are not to be missed, nor a wander around the one-time **Ukrainian quarter**.

The Beliy Gorod's web-like layout and hilly topography make orientation quite difficult. This account starts with Manezhnaya ploshchad and the **central axis** of Tverskaya ulitsa, before covering the remainder of the Beliy Gorod in **wedge-shaped sections** – first the western and then the eastern sectors. Each itinerary starts from the point nearest the Kremlin or the Kitay-gorod and works outward to the Boulevard Ring – a distance of between one and two kilometres. In practice, you'll probably zigzag across several "wedges" rather than follow a single one to the end.

Manezhnaya ploshchad and Okhotniy ryad

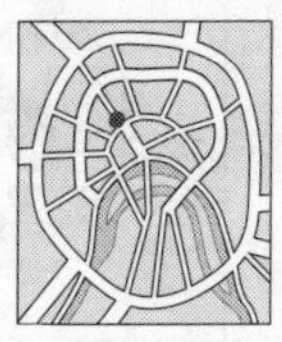

Since 1995, billions of rubles have been spent on humanizing **Manezhnaya ploshchad**, a bleak expanse created by the demolition of shops and houses in the late 1920s, where columns of tanks and marchers assembled prior to entering Red Square for the great parades of the Soviet era. To give the square and the centre of Moscow a new image, Mayor Luzhkov blew $350 million on a deluxe **underground shopping mall** (daily 11am–10pm), adorned with creations by his favourite sculptor, Tsereteli, who clad its three levels in fake marble and gilt, capped by a dome-map of the northern hemisphere with a model Kremlin distinguishing Moscow from other capitals (merely marked by dots). The roof segues into the Alexander Gardens via a Disneyesque melange of statues and balustrades, thronged with people hanging out and drinking beer whenever the weather is fine.

Somewhat ironically, the mall bears the name of the **Okhotniy ryad** (Hunters' Row), a malodorous meat and pie market that once sprawled from Manezhnaya ploshchad to the Bolshoy Theatre, serving hot food and drinks all night. This convivial fixture of city life was swept away in the 1930s, when the avenue of that name was built together with the *Moskva Hotel* and the Gosplan building, as part of Stalin and Kaganovich's scheme to transform Moscow. The avenue is basically just for traffic, circumvented by pedestrian subways linking the Kremlin and Tverskaya sides of Manezhnaya ploshchad and the disunited halves of Teatralnaya ploshchad, which contain kiosks, buskers and souvenir sellers, and have long been a gay cruising ground.

The Manège

Starting from the Alexander Gardens, the nearest thing on Manezhnaya ploshchad is its namesake, the one-time **Manège** (*Manezh*), or military riding school, where Tolstoy had his first riding lessons. Built in only six months to the plans of the engineer General Betancourt, it was opened by Alexander I in 1817, on the fifth anniversary of Napoleon's defeat. Contemporaries marvelled at how its 45-metre-wide roof was unsupported by interior columns, allowing two cavalry regiments to manoeuvre indoors – but in the 1930s Soviet engineers had to prop up the sagging roof with steel columns, spoiling the effect. Before then, the Manège also served as a concert hall (where Berlioz once conducted), and after the Revolution became the

To enquire about exhibitions, ☎202 89 76 (Mon–Fri 10am–1pm & 2-6pm).

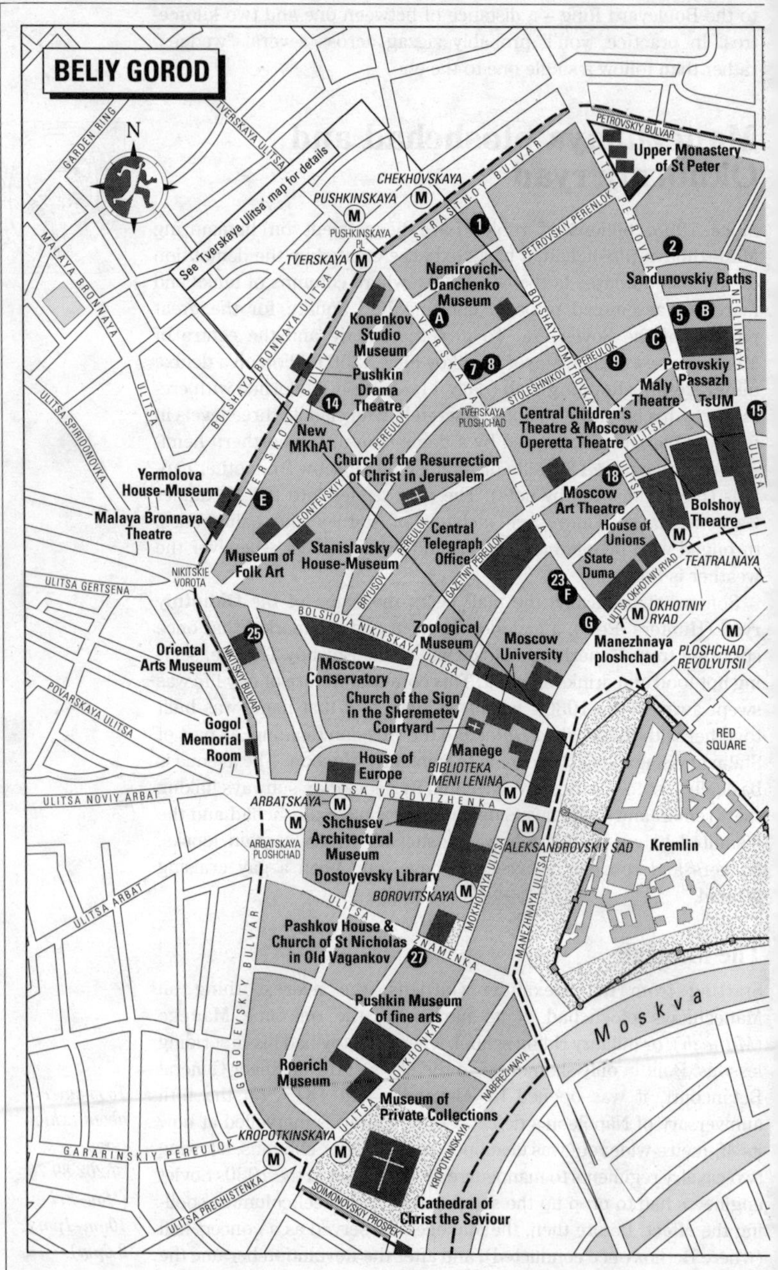
BELIY GOROD
N
Upper Monastery of St Peter
Sandunovskiy Baths
Nemirovich-Danchenko Museum
Konenkov Studio Museum
Pushkin Drama Theatre
New MKhAT
Petrovskiy Passazh
Maly Theatre
TsUM
Central Children's Theatre & Moscow Operetta Theatre
Church of the Resurrection of Christ in Jerusalem
Yermolova House-Museum
Malaya Bronnaya Theatre
Museum of Folk Art
Stanislavsky House-Museum
Central Telegraph Office
Moscow Art Theatre
House of Unions
Bolshoy Theatre
State Duma
Zoological Museum
Moscow University
Manezhnaya ploshchad
Oriental Arts Museum
Moscow Conservatory
Church of the Sign in the Sheremetev Courtyard
Gogol Memorial Room
Manège
House of Europe
Shchusev Architectural Museum
Dostoyevsky Library
Kremlin
RED SQUARE
Pashkov House & Church of St Nicholas in Old Vagankov
Pushkin Museum of fine arts
Roerich Museum
Museum of Private Collections
Cathedral of Christ the Saviour
Moskva
See 'Tverskaya Ulitsa' map for details
GARDEN RING
TVERSKAYA ULITSA
CHEKHOVSKAYA
PUSHKINSKAYA
PUSHKINSKAYA PL
TVERSKAYA
STRASTNOY BULVAR
PETROVSKIY BULVAR
ULITSA PETROVKA
PETROVSKIY PERENLOK
BOLSHAYA DMITROVKA
NEGLINNAYA
STOLESHNIKOV PEREULOK
TVERSKAYA PLOSHCHAD
BOLSHAYA BRONNAYA ULITSA
TVERSKOY BULVAR
MALAYA BRONNAYA
ULITSA SPIRIDONOVKA
LEONTEVSKIY
BRYUSOV PEREULOK
GAZETNIY PEREULOK
NIKITSKIE VOROTA
ULITSA GERTSENA
BOLSHOYA NIKITSKAYA ULITSA
NIKITSKIY BULVAR
POVARSKAYA ULITSA
TEATRALNAYA
ULITSA OKHOTNIY RYAD
OKHOTNIY RYAD
PLOSHCHAD REVOLYUTSII
ULITSA NOVIY ARBAT
ARBATSKAYA
ARBATSKAYA PLOSHCHAD
BIBLIOTEKA IMENI LENINA
ULITSA VOZDVIZHENKA
ALEKSANDROVSKIY SAD
MOKHOVAYA ULITSA
MANEZHNAYA ULITSA
BOROVITSKAYA
ULITSA ARBAT
ZNAMENKA
GOGOLEVSKIY BULVAR
VOLKHONKA
KROPOTKINSKAYA NABEREZHNAYA
KROPOTKINSKAYA
GAGARINSKIY PEREULOK
ULITSA PRECHISTENKA
SOIMONOVSKIY PROSPEKT

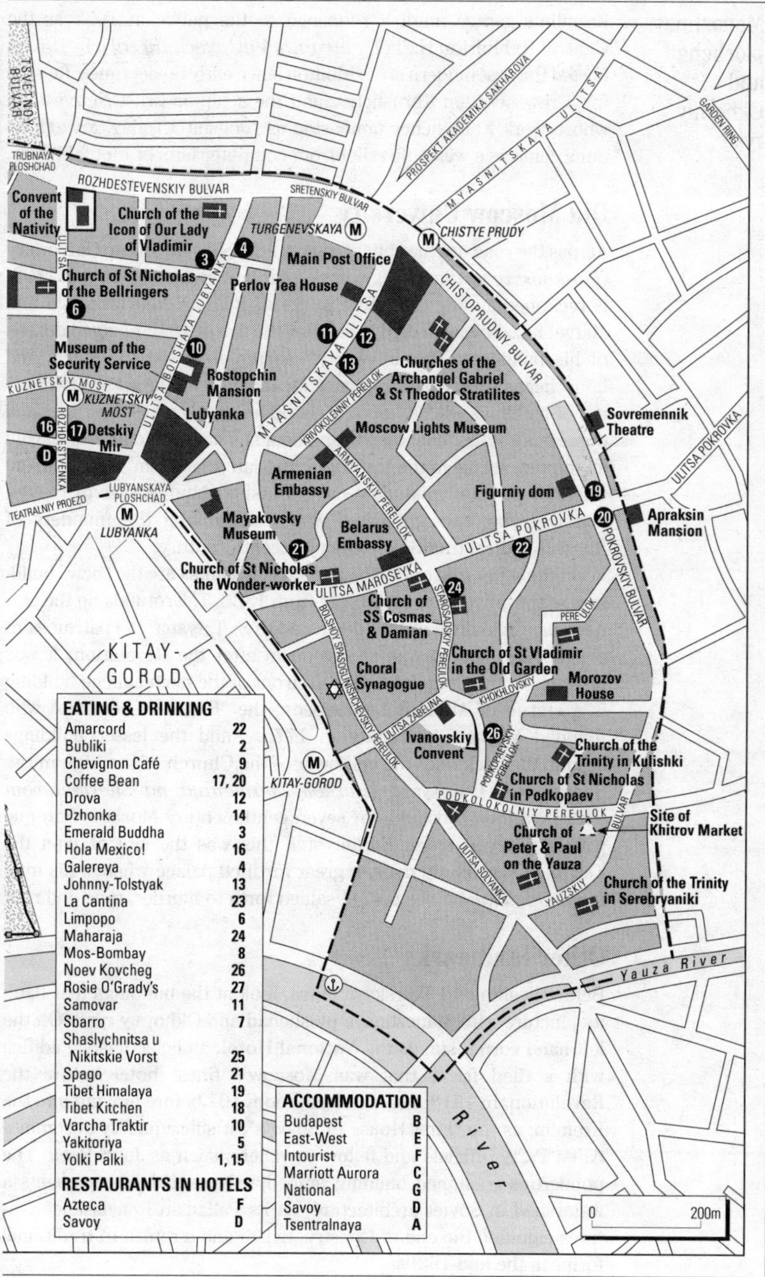
TSVETNOY BULVAR
TRUBNAYA PLOSHCHAD
ROZHDESTEVENSKIY BULVAR
SRETENSKIY BULVAR
PROSPEKT AKADEMIKA SAKHAROVA
MYASNITSKAYA ULITSA
GARDEN RING
Convent of the Nativity
Church of the Icon of Our Lady of Vladimir
TURGENEVSKAYA
CHISTYE PRUDY
Main Post Office
Church of St Nicholas of the Bellringers
Perlov Tea House
CHISTOPRUDNIY BULVAR
Museum of the Security Service
Rostopchin Mansion
Churches of the Archangel Gabriel & St Theodor Stratilites
KUZNETSKIY MOST
Lubyanka
ULITSA BOLSHAYA LUBYANKA
Sovremennik Theatre
Detskiy Mir
ROZHDESTVENKA
Moscow Lights Museum
KRIVOKOLENNIY PEREULOK
ARMYANSKIY PEREULOK
Armenian Embassy
ULITSA POKROVKA
Figurniy dom
LUBYANSKAYA PLOSHCHAD
TEATRALNIY PROEZD
LUBYANKA
Mayakovsky Museum
Belarus Embassy
Apraksin Mansion
POKROVSKIY BULVAR
Church of St Nicholas the Wonder-worker
ULITSA MAROSEYKA
Church of SS Cosmas & Damian
STAROSADSKIY PEREULOK
PEREULOK
KITAY-GOROD
BOLSHOY SPASOGLINISHCHEVSKIY PEREULOK
Church of St Vladimir in the Old Garden
Choral Synagogue
Morozov House
KHOKHLOVSKIY
ULITSA ZABELINA
Ivanovskiy Convent
PODKOPAEVSKIY PEREULOK
Church of the Trinity in Kulishki
Church of St Nicholas in Podkopaev
PODKOLOKOLNIY PEREULOK
Site of Khitrov Market
BULVAR
Church of Peter & Paul on the Yauza
ULITSA SOLYANKA
YAUZSKIY
Church of the Trinity in Serebryaniki
Yauza River
River
0
200m
EATING & DRINKING
Amarcord 22
Bubliki 2
Chevignon Café 9
Coffee Bean 17, 20
Drova 12
Dzhonka 14
Emerald Buddha 3
Hola Mexico! 16
Galereya 4
Johnny-Tolstyak 13
La Cantina 23
Limpopo 6
Maharaja 24
Mos-Bombay 8
Noev Kovcheg 26
Rosie O'Grady's 27
Samovar 11
Sbarro 7
Shaslychnitsa u Nikitskie Vorst 25
Spago 21
Tibet Himalaya 19
Tibet Kitchen 18
Varcha Traktir 10
Yakitoriya 5
Yolki Palki 1, 15
RESTAURANTS IN HOTELS
Azteca F
Savoy D
ACCOMMODATION
Budapest B
East-West E
Intourist F
Marriott Aurora C
National G
Savoy D
Tsentralnaya A

Kremlin's garage, until it reopened to the public in 1957 as the **Central Exhibition Hall** (*Tsentralniy Vystavochniy zal*). In 1962 it hosted the first modern art exhibition since early Soviet times, famous for a row between Khrushchev and the sculptor Ernst Neizvestniy, whose work Khrushchev lambasted as "dogshit". Today, art exhibitions come as a welcome relief from computer fairs or motor shows.

Old Moscow University

Across the road are the canary-yellow edifices of **Moscow University** (*Moskovskiy universitet*), whose "old" building, completed in 1793, is reckoned among the finest works of Russian Neoclassicism and Matvei Kazakov, who died soon after the fire of 1812 ravaged dozens of his buildings. The university was repaired and bas-reliefs and lions' heads added to its imposing facade. Behind the scenes is a warren of buildings whose "gloomy corridors, grimy walls, bad light and depressing stairs, coat stands and benches have undoubtedly played an important role in the history of Russian pessimism" – or so wrote Chekhov of his own student days. Outside stand statues of Herzen and Ogaryov, two graduates who were among the founders of Russia's radical tradition in the nineteenth century.

On the other side of Bolshaya Nikitskaya ulitsa are the "new" buildings of the university, which date from 1836. The rotunda on the corner was originally a chapel dedicated to St Tatyana, the patron saint of students, until it was closed down after the Revolution; it was returned to the Church in 1994. In front of the main college building is a **statue of Mikhail Lomonosov**, the "Russian Leonardo" who founded Moscow University in 1775. Amid the lesser buildings around the back rises the belltower of the **Church of the Sign in the Sheremetev Courtyard** (*tserkov Znameniya na Sheremtevom dvore*), a lovely example of seventeenth-century Moscow Baroque with a filigreed spire. Earlier still, this was the site of Ivan the Terrible's **Oprichniy dvor**, a great fortified palace whence his infamous *Oprichniki* (see p.421) sallied forth to murder, rape and rob.

Other landmarks

Before heading up Tverskaya ulitsa, look at the buildings that flank its juncture with Manezhnaya ploshchad and Okhotniy ryad. On the left-hand corner stands the **National Hotel**, an eclectic-style edifice with a tiled frieze that was Moscow's finest hotel before the Revolution. In 1918, Lenin lived in room 107 before moving into the Kremlin; as the "First House of Soviets", it subsequently accommodated Party officials and fellow travellers, such as John Reed. The ponderous columned building immediately next door represents a watershed in Soviet architecture, as its Palladian Renaissance features signified the end of Constructivism and a return to traditional forms in the mid-1930s.

On the other side of the road, facing the *Moskva Hotel*, looms a grey 1930s building erected for Gosplan, the agency that oversaw the Soviet economy, which is now used by the **State Duma**, or lower house of the Russian parliament – known for its brawls, and reputedly the scene of after-hours orgies. It totally dwarfs the adjacent **House of Unions**, a green-and-white Neoclassical edifice built in the 1780s, which served as the Club of the Nobility until the Revolution. In Soviet times its glittering Hall of Columns was used for the show trials of veteran Bolsheviks like Bukharin (see p.433), and the lying in state of Lenin and Stalin, which occasioned mass demonstrations of genuine grief. The queue to bid farewell to Lenin lasted for three days and nights, despite arctic weather conditions; while nobody knows how many people were crushed to death in the crowd at Stalin's funeral – estimates range as high as 1500 victims. The poet Yevtushenko (who was there) later wrote:

Manezhnaya ploshchad and Okhotniy ryad

Judgement was passed on the
day of the funeral
when the people came to Stalin
over people
for he taught them to
walk over people.

Tverskaya ulitsa

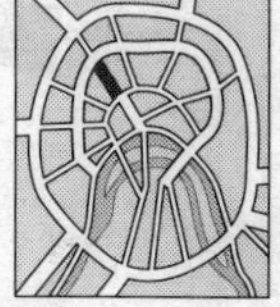

As its name suggests, **Tverskaya ulitsa** originated as the road leading to the old town of Tver, continuing to Novgorod and (after 1713) on to St Petersburg. Inns and smithies soon grew up alongside, until they were displaced during the sixteenth century by the stone palaces of the boyars and merchants. The road was surfaced with logs and varied in width from eight to fifteen metres along its zigzag course. As Moscow's main thoroughfare from the seventeenth century onwards, it boasted two monasteries and four churches, past which the tsars proceeded on arrival from St Petersburg; for victory parades, Tverskaya was bedecked with carpets, flowers and icons. During the nineteenth century it became more commercial, as the point of departure for stagecoaches to St Petersburg, and notable for being the first street in Moscow to be lit by lampposts and feature billboards.

Its present form owes to a massive reconstruction programme during the mid-1930s, when Tverskaya was also renamed in honour of the writer Maxim Gorky (it reverted to its old name in 1990). To straighten and widen the street, rows of houses were demolished, while other buildings were moved back to create a new avenue forty to sixty metres wide, lined with gargantuan buildings. Despite their scale, the variety of ornamentation and the older, often charming

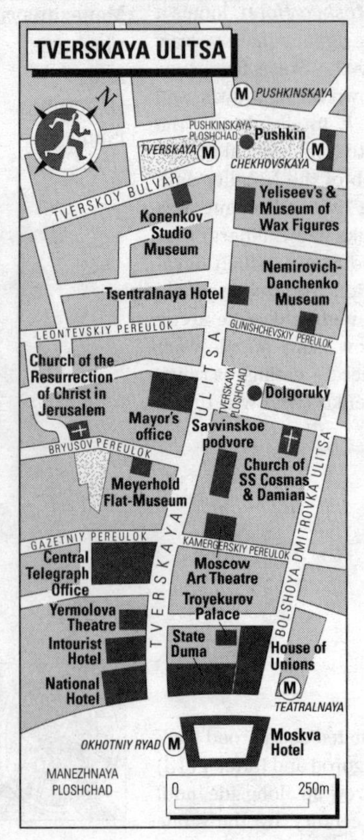

side streets that are visible through their huge archways give the avenue a distinctive character. Its **sights** are best appreciated by walking up the eastern side as far as Pushkinskaya ploshchad and then crossing over and backtracking a bit to check out a few side streets to the west.

Uphill to Tverskaya ploshchad

The initial uphill stretch of Tverskaya boasts several landmarks and various curiosities tucked away off the street. On the left-hand side stands the ugly 22-storey **Intourist Hotel**, aptly known as the "glass box", followed by the diminutive **Yermolova Theatre**. Across the road, a huge archway leads through to Georgievskiy pereulok, where the fence behind the State Duma building allows a glimpse of the modestly sized **Troyekurov Palace**, a rare surviving example of a seventeenth-century boyar's townhouse. Sticking to the main road, you can't miss the dour **Central Telegraph Office**, with its illuminated globe. In Brezhnev times its ill-paid female staff were renowned for moonlighting as prostitutes, imbuing the globe with the significance of a red light in a seedy neighbourhood; street-walkers remained a feature of Tverskaya until the late 1990s, when they were obliged to move down to Teatralnaya ploshchad, or out to the further reaches of Leningradskiy prospekt.

MKhAT and the Savvinskoe podvore

On pedestrianized Kamergerskiy pereulok, to the east of Tverskaya, a **statue of Chekhov** presages the famous **Moscow Art Theatre**, known here by its Russian initials as **MKhAT** (pronounced "Em-*Khat*"). Founded in 1898 by Konstantin Stanislavsky and Vladimir Nemirovich-Danchenko, MKhAT pioneered the methodical training of actors and directors, and the doctrine that acting should express inner feelings, rather than merely consist of gestures and vocal tricks. Its foundation coincided with the advent of Chekhov's plays, the first modern drama, which required a new style of acting. Having flopped in St Petersburg when first performed by hammy old thespians, *The Seagull* became an overnight sensation thanks to MKhAT's

Tverskaya ulitsa

production; Chekhov's congratulatory telegram to Stanislavsky read: "You have brought my seagull back to life".

In Soviet times, MKhAT specialized in the plays of Gorky and grew increasingly conservative, but nevertheless produced outstanding directors like Meyerhold and brilliant actors such as Inokennty Smoktunovsky, famous for his portrayal of Hamlet in particular. The theatre building itself was converted by Fyodor Shekhtel according to Stanislavsky's belief that nothing should distract audiences from the stage. Its foyer and auditorium are extremely simple, and the exterior decorations are limited to a stylized seagull on the pediment and a bas-relief wave above the doorway.

For more on MKhAT, see "The Arts", p.362.

Returning to Tverskaya, check out the courtyard of no. 6, which harbours a spectacular Neo-Russian residential complex whose silver tent-roofed towers and pale-green-and-lilac-tiled frontage contrast with the Stalinist gloom that now surrounds it. Built in 1905–07 as a speculative venture by the Orthodox Church, the **Savvinskoe podvore**'s huge apartments, turned into communal flats after the Revolution, have now been converted back into luxury residences and offices.

Opposite are two mammoth brownstone buildings (nos. 9–11) erected just after the war, united by a great **arch** made from granite intended for a Nazi victory memorial, captured in 1941. Passing through the arch you can find the **Meyerhold Flat-Museum** (Wed, Thurs, Sat & Sun noon–6pm; $1) in a Constructivist block built for Soviet actors and theatre directors, at Bryusov pereulok 12. It preserves his living quarters as they were before Meyerhold was arrested and tortured to death in 1937, and exhibits pictures and designs from his avant-garde productions, that proved too revolutionary for the Party. Further down the lane, the pretty orange-and-white **Church of the Resurrection of Christ in Jerusalem**, dating from 1629, was one of the few Moscow churches that functioned throughout Soviet times.

Tverskaya ploshchad to the Boulevard Ring

Soon afterwards the avenue levels out at **Tverskaya ploshchad**, as if in awe of the **Mayor's Office**, a crimson edifice with a golden crest that bears little relation to Kazakov's original design of 1782, for when the avenue was widened in Stalin's time the building was moved back fourteen metres, its wings were removed, and two storeys and a new entrance added. Originally the residence of Moscow's Tsarist governor generals, it was "sold" sometime in the nineteenth century to an English lord by a gang of con men, with the help of the notoriously gullible Governor Dolgorukov. After the October Revolution it housed the Moscow Soviet of Workers' and Soldiers' Deputies and the Military-Revolutionary Committee, which Lenin addressed on occasions now commemorated by sculpted plaques. Before perestroika, it was traditional to register him as deputy no. 1 whenever a newly elected City Council convened. Since its powers were vested in a Mayor, the office has become synonymous with **Yuri Luzhkov**, who has been elected three times in succession and likens himself to Mayor Daley of Chicago. Yet Luzhkov's undoubted achievements and popularity in Moscow won him few votes in the 2000 Presidential elections, and the unfettered powers that he enjoyed in Yeltsin's time are now being clawed back by the Kremlin.

Across the road prances an equestrian **statue of Yuri Dolgoruky**, the founder of Moscow, belatedly unveiled seven years after the city's 800th anniversary in 1947. The large building on the right, with a fruity cornice, was once the *Dresden Hotel*, where Schumann, Chekhov and Turgenev stayed. Since Soviet times it has housed the **Aragvi Restaurant**, giving rise to a Georgian joke that Dolgoruky had the sense to found his city near a good place to eat. Next door to the *Aragvi* is the small seventeenth-century **Church of SS Cosmas and Damian** (*tserkov Kosmy i Damiana*) whose congregation includes many dissidents from the Brezhnev era, vindicated by the demise of the Institute of Marxism-Leninism at the end of the square.

Off to the east

Running downhill from the SS Cosmas and Damian, the cobbled **Stoleshnikov pereulok** takes its name from the tablecloth weavers (*Stoleshniki*) who resided here in the sixteenth century. Towards the end of the last century, no. 9 was inhabited by Vladimir Gilyarovsky, whose book *Moscow and the Muscovites* brilliantly portrayed the city's life before the Revolution. He would surely welcome the return of stylish shops and cafés to the street, which is now one of the most elegant in Moscow, with a tiny chapel in the middle at the far end.

Returning to Tverskaya ulitsa and continuing northwards, you'll pass the dingy **Tsentralnaya Hotel**, which served as a residential hostel for many members of the Communist International during the 1930s, when their ranks were decimated by Stalin's purges. Victims were arrested at night and hustled out through the kitchens into a waiting prison van, disguised as a bread delivery van, whereupon their families were moved into worse rooms and shunned by everyone else in the hostel.

At that time, the street around the corner was home to many esteemed People's Artists, including the co-founder of the Moscow Art Theatre. MKhAT fans can track down the **Nemirovich-Danchenko Museum** (no regular hours, ☎209 53 91) in the huge labyrinthine apartment block at Glinishchevskiy pereulok 5–7: go through the heroic arch, head upstairs to the left, through the door beneath the pipes to a second lift shaft and take the elevator to the third floor to find his former flat (#52), whose contents have been lovingly preserved. Chekhov's widow, the actress Olga Knipper-Chekhova, lived in a similar apartment further downhill from 1938 until her death in 1959.

As yet, there is no plaque to mark the flat where Solzhenitsyn lived before his expulsion from the Soviet Union: apartment 169, in the block behind Tverskaya 12.

Tverskaya ulitsa

Yeliseev's, the Wax Figures and Ostrovsky museums

Nearer Pushkinskaya ploshchad, Tverskaya 14 houses a disparate trio of institutions. **Yeliseev's** (Mon–Sat 8am–9pm, Sun 10am–7pm) used to be Moscow's foremost delicatessen and still boasts the finest interior of any shop in the city, replete with stained-glass skylights, floral chandeliers and mahogany counters, its lofty ceiling upheld by voluptuous buttresses. The entrance hall displays a bust of Pyotr Yeliseev, a serf and gardener who won his freedom by growing a perfect strawberry, and traded so successfully in St Petersburg that in 1843 his sons were able to found the *Brothers Yeliseev*, opening branches in Moscow and Kiev. After the Revolution, they reputedly tried to save their gold by making it into rods and connections for the lamps in the chandeliers that illuminated their stores.

The entrance just up the road leads to the **Nikolai Ostrovsky Museum** and a **Humanitarian Centre** in his name. Ostrovsky (1904–36) was a true believer who sacrificed everything for Communism, becoming a Party activist at the age of thirteen, and contracting a wasting disease while laying a railway line after the Civil War. By the age of 25 he was blind and paralyzed; having contemplated suicide, he dictated his semi-autobiographical novel, *How the Steel was Tempered*, a classic of Stalinist literature. The museum preserves his Spartan study and bedroom, while the centre showcases the achievements of disabled people like Ludmilla Rogova, who overcame multiple sclerosis by devising exercises that she later taught to children with cerebral palsy, and Nikolai Fenomenov, who built more than ten metro stations despite being severely injured in the war.

The Ostrovsky Museum is open Tues–Sun 11am–7pm, $1; the Wax Figures Museum Tues 11am–7pm, Wed–Sun 11am–6pm, $1.

On the same floor is a **Museum of Wax Figures** from Russian history and the arts, changed at intervals and grouped into didactic tableaux. Depending on who's on show, you might find anyone from Putin to Chekhov. As wax figures go, the most convincing are Luzhkov's and Zhirinovsky's (dressed in one of his own quasi-military tunics); the figure of the rock star Viktor Tsoy wears the clothes that he died in, donated by his fans.

Another, separate exhibit covers the **salon of Zinaida Volkonskaya** that existed here in the 1820s. After her brother, Prince Volkonsky, was exiled for life to Siberia for his part in the Decembrist revolt, his wife Maria set an example to other wives by joining him and enduring the same hardships for thirty years – before running off with another man. The prince's second cousin, Tolstoy, possibly had this tale in mind when he invented Anna Karenina, a woman prepared to sacrifice all for love. In real life, another fate was sealed when Pushkin met his future wife, Natalya, at the salon in 1830 (for more about them, see p.187).

Tverskaya ulitsa

To Pushkinskaya ploshchad

Further on, Tverskaya crosses the heavily trafficked Tverskoy and Strastnoy sections of the Boulevard Ring at **Pushkinskaya ploshchad**. The maze of underpasses beneath the square is notorious for the bomb that exploded on August 8, 2000, killing twelve people and injuring scores more. One of its exits emerges on the corner of Tverskoy bulvar near the **Konenkov Studio Museum** (Wed–Sun 11am–5pm; closed every Mon & Tues & the last Fri of each month; $0.50), commemorating the sculptor Sergei Konenkov (1874–1971), who left Russia following the Revolution but returned from America in 1945, ensuring himself a warm welcome by bringing busts of Stalin and his Marshals sculpted from photographs. The studio contrasts such orthodox works (which eventually won him a Stalin Prize) with busts of Jesus and Einstein and playfully private creations using roots and tree trunks, in the form of figures from Russian folklore.

Pushkinskaya ploshchad and the section of Tverskaya ulitsa beyond the Boulevard Ring are covered on p.169.

Bolshaya Nikitskaya, Nikitskie vorota and Tverskoy bulvar

Another promising route from Manezhnaya ploshchad to the Boulevard Ring is **Bolshaya Nikitskaya ulitsa**, a narrow street lined with university buildings in various shades of yellow, which looks fetchingly nineteenth-century when blanketed with snow. In Soviet times the street was named after the radical journalist Alexander Herzen, who set Ogaryov's salon at no. 23 buzzing in the early 1820s. Today, the initial stretch is notable for the **Zoological Museum** (Tues–Sun 10am–5pm; closed the last Sun of each month; $0.30), recognizable by its mural and stucco frieze of animals cavorting in flora. The collection includes a mammoth's skeleton from Yakuta, stuffed bison and bears, and a mongoose fighting two cobras at once.

Most of the university's science faculties are in the University skyscraper in the Sparrow Hills, covered on p.224.

The Moscow Conservatory

Across the road further on is Russia's foremost music school, the **Moscow Conservatory** (*Moskovskaya konservatoriya*). Founded in 1866 by Nikolai Rubenstein, the Conservatory occupies an eighteenth-century mansion fronted by a statue of Tchaikovsky waving his hands as if to conduct an orchestra – its railing is in the form of notes from six of his works, including *Swan Lake*. Tchaikovsky taught for twelve years at the Conservatory, which now bears his name. Although some Western biographers have argued that he committed suicide to avoid a scandal over an affair with his nephew, it is now reckoned that he actually died from cholera, which was the cause of death recorded at the time.

Try to attend a concert in the **Grand Hall** (*Bolshoy zal*), decorated with giant medallions of composers. It was here that one of Shostakovich's most virulent critics suffered a fatal heart attack dur-

Tverskaya ulitsa

ing the premiere of a symphony that expressed the composer's torment at the years when his works were branded "formalist perversions". Every four years, it hosts the Tchaikovsky Competition, one of the most prestigious contests in the world of classical musicianship; the winner's professional success is assured.

Nikitskie vorota and the Stanislavsky Museum

Just beyond the Conservatory, Bolshaya Nikitskaya ulitsa meets the Boulevard Ring, as a dozen roads converge on the site of the medieval St Nicholas Gate – still called **Nikitskie vorota**, although the gate was demolished in Stalin's time. While the junction itself has no appeal, it's close to the amazing Gorky House (see p.179) and the Oriental Arts Museum (p.140), plus two museums on Leontevskiy pereulok, off beside the ITAR-TASS news agency.

A short way along this quiet street of embassies you'll find the **Stanislavsky House-Museum**, occupying a Neoclassical mansion that was allocated to Stanislavsky after his own home on Karetniy ryad was requisitioned as a chauffeurs' club. Here he tutored actors from the Moscow Art Theatre and Bolshoy opera studio, who signed in at the top of the stairs before applying their make-up in the Red Room and setting to work in his study, bisected by bookcases that served as "wings". Performances were staged in the Onegin Hall, named after the premiere of Tchaikovsky's opera *Yevgeny Onegin*, which took place in 1922. You can still see the armchair from which he oversaw rehearsals, and the bedroom where the ailing director wrote *An Actor Prepares* – the bible of the Method school of acting.

The Stanislavsky House-Museum is open Wed & Fri 2–8pm, Thurs, Sat & Sun 11am–6pm; admission free.

Diagonally across the road stands a Neo-Russian style building with a church-like porch, housing a small **Museum of Folk Art** (Tues–Sun 11am–6pm; $1), which mounts temporary exhibitions of ethnic crafts from across the former Soviet Union.

Along Tverskoy bulvar

To slog the whole length of Tverskoy bulvar between Nikitskie vorota and Pushkinskaya ploshchad isn't recommended due to the heavy traffic either side of the wooded central strip, but it's worth a 250m walk to the **Yermolova House-Museum** at no. 11. Its decrepit Empire frontage hides a charming period interior that conveys how affluent Russians lived before the Revolution. While her lawyer husband fled into exile, the Maly Theatre actress Maria Yermolova remained here from 1880 till 1928, dying a People's Artist of the USSR. Her personality pervades the house upstairs, especially the study, filled with statues and biographies of Joan of Arc, her favourite role. There are two grand pianos, a palmy conservatory, and a covered balcony from which she greeted admirers. Head straight upstairs, leaving the exhibition on the ground floor till last, but don't miss seeing its clockwork puppet-stage, nor the diorama of Teatralnaya ploshchad in the early nineteenth century.

The Yermolova House-Museum is open Mon & Wed–Sun noon–6pm; closed the last Wed of each month; $1.

Tverskoy bulvar's theatrical connections go way beyond this, what with the **Pushkin Drama Theatre** and the **New MKhAT** playhouse midway along, and the **Malaya Bronnaya Theatre** close to Nikitskie vorota. It was in the Chamber (now the Pushkin) Theatre that Tairov and Meyerhold pioneered Expressionist drama and Constructivist stage designs, and introduced the plays of Brecht, Shaw and O'Neill to Russia, while Malaya Bronnaya occupies the building that once housed the State Yiddish Theatre, whose brilliant actor-director Solomon Mikhoels was murdered by the NKVD as a prelude to its dissolution in 1948.

Towards the Arbat

Another route to the Boulevard Ring – and the Arbat beyond it – is to head along **ulitsa Vozdvizhenka**, which starts beside the gigantic Dostoyevsky Library (see p.140). On the right-hand side at no. 10 is the now-empty **Military Department Store** or *Voyentorg*, an eclectic-style edifice decorated with peacock and camel bas-reliefs and statues of medieval Slav warriors, that once catered to officers of the Imperial Army and then to their Soviet counterparts. Across the road from *Voyentorg*, the eighteenth-century Talyzin mansion still nominally houses the **Shchusev Architectural Museum**, boasting a host of models and photos of buildings from medieval times to the Soviet era, when its namesake, Alexei Shchusev (1873–1949), designed such varied structures as the Lenin Mausoleum and the *Moskva Hotel*. At present, however, the museum has been reduced to an exhibition hall (Tues–Sun 10am–6pm; $0.50) in the converted Apothecary's Palace around the back, while the mansion is being slowly refurbished. The whitewashed palace once served the German apothecaries who laid out the tsar's medicinal herb garden on Vagankov Hill, further along Starovagankovskiy pereulok, a backstreet that leads past the Pashkov House (see p.141) towards the Cathedral of Christ the Saviour in the distance.

The "Pentagon" and the House of Europe

Slightly further along Vozdvizhenka on the corner of Bolshoy Znamenskiy pereulok stands a two-storey house with a floral cornice (no. 9) that once belonged to **Tolstoy's grandfather**. Though he died before Tolstoy's birth, in 1821, Prince Nicholas Volkonsky was imaginatively resurrected in *War and Peace* as the irascible Prince Bolkonsky, with his "gloomy house on the Vozdvizhenka". He should not be confused with Tolstoy's second cousin, the other real-life Prince Volkonsky, who was exiled to Siberia for his part in the Decembrist revolt.

Immediately beyond are the marble-clad modular offices of the Armed Forces **General Staff** (*Generalniy Shtab*), familiarly known to Muscovites as the "Pentagon". Its concrete bowels contain the decorative 1930s **Arbatskaya metro** station on the Arbatsko-Pokrovskaya line, whose exit brings you out opposite the **House of Europe** (*dom Yevropy*). This amazing mansion was built in 1898 for a dissipated heir, Arseny Morozov, who shot himself in the foot to see whether he could bear the pain and died of septicemia at the age of 24. Its lace-trimmed towers and sculpted seashells were inspired by the Casa de las Conchas in Salamanca, seen during Arseny's travels. After the Revolution it was briefly taken over by Anarchists before becoming the headquarters of Proletcult, an organization involving Mayakovsky and Meyerhold that aimed to turn workers and peasants into agitprop artists – one of whom made himself a home in Morozov's bathroom. Since the 1950s the building has housed the Union of Friendship Societies – recently renamed the Centre for Scientific and Cultural Co-operation – which during Soviet times was responsible for staging meetings between foreign visitors and approved artists. Try to bluff your way in to see its wildly opulent interior (Mon–Fri 10am–6pm).

Towards the Arbat

Arbatskaya ploshchad and Nikitskiy bulvar

Further up the road, **Arbatskaya ploshchad** (Arbat Square) bears the scars of several bouts of redevelopment. It has a 1950s underpass serving traffic on the Boulevard Ring, and another, multi-branched pedestrian **subway** whose steps are lined with people selling puppies, while thrash rockers busk in its depths till late at night. On the surface, you'll also notice the pavilion of **Arbatskaya metro** station on the Filyovskaya line, built in the shape of a five-pointed star (a favourite architectural conceit of the 1930s), and the **Praga Restaurant**. Founded before the Revolution, it was long regarded as Moscow's top restaurant and hosted diplomatic banquets in Soviet times till it fell out of fashion in the 1980s. Having hit rock bottom in the early 1990s, the *Praga* was refurbished by Ismailov Telman, a magnate whose astrological sign is emblazoned on all the plates and rugs. Its Brazilian Room is festooned with fake parrots and attended by thirty waiters dressed as caballeros; other sections are equally over the top, and the prices astronomical – but the food is nothing special.

The Arbat district is covered on p.184.

While visitors are usually drawn into the Arbat district beyond the *Praga*, a few sights beg a detour **along the Boulevard Ring** itself. At the head of Gogolevskiy bulvar, beside the square, stands what locals call the **Happy Gogol statue**, since it replaced a statue that the Soviet authorities deemed too gloomy for the late 1940s. The original, by the sculptor Andreev, was banished to the courtyard of no. 7 Nikitskiy bulvar, just off the square, where the **Sad Gogol statue** huddles in a cape, eyes downcast, while the plinth bears a jolly frieze of characters from *The Government Inspector* and *Taras Bulba*. In the public library on the right, devoted scholars have created the

Towards the Arbat

Gogol's grave is in the Novodevichiy Cemetery (p.222).

Gogol Memorial Room (Mon–Fri noon–7pm; Sat & Sun noon–5pm; closed on the 30th of each month; free) in what was Nikolai Gogol's study during his last years. Here he burned the second part of *Dead Souls* and lapsed into religious melancholia, eating only pickled cabbage. A sufferer from cataleptic fits, he was mistakenly buried alive in 1852.

Across the road and 150m further north at no. 12a Nikitskiy bulvar, a pale yellow, Corinthian-pilastered mansion contains the **Oriental Arts Museum** (Tues–Sun 11am–8pm; $2). Its superb collection includes Caucasian rugs, Indonesian shadow-puppets, Vietnamese silver Buddhas, Samurai swords, lacquer-ware, porcelain, Chinese screens and robes. As the museum is located south of Nikitskie vorota, it's also feasible to reach it from there.

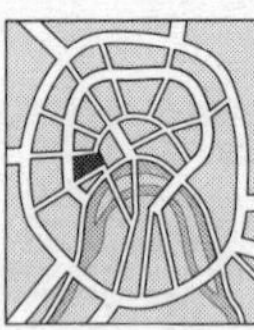

From the Dostoyevsky Library to the Pushkin Museum

The corner of Vozdvizhenka and Mokhovaya streets is dominated by the immense **Dostoyevsky Library** – better known by its former title, the **Lenin Library** (*Biblioteka imeni Lenina*) or "Leninka" – where some forty million books and periodicals repose on two hundred kilometres of shelving. Looming above a hillock behind a lanky arcade of black pillars, the library's main building was actually a reworking of a design for a hydroelectric power station, which became progressively more encrusted with reliefs and statues as its construction (1928–50) was influenced by the Palace of Soviets that was supposed to arise in the vicinity (see p.150). The black marble **statue of Dostoyevsky** at the top of the steps was added in 1997, and his name bestowed upon the building three years later.

Although you can't go beyond the cloakrooms without a reader's pass, have a look at the grand staircase (entrance #1) that ascends to the library's four main halls, decorated in the apogee of Soviet Neoclassicism (Mon–Sat 9am–9pm, Sun 9am–8pm; closed the last Mon of each month). Keen bibliophiles can also visit the **Museum of Books** (Mon–Fri 10am–5pm, Sat 10am–4pm; closed Sun & the last Mon of each month; free) on the third floor of the wing (entrance #3). Its collection includes a cuneiform tablet from ancient Mesopotamia; *The Gospel of the Archangel*, one of Russia's earliest handwritten books (1092); and the first book ever printed in Russia, Fyodorov's *The Apostle* (1564).

Sadly, since perestroika the library has fallen on hard times and now lacks the money to heat its rooms, let alone modernize its facilities and replenish its stocks. Its troubles date back to the opening of **Borovitskaya metro station** in 1985, which caused subsidence beneath the library's huge depository and the loss of some forty thousand books. Ensuring its structural integrity had to come before anything else, at a time of shrinking budgets.

The Pashkov House and Mokhovaya ulitsa

From the Dostoyevsky Library to the Pushkin Museum

Subsidence also badly affected the impressive **Pashkov House** (*dom Pashkova*) that overlooks the Kremlin's Borovitskiy Gate from a hill-top, and once had a garden running down to the Kremlin moat, where peacocks strutted. When built by Bazhenov in the 1780s it was the finest private house in Moscow, and constituted a bridge between Baroque and Neoclassical architecture. Mortgaged away by the gambling-mad Count Pashkov, it was purchased by a book-loving Marshal and turned into the Rumyantsev Library, whose collection of one million volumes later formed the core of the Lenin Library, located on the premises until 1950. It was from the rooftop of this building that the Devil and his entourage surveyed the chaos they had sown across Moscow in Bulgakov's *The Master and Margarita*.

Despite its grand facade facing the Kremlin, the main entrance actually lies round the back on Starovagankovskiy pereulok, where the adjacent walled **Church of St Nicholas in Old Vagankov** (*tserkov Nikolaya v Starom Vagankove*) sports a plaque boasting that Gogol was a regular worshipper in the 1840s. While the church's title recalls the village of Vagankov that existed here in the Middle Ages, the main road below the library, **Mokhovaya ulitsa**, is named after the moss (*mokh*) once sold here for caulking the chinks in wooden houses, and later for inserting between the panes of double-glazed windows to prevent fogging from condensation. If you're heading for the Pushkin Museum of Fine Arts, crossing the busy intersection of Mokhovaka ulitsa and Borovitskaya ploshchad will require an irksome detour up ulitsa Znamenka, since there are no underpasses in the vicinity.

The Pushkin Museum of Fine Arts, and other collections

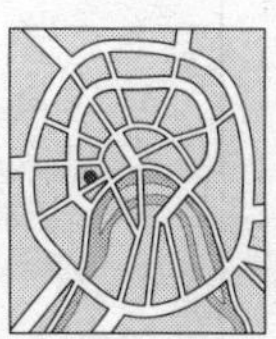

Like the Hermitage Museum in St Petersburg, Moscow's **Pushkin Museum of Fine Arts** (*muzey Izobrazitelnykh Iskusstv imeni A.S. Pushkina*) boasts a collection that ranges from Greek antiquities to Picasso, and is so vast that only a fraction can be displayed. Besides the constraints imposed by lack of space, politics have also played a part, as in the decades when abstract works were ideologically taboo. In recent years, the museum has also revealed much of the "Trophy Art" that was seized from the Nazis in 1945 and hidden for decades afterwards, such as the Treasure of Troy.

The Pushkin Museum of Fine Arts is open Tues–Sun 10am–6pm; last tickets sold 5pm; $6.

The museum was founded in 1912 on the initiative of the father of the poetess Marina Tsvetaeva, its collection of casts of antique, medieval and Renaissance sculptures being augmented by works

The Pushkin Museum of Fine Arts, and other collections

confiscated from private collections after the Revolution. Renamed the Pushkin Museum in 1937, it subsequently bore the indignity of being turned over to an exhibition of gifts received by Stalin, prompting the resignation of the director – and understandably prefers to recall hosting exhibitions of Tutankhamun's treasures and works from the Louvre and the Prado. For a preview of some of its collection and news of temporary exhibitions, visit the museum's **Web site** at *www.museum.ru/gmii/*.

Besides the Pushkin Museum of Fine Arts there are two other intriguing museums close by. The **Museum of Private Collections** has a diverse mix of Russian and foreign, mostly modern, art, while the **Roerich Museum**, in a backstreet around the corner, is dedicated to the Roerich family of mystics, painters and explorers.

Visiting the Pushkin Museum

The museum is at ulitsa Volkhonka 12, a short walk from Kropotkinskaya metro. Although not as dauntingly large as the

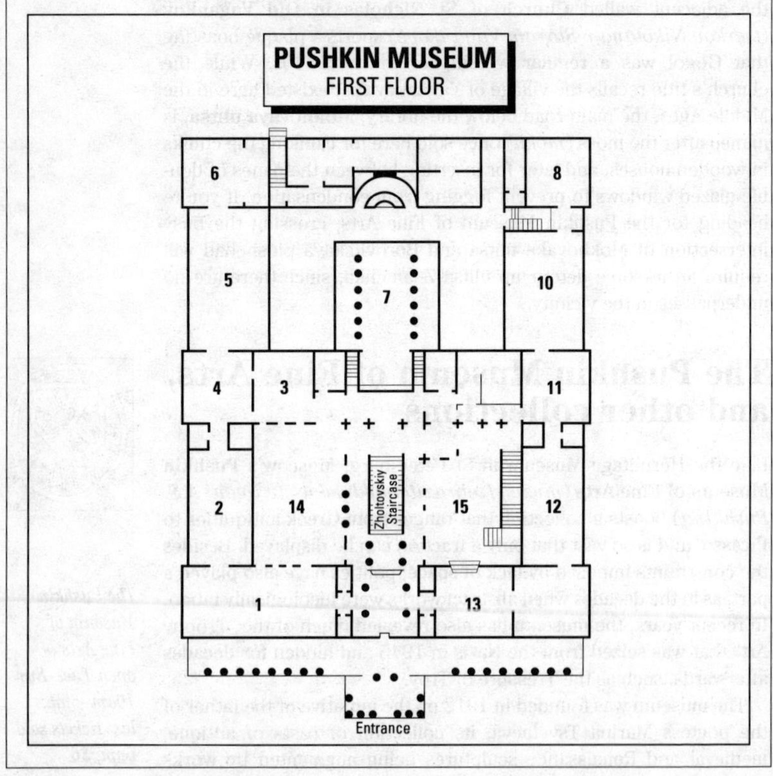

Hermitage, it's still wise to see what appeals first, lest you run out of steam midway through the rooms full of plaster casts. A bigger problem is that the contents of certain sections are liable to change depending on the space allotted to **temporary exhibitions**, so that paintings that one expects to find are nowhere to be seen, or whole rooms may be off-limits while their contents are rearranged.

Identifying the exhibits is less of a problem, as most are captioned in English, and **guide tapes** ($3.50) can be rented in the basement. Alternatively, sign up for the **guided tour** offered by Patriarsky Dom Tours (see p.43). **Photography** is not allowed. Since the rooms are numbered in a way that bears little relation to their **layout** in terms of access, the following account is loosely structured on a thematic basis, starting on the first (or ground) floor, which is approached from the basement, where the cloakrooms are located.

The museum is also the venue for annual concerts of classical music, known as the **December Evenings**.

Antiquities and Byzantine art

Coming up from the basement, most visitors head straight for **Room 7**, displaying the famous **Treasure of Troy** (*Sokrovishcha Troy*) found by Schliemann, that vanished from a Berlin bunker to surface at the Pushkin Museum fifty years later. As Russian legislators are at one with public opinion in opposing the return of any "Trophy Art" to Germany until Russian claims for treasures despoiled by the Nazis are settled, it's set to remain here for some time. The gold diadems, torques and nephrite axeheads come from Hissarlik in Turkey, where Schliemann believed that he had found the Troy of Homer's Iliad but actually uncovered the Mycenean-era city. By coincidence, he made the fortune that financed his excavations while trading as an indigo merchant in Russia during the Crimean War.

The other eye-grabber – though hardly valuable or controversial – is the life-sized plaster casts of **ancient monuments** in **Room 14**, including a corner of the Parthenon and a gigantic bull-headed capital from the palace of Artaxerxes II in Susa.

Alternatively, you can enter **Room 3**, which opens with a fine display of **Coptic textiles** and funerary masks, and sixteen amazingly vivid **Fayoum portraits**, which were painted while their subjects were alive and then pasted onto their mummies – all from Egypt, between the first and sixth centuries AD. On the far wall are several glorious **Byzantine icons**, most notably a serene *Christ Pantokrator* from the fifteenth century.

From here, you can proceed through the Italian art in Room 4 (see below) to reach **Room 2**, which contains some Pre-Columbian and Hindu sculptures but is largely devoted to magnificent limestone **Babylonian bas-reliefs** from the Palace of Ashurnaziral (885–860 BC), whose portal flanked by winged bulls forms the entrance to the hall. At the far end lies Room 1, decorated like an Egyptian temple and filled with **Pharaonic artefacts** from the Old, Middle and New Kingdoms, collected by the orientalist Golenischev. They include funerary figures, Canopic chests, a mummified woman's head and the mummy of Hor-Ha (in the far corner).

Gothic and Renaissance art

Room 4 exhibits **Italian art** from the thirteenth to the fifteenth centuries, as it evolved from Byzantine to Gothic forms. On the wall as you enter is a splendid *Madonna and Child Enthroned* with a gem-studded halo, framed with scenes from Christ's life, by an anonymous Florentine artist (c.1280). Two exquisite altar triptychs from the second half of the fourteenth century hang at the left side of the partition, whose other side features a skeletal *Crucifixion* by Jacobello del Fiore. Notice the jealous expressions in Pietro di Giovanni Lianori's rose- and yellow-hued triptych of the *Virgin and Child with Saints*, and the brilliantly coloured *Madonna Enthroned with Angels* by Giovanni di Bartolomeo Cristiani.

Room 5 features **Italian**, **German and Dutch art** of the fifteenth and sixteenth centuries. Left of the doorway hangs Vittore Crivelli's sumptuously decorative *Virgin and Child with Saints*, while on the partition and wall to the right are a sadistic *Flagellation of Christ* by Johann Koerbecke, and St Michael trampling a hairy demon, attributed to the Catalonian master Pedro Espalargves. In the next section, Giulio Romano's *Woman at her Toilet* faces an exquisite *Annunciation* by **Sandro Botticelli** and a lovely *St Sebastian* by da Vinci's pupil and assistant, Giovanni Boltraffio; while across the way is a magnificently pain-wracked *Golgotha* by the mysteriously named Master of the Prodigal Son.

The following section features four small works by **Lucas Cranach the Elder**, the most striking being *The Fall of Man* and *The Results of Jealousy*. On the right-hand wall of the final section hangs a *Winter Landscape with Bird Trap* by **Pieter Brueghel the Younger** – actually a copy of a like-named painting by his father, Brueghel the Elder, in Brussels – while beside the doorway is an over-the-top *Solomon and the Queen of Sheba* by Hans Vredman de Vries, where figures in Renaissance dress are posed against an oddly metallic-looking palazzo.

Italian art of the sixteenth century enjoys a final fling in **Room 6**, where a diminutive *Minerva* by **Paolo Veronese** is accompanied by larger works of his school. Here too you'll find a sinuous *St John the Baptist* by **El Greco**, that was thought to have vanished during World War II, and a *Portrait of a Man* in an ermine-trimmed robe by **Tintoretto**.

Rubens, Rembrandt and Baroque art

Crossing the lobby to reach the seventeenth-century **Flemish and Spanish art** in **Room 11**, you'll be greeted by the gigantic *Still Life* *with Swans* by **Frans Snyders**, beside a portrait of the corpulent merchant Adriaen Stevens, by **Anthony van Dyck**. Both Snyders and Van Dyck worked as assistants at the studio of **Peter Paul Rubens**, whose three works owned by the Pushkin Museum (on the partition wall) include *Bacchanalia*, featuring an intoxicated Bacchus supported by his slaves while a cloven-hoofed woman suckles a brood of baby satyrs. To the right of the door is a trio of paintings by the Spaniard **Bartolomé Murillo**, whose *Archangel Raphael and Bishop Domonte* was commissioned to adorn the bishop's own cathedral.

The far door leads into **Room 10**, devoted to **seventeenth-century Dutch art**, where everyone makes a beeline for six works by **Rembrandt**. His mastery of dark tones and free brushwork is evinced by *Ahasuerus, Haman and Esther*, where the males are almost lost in the shadows, while Esther's embroidered bodice is rendered by merely scratching the paint's surface. On the other side of the partition, two religious works – *Christ Cleansing the Temple* and *The Incredulity of Thomas* – face a trio of portraits depicting Rembrandt's mother (*An Old Woman*), brother (*An Old Man*) and sister-in-law (*An Elderly Woman*), all painted in 1654, when the artist was struggling to come to terms with bereavement and poverty.

Room 12, reached by the door nearest the Murillos, contains **Italian art** of the seventeenth and eighteenth centuries. On the right as you enter are Salvatori Rossa's cruel *Old Coquette*, followed by Domenico Gargiulo's action-packed *The Ark brought by King David to Jerusalem*, which leads one towards the large *Betrothal of the Doge and the Sea* at the far end – a sumptuous vista of gilded barges and Venetian palazzi attributed to **Canaletto**.

Room 13 covers **French art** of the same period, which was much favoured by Catherine the Great. A misty-eyed *Voluptuousness* is the most memorable of three works by **Jean-Baptiste Greuze**, while portraits of the Prince and Princess Golitsyn strike a Russian note. More interesting than the small genre paintings by **Jean-Honoré Fragonard** and two miniatures by **Jean-Antoine Watteau** are the Classical scenes by **François Boucher**, notably his explicitly erotic *Hercules and Omphale*. Along the main wall hang four works by **Nicolas Poussin**, including a surreal *Landscape with Hercules and Cacus* and a frenzied *Battle of the Israelites and Amorites*.

Copies of masterpieces

The large hall designated as **Room 15** contains bronze and plaster **copies of Medieval and Renaissance masterpieces** such as the Golden Arch of Freiburg Cathedral, the Bishop's Seat of Ulm Cathedral, Michelangelo's *David*, and the famous *condottieri* statues from Padua and Venice.

Its stairway leads **upstairs** into a gallery used for **temporary exhibitions**, which often extend into the lobby of the main Zholtovskiy

Staircase, flanked by Grecian friezes and red marble columns, whence an arrow directs you into **Room 16**, filled with plaster casts of ancient Greek sculptures and friezes. This marks the start of a series of rooms devoted to copies of statues by Michelangelo (**Room 29**); other Renaissance masterpieces, such as Ghiberti's "Doors of Paradise" from the Florentine Baptistry (**Room 28**); medieval cathedral art from France and Germany (**Room 26**); and Greek and Roman statuary (**Rooms 24 & 25**) – whose period decor complements the exhibits.

Barbizon, Orientalist and Academic painters

Room 23 exhibits a fraction of the museum's huge collection of **Barbizon painters**, which rivals the Louvre's. Though nowadays unfashionable, they paved the way for the Impressionists by abandoning the studio in favour of *plein air* painting. The emphasis on spontaneity and naturalism is particularly evident in landscapes by **Jean-Baptiste-Camille Corot**, such as *Stormy Weather* and *A Gust of Wind*.

In the same room you will also find picturesque **Orientalist paintings** like Jean Fromentin's *Awaiting the Boat to Cross the Nile*, and a small *View of the Mountains* by one of the greatest German Romantic painters, **Caspar David Friedrich**.

At the far end of the room is a host of works in the **Academic style** that Russian artists were obliged to ape during the eighteenth and nineteenth centuries, including a serene *Virgin with the Host* by **Ingres**, commissioned by Tsar Alexander II; an equestrian *Portrait of Prince Yusupov* by **Antoine-Jean Gros**; and *After the Shipwreck* by **Eugène Delacroix**.

French Impressionism

In the early 1900s, the Moscow millionaires Sergei Shchukin and Ivan Morozov bought scores of paintings by Picasso, Matisse and the French Impressionists, which now form the core of the modern European art collections of the Hermitage and the Pushkin Museum. The latter generally devotes **Rooms 21 and 22** to its **French Impressionists**, rotating them so as to show different works by various artists.

Of several paintings by **Claude Monet**, you're likely to find *Rouen Cathedral at Sunset* (one of a series that captured the changing light on the cathedral's facade throughout the day), and foggy views of the River Thames. The most striking of those by **Van Gogh** are *Prisoners at Exercise* and the coruscating *Red Vineyard at Arles*. The latter was the only painting he sold in his lifetime, about which he wrote: "Oh, the beautiful sun of midsummer! It beats upon my head, and I do not doubt that it makes one a little queer" – shortly before cutting off his ear and leaving it in a brothel.

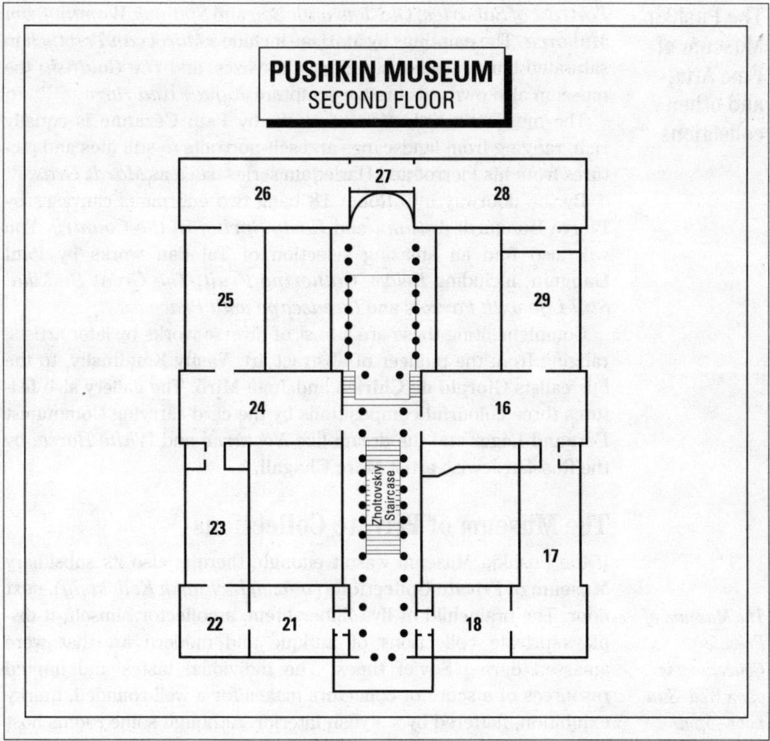

The museum also owns several landscapes and Parisian street scenes by **Camille Pissarro**; vivid pastels by **Edgar Degas**, such as *Ballet Rehearsal* and *Dancers in Blue*; and a *Portrait of Yvette Guilbert* by **Henri de Toulouse-Lautrec**, who often sketched this chanteuse at the Moulin Rouge. Its large collection of works by **Auguste Renoir** includes various portraits of actresses and a gorgeous plump nude known as "The Pearl", while versions of *The Burghers of Calais* and *The Kiss* are numbered among its sculptures by **Auguste Rodin**.

Post-Impressionism and Modernism

Rooms 17 and 18 are usually reserved for **Post-Impressionist and Modernist art**, mostly originating from the collections of Morozov and Shchukin, both of whom bought more than fifty works apiece by Picasso and Matisse.

Those by **Picasso** range from a Cézanne-like *Cottage with Trees* and the *Cubist Violin* and *Queen Isabeau*, to paintings from his Blue, Rose and Spanish periods, such as *Young Acrobat on a Ball*,

Portrait of Sabartès, *Old Jew with Boy* and *Spanish Woman from Mallorca*. The paintings by **Matisse** include a *Moroccan Triptych* in saturated blues, several still lifes with vases, and *The Goldfish*; the museum also owns his bronze sculpture *Jaguar and Hare*.

The museum's collection of works by **Paul Cézanne** is equally rich, ranging from landscapes and self-portraits to still lifes and pictures from his Pierrot and Harlequin series, such as *Mardi Gras*.

By the doorway into Room 18 hang two enormous canvases by **Pierre Bonnard**: *Autumn* and *Early Spring in the Country*. You will also find an amazing selection of Tahitian works by **Paul Gauguin**, including *Relax*, *Gathering Fruit*, *The Great Buddha*, *Still Life with Parrots* and *Landscape with Peacocks*.

Complementing these are a host of diverse works by later artists, ranging from the pioneer of abstract art, **Vasily Kandinsky**, to the Surrealists **Giorgio de Chirico** and **Juan Miró**. The gallery also features three colourful compositions by the card-carrying Communist **Fernand Léger** and the dream-like *Nocturne* and *White Horse*, by the Russian-Jewish artist **Marc Chagall**.

The Museum of Private Collections

The Museum of Private Collections is open Wed–Sun noon–6pm, last admission 5pm; $1.50.

If the Pushkin Museum wasn't enough, there is also its subsidiary **Museum of Private Collections** (*muzey Lichnykh Kollektsiy*), next door. The brainchild of Ilya Zilbershtein, a collector himself, it displays private collections of antique and modern art that were amassed during Soviet times. The individual tastes and limited resources of a score of collectors makes for a well-rounded, quirky exhibition, flattered by a stylish interior. Although some rooms host temporary exhibitions, the rest shouldn't change much. All the artworks are clearly labelled in English.

The exhibition

The permanent exhibition begins on the **second floor** with **Salvador Dalí**'s pen and wash drawings from the series *Mythology* and *The Hippies*, and anthropophagic illustrations to *Faustus* and *The Songs of Maldoror*. Next door features drawings of vases and women by **Matisse**, and the artist's own palette. Look out for the portraits of Lydia Delektorskaya, Matisse's model and secretary from 1928 until his death, who donated many of his works to Russian museums.

The **third floor** is more Russian in spirit, with nineteenth-century works by the Wanderers, such as **Ilya Repin**, whose lurid pink and gold *Duel* is counterposed by **Vasily Polonev**'s gentle *Christ* musing over the Sea of Galilee. You will also find set designs by **Boris Kustodiev** and **Alexander Benois** from the golden age of Russian ballet; views of Moscow and St Petersburg in the eighteenth century; and a score of sixteenth- and seventeenth-century icons. Of historical interest are the tiny **portraits of the Decembrists** exiled to

Siberia in 1825, drawn by fellow prisoner Nikolai Bestuzhev, and a painting of Countess Maria Volkonskaya, who followed Tolstoy's second cousin into exile (see p.135).

The Pushkin Museum of Fine Arts, and other collections

The **fourth floor** offers a feast of twentieth-century art, to which the concert pianist Svatoslav Richter contributed his own pastels and grand piano, and still lifes by **Robert Falk**. Look out for Kustodiev's *After the Storm with a Rainbow* and Grabar's *Women Merchants*, in the room that brings together *fin-de-siècle* artists fascinated by Parisian nightlife, and rural Russia. Beyond a horde of whimsical canvases and woodcarvings by **Alexander Tyshler** are two rooms devoted to **Alexander Rodchenko** and his wife **Varvara Stepanova** – arguably the museum's prime attraction. Rodchenko pioneered photo-collage and unorthodox perspectives, and his photos, posters and Constructivist book jackets are now classics of the genre, while Stepanova's textile designs have equal retro appeal. You can also see a snazzy red-and-black chess table, designed by Rodchenko for a workers' club.

The Roerich Museum

The odd one out of the trio of art collections in this part of town is the **Nikolai Roerich Museum** – or "International Centre of the Roerichs" – which has to be the only museum in Moscow that is scented by joss sticks. Opened in 1997, it is dedicated to the ideals of Nikolai Roerich (1874–1947), an artist and scholar whose passion for Eastern philosophy led him to Central Asia, Tibet and India in the 1920s, and Manchuria and Mongolia in the 1930s. Another aspect of his idealism was the Roerich Pact for the preservation of cultural values during wartime, which became the basis of the Hague Convention of 1954. The museum displays his paintings of mystics, steppes and the Himalayas, intermingled with photos of Ladekh and Tibet and items of gear from his expeditions, on which Roerich was accompanied by his wife Helene and their son Georgi (the only one of the family to return to Soviet Russia, and be buried in the Novodevichiy Cemetery). There's also a shop in the grounds selling Asian handicrafts and philosophical tracts.

The Roerich Museum is open Tues–Sun 11am–6pm, last admission 5.15pm; $1.

The Cathedral of Christ the Saviour

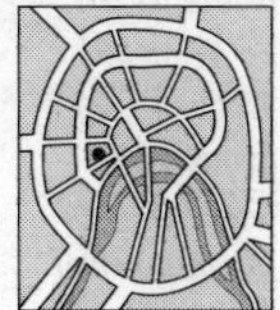

One of the newest and most conspicuous additions to Moscow's skyline is the gigantic **Cathedral of Christ the Saviour** (*khram Khrista Spasitela*), near the Pushkin Museum, whose gilt onion domes are visible from as far away as Manezhnaya ploshchad. Clad in marble and granite, with huge bronze doors covered in repoussé saints, the cathedral is an awesome statement of the refound power and prestige of the Orthodox Church – and Mayor Luzhkov's intention to

The Cathedral of Christ the Saviour

leave his mark on Moscow as surely as Stalin did. It was Stalin who was responsible for destroying the original Cathedral of Christ the Saviour that Luzhkov rebuilt, in tandem with the erection of an equally vast monument to Peter the Great.

The re-creation of Christ the Saviour has struck a chord in the national psyche as an act of atonement for the sins of Communism and the reaffirmation of spiritual values; "Russia is freeing itself from evil. Good is triumphing!" was a typical comment in the visitors' book on the construction site. Only a small minority were opposed for aesthetic reasons; arguing that the original cathedral was regarded as an eyesore when it was built (1839–83) to commemorate Russia's victory over Napoleon; and that it entailed the destruction of the medieval Alexeevsky convent (whose abbess reputedly cursed the site) – so that the Orthodox Church and Alexander II were guilty of the same vandalism that the Communists are now accused of.

Stalin's destruction of the cathedral in 1933 was intended to make way for the centrepiece of his new Moscow – a gargantuan **Palace of Soviets**, envisaged as the most important building in the USSR. As conceived by its architects, it was to be 315 metres high and crowned by a one-hundred-metre-tall aluminium statue of Lenin that would make it higher than the Empire State Building and the Statue of Liberty combined. Legend has it that the statue was added at Stalin's bidding, and its eyes were intended to emit a bright red beam. Work progressed as far as sinking the foundations, but the girders were ripped out to make anti-tank "hedgehogs" in 1941, and when construction resumed after the war it was with less conviction. Ultimately the palace was never realized because the high water table made the ground unstable, so in 1959 the plan was dropped and an open-air **swimming pool** was built instead. Pious Russians whispered that it was God's revenge that smote Stalin's Tower of Babel, while the pool itself was later believed to be accursed after several swimmers drowned or were stabbed to death in the fog that shrouded its surface (which also threatened art works in the Pushkin Museum).

Guided cathedral tours in Russian (Mon–Fri 10am–6pm) must be booked the day before ☎201 28 47 or 201 45 65; $5–16 group rate, depending on the number of people. Admission to the museum (same hours) is free.

Today's cathedral was built between 1995 and 1997; the **interior** took another three years to decorate, and bought the total cost to an estimated $360 million. According to Tsereteli, its murals are an exact replica of the originals, "only better", and gilded with 103 kilos of gold leaf. The centerpiece is a Holy Trinity spread over 1100 square metres of the main cupola. Alas, it is only viewable on **guided tours**, which include access to an observation platform 40m above the ground, with a **panoramic view** of the Kremlin and the waterfront. Otherwise, you're limited to visiting the **Church of the Resurrection** and the **museum** beneath the cathedral, entered from Soimonovskiy proezd. The museum exhibits relics and plans of the original cathedral and a gouache of the Palace of Soviets, plus many pictures on religious themes which look like they were painted in the nineteenth century but actually date from the 1990s – affirming the regressive spirit underlying the whole project.

The Cathedral of Christ the Saviour

East of Tverskaya – theatreland to Lubyanka

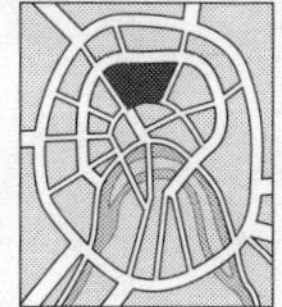

East of Tverskaya is a wedge of the Beliy Gorod that encompasses some of Moscow's oldest monasteries and most treasured cultural landmarks. The Bolshoy Theatre and the fashionable shops of ulitsa Kuznetskiy most and ulitsa Petrovka were the hub of Moscow's social life before the Revolution; and the whole area seethes with activity today. Although its hot-dog vendors and renovation work might seem a far cry from how you'd imagine it in Anna Karenina's day, rubbish and mud were a bigger problem then, as the Neglina River – channelled into an underground pipe – often flooded the whole area with putrid sludge. The wealth flaunted by the banks, bars and boutiques that mushroomed here in the 1990s is something that Tolstoy's heroine would have recognized as a familiar aspect of Moscow.

The Bolshoy Theatre

Bolshoy means "big" or "great", and the **Bolshoy Theatre** (Bolshoy *teatr*), dominating Teatralnaya ploshchad, is both – with a massive eight-columned portico, surmounted by Apollo's chariot. Alas, its problems are also on a grand scale, for the building is in danger of collapse due to its position above the underground Neglina River, and **reconstruction work** will oblige the company to perform at other venues until 2005. While audiences will miss the magnificent 2000-seat auditorium with its glittering chandeliers and tiers of gilded red-velvet boxes, no one can deny the gravity of the problem, which first appeared in 1906 (when part of the auditorium sagged during a matinee) but remained untreated until 1921. Subsidence returned in the late 1980s when the state was unable to afford repairs – so matters got worse, till a spate of national disasters impelled Putin to purge the Bolshoy's bosses and appoint new ones to implement a rescue plan. Although the spotlight will fall on the veteran conductor **Gennady Rozhdestvensky** as artistic director, it's the general director Anatoly Iksanov who'll call the shots until reconstruction is finished – though where the estimated $200 million will come from is anybody's guess.

See p.359 for details of performances and how to obtain tickets.

Some history

The Bolshoy's origin goes back to 1776, when the English showman Michael Maddox founded a company that became established on the corner of ulitsa Petrovka as the first permanent theatre in Moscow. The company's ballet tradition was firmly established after it came under state control in 1806, while some of the first Russian operas were performed here in the 1890s. However, the Bolshoy played second fiddle to St Petersburg's Mariinskiy Theatre until the early 1900s and only became supreme following the return of the capital to Moscow in 1918. Its international reputation was gained in the period from the 1950s to the 1970s by new works such as Khachaturian's *Spartacus* and star dancers like **Maya Plisetskaya** and **Vladimir Vasilev**. It is also famous for defections in protest at the autocratic management and conservative choreography associated with **Yuri Grigorovich**, the artistic director for thirty years until his abrupt dismissal in 1995. His successor, the revered dancer Vasilev, failed to arrest the Bolshoy's decline, and five years later he too was fired – only hearing the news from the radio.

Besides opera and ballet, the Bolshoy has been a stage for **political dramas**, the stormiest of which was the Fifth Party Congress of July 1918, which witnessed the final split between the Bolsheviks and the Left Socialist Revolutionaries, whose leader Maria Spiridonova denounced Lenin for treating the peasantry like "dung" and called for war. The Left SR delegation were held prisoner in the Bolshoy while the Bolsheviks put down an uprising by their followers; in the words of Bruce Lockhardt, "the revolution, which was conceived in a theatre, ended in the same place".

Other theatres and TsUM

Some of the opera set designs are in the Museum of Private Collections (p.148). Mamontov's activities as a patron are described under "Abramtsevo" (p.394).

The long, low-slung **Maly Theatre** (*Maliy teatr*) on the eastern side of the square was originally built as a warehouse for Moscow's only honest army provisioner. After he was jailed on false charges, it was sold off and converted into a theatre in 1838. Its drama company traces its history back to the university theatre founded in 1757, but really came of age in tandem with the playwright Alexander Ostrovsky (1823–86), who is honoured by a seated statue outside. The actress Maria Yermolova (1853–1928) spent five decades at the Maly, providing a continuity from the age of Ostrovsky into the Soviet era, when she was the first person to be awarded the title of People's Artist. Across the square is a florid yellow Empire-style edifice occupied by the **Central Children's Theatre** (*Tsentralniy Detskiy teatr – TsDT*), founded in 1921. Opera buffs should also note the **Moscow Operetta Theatre** (*Moskovskiy teatr Operetty*), tucked away just off the square on the corner of Pushkinskaya ulitsa. In the 1890s, the composer Rachmaninov and the singer Chaliapin began their careers at what was then the avant-garde Private Opera of Savva Mamontov, which hired leading artists to design the costumes and sets.

There's also something theatrical about the **TsUM** (pronounced "tsoom") department store, sandwiched between the Maly Theatre and ulitsa Petrovka. Built as Moscow's first modern store in 1908 by the Scottish trading firm Muir & Mirrielees, its spiky Neo-Gothic exterior conceals the pioneering use of reinforced concrete and curtain walls; it was also the first building in Russia to be fitted with lifts. Chekhov bought his writing paper here and named his dogs Muir and Mirrielees. Behind the store's 1960s rear extension, boutiques herald the proximity of ulitsa Kuznetskiy most and the Petrovskiy Passazh (see below).

Ulitsa Kuznetskiy most

As a connoisseur of bookshops, cafés and scandal, Mayakovsky wrote: "I love Kuznetskiy most . . . and then Petrovka" – two streets whose buzz is definitely back. **Ulitsa Kuznetskiy most** is where the aristocracy used to take their afternoon promenade and browse in shops selling everything from Fabergé bracelets to English woollens. Tolstoy listened to an early phonograph in what used to be the music shop at no. 12, and wrote of Anna Karenina shopping in Gautier's at no. 20.

Today, the street still meanders picturesquely over hills and across thoroughfares, past arresting buildings like the crested Style Moderne structure on the corner of Neglinnaya ulitsa. The rich are pulled in by foreign **airlines** and home appliances, the **banks** are back in force, and the **bookshops** and the House of Artists exhibition hall are as busy as ever. Cruder commerce in CDs, liquor and peepshows flourishes in the arcades that screen Kuznetskiy Most metro station from ulitsa Rozhdestvenka.

Ulitsa Petrovka

Long before the Bolshoy was built, **ulitsa Petrovka** was one of the most aristocratic streets in Moscow, as the boyars emulated Grand Duke Vasily III, who built a palace here with grounds extending between today's Boulevard and Garden Rings. It was also a major thoroughfare leading to the St Peter's Gate in the city's walls, which was protected by a medieval fortified monastery.

Gradually, the aristocracy moved out and merchants took over – a process culminating with the opening in 1903 of the **Petrovskiy Passazh** (Mon–Sat 10am–8pm, Sun 11am–6pm), an elegant twin-arcaded mall along the lines of GUM. Restored by Turkish contractors in the early 1990s, the Passazh set a benchmark for retailing in Moscow that newer rivals like the mall beneath Manezhnaya ploshchad have tried to surpass. The figure of the heroic proletarian outside the Petrovka entrance is a rare surviving example of the "Monumental Propaganda" decreed by Lenin in 1920. In Ilf and Petrov's satire *The Twelve Chairs*, it was in the Passazh that most of the said objects were auctioned off to buyers unaware of the diamonds secreted within them.

The Upper Monastery of St Peter and beyond

From the Passazh, you can walk 600m uphill to the former **Upper Monastery of St Peter** (*Vysoko-Petrovskiy monastyr*). Enclosed by

East of Tverskaya – theatreland to Lubyanka

a high red-brick wall whose blank lower half contrasts with the ornately framed windows above, the fortified complex is a superb example of late Moscow Baroque architecture – a style promoted by the Naryshkin relatives of Peter the Great who financed its reconstruction in the 1680s.

The monastery is open daily 9am–7pm; free.

Passing through the gateway of its Baroque **belltower**, you'll see the multi-domed **Church of the Icon of the Virgin of Bogolyubovo** (*tserkov Bogolyubskoy Bogomateri*), commemorating three of Peter's uncles killed in the 1682 Streltsy revolt, who are buried in its vaults. Other Naryshkins lie beneath the low stone building alongside, beyond which stands the single-domed **Church of Metropolitan Peter** (*tserkov Petra-Mitropolita*), which Peter's mother Natalya founded to celebrate their defeat of the Regent Sofia in 1689. The ensemble is completed by a **Refectory Church** with five blue cupolas on tall drums, linked by a shadowy arcade to the **Naryshkin Palace** inside the outer walls. In Soviet times the palace was turned into a workers' hostel and a factory, and many rooms are still occupied by workshops. Since being returned to the Church, the complex now houses the Moscow Patriarchate's Department for Religious Education and Catechism, and is gradually being restored by volunteers.

The junction with the Boulevard Ring just beyond the monastery is named **ploshchad Petrovskiy vorota**, after the St Peter's Gate that stood here in medieval times, near a large market called the *Skorodom* (literally "quick house"), specializing in everything needed to assemble a house within two or three days. Business thrived thanks to the fires that regularly gutted whole districts of Moscow; citizens preferred their traditional wooden houses to European-style stone dwellings, which were colder and damper in winter. Today there is nothing much to see but a hideous **statue of Vysotsky**, that does no justice to the memory of the beloved bard (see p.274).

Neglinka and Rozhdestvenka ulitsa

Neglinka is the popular diminutive for the Neglina River that once flowed into the heart of Moscow, encircling the Kremlin and the Kitay-gorod; *neglina* means "without clay". In Catherine the Great's time the river was channelled into a pipe running underneath what is now Neglinnaya ulitsa, but continued to flood due to infrequent cleaning and the locals' habit of dumping rubbish – and victims of robberies – into the storm drains. Today, this hilly area is only hazardous for its icy slopes in winter, and otherwise invites a wander ending at the Convent of the Nativity near the Boulevard Ring. As you ascend the hill, banks and sushi bars gradually give way to small shops, such as characterized the area during Soviet times.

The Sandunovskiy Baths

One establishment spanning the pre- and post-Communist eras with ease is the **Sandunovskiy Baths** (*Sandunovskie bani*), two blocks north of Kuznetskiy. Traditionally favoured by merchants, and writers like Tolstoy and Chekhov, the baths grew shabby during Soviet times but were fully refurbished for the centenary of their inauguration (in 1896). You first notice a grandiose Beaux Arts facade, whose great arch fronts a courtyard modelled on the Moorish Alhambra Palace in Andalucía, that originally formed the main entrance but is now off-limits. The baths occupy the red-brick building behind it, and are entered by an alley with separate doors for either sex, leading to foyers rich in majolica. While most punters opt for the "first-class" *banya* on the floor above, wealthy Muscovites patronize the "luxe" ones on the top floor, with their vaulted pool and private rooms, stained-glass windows and mahogany benches.

East of Tverskaya – theatreland to Lubyanka

Bathing details appear on p.376.

Up ulitsa Rozhdestvenka to the Convent of the Nativity

Running parallel to Neglinnaya ulitsa along what was once a high riverbank, a steeper road, **ulitsa Rozhdestvenka**, ascends to the Convent of the Nativity. At the lower end of the street is the **Savoy Hotel**, whose Style Moderne and Baroque interior rivals the Metropol's for splendour, where the French socialist Barbusse stayed while writing his sycophantic biography of Stalin.

Further uphill stands the seventeenth-century **Church of St Nicholas of the Bellringers** (*tserkov Sveta Nikolay v Zvonaryakh*), whose name refers to the street's old settlement of bellringers from the Ivan the Great Belltower in the Kremlin. In medieval Russia, holy days were celebrated by ringing all the bells of Moscow's "forty times forty" churches in unison, until "the earth shook with their vibrations like thunder".

At the end of Rozhdestvenka a gilt-spired Baroque belltower proclaims the **Convent of the Nativity** (*Rozhdestvenskiy monastyr*), which otherwise retires behind a wall. Duck in through the arch to find a complex of nuns' cells surrounding the sixteenth-century **Cathedral of the Nativity** and the eighteenth-century **Church of St John Chrysostom**. Both are small and currently being repaired by black-cowled nuns and architectural students. In medieval times, the convent had a dual role as a perimeter fortress, as a corner turret and brick ramparts along Rozhdestvenskiy bulvar attest.

Lubyanka and around

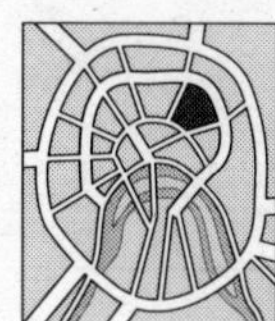

The name Lubyanka resounds like a gunshot at the far end of a darkened corridor – the traditional method of killing prisoners in the **headquarters of the secret police** on Lubyanka Square. For Russians, the building represents a historically malevolent force that's best ignored whenever possible, whereas foreigners can afford to be curious and genuinely blasé – in the old days it was almost a sport for foreigners to bait Intourist guides with awkward questions

Spying

Spying has played a big part in Russian history since the time of Ivan the Terrible; every tsar had a Secret Office or Third Section to sniff out intrigues and spy on foreign powers. Its apotheosis came with Soviet rule, as the "organs" waxed all-powerful at home and seemingly omniscient abroad. When establishing the Extraordinary Commission for the Struggle against Counter-Revolution, Speculation and Sabotage – or **Cheka** – in December 1917, Dzerzhinsky asserted that "every Chekist should have clean hands, a cool head and a warm heart". Such perverted idealism soon faded, but its myth helped sustain the organization through decades of bloodshed and fabricated conspiracies.

As the **NKVD** it controlled the slave empire of the Gulag and a large private army, making its boss, Beria, the prime contender for supremacy after Stalin's demise – a prospect that galvanized the rest of the Politburo into having him shot and pruning the ministry's powers. As a pillar of the establishment, the **KGB** proved more durable than the Communist Party, effecting cosmetic changes under Gorbachev and enduring several shake-ups by Yeltsin, from which it emerged as two agencies. The Lubyanka is occupied by the **Federal Security Service** (FSB) that monitors the home front, while the **External Intelligence Service** (SVR) is based in a modern block at Yasenevo, beyond the Moscow Ring Road.

Both the FSB and SVR have greatly improved their image in recent years, thanks to Russians' fear of terrorism and organized crime, and their suspicion of Western meddling. While catching CIA and MI6 agents makes for good publicity, the FSB's strongest card has been the threat of **Chechen terrorism**, epitomized by the apartment-block bombings of 1999. (Few Russians believe the theory that they were carried out by the FSB, to provide a pretext for invading Chechnya.) Even before becoming President, **Putin** vowed to strengthen the FSB, whose boss he had been from 1998 to 1999, having spent sixteen years in its Soviet predecessor – although his former colleagues sniffily recall him as a mere administrator, rather than a proper *razvedchik* (spy).

whenever KGB HQ came into sight at the top of the long rise from Okhotniy ryad. The secret police are still ensconced here – though nowadays called the FSB.

While it's common knowledge that the building is named after its location on **Lubyanskaya ploshchad**, few Muscovites know that Catherine the Great's secret police had its headquarters on the same spot – its memory having been effaced in the nineteenth century, when the square was surrounded by stables and dens for the refreshment of coachmen, until the 1890s, when insurance companies transformed the neighbourhood with residential and office buildings. Expropriated after the Revolution, these formed the nucleus of a 1930s redevelopment plan that included the demolition of the Kitay-gorod's Vladimir Gate.

Today, you're struck by the grotesque decision to construct in 1957 Moscow's largest toy shop just across the square from the Lubyanka – supposedly as a tribute to the founder of the Soviet secret police, who also chaired a commission on children's welfare. Located on the site of the medieval cannon foundry where the giant Tsar Cannon in the Kremlin was cast, the **Detskiy Mir** (Children's World) now sells everything from Barbie to woolly tights from Omsk, while women loitering outside offer cut-price Chinese prams, computer programs and fake designer kidswear.

The Lubyanka

The Lubyanka rises in sandstone tiers from a granite-faced lower storey emblazoned with Soviet crests. Built as the head office of the Rossiya Insurance Company in 1897, it was taken over by the Bolshevik Cheka in March 1918, only months before the repression of the Anarchists and Left SRs. In Stalin's time, generations entered its maw via the infamous Lubyanka "kennel", a whitewashed cellar used for body searches. Such was the volume of arrests that the versatile Shchusev was commissioned to design an extension that doubled its size by 1947. Even so, its bureaucracy engulfed neighbouring buildings as the security service burgeoned through successive name changes, into the KGB of Cold War notoriety (see box).

For several decades, a six-metre-tall statue of "Iron Felix" **Dzerzhinsky**, the Cheka's founder, loomed from its massive pedestal on the grassy knoll in the middle of Lubyanskaya ploshchad. The night after the collapse of the 1991 putsch, crowds cheered as the statue was toppled by a crane, its head in a wire noose, a symbol of the end of Soviet Communism. It's a sign of how far Russia has travelled since then that the Duma recently debated (but rejected) a motion to replace Dzerzhinsky's statue there. However, the organization that he created is still going strong, as you can see from the hordes of people that leave its headquarters at 5pm. The FSB is actually based in the sinister-looking 1980s block to the west of the "old" Lubyanka (which now houses the Border Police); their computer centre is above a bookstore on Myasnitskaya ulitsa, and their social club and private museum are beside a supermarket on Bolshaya Lubyanka ulitsa.

Dzerzhinsky's statue is now in the sculpture park behind the New Tretyakov Gallery (p.250).

The Museum of the Security Service

The **Museum of the Security Service** (as it's now called) was set up in 1984 to give recruits an idea of the KGB's history, but was soon applied to recasting the organization's image, with **guided tours** for Russians under glasnost and foreigners allowed in since 1991. As the exhibits are captioned in Cyrillic only, one hears a spiel from a colonel that combines droll revelations with barefaced lies. A reference to Tsarist espionage underscores the message that Russia has always been threatened by subversion and foreign foes, so spying in her defence is inevitable – and honourable. Examining photos of bygone KGB bosses, you're told that five were shot for "violations of socialist norms of legality", as if they weren't typical of the organiza-

Visits to the "KGB Museum" ($15 per person) are scheduled every week or so by Patriarshy Dom Tours (☎ 795 09 27).

tion. A coy admission that it incarcerated 3.7 million citizens and shot 700,000–800,000 others is mitigated by the absurd claim that 21,000 of its own were killed for "refusing to commit acts of repression".

Dzerzhinsky's desk and his bizarre funerary wreath of bayonets set the tone for exhibits from the "heroic" days of the Cheka, such as the pistol belonging to the captured British "Ace of Spies", Sidney Reilly. Much is made of Soviet master-spies in Germany and Switzerland who gave warning of Hitler's invasion (which Stalin ignored), and the Cambridge Ring of British traitors, also active during WWII, and afterwards – but there's nothing about Russian espionage since then. Instead, you get to chuckle over the secret cameras and other gadgets used by foreign spies caught by the KGB; while contraband weapons, drugs and art intercepted since the break-up of the Soviet Union leave visitors with the image of a responsible, caring agency, "like the American FBI".

The museum is located on the premises of the secret police **social club**, whose gloomy foyer resembles that of any other *dom kultury* but for a giant wall-relief of Dzerzhinsky. Named Lubyanka 12 after its address, the club's unlabelled glass doors are easily overlooked between the Central Gastronom and the Rostopchin mansion.

Behind the Lubyanka

The **Central Gastronom**, behind the Lubyanka, was created as a food store for the secret police and opened to ordinary citizens after the war. Like several former flagship stores, its counters where citizens queued to buy fish or butter have now been replaced by self-service aisles crammed with imported goods, while the original Stalinist decor of marble, friezes and chandeliers has been refurbished to pander to nouveau riche Muscovites.

Just uphill past the entrance to Lubyanka 12, a fence topped by urns preserves the privacy of the **Rostopchin mansion**, a longtime haunt of the secret police whose exterior matches the colour of the epaulettes worn by the KGB. It once belonged to Count Rostopchin, the governor who ordered Moscow to be burned in 1812, and escaped from a mob besieging his home by throwing them an alleged traitor. During the first night of the French occupation, Rostopchin's agents set fire to wine stalls in the Kitay-gorod and the carriage-workshops on Karetniy ryad. By the next morning, a powerful wind had fanned the flames and the fire had spread to engulf half of Moscow – Lubyanka was one of the few quarters to survive, owing to vigorous fire-fighting by its residents.

From the Rostopchin mansion, Bolshaya Lubyanka runs 500m uphill to the Boulevard Ring, where the small white **Church of the Icon of Our Lady of Vladimir** is all that remains of the fortified Sretenskiy Monastery, erected on the spot where Muscovites had welcomed the arrival of a miraculous icon of the Virgin in 1395 (see p.239).

The only inducement to walk along Sretenskiy bulvar is the **statue of Nadezhda Krupskaya** (1869–1939), Lenin's wife. The lithe, gamine figure bears little resemblance to the real dumpy, fish-eyed Krupskaya – just like the hagiographies that failed to mention Lenin's infidelity before the Revolution, or how Krupskaya was browbeaten by Stalin after Lenin's death.

The Mayakovsky Museum

Across the road to the east of the Lubyanka, beneath an anonymous superstructure containing its computer centre, a granite head gazing from a portal at ulitsa Myatninskaya 3–6 betrays the **Mayakovsky Museum** in the courtyard behind. **Vladimir Mayakovsky** (1893–1930) was an enthusiastic supporter of the Bolsheviks from an early age, who got into Futurism at the Moscow School for Painting and Sculpture after meeting the Burlyuk brothers. Together they published a manifesto called *A Slap in the Face for Public Taste* and embarked on a publicity tour, Mayakovsky wearing earrings and a waistcoat with radishes in the buttonholes. In 1917 he threw himself into the October Revolution, founding the Left Front of Art with Alexander Rodchenko and Osip Brik, and producing more than six hundred giant cartoon advertisements with pithy verse captions for the Russia Telegraph Agency. Mayakovsky's suicide at the age of 37 has been variously ascribed to despair over his love for Osip's wife, Lili; to disillusionment with Soviet life and its censors; or to hostile reviews of his last exhibition. Thousands filed past his open coffin at the Writers' Union, and Stalin would later decree that "Mayakovsky was and remains the most talented poet of our Soviet epoch. Indifference to his memory and to his work is a crime."

The Mayakovsky Museum is open Mon, Tues & Fri–Sun 10am–6pm, Thurs 1–9pm; closed Wed and the last Fri of each month; $2. To arrange a guided tour in English ($42 group rate) ☎928 25 69.

Opened in 1990, and run by the poet's granddaughter, the Mayakovsky Museum is quite unlike other memorial museums in the ex-residences of writers or artists, with their period decor and display cases. Rather, it feels like walking around inside Mayakovsky's head during a brainstorm. Melting chairs and Constructivist vortices breathe life into editions of his poetry and agitprop posters, mixed in with personal effects and symbolic *objets* – viewed as you ascend a spiral ramp towards the upper floor. Although nothing remains of the original flat, it was here that Mayakovsky lived from 1919 onwards, and ultimately committed suicide with a stage prop revolver, leaving an unfinished poem beside him.

Towards Chistye prudy

The section of the Boulevard Ring known as **Chistye prudy** is notable for several architectural curiosities, mostly within five minutes' walk of Chistye Prudy or Turgenevskaya metro stations. Another approach is to walk up **Myasnitskaya ulitsa**, where at no. 19, on the left, you'll recognize the **Perlov Tea House** (Mon–Fri

8am–1.15pm & 1.45–7.30pm, Sat 9am–6pm) by its facade crawling with bronze dragons and pagoda-like flourishes, matched inside by lacquered columns and Chinese vases. Legend has it that the shop was decorated in this fashion by the wealthy tea merchant Perlov, who desired to impress the young emperor of China during his visit to Russia in 1893. Sadly for Perlov, the emperor chose to visit a rival tea merchant instead. There's a wonderful aroma of tea and coffee inside.

The pale-peach-and-white building next door played an important role in Russian art after the Moscow School of Painting and Sculpture was established here in 1844. By 1872, when it hosted the first major exhibition of the Wanderers movement, the Moscow School had begun to outshine the Academy of Arts in St Petersburg; four decades later, it was at the forefront of the avant-garde. The teaching staff included Leonid Pasternak, whose son Boris – the future author of *Doctor Zhivago* – spent his childhood in a nearby annexe. In 1920, it was transformed into the Higher Technical-Artistic Workshop or VKhuTeMas, the short-lived Soviet equivalent of the Bauhaus, whose radical Futurism dismayed Lenin.

Apart from the Tea House, the best sights are located along or just off Chistoprudniy bulvar, round the corner from the **Main Post Office** (*Glavpochtamt*). The boulevard and the locality are named after the pond at the far end, which was used for the disposal of butchers' waste until 1703, when it was mucked out on the orders of Prince Menshikov and henceforth known as Chistye prudy (Clean Ponds). Given Menshikov's notorious corruption, it seems fitting that the far side of the boulevard is now dominated by the **headquarters of LUKoil**, the scandal-prone oil company created during the privatization binge of the 1990s. At the entrance to the park that runs along the boulevard stands a **statue of Alexander Griboedov**, an army officer turned playwright and diplomat who was murdered by a mob in Teheran. The pedestal is decorated with reliefs of characters from his celebrated drama, *Woe from Wit*.

Menshikov's Tower

In the early eighteenth century, this part of Moscow belonged to **Prince Menshikov** (1673–1729), who rose from being a humble pie-lad to fortune and power, owing to Peter the Great's appreciation of his ruthless ability and artful blend of "servility, familiarity and impertinence". Menshikov understood Peter's impatience with Muscovite conservatism and the Orthodox Church, and surpassed the tsar in ostentatious gestures. Accordingly, he commissioned Ivan Zarudny to build (1705–07) an outstanding edifice that incorporated secular Western forms into Orthodox architecture – the **Church of the Archangel Gabriel** (*tserkov Arkhangela Gavriila*).

Popularly known as **Menshikov's Tower** (*Menshikova bashnya*), this boasted a wooden-spired belfry holding fifty bells and crowned by a gilded statue of the Archangel, three metres higher than the Ivan the Great Belltower in the Kremlin – hitherto the tallest building in all Russia. His hubris was punished in 1723, when lightning set the spire ablaze. Since Menshikov was then living at Oranienbaum, and shortly had to fight for survival following Peter's death, no rebuilding took place until 1766–80, when the Freemason Izmaylov devised a belfry with only two of the three original octagonal tiers and a gilded coronet instead of a spire. However, many features of Zarudny's design remain, such as the Bible-clutching seraphim that flit across the facade, and the massive buttresses scrolling upwards beside the door on the left-hand side. The **interior** looks more Catholic than Orthodox, its frescoes offset by swags and cherubs – but Izmaylov's Masonic symbols were removed after the Freemasons were banished from the church in 1863. The tower is set back from the street directly behind the lower Neoclassical **Church of St Theodor Stratilites** (*tserkov Fyodora Stratilita*).

By turning right after both churches, you'll find yourself in **Krivokolenniy pereulok** (Double Knee-Bend Lane), so-called because it has two sharp bends instead of one. Its cute name aside, this is a nice, quiet way into the Ukrainian quarter, coming out on Armyanskiy pereulok (see opposite).

Along the Ring to the Apraksin Mansion

Alternatively, you can return to the Boulevard Ring and carry on to the limpid pond that gives Chistye prudy its name. On the far side stands the **Sovremennik Theatre**, occupying a former cinema with an elegant, rounded portico flanked by bas-reliefs of Greek deities. Further along at no. 23 is a florid sky-blue apartment building where the film director Sergei Eisenstein lived from 1920 to 1934. On the near side of the boulevard, don't miss the **Figurniy dom** (Figured House) at no. 14, built by Sergei Vashkov at the beginning of this century, whose frontage crawls with a bestiary of supernatural creatures.

While in the area, it's worth a short detour beyond the Ring to see the former **Apraksin Mansion** near the corner of ulitsa Pokrovka. Erected in the 1760s, overlooking the Pokrovka Gate and the road leading to the royal palaces in the old foreigners' quarter, the mansion was Moscow's ultimate in decorative Baroque: a rambling mass of bay windows and scalloped niches, clusters of angels and Corinthian pilasters, modelled on the Winter Palace in St Petersburg. The archway into its courtyard is lined with plaques listing technical journals based at the premises – a legacy of the Industrial Academy for "Red managers" that existed here after the Revolution. Its students included Stalin's wife Nadezhda Allilueva, and Nikita Khrushchev, who was the school's Party secretary.

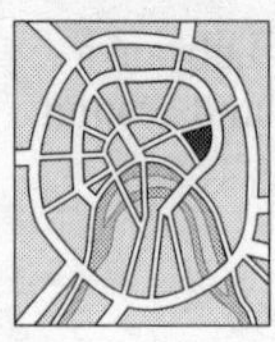

The Ukrainian quarter

The erstwhile **Ukrainian quarter** to the east of the Kitay-gorod no longer has a distinct ethnic flavour, but its hilly, winding lanes are a reminder of the time when Moscow's residential quarters consisted of "quiet lanes where wooden gates open into courtyards planted with lilacs, acacias and senna".

In late medieval times this area was prosperous and cosmopolitan, for scores of Westerners chose to settle here after Tsar Mikhail Romanov allowed non-Orthodox believers to live where they pleased. But as income for local Orthodox churches declined, protests impelled the tsar to order the demolition of their chapels and a ban on further settlers; his successor, Alexei, later banished them to a colony beyond the city walls. Ukrainians began moving in after the Russo-Polish war of 1654–67 left Ukraine under Russian control, followed by other races as the empire grew. Today, embassies and diverse places of worship maintain something of this tradition, but the area's real charm lies in its meandering backstreets and odd juxtapositions of medieval, nineteenth-century and Soviet architecture. The nearest metro stations are Kitay-gorod and Chistye Prudy.

Along Maroseyka

Running from the edge of the Kitay-gorod through the heart of the quarter, **ulitsa Maroseyka** takes its name from *Malorosseyka* or "Little Russia", the old Tsarist title for Ukraine, which came under the jurisdiction of the Little Russian Office. During Soviet times, the street was patronizingly named after Bogdan Khmelnitskiy, the Cossack Hetman who transferred control of Ukraine from Poland to Russia in 1653. Nowadays far too narrow for its heavy traffic, Maroseyka is shabby and congested, but redeems itself with some fine old buildings and picturesque lanes before becoming ulitsa Pokrovka, nearer the Boulevard Ring.

Starting from the vicinity of Staraya ploshchad, the first sight is the small salmon-pink **Church of St Nicholas the Wonder-worker** (*tserkov Nikolay Chudotvortsa*), characterized by chunky *nalichniki*, green roofs and a cobalt onion dome. The church dates from 1687, its belltower from 1748. Further on at no. 17 stands a sky-blue-and-white mansion dripping with caryatids. Originally the Little Russian Office, it now contains the **Belarus Embassy**, which maintains a hotel for visiting dignitaries around the corner. Across the main road is the sage-green **Church of SS Cosmas and Damian** (*tserkov Kosmy i Damiana*), built by Kazakov in 1791–1803, which is unique among Moscow churches for its central cylinder, topped by a gilt-knobbed cupola and abutted by several rounded chapels.

Armenians' Lane

The Ukrainian quarter

Around the corner from the embassy lies the original heart of the foreign quarter, **Armyanskiy pereulok** (Armenians' Lane), whose security was half-assured by the fact that Artamon Matveev, Tsar Alexei's foreign minister, lived here with his Scottish wife, Mary Hamilton, surrounded by mirrors, clocks and paintings that attested to his fascination with European ways. Although this didn't stop Alexei from evicting all the foreigners in 1652, it was here that he later met his second wife, Natalya Naryshkina – the upshot being a child who upset the dynastic ambitions of the **Miloslavsky boyars**, whose intrigues against Matveev and Natalya led to the Streltsy revolt of 1682. The rival families lived directly opposite each other: Matveev where the Belarus Embassy stands today; the Miloslavskys in a pale-grey house that still exists (albeit much remodelled) around the corner. During the late nineteenth century this was inhabited by the Slavophile poet Fyodor Tyutchev, who famously wrote that you cannot understand Russia, only believe in her.

At the far end of the lane, the **Armenian Embassy** occupies a pale yellow mansion (no. 2) that retires behind an elegant portico and wrought-iron gates, which was formerly the Lazarev Institute for Oriental Languages, established by a wealthy Armenian family. Armenians have lived here since the time of the Miloslavskys, who also owned a house across the road at no. 3. Unlike their other place, this looks more of its time, having low brick vaulted rooms at several levels, and is now given over to a **Moscow Lights Museum** (Mon–Fri 9am–5pm; free), covering the history of illuminating the city. If antique gas lamps don't get you going, there are switchboards from the metro and an album of photos showing Moscow ablaze with neon and fireworks at the victory celebrations in 1945.

To the Ivanovskiy Convent

By turning off ulitsa Maroseyka beside SS Cosmas and Damian, you can follow **Starosadskiy pereulok** (Old Garden Lane) downhill to the **Church of St Vladimir in the Old Garden** (*tserkov Vladimira v Starykh sadakh*), the only surviving example of the dozen or so stone parish churches erected under Grand Duke Vasily III. Built in 1514 by the Italian Alevisio Novi (creator of the Archangel Cathedral in the Kremlin), it was altered and truncated in the 1680s and thereafter nicknamed "domeless" (*bez glavy*) – though it actually has six small domes, resting on drums carved with anthropomorphic figures.

Across the slope looms the high-walled **Ivanovskiy Convent** (*Ivanovskiy monastyr*), whose fanged belltowers and scabrous cupolas reflect its sinister history. Founded in the sixteenth century, it was used as a dumping ground for unwanted wives and daughters and as a prison for noblewomen guilty of heinous crimes or vaguely

The Ukrainian quarter

The story of Princess Tarakanova is told on p.280. Countess Saltykova is buried in the Donskoy Monastery (p.256).

defined political offences. Among those detained in the reign of Catherine the Great were the notorious Countess Dariya Saltykova – confined for thirty years in an underground cell for murdering 139 of her serfs – and the tragic Princess Tarakanova, who fell foul of the empress. In Soviet times the convent was disbanded and the complex turned into a police training school, onto which a modern block was grafted. Now back in Orthodox hands, it is slowly being restored as a working convent, which isn't open to outsiders.

If you want to head back towards the centre at this point, ulitsa Zabelina provides a quick route to the Kitay-gorod, with the option of a detour near the bottom of the hill to the **Choral Synagogue** on Bolshoy Spasoglinishchevskiy pereulok. Moscow's oldest and largest Jewish place of worship, it has been under 24-hour guard since another synagogue was burned down in 1993, so unless you're seriously interested it's not worth facing the scrutiny by trying to enter or taking photographs outside.

Down towards the Yauza River

If you're still keen on exploring, try the lane running uphill to the east of St Vladimir's Church, whose name, **Khokhlovskiy pereulok**, comes from *khokhli*, an old Russian nickname for Ukrainians, derived from their traditional hairdos (*khokhol* means "tuft" or "crest").

At the triple fork beyond the first bend you'll see a terraced garden, overlooked by a turquoise mansion whose ornamental Neo-Russian archway invites a closer look. The **Morozov House** once belonged to Maria Morozova, a fervent Old Believer who inherited her husband's textile empire and ran it regardless of her sons, leaving them to patronize the arts. While Savva bankrolled the Moscow Art Theatre and resided elsewhere, Sergei lived here with mother and her ban on baths and electricity. However, he did sponsor a museum, took up art himself and built a studio in the garden, which he later gave as a sanctuary to the painter Isaak Levitan, who would otherwise have been included in the expulsion of twenty thousand Jews from Moscow in 1891. After the Revolution the Morozovs fled and the house was seized by Left SRs, who transformed it into a fortress. During their abortive "Bolshoy coup" of July 6, 1918, they held Dzerzhinsky a prisoner here until he was freed by Latvian sharpshooters. It now serves as a playschool.

On a parallel side street stands the **Church of the Trinity in Kulishki** (*tserkov Trekh Svyatiteley na Kulishkakh*), whose deep undercroft supports a nest of chapels and shingled domes, their ogee-gables picked out in red. Finished in 1674, this multi-level structure once contained an upper "summer" church, and a smaller, warmer one for winter worship, below – a functional division common in those times. Turned into an NKVD prison in the 1930s and more recently used as offices, it is now again a place of worship.

The Khitrov Market

No description of the Beliy Gorod quarter would be complete without a mention of the **Khitrov Market** (*Khitrovskiy rynok*) that existed on the corner of the Boulevard Ring from 1826 to 1923. Sited in a dell surrounded by flophouses and mud banks awash with sewage, this so-called labour market constituted an underworld of ten thousand beggars, orphans, thieves and whores, which Stanislavsky took as a model when staging Gorky's play *The Lower Depths*. Its robbers and pimps drank in dives called "Siberia" and "Hard Labour", while local kids were raised to steal or sell their bodies by the age of ten. The whole area was unlit and shrouded in fog, so the police never ventured in after dark; outsiders who did were found stabbed to death and stripped naked the next morning. After the Civil War, this urban sore was cauterized by bulldozing away the slums and erecting a huge model apartment building entered by an arch flanked by **statues of an armed worker and peasant**, which can still be seen at the far end of Podkolokolniy pereulok.

From here there's a choice of routes down to **Podkolokolniy pereulok** (Under the Bells Lane), which slopes gently uphill from ulitsa Solyanka to the Boulevard Ring. Khitrovskiy pereulok, running off behind the Church of the Trinity, gets its name from the infamous Khitrov Market that once existed in the vicinity (see box above), while Podkpaevskiy pereulok lends its name to the **Church of St Nicholas in Podkopaev** (*tserkov Nikoly v Podkopae*), which blithely defies the rules of Classical harmony by juxtaposing a tiny church with a bulbous dome and a chunky freestanding belfry.

Across the main road from St Nicholas, the first turning to the east (Petropavlovskiy pereulok) will lead you to the **Church of Peter and Paul on the Yauza** (*tserkov Petra i Pavla chto na Yauze*). Erected on a hill near one of the city gates in 1700, this once enjoyed a lovely view across the river to the churches of Zayauze, extending upstream as far as the Andronikov Monastery. Though its view has been curtailed by high-rise apartments, the church remains peacefully aloof from the city, its visual appeal enhanced by a deep red paint job, against which its crested *nalichniki* and golden domes stand proud.

One final church worth seeing rises just beyond the Boulevard Ring near ploshchad Yauzkie vorota, where the gate once stood. The **Church of the Trinity in Serebryaniki** (*tserkov Troitsy v Serebryanikakh*) takes its name from the quarter of silversmiths (*serebryanki*) that existed here when Karl Blank built the church in 1781. Its lofty freestanding belfry of three tiers buttressed by Corinthian pilasters and jutting pediments is a local landmark, painted a bright cerulean blue; the refectory and chapel are secluded behind it. At this point, you might be drawn across the Yauza by the looming mass of the Stalin-Gothic Kotelnicheskaya Apartments, described on p.276.

Streets and squares

Arbatskaya ploshchad	Арбатская площадь
Armyanskiy pereulok	Армянский переулок
Bolshaya Nikitskaya ulitsa	Большая Никитская ўлица
Bolshoy Spasoglinishchevskiy pereulok	Больой Спасоглищевский переулок
Chistoprudiy bulvar	Чистопрудный бульвар
Georgievskiy pereulok	Георгиевский переулок
Gogolevskiy bulvar	Гоголевский бульвар
Kamergerskiy pereulok	Камергерский переулок
Khokhlovskiy pereulok	Хохловский переулок
Krivokolenniy pereulok	Кривоколенный переулок
Lubyanskaya ploshchad	Лубянская площадь
Manezhnaya ploshchad	Манежная площадь
Mokhovaya ulitsa	Моховая улица
Myasnitskaya ulitsa	Мясницкая улица
Neglinnaya ulitsa	Неглинная улица
Nikitskiy bulvar	Никитский бульвар
Nikitskie vorota ploshchad	Никитские ворота площадь
Petrovskiy vorota ploshchad	Петровские ворота площадь
Podkolokolniy pereulok	Подколокольный переулок
Pokrovskiy bulvar	Покровский бульвар
Pushkinskaya ploshchad	Пушкинская площадь
Rozhdestvenskiy bulvar	Рождественский бульвар
Serebryanicheskiy pereulok	Серебрянический переулок
Starosadskiy pereulok	Старосадский переулок
Stoleshnikov pereulok	Столешников переулок
Tverskaya ploshchad	Тверская площадь
Tverskaya ulitsa	Тверская улица
Tverskoy bulvar	Тверской бульвар
Teatralnaya ploshchad	Театральная площадь
ulitsa Bolshaya Lubyanka	улица Большая Лубянка
ulitsa Malaya Lubyanka	улица Малая Лубянка
ulitsa Kuznetskiy most	улица Кузнецкий мост
ulitsa Maroseyka	улица Маросейка
ulitsa Petrovka	улица Петровка
ulitsa Pokrovka	улица Покровка
ulitsa Rozhdestvenka	улица Рождественка
ulitsa Vozdvizhenka	улица Воздвиженка
ulitsa Zabelina	улица Забелина
ulitsa Znamenka	улица Знаменка

The Ukrainian quarter

Metro stations

Arbatskaya	Арбатская
Biblioteka imeni Lenina	Библиотека имени Ленина
Borovitskaya	Боровицкая
Chekhovskaya	Чеховская
Chistye Prudy	Чистые пруды
Kropotkinskaya	Кропоткинская
Lubyanka	Лубянка
Okhotniy Ryad	Охотный ряд
Ploshchad Revolyutsii	Площадь Революции
Pushkinskaya	Пушкинская
Teatralnaya	Театральная
Turgenvskaya	Тургеневская
Tverskaya	Тверская

Museums

Konenkov Studio Museum	музей-мастерская С.Т. Конёнкова
Mayakovsky Museum	музей В.В. Маяковского
Meyerhold Flat-Museum	музей-квартира В.И. Мейерхольда
Moscow Lights Museum	Московский музей свтеа
Museum of Books	музей Книги
Museum of the Security Service	музей Службы Безорасности
Museum of Folk Art	музей Народново искусства
Museum of Private Collections	музей Личных Коллекций
Museum of Wax Figures	музей Восковых Фигур
Nemirovich-Danchenko Museum	музей-квартира Немировиф-Данченка
Nikolai Ostrovskiy Museum	музей-квартира Николя Островского
Pushkin Museum of Fine Art	музей изобразительных искусств им. А.С. Пушкина
Shchusev Architectural Museum	музей архитктуры им. А.В. Щусева
Stanislavsky House-Museum	дом-музей К.С. Станиславского
Yermolova House-Museum	дом-музей М.Н. Ермоловой
Zoological Museum	Зоологический музей

Chapter 5

The Zemlyanoy Gorod

In medieval times, the white-walled Beliy Gorod was encircled by a humbler **ZEMLYANOY GOROD**, or "Earth Town", ringed by an earthen rampart fifteen kilometres in diameter. Its wooden houses and muddy lanes proved impervious to change until its total destruction in the fire of 1812. Reconstruction presented an ideal opportunity for gentrification, as former artisans' quarters were colonized by the nobility and the old ramparts were levelled to form a ring of boulevards, where anyone building a house was obliged to plant trees – the origin of the **Garden Ring** (*Sadovoe koltso*) that marked the division between the bourgeois centre and the proletarian suburbs.

Although Moscow's growth eroded this distinction and the Revolution turned it inside out, the area's cachet endured. Its roll call of famous residents includes Pushkin, Lermontov, Chekhov, Gorky and Bulgakov, all of whom are associated with certain neighbourhoods – in particular, Bulgakov and the **Patriarch's Ponds**. Besides its **literary associations**, this is one of the best-looking parts of Moscow, with Empire and Art Nouveau **mansions** on every corner of the backstreets off the **Arbat**. This quarter has inspired poet-musicians like Bulat Okudzhava, giving rise to a vibrant **streetlife** that was unique in Moscow during the 1980s and is still more tourist-friendly than anything else currently on offer, though the future lies with the malls of the **New Arbat**.

The modern Garden Ring is a Stalinist creation whose name has been a misnomer since all the trees were felled when it was widened to an eight-lane motorway in the 1930s. Vast avenues, flanked by leviathan blocks and the **Stalin-Gothic skyscrapers** whose pinnacles and spires dominate Moscow's skyline, exude power and indifference. In 1944, hordes of German POWs were herded along the Ring en route to Siberia; some Muscovites jeered, others threw them bread. The Ring witnessed **barricades** and bloodshed during the crises of 1991 and 1993 and seems guaranteed a role in any future troubles – though under normal circumstances, traffic is the only real hazard.

Approaches

The size of the Zemlyanoy Gorod and its uneven distribution of sights call for two approaches. Whereas the western half – particularly the Arbat district – repays exploration **on foot**, the rest is best tackled on a hit and run basis, making forays from the nearest **metro** station. Some Circle line stations coincide with the Garden Ring, but most are sited further out. Travelling overground is an experience in itself. Despite the Ring's heavy traffic and brutal functionalism, its sheer width and rollercoaster succession of underpasses and flyovers make for a dramatic ride by car, or a slow parade of skyscrapers aboard **trolleybus** Б which takes about an hour to circle the Ring, stopping at all the main intersections.

Each section of the Ring is individually named (eg Bolshaya Sadovaya ulitsa, Sadovaya-Triumfalnaya ulitsa) and numbered in a clockwise direction with the odd numbers on the rim. Our account follows the pattern of the previous chapter by starting with Tverskaya ulitsa and dividing the rest into wedge-shaped sectors. Many of these tie in with points on the Boulevard Ring, mentioned in the previous chapter, although in other cases the starting point is the Garden Ring or a metro station.

Around Pushkinskaya ploshchad

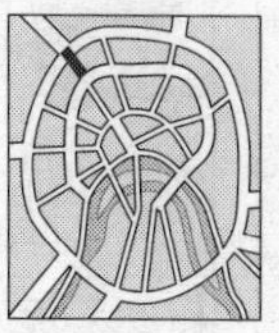

The long, flat stretch of Tverskaya ulitsa beyond the Boulevard Ring starts with an elongated slab of greenery underlaid by pedestrian subways and three metro stations (Pushkinskaya, Tverskaya and Chekhovskaya), one of which takes its name from the statue of the poet that gazes over **Pushkinskaya ploshchad** (Pushkin Square).

The lower end of Tverskaya ulitsa is covered on pp.131–136.

Alexander Opekushin's bronze **statue of Pushkin** is Moscow's best-loved monument. Paid for by public donations and unveiled in 1880 to eulogies by Ivan Turgenev and other writers, the statue was moved from its original location on the other side of Tverskaya ulitsa to its present site in 1950. Floral tributes always lie at the foot of its plinth, while on Pushkin's birthday (June 6), thousands of admirers gather to recite his poetry. In the 1970s and 1980s, the statue was also a focal point for demonstrations, as Russians regard Pushkin as the embodiment of moral honesty, and the protesters hoped that the police would be too ashamed to wade in (they weren't). The lines on the monument's plinth read:

Long will I be honoured by the people
For awaking with my lyre kind impulses
For praising, in this fallen age, freedom
And advocating mercy to the fallen.

Behind Pushkin's statue looms the bronzed pediment and glass facade of a **cinema** that was one of the first daringly modern buildings in postwar Moscow when it was erected in 1961, on the site of

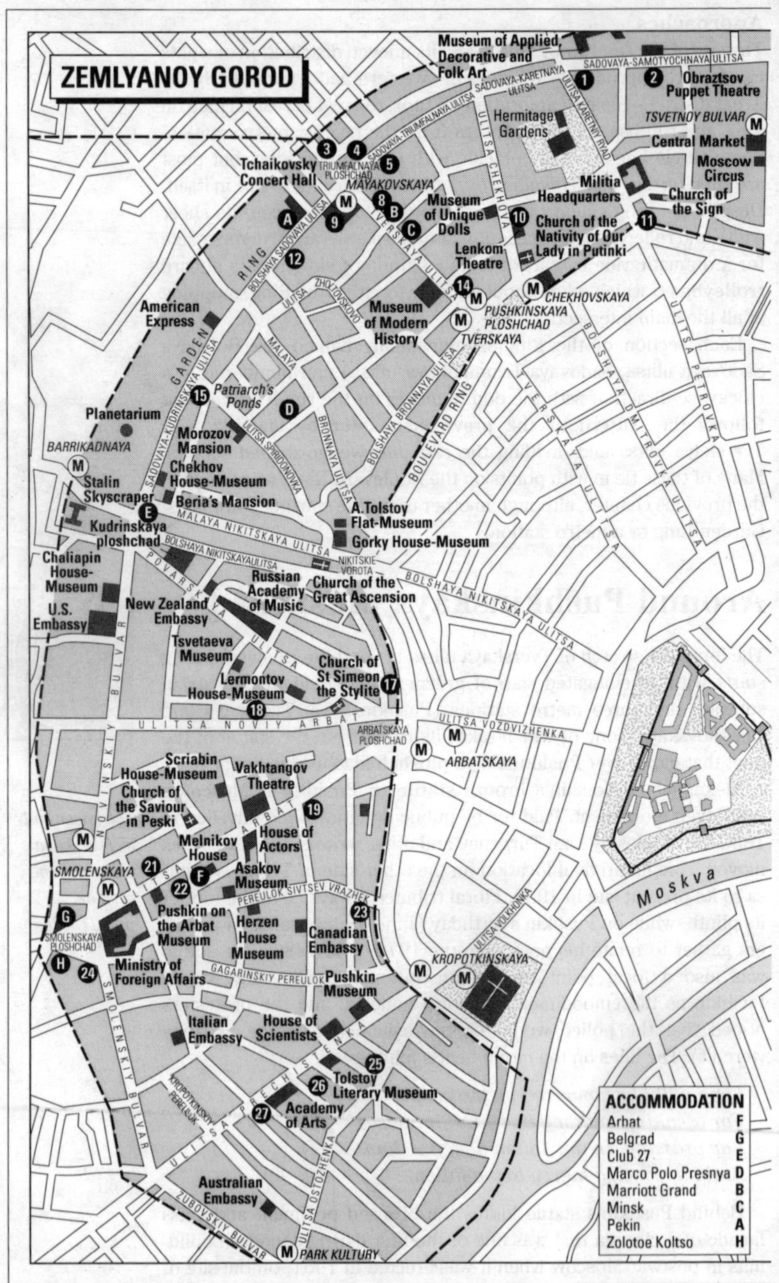
ZEMLYANOY GOROD
Museum of Applied, Decorative and Folk Art
SADOVAYA-SAMOTYOCHNAYA ULITSA
SADOVAYA-KARETNAYA ULITSA
Obraztsov Puppet Theatre
Hermitage Gardens
TSVETNOY BULVAR
Central Market
Moscow Circus
Militia Headquarters
Church of the Sign
ULITSA KARETNIY RYAD
ULITSA CHEKHOVA
SADOVAYA-TRIUMFALNAYA ULITSA
TRIUMFALNAYA PLOSHCHAD
Tchaikovsky Concert Hall
MAYAKOVSKAYA
Museum of Unique Dolls
Church of the Nativity of Our Lady in Putinki
Lenkom Theatre
TVERSKAYA ULITSA
BOLSHAYA SADOVAYA ULITSA
RING
GARDEN
ULITSA ZHOLTOVSKOVO
MALAYA
American Express
Museum of Modern History
CHEKHOVSKAYA
PUSHKINSKAYA PLOSHCHAD
TVERSKAYA
SADOVAYA-KUDRINSKAYA ULITSA
Patriarch's Ponds
Planetarium
Morozov Mansion
ULITSA SPIRIDONOVKA
BRONNAYA ULITSA
BOLSHAYA BRONNAYA ULITSA
BOULEVARD RING
TVERSKAYA ULITSA
BOLSHAYA DMITROVKA
ULITSA PETROVKA
BARRIKADNAYA
Chekhov House-Museum
Stalin Skyscraper
Beria's Mansion
A.Tolstoy Flat-Museum
Gorky House-Museum
Kudrinskaya ploshchad
MALAYA NIKITSKAYA ULITSA
BOLSHAYA NIKITSKAYA ULITSA
NIKITSKIE VOROTA
Chaliapin House-Museum
POVARSKAYA ULITSA
Russian Academy of Music
Church of the Great Ascension
U.S. Embassy
New Zealand Embassy
Tsvetaeva Museum
Church of St Simeon the Stylite
Lermontov House-Museum
NOVINSKIY BULVAR
ULITSA NOVIY ARBAT
ARBATSKAYA PLOSHCHAD
ULITSA VOZDVIZHENKA
ARBATSKAYA
Scriabin House-Museum
Vakhtangov Theatre
Church of the Saviour in Peski
ARBAT
House of Actors
Melnikov House
SMOLENSKAYA
Asakov Museum
PEREULOK SIVTSEV VRAZHEK
Pushkin on the Arbat Museum
Herzen House Museum
Canadian Embassy
SMOLENSKAYA PLOSHCHAD
Ministry of Foreign Affairs
GAGARINSKIY PEREULOK
Pushkin Museum
ULITSA VOLKHONKA
KROPOTKINSKAYA
Moskva
SMOLENSKIY BULVAR
Italian Embassy
House of Scientists
PRECHISTENKA
Tolstoy Literary Museum
KROPOTKINSKIY PEREULOK
Academy of Arts
ULITSA OSTOZHENKA
Australian Embassy
ZUBOVSKIY BULVAR
PARK KULTURY
ACCOMMODATION
Arbat F
Belgrad G
Club 27 E
Marco Polo Presnya D
Marriott Grand B
Minsk C
Pekin A
Zolotoe Koltso H

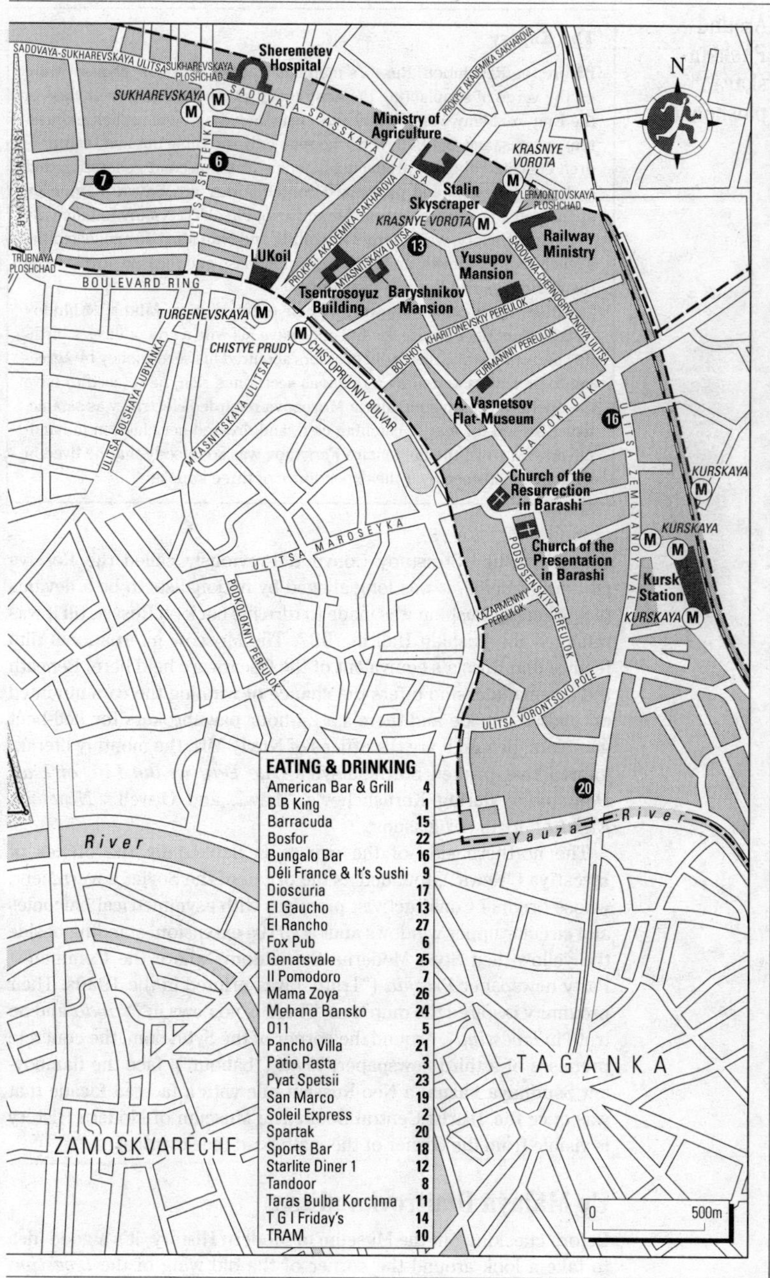

N
Sheremetev Hospital
SADOVAYA-SUKHAREVSKAYA ULITSA
SUKHAREVSKAYA PLOSHCHAD
SUKHAREVSKAYA
M
SADOVAYA-SPASSKAYA ULITSA
PROKPET AKADEMIKA SAKHAROVA
Ministry of Agriculture
TSVETNOY BULVAR
ULITSA SRETENKA
6
7
KRASNYE VOROTA
Stalin Skyscraper
LERMONTOVSKAYA PLOSHCHAD
KRASNYE VOROTA
Railway Ministry
TRUBNAYA PLOSHCHAD
LUKoil
MYASNITSKAYA ULITSA
13
Yusupov Mansion
SADOVAYA-CHERNOGRYAZNOYA ULITSA
BOULEVARD RING
Tsentrosoyuz Building
Baryshnikov Mansion
TURGENEVSKAYA
CHISTYE PRUDY
CHISTOPRUDNIY BULVAR
BOLSHOY KHARITONEVSKIY PEREULOK
FURMANNIY PEREULOK
ULITSA BOLSHAYA LUBYANKA
MYASNITSKAYA ULITSA
A. Vasnetsov Flat-Museum
ULITSA POKROVKA
16
ULITSA ZEMLYANOY VAL
Church of the Resurrection in Barashi
KURSKAYA
ULITSA MAROSEYKA
PODSOSENSKIY PEREULOK
Church of the Presentation in Barashi
KURSKAYA
Kursk Station
KURSKAYA
PODKOLOKNIY PEREULOK
KAZARMENNIY PEREULOK
ULITSA VORONTSOVO POLE
EATING & DRINKING
American Bar & Grill 4
B B King 1
Barracuda 15
Bosfor 22
Bungalo Bar 16
Déli France & It's Sushi 9
Dioscuria 17
El Gaucho 13
El Rancho 27
Fox Pub 6
Genatsvale 25
Il Pomodoro 7
Mama Zoya 26
Mehana Bansko 24
011 5
Pancho Villa 21
Patio Pasta 3
Pyat Spetsii 23
San Marco 19
Soleil Express 2
Spartak 20
Sports Bar 18
Starlite Diner 1 12
Tandoor 8
Taras Bulba Korchma 11
T G I Friday's 14
TRAM 10
20
River
Yauza River
TAGANKA
ZAMOSKVARECHE
0 500m

The Kuptsy

Before the Revolution, Russia's merchant-industrialists, or **Kuptsy**, were on the verge of supplanting the aristocracy as the most powerful class in the Empire. Many were former serfs who ended up owning their ex-masters' estates, and Old Believers who read only the Bible but had their children educated abroad, producing a sophisticated second generation that endowed hospitals and patronized contemporary art. **Savva Mamontov** sponsored an artists' colony at Abramtsevo, **Pavel Tretyakov** founded the Tretyakov Gallery, while **Sergei Shchukin** and **Ivan Morozov** collected the French Impressionists, and the works of Matisse and Picasso now held by the Hermitage and Pushkin museums.

Others were chiefly known for their eccentricities. **Mikhail Khludov** walked a pet tiger on a leash and once gave his wife a crocodile as a birthday present. One of the **Lapin** brothers acquired his seed-money by agreeing to be half-castrated by a religious sect; once rich, he refused to have the operation completed. **Maria Morozova** regarded electricity as satanic, never bathed for fear of catching cold, and dressed her children in hand-me-downs, while the millionaire **Fersanov** was so miserly that he lived in a hut and lost sleep over the expenditure of three kopeks.

the demolished Strastnoy Convent. Previously called the Rossiya (Russia) Cinema, it was long alleged by nationalists to be a devious ploy whereby Pushkin was made to turn his back on Russia, till it was renamed the Pushkin Hall in 1997. The Moscow international film festival and Russia's equivalent of the Oscars are held here. Beneath the cinema, a casino offers the chance of winning the cars mounted on plinths outside and there's a 24-hour pawnbrokers for hell-bent gamblers; behind it are the offices of **Noviy Mir**, the monthly literary journal that printed Solzhenitsyn's *One Day in the Life of Ivan Denisovich* during Khrushchev's "thaw", and Orwell's *Nineteen Eighty-four* under glasnost.

The northern side of the square is flanked by the offices of **Izvestiya** ("News"), founded as the organ of the Soviet government, whose original Constructivist premises with asymmetrical balconies and circular upper windows abut a 1970s extension, standing beside the yellow-tiled Style Moderne **Sytin dom**, where the Communist Party newspaper *Pravda* ("Truth") was printed in the 1920s. Their proximity inspired the quip that "There is no news in *Pravda* and no truth in *Izvestiya*". Around the corner of the Sytin dom, the concrete premises of a third newspaper, *Trud* ("Labour"), face the flamboyant **Ssudnaya kazna**, a Neo-Russian pile with a faceted facade that was once the Tsarist Central Bank. The Museum of Modern History is visible from the corner of the main road (see overleaf).

Up Malaya Dmitrovka ulitsa

Before checking out the Museum of Modern History, it's a good idea to take a look around the corner of the old wing of the *Izvestiya* building, where a delightful church stands at the beginning of **Malaya Dmitrovka ulitsa**. During Soviet times the street was named after Chekhov because he liked it so much that he lived in three separate houses here (nos. 11, 12 and 29) over the years.

Entirely white, with gold-frilled azure onion domes, the **Church of the Nativity of Our Lady in Putinki** (*tserkov Rozhdestva Bogroditsy shto v Putinkakh*) was the last church to be built with tent-roofs before Patriarch Nikon banned them in 1652. Its complex form includes three steeples atop the church proper; a protruding chapel crowned with a tent-roof and a pyramid of ogival *kokoshniki*; an arched, open belfry; and a one-storey narthex and porch, the latter also decorated with a tent-roof and *kokoshniki*. Alas, the interior is as plain as the exterior is lavish, retaining only a portion of the original iconostasis.

Up the road at no. 6, the **Lenkom Theatre** occupies the former Merchants' Club, built in 1909. Its sedate facade hides a slick Style Moderne interior whose doorways are framed in marble and rare hardwoods, where Moscow's *Kuptsy* (see box above) gathered every Tuesday to feast on sturgeon, milk-fed lamb, sucking pigs and twelve-layer pancakes, accompanied by Russian, Magyar and Gypsy orchestras. Afterwards, they would gamble at the English Club or rent horse-drawn sledges and drive singing and shouting to the *Yar* restaurant on Moscow's outskirts, returning to the club at dawn to start planning next week's binge. Following the Revolution, it was taken over by Anarchists, until they too were evicted from their luxurious base by the Bolshevik secret police.

The Museum of Unique Dolls is open Tues–Sun 10am–2pm; free. To arrange a guided tour ☎299 28 00.

Finally, don't overlook the **Museum of Unique Dolls**, across the road at no. 9. Opened in 1996, it displays some 250 dolls from the huge private collection of Yulia Vishnevskaya, manufactured in Russia, France, England and Germany between the 1830s and the 1950s. The rarest is one made by the pre-revolutionary Russian firm Zhuravlov & Kocheshkov, whose dolls were banned by the Bolshevik Commissariat of Enlightenment for being "excessively bourgeois". Bonnets, frills and big hair are certainly ubiquitous, but there are also such cute exceptions as a "granny doll" doing her knitting.

The Museum of Modern History

The Museum of Modern History is open Tues–Sat 10am–6pm, Sun 10am–5pm; closed the last Fri of each month; $0.30. To arrange a guided tour in English ($14 group rate) ☎299 52 17.

What is now called the **Museum of Modern History** was, until recently, the Museum of the Revolution, housed with a crude sense of irony in the former English Club, a pre-Revolutionary haunt of aristocrats and *bon viveurs*. Built by the poet Kheraskov in 1722, the orangey-red mansion was one of the few secular buildings to survive the fire of 1812 and is noted for the hyena-like stone lions on top of its gatehouses, mentioned in Pushkin's *Yevgeny Onegin*.

Originally used for Masonic meetings, in 1831 it became the **English Club** ("so called because hardly any Englishman belongs to it"), virtually the only place where political discussions were tolerated during the reign of Nicholas I. The club soon turned into a "cathedral of idleness" where Tolstoy lost 1000 rubles and Mikhail Morozov blew more than a million in one night, in the card room called "Hell". In 1913 it hosted a costume ball in honour of the tricentenary of the Romanov dynasty that was the last truly grand social event before the Revolution.

The museum's exhibits reflect its uneasy transformation from a bastion of ideological rectitude to an "objective chronicle of modern Russian history", and a cash crisis that has thwarted hopes of attracting more visitors by revamping the displays. In the absence of captions in English, or even a coherent layout, non-Russian speakers who haven't arranged a guided tour are left floundering among banners, proclamations and weapons, with little sense of their context. Among the more memorable items are cobblestones thrown at the police in 1905, an armoured car from the street battles of 1917, numbered grave posts from the Karaganda labour camp, masses of Stalin kitsch, and a glasnost-era room highlighting social problems. A re-creation of the English Club's library and a room devoted to the club's history round off the permanent display, but you may also find arresting temporary exhibitions.

The museum shop stocks Soviet posters, stamps and badges, at collectors' prices.

On to Triumfalnaya ploshchad

The final stretch of Tverskaya ulitsa is fairly unremarkable, featuring the **Moscow Dramatic Theatre** (next to the Museum of Modern History), the swanky **Marriott Grand Hotel**, and pretentious shops for nouveaux riches.

For coverage of the other side of the Garden Ring, see p.191. Triumfalnaya ploshchad is also within walking distance of the Museum of Musical Culture (p.294).

Shortly afterwards, Tverskaya ulitsa meets the Garden Ring at **Triumfalnaya ploshchad**, named after the festive arches that were erected here to greet monarchs in the eighteenth century. As these were surmounted by a statue of a charioteer, Muscovites joked that there were only two coachmen in Moscow who weren't drunk: the one on the arch and the one on top of the Bolshoy Theatre.

The square is, in fact, better known by its former Soviet name – ploshchad Mayakovskovo – and for its craggy **statue of Mayakovsky**, unveiled in 1958. Its truculent pose and baggy trousers call to mind Mayakovsky's eulogy on the first Soviet passport, issued in the 1920s: "I take from the pocket of my wide trousers my red-skinned passport, the priceless object I carry. Read it and envy me! I am a citizen of the Soviet Union." Beyond the statue rises the **Pekin Hotel**, a yellow-and-white wedding cake from the era of Sino-Soviet Friendship.

Above the main entrance to Mayakovskaya metro looms the massive square-pillared portico and diamond-patterned facade of the **Tchaikovsky Concert Hall**. Originally built as a theatre for the avant-garde director Meyerhold, who wished to design it "for the wonderful future a hundred years ahead", it was to have two circular stages – able to revolve, descend or rise as the director wished – and a "creative tower" on the corner of Tverskaya ulitsa, for artistic experiments. Then Meyerhold was arrested and tortured to death, and in 1938 the theatre was converted into a concert hall, now used by the State Symphony Orchestra.

That same year saw the completion of **Mayakovskaya metro station**, internationally acclaimed for its light and silvery ribbed hall. As one of the deepest stations on the metro, this hosted a dramatic wartime meeting on the eve of the anniversary of the Revolution in November 1941, when the Nazis were on the outskirts of Moscow, at which Stalin gave a sombre briefing to the assembled generals and Party activists. It also served as a public air raid shelter.

Beside the concert hall are the **Satirical Theatre** and the **Aquarium Gardens**, containing the Mossovet Theatre. If you're heading in this direction you're on the right track for the next stage of the itinerary.

Around the Patriarch's Ponds, Kudrinskaya and Nikitskie vorota

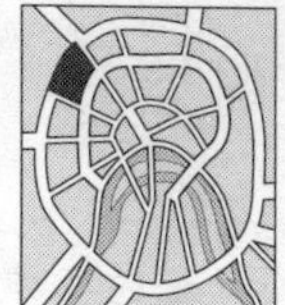

The quarter to the southwest of Tverskaya is notable for its pretty, leafy backstreets and **literary associations**, which make the Patriarch's Ponds one of the priciest neighbourhoods in Moscow. Admirers of Chekhov, Gorky, Pushkin or Alexei Tolstoy will find their former homes preserved as museums, while fans of **Style Moderne** and **Stalinist architecture** can revel in the Ryabushinskiy mansion near Nikitskie vorota or the Stalin-Gothic skyscraper on Kudrinskaya ploshchad (visible from Triumfalnaya ploshchad, around the curve of the Ring).

Bulgakov and the Patriarch's Ponds

Past a row of kiosks beyond the Aquarium Gardens, a plaque beside the archway of no. 10 Bolshaya Sadovaya ulitsa attests that **Mikhail Bulgakov** (see box overleaf) lived here from 1921 to 1924. His satirical fantasy *The Master and Margarita* is indelibly associated with Moscow – and this area in particular – as Bulgakov transposed his own flat to "302a Sadovaya Street" and made it the setting for Satan's Ball and other events in the novel. During the 1980s it became a place of pilgrimage, to the annoyance of residents, who grew sick of fans gathering on the stairway and covering the walls with graffiti and images of the impish cat Behemoth. To pay a visit, go into the courtyard and look for entrance 6, on the left; the flat (no. 50) is at the very top of the stairs, which aren't lit. There were plans to turn it into a Bulgakov Museum, but they never came to anything.

Around the Patriarch's Ponds, Kudrinskaya and Nikitskie vorota

The **Patriarch's Ponds** (*Patriarshiy prudy*) are actually one large pond, derived from three fishponds dug from the medieval Goat's Marsh. Surrounded by wrought-iron railings and mature trees, this beautiful pond forms the heart of a square flanked by tall apartment blocks, which before the Revolution were largely inhabited by students, earning it the sobriquet of Moscow's "Latin Quarter". Today its flats are rented out to foreigners at premium rates, and often owned by Mafiosi, which keeps the neighbourhood looking respectable, if not exactly safe.

Readers of *The Master and Margarita* will know the Ponds from its opening chapter as the place where two literary hacks meet the Devil in the guise of a stage magician. His prediction that one of them will die soon is borne out when the editor Berlioz slips on spilt sunflower oil just outside the park on the corner of Malaya Bronnaya and Yermolaevskiy streets, and falls under a tram. The park's literary credibility is enhanced by a **monument to Ivan Krylov** (1769–1844), a pensive bronze figure surrounded by creatures from his popular fables.

To see more of the area, follow **Malaya Bronnaya ulitsa** off to the south. Like Bolshaya Bronnaya, it is named after the quarter of armourers (*bronoviki*) which existed here in medieval times. Alternatively, you can head down Vspolniy pereulok and turn off into ulitsa Spiridonovka to reach the impressive Morozov and Ryabushinsky houses, or follow the pereulok to the end to emerge near Beria's mansion and Kudrinskaya ploshchad (see below).

Around Kudrinskaya ploshchad

From Kudrinskaya you can also head south to Chaliapin's house or back into the centre along Povarskaya ulitsa (see p.181), or westwards into Krasnaya Presnya (covered in Chapter 6).

Kudrinskaya ploshchad (still widely known as ploshchad Vosstaniya) is a jumping-off point for several sights in the vicinity and one of the most distinctive junctions on the Garden Ring – but you'll probably think twice about getting there from Triumfalnaya ploshchad. It's a bit far to walk (1.2km) and you can wait ages for a trolleybus 6 around the Ring; while the metro journey involves changing at Belorusskaya station.

As you can see from afar, Kudrinskaya is dominated by a 22-storey **Stalin skyscraper** laden with pinnacles but relatively free of reliefs and statuary. Built in 1950–54, it was the last of Moscow's skyscrapers. According to Khrushchev, Stalin justified their erection on the grounds that "We've won the war and are recognized the world over as the glorious victors. We must be ready for an influx of foreign visitors. What will happen if they walk around Moscow and find no skyscrapers? They will make unfavourable comparisons with capitalist cities." The Kudrinskaya block was originally reserved for Party bigwigs, but its large, stylish flats are now favoured by rich New Russians, who patronize the casino (owned by Chuck Norris) and French restaurant on the ground floor.

Shortly before Kudrinskaya you'll glimpse the **Planetarium** set back on the right. Built by Barshch and Sinyavskiy, its aluminium

> **Bulgakov and The Master and Margarita**
>
> Born in Kiev in 1891, **Mikhail Bulgakov** practised medicine and experienced the Civil War in Ukraine and the Caucasus before he settled in Moscow in 1921 and became a full-time writer. His early success as a satirist and playwright aroused a backlash from RAPP (Russian Association of Proletarian Artists), which attacked his sympathetic portrayal of White characters in *The Days of the Turbins*, and his anti-Bolshevik allegory, *The Heart of the Dog*. Luckily for Bulgakov, *The Days of the Turbins* was Stalin's favourite play, so despite being blacklisted his life was spared. Eventually, he asked Stalin's permission to emigrate; Stalin refused, but authorized the staging of his play *Molière*.
>
> Bulgakov began **The Master and Margarita** in 1928, knowing from the outset that it wouldn't be published for political reasons. The book was completed just days before his death in 1940, and his widow was obliged to hide the manuscript, which wasn't published in Russia until 1966. Its huge popularity in the 1980s owed much to the Taganka Theatre's amazing production of the novel – but its enduring fame rests on its piquant absurdities, as the Devil and his gang sow chaos across Moscow. Tellingly, it contains many instances of behaviour and dialogue which ring as true in the New Russia as they did when Bulgakov satirized *Homo Sovieticus* in the 1920s and 1930s.

and ferroconcrete structure was considered revolutionary in 1928; another novelty was the planetarium's theatrical troupe, performing plays about Galileo and Copernicus. Alas, after its silvery ovoid dome began to leak the planetarium was forced to close in 1994, since when funding for repairs has been intermittent. At present it is only open to visitors at weekends and on public holidays (noon–6pm), when one can observe sunspots and other solar activity through its Zeiss telescope – but phone (☎252 02 17) to make sure. Besides the main entrance on the Garden Ring, it is also accessible from the Children's Zoo (see p.202).

Chekhov's house

Diagonally across the road at Sadovaya-Kudrinskaya ulitsa 6, a pink two-storey dwelling sandwiched between two taller buildings has been preserved as the **Chekhov House-Museum**. Here, Anton Chekhov, his parents and his brother lived from 1866 to 1890, during which time he wrote *Ivanov*, three one-act farces and over 100 short stories, while practising as a doctor. He also found time for an active sex life, as evinced by letters that discuss the pros and cons of making love on the floor, in bed, or over a trunk – and what to do if the servants walked in.

The Chekhov House-Museum is open Tues–Sat 11am–4pm, Sun 11am–5pm; closed the last day of each month, or if the temperature falls much below zero; $0.30.

Despite Chekhov's lifestyle, the house looks as prim as the "Doctor A.P. Chekhov" nameplate by its front door. The second room was Chekhov's study and consulting room; notice his doctor's bag. While Chekhov's bedroom and that of his student brother are small and Spartan, the family salon upstairs is replete with gold-brocaded sofas and chairs. Next to the salon are his mother's room with her easel and sewing machine, and the dining room, now given over to exhibits of playbills and first editions of Chekhov's works. An old photograph of Chekhov with Tolstoy hangs by the window.

Beria's mansion

One of several streets leading back towards the Beliy Gorod, **Malaya Nikitskaya ulitsa** is the site of the **Tunisian Embassy**, on the corner of the Garden Ring, which was abashed to make news in 1993 when workmen found a dozen skeletons buried outside, reminding Muscovites that this was once **Beria's mansion**. The most odious and feared of Stalin's cohorts, Lavrenty Beria headed the secret police from 1938 onwards, and oversaw high-priority projects such as the construction of Moscow's skyscrapers and the development of the Soviet atomic bomb. His favourite recreation was raping pre-pubescent girls, in his mansion. After Stalin's death, Beria's Politburo colleagues feared for their lives and had him arrested at a meeting in the Kremlin. It's unclear whether he was shot at once, or first tried *in camera* as a "foreign agent", but the outcome was the same. Recently, in a grotesque twist, Russia's Supreme Court debated whether to posthumously pardon him as the victim of false charges, but decided that his genuine crimes made any such absolution risible. The mansion features in Robert Harris's thriller *Archangel*.

To Nikitskie vorota

There are several possible routes from the Patriarch's Ponds or the Garden Ring **to Nikitskie vorota**, not to mention approaching it from the Boulevard Ring (see p.137). Perhaps the most obvious – and nicest – is **ulitsa Spiridonovka**, a long, quiet, residential street. Walking down from the Patriarch's Ponds, you'll pass the former Savva Morozov mansion at no. 17. The first of over a dozen mansions designed by the prolific architect Shekhtel, this yellow Neo-Gothic edifice with mock crenellations was built (1893–98) for a liberal scion of the Morozov textiles dynasty, who sponsored the Moscow Art Theatre and funded Lenin's newspaper *Iskra*. In 1905, with revolution raging in Russia and his own contradictions pulling him apart, Morozov committed suicide while on a visit to France. The mansion now belongs to the Ministry of Foreign Affairs, which holds press conferences in its Neo-Gothic grand hall.

Further along the street are several mid-rise blocks that look nothing special from outside, but are finished to a high standard within. When **Gorbachev** joined the Politburo as a candidate member in 1979, he and Raisa were allotted an apartment in one of these enclaves; after he became Soviet leader, they moved to the Lenin Hills. Soon afterwards, you'll reach a small park containing a statue of Alexander Blok (1880–1921) looking every inch the Symbolist poet that he was, in a flowing overcoat and cravat. Just beyond stands the house where Blok lived before World War I, while a little further on you'll come to two literary museums.

Alexei Tolstoy's flat

The **Alexei Tolstoy Flat-Museum** is tucked away around the back of the Gorky Museum (see below), mirroring the way its owner lived in the shadow of his illustrious distant relative, Lev Tolstoy. Count Alexei Tolstoy (1882–1945) was a White émigré who returned in 1923 to establish himself as a popular author and later as a Deputy of the Supreme Soviet, occupying this flat from 1941 until his death.

The Tolstoy Flat-Museum is open Thurs, Sat & Sun 11am–6pm, Wed & Fri 1–8pm; closed the last Wed of each month; $1.

It is decorated in the *haut-bourgeois* style of the previous century, making the copy of *Pravda* in the drawing room seem an anachronism. In his columned salon, Tolstoy entertained friends at the grand piano or Lombard table like an aristocrat, while his study was a cosy world of history books, Chinese tea urns and pipes, with a copy of Peter the Great's death-mask for inspiration. Here he wrote *Peter I*, *Darkness Dawns* and half an epic about the time of Ivan the Terrible. In the hallway hangs a tapestry picture of Peter crowning Catherine I, and a portrait of the tsar made of seeds.

Gorky's house

Unlike Tolstoy's flat, the **Gorky House-Museum** next door is worth seeing purely for its amazing decor, both inside and out. Still widely known as the **Ryabushinskiy mansion**, the house was built in 1900 for the art-collecting chairman of the Stock Exchange, Stepan Ryabushinsky, who fled after the Revolution. If not unquestionably the finest Style Moderne creation of the architect Fyodor Shekhtel, it is certainly his most accessible, as the others are now embassies.

The Gorky House-Museum is open Thurs, Sat & Sun 10am–5pm, Wed & Fri noon–7pm; closed the last Thurs of each month; admission free.

Its glazed brick exterior has sinuous windows and a shocking-pink floral mosaic frieze, while inside there's hardly a right angle to be seen, nor a square foot unadorned by mouldings or traceries. It seems ironic that this exotic residence should have been given to such an avowedly "proletarian" writer as Maxim Gorky (see box overleaf), who lived here from 1931 to 1936. The first room you encounter belonged to his secretary, who screened his visitors and reported to the NKVD. In Gorky's own study, notice the thick coloured pencils that he used for making notes and revisions. His library is installed in Ryabushinsky's salon, whose ceiling is decorated with stucco snails and flowers. Repeated wave-like motifs are a feature in both the parquet flooring and the ceiling of the **dining room**, while the crowning glory is a limestone **staircase** that drips and sags like molten wax, as if melted by the stalactite-lamp atop its newel post. The ugly wooden cabinets on the stairs were installed at Gorky's request; as he confessed to his daughter, Style Moderne was

Maxim Gorky

Orphaned and sent out to work as a young boy, Alexei Peshkov achieved literary success in his thirties under the *nom de plume* of **Maxim Gorky**, and took a leading role in the 1905 revolution. After protests from Western writers, his subsequent prison sentence was commuted to exile abroad, where he raised funds for the Bolsheviks from his hideaway on Capri. Returning home in 1913, Gorky's joy at the overthrow of Tsarism soon turned to apprehension and disgust at the savagery unleashed by the Revolution, and the violence and cynicism of the Bolsheviks, whom he fiercely criticized in articles.

Having left Russia in 1921 – ostensibly on the grounds of ill health – Gorky was wooed back home by Stalin in 1928 to become chairman of the new Union of Soviet Writers. His own novel *Mother* was advanced as a model for **Socialist Realism**, the literary genre promulgated by the Union in 1932, and he also collaborated on a paean to the White Sea Canal, built by slave labour. As a murky finale, his death in 1936 was used as a pretext for the arrest of Yagoda, the head of the NKVD, who was charged with killing Gorky by seating him in a draught until he caught pneumonia. Despite allegations of foul play, it is now thought that Gorky really did die of natural causes.

not to his taste. Notice the pillar on the landing, whose capital is decorated with giant lizards. The upstairs rooms are plainer and devoted to Gorky memorabilia, including his Chinese gown and skull cap.

Lastly, you can visit a tiny Old Believers' **chapel** secreted in the attic (reached by a stairway just inside the mansion's entrance), which contains an exhibition on Stepan Ryabushinsky and his eight brothers. Their father was an industrialist who had eight daughters by his first wife, before divorcing her to marry another woman, in order to have male heirs.

The Church of the Great Ascension and the embassy quarter

Across the road from Gorky's house stands the bronze-domed **Church of the Great Ascension** (*tserkov Bolshovo Vozneseniya*), where Pushkin, aged 32, married 17-year-old Natalya Goncharova on February 18, 1831. During the ceremony one of the wedding rings was dropped and the candle that he was holding blew out, causing the superstitious writer to mutter in French, "All the omens are bad" – as indeed they were, for he was killed in a duel over his wife's honour six years later (see p.187). On the Nikitskie vorota side of the church stands the recently erected **Natalya and Alexander fountain**, with a gilded cupola surmounting bronze statues of the newly-weds, who don't look very happy. From here, you can orientate yourself vis-à-vis Nikitskie vorota and cross over to the south side, where any lane will take you into an **embassy quarter** full of Style Moderne and Neo-Gothic mansions, whence you should emerge somewhere along Povarskaya ulitsa.

Povarskaya and the New Arbat

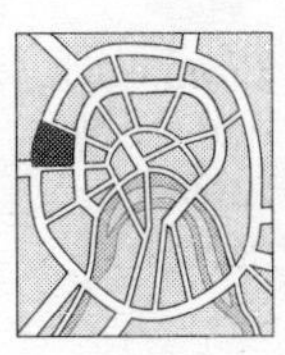

The area to the south of Kudrinskaya ploshchad and Nikitskie vorota bears the stamp of two distinct epochs: the twilight of the Romanov era and the apogee of the Soviet period.

Povarskaya ulitsa and its side streets reflect a time when the old aristocracy was being supplanted by a new class of merchants and financiers, whose preference for Style Moderne and Neo-Gothic was a rejection of the classical aesthetic revered by the nobility. Picturesque and on a human scale, it is one of the nicest areas in Moscow to wander around.

By contrast, the New Arbat, south of Povarskaya, is a brutal 1960s slash of traffic lanes, mega-blocks and stores, meant to prove that the Soviet capital was as racy, modern and consumerist as anywhere in the West, but only now realizing those Brezhnevite aspirations in the post-Soviet era. Though there's little to see as such, anyone staying a week in Moscow will probably go drinking or shopping here at some point.

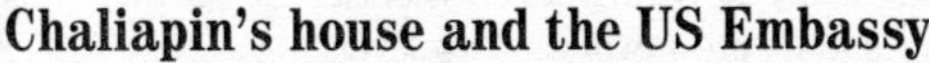

Chaliapin's house and the US Embassy

Before delving into the backstreets, it's worth mentioning two places just south of **Kudrinskaya ploshchad**, on the same side of the Ring as the Stalin skyscraper, from which they're a few minutes' walk.

At Novinskiy bulvar 25, the **Chaliapin House-Museum** is recognizable by a bas-relief of the singer outside the yellow house where he lived from 1910 to 1922. Fyodor Chaliapin's family life was as remarkable as his career – from riverboat stevedore to the foremost opera singer of his age. In Moscow, he married a ballerina who gave up dancing to be a housewife, while in St Petersburg he had another family by a woman whom he bigamously wed in 1927. His first wife had to move upstairs after their house was turned into a *komunalka*, and their children emigrated to the West. It was they who financed the house's restoration and supplied the mementos, leading to the opening of the museum in 1988; it also hosts **concerts** in September.

The Chaliapin House-Museum is open Tues & Sat 10am–5pm, Wed & Thurs 11.30am–7pm, Sun 10am–4pm; $1. For details of concerts ☎205 62 36.

The house is richly decorated in a mixture of French Empire and Style Moderne. His **wife's room** is papered with silk, and enshrines the candles from their wedding. After his operatic performances, Chaliapin loved to throw parties in the gilded white **ballroom**, but hated to be beaten in the **billiard room**. When he was feeling low, his wife would invite friends over who would deliberately lose. You can see his costumes from *Prince Igor*, *Faust* and *Judith*; his blue **study** hung with self-portraits of him as Don Quixote; and a replica of his **green room**, awash with wigs, cosmetics and trunks. Upstairs is an exhibition of dull portraits by his son Boris, who worked as an illustrator for *Time* magazine in the 1950s.

Immediately beyond, the **US Embassy** occupies a massive block whose Soviet-crested pediment and custard- and bile-coloured paint job might have been designed to make its occupants feel nauseous. In fact, they had worse reasons for feeling so, as from the 1970s the embassy was subjected to a constant bombardment of microwaves from KGB listening posts in the vicinity. The Americans' discovery of this coincided with the fiasco over their new embassy annexe, which was found to be riddled with bugs from the outset (see p.203).

Povarskaya ulitsa

Povarskaya ulitsa (Cooks' Street) once served the royal household, together with nearby settlements on Khlebniy (Bread), Stoloviy (Table) and Skaterniy (Tablecloth) lanes. During the eighteenth century it became as fashionably aristocratic as the Old Equerries' quarter beyond the Arbat – and enjoyed the same complacent decline until revitalized by an influx of Kuptsy in the late nineteenth century. In 1918, a dozen local mansions were seized by Anarchists, who held wild orgies there until flushed out by the Bolshevik Cheka, leaving the interiors riddled with bullet holes and smeared with excrement. Under Soviet rule the mansions were refurbished and put to institutional uses; today many have privatized themselves, as their real estate value reverts to its pre-Revolutionary level.

From the House of Writers to the New Arbat

Near the Kudrinskaya ploshchad end of the street, the graceful Neoclassical mansion with a horseshoe-shaped courtyard (no. 52) is thought to have been the model for the Rostov family house in Tolstoy's *War and Peace*. In 1932 it became the **House of Writers**, the headquarters of the Writers' Union that dispensed *dachas* and other perks to authors who toed the Party line. They also enjoyed a subsidized restaurant next door, which features in Bulgakov's *The Master and Margarita*. "Lovely to think of all that talent ripening under one roof," muses the Devil's henchman to the magical cat Behemoth, before their supper ends in mayhem, with the restaurant in flames.

Across the road stands an asymmetrical Constructivist building created (1931–34) by the Vsenin brothers for the Society of Former Political Prisoners. After the Society was dissolved a few years later it became the **Studio Theatre of Cinema Actors** (*Kinoakter*). Further along at no. 25, the pink and white Empire-style Gagarin mansion is notable for its stucco eagles and a statue of Gorky in peasant dress outside. It houses the **Gorky Institute of World Literature**, which he founded to publish cheap translations of foreign classics, and provide a livelihood for starving intellectuals after the Revolution.

The Count's romance with Zhemchugova is related under "Ostankino", in Chapter 9.

The corner of Povarskaya and the New Arbat juxtaposes a huge, striking 24-storey block and the small white **Church of St Simeon the Stylite** (*tserkov Simeon Stolpnika*). Built in the mid-seventeenth century on the model of the Church of the Trinity on Nikitinov (see p.121), the nave is capped by tiers of *kokoshniki* and green domes. It was here that Count Sheremetev secretly married the serf actress Parasha Kovalyeva-Zhemchugova, and Gogol was a regular worshipper when he lived in the vicinity (see p.140).

Before emerging onto the New Arbat, consider a brief detour off to the right to view the **wooden house** at ulitsa Malaya Molchanovka 2 where the poet **Mikhail Lermontov** lived from 1829 until 1832. Then enrolled at Moscow University, he spent so much time writing poems and dramas that he never sat his exams. Among these was an early version of *The Demon*, a theme that haunted Lermontov for years. The interior of the house is currently being repaired; ☎291 52 98 to enquire when it will reopen.

The Tsvetaeva Museum

Lovers of Russian literature may embrace a longer detour to the **Tsvetaeva Museum** on Borisoglebskiy pereulok, an earlier turning off Povarskaya. The two-storey house at no. 6 doubles as a literary centre and shrine to Marina Tsvetaeva (1892–1941), one of the finest poets of the Silver Age, whose tragic life enhanced her iconic status as the symbol of a generation who supported the Whites. Flat #3 partially reconstructs the six-room apartment that Tsvetaeva's family enjoyed before the Revolution – with a grand piano in the salon and a stuffed eagle in her husband Sergei's study – rather than the bare, unheated *kommunalka* that it became during the Civil War, when Sergei fought in the White Army while she struggled to feed their two daughters, whom she finally placed in an orphanage, where one died. After Marina, Sergei and their remaining daughter emigrated to Paris in 1922, Sergei became a Soviet spy and she left him after discovering his treachery, returning to Russia where she lived in desperate poverty and killed herself during the war. Tsvetaeva's work was banned but circulated in underground literature until glasnost restored her to her rightful place in the literary pantheon; the museum was opened on the centenary of her birth.

The Tsvetaeva Museum is open Mon & Fri–Sun noon–5pm; free. Pre-booked tours Tues–Thurs noon–5pm ☎202 35 43.

The New Arbat (Noviy Arbat)

Among its many changes to the capital, the 1935 General Plan for Moscow envisaged an arterial avenue linking the Boulevard and Garden Rings to create a cross-town route between the Kremlin, Kiev Station and points west. By Khrushchev's time this had become imperative since the narrow Arbat could no longer cope with the volume of traffic. Between 1962 and 1967, a one-kilometre-long swathe was bulldozed through a neighbourhood of old wooden houses, and a wide avenue flanked by high-rise complexes was laid out. Though officially named prospekt Kalinina (after the Bolshevik head of state, Kalinin) until 1991, Muscovites called it the **Noviy Arbat** – or **New Arbat** – from the outset.

Trolleybus #2 runs the length of the Noviy Arbat.

Its inhuman scale and assertive functionalism won the architects a prize in 1966. Along the northern side are ranged five 24-storey apartment blocks awarded to People's Artists and other favoured citizens, which featured in 1970s Soviet films as symbols of *la dolce vita*; the gap-toothed appearance that they gave to the street led to it being nicknamed "The Dentures". Moscow's largest bookshop, the **Dom knigi** (House of Books), is located between the first and second blocks, while the newly revamped multiplex **Oktyabr Cinema** fills the gap between the penultimate and final blocks, its entire facade covered with a Revolutionary mosaic.

The other side of the avenue is flanked by four 26-storey administrative blocks shaped like open books, which tower above an 850-metre-long glass-fronted gallery that briefly embodied Moscow's mall culture, before other, fancier emporiums stole its limelight. Further along are **Metelitsa** – Moscow's highest-rolling gambling den – and a large rooftop **globe** that once showed Aeroflot's routes and now advertizes Alfa Bank.

At the far end of the avenue, beyond the Garden Ring, the Mayoralty building presages the White House beside the river (see pp.203–205).

On and off the Arbat

Oh Arbat, my Arbat, you are my destiny,
You are my happiness and my sorrow

Bulat Okudzhava

Celebrated in song and verse, the **Arbat** once stood for Bohemian Moscow in the way that Carnaby Street represented swinging London. Narrow and cobbled, with a tramline down the middle, it was the heart of a quarter where writers, actors and scientists frequented the same shops and cafés. This cosy world of the Soviet intelligentsia drew strength from the neighbourhood's identity a century earlier, when the **Staraya Konyushennaya** or **Old Equerries' quarter** between the Arbat and Prechistenka streets was the home of the *ancien* nobility, later supplanted by *arriviste* dynasties from St Petersburg, who still measured their wealth by the number of "souls" (male serfs) that they owned (women didn't count), training them to cook French pastries or play chamber music so as to be able to boast that their estate provided every refinement of life.

Divided into communal flats after the Revolution, each household felt Stalin's Terror, as recalled in Anatoly Rybakov's novel *Children of the Arbat*, which wasn't published until glasnost. By then, the Arbat was established as the hippest place in Moscow, having been pedestrianized in the early 1980s (for the worse, many thought). Perestroika made it a magnet for young Muscovites and tourists in search of something happening, while the Yeltsin years saw its real estate value soar as businesses moved in and residents left. At street level, however, it's anything but staid, with lots of cafés and beer tents; souvenir stalls catering to both Russians and foreigners; and people of all ages strolling or hanging out, watching the street performers and singsongs over a few bottles of Baltika until midnight or later.

Getting to the Arbat

Most visitors approach the Arbat via the pedestrian underpass on **Arbatskaya ploshchad** (p.139). If you're coming by metro, bear in mind that there are two pairs of identically named stations on separate lines. On the Arbatsko–Pokrovskaya line, Arbatskaya station exits opposite the House of Europe on ulitsa Vozdvizhenka, while Smolenskaya brings you out behind *McDonald's* at the far end of the Arbat. Arbatskaya station on the Filyovskaya line is also conveniently situated, but the other Smolenskaya is way off on the Garden Ring and best avoided.

Beyond the Peace Wall

The Arbat begins with an array of fast-food outlets and antique shops, but there's nothing especially remarkable until you reach the **Peace Wall**. A cute example of propaganda against Reagan's Star Wars, the wall consists of scores of tiles painted by Soviet schoolchildren, expressing their hopes for peace and fears of war. The names of the side streets beyond recall the era when the neighbourhood served the tsar's court: Serebryaniy (Silver) and Starokonyushenniy (Old Stables) lanes. As you pass by the latter, notice the green **wooden house** with carved eaves, dating from 1872, a model of which won a prize at the Paris Exhibition as the epitome of the "Russian Style".

Thereafter, the Arbat gets busier with portrait artists, buskers, and photographers offering a range of props, while the buildings bloom with bright colours and quirky details. Stuccoed ivy flourishes above the lilac Style Moderne edifice at no. 27, while the next block consists of a Neo-Gothic apartment complex guarded by statuesque knights and containing the **House of Actors**. Opposite stands the **Vakhtangov Theatre**, named after its founder, Yevgeny Vakhtangov (1883–1922), who split from MKhAT to pursue a fusion of Realism and the Meyerhold style. The postwar building is notable for its heavy Stalinist facade, and a grey marble and gilt fountain representing Turandot, that was built alongside in the mid-1990s.

Around the backstreets

While Vakhtangov himself lived on the Arbat, the neighbouring Bolshoy Nikolopeskovskiy pereulok is more tangibly associated with the composer Alexander Scriabin (1872–1915), who spent his last

On and off the Arbat

The Scriabin House-Museum is open Thurs, Sat & Sun 10am–4.30pm, Wed & Fri noon–6.30pm; closed the last Fri of each month; $0.80. For details of concerts ☎241 03 02.

years at no. 11 before dying of a septic boil on his lip. The **Scriabin House-Museum** preserves his sound and light laboratory, an apparatus with which he tried to match notes with colours, in accordance with his musical and philosophical theories, which the curators are happy to explain if you're interested (and speak Russian). They also hold **concerts** in the house, which sometimes feature the apparatus in action.

The next lane on the right – Spasopeskovskiy pereulok – retains a seventeenth-century church with a tent-roofed belfry and an ornamental gate. The **Church of the Saviour in Peski** (*tserkov Spasa na Peskakh*) gets its name from the site (*peskiy* means "sandy") of an earlier wooden church that caught fire from a votive candle in 1493; igniting the neighbourhood, it grew into a city-wide conflagration. The locality still looked rural as late as the nineteenth century, as depicted by Vasily Polonev in his popular painting *A Moscow Courtyard*. At the far end is a guarded green dignified by the Neoclassical **Spaso House**, the residence of US ambassadors since 1933.

Polonev's painting can be seen in Room 35 of the Tretyakov Gallery (p.245).

More immediately grabbing is Krivoarbatskiy pereulok (Crooked Arbat Lane), around the far side of the House of Actors. The walls of the building are luridly covered in **graffiti about Viktor Tsoy**, the lead singer of the group Kino (Film), whose fatal car crash in 1990 ensured his immortality as a cult hero. Though fans gather here to sing his songs and contemplate (or add to) the graffiti, nobody seems to know why this spot became a shrine in the first place.

The Melnikov House

Around the corner past the Tsoy graffiti, the lane's Art Nouveau buildings are interrupted by the defiantly Constructivist **Melnikov House** (no. 10). Konstantin Melnikov (1890–1974) was one of the most original architects of the 1920s, who was granted a plot of land to build a house after winning the Gold Medal at the Paris World Fair in 1925. Though his career nose-dived once the Party spurned Modernism, he was allowed to keep his home – the only privately built house in Moscow after the Revolution – but died in obscurity. Belatedly honoured owing to the efforts of his children, his unique house was declared a historic monument in 1987 and has now been repaired, though it isn't open to visitors.

Consisting of three interlocking cylinders pierced by scores of hexagonal windows, it predated (1927–29) the breakthroughs of Melnikov's contemporaries, Le Corbusier and Mies van der Rohe, with self-reinforcing floors that eliminated the need for internal load-bearing walls. The rooms are divided up by slim partitions and feature built-in furniture (as in peasant cottages), while the intersection of the cylinders creates a space for the staircase that spirals up through the core of the house. Despite its revolutionary design, the materials are simple and traditional: timber, brick and stucco.

Its cylindrical rear can only be seen from the courtyard of no. 43 on the Arbat. This was once the home of Bulat Okudzhava, whose song about the Arbat made its name; when he died, hundreds of thousands of Muscovites sang it as they queued to pay their last respects.

On and off the Arbat

Pushkin and Bely on the Arbat

Beyond the childhood home of the novelist Anatoly Rybakov (no. 51) – marked by a bronze plaque – a sky-blue Empire-style house enshrines the fleeting domicile of Russia's most beloved writer as the **Pushkin on the Arbat Museum**. In the spring of 1831, it was here that Pushkin held his stag night and spent the first months of married life with Natalya Goncharova. They then moved to St Petersburg, where Pushkin was later killed in a duel with a French officer whose advances to Natalya were the talk of the town. After Pushkin's death their apartment was preserved as an evocative museum, which is worth seeing should you visit St Petersburg. The Arbat Museum, however, is strictly for manuscript buffs, offering few insights into their lifestyle other than a taste for gilded chairs – and they would probably have been embarrassed by the bronze **statue of Natalya and Pushkin** that now stands on the other side of the street, resembling Barbie and Ken dressed for a costume ball.

Given that Moscow fondly devotes two museums to him, it's ironic that Pushkin scorned the city as a "Tatar nonentity" where "nobody receives periodicals from France", and lamented being "condemned to live among these orang-utans at the most interesting moment of our century". Worse for newly-weds, he wrote, "here you live, not as you wish but as aunties wish. My mother-in-law is just such an auntie. It's a quite different thing in Petersburg! I'll start living in clover, as a petty bourgeois, independently, and taking no thought of what Maria Alexeevna will say."

Both Pushkin and Bely museums are open Wed–Sun 11am–7pm; closed the last Fri of every month; $0.50 each.

The *kassa* for the Pushkin Museum also sells tickets for the sparsely furnished **Bely Memorial Room** in the house next door, where the Symbolist writer Andrei Bely was born and grew up. Originally named Boris Bugaev, he adopted the pseudonym Bely (White) to disassociate himself from his father – a well-known professor – and express his identification with spiritual values. Most of his novels were autobiographical and concerned with consciousness; visitors can see four graph-like charts, representing his material and spiritual lives, his friends and his influences (classified as good or evil), drawn by Bely. Surprisingly, his novels continued to be published after the Revolution, and he wasn't persecuted by the authorities – not least because he died in 1934, before the Great Terror began.

Smolenskaya ploshchad and further south

Smolenskaya ploshchad, at the far end of the Arbat, was once Moscow's haymarket, ankle-deep in straw and dung and thronged with ostlers and farriers. Today, it bears the stamp of Stalinist planning, dominated by 1940s monoliths and the Stalin-Gothic skyscraper of the **Ministry of Foreign Affairs**. Known by its initials as the **MID**, the central block is 172m high, with three portals surmounted by bas-reliefs of furled flags, fronted by granite propylaea and lamps. Having been led by Molotov (known to Western diplomats as "Old Stony-face") and Gromyko ("Mr Nyet") during the Cold War, and at the forefront of perestroika with Sheverdnadze ("The Silver Fox"), the ministry enjoyed its last spell in the limelight under the veteran spymaster Primakov, since when its bosses have been relative nonentities.

In October 1993, Smolenskaya ploshchad witnessed two days of clashes between riot police and supporters of the White House, which ended with the police surrendering en masse, the breaking of the blockade of Parliament, and a victory rally where Khasbulatov urged the seizure of the TV Centre and the Kremlin. Though the "desertion" of the police seemed a sign of Yeltsin's weakness at the time, it may actually have been a ruse to make the rebels overconfident, and tempt them into a rash move that would ensure their downfall (see p.205).

South towards Prechistenka

To explore the Old Equerries' quarter and link up with the next itinerary, you can follow almost any street running off the Arbat and emerge on ulitsa Prechistenka.

Although a bit of a detour, **pereulok Sivtsev Vrazhek** (Grey Mare's Gully) boasts an array of stuccoed wooden houses with literary connections. The poet Maria Tsvetaeva and her fiancé Sergei Efron stayed in a "huge, uncomfortable flat" at no. 19; Tolstoy made his first attempts at writing fiction at no. 34; and there are two house-museums dedicated to other literary figures. The **Herzen Museum** (Tues, Thurs, Sat & Sun 11am–5.30pm, Wed & Fri 1–5.30pm; $0.30) at no. 27 records Alexander Herzen's odyssey around Europe, during which he was expelled from France after the 1848 Revolution, moved to London and founded the radical newspaper *Kolokol* (The Bell) which, although published in London, had a great impact in Russia despite being banned – even the tsar read it. The best exhibit is a picture of a giant bell borne aloft over unenlightened Russia. Over the road at no. 30, the **Asakov Museum** (Wed–Sun 10am–5pm, closed the last day of the month; $0.50) calls itself an "almanac of literary life in the 1840s–1880s" and gives an idea of how such writers as Dostoyevsky, Gogol, Tolstoy and Turgenev once lived, with pictures of nineteenth-century estates and household interiors. The house once belonged to the Slavophile writer Sergei Asakov (see p.394).

One direct route to ulitsa Prechistenka is **Denezhniy pereulok**, which turns off the Arbat just before the MID and brings you to a typical wooden house of the early nineteenth century (no. 9), painted turquoise and white. Halfway down the next block, the **Italian Embassy** (no. 5) occupies the former Berg mansion, a sandstone pile whose interior manifests every style from Baroque to Neo-Gothic. Confiscated from its owner after the Revolution, the mansion was given to Imperial Germany as an embassy just after the Bolsheviks signed the humiliating Peace of Brest-Litovsk. By following the road to the very end, across Lyovshinsky pereulok, you'll emerge on ulitsa Prechistenka.

Along Prechistenka

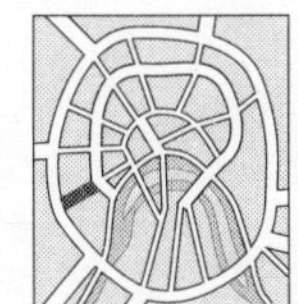

Ulitsa Prechistenka, the medieval road leading from the Kremlin to the Novodevichiy Convent, delineating the southern edge of the Old Equerries' quarter, has been one of Moscow's poshest avenues since the sixteenth century. The quarter's array of mansions in the Russian Empire style – newly built after the fire of 1812 – can really only be appreciated by walking along Prechistenka. If you're not coming from the direction of the Arbat, the best starting point is **Kropotkinskaya metro**, whose stylish platform is itself an attraction. In Soviet times, the avenue was also named "Kropotkinskaya", after the Anarchist Prince Kropotkin, who was born nearby.

Prechistenka starts at the bottom of the hill with a **statue of Friedrich Engels**, erected in 1976. The idea was that this would be "united" with the statue of Marx on Teatralnaya ploshchad by prospekt Marksa, to form a kind of Communist ley line. Behind the statue rises the **Golovin palace**, a simple brick structure with barred windows, built at the end of the seventeenth century by a family associated with Peter the Great.

The Pushkin and Tolstoy museums

The Pushkin Museum is open Tues–Sun 11am–7pm, winter 10am–7pm; closed the last Fri of each month; $0.50.

Further uphill and across the road at no. 12, the former Khrushchev mansion contains the **Pushkin Museum**, with ten rooms devoted to the life and works of the poet. Besides his sketches and first editions, the mansion's interior is notable for its elegant fireplaces and ceiling frescoes. Built of wood covered in stucco, its exterior is colonnaded on two sides; the entrance is on Khruschevskiy pereulok, around the corner. On the next block is another impressive pile whose gatehouses are topped by lions, which now serves as the **House of Scientists** and is an occasional venue for classical concerts.

The Tolstoy Museum is open Tues–Sun 11am–5pm; closed the last Fri of each month; $1.50.

Directly opposite at no. 11, the former Lopukhin mansion has been turned into a **Tolstoy Literary Museum** which, like the Pushkin Museum, exhaustively documents the man and his times. Though its engravings and photos are less interesting than Tolstoy's actual residence in the Khamovniki district (p.215), the ceiling decorated with sphinxes rates a look. Like the Khrushchev mansion, the house was built by Afanasy Grigoriev, one of the most prolific architects of the Russian Empire style.

Mansions and personages

The remainder of Prechistenka has several addresses associated with diverse personages. The Ushakov mansion at no. 20 once belonged to the vodka magnate **Pyotr Smirnov**, and was **Isadora Duncan**'s residence after she arrived in Moscow in 1921. She lived with the poet Yesenin, whom she married despite the fact that she spoke little Russian and he no English (though he reputedly managed to scrawl "I love you" in lipstick on a mirror). On the other side of the road, the house at no. 17 once belonged to **Denis Davydov** – the partisan leader of 1812 who inspired the character Denisov in *War and Peace* – while the old Dolgorukov mansion (no. 19) contains the **Academy of Arts**, whose gallery hosted Mayakovsky's last exhibition, *Twenty Years of Work*.

If you're still in the mood for walking, check out the extremities of an attractive lane called Kropotkinskiy pereulok, which crosses Prechistenka. Off to the south at no. 13, the **Australian Embassy** occupies a Style Moderne masterpiece by Shekhtel – the former Derozhinskaya mansion, built for a textile manufacturer's daughter in 1901. Less florid than the Ryabushinskiy mansion (p.179), its superb woodwork is sadly hidden from view, though Australian citizens might stand a chance of admission. At the other end of the lane, north of Prechistenka, the building that is now the Palestinian Embassy (no. 26) was once the **birthplace of Prince Kropotkin** (see box). After the Revolution, his sister continued to live there in abject poverty, depending on the charity of the family's former serfs.

Prince Kropotkin

The life of **Prince Pyotr Kropotkin** (1842–1921) spanned the most tumultuous years of Russian history, from the reign of Nicholas I to that of Lenin. Born into the old Moscow nobility and a graduate of the elite Corps des Pages, Kropotkin's service with a Cossack regiment in Siberia established his reputation as a geographer and opened his eyes to the injustices of Tsarism. In 1872, he joined the International Working Men's Association in Geneva and adopted **Anarchism** as his creed, expounding a pacifist version that advanced such models of non-statist co-operation as the British Lifeboat Association. Upon returning home in 1874, Kropotkin was imprisoned in the Peter and Paul Fortress (where he spent a week tapping out the story of the Paris Commune to a prisoner in the next cell) and then exiled to Siberia. In 1896 he escaped to England, where he was elected to the Royal Geographical Society. After the Revolution he returned to Russia, but was too ill to play an active role in politics and died in poverty. On Lenin's orders, Kropotkin was accorded a lying in state in the Hall of Columns as an honorary Marxist, and buried in the prestigious Novodevichiy Cemetery.

Between Triumfalnaya ploshchad and Tsvetnoy bulvar

Halfway around the Garden Ring from Prechistenka, the flyover- and underpass-ridden stretch **between Triumfalnaya ploshchad and Tsvetnoy bulvar** musters a few low-key sights along its outer edge, but you're more likely to be tempted in by the leafy streets adjacent to the Boulevard Ring – Karetniy ryad or Tsvetnoy bulvar itself.

Along the Garden Ring

There's nothing along the initial stretch – called Sadovaya-Triumfalnaya and Sadovaya-Karetnaya – so you should take trolleybus 6 directly to the **Museum of Applied, Decorative and Folk Art**, on the corner of Delegatskaya ulitsa (Mon–Thurs, Sat & Sun 10am–5pm; closed the last Thurs each month; $1). Its diverse collection occupies the main wing of the eighteenth-century Osterman mansion, and an annexe off to the right of the courtyard – wherever you begin, keep your ticket for the other bit. The star attraction (in the annexe, upstairs) is Soviet porcelain of the 1920s and 1930s, decorated with Futurist designs or metro-building motifs; among the figurines, notice the Uzbek family rejoicing over the Stalin Constitution. Downstairs are scores of Palekh boxes, painted with fairytale scenes, along with nineteenth-century folk costumes and contemporary tapestries.

Thereafter, the Ring is designated as Sadovaya-Samotyochnaya ulitsa and known to all motorists for the **headquarters of the GIBDD**, or traffic police. The next city block (no. 3) contains the famous **Obraztsov Puppet Theatre**, founded by Sergei Obraztsov, whose concrete facade is enlivened by a decorative clock consisting of twelve little houses. Every hour one of them opens to reveal an animal puppet; at noon all the figures dance to a Russian folk song. Before glasnost, dissidents and Western reporters often arranged to meet here to clandestinely hand over news stories or underground literature.

The spot was convenient for the journalists since many of them lived nearby on the other side of the Ring, where a spacious postwar block (no. 12) known as **"Sad Sam"** still houses CBS, the *Christian Science Monitor*, the *Daily Telegraph* and the *Los Angeles Times*. A 677-metre-long flyover carries the Ring across the old valley of the Neglina River at Samotyochnaya ploshchad, with Tsvetnoy bulvar on the right (see below), and the wonderful Viktor Vasnetsov house in the other direction.

The Vasnetsov house is described on p.295.

Karetniy ryad

The wide **Karetniy ryad** (Coach Row) gets its name from the carriage- and coach-making workshops that lined the road during the nine-

Between Triumfalnaya ploshchad and Tsvetnoy bulvar

teenth century, whose artisans burned their vehicles rather than let them be stolen by the French in 1812. Turned into state garages after the Revolution, they are still recognizable behind the arched houses along the eastern side. No. 4 was the family mansion of the director Stanislavsky until it was requisitioned as a chauffeurs' club in 1918.

Ironically, Stanislavsky first achieved professional success in the **Hermitage Gardens**, opposite, where his Moscow Art Theatre premiered *The Seagull* in 1898. The Hermitage pleasure-garden was founded by Yakov Shchukin, an ex-manservant who ensured that it remained respectable by spreading rumours that he threw drunks into the pond; he later invited the Lumière brothers to screen the first film in Moscow there.

The southern end of the avenue is designated as a continuation of ulitsa Petrovka (p.153) and dominated by the vast beige **headquarters of the Militia** and the Criminal Investigations Department. "**Petrovka 38**" is as famous in Russia as Scotland Yard is in Britain, having been acclaimed in Soviet pulp fiction and TV dramas since the 1970s, and more recently featured in the best-selling novels of Alexandra Marinina (a former police criminologist) and Nikolai Leonov.

Around the corner on 2-y Kolobovskiy pereulok stands a battered relic of law enforcement from the years before Peter the Great. The multi-domed **Church of the Sign** was erected by a company of Streltsy in the late seventeenth century, when several companies were settled in this quarter to defend the ramparts and keep order in the Earth Town.

Tsvetnoy bulvar

Tsvetnoy bulvar is the prettiest radial avenue along this stretch of the Ring, having a wooded park with wrought-iron railings running up the middle from Trubnaya ploshchad. From 1851, when flowers (*tsvety*) began to be sold on Trubnaya ploshchad, the boulevard became Moscow's flower market, and its red-light district. The side streets to the east harboured dozens of brothels coyly referred to in the 1875 *Murray's Handbook* as "several *guinguettes* where the male traveller may study 'life'". There, Chekhov wrote from personal experience: "No one hurried, no one hid his face in his coat, no one shook his head reproachfully. This unconcern, that medley of pianos and fiddles, the bright windows, wide open doors – it all struck a garish, impudent, dashing, devil-may-care note."

Today, the boulevard takes its tone from a trio of places near Tsvetnoy Bulvar metro station, where a few disconsolate vendors linger outside the padlocked **Central Market**. Formerly a pungent Aladdin's cave of produce, where shoppers were tempted with morsels of sturgeon and caviar, melons and dried fruits from Central Asia, the market has been closed for years, while speculators squabble over turning it into a mall.

Next door stands the Yuri Nikulin Circus, better known abroad as the **Moscow State Circus**. It now bears the name of its former director and Russia's most popular clown, who died in 1997 and lay in state beneath its big top before being buried with honours in the Novodevichiy Cemetery. It is also familiarly known as the "Old Circus", since there is another, "New" Circus on prospekt Vernadskovo in the Sparrow Hills, inaugurated in 1986 to mark the centenary of the original institution.

Between Triumfalnaya ploshchad and Tsvetnoy bulvar

To Krasnye vorota

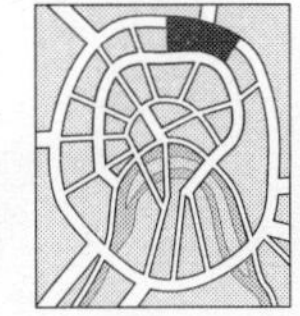

The **eastern half of the Garden Ring** – from Tsvetnoy bulvar to Krasnye vorota, and on to Kursk Station – is the least appealing part of the Zemlyanoy Gorod, unless you're mad about Constructivist and Stalinist architecture, in which case it merits a trolleybus б ride around the Ring as far as Krasnye vorota. A seat on the left of the vehicle affords the best view.

Otherwise, the quarter's attractions boil down to the archaic Yusupov mansion, a flat-museum devoted to the historical painter Apollinarius Vastnetsov, and a couple of churches – all best reached on foot from Krasnye Vorota or Chistye Prudy metro stations. You can also walk there from the Boulevard Ring in about ten minutes.

Sukharevskaya ploshchad and Sadovaya-Spasskaya ulitsa

If you opt for a trolleybus ride, the first notable junction is **Sukharevskaya ploshchad** which – like the local metro station – is named after the bygone **Sukharev Tower** (*Sukhareva bashnya*). Erected in honour of Colonel Sukharev – whose soldiers had escorted the young Peter the Great and his mother to safety during the Streltsy mutiny of 1682 – this was designed in the form of a ship, with the tower representing a mast and its surrounding galleries a quarterdeck. Reputedly, Peter's private Masonic lodge held rituals in the tower, which was thereafter regarded as unlucky. It was converted in 1829 into an aqueduct-cum-fountain for supplying Moscow with water piped in from ten miles away, and subsequently demolished during the widening of the Garden Ring in the 1930s. A small **replica** of the tower rises above one of the buildings on the northern side of Sukharevskaya ploshchad. Before and after the Revolution the square was known for its huge flea market for stolen goods, causing Lenin to lament that in the soul of every Russian there was "a little Sukharevka".

Far easier to spot is the former **Sheremetev Hospital**, a huge curved building painted sea-green and turquoise. Founded by Count Nikolai Sheremetev, the hospital was built (1794–1807) by the serf architect Elizvoi Nazarov, and had a poorhouse in its left wing. After

To Krasnye vorota

the death of his beloved serf actress wife, the Count commissioned Catherine the Great's court architect Quarenghi to change the hospital's church into a memorial chapel, which he enhanced by adding a semicircular portico. Since Soviet times the building has housed the Sklifosovskiy Institute, named after a pioneering surgeon of the late nineteenth century.

The next stretch of the Ring – **Sadovaya-Spasskaya ulitsa** – bears no resemblance to the gracious avenue that it was in Tsarist times, and nowadays business and administration are the keynotes, with the triple bronzed-glass towers of the **International Banking Centre** visible off to the right, just before you sight the rust-red **Ministry of Agriculture**. One of the last Constructivist edifices built (1928–33) in Moscow, the ministry was designed by Shchusev, the architect of Lenin's Mausoleum.

This thoroughfare is named after Dr Andrei Sakharov (1921–90), the nuclear physicist and human rights campaigner who lived at no. 47 after he and his dissident wife, Yelena Bonner, were allowed to return from exile by Gorbachev. The 1980s Banking Centre opposite their flat is a logical outgrowth of the older economic administration blocks that flank the section of the prospekt nearer the Boulevard Ring, where fans of Brutalist architecture will go for the **Tsentrosoyuz building** designed by Le Corbusier. Built in 1929–36 for the Union of Consumer Societies, this hideous clinker-block structure is now occupied by the State Statistical Commission, which produced 30,000 million forms a year during Soviet times.

The building also overlooks ulitsa Myasnitskaya, where the former **Baryshnikov Mansion** at no. 42 houses the editorial staff of the magazine *Argumenty i Fakti* ("Arguments and Facts"), a torch-bearer of glasnost in the mid-1980s.

Krasnye vorota

The junction known as **Krasnye vorota** (Beautiful Gate) takes its name from a Baroque triumphal arch erected in honour of Empress Elizabeth in 1742. For the coronation of Tsar Paul in 1796 the streets were lined with tables spread with food and drink for the populace all the way from here to the Kremlin. Although the arch was demolished in 1928, the locality is still popularly called Krasnye vorota – which means "Red Gate" in modern Russian and seems an apt name for a square dominated by a **Stalin skyscraper** with a huge red-granite portal. Erected in 1947–53, its 24-storey central block is shared by the Transport Construction Ministry and the Directorate for the Exploitation of Tall Buildings, while the wings contain communal flats. Typically, the portal is flanked by propylaea and urns, and the towers festooned with heroic statuary.

A plaque on the wall around the southeast corner attests that the Romantic poet Mikhail Lermontov was born on this spot in 1814, which accounts for the triangular-shaped square being named

Lermontovskaya ploshchad, and its **monument to Lermontov**. Behind his frock-coated statue is a concrete frieze of a man wrestling a lion, inscribed with Lermontov's words:

Moscow, my home – I love you as a son,
Love like a Russian, strong and fierce and gentle!

To Krasnye vorota

Around the backstreets – and Kursk Station

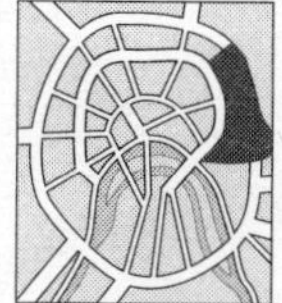

The **backstreets** between the Garden and Boulevard Rings represent an older Moscow that turns its back on Stalinist giganticism, preserving an intimate, residential character. Once-elegant mansions turned into institutes or communal flats are juxtaposed with postwar low-rises, schools and clinics. Though specific sights are limited, it's a nice area to wander around. Sticking to the Garden Ring, instead, inevitably leads to Kursk Station, the largest train terminal in Moscow.

The Yusupov Mansion

By heading 500m south from Krasnye Vorota metro and turning off onto Bolshoy Kharitonevskiy pereulok, you'll find the **Yusupov Mansion** behind a swirly iron fence and a grove of trees. Painted a deep red, with its pilasters and *nalichniki* picked out in white, the mansion's melange of undercrofts, wings and annexes typifies the multi-cellular architecture of the late seventeenth century, unified by a checkerboard roof. One of its earliest occupants was Peter Tolstoy, the head of Peter the Great's Secret Chancellery. It is entered via an enclosed porch around the back, added in the 1890s, like the ceremonial gateway that bears the Yusupov crest. An immensely rich family descended from the Nogai Tatar Khans – now chiefly remembered for the last of the dynasty, Prince Felix, who murdered Rasputin – the Yusupovs acquired the mansion in 1727, but preferred to live in St Petersburg and rent it out; Pushkin lived here as a child. After the Revolution it became the Academy of Agriculture, where the eminent geneticist Vavilov worked from 1929 to 1935. Though it's not open to the public, you could try begging a peep at its romantic interior, a warren of pseudo-medieval chambers furnished with tiled stoves.

The Vasnetsov Flat-Museum is open for group visits Tues, Thurs & Sat 11am–5pm, Wed & Fri noon–6pm (☎208 90 45) and for individual visits Sat 11am–4pm; $3. Viktor Vasnetsov's house has also been preserved as a museum, which shouldn't be missed. *See p.295 for details.*

The Vasnetsov Flat-Museum

More accessible is the **Apollinarius Vasnetsov Flat-Museum** at Furmanniy pereulok 6, a few minutes' walk from the Yusupov mansion. The historical artist Apollinarius Vasnetsov (1856–1933) lived here from 1903 until his death, an "internal exile" from Soviet life and Socialist art. Flat no. 22 displays his carefully researched drawings of Old Muscovy and the Simonov Monastery, plus a portrait of Apollinarius by his artist brother Viktor. His living quarters are preserved across the landing, where the drawing room is festooned with pictures given as gifts by Sarasov, Polonev and other artist friends, while the study contains an ingenious chair that "changes sides" (demonstrated by the curator). The tour ends in Vasnetsov's studio, hung with cloud and light studies; notice his travelling painting kit, and the preparatory drawing for his last work, on the easel.

On towards Kursk Station

From the Vasnetsov Flat-Museum you could follow the backstreets southwards into the quarter where the tsar's tent-makers (*Barashi*) lived in the fifteenth century, which gives its name to the former

Streets and squares

Bolshaya Nikitskaya ulitsa	Большая Никитская улица
Bolshoy Nikolopeskovskiy pereulok	Большой Николопесковский переулок
Bolshaya Sadovaya ulitsa	Большая Садовая улица
Bolshoy Kharitonevskiy pereulok	Большой Харитоньевский переулок
Delegatskya ulitsa	Делегатская улица
Denezhniy pereulok	Денежный переулок
Furmanniy pereulok	Фурманный перулок
Karetniy ryad	Каретный ряд
Krivoarbatskiy pereulok	Кривоарбатский переулок
Kropotkinskiy pereulok	Кропоткинский переулок
Kudrinskaya ploshchad	Кудринская площадь
Lermontovskaya ploshchad	Лермонтовская площадь
Malaya Bronnaya ulitsa	Малая Бронная улица
Malaya Dmitrovka ulitsa	Малая Дмитровка улица
Malaya Nikitskaya ulitsa	Малая Никитская улица
Novinskiy bulvar	Новинский бульвар
pereulok Sivtsev Vrazhek	переулок Сивцев Вражек
Povarskaya ulitsa	Поварская улица
Pushkinskaya ploshchad	Пушкинская площадь
Sadovaya-Karetnaya ulitsa	Садовая-Каретная улица
Sadovaya-Kudrinskaya ulitsa	Садовая-Кудринская улица
Sadovaya–Triumfalnaya ulitsa	Садовая-Триумфальная улица
Sadovaya-Samotyochnaya ulitsa	Садовая-Самотёчная улица
Sadovaya-Spasskaya ulitsa	Садовя-Спасская улица
Spasopeskovskiy pereulok	Спасопесковский переулок
Smolenskaya ploshchad	Смоленская площадь
Sukharevskaya ploshchad	Сухаревская площадь
Triumfalnaya ploshchad	Триумфальная площадь
Tsvetnoy bulvar	Цветной бульвар
Trubnaya ploshchad	Трубная площадь
Tverskaya ulitsa	Тверская улица
ulitsa Arbat	улица Арбат

Around the backstreets – and Kursk Station

Church of the Resurrection in Barashi, where Empress Elizabeth is said to have secretly married her lover Alexei Razumovsky in 1742. Much altered since then and now a fire station, the shocking-pink edifice will set you in the direction of the **Church of the Presentation in Barashi** (*tserkov Vvedeniya v Barashakh*), down a lane to the right. Built in 1701, its strawberry facade is decorated with cable-mouldings, and crested, scalloped *nalichniki*, while ventilation flues and builders' rubble attest to the church's use as a factory in Soviet times, and efforts to restore it.

Modernized in 1972, the vast steel-and-glass shed of **Kursk Station** (*Kurskiy vokzal*) might have been even larger, under a 1930s plan to combine all of Moscow's mainline stations into a single mega-terminal serving every point in the USSR. Fortunately this never happened; the existing station (for Vladimir, Crimea, the

ulitsa Malaya Molchanovka	улица Малая Молчановка
ulitsa Noviy Arbat	улица Новый Арбат
ulitsa Petrovka	улица Петровка
ulitsa Prechistenka	улица Пречистенка
ulitsa Spriridonovka	улица Спиридоновка
Vspolniy pereulok	Вспольный переулок
Metro stations	
Arbatskaya	Арбатская
Chkalovskaya	Чкаловская
Krasnye Vorota	Красные ворота
Kurskaya	Курская
Mayakovskaya	Маяковская
Pushkinskaya	Пушкинская
Smolenskaya	Смоленская
Tsvetnoy Bulvar	Цветной бульвар
Tverskaya	Тверская
Museums	
Apollinarius Vasnetsov Flat-Museum	музей-квартира А.М. Васнецова
Alexei Tolstoy Flat-Museum	музей-квартира А.Н. Толстого
Chekhov House-Museum	дом-музей А.П. Чехова
Gorky House-Museum	дом-музей А.М. Горького
Herzen House-Museum	дом-музей А.И. Герцена
Museum of Applied, Decorative and Folk Arts	музей декоративно -прикладного и народного искусства
Museum of the Revolution	музей Революции
Pushkin Museum	музей А.С. Пушкина
Pushkin on the Arbat Museum	музей-квартира А.С. Пушкина
Scriabin House-Museum	дом-музей Скрябина
Tolstoy Literary Museum	музей Л.Н. Толстого

Around the backstreets – and Kursk Station

Caucasus and eastern Ukraine) is bad enough, with a dank labyrinth of underpasses where travellers slump amid their baggage. In spirit, little has changed since it featured in Yerofeev's 1970s novel *Moscow Stations* as the starting point of his hero's alcoholic odyssey (see "Books", p.448). Beneath the station lies **Kurskaya metro**, whose splendid vestibule upheld by massive ornamental pillars almost justifies a visit using the Circle line.

Chapter 6

Krasnaya Presnya, Fili and the southwest

Beyond the Garden Ring, Moscow seems an undifferentiated sprawl of blocks and avenues, attesting to its phenomenal growth in Soviet times. Yet on closer inspection, each arc of the city contains a scattering of monuments and institutions that command attention. This is particularly true of **KRASNAYA PRESNYA, FILI AND THE SOUTHWEST** – a swathe of the city defined by the loops of the Moskva River and the approaches to the Sparrow Hills.

Krasnaya Presnya is chiefly notable for the ex-Parliament building known as the **White House** – whose role in the crises of the 1990s invested it with symbolic potency – but also harbours the lovely **Vagankov Cemetery**. Over the river, a showpiece avenue that epitomizes Stalinist planning forges out past the **Borodino Panorama Museum** and a **Victory Park** commemorating the USSR's triumphs and sacrifices during World War II. The lovely **Church of the Intercession at Fili** is a sole reminder of the estates and villages that once flanked Moscow's western approaches, where Napoleon marched into the city in 1812, and the Red Army advanced to confront the Nazis in 1941.

Closer to the centre, a peninsula defined by the Moskva River boasts **Tolstoy's House** and the fairytale **Church of St Nicholas of the Weavers** in the Khamovniki district, while further out lies the **Novodevichiy Convent and Cemetery**, the grandest of Moscow's monastic complexes. Across the river from the Luzhniki Stadium, further south, a magnificent view of the city is afforded by the **Sparrow Hills**, dominated by the titanic Stalin skyscraper of **Moscow State University** (MGU). And if science museums are your thing, don't miss the **Darwin and Palaeontology Museums** out beyond the university.

This chapter is largely structured with **transport** in mind, each major section corresponding to a metro line used to reach the sights. All of them connect with the Circle line, enabling you to switch from

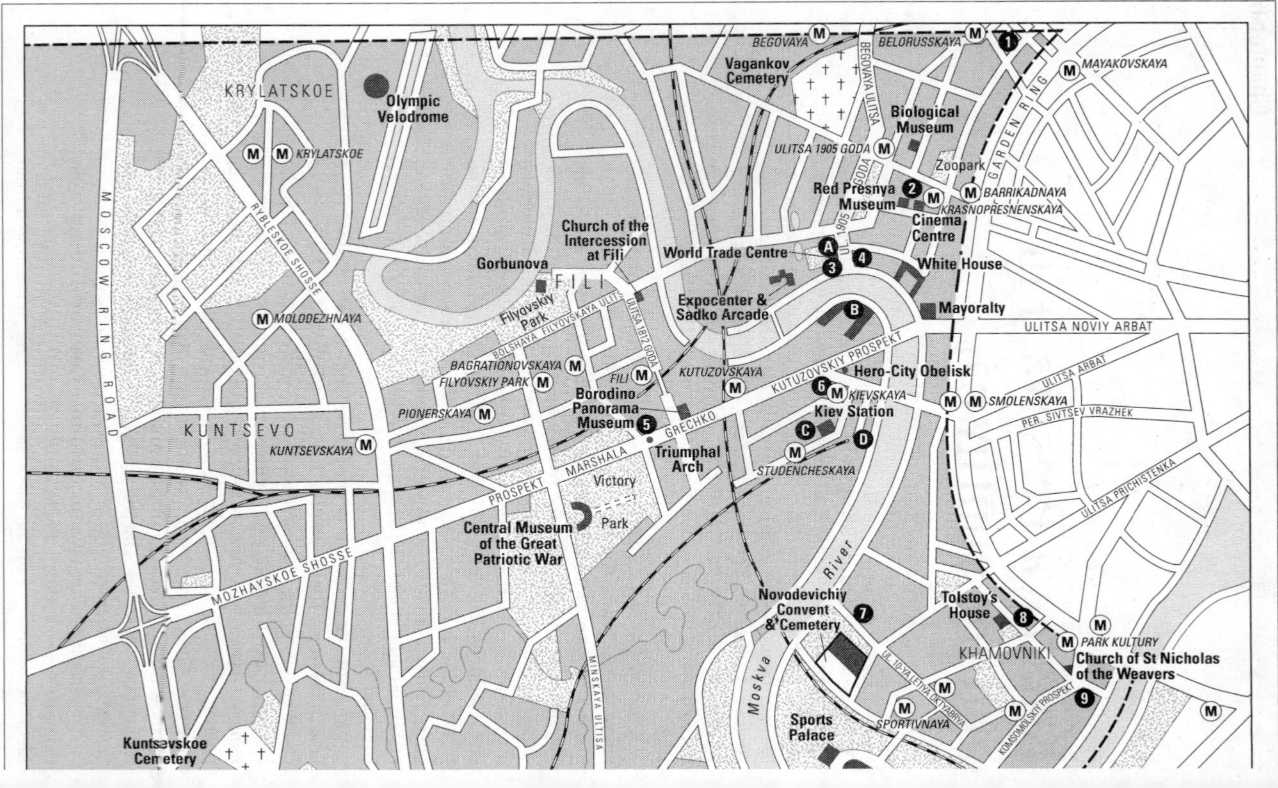

KRYLATSKOE
Olympic Velodrome
KRYLATSKOE
BEGOVAYA
BELORUSSKAYA
Vagankov Cemetery
BEGOVAYA ULITSA
MAYAKOVSKAYA
GARDEN RING
Biological Museum
ULITSA 1905 GODA
Zoopark
Red Presnya Museum
BARRIKADNAYA
KRASNOPRESNENSKAYA
Cinema Centre
UL. 1905 GODA
Church of the Intercession at Fili
World Trade Centre
Gorbunova
FILI
White House
Expocenter & Sadko Arcade
Mayoralty
MOSCOW RING ROAD
RYBLESKOE SHOSSE
Filyovskiy Park
BOLSHAYA FILYOVSKAYA ULITS
ULITSA 1812 GODA
MOLODEZHNAYA
ULITSA NOVIY ARBAT
KUTUZOVSKIY PROSPEKT
BAGRATIONOVSKAYA
FILI
KUTUZOVSKAYA
Hero-City Obelisk
FILYOVSKIY PARK
ULITSA ARBAT
Borodino Panorama Museum
KIEVSKAYA
SMOLENSKAYA
Kiev Station
PIONERSKAYA
PER. SIVTSEV VRAZHEK
GRECHKO
KUNTSEVO
KUNTSEVSKAYA
Triumphal Arch
MARSHALA
STUDENCHESKAYA
PROSPEKT
Victory Park
ULITSA PRICHISTENKA
Central Museum of the Great Patriotic War
MOZHAYSKOE SHOSSE
River
Novodevichiy Convent & Cemetery
Tolstoy's House
PARK KULTURY
KHAMOVNIKI
Church of St Nicholas of the Weavers
Moskva
UL. 10-YA LETIYA OKTYABRYA
MINSKAYA ULITSA
SPORTIVNAYA
KOMSOMOLSKIY PROSPEKT
Sports Palace
Kuntsevskoe Cemetery

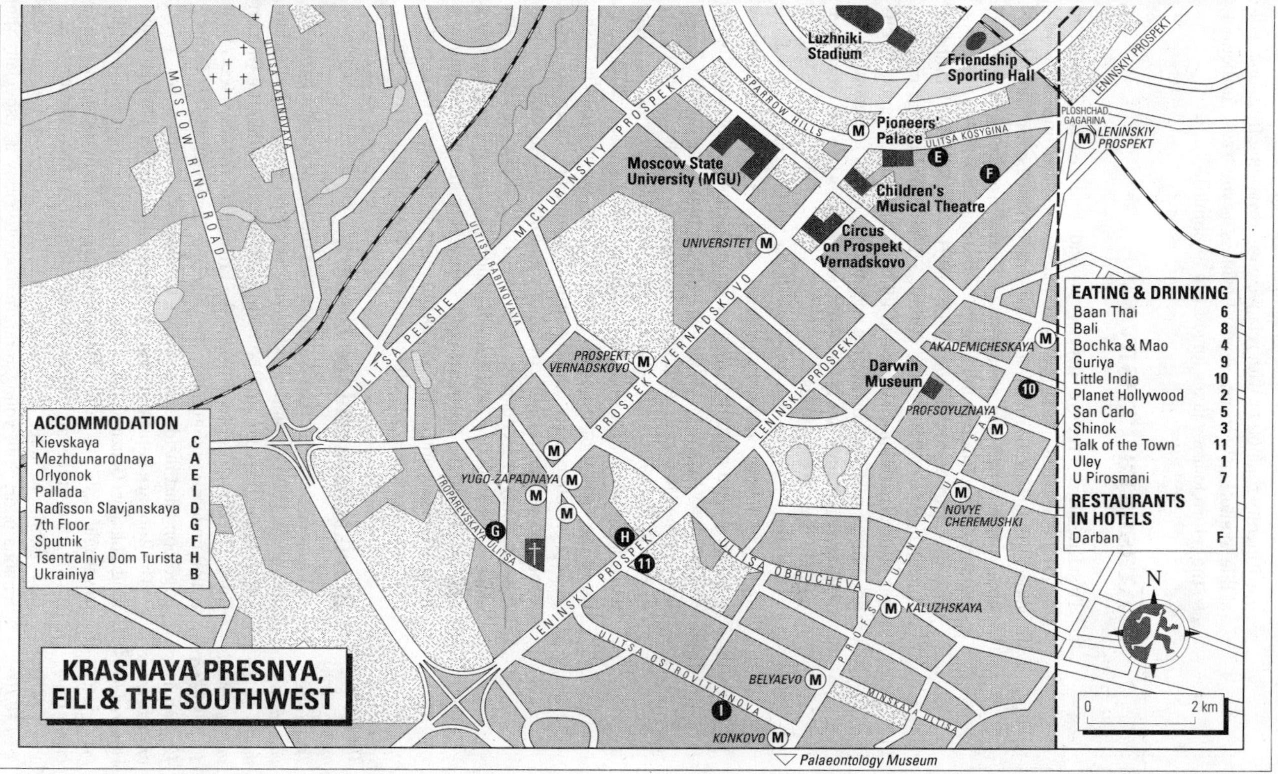
KRASNAYA PRESNYA,
FILI & THE SOUTHWEST
ACCOMMODATION
Kievskaya C
Mezhdunarodnaya A
Orlyonok E
Pallada I
Radîsson Slavjanskaya D
7th Floor G
Sputnik F
Tsentralniy Dom Turista H
Ukrainiya B
EATING & DRINKING
Baan Thai 6
Bali 8
Bochka & Mao 4
Guriya 9
Little India 10
Planet Hollywood 2
San Carlo 5
Shinok 3
Talk of the Town 11
Uley 1
U Pirosmani 7
RESTAURANTS IN HOTELS
Darban F
N
0
2 km
Luzhniki Stadium
Friendship Sporting Hall
Pioneers' Palace
Children's Musical Theatre
Circus on Prospekt Vernadskovo
Moscow State University (MGU)
Darwin Museum
Palaeontology Museum
SPARROW HILLS
LENINSKIY PROSPEKT
PLOSHCHAD GAGARINA
ULITSA KOSYGINA
AKADEMICHESKAYA
PROFSOYUZNAYA
NOVYE CHEREMUSHKI
KALUZHSKAYA
BELYAEVO
KONKOVO
UNIVERSITET
PROSPEKT VERNADSKOVO
YUGO-ZAPADNAYA
ULITSA PROFSOYUZNAYA
ULITSA OBRUCHEVA
ULITSA OSTROVITYANOVA
MINSKAYA ULITSA
MICHURINSKIY PROSPEKT
ULTISA RABINOVAYA
ULITSA PELSHE
TROPAREVSKAYA ULITSA
MOSCOW RING ROAD

one itinerary to another with relative ease. Swapping from one radial line to another becomes slower business as you travel further out, so the return journey takes longer (up to 25min).

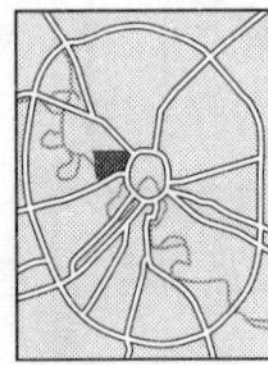

Krasnaya Presnya

The **Krasnaya Presnya** district beyond Kudrinskaya ploshchad (p.176) is a former working-class quarter that was once Moscow's most radical and has now become one of its "better" neighbourhoods, with shops and restaurants catering to wealthy Muscovites and foreigners. Besides amenities, the district has political and financial clout, harbouring the Russian White House, the new US Embassy annexe and the World Trade Centre. These all seem a far cry from the proletarian militancy evoked by huge sculptures, faded murals and names bestowed on streets and metro stations in honour of the 1905 uprising, until one remembers how Russia's fate has twice been decided here in the 1990s.

The district's early history reads like a Marxist tract, as the local textiles industry boomed and slum landlords made fortunes by exploiting rural migrants, creating an urban proletariat receptive to revolutionary agitation. Originally called simply Presnya after a tributary of the Moskva River running through the district, it earned the name "Red" (*Krasnaya*) during the December uprising of 1905, when local workers heeded the Moscow Soviet's rash call to overthrow the Tsarist government, which had just suppressed the Soviet in St Petersburg. The poorly armed insurgents failed to break through into central Moscow and withdrew behind barricades in Presnya, only surrendering after nine days of bombardment and close-quarter fighting, whereupon hundreds more fell to army firing squads. During the Brezhnev era, Presnya's profile was transformed by new housing and amenities, as bureaucrats awoke to the potential of a waterfront site only fifteen minutes' drive from the Kremlin.

The Zoopark is open Tues–Sun 9am–6pm; adults $2, 12- to 16-year-olds $0.30, under-12s free. A separate ticket is required for the Exzotarium; adults $2, children $0.10.

Barrikadnaya and the Zoopark

As its name suggests, **Barrikadnaya** was the site of a major barricade during the 1905 revolution, where the workers retrenched after failing to break through into the bourgeois districts within the Garden Ring. The barricade stood beside the Presnya River, which was channelled underground in 1908; the only part that's still visible forms a large pond just inside the entrance to Moscow's Zoopark.

The **Zoopark** consists of two sections connected by a bridge spanning Bolshaya Gruzinskaya ulitsa; its main entrance sports a fairytale tower and rusticated arch. Though money has been spent on a facelift for some of the enclosures and building a new **Exzotarium** to display exotic wildlife, the environment for many of the animals remains poor. Still, youngsters are likely to enjoy it, especially the touchy-feely encounters in the children's zoo on the eastern side of Bolshaya Gruzinskaya. On a more macabre note, during the Zoopark's refurbishment in the mid-1990s, the skeletons of several hundred Muscovites secretly killed in Stalin's time were discovered.

Down towards the river

Emerging from the Krasnopresnenskaya metro pavilion across the road from the zoo, turn left around the corner to find the **Cinema Centre**, a traditional venue for art-house movies that includes a small **Film Museum** (Mon–Fri 10am–10pm, Sat & Sun noon–10pm) featuring temporary exhibitions on diverse aspects of Russian cinema. To reach the White House from here, you can either head down Druzhinnikovskaya ulitsa, directly behind the Cinema Centre – past the shrine to the "martyrs" of 1993 (see p.204) – or south along Konyushovskaya ulitsa, the main road running down towards the Moskva River.

The latter route passes the **Krasnaya Presnya Stadium** and the red-brick blocks of the **new US Embassy**, across the road. In the mid-1980s, this caused grave embarrassment when it was found to be riddled with KGB bugs, implanted during construction. The US reckoned that it would be cheaper to tear the whole place down and start afresh rather than de-bug it, until Gorbachev handed the Ambassador a wodge of plans six inches thick. Naturally, the Americans never believed that *all* the bugs had been exposed, so the building remains largely empty, and most embassy business is still conducted at the old embassy block on the Garden Ring (p.181).

The White House

The **White House** or **Beliy dom** is a marble-clad hulk crowned by a gilded clock and the Russian tricolour, that's known around the world for its starring role in two confrontations telecast by CNN. When the building was completed in 1981 to provide spacious offices for the Council of Ministers of the Russian Federation, nobody dreamed that its windowless Hall of Nationalities would serve as a bunker ten years later, despite the paranoid foresight that specified the construction of a network of escape tunnels from the building. All this changed after the Russian Parliament took up residence and Yeltsin was elected president with a mandate to take on the *apparat*. When the old guard staged a putsch against Gorbachev on August 19, 1991, the democratic opposition made the White House their rallying point.

The **August putsch** was an epic moment of self-discovery, as a hundred thousand Russians from all walks of life found the courage to form human barricades fifty layers deep around the building, where Yeltsin, Rutskoy and Khasbulatov were holed up on the third floor, phoning around the garrisons and broadcasting defiance. The expected assault on August 20 never materialized, as the KGB unit assigned to storm the White House baulked, and the putsch leaders lost their nerve. This brought the whole edifice of Soviet power crashing down, as symbolized by the toppling of Dzerzhinsky's statue outside the Lubyanka. At the time, it was easy to agree with poet Yevtushenko's declamation that "the Russian Parliament, like a wounded marble swan of freedom defended by the people, swims into immortality".

Two years later the myth was turned inside out, as the White House became the crucible of conflict between Parliament and the President, culminating in what Russians call the **October events**, a neutral tag for something tragic and divisive. The dubious legality of Yeltsin's dissolution of parliament and his sanctions against the deputies who occupied the White House enabled Khasbulatov and Rutskoy to claim that they were only defending the constitution when they urged a mob of supporters to seize the Ostankino TV centre on October 3. Next day, the army bowed to Yeltsin's orders and shelled the White House into submission. Yet, having smashed a hostile Parliament to create a favourable one, Yeltsin found that the elections resulted in a majority of deputies who sympathized with the rebels, and voted an amnesty for all those arrested in October, and the plotters of the August putsch too.

Since then the building has been renamed the **House of Government** (*Dom Praiteltsva*) and its occupants have taken precautions against future trouble by erecting a tall ornamental fence around the perimeter. The White House is best seen from the embankment side, where an outpost flying the Iraqi flag added a bizarre touch to the defences in 1993. From here you also have a striking view of the Stalin-Gothic *Ukrainiya Hotel* (p.208) across the river, and the World Trade Centre, 700m west along the embankment (p.207).

The Gorbaty most and shrine to the October events

Beside the main road behind the White House lies the **Gorbaty most** (Hunchback Bridge), a small cobbled structure that's used to trouble. In December 1905, workers barricaded it to bar Tsarist troops from Presnya, until artillery blew them away. Later, the bridge was covered over and forgotten till it was unearthed and restored in 1979, when a **monument** showing three generations of workers fighting side by side was erected nearby. This proved apposite when the barricades went up again in the 1990s, as people gathered to defend the White House. In 1991, bikers mingled with ruble millionaires and professors, while over the weeks leading up to the bloodshed of 1993 one saw a "Red-Brown" alliance of Cossacks, Nazi paramilitaries, and "Red *babushki*" with photo-collages illustrating the depravity of Yeltsin's Russia.

"Patriots were killed here" reads the inscription on a cross behind the White House, a belief manifest in an **outdoor shrine** on

Druzhinnikovskaya ulitsa, where the flags of the Soviet Union and the Tsarist army and navy fly above the portraits of 100 "martyrs", accompanied by photos of bullet-riddled corpses and a miniature barricade. An annual remembrance service (October 2–4) charged with grief and hatred symbolizes the pain of Russia's change from communism to "democracy". Foreigners who wish to attend should be careful and may not feel very welcome. At other times the shrine is deserted, so you can look around without being approached by old ladies who declare themselves to be "patriots, not Communists", before ranting about how Russia was plundered by the Americans with the connivance of Yeltsin, Luzhkov and Patriarch Alexei – all of whom are "really Jews". They also maintain that as many as 500 defenders of the White House were summarily shot in the Krasnaya Presnya Stadium, after Parliament fell to the army.

The Mayoralty

To the east of the White House looms a glassy 31-storey block housing Moscow's **Mayoralty**, which also played a part in the bloody events of 1993. On the afternoon of October 3, Rutskoy and Khasbulatov's supporters were holding a triumphal rally outside the White House to celebrate the breaking of the police blockade when they were fired on by snipers from the Mayoralty and the adjacent *Mir Hotel*. At that point, the rebels were on the verge of a political victory, as the Federation Council had just agreed on a compromise solution to the crisis that would have cast Yeltsin in the role of provocateur and his opponents as moderates. Instead, the sniping goaded them into storming the Mayoralty – whose lower floors were set ablaze – and this easy victory convinced them that power was ripe for the taking, causing Rutskoy and Khasbulatov to issue the fateful order to seize the TV Centre (see p.309).

Around ulitsa 1905 goda

The other main jumping-off point for exploring Krasnaya Presnya is Ulitsa 1905 goda (1905 Street) station, 1km west of Krasnopresnenskaya metro. Should you decide to walk from one metro station to the other, **Krasnaya Presnya ulitsa** sports a rash of nightclubs and restaurants whose owners were killed so regularly in the mid-1990s that it was dubbed the "Murder Strip", while the side streets to the north and south harbour a couple of museums that might appeal. Roughly midway along, you can turn off to the right to find the **Biological Museum** at Malaya Gruzinskaya ulitsa 15 (Tues–Sun 10am–6pm; closed the last Tues of each month; $0.30), where school kids gawp at the deformed foetuses in room six. Named after the biologist Timiryazev, the museum also celebrates the work of Darwin, Pavlov and the plant breeder Michurin.

Alternatively, there's the **Red Presnya Museum** at Bolshoy Peredtechenskiy pereulok 4, whose first floor displays photos of the

Krasnaya Presnya

The Red Presnya Museum is open Tues–Sat 10am–6pm, Sun 10am–5pm; closed Sun in summer; $0.30.

1905 Revolution and the 1991 putsch. Exhibits upstairs represent the triumphs and tragedies of the Soviet era, from the flying suit worn by Chkalov on his pioneering flight across the North Pole in 1937, to a prisoner's mug and spoon from the Sakhalin labour camp and the rehabilitation certificates posthumously issued to victims of the purges. From World War II are prisoners' clothes from Auschwitz and the personal telephone of Field Marshal von Paulus, captured at Stalingrad. You can also see Gagarin's overcoat and the spacesuit used to send a dog into orbit prior to his epic voyage. Last but not least, there's a huge **diorama** of the barricade at the Hunchback Bridge in 1905, with commentary in diverse languages, complete with the sound of shell fire and the strains of the *Internationale* – clearly unchanged since the museum opened in the 1970s.

If you choose to get there by metro instead, beware of the multiple exits around this major intersection. The main one brings you out on Krasnopresnenskiy Zastavy ploshchad, where shoppers ignore a huge Brezhnev-era **Monument to the 1905 Revolution**, featuring workers unhorsing a gendarme and waving rifles. Another surfaces near Bolshaya Dekabrskaya ulitsa, which is the one to take if you're aiming for the Vagankov Cemetery (see below), while a third emerges on a verge to the south of the intersection.

Vagankov Cemetery

The cemetery is open daily, 9am–7pm in summer, 9am–6pm in winter; admission free. There's a kiosk across the road from the entrance devoted to Vysotsky tapes and videos.

Sited at the end of Bolshaya Dekabryskaya ulitsa, five minutes' walk from Ulitsa 1905 goda metro, the **Vagankov Cemetery** (*Vagankovskoe kladbishche*) is an oasis of mournful beauty, redolent of another age. In Moscow's hierarchy of prestigious burial grounds, it runs a close second to the Novodevichiy cemetery, which takes people who never quite made it into the Kremlin Wall. Though it doesn't have such a profusion of sculptural monuments, there are enough surprises to make wandering around a pleasure. The cemetery itself dates from 1771, when an outbreak of plague impelled the authorities to dig up all the graveyards in central Moscow and establish new ones beyond the city limits. It takes its name from the parish cemetery that belonged to the Church of St Nicholas in Old Vagankov, near the Borovitskiy Gate of the Kremlin.

Off to the right just inside the entrance is the flower-strewn grave of **Vladimir Vysotsky**, the maverick actor-balladeer of the Brezhnev era (see p.274). Though hundreds of fans braved police cordons to attend his hushed-up funeral in 1980, no monument was permitted until the advent of perestroika, five years later. It portrays Vysotsky garbed in a shroud like a martyr, his guitar forming a halo behind his head. Nearby lies the grave of the Mafia boss **Otari Kvantrishvili**, shot by a contract sniper as he left a local bathhouse in 1994, whose funeral was shown on TV accompanied by the theme tune from *The Godfather*. His brother (killed the year before) is buried alongside, with a sculpted angel watching over their graves.

Further in, you can head down a path to the left of the **Church of the Resurrection** to find Plot 17, where a tender sculpture marks the grave of the heart-throb poet **Sergei Yesenin**, who in 1925 apparently cut his wrists and hanged himself, leaving a final poem written in his own blood. An admirer, **Galina Benislavskaya**, shot herself on his grave a year later and is buried behind him. In the same neck of the woods are the graves of the historical painter **Vasily Surikov** – marked by a palette and brushes – the biologist **Nikolai Timiryazev** (Plot 14), and the lexicographer **Vladimir Dal**, whose work is known to every student of the Russian language (signposted off Timiryazevskaya alleya).

It's also worth seeing the graves of various **Soviet sporting heroes** – marked with footballs, ice hockey sticks and such like – on the alley leading to the modern Columbarium at the centre of the cemetery.

The World Trade Centre and the Mezh

The last place worth noting in Krasnaya Presnya is the riverside enclave comprising the World Trade Centre, the Mezhdunarodnaya Hotel, the Expocenter and Sadko's Arcade. Moscow's **World Trade Centre** (*Tsentr Mezhdunarodnoy Torgovli*, or TsMT) was initiated by Armand Hammer, the founder of Occidental Petroleum, who began doing business with the USSR in the 1920s and personally knew every Soviet leader from Lenin to Gorbachev. Inaugurated in 1980, the glass and concrete complex was an early beachhead of Western business culture, in tandem with the adjacent *Mezhdunarodnaya* (International) **hotel**, whose expatriate clientele dubbed it "the Mezh" – both of which were later subsumed into the **Sovincentre**, whose director was murdered in 1997, supposedly by Mafia groups trying to gain control of the conference centre.

Further east across a park stands the **Expocenter**, and the pyramid-roofed **Sadko Arcade**, one of Moscow's earlier malls. A post-modernist **footbridge** links this area to the vicinity of Kutuzovskiy prospekt, across the river – one of Mayor Luzhkov's less egregious follies.

To Victory Park, Fili and beyond

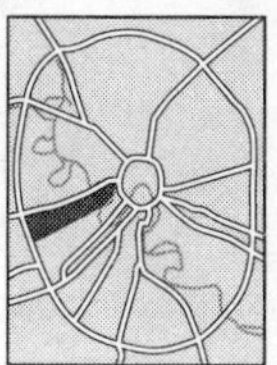

Across the river from Presnya, the hand of Stalinist planning is writ large in gigantic avenues and residential blocks whose pomposity is underscored by the vibrant Church of the Intercession in Fili and a string of Napoleonic and World War II memorials culminating in a grandiose Victory Park. Though relatively low on Moscow's list of tourist attractions, they say much about Soviet aesthetics and Russian patriotism. Almost every sight is within walking range of a metro station on the Filyovskaya line, but so far apart that you're obliged to retrace your steps before riding on to the next place. Further out towards the Moscow Ring Road are the suburb of Kuntsevo, where Stalin had his *dacha*, and the stunning Olympic Velodrome at Krylatskoe.

Around Kiev Station

Kievskaya metro is the obvious starting point, being close to a few places worth noting, and an interchange onto the metro line that serves everywhere else. Its name comes from the **Kiev Station** (**Kievskiy vokzal**) that handles trains from Ukraine and Moldova, built by Ivan Rerberg in 1913–17 and modernized in the 1980s; its tall clocktower overlooks a monument commemorating the unification of Ukraine and Russia in the seventeenth century. A short distance away on the embankment is a boat pier for **river cruises** which also offers a fine view of the monument to Peter the Great (see p.232). The nearby **Radisson Slavjanskaya Hotel** is notorious among Moscow's expat community for the feud between the US entrepreneur Paul Tatum and his Russian partners in the $50-million venture, which led to Tatum's assassination outside Kievskaya metro in 1996. Although Moscow's expats harboured suspicions, nothing was said until a spate of TV "exposés" on Mayor Luzhkov's links with organized crime suggested that Luzhkov sanctioned the murder – claims that destroyed his credibility in the run-up to the presidential election that saw Putin coast to victory.

Kutuzovskiy prospekt

Kutuzovskiy prospekt was laid out in the mid-1950s as a prestigious residential area for diplomats, top scientists, and even the Soviet leadership, whose town apartments were conveniently located midway between the Kremlin and their suburban *dachas* to the west of Moscow – all rapidly accessible by the Chaika Lane (see box opposite). The avenue is named after Field Marshal Kutuzov, whose troops marched this way to confront Napoleon's *Grande Armée* at Borodino and retreated back along the road after Kutuzov's fateful decision to abandon Moscow. In 1941, Stalin evoked the shades of 1812 as Soviet regiments streamed towards the advancing *Wehrmacht*; the sacrifices and victories of both wars are commemorated by a series of monuments along several miles of the avenue.

Kutuzovskiy's initial stretch is notable for the **Ukrainiya Hotel**, a tawny-coloured Stalin-Gothic leviathan that boasts one thousand rooms. Completed in 1956, its 36-storey central tower is flanked by turreted wings and culminates in a 72-metre-high spire crowned with a Soviet star. During the crises of 1991 and 1993, the hotel's guests had a ringside view of events at the White House, across the river.

If you want to see more of the prospekt, trolleybus #39 or any bus going west will take you past the **Moscow-Hero-City Obelisk** erect-

The Chaika Lane

The **Chaika Lane** is the nickname given to the central lane of Moscow's main avenues, reserved for the cars of the elite to travel at high speed as the police wave other traffic aside. In Soviet times, cars were allotted to the Party *nomenklatura* according to a strict protocol. Politburo members rated armoured **ZiLs** – a kind of stretch limo – and often travelled together in convoys. Stalin used six cars, riding a different vehicle each time as a precaution (but sometimes offered lifts to pensioners), while Khrushchev reduced the motorcade to four vehicles. Far commoner were the chauffeur-driven **Chaikas** of the second echelon cadres – hence the Chaika Lane – and the vast fleet of black **Volgas** used by lower-ranking bureaucrats. Nowadays, the Chaika Lane is supposedly for top state officials only, but in practice the requisite licence can be bought for $10,000, as many nouveaux riches have done. While Yeltsin shared their taste for foreign cars, Putin has patriotically opted for the latest model ZiL, a two-ton armoured limo capable of 120 mph, which guzzles gas like a tank.

To Victory Park, Fili and beyond

ed at the junction of Bolshaya Dorogomilovskaya ulitsa in 1977. The Stalinist blocks on either side of the prospekt contain high-ceilinged apartments of up to a dozen rooms that are each the size of an entire flat for the average Muscovite family. Notice no. 26, which used to be known as the Politburo block, where Brezhnev had an opulent two-floor apartment and his Interior Minister, Shchelokov, an entire floor – in contrast to the ascetic KGB chief, Andropov, with his one-bedroom flat.

The Borodino Panorama

The *War and Peace* trail begins beyond Kutuzovskaya metro station; take the exit near the front of the train, turn right outside and head towards the Triumphal Arch 500m away. Shortly before this is the circular blue pavilion of the **Borodino Panorama Museum** (*muzey Panorama Borodinskaya Bitva*), inaugurated in 1962 on the 150th anniversary of Borodino. Its 115-metre-long circular painting by Franz Roubaud depicts a critical moment in the battle, which occurred 129km west of Moscow on August 26, 1812. Casualties were unprecedented in world history, with forty thousand Russians and thirty thousand French killed in fifteen hours – but neither side emerged the winner. Visitors admiring the painting survey the battle raging all around from the standpoint of Russian troops holding the village of Semyonovskaya. Napoleon can be identified in the distance by his white horse. Real cannons, carts and stuffed horses have been placed at strategic points, for a 3-D effect.

The Panorama is open Mon–Thurs 10am–6pm, tours every 15min; Sat & Sun 11am–2pm & 2.45–4.45pm individual entry; closed the last Thurs of each month; $ 0.75.

Outside the pavilion, an equestrian **statue of Kutuzov** bestrides a pedestal flanked by bronzes of Russian soldiers and peasant guerillas. Mikhail Kutuzov (1745–1813) was a one-eyed giant who used to close his good eye and pretend to be asleep so that his aides could express their opinions freely. Five days after Borodino, with the French still advancing, a council of war was held in the *izba* (hut) of a peasant named Frolov, at which Kutuzov resolved to withdraw from Moscow to avoid being outflanked. His decision aroused anger but was soon vindicated by events: the burning of Moscow left Napoleon's *Grande Armée* bereft of shelter as winter approached, and obliged to retreat under the constant threat of Russian attacks.

In 1887, a supposedly exact copy of the historic *izba* was opened as a museum. Located in a park behind the pavilion, the **Kutuzov Hut** (Tues–Thurs 10am–6pm, Sat & Sun 10.30am–5.30pm; closed the last Thurs of each month; $1) musters an array of weapons, banners and oil paintings of the battle. Tickets are sold at the brick hut next door.

The Triumphal Arch

Russia's victory over Napoleon is commemorated on a grander scale by a **Triumphal Arch** designed by Osip Bove, originally erected (1829–34) where the St Petersburg road entered Moscow, near what is now Belarus Station; imperial processions passed beneath it and along Tverskaya ulitsa, towards the Kremlin. Like the Triumphal Arch in Leningrad, this was deemed an impediment to traffic and demolished in the 1930s, but Vitali's sculptures were preserved at the Donskoy Monastery until it was decided to reconstruct the arch in the patriotic upsurge that followed World War II. Completed in 1968, the stone arch is bracketed by Corinthian columns flanking Classical warriors, decorated with the coats-of-arms of 48 Russian provinces and surmounted by the winged figure of Glory urging his chariot westwards. To inspect it at closer quarters, follow the underpass that surfaces near the arch in the middle of the avenue – which will also enable you to cross over to the Victory Park.

Victory Park

Patriotic ardour reaches a climax at the sprawling **Victory Park** (*Park Pobedy*) on the far side of the highway. The idea for this memorial complex to the Soviet victory in World War II goes back to the Era of Stagnation, when the Party erected ever larger war memorials in an effort to overcome ideological apathy among the masses.

In 1983 the Politburo gave its approval to a design by Nikolai Tomsky that involved levelling the **Poklonnaya gora** (Hill of Greetings), where generations of travellers had exclaimed with joy as they reached its summit to suddenly behold Moscow ahead of them, and where Napoleon had waited in vain to be presented with the keys to the city. The intention was to erect a 250-foot-high monument to Mother Russia, supported by a host of allegorical figures. With the advent of glasnost the project aroused a public outcry and was cancelled, only to be revived in a toned-down form by Yeltsin's government. Billions of rubles and battalions of conscripts were committed to "storm" the final stage, so that the park could be ready for the 49th anniversary of Victory Day, in 1994, while the 50th anniversary saw yet more additions to the complex, and the grandest military parade since Stalin's days.

Indeed, it's best to come here on **Victory Day** (May 9) – the only anniversary in Soviet times that was genuinely heartfelt – when crowds stream towards the park carrying bouquets. Bemedalled old women and bow-legged ex-cavalrymen in archaic uniforms reminisce, weep, sing and dance to accordion music. The mood is deeply sentimental, dwelling less on the triumphs of Stalingrad and Berlin than on the terrible autumn of 1941, when the Red Army was repeatedly savaged and forced back towards Moscow – as in a poem by Konstantin Simonov, whose opening lines are known to every Russian:

Do you remember, Alyosha
The Smolensk roads
Where the dank rains fell unending.

The park's fountain-lined axis runs past a memorial **church**, **mosque** and **synagogue** to a lofty **obelisk** topped by an angel and cherubs blowing trumpets, with St George beheading a Nazi dragon at its base – a typically kitsch design by Tsereteli. Behind it looms the **Central Museum of the Great Patriotic War**, a vast concave structure raised on stilts and surmounted by a spiked bronze dome, containing the ultimate exposition of World War II from the Soviet perspective. What Russians call the Great Patriotic War is only deemed to have begun in 1941 with Hitler's invasion of the USSR, and ended with the liberation of Prague two days *after* the formal German surrender that's taken in the West as VE Day. This ethnocentric bias is more excusable than most, since Soviet losses were greater than any other country's and even Churchill acknowledged that it was the Red Army that "tore the guts from the Nazi war machine". Don't miss the **dioramas** behind the Hall of Memory in the basement, depicting the critical battles of Moscow, Stalingrad, Kursk and the Dniepr, the siege of Leningrad and the fall of Berlin. Upstairs, the main exhibition is arranged in chronological order round the outside of a Hall of Glory whose dome is 50m in diameter.

The museum is open Tues–Sun 10am–6pm; closed the last Thurs of each month; $1.50.

Behind the museum are outdoor displays of **anti-tank traps** and **trenches** of the kind that once defended Moscow, while on Victory Day elders nod sagely as loudspeakers play wartime radio broadcasts, such as the famous call to arms by Stalin that opened with the Orthodox salutation "Brothers and Sisters", and went on to invoke the warrior-saints of Holy Russia. One legacy of the military that isn't trumpeted is the **nuclear waste** that was secretly buried beneath Poklonnaya gora in the 1950s and 1960s, and whose present whereabouts is a mystery.

These days, the park is a popular **meeting place** for young Muscovites, with rollerbladers taking advantage of its ramps and paved expanses, and groups of friends drinking and hanging out till the small hours.

Fili

While the estates and villages that once flourished to the west of Moscow vanished long ago, an outstanding church of the pre-Petrine era survives in the 1950s suburb of **Fili**. It can be reached on foot from the Borodino Panorama via ulitsa 1812 goda (1.5km; no access to cars), though it's easier to catch the metro to Fili station instead. Leaving by the exit nearest the front of the train and turning left outside, you'll be lured by a golden dome above the treetops just 350m down an avenue towards the junction with Bolshaya Filyovskaya ulitsa.

The church is open Mon & Thurs–Sun 11am–5pm; closed the last Fri of each month; $1.

The **Church of the Intercession at Fili** (*tserkov Pokrova v Filyakh*) is the first real masterpiece of Naryshkin Baroque. Delightfully exuberant yet firmly controlled, it seems a world apart from the gloomy, rambling Upper Monastery of St Peter that the Naryshkins endowed a few years earlier. Nobody knows the identity of the architect who was commissioned by Prince Lev Naryshkin, but his design was inspired. Constructed (1690–93) in the form of a Greek cross with short rounded arms, the church rises in wedding-cake tiers of red brick ornamented with engaged columns and "cockscomb" cornices, offset by gilded rhomboids above the second level and a larger dome crowning the belltower. The locked summer church is reached by three stairways incorporating sharp turns that were intended to heighten the drama of processions. In 1812, the French turned it into a tailors' workshop and stabled their horses in the lower winter church, which now contains some fragmentary murals and **temporary exhibitions of religious art**. You may feel it's not worth buying a ticket from the hut nearby, as the church's exterior can be admired for free. Occasional **concerts** in the summer are advertised on the spot.

Though you wouldn't notice it, Fili is also the site of the **Khrunicheva space centre**, which reportedly contains a nuclear reactor – there are ten (seven of them still functioning) in Moscow, according to official figures.

Filyovskiy Park and the Gorbunov market

The Gorbunov market is held on Sat & Sun from 9am to around 4pm. The clubhouse is also a venue for live music (see p.352).

While in this neck of the woods, it would be a shame not to visit **Filyovskiy Park**, which hugs a bend in the Moskva River further along Bolshaya Filyovskaya ulitsa. Besides the obvious attraction of greenery and breezes, there is the weekly **Gorbunov market**, where enthusiasts trade vintage albums, CDs, videos and software at the D/K Gorbunova clubhouse near the northern edge of the park. Known to regulars as the *Gorbushka* or the *tolkuchka* (crowd), it is better-natured than most of Moscow's other flea markets and offers some real bargains – though sometimes raided by the OMON in search of pirate CDs and software. You can reach the park from the church by riding trolleybus #54 along Bolshaya Filyovskaya, or by catching the metro to Bagrationovskaya station and walking from there.

Further out: Kuntsevo and Krylatskoe

West of Fili, the former village of **KUNTSEVO** rates a mention for having once been the site of **Stalin's dacha**, *Blizhnoe*, where he largely spent his final years and died of a brain hemorrhage in 1953. Stalin, who hated being alone, obliged his cronies to watch films until the small hours, or drink endless alcoholic toasts while he consumed mineral water and jovially accused them of being British agents, or snarled: "Why are your eyes so shifty?" Yet only belatedly did Stalin realize that he was surrounded by Georgian staff chosen by Beria, a skilled dissembler who later danced beside his corpse. As they feared to disturb him, hours passed before Stalin was found unconscious in his bedroom on March 1, and a further ten elapsed before any treatment (with leeches) was authorized, which kept him barely alive until March 5. At 4am the next day, Moscow Radio announced that "the heart of the comrade-in-arms and continuer of the genius of Lenin's cause, of the wise leader and teacher of the Communist Party and the Soviet Union, has ceased to beat". Within a few years, the Party elite had abandoned Kuntsevo for Zhukovka – a new *dacha* colony beyond the Ring Road – leaving Kuntsevo to be swallowed up by the city.

Further upriver lies the leafy suburb of **KRYLATSKOE**, where apartment blocks have sprouted around a 130-hectare sports complex that was beefed up for the 1980 Olympics. Spread across the Tartarovo Flats are a 2300-metre-long artificial **rowing canal**, archery facilities, a thirteen-kilometre outdoor **cycling track** and the hi-tech indoor **Olympic velodrome**. Designed by a team under Natalya Voronina, the velodrome resembles a giant silvery-white butterfly, enclosing a steeply banked cycling track of Siberian larch, flanked by seating for six thousand spectators. The track's sweeping lines are mirrored by the plunging and soaring roof, held taut by steel filaments stretched between pairs of arches, supported by a truss-frame system. In 1992, the velodrome hosted one of Moscow's first raves, whose theme – sport, energy and strength – was expressed by cyclists racing around the track as people danced in the middle until dawn. To get there, ride the metro to Molodezhnaya and then bus #286 to the end of the line, or travel to Krylatskoe station and walk (10min).

Lastly, amid a high-rise district to the south of the Mozhaysk highway, the **Kuntsevskoe Cemetery** (daily: 9am–7pm summer, 9am–5pm winter) contains the grave of Kim Philby, the KGB mole within British Intelligence who was dubbed the "Third Man" in the 1960s. His headstone is simply marked in Russian: *Kim Philby*

11.1.1912–11.5.1988. The cemetery is accessible by bus #612 from Kuntsevskaya metro. Another British traitor, George Blake, still lives in Moscow.

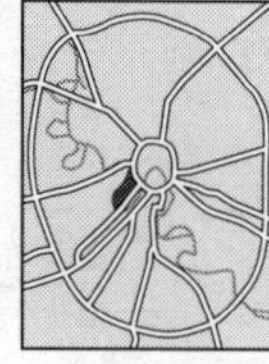

Khamovniki and Luzhniki

The **Khamovniki** and **Luzhniki** districts are somewhat removed from the rest of the city, covering a peninsula bounded by the Moskva River and the Garden Ring, and best approached by metro. From Park Kultury station, it's a short walk to the lovely Church of St Nicholas of the Weavers and thence to Tolstoy's House. But the star attraction has to be the Novodevichiy Convent and Cemetery, a magnificent fortified complex with a history of intrigues, next to a necropolis that numbers Gogol and Shostakovich among its dead. This lies a bit further from Sportivnaya metro, which also serves for reaching the Luzhniki sports complex at the far end of the peninsula. When deciding what to see, it's worth considering how you can tie the sights in with **other itineraries**. Park Kultury station lies across the river from Gorky Park and the New Tretyakov Gallery (see p.248), while the Sokonicheskaya metro line runs southwest to Moscow University in the scenic Sparrow Hills (covered later in this chapter).

The Church of St Nicholas of the Weavers

Emerging from Park Kultury station, the 200m of flyover and kiosks along Komsomolskiy prospekt make the **Church of St Nicholas of the Weavers** (*tserkov Nikolay v Khamovnikakh*) appear even more striking by contrast. A fine example of the colourful parish churches of the mid-seventeenth century, its long refectory and elaborate tent-roofed belltower are painted a snowy white, while all the *nalichniki*, gables, drums, pendentives and columns are outlined in dark green or Day-Glo red, like a chromatic negative of a Russian church in winter. The exterior is rounded off with wrought-iron porches and strategically placed images of St Nicholas the Wonderworker. A protector of those in peril (and the saint from whom Father Christmas originated), St Nicholas is regarded in Russia as the patron of weavers, farmers and sailors. His name day (December 19) and the day on which his relics were removed to Bari in Italy (May 22) are both celebrated here.

The church was founded by a weavers' (*khamovniki*) settlement that was established in the 1620s. One of many settlements (*slobody*) in Moscow based on crafts guilds, it forbade non-weavers from living there and marriages outside the community. Their prized looms occupied the **Palace of Weavers**, up a side road from the church. This whitewashed brick edifice with a wooden roof counted as a palatial workplace by the standards of seventeenth-century

Moscow. On the way, you'll pass two wooden houses from the last century, when such dwellings were still the norm in Moscow's suburbs.

Tolstoy's House

Slightly further north, on the left-hand side of ulitsa Lva Tolstovo, a tall brown fence with a plaque announces **Tolstoy's House** (*muzey-usadba L.I. Tolstovo*). Count Lev Tolstoy purchased the wooden house in October 1882 to placate his wife, Sofia Andreevna, who was tired of provincial life at Yasnaya Polyana and feared that their children's education was suffering. By this time, Tolstoy had already written *War and Peace* and *Anna Karenina*, and seemed bent on renouncing his wealth and adopting the life of a peasant – to the fury of Sofia. The children generally sided with her but felt torn by love for their father, who found it hard to reconcile his own paternal feelings with the dictates of his conscience. To strain family relations further, Tolstoy alternated between anguished celibacy ("I know for certain that copulation is an abomination") and boundless lust for his wife, who bore thirteen children (eight of whom lived) and wrote: "I am to gratify his pleasure and nurse his child, I am a piece of household furniture, a *woman*!"

Tolstoy's House is open Tues–Sun 10am–6pm (Oct–March till 4pm); closed the last Fri of each month; $4.

Around the house

Although this psychodrama was played out over the twenty winters that the Tolstoys lived in Khamovniki, the house-museum enshrines the notion of one big happy family. Its cheery ground-floor **dining room** has a table laid with English china, oilcloth wallpaper and a painting of their daughter Maria by her sister, Tatyana. Tatyana's own portrait (by Repin) hangs in the **corner room** that belonged to the older sons, Sergei, Ilya and Lev, where Tolstoy once wept with relief upon learning that Ilya was still a virgin at the age of twenty.

The **Tolstoys' bedroom** doubled as Sofia's salon and study, with a sofa for guests and a mahogany bureau where she made fair copies of his draft manuscripts; their walnut bed is hidden behind a screen. Down the corridor, their youngest, Vanichka, slept in a truckle bed with his rocking horse at hand, within earshot of his foreign governess and the scullery where the maids took tea. While Andrei and Mikhail leave little impression, **Tatyana's room** bespeaks a bright, artistic young woman who often chafed at Tolstoy's strictures. Hung with her paintings and sketches, it contains a table covered with black cloth that she got family and friends to sign, embroidering their signatures in coloured thread. Everyone drank tea constantly, so the **buffet**'s samovar was rarely cold.

Upstairs in the **salon** Scriabin, Rachmaninov and Rimsky-Korsakov played on the piano and Tolstoy read his latest works to Chekhov and Gorky (an early recording can be heard). The carpeted **drawing room** full of knick-knacks was favoured by Sofia

Andreevna, who read Tolstoy's proofs by the window; her portrait (by Serov) hangs on the opposite wall. Conversely, **Maria's room** is low and Spartan, in keeping with her Tolstoyan ideals; she taught at the Yasnaya Polyana peasants' school every summer. Further down the passage are the tiny housekeeper's room (she was with them for thirty years), and the room of Tolstoy's valet, who cared devotedly for his ailing master but avoided other work as demeaning.

Tolstoy's study with its heavy desk and dark leather furniture fits his gloomy literary output in the 1880s. Here he penned *The Death of Ivan Ilyich* and *The Power of Darkness*; the moral treatises *On Life* and *What Then Are We to Do?*; and began his famous polemic against sex and marriage, *The Kreutzer Sonata* (which Sofia read aloud to the family without a blush). Next door is a small room devoted to Tolstoy's enthusiasms: weightlifting, boot-making and bicycling (which he took up at the age of 67). Tolstoy usually reached his study by the back stairs near the pickling-room. Sadly, the house's large back **garden** is only accessible to groups; off to one side of the yard are the former stables.

The Maidens' Field

At the far end of the street lies a triangular wooded park known as the **Maidens' Field** (*Skver Devichovo pole*), where teenage girls were once left as tribute to the Tatars. Nearby, Tolstoy set the scene in *War and Peace* where Pierre Bezhukov witnesses the execution of prisoners by the French. A seated **statue of Tolstoy** broods beside the entrance to the park.

Novodevichiy Convent

The convent is open 10am–5pm, closed Tues. Admission to the grounds $1; a combined ticket including the various exhibits costs $12.

Where the Moskva River begins its loop around the marshy tongue of Luzhniki, a cluster of shining domes above a fortified rampart proclaims the presence of the **Novodevichiy Convent** (*Novodevichiy monastyr*) – one of the loveliest monasteries in Moscow, and a perennial favourite with tour groups. Though purists might prefer the Donskoy Monastery for its tourist-free ambience, Novodevichiy is undeniably richer in historical associations and a more coherent architectural ensemble, with the added attraction of being right next to Moscow's most venerable cemetery.

The Novodevichiy, or New Maidens', Convent was founded in 1524 to commemorate Vasily III's capture of Smolensk from the Poles a decade earlier. It had many high-born nuns and often played a role in politics – one of its own nuns prevented the convent from being blown up by the French in 1812, by snuffing out the fuses. Here, Irina Godunova retired after the death of her imbecilic husband, Fyodor I, and her brother Boris Godunov was proclaimed Tsar. Ravaged during the Time of Troubles, the convent was rebuilt in the 1680s by the Regent Sofia, who was later confined here by Peter the Great, along with his unwanted first wife. Bequests made

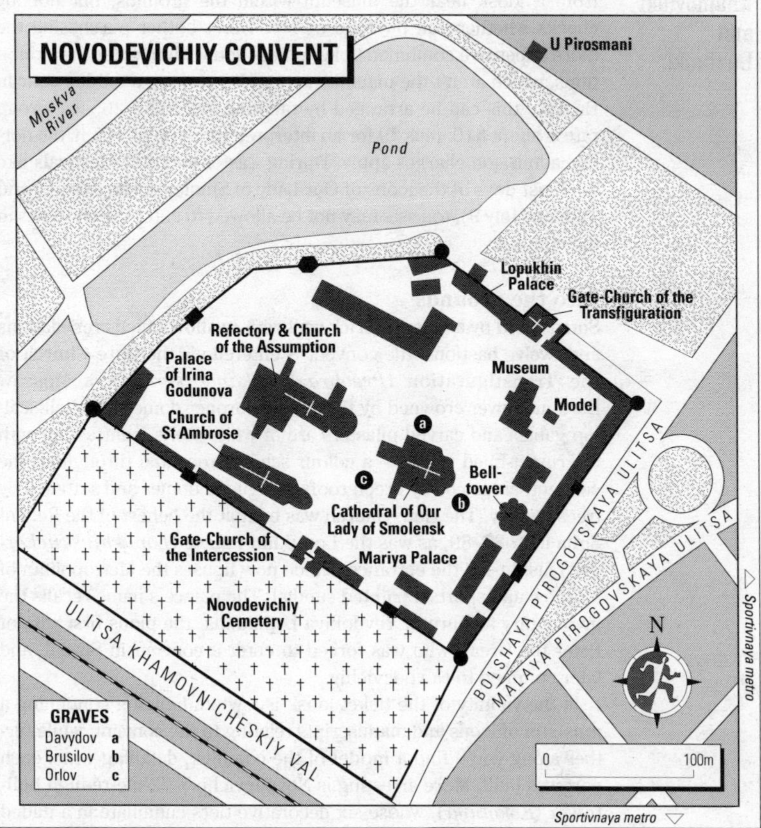

Novodevichiy a major landowner with fifteen thousand serfs, but after the Revolution its churches were shut down and in 1922 the convent was turned into a museum, which spared it from a worse fate until the cathedral was returned to the Church in 1945 as a reward for supporting the war effort. Restoration work began in the 1960s under the architect Makarov, and in 1988 an episcopal see was established here. Though still officially a museum, Novodevichiy is once again a convent, whose twenty nuns and novices keep a low profile.

Practicalities

Getting there entails riding the metro out to Sportivnaya station. Using the Luzhniki Stadium exit, turn right outside the station, right again at the end of the road, and then take the first left; the convent's domes are visible at the end of the road. Admission **tickets** are sold from a kiosk near the museum within the grounds, but nobody checks whether you buy one or not. Don't bother purchasing the more expensive combined ticket unless you wish to enter the exhibitions, which aren't the main attraction. If you want a **guided tour** in English, this can be arranged by phoning ☎246 85 26. The group rate is about $10, plus $9 for an interpreter; on top of which, the normal admission charges apply. During Easter and other festivals like the **feast days** of the icons of Our Lady of Smolensk (August 10) and Tikhvin (July 9), tourists may not be allowed to enter the churches in the convent.

Into the grounds

Surrounded by a massive brick wall with swallow-tailed crenellations and twelve bastions, the convent is entered via the **Gate-Church of the Transfiguration** (*Preobrazhenskaya tserkov*), a Moscow Baroque tower crowned by five gilded coronet-domes. Its shell-scallop gables and carved pilasters are of white stone, contrasting with the russet-hued stucco – a colour scheme repeated throughout the convent, enhanced by green roofs and gilded domes and softened by trees and ivy. The Gate-Church was built at the behest of the Regent Sofia in 1687–89, as was the **Lopukhin Palace** (*Lopukhinskiy korpus*) just inside the entrance, which now houses the Metropolitan of Moscow and sports a painted sundial. The palace's name recalls the involuntary sojourn of Yevdokiya Lopukhina, the pious first wife of Peter the Great, who was forced to enter a convent in Suzdal, and later confined to Novodevichiy.

In the vicinity of the ticket kiosk is a white building containing a **museum** of icons and manuscripts relating to the convent, while further along you'll find a **model** of the complex, detailing when each part was built. More arresting is Novodevichiy's 72-metre-high **belltower** (*Kokolnya*), whose six decorative tiers culminate in a gilded onion dome on a slender drum, all so perfectly proportioned that many reckon it to be the finest belltower in Moscow. Unusually, it is situated near the east wall rather than on the western side, as was customary with Russian monasteries. The Futurist Tatlin is said to have retreated to this tower to design his famous articulated glider, *Letatlin*, which never flew.

The Cathedral of Our Lady of Smolensk

At the heart of the convent stands the white **Cathedral of Our Lady of Smolensk** (*sobor Smolenskoy Bogomateri*), whose tall *zakomary* gables give it a strong resemblance to the Cathedral of the Assumption in the Kremlin. Constructed in 1524–25 on the orders of Vasily III, its architects borrowed a device from the Kremlin's Church of the Deposition of the Robe, by sitting the cathedral on top of a high *podklet* or undercroft, to enhance its majesty. But what really makes it are the massed onion domes, added in the seventeenth century: the central one gilded and the others green with gold frills, supporting tall crosses that glitter in the sunlight.

The interior is worth seeing if you get the chance. Its **frescoes** weren't painted until 1684 (reflecting the troubled century after the completion of the cathedral), executed in only three months by a team of 35 painters under Dmitry Grigorev of Yaroslavl. The enormous five-tiered **iconostasis** also dates from Petrine times, but was salvaged from the Church of the Assumption in Pokrovka, demolished in the Soviet era. Flowers and ribbons garland the icons of the Smolensk and Tikhvin Virgins on feast days. Notice the large copper font and wooden ciborium, dating from the latter half of the seventeenth century. Regent Sofia and the two other sisters of Peter the Great are buried in the (inaccessible) vaults underfoot.

Somewhat incongruously, Novodevichiy is the burial place of Tsarist military heroes, whose **tombs** cluster around the cathedral. A bronze moustachioed bust honours **Denis Davydov**, a poet and Hussar slain battling the French in 1812, who was immortalized in verse by Pushkin, and by Tolstoy in *War and Peace*; while **General Orlov**, who accepted the surrender of Paris from Napoleon, lies beneath a jet-black slab. Beside the grave of **General Brusilov** – the only successful Tsarist general of World War I, who later joined the Reds – is a plaque added by the far-right group Pamyat, dedicated to the generals of the Imperial Army and the "Russian Resistance" against Communism. Nearby you'll see a beautiful Neo-Russian **mausoleum** whose stone base, carved with birds and flowers, rises in tiers of gilded wings.

Other sights within the grounds

The red-and-white **Church of the Assumption** (*Uspenskaya tserkov*) and its adjacent **Refectory** were constructed at Sofia's behest in the 1680s. Access to the church is by the far stairway; between services (8am & 5pm) you can only peer through the doors at its rows of vaulted windows interspersed by icons, and the gilded iconostasis fronted by tall candleholders. Lurking in a dell around the back is the lower, all-white **Church of St Ambrose**, which contains an exhibition of cloth-of-gold cassocks and eighteenth-century icons.

Further west you'll see the modest two-storey **Palace of Irina Godunova**, where the widow of the last of the Rurik monarchs retired in 1598. State business continued to be transacted in her monastic name of Alexandra until Patriarch Job and the clergy came en masse to the convent, to implore her brother, Boris Godunov, to assume the vacant throne – a show of popular support that he had orchestrated himself.

The southern wall of the convent is breached by the triple-domed **Gate-Church of the Intercession** (*Pokrovskaya tserkov*), whose red-and-white facade surmounts a gateway wide enough to drive a

The Regent Sofia

Tsarevna **Sofia** (1657–1704) was remarkable for ruling Russia at a time when noblewomen were restricted to the stultifying world of the *terem*. As a child, she persuaded her father Tsar Alexei to let her share lessons with her brother, the future Fyodor III, and from the age of nineteen attended the boyars' council. After Fyodor's death she feared being relegated by the Naryshkin relatives of the new heir, Peter, and manipulated the Streltsy revolt of 1682 in order to get another sibling, Ivan, recognized as co-tsar, and make herself **regent**. As Ivan was half-witted and Peter only ten years old, she prompted them by whispering from a grille behind their specially made double throne, and privately received ambassadors in person, seated on the Diamond Throne. The diplomat De Neuville noted that "though she has never read Machiavelli, nor learned anything about him, all his maxims come naturally to her".

Nonetheless, Sofia's regency was inevitably threatened as Peter came of age. In August 1689, rumours that she was about to depose him and crown herself empress impelled the 17-year-old tsar to flee to a monastery outside Moscow and rally supporters. By October, Sofia's allies had deserted her and she was ceremonially escorted to the convent. When the Streltsy rebelled again, nine years later, Peter was sure of her involvement but refrained from executing her through admiration, confessing: "What a pity that she persecuted me in my minority, and that I cannot repose any confidence in her, otherwise, when I am employed abroad, she might govern at home." She died of natural causes as the nun Susanna.

hearse into the adjacent Novodevichiy Cemetery. Alongside stands the three-storey **Mariya Palace** (*Mariinskiy korpus*) where it is popularly believed that Peter the Great confined his half-sister Sofia, after deposing her as Regent (see box). Sofia was allowed no visitors except her aunts and sisters, but wasn't obliged to forego any comforts until after the Streltsy revolt of 1698, when she was forced to take religious vows, making her "dead" to the world. According to popular history, 195 rebels were hanged in full view of the palace, while three ringleaders who had petitioned her to join them were strung up outside her window and left hanging all winter. However, the convent's curators maintain that Sofia probably lived in the green-roofed building behind the **Naprudnaya Tower**, and the Streltsy were executed outside the city walls – visible from the tower but not so close as legend has it.

Novodevichiy Cemetery

The cemetery is open daily: summer 9am–7pm, winter 9am–6pm; $0.75.

Beyond the convent's south wall lies the fascinating **Novodevichiy Cemetery** (*Novodovicheskoë kladbische*), where many famous writers, artists and politicians are buried – only burial in the Kremlin Wall is more prestigious. It seems fitting that Novodevichiy was the site of Trotsky's last public speech in Russia, at the graveside of an Old Bolshevik who committed suicide in protest against Stalin's dictatorship. During the Brezhnev era, the disgraced former leader Khrushchev was buried here, after which the cemetery was closed to prevent any demonstrations at his grave. Now that visiting restrictions have been lifted, Russians of all ages come to grave-spot, laying flowers on the tombs of some, tutting or cursing over others.

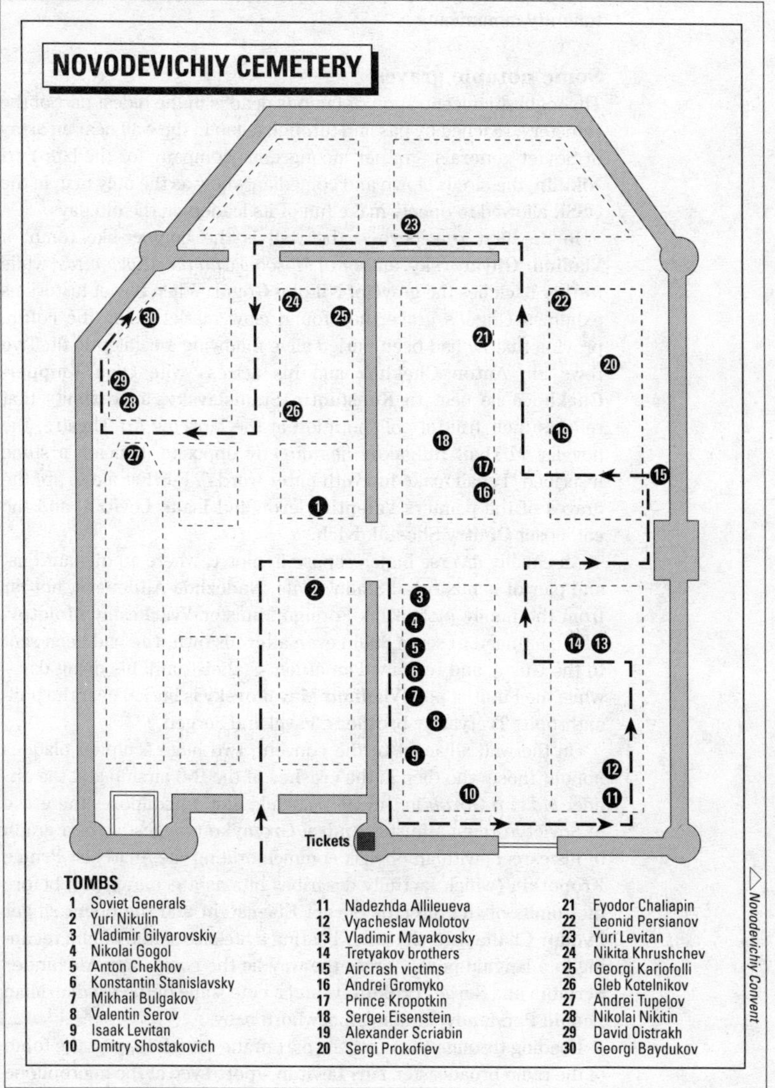

Admission **tickets** are sold just outside the gates, 100m south of the convent. Once inside, try to make sense of the cemetery's division into three main sections, each composed of two or more plots with numerous rows of graves. Though some of the tombs can be hard to find, you're sure to stumble on plenty of interest just wandering around – but the route in this book is as good a way as any of visiting the "top thirty" graves, distinguished by their occupants or funerary monuments.

Some notable graves

The highest concentration of famous dead is in the oldest part of the cemetery, reached by passing through a gap in the wall near an array of **Soviet generals** – rather incongruous company for the late **Yuri Nikulin**, the circus clown and comedian who was the only man in the USSR allowed to openly make fun of its leaders in the old days.

In the first row beyond the wall is the boulder-like tomb of **Vladimir Gilyarovsky**, author of *Moscow and the Muscovites*, while further back lies the grave of **Nikolai Gogol**. When Soviet historians exhumed Gogol's grave they found claw marks inside the coffin, proving that he had been buried alive following a cataleptic fit. Two rows on, **Anton Chekhov** and his actress wife **Olga Knipper-Chekhova** lie near to **Konstantin Stanislavsky**, a proximity that reflects their fruitful collaboration at the Moscow Art Theatre; the novelist **Mikhail Bulgakov** lies directly opposite, beneath a stone inscribed "I shall make fun with bitter words". Further along are the graves of the painters **Valentin Serov** and **Isaak Levitan**, and the composer **Dmitry Shostakovich**.

An equally diverse bunch repose in plot 1, where a poignant bust and pair of hands recall Stalin's wife, **Nadezhda Allileueva**, not far from the family plot of his Foreign Minister **Vyacheslav Molotov**, who continued to serve Stalin even after his own wife had been sent to the Gulag, and remained an ardent Stalinist until his dying day – while the Futurist poet **Vladimir Mayakovsky** is buried near the philanthropist **Tretyakov brothers**, Pavel and Sergei.

On the wall adjacent to the convent, two huge sculpted plaques honour those who died in the **crashes** of the B-6 airship and the airliner *Maxim Gorky* in the 1930s, while plot 4 juxtaposes the grave of Soviet Foreign Minister **Andrei Gromyko** (suggestive of a graph of his career) with an obelisk commemorating the Anarchist **Prince Kropotkin** (which tactfully describes him as a geographer), before the tombs of the director **Sergei Eisenstein** and the opera singer **Fyodor Chaliapin** – the latter bearing a life-size statue of him reclining in a languid pose. Across the way lie the composers **Alexander Scriabin** and **Sergei Prokofiev**, and a cute staue of the paediatrician **Leonid Persianov**, cradling a newborn baby.

Heading through the northern part of the cemetery, past the tomb of the radio broadcaster **Yuri Levitan** – portrayed at the microphone

– you arrive at the grave of **Nikita Khrushchev**, the Soviet leader who risked de-Stalinization and reform, was ousted by his colleagues and died in obscurity in 1971. (*Pravda* reported the death of "pensioner N.S. Khrushchev" in one line, 36 hours after the news broke.) The striking headstone was designed by Ernst Neizvestny, whom Khrushchev had once lambasted, but posthumously requested to create his memorial – a bronze cannonball headlocked between jagged white and black monoliths, symbolizing the good and bad in Khrushchev's life.

Other plots are devoted to inventors and designers, whose works adorn their tombstones, from the salvo of Katyusha rockets above **Georgi Kariofolli**'s bust to the billowing parachute on **Gleb Kotelnikov**'s grave, or the bird's wings and jet on the tomb of **Andrei Tupelov**, and the image of the Ostantinko TV Tower on the grave of **Nikolai Nikitin**. You'll also find a bust of **David Oistrakh** playing his violin, and the grave of the pilot **Georgi Baydukov**, with a model of the globe showing his trans-polar flight from Moscow to Vancouver in 1937.

Luzhniki Sports Complex

The busy Khamovnicheskiy val and an elevated railroad separate the cemetery from the 180-hectare **Luzhniki Sports Complex**, laid out in the 1950s and modernized for the 1980 Olympics. Its parking lot has since provided a setting for the funeral service of Andrei Sakharov – which drew fifty thousand mourners – and for Moscow's annual **beer festival**. En route there or back, it's possible to visit the **Metro Museum** attached to the southern exit of Sportivnaya metro station, if you take the trouble to call ahead. You can check out a driver's cab and get a good idea of how the metro is controlled from various working models. Evocative photos of the construction of the earliest lines highlight the role played by Komsomol volunteers and gloss over the contribution of the slave-labourers who toiled alongside.

The Metro Museum is open Mon 11am–6pm, Tues–Fri 9am–4pm; free. Call ☎222 73 09 to arrange a visit.

Ironically, the Lenin Central Stadium – now called **Luzhniki Stadium** – was one of the first assets in Moscow to be privatized. Its new owners refurbished the stadium to meet UEFA standards and purchased the bankrupt club Torpedo to play there, since when it has muscled into the premier league and become Mayor Luzhkov's favourite club. The stadium's $200 million refit has laid the ghost of Europe's worst-ever stadium disaster, in 1982, when 340 Spartak fans were crushed to death at Luzhniki during a UEFA Cup match against Holland – though due to Soviet censorship details of the tragedy took seven years to emerge.

See p.380 for details of football matches at Luzhniki and other stadiums in Moscow.

To the east of the stadium are the 13,000-seater **Sports Palace** and a **Museum of Physical Culture and Sport** (currently closed). On the far side of Komsomolskiy prospekt can be seen one of the most successful buildings constructed for the 1980 Olympics, the multipurpose **Friendship Sporting Hall** that Muscovites nicknamed the "Golden Tortoise" – though its gold-coloured epoxy roofing actually looks more like a giant sunflower that has wilted over the complex. From here you can see the enclosed bridge that carries the metro across the river towards the Sparrow Hills and Moscow University. Since the long-ago closure of Vorobyovie Gory station (which has exits on both sides of the river), the only feasible approach has been to ride on to the next stop, Universitet.

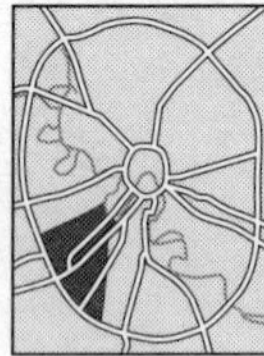

The Sparrow Hills and beyond

A wooded ridge overlooking the city, the ex-Lenin Hills have now reverted to their Tsarist-era name, the **Sparrow Hills** (*Vorobyovie gory*), but still look quintessentially Soviet. The main reason is the Moscow State University, whose stupendous Stalin-Gothic skyscraper dominates the plateau, its formal gardens extending to the granite esplanade where newly-weds come to be photographed and rollerbladers risk their necks. Besides the university, the attraction is quite simply the **panoramic view of Moscow**, with Luzhniki stadium and the Novodevichiy Convent (left) in the foreground, the White House and the Kremlin in the middle distance, and six Stalin skyscrapers ranged across the city. It made the perfect setting for a Jean-Michel Jarre concert during Moscow's 850th anniversary bash, but has since settled back into its familiar pattern of souvenir vendors, desolate **ski jumps** reached by rickety stairways, and newlyweds being photographed with Moscow or MGU as a backdrop.

The most direct way of **getting there** is to travel to Universitet metro and exit near the back of the train; you'll see the University tower above the trees to the left, and the silvery dome of the New Circus off to the right. A less direct approach is to take the metro to Leninskiy Prospekt station, and then a trolleybus #7 from ploshchad Gagarina out along ulitsa Kosygina, past Gorbachev's residence and the Pioneers' Palace.

MGU

Moscow State University – known by its initials as **MGU** (pronounced "em-gay-oo") – occupies the largest of the city's skyscrapers. When the Supreme Soviet decreed in 1947 that Moscow's skyline should be embellished by eight such buildings (of which seven were raised), grouped around the colossal (but never built) Palace of Soviets, it affirmed faith in the Communist future at the cost of the more pressing tasks of postwar reconstruction. Sixty trains were required to transport the building's steel frame from Dneiprpetrovsk, and thousands of free and slave workers toiled night and day from 1949 to 1953 – a construction period that almost matched the duration of the whole skyscraper programme, overseen by Beria from the half-built main hall of MGU. One wonders if he ever knew that Ivan the Terrible had forbidden building on the site, deeming it "too windy".

The MGU building consists of a 36-storey teaching block flanked by four huge wings of student accommodation, said to have 33km of corridors. Wheatsheaf pinnacles cap the side towers, which bear giant clocks and temperature/humidity indicators, while the central tower is festooned with swags and statues, carved with the Soviet crest, and surmounted by a gilded spire that looks small and light but is actually 240m tall with a star that weighs twelve tons. The most impressive facade faces northeast towards the city, across a terrace with heroic statues of a male and female student gazing raptly not at each other, nor at the books in their laps, but apparently into the future.

Try to plead or bluff your way past the guard outside its massive columned portico, to see the fabulous green-marbled, colonnaded foyers lined with medallions of world-famous scientists, culminating in bronze figures of illustrious Soviet ones. On the wall is a quote from the plant breeder Ivan Michurin: "We cannot await charity from Nature. To take it from Nature is our task." As yet, there is no statue of Gorbachev, who graduated from MGU with a law degree in 1955.

MGU's thirty thousand-plus residents include many "illegals" who lack a Moscow *propiska* (residency permit). In an attempt to control the situation, anyone entering or leaving the building is obliged to produce a pass. Yet the crumbling dormitories and classrooms rented out to shady businesses point to a deeper crisis, reflected in the low morale all round. While students struggle to survive on grants of $15 a month, academics try to salvage what they can of departments that once enjoyed lavish funding, unrivalled prestige in their own country and a high regard abroad.

Other sights

Ranged **along prospekt Vernadskovo** as it runs past the grounds of MGU are three buildings devoted to the amusement and education of children. If you have **kids**, a performance at the Circus or the Children's Musical Theatre could be just the ticket; see p.364 for details.

The **Circus on prospekt Vernadskovo** is visible from Sportivnaya metro, but rates a closer look for its silvery, wavy-edged cupola, resembling a giant jelly-mould. The glass curtain walls allow a glimpse of the ring, which has four interchangeable floors that can be switched in five minutes (including a pool for aquatic events and a rink for ice shows), with seating for 3400 spectators. Its opening in 1971 coincided with the closure (for refurbishment) of the original Moscow State Circus on Tsvetnoy bulvar.

Further up the prospekt stands the **Children's Musical Theatre**, named after its creator, the late Natalya Sats, who founded Moscow's

Central Children's Theatre as a teenager, inspired Prokofiev to write *Peter and the Wolf* in 1936, and spent sixteen years in the Gulag after the execution of her husband, Marshal Tukhachevsky. Initially set up in a tiny hall in 1965, the company now enjoys a purpose-built theatre with a giant filigree birdcage and a Palekh Room painted with fairytale scenes, where actors costumed as animals mingle with the children before each performance.

From here, trolleybus #28 trundles up the prospekt to the **Pioneers' Palace** on the corner of ulitsa Kosygina. Recognizable by its tall flagstaff, the complex's main block bears a mosaic of Pioneers blowing bugles and pursuing hobbies under the benign gaze of Lenin, as befits the variety of studios and workshops within – and the Lenin Hall, where children used to be sworn into the Young Pioneers. Founded in 1922 to "socialize" 9- to 14-year-olds, the organization eventually had over 25 million members. Though few Russians mourn its demise on ideological grounds, its provision of cheap facilities is sorely missed; the Palace now charges premium rates.

Should you opt to reach MGU by trolleybus #7 from ploshchad Gagarina, this will take you past ulitsa Kosygina 10, a guarded yellow building that has been **Gorbachev's residence** in Moscow since 1984. In the days when he was Party leader, the rumour was that the

Streets and squares	
Bolshaya Dekabrskaya ulitsa	Большая Декабрьская улица
Bolshaya Dorogomilovskaya ulitsa	Большой Дорогомиловская улица
Bolshaya Filyovskaya ulitsa	Большая Филёвская улица
Bolshaya Gruzinskaya ulitsa	Большая Грузинская улица
Bolshoy Predtechenskiy pereulok	Большой Предтеченский переулок
Druzhinnikovskaya ulitsa	Дружинниковская улица
Komsomolskiy prospekt	Комсомольский проспект
Krasnopresnenskiy Zastavy ploshchad	Краснопресненский Заставы площадь
Kutuzovskiy prospekt	Кутузовский проспект
ulitsa Lva Tolstovo	улица Льва Толстого
prospekt Vernadskovo	проспект Вернадского
Timiryazevskaya alleya	Тимирязевская аллея
ulitsa 1905 goda	улица 1905 года
ulitsa Khamovnicheskiy val	улица Хамовнический вал
ulitsa Kosygina	улица Косыгина
ulitsa Krasnaya Presnya	улица Красная Пресня
Metro stations	
Akademicheskaya	Академическая
Bagrationovskaya	Багратионовская
Barrikadnaya	Баррикадная

house had five sub-levels and was connected to the Kremlin by an underground railway. Secret tunnels often feature in the mythology of Russia's leaders. Ivan the Terrible supposedly had one from the Kremlin to his palace 100 miles from Moscow, and others beneath Kolomenskoe, while Mayor Sobchak of St Petersburg was said to *fly* to the capital through a tunnel 400 miles long and hundreds of metres wide.

The Darwin and Palaeontology Museums

The vast arc of Moscow to the **east of Leninskiy prospekt** contains numerous institutes, student hostels and flats owned by scientists and academics – making it an apt setting for two science museums.

The **Darwin Museum** at ulitsa Vavilova 7 extols the evolutionary vision that provided an underpinning for the Marxist-Leninist theory of history. Though you need to understand Russian to get the most out of it, there are displays such as a reconstruction of an alchemist's laboratory and Darwin's cabin aboard *HMS Beagle* that transcend the language barrier – not to mention automated dinosaurs, a section on urban ecology, and a collection of stuffed foxes, wolves, bears and tigers on the third floor. The museum is located a short bus ride (#57 or #119) from Akademicheskaya metro on the Kaluzhskaya-Rizhskaya line.

The Darwin Museum is open Tues–Sun 10am–6pm, closed the last Fri of each month; $1. To reach this and the Palaeontology Museum (see below), you'll have to transfer onto the Kaluzhsko-Rizhskaya metro line.

Fili	Фили
Kievskaya	Киевская
Krasnopresnenskaya	Краснопресненская
Krylatskoe	Крылацкое
Kuntsevskaya	Кунцевская
Kutuzovskaya	Кутузовская
Molodezhnaya	Молодежная
Park Kultury	Парк Культуры
Sportivnaya	Спортивная
Tyopliy Stan	Тёплы Стан
Ulitsa 1905 Goda	Улица 1905 года
Universitet	Университет
Museums	
Biological Museum	Биологический музей
Borodino Panorama Museum	музей-панорама Бородинска Битва
Central Museum of the Great Patriotic War	Центральный музей Великой Отечественной войны
Darwin Museum	Дарвиновский музей
Metro Museum	музей Московского Метрополитена
Museum of Physical Culture and Sport	музей физицеской культуры
Palaeontology Museum	Палеонтологический музей
Red Presnya Museum	музей Красная Пресня
Tolstoy House-Museum	музей-усадьба Л.Н. Толстого

The Sparrow Hills and beyond

The Palaeontology Museum is open Wed–Sun 11am–7pm; $1.50.

By travelling six stops further on to Tyopliy Stan metro and then riding any bus or trolleybus one stop back towards the centre you can reach the **Palaeontology Museum** at Profsoyuznaya ulitsa 123, a stylishly designed 1970s showcase for some amazing fossils, such as **dinosaur skeletons** found near the Severnaya Dvina River in the late nineteenth century, including a Tardosaurus – a relative of Tyrannosaurus Rex dubbed the "Russian Godzilla". If you're interested, bear in mind that the museum closes for several weeks during the summer – so phone (☎339 15 00) to check first. It's possible to arrange a guided tour in English (☎339 45 44).

Chapter 7

Zamoskvareche and the south

ZAMOSKVARECHE AND THE SOUTH are clearly defined by geography and history. The Zamoskvareche district dates back to medieval times and preserves a host of colourful **churches** and the mansions of civic-minded merchants. The same merchants founded the **Tretyakov Gallery**, Moscow's pre-eminent gallery for Russian art, with a superlative collection of paintings. In pre-Petrine times, Moscow ended at its earthen ramparts (now the Krymskiy and Vatsepskiy val), beyond which the fortified **Donskoy and Danilov monasteries** overlooked fields and orchards.

By the mid-eighteenth century, Moscow had expanded as far as the Kamerkollezhskiy boundary, drawn by the tsar's tax collectors; over the next century, slums and factories surrounded what had been suburban estates. In the Soviet era, these were collectivized into Gorky Park, vast new thoroughfares were laid out, and the city spread out past the magical summer retreats of **Kolomenskoe** and **Tsaritysno**, to what is now the Moscow Ring Road.

Zamoskvareche

Zamoskvareche simply means "Across the Moskva River", a blunt designation in keeping with the character of its original inhabitants. As the part of Moscow most exposed to Tatar raids, it was once guarded by twenty companies of Streltsy, settled here with their families, and separated from the other, civilian settlements by meadows and swamps. In the long term, these communities of skilled artisans and shrewd merchants did more for Zamoskvareche than the riotous Streltsy. The artisans erected the parish churches that are still its glory, while the merchants' lifestyle provided inspiration for the playwright Ostrovsky and the artist Tropinin in the nineteenth century. By the 1900s, Zamoskvareche had become a major industrial district, with a fifth of Moscow's factories and a third of its workers.

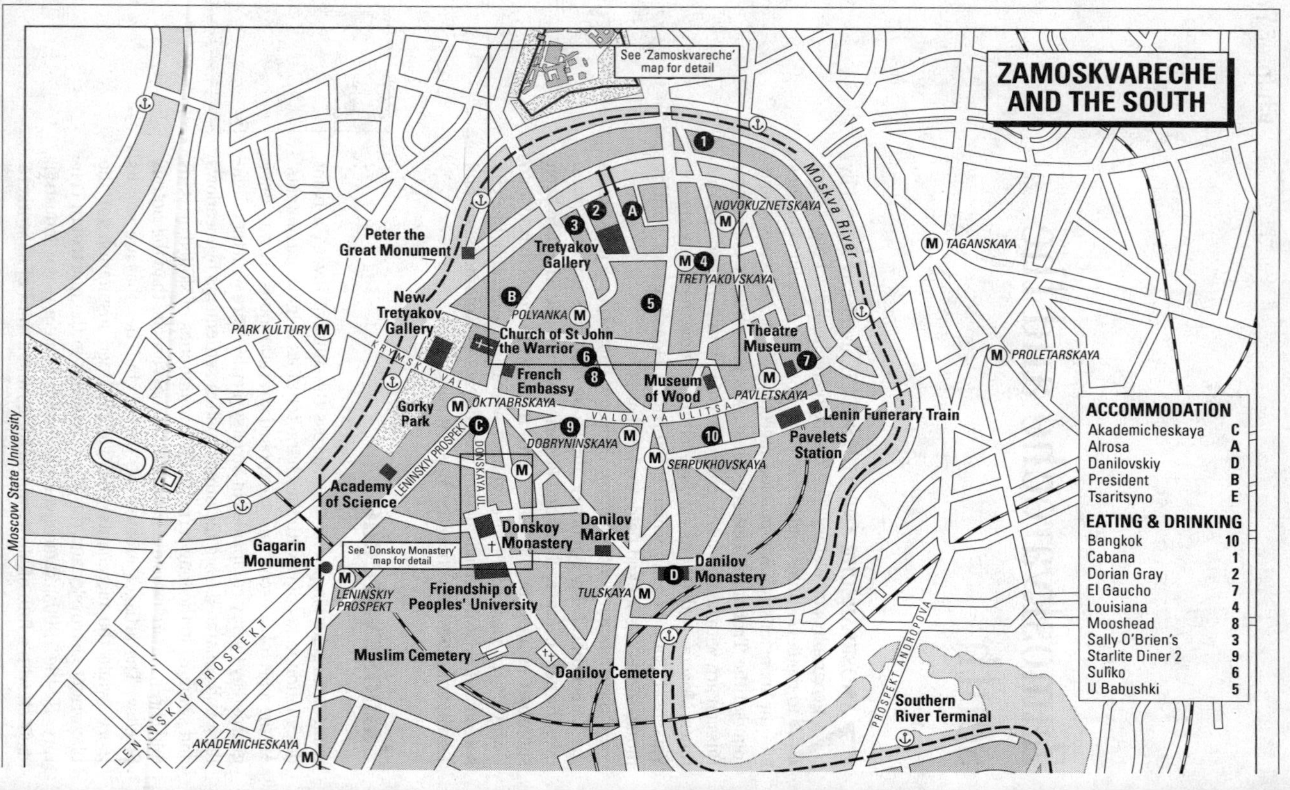

ZAMOSKVARECHE AND THE SOUTH
ACCOMMODATION
Akademicheskaya C
Alrosa A
Danilovskiy D
President B
Tsaritsyno E
EATING & DRINKING
Bangkok 10
Cabana 1
Dorian Gray 2
El Gaucho 7
Louisiana 4
Mooshead 8
Sally O'Brien's 3
Starlite Diner 2 9
Sulîko 6
U Babushki 5
See 'Zamoskvareche' map for detail
See 'Donskoy Monastery' map for detail
Moskva River
TAGANSKAYA
PROLETARSKAYA
NOVOKUZNETSKAYA
TRETYAKOVSKAYA
PAVLETSKAYA
SERPUKHOVSKAYA
DOBRYNINSKAYA
POLYANKA
OKTYABRSKAYA
TULSKAYA
LENINSKIY PROSPEKT
PARK KULTURY
AKADEMICHESKAYA
VALOVAYA ULITSA
KRYMSKIY VAL
LENINSKIY PROSPEKT
DONSKAYA UL.
PROSPEKT ANDROPOVA
Lenin Funerary Train
Pavelets Station
Theatre Museum
Museum of Wood
Danilov Monastery
Danilov Market
Danilov Cemetery
Southern River Terminal
Tretyakov Gallery
Church of St John the Warrior
French Embassy
Donskoy Monastery
Friendship of Peoples' University
Muslim Cemetery
Peter the Great Monument
New Tretyakov Gallery
Gorky Park
Academy of Science
Gagarin Monument
Moscow State University

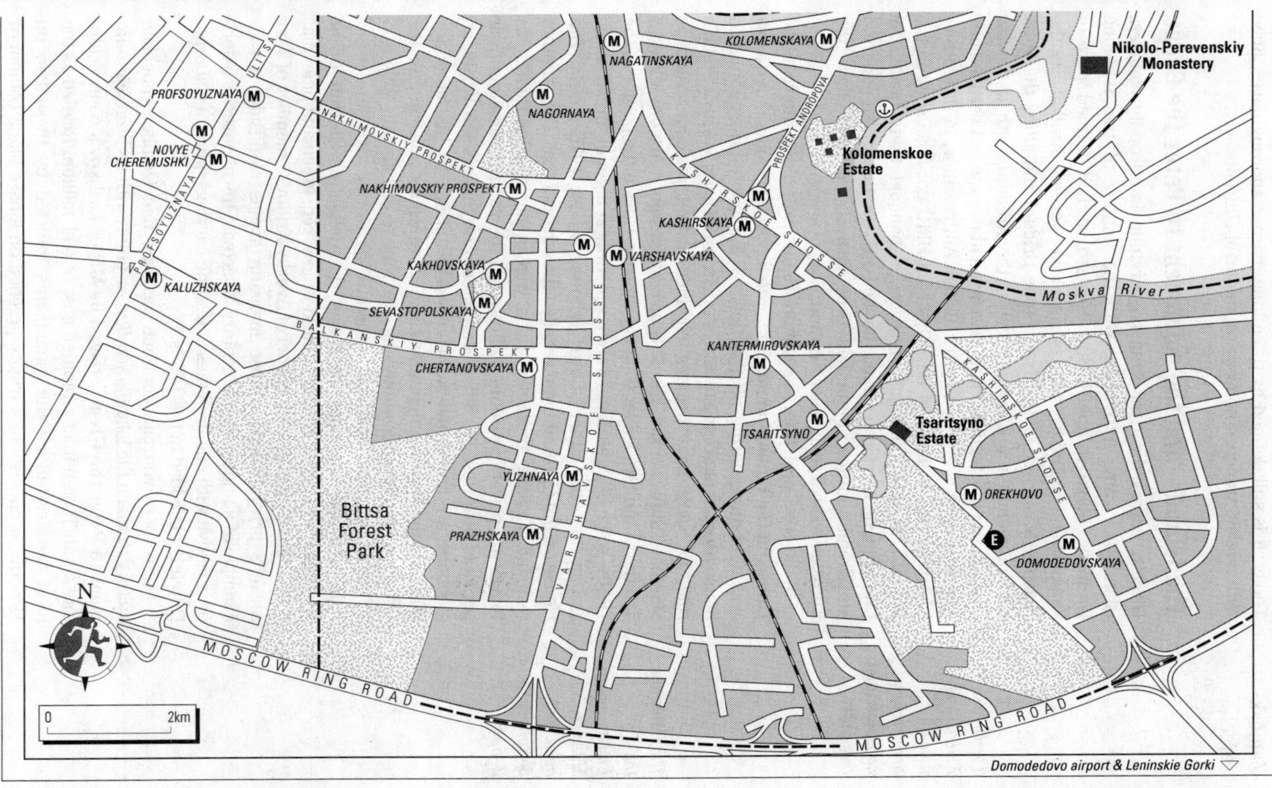
Nikolo-Perevenskiy Monastery
KOLOMENSKAYA
NAGATINSKAYA
PROFSOYUZNAYA
ULITSA
NAGORNAYA
NOVYE CHEREMUSHKI
NAKHIMOVSKIY PROSPEKT
PROSPEKT ANDROPOVA
Kolomenskoe Estate
KASHIRSKOE SHOSSE
KASHIRSKAYA
VARSHAVSKAYA
PROFSOYUZNAYA
KAKHOVSKAYA
KALUZHSKAYA
Moskva River
SEVASTOPOLSKAYA
BALKANSKIY PROSPEKT
KANTERMIROVSKAYA
CHERTANOVSKAYA
TSARITSYNO
Tsaritsyno Estate
YUZHNAYA
OREKHOVO
Bittsa Forest Park
PRAZHSKAYA
VARSHAVSKOE SHOSSE
DOMODEDOVSKAYA
N
MOSCOW RING ROAD
0
2km
Domodedovo airport & Leninskie Gorki

Today, it is still defined by three long, narrow thoroughfares, lined with modest stuccoed houses and colourful churches.

The island – and the monument to Peter the Great

Directly across the river from the Kremlin is an oddly nameless island that came into being with the digging of the 4km-long Drainage Canal in the 1780s; hitherto, it had formed part of Zamoskvareche and been the tsar's market garden. Stroll across the Bolshoy Kamenniy most (Great Stone Bridge) and along the Sofia Embankment for a glorious view of the Kremlin, with its yellow palaces and thirty golden domes arrayed above the red battlements. The best view is enjoyed by the British Ambassador, in the former Kharitonenko mansion at no. 14, which HMG got for a song in the 1920s. Though Stalin once attended a banquet there hosted by Churchill, he was always irked that he could see the British flag from his Kremlin office; Putin has been spared the sight since the Embassy moved to another location.

The British Embassy is now on Smolenskaya naberezhnaya (see p.24).

In the other direction, the vast grey apartment block known as the **House on the Embankment** (*dom naberezhnoy*) looms above a torrent of traffic pouring off the Bolshoy Kamenniy bridge. Built to house prominent scientists and officials in the early years of Stalin's rule, its walls bear plaques commemorating residents such as Marshal Tukhachevsky, the MiG aircraft designer Artyom Mikoyan and the Comintern leader Georgi Dimitrov. During the purges of the 1930s, some 600 residents were taken away at night in "bread" vans, among them the father of Yuri Trifonov, whose 1976 novella *The House on the Embankment* recalled the terror of that time. Another resident, Tamara Andreevna (who was in her thirties then), has founded a private **museum** dedicated to the victims, detailing their personal histories. There is even material on Stalin's son Vasily, an alcoholic Air Force general who was dismissed by his father for bungling the May Day flypast in 1952. To reach the museum, use the entrance on ulitsa Serafimovicha. It's wise to call ahead (☎959 03 17) to ensure that somebody is there.

The House on the Embankment Museum is open Wed 5–8pm & Sat 2–5pm; free.

Beyond the infamous House is the delightful **Church of St Nicholas**, a fairytale edifice painted yellow, red, green and blue, that was originally the private chapel of Averky Krillov, a member of Tsar Alexei's privy council, whose **mansion** stands alongside. A rare example of a mid-sixteenth-century Muscovite townhouse, its exterior is festive with coloured tiles and stone carvings, plus an elaborate Dutch gable added in the 1750s.

From there you can continue past the Red October chocolate factory to reach the island's *strelka*, or point, with its bizarre **monument to Peter the Great**, created by Mayor Luzhkov's court sculptor, Zurab Tsereteli, at a reputed cost of $11 million. Reviled as the most tasteless of all the monuments inflicted by these two on Moscow, it consists of a frigate perched on a base like a column of

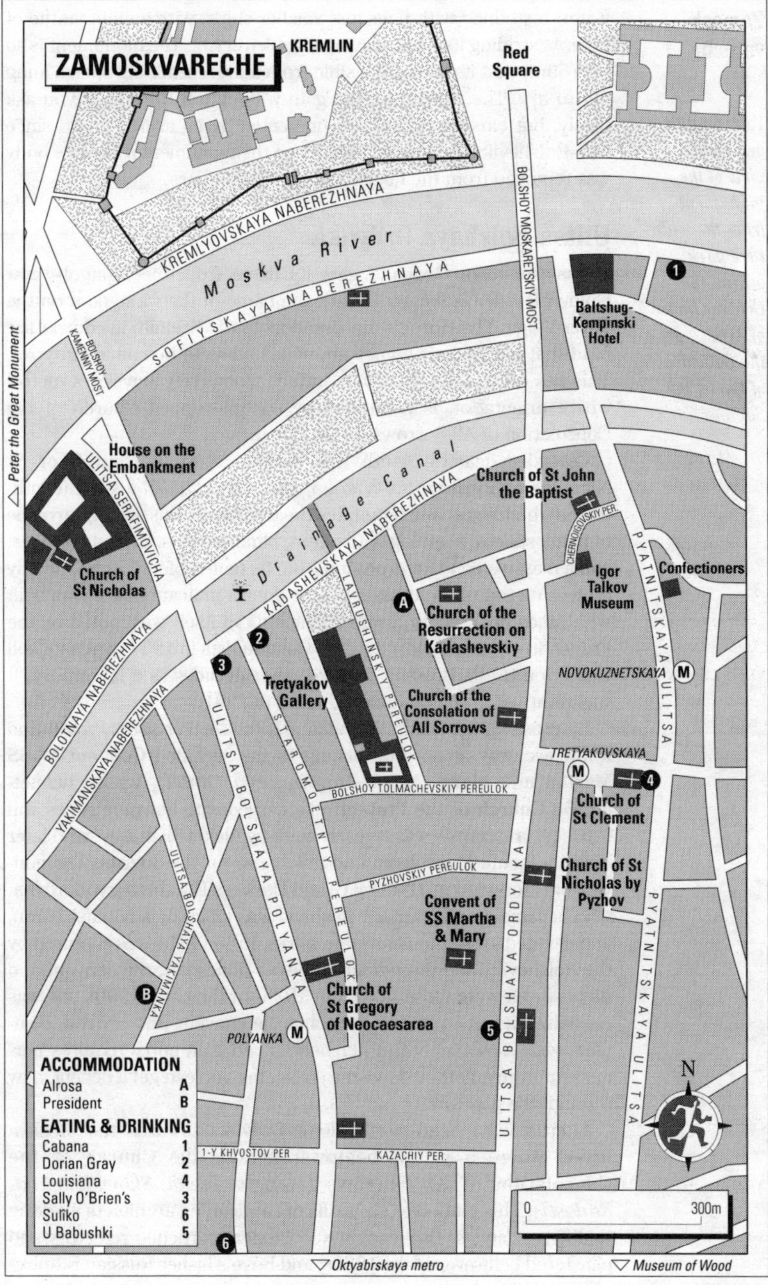
ZAMOSKVARECHE
KREMLIN
Red Square
KREMLYOVSKAYA NABEREZHNAYA
Moskva River
SOFIYSKAYA NABEREZHNAYA
BOLSHOY MOSKARETSKIY MOST
BOLSHOY KAMENNIY MOST
Baltshug-Kempinski Hotel
Peter the Great Monument
House on the Embankment
ULITSA SERAFIMOVICHA
Drainage Canal
KADASHEVSKAYA NABEREZHNAYA
Church of St John the Baptist
CHERNIGOVSKIY PER.
Church of St Nicholas
Igor Talkov Museum
Confectioners
Church of the Resurrection on Kadashevskiy
LAVRUSHINSKIY PEREULOK
PYATNITSKAYA ULITSA
NOVOKUZNETSKAYA
BOLOTNAYA NABEREZHNAYA
YAKIMANSKAYA NABEREZHNAYA
Tretyakov Gallery
Church of the Consolation of All Sorrows
STAROMONETNIY PEREULOK
TRETYAKOVSKAYA
ULITSA BOLSHAYA POLYANKA
BOLSHOY TOLMACHEVSKIY PEREULOK
Church of St Clement
ULITSA BOLSHAYA YAKIMANKA
PYZHOVSKIY PEREULOK
Church of St Nicholas by Pyzhov
Convent of SS Martha & Mary
ULITSA BOLSHAYA ORDYNKA
Church of St Gregory of Neocaesarea
POLYANKA
ACCOMMODATION
Alrosa A
President B
EATING & DRINKING
Cabana 1
Dorian Gray 2
Louisiana 4
Sally O'Brien's 3
Suliko 6
U Babushki 5
1-Y KHVOSTOV PER
KAZACHIY PER.
N
0 300m
Oktyabrskaya metro
Museum of Wood

water, festooned with flags and smaller ships, with a giant statue of Peter bestriding its deck, waving a golden scroll. The monument is so tall (59m) that its sails are visible from afar, resembling sheets hung out to dry. The woman on the gate will let you through if you ask nicely, but closer proximity is prevented by an armed guard since Neo-Bolsheviks threatened to blow up the monument if Lenin's body was removed from the mausoleum on Red Square.

You can also get a good view of the monument from the sculpture park behind the Central House of Artists, or the Cathedral of Christ the Saviour.

Ulitsa Bolshaya Ordynka

Ulitsa Bolshaya Ordynka gets its name from the Mongol–Tatar Golden Horde (*Zolotaya Orda*), the name of their kingdom on the lower Volga. The Horde's ambassadors to the Kremlin lived near the road that led to their homeland, which came to be called Ordynka. This lies off to the left as you surface from Tretyakovskaya metro, where orientation is facilitated by the gilt-topped Church of the Consolation of All Sorrows, to the north.

Consider heading south first to the all-white **Church of St Nicholas by Pyzhov** (*Sv. Nikolay shto v Pyzhakh*), a seventeenth-century building that exemplifies the traditional Russian abhorrence of blank spaces, seething with ogees, blind arcades, fretted cornices, and a massive pendant drooping from its tent-roofed porch. The tiny crowns on top of the crosses on the domes indicate that it was built with funds donated by Streltsy. The church itself was looted by the French in 1812 and closed by the Communists in 1934, when its bell was given to the Bolshoy Theatre. After decades as a laboratory, it was returned to the Orthodox Church in 1991.

By crossing the road and walking 150m further south, you'll find a low archway at no. 36, leading to the secluded **Convent of SS Martha and Mary** (*Marfo–Mariinskaya Obitel*), whose helmet-domed **Church of the Protection** – carved with Slavonic runes and mythical creatures – was an early work by Alexei Shchusev, who later built the Lenin Mausoleum and much else for the Soviets. The convent was founded in 1908 by Grand Duchess Elizabeth Fyodorovna, who became a nun after her husband was killed by a Nihilist bomb, and devoted herself to charitable works. In 1917 she was captured by the Bolsheviks and thrown alive down a mineshaft; the convent and its hospices were closed down in 1926. In the early 1990s she was canonized as an Orthodox saint and the convent was revived, complete with a monument in her honour. To gain entry requires permission from an office down the street, but you can get a decent view through the gateway.

Alternatively, head north along Ordynka towards the Moskva River, where a yellow belltower heralds the **Church of the Consolation of All Sorrows** (*tserkov Vsekh Skoryashchikh Radosti*). This embodies the skills of two leading architects working in different styles: Bazhenov's Neoclassical porticoed refectory and pilastered belltower of the 1780s; and Bove's lusher Russian Empire-style rotunda (1828–33). The narthex contains more oil paintings than frescoes, while a ring of thick Ionic columns defines the pale blue, white and gold sanctuary, partly obscuring its iconostasis. The feast day of the church's sacred icon of the Madonna of Tenderness is on November 6.

Slightly further north, a lane on the left called 1-y Kadashevskiy pereulok provides a fine view of the awesome **Church of the Resurrection on Kadashevskiy** (*tserkov Voskresenie v Kadashakh*). Built in 1687, in the Naryshkin Baroque style, it is rich in limestone ornamentation, with a fancy parapet instead of the usual pyramid of *kokoshniki*, while the belltower, added in 1695, rises from a ponderous base through delicate tiers emblazoned with flame-shaped mouldings. Although its name alludes to the Kadeshi quarter of barrel-makers that existed here in the fifteenth and sixteenth centuries, the church's construction was actually funded by factory workers in what had by then become a textile-producing quarter. True to its industrial pedigree, the church now serves as a restorers' workshop within the grounds of a furniture factory, which makes access impossible.

By following 2-y Kadashevskiy pereulok eastwards, you can re-emerge on Bolshaya Ordynka opposite Chernigovskiy pereulok, leading through to Pyatnitskaya ulitsa (see below), with an unexpected view of the Kremlin towers and St Basil's Cathedral, to the north.

Pyatnitskaya ulitsa

Zamoskvareche's busiest thoroughfare and traditional marketplace, **Pyatnitskaya ulitsa** remains the heart of the neighbourhood, flushed with kiosks and shops in the vicinity of Novokuznetskaya metro – a palatial 1950s station smothered in bas-reliefs and murals of military heroes.

If you don't start there, the best approach is via the **Church of St Clement** (*tserkov Klimenta*), to the east of *McDonald's* near Tretyakovskaya metro. Looming above the stalls on Klimentovskiy pereulok, this was Moscow's last great monument of Baroque religious architecture, built sometime between 1740 and 1770. Corinthian pilasters and seraphim-topped windows rise from a lower level clad in fretted stucco to a parapet with flame-patterned railings. Its five black domes rest on sienna-red drums of equal height; the four corner ones are spangled with gold stars. Unfortunately the church is locked and derelict, so there's no need to linger.

Up the road past Novokuznetskaya metro, keep an eye out for the **Confectioners** (*Konditerskaya*) at no. 9, on the right. Its interior dates from the early 1900s and remains intact: pale-blue-and-lavender stucco overlaid by swags and urns, walnut counters with brass fittings, and faceted lights that wouldn't look amiss in a disco. From here you can see the urn-festooned green-and-white belltower of the

Church of St John the Baptist (*tserkov Ioanna Predtechi*), on the corner of Chernigovskiy pereulok. While this was raised in 1758, the church proper is exactly a century older, and less ambitious: a red-and-white refectory allied to a small sanctuary, nowadays lit by stainless steel chandeliers from the time that it was a museum of glassware. St John "the Forerunner" (as Russians call him) is honoured by two feast days, on August 7 and September 11.

Around the corner of the lane is an old mansion housing a Slav Cultural Centre whose outbuildings harbour the tiny **Igor Talkov Museum** (Tues–Sat noon–6pm, Sun 11am–5pm; $0.50). Known for his nationalistic pop songs during the latter years of perestroika, Talkov achieved cult status when he was shot dead in 1991 by the bodyguard of another singer, during an argument over who should take precedence at a concert – though his right-wing fans blamed a "Jewish conspiracy". Talkov's Soviet army uniform takes pride of place amongst the memorabilia, and one can buy recordings of his songs.

Ulitsa Bolshaya Polyanka

Though quite close to Ordynka, **ulitsa Bolshaya Polyanka** is quite awkward to reach from there, involving a zigzagging walk through the backstreets, or two changes of line to get there by metro from Tretyakovskaya or Novokuznetskaya.

Emerging from Polyanka station, you can't miss the silvery domes and luridly coloured towers of the **Church of St Gregory of Neocaesarea** (*tserkov Grigoriya Neokesariiskovo*), built in 1667–69 by Peter the Great's father, Alexei. This lovely church is unusual on two counts: the porch at the base of its belfry straddles the pavement out to the kerb, while the main building is girdled by a broad frieze of dark blue, turquoise, brown and yellow tiles, whose floral motifs so resemble plumage that Muscovites dubbed the church "the Peacock's Eye". Even without the tiles, its facade would be striking: the walls are painted bright orange with a sky blue trim, and the roofs turquoise. After decades of being occupied by the Soviet Department of Art Exports – which bought valuable icons cheaply and sold them abroad for hard currency – St Gregory's is now used by a group of nuns that helps war refugees.

Still more luridly, the flat beneath the sign of the *El Dorado* restaurant at the northern end of the street was the site of State Prosecutor Skuratov's infamous *ménage a trois* with two teenage prostitutes, that was secretly videotaped and later broadcast on national television, thereby aborting his investigation into the Mabetex scandal (see box on p.93).

The Tretyakov Gallery

Located in the heart of Zamoskvareche, the **Tretyakov Gallery** (*Tretyakovskaya galereya*, familiarly known as the *Tretyakovka*)

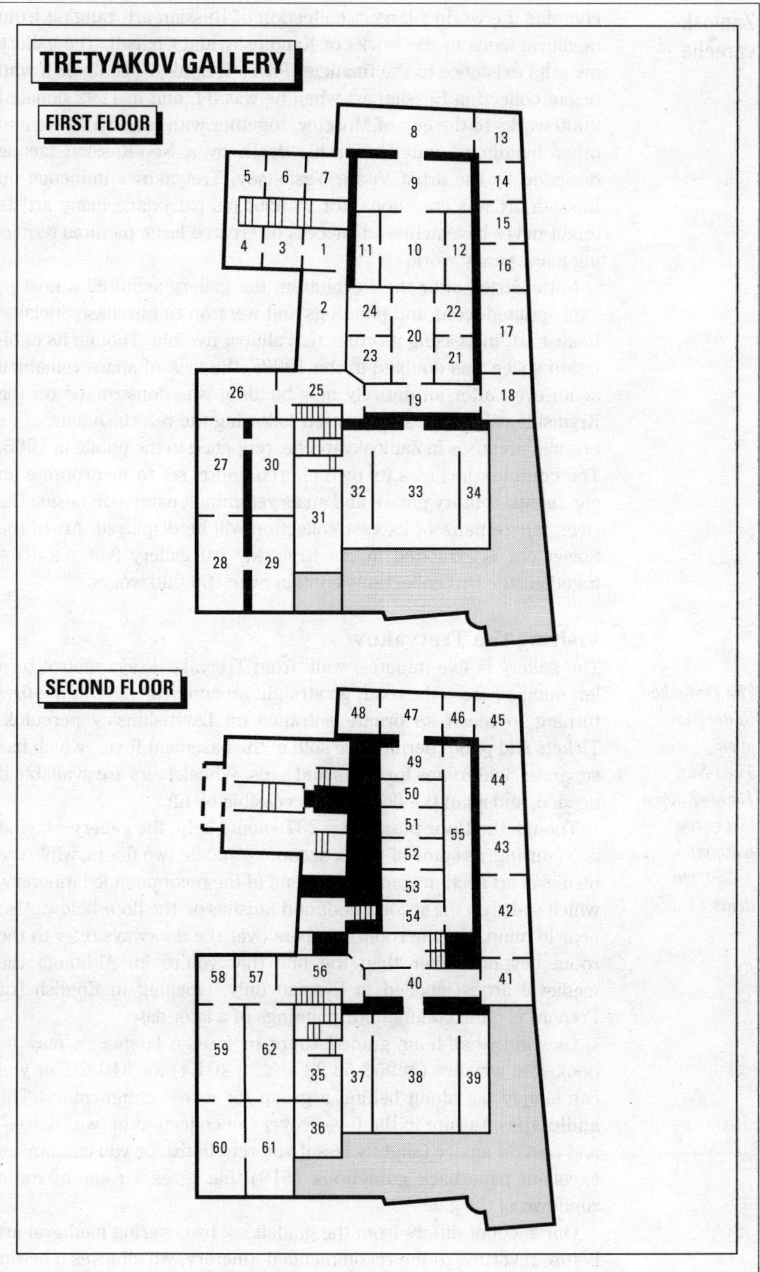
TRETYAKOV GALLERY
FIRST FLOOR
1
2
3
4
5
6
7
8
9
10
11
12
13
14
15
16
17
18
19
20
21
22
23
24
25
26
27
28
29
30
31
32
33
34
SECOND FLOOR
35
36
37
38
39
40
41
42
43
44
45
46
47
48
49
50
51
52
53
54
55
56
57
58
59
60
61
62

Zamoskvareche

contains the world's largest collection of Russian art, ranging from medieval icons to the works of Kandinsky and Chagall. The gallery owes its existence to the financier Pavel Tretyakov (1832–98), who began collecting Russian art when he was 34, and in 1892 donated 2000 works to the city of Moscow, together with his own house and other buildings, united after his death by a Neo-Russian facade designed by the artist Viktor Vasnetsov. Tretyakov's influence on Russian art was enormous, for without his patronage many artists might never have achieved success or created large pictures requiring many years' work.

Nationalized after the Revolution, the gallery acquired a host of expropriated icons and paintings and went on to purchase Socialist Realist art, increasing its collection almost fivefold. Though its exhibition space was doubled in the 1930s, the lack of space remained acute even after an entirely new building was constructed on the Krymskiy val, and has only eased following the refurbishment of its original premises in Zamoskvareche, reopened to the public in 1995. The **complex** includes its own church and is set to incorporate an eighteenth-century palace and an as yet unbuilt extension beside the river, where more of its vast collection will be displayed. Art of the Soviet era is exhibited in the Krymskiy val gallery (see p.249) – together, the two collections contain over 100,000 works.

Visiting the Tretyakov

The Tretyakov Gallery is open Tues–Sun 10am–7.30pm, last entry 6.30pm; $ 7.50, students $4.

The gallery is five minutes' walk from Tretyakovskaya metro: turn left outside, cross the road, go straight on and bear right at the first turning to reach its ornate entrance on Lavrushinskiy pereulok. Tickets and photo permits are sold in the basement foyer, which has separate cloakrooms for coats and bags. Wheelchairs are available if needed, and all of the floors are accessible by lift.

Though the **floor plans** on p.237 should help, the gallery's layout is confusing, as some of its six sections straddle two floors, while the medieval art section comes at the end of the recommended itinerary, which starts on the second floor and finishes on the floor below. Also bear in mind that the room numbers over the doorways refer to the room beyond rather than the one that you're in. Although the medieval art is labelled in Russian only, labelling in English (or French) is quite common for paintings of a later date.

One-and-a-half-hour **guided tours** in foreign languages may be booked in advance (☎953 52 23 or 238 20 54) for $10–20, or you can simply tag along behind a group for a free commentary. The **audiotapes** for hire in the foyer cover the collection in two "halves" and cost $4 apiece (slightly less if you rent both), or you can buy an excellent paperback **guidebook** ($10) that gives a room-by-room rundown of the gallery.

Our account differs from the guidebook by covering medieval art before reverting to the recommended itinerary, which gives a better sense of the development of Russian art and doesn't involve too much backtracking. There is also advice on how to reach sections directly, using the backstairs, rather than plodding through the whole tour.

Medieval Russian art (rooms 56–62)

For 600 years, almost the only form of pictorial art in Russia was religious art – mosaics, murals and, above all, icons. **Icons** (from the Greek *eikon*, "image") came to Russia from Byzantium, like Orthodox Christianity. Painted on wooden panels varnished with linseed oil and amber, their patina darkened by candle smoke, these holy images were mounted in tiers to form iconostases in churches, or hung in the *krasniy ugol* ("beautiful corner") of every Russian household. While generally venerated, those that failed to "perform" were sometimes beaten by their irate owners.

Icons were valued for their religious and spiritual content rather than artistic merit. One Russian critic argues that their visual flatness reflects a view of each human soul as the centre of the universe, unlike the spatial and moral distancing implied by Renaissance perspective. Anatomical realism was initially taboo as a reminder of mortal imperfections, but gradually became more accepted. The Tretyakov owns works from all the main schools (see box overleaf), including several that are deeply revered by believers, who can be seen praying before *Our Lady of Vladimir* or Rublev's *Old Testament Trinity*.

Room 56 displays the **oldest examples** of Russian art, predating the Mongol invasion. To the left as you enter are a mosaic of St Demetrius of Salonika and a fresco of St Nicholas from the Church of the Archangel Michael in Kiev, opposite a rare stone relief of two horsemen from the same church. A glass case displays the double-sided *Image of the Saviour Not Made by Human Hands*, relating to a legend that Christ imprinted his visage on a cloth to cure the ailments of the King of Edessa. At the far end of the room are life-sized panels of *St George* and the *Ustyug Annunciation*, the oldest icons (c.1130–1140) extant from Novgorod.

To reach these rooms (56–62) use the stairs off the right-hand side of the foyer and bear right through Room 40. Afterwards, you either view the early twentieth-century art nearby, or return to the foyer and ascend the main stairs to Room 1.

Russia inherited from Byzantium six conventions for depicting the **Mother of God**, of which the two most popular were the Hodegetria, who sits serenely unrelated to the miniature adult in her lap; and the Eleousa, or Madonna of Tenderness, who lovingly embraces the Christ child. Russians have always preferred the latter, and referred to Mary as the Mother of God (*Bogomateri* or *Bogroditsa*) rather than the Virgin. The most revered icon is *Our Lady of Vladimir* (**Room 57**), reputedly painted by St Luke but actually from the early twelfth century. Brought from Constantinople to Kiev, then to Vladimir and in 1395 to the Kremlin's Cathedral of the Assumption, it became a symbol of national unity and was credited with saving Moscow from the army of Timerlane. Another notable icon in Room

57 is the *Virgin Great Panagia*, representing her as the Heavenly Sovereign with Christ Emmanuel, which was discovered in the lumber room of a monastery in Yaroslavl in 1919.

Room 58 displays icons of the **Novgorod and Pskov schools** of the thirteenth to the fifteenth centuries. To the left of the door are *SS Boris and Gleb*, who let themselves be killed by their brother rather than fight for their inheritance, while on the right is the *Battle of the Men of Novgorod and Suzdal*, commemorating the siege of Novgorod (1170) and its deliverance by an icon of the Virgin of the Sign which, hit by an enemy arrow, recoiled, so outraging the Novgorodians that they stormed out of the city and routed the Suzdalians. Also notice the typically Pskovian icon of *St Paraskeva and the Three Hierarchs*, in white surplices emblazoned with black crosses.

One of many craftsmen and scholars who fled to Russia before the fall of Constantinople, **Theophanes the Greek** (c.1340–1405) has been justly called the "Russian El Greco". Though he is said to have decorated forty churches before coming to Moscow, all that survive in situ are his murals in the Church of the Transfiguration in Vladimir, and his icons in the Cathedral of the Annunciation in the Kremlin. **Room 59** exhibits his *Our Lady of the Don*, and attributes to the school of Theophanes the early fifteenth-century *Transfiguration*, showing Christ atop Mount Tabor, with unbelievers smitten by rays emanating from its summit. Another superb icon is the so-called "Blue" *Dormition* from Tver, featuring the apostles floating on clouds accompanied by angels.

Room 60 is devoted to the two greatest icon painters of medieval Russia. **Dionysius** (c.1440–1508) was the first famous lay-painter, whose career coincided with a rising demand for icons, which spread from the noble and mercantile classes to the peasantry. His *Christ Enthroned* (framed by a red rhombus, a dark green oval and a red quadrangle, symbolizing Christ's glory, his earthly and heavenly powers) was once the centrepiece of the Deisis tier in the Pavlovo-Obnorskiy Monastery, while the icons beside it were painted with the help of Dionysius's sons and belonged to the Deisis row of the Therapont Monastery.

The work of the monk **Andrei Rublev** (c.1360–1430) is more searching and mystical, its draughtsmanship at once bold and gossamer-fine. To contemporaries, the huge faces of *Our Saviour*, the *Archangel Michael* and the *Apostle Paul* that he painted for Zvenigorod Cathedral seemed "as though painted with smoke". Alongside are *The Descent into Hell*, *The Annunciation* and *The Assumption* from the festival tier of the Cathedral of the Assumption in Vladimir, where Rublev and **Daniil Cherniy** also created a Deisis tier of larger-than-life figures, including *Christ Enthroned*. The Tretyakov also owns Rublev's *Old Testament Trinity*, a later icon whose gold and blue angels seem "full of joy and brightness", as

Rublev himself was said to be; he painted it at the request of the Trinity Monastery, where he had served his novitiate.

Zamoskvareche

Room 61 contains sixteenth-century works of the **Moscow school** and northern Russia. The large horizontal icon *Blessed be the Host of the King of Heaven* celebrates Ivan the Terrible's capture of Kazan, with the tsar and his army returning from a burning fortress to the holy city of Jerusalem, symbolizing Moscow. Nearby hang two fine icons of *St George and the Dragon*, which was adopted as the emblem of the Muscovite state by Ivan III. Also notice the *Last Judgement* from Novgorod, showing Christ presiding over the weighing of souls and a green snake writhing down to a winged Satan and the child Antichrist.

The exhibition ends in **Room 62** with icons from the seventeenth century, when the appearance of lay figures in icons (such as the Stroganovs in *The Cherubic Hymn "We, the cherubim")* and a stylized form of portraiture called the **parsuna** (represented by an early one of the boyar Skopin-Shuisky) presaged the emergence of secular forms of art. Arguably the last great icon painter was **Simon Ushakov** (1626–86), who headed the icon-painting studio in the Kremlin Armoury, and was also a muralist and art theorist. His *Tree of the Muscovite State* shows the Virgin of Vladimir conferring her

Ushakov's finest frescoes are in the Church of the Trinity on Nikitinov Lane (see p.121).

A brief history of Russian icons

While it's true that much **icon painting** was done by monks and priests as a spiritual devotion, artels of decorators who specialized in churches and produced icons to order were equally active – if not more so.

Kiev, where Christianity took root in 988, was the main centre of icon production until its devastation by the Mongols in 1240. What little survives from this era shows a taste for figures in dark, earth colours, against a plain background, often of gold (representing the Holy Ghost). After Kiev's fall, other schools began to develop regional identities. **Novgorod** icons were painted in emerald green, vermilion and other bold colours, with figures defined by resolute, angular lines, their faces given character by highlighting and shading. The "Northern School" of **Vladimir-Suzdal**, **Yaroslavl** and **Pskov** combined bright colours and rhythmical patterning with simpler forms and more gestural symbolism, while **Tver** icon painters preferred paler, more delicate hues.

The **Moscow school** developed in the late fifteenth century after Ivan the Terrible ordered artists to reside and work in the Kremlin; only then did this style become the most prevalent. However, the Kremlin had been employing the finest artists ever since the dawn of the **golden age** of Russian icon painters such as Rublev and Theophanes, in the 1370s.

Theophanes the Greek made his mark in Novgorod sometime in the latter half of the fourteenth century, starting an illustrious career that overlapped with those of the earliest known native masters, **Andrei Rublev** and **Daniil Cherny**. The torch was carried on by **Dionysius**, and handed down to **Simon Ushakov** in the seventeenth century, after which it never shone as brightly again. So far as is known, there were no women icon painters until the late nineteenth century.

protection on its rulers. Nearby hangs a rare icon of *St Basil the Blessed* by an unknown artist, depicting the holy man wandering naked outside the Kremlin walls.

Several **other icons** can be seen in the Jewellery section (Room 55) on the same floor (see p.247).

Portraiture and the Academy (rooms 1–15)

This marks the start of the official itinerary, on the second floor. Access is via the main staircase to the left of the foyer entrance.

The **eighteenth century** was a great watershed in Russian art, as secular painting and sculpture supplanted icons, with **portraiture** leading the way. While Peter the Great was the first to collect foreign paintings and sent native artists to be trained in Europe, it was his daughter Elizabeth who established the **Academy** (1757) that was to dominate Russian art until the second half of the nineteenth century. Its curriculum was modelled on the French Academy's and further circumscribed by Tsarist censorship: artists were told to stick to Classical themes, safe genre scenes or flattering portraits. Since state commissions accounted for much of their earnings, most obliged – or worked abroad.

Room 1 displays work by foreign artists who worked in Russia and early native painters such as **Ivan Nikitin** (c.1680–1742), whose vivid portraits of Peter the Great's sister Natalya and Chancellor Golovkin didn't save him from being denounced as a traitor during the reign of Empress Anna. **Sculpture** was slower to develop, the first real Russian master being **Fedot Shubin** (1740–1805), whose busts of aristocrats appear in **Room 2**.

Alexei Antropov (1716–95) was a trained icon painter who turned to portraiture under the tutelage of the Italian Pietro Rotari. His flamboyant *Peter III*, in **Room 3**, stands comparison with the work of another pupil of Rotari's, **Fyodor Rokotov** (1736–1808), whose later use of soft indirect lighting and silvery olive hues has been likened to Gainsborough. Of the many serf artists trained at the expense of the Sheremetevs, the most talented was **Ivan Argunov** (1729-1802), whose *Unknown Woman in Russian Dress* (**Room 4**) was said to embody the Russian ideal of feminine beauty.

A better-known subject is Catherine the Great, an enthusiastic patron of the arts whom the Ukrainian-born **Dmitry Levitsky** (1732–1822) depicted as the law-giver against a backdrop of drapery and smoke (**Room 5**). Typical of the state portraits that she gave as gifts to other monarchs, it's less revealing than the picture of the Empress walking her dog at Tsarskoe Selo in a dressing gown, by Levitsky's pupil, **Vladimir Borovikovsky** (1735–1825), which hangs in **Room 7**. Of historical interest are the views of Red Square and the Neva in St Petersburg by **Fyodor Alexeev** (1753–1824), and the *Portrait of Paul I* by **Stepan Shchukin** (1762–1828), in **Room 6**.

Russia's first Romantic painter was **Orest Kiprensky** (1782–1836), the illegitimate son of a nobleman and a serf, who became involved with the Decembrists while painting his *Portrait of*

Pushkin and died in exile from tuberculosis (**Room 8**). Two of his contemporaries who also spent many years in Italy but managed to become Academicians in Russia were **Karl Bryullov** (1799–1852) and **Alexander Ivanov** (1806–58). Bryullov is best known for his *The Last Day of Pompeii*, in the Russian Museum, but his love of melodrama is apparent from a sketch for *Gaiseric's Invasion of Rome* (**Room 9**). Ivanov's monumental *Christ Among the People*, which dominates **Room 10**, was the result of years of preparatory sketches, exhibited alongside mementos of his Italian sojourn such as *Apollo with Youths* and *Olive Trees at Albano* in **Room 11**.

Room 13 exhibits sugary genre portraits by **Vasily Tropinin** (1776–1857), who trained as a confectioner before graduating from the Academy at the age of 48. More interesting – though not as bitingly satirical as some of his other works – are three pictures by **Pavel Fedotov** (1815–52), who was censored and finally expelled by the Academy, went mad and died in an asylum. *The Major's Courtship* depicts a merchant's daughter recoiling from the attentions of a preening soldier, *The New Chevalier* a minor official exalting over a medal in his dressing gown, and *The Aristocrat's Breakfast* a dissolute youth surprised by visitors (**Room 15**).

Realists and Wanderers (rooms 16–31, 35–37)

This section (rooms 16–31) is accessible from Room 15 on the second floor, and continues on the floor below (rooms 35–37), which can be reached by a staircase off Room 32.

The **second half of the nineteenth century** saw genre painting become increasingly infused with **realism** and concern for social issues, reflecting a growing civic consciousness in society. In 1863 fourteen of the Academy's most talented pupils refused to paint the mythological subject set by their examiners, and left to set up an artists' co-operative that was the genesis (1870) of the Society for Travelling Art Exhibitions, known as the **Wanderers** (*peredvizhniki*), which evaded censorship by exhibiting in the provinces, and heralded a wave of artistic movements that washed over Russia as the Revolution approached.

Room 16 suggests that the Tsarist censors tolerated criticism of society but not of autocracy itself. **Vasily Pukirev** (1832–90) could highlight the plight of a maiden forced to marry an old roué in *The Unequal Marriage*, and **Valery Yakobi** (1834–92) the brutality of the penal system in *A Halt for Convicts on the Road to Siberia*, whereas **Konstantin Flavitsky** (1830–66) took refuge in allegory by portraying Princess Tarakanova, drowning in her cell, as an innocent victim of state oppression.

Princess Tarakanova's story is related on p.280.

The Siberian **Vasily Perov** (1834–82) caused a furore with his *Village Easter Procession* – showing a drunken priest lurching from an inn – but silenced critics with his penetrating *Portrait of Dostoyevsky* and large-scale historical works such as *The Dispute on Faith* and *The Judgement of Pugachov* (**Room 17**).

Rooms 18 & 19 show the emergence of **landscape painting** as a lyrical genre. The leader of the Moscow school was **Alexei Sarasov**

(1830–97), whose *The Rooks Have Returned* is to Russian landscape painting what Pushkin's *Yevgeny Onegin* is to Russian literature, while **Fyodor Vasiliev** (1850–73) was akin to Lermontov in his romanticization of the Crimea. **Ivan Aivazovsky** (1817–1900) captured the essence of storms in his *Black Sea* and *The Rainbow*, while **Alexei Bogolyubov** (1824–96) made his name with views of St Petersburg.

The moving spirit of the Wanderers was **Ivan Kramskoy** (1837–87), renowned for his portraits of Tolstoy, for a pert *Nameless Lady* who is thought to have been the model for Anna Karenina, and for a melancholy Slavic *Christ in the Wilderness* which Kramskoy painted because "The Italian Christ is handsome, one may say divine, but he is alien to me" **(Room 20)**.

While most of the Wanderers agreed with the socialist Chernyshevsky that art is only valid if socially engaged, the Academy venerated the cult of beauty and antiquity, epitomized by the titillating *Sword Dance* and *An Orgy in Tiberius' Day* in **Room 22**, by **Genrikh Semiradsky** (1843–1902). Conversely, **Vasily Maximov** (1844–1911) quit the Academy to paint peasant life, treating the twilight of the gentry as sympathetically as the plight of landless labourers **(Room 23)**.

The 1860s and 1870s were a time of soul-searching over Russia's national identity. **Viktor Vasnetsov** (1846–1926) was a founder of the Neo-Russian style and avowed Russia's Slavic heritage in scenes like *Three Warriors* and *After the Battle of Igor and Svyatoslavich with the Polovtsians* **(Room 26)**, while **Vasily Vereshchagin** (1842–1904) dwelt on the horrors of warfare and the barbaric splendours of Central Asia before the "civilizing" rule of the Tsars **(Room 27)**.

Russia's foremost historical painter, **Vasily Surikov** (1846–1916), is represented by four huge canvases in **Room 28**. While *The Morning of the Execution of the Streltsy on Red Square*, the *Boyaryna Morozova* being dragged away to meet her death for heresy and *The Conquest of Siberia by Yermak* all depict famous events, *Menshikov in Berezovo* shows the disgraced ex-Prince brooding in a Siberian hut on his days of fortune under Peter the Great.

Rooms 29 & 30 are devoted to the great realist **Ilya Repin** (1844–1930), whose populist sympathies were expressed in *Barge-Haulers on the Volga* (in the Russian Museum) and narrative works like *They Did Not Expect Him*, portraying a dissident's return from exile. Notice, too, the anguished Ivan the Terrible cradling his dying son, and Repin's frank portrait of the alcoholic composer Mussorgsky.

Although **Nicholas Ge** (1831–94) reinterpreted biblical themes like Calvary and the Garden of Gethsemane in a strikingly original style that prefigured Expressionism, the public preferred his

Academic historical works, particularly *Peter the Great Interrogating Tsarevich Alexei at Peterhof* (**Room 31**).

At this point one is meant to go **downstairs** to view the remainder of the Wanderers on the floor below – but as this entails passing through the Vrubel hall (Room 32/33) you're likely to get sidetracked (see below).

Sticking to the itinerary, you'll wind up in **Room 35**, displaying genre landscapes by **Vasily Polonev** (1884–1927), including his popular favourites *Moscow Courtyard* and *Grandmother's Garden*. **Room 36** is notable for scenes of medieval Moscow by **Apollinarius Vasnetsov** (1856-1933), the brother of Viktor (see above), and a vivid portrait of Tchaikovsky by **Nikolai Kuznetsov** (1850–1929).

The Wanderers section concludes in **Room 37** with **Isaak Levitan** (1860–1900), the finest Russian landscapist of the nineteenth century, revered for his limpid rivers and soft light, in works like *The Evening Bells* and *Eternal Peace*.

Zamosk-vareche

Romantics, Symbolists and the avant-garde (rooms 32–34, 38–48)

Many artists who began as Wanderers subsequently became Slav **Romantics**, in thrall to the Russian countryside or ancient legends, while the following generation tended towards **Symbolism**. Post-Impressionism, Symbolism and Expressionism reached Russia almost simultaneously, producing a heady brew whose ferment equalled that of Western European art, but also coincided with a political avalanche. The Russian **avant-garde** was the most dynamic in Europe – and the shortest lived; its exponents either emigrated and became absorbed into other cultures, or remained in Russia to see their ideas stifled.

This section is divided between two floors. Rooms 32–34 are reached by a short flight of steps from room 31, while a parallel staircase near-by leads down-stairs to rooms 38–48, which are also acces-sible by the stairs off the right-hand side of the basement foyer.

Mikhail Vrubel (1856–1940) had an impact on Russian art akin to that of Cézanne in the West, founding the Symbolist and Art Nouveau movements that began the revolt against realism. A lofty hall (**Room 33**) displays giant canvases and panels designed for the mansions of wealthy patrons like Morozov. *The Demon* is one of a series inspired by Lermontov's poem of the same name, which obsessed Vrubel to the point of madness. In 1902, on the night before the opening of the fourth World of Art exhibition, he locked himself in the gallery with a bottle of champagne and totally repainted it; the next morning he was found gibbering incoherently and committed to an asylum.

By contrast, **Mikhail Nesterov** (1862–1942) was inspired by Orthodox spirituality. *The Child Bartholomew's Vision* depicts the moment when St Sergei of Radonezh first felt the touch of God (see p.388), the life of the monks of Solovetskiy Monastery is captured in *Silence* and *The Hermit*, while *The Soul of the People* embodies Nesterov's view of Russia as a spiritual ethnos (**Room 34**).

Zamosk-
vareche

Roerich's work is better represented in the Roerich Museum (p.149).

To check out the rest you must go downstairs, where **Room 38** displays the varied work of Romantics such as **Nikolai Roerich** (1874–1947), for whom the Kievan Rus and Eastern civilizations were spiritual lodestars; **Andrei Ryabushkin** (1861–1904), who depicted medieval Muscovy; the landscapist **Konstantin Yuon** (1875–1958); and **Filipp Malyavin** (1869–1940), whose electrifying crimson *Whirlwind* dominates the room.

Symbolism and Art Nouveau (called Style Moderne in Russia) originally centred on the **World of Art** (*Mir istkusstva*) movement in St Petersburg, led by Diaghilev and Benois, the creators of the *Ballet Russe*. Many of its sets were designed by **Leon Bakst** (1866–1924) and **Alexander Golovin** (1863-1930), who applied the techniques of the stage to easel painting, as in Bakst's *Siamese Sacred Dance* and Golovin's splendid portrait of Chaliapin in the role of Holofernes (**Room 40**).

Room 40 is next door to the Medieval art section.

After Vrubel, the most influential Symbolist was **Viktor Borissov-Mussatov** (1870–1905), who was crippled in childhood and secretly lusted after his sister; his *Phantoms*, *The Pool* and *Sleep of the Gods* are brooding meditations on young womanhood (**Room 41**).

By the early 1900s Russian and Western art were evolving in tandem and mutually indebted, with Kandinsky and Chagall teaching in Munich and Paris, and international Symbolist exhibitions held in Moscow. The leading lights of Russia's Blue Rose movement of Symbolists were **Pavel Kuznetsov** (1878–1968) and the Armenian **Martiros Saryan** (1880–1972), whose mysterious, static landscapes influenced the German *Blaue Reiter* school (**Room 42**).

The progenitors of the Russian avant-garde were **Mikhail Larionov** (1881–1964) and **Natalya Goncharova** (1881–1962), whose **Primitivism** assailed conventional values by depicting whores and soldiers in a style akin to traditional woodcuts, scrawled with doggerel and obscenities (**Room 43**). Influenced by Italian Futurism, Larionov then launched a new style called **Rayonism**, whose manifesto declared that the genius of the age consisted of "trousers, jackets, shoes, tramways, buses, aeroplanes . . .".

Larionov also organized the Jack of Diamonds exhibition of 1910, uniting young artists who rejected all previous trends in art, and stressed colour and texture over form and meaning. Their journey from Primitivism to analytical Cubism was anticipated by **Aristakh Lentulov** (1882–1943), whose coruscating *St Basil's Cathedral* is the star attraction of **Room 44**. However, Symbolism remained a vital force till the outbreak of war, especially in St Petersburg, where **Kozma Petrov-Vodkin** (1878–1939) painted his iconic *Bathing the Red Horse* (**Room 45**).

Marc Chagall (1887–1985) created a uniquely personal style that set him apart from the avant-garde. Chagall made the ordinary phantasmagoric, with scenes from family life and his provincial home town pervaded by angels, miracles and portents from Jewish folklore. **Room 46** also contains a couple of works by **David Burlyuk** (1882–1967), the flamboyant "father of Russian Futurism".

Futurism is a catch-all term for a plethora of styles and theories from 1910 to 1925, from the prankish "happenings" of Mayakovsky and the Burlyuk brothers to the cerebral works of Tatlin and Kandinsky. **Vladimir Tatlin** (1885–1953) moved beyond Primitivism to the concept of a "Culture of Materials" whose junk collages anticipated Dada. What came to be called **Constructivism** owed much to his experiments in theatre design with the director Meyerhold and the Cubist-Futurist painter **Lyubov Popova** (1889–1924), whose work hangs beside Tatlin's in **Room 47**.

The exhibition concludes in **Room 48** with a bravura show by the pioneers of **abstract art**, Kandinsky and Malevich. **Vasily Kandinsky** (1866–1944) saw art as a spiritual quest and painting as a cure for the angst of materialism, so it is hardly surprising that Bolshevik commissars branded his abstract *Compositions* and *Improvisations* "empty formalism". **Kazimir Malevich** (1878–1935) derived his Cubism-Futurism from the bold lines and colours of icons and woodcuts, and developed both to a pitch of theory that he termed **Suprematism**, the "art of pure sensation". His *Black Square* and *White On White* were first shown at an exhibition called "The Last Picture Has Been Painted".

In fact it was Futurism that perished, as Socialist Realism replaced abstractionism, and experiments in form gave way to traditional motifs in architecture and easel painting. That the Tretyakov owns any Futurist art at all is largely due to George Costakis (1921–1990), a Russian-born Greek who began collecting it in the 1940s when it was all but forgotten, and amassed nearly 300 paintings which he exhibited in his flat as the climate thawed, and finally sold to the state.

Graphic art and jewellery (rooms 49–55)

The last two sections of the Tretyakov are usually overlooked by visitors unless they end up there by accident, but it's worth seeing what's there as some of it is top class. If you only have an hour to spend in the gallery, the **Graphic art** section (Rooms 49–54) on the first floor offers a speeded-up *tour d'horizon* of Russian art, with engravings, drawings and watercolours by many of the artists whose oils hang in other rooms. Its highlights include Levitan's *Autumn*, Surikov's Spanish watercolours, scads of gouaches by the World of Art crowd, and studies from the folios of Chagall, Malevich, Kandinsky and Popova.

Room 54 gives access to the **Jewellery** gallery, a single long room of showcases displaying pearl-embroidered veils that shrouded icons of the Virgin in the sixteenth century, the icon of St Nicholas of Mozhaisk that once stood above the Kremlin's St Nicholas Gate, and others set in magnificent silver frames. You can also see items of jewellery made by rival workshops to the House of Fabergé.

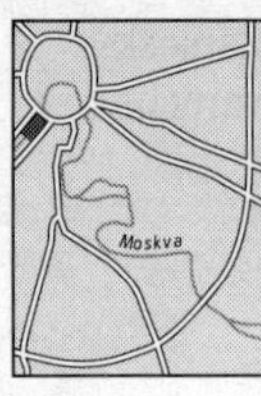

Krymskiy val and Gorky Park

Named after the bygone "Crimean Rampart" of the Zemlyanoy Gorod, the Krymskiy val is the only part of the Garden Ring's southern arc that tourists are likely to be concerned with, running as it does past Gorky Park, the new Tretyakov Gallery and the Central House of Artists. Aside from these, there's the attraction of the riverside vistas of Stalinist monoliths and Tsereteli's colossal monument to Peter the Great.

Both ways of **getting there** involve a ten- to fifteen-minute walk from a metro station. It's better to start from Park Kultury (below) and cross over the bridge rather than begin at Oktyabryskaya (see p.250). That way, your appetite for Soviet leisure culture is whetted by the bas-reliefs in Park Kultury station, and further aroused by the grand arch at the entrance to the park, as its planners intended. During summer, you can also get there by boat from Kiev Station (see p.376).

Gorky Park (Park Kultury)

Gorky Park is open daily: summer 10am–10pm; winter 10am–9pm. Adults $1.50, children (5–17 years) $1.

Better known to Muscovites as Park Kultury, **Gorky Park** is famous abroad from Martin Cruz Smith's classic thriller of the same name, which opens with the discovery of three faceless corpses in the snow, setting investigator Renko on the trail of a wealthy American. The reality is less sinister but still a bit creepy in another way, as Pepsi culture flourishes amid the relics of a totalitarian regime's fun side.

Inaugurated in 1928, the Soviet Union's first "Park of Culture and Rest" was formed by uniting an exhibition zone near the Krymskiy val with the vast gardens of the Golitsyn Hospital and the Neskuchniy Palace, totalling 300 acres. In winter, recalled Fitzroy Mclean, "the whole of it was flooded, and on skates one could go skimming along for miles over brilliantly lighted frozen avenues to the strains of Vienna waltzes and Red Army marches".

Nowadays, three funfairs constitute the main attraction, though not all the rides operate over winter. Thrill-seekers go for the one beside the river, offering **bungee-jumping** ($15) from 50m, two **roller coasters** and a **water chute**, whose rides ($4–5) are more exciting than a "flight" in the *Buryan*, a retired Soviet **space shuttle** linked to a series of domes offering a "cosmic experience". The build-up to the ride is fun, but its gyroscopic chairs do a poor job of simulating zero gravity, so you basically pay to see thirty minutes of videos, and some spacesuits. It seems an ignominious end for the *Buryan*, which made a trial orbit of the earth under remote control in 1988 and might have carried cosmonauts into space had not the Soviet space programme virtually collapsed a few years later.

During summer kids can enjoy the Wondertown and Fantastic Journey fun houses; the carousels and electronic games work all year; and rollerbladers turn out in force whenever the weather's fine.

Nor does winter dampen spirits: the **ice disco** is jumping at weekends and most evenings, and in February the park hosts a **festival of ice sculptures**. On national holidays and at weekends over summer, hydrofoils depart from the landing stage beside Gorky Park on sightseeing cruises through the heart of Moscow (see p.376). However, **beware of visiting** on the days dedicated to Russia's Border Guards (May 28), Navy (last Sun in July) or Airborne Forces (Aug 2), or whenever Luzhniki Stadium hosts a match between Spartak, Dinamo or TsKA, as the park is full of drunken servicemen or football fans, spoiling for a fight.

Krymskiy val and Gorky Park

The Central House of Artists and the new Tretyakov Gallery

On the other side of Krymskiy val, Vuchetich's "Swords into Ploughshares" (a copy of the original sculpture presented to the UN in 1957) and other allegorical statues greet visitors to a vast, box-like complex that houses two large galleries under one roof. The **Central House of Artists** (*Tsentralniy dom Khudozhnikov*) is Moscow's main showcase for international exhibitions and modern art from all over the former USSR (Tues–Sun 11am–8pm; $0.50), with several shows running concurrently. It also contains furniture showrooms, so don't be surprised if paintings suddenly give way to sofas and sideboards.

Around the east side of the building is the entrance to the **new Tretyakov Gallery**, which takes up where the old Tretyakov left off. As the works in its collection are rotated at intervals, or moved around to make space for temporary exhibitions, it's impossible to say what you'll find where – but it's worth looking out for certain artists and paintings.

The new Tretyakov Gallery is open Tues–Sun 10am–7.30pm; $7.50. To arrange a guided tour in English ($14 plus admission ticket) ☎ 953 52 23 or 238 20 54.

Among the pre-revolutionary artists obliged to change their style or subject matter under the Soviet regime, **Mikhail Nesterov** turned to painting portraits of scientists, and **Konstantin Yuon**'s sci-fi visions of the Revolution soon gave way to more prudent scenes like *A Parade on Red Square*. Of the new generation of Soviet artists, **Alexander Deineka** and **Yuri Pimenov** each produced a gritty masterpiece – *The Defenders of Petrograd* and *Heavy Industry* – but subsequently depicted athletes with far less verve, while others welcomed the return of academic art. Were it not for the Red Stars on the locomotives, **Boris Yakovlev**'s *Transport Siding* could pass for an Impressionist's view of a train station. Alexander Gerasimov's *Stalin and Vorishilov in the Grounds of the Kremlin* and **Boris Ioaganson**'s *Interrogation of the Communists* are more overtly ideological (Ioganson succeeded Gerasimov as president of the Academy), while the cloying optimism associated with Socialist Realism is epitomized by **Andrei Mylnikov**'s *In Peaceful Fields*.

In the Brezhnev era the gulf between official and "underground" art became a point of reference for conformists and non-conformists

Krymskiy val and Gorky Park

alike, with a "dissident" subculture typified by the bohemian **Mytki**, whose paintings and rhymes were reminiscent of Primitivism – but also by **Ilya Glazunov**, whose works exalting Tsarism and Orthodoxy were privately admired by nationalists in the Politiburo and anticipated the reactionary art beloved of Mayor Luzhkov. Perestroika saw the rise of SotsArt – subverting the genre of Socialist Realism – and the absurdities of the Yeltsin era were mirrored by the Actionists, who aimed to shock with stunts, about which the Tretyakov is understandably reticent. **Oleg Kulik** was arrested for chaining himself naked to a kennel, while **Alexander Brener** made headlines by spraying a dollar sign on a Malevich in protest against the commercialization of art – though cynics noted that he defaced one in Holland, where his crime rated some months in an open prison, rather than in Russia, where he would have been punished by fifteen years in a hard-labour camp.

Current exhibitions are listed on Saturdays in the Moscow Times.

Less likely to be under wraps is the outdoor **Sculptural Park** (daily 10am–9pm; free) out back. This started out as a graveyard of Communist monuments that gave pride of place to the statue of "Iron Felix" Dzerzhinsky that stood outside the Lubyanka until it was toppled in 1991, but has since become a refuge for all kinds of figures, including a sappy-looking Einstein, and Niels Böhr. The big daddy of them all is Tsereteli's Peter the Great (p.232), which towers in the background, spectacularly floodlit at night.

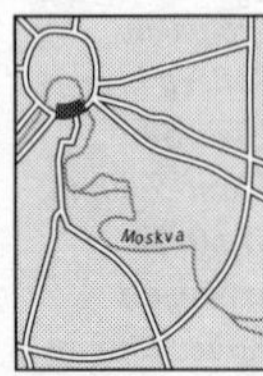

Oktyabrskaya, Leninskiy prospekt and Pavelets Station

For tourists, everywhere beyond Gorky Park is reducible to a few clusters of attractions miles apart, and the avenues and metro lines that connect them. **Oktyabrskaya ploshchad** (October Square) is an urban showpiece from the Era of Stagnation: ugly blocks that count as prestigious accommodation, frowning over an arterial junction and the last **statue of Lenin** to be erected in Moscow (in 1985). Bestriding a plinth embossed with peasants and workers fired by his vision, he is cast as a Titan of world history – now reduced to insignificance by the giant satellite dishes and neon hoardings on Oktyabrskaya's skyline. However, he still attracts followers: the National Bolshevik Party **rallies** here on November 7, in honour of the October Revolution (arrive by 9am to witness the spectacle).

There are two fine sights 150m north of here, on ulitsa Bolshaya Yakimanka. The **Igumnov House**, built for a rich merchant in 1893, is a Neo-Russian fantasy of peaked roofs and gables, pendant arches, coloured tiles and a blend of Gothic, Byzantine and Baroque decor. While tales that Igumnov buried his mistress in one of the walls and the architect hanged himself in the hallway are probably untrue, the mansion did later contain the Institute of the Brain, where Lenin's brain was cut into thirty thousand slices and studied, with the aim of discovering the source of his genius – a procedure later applied to the brains of Stalin, Pavlov, Gorky, Eisenstein, Mayakovsky and Sakharov. In 1938 the house became the **French Embassy**, a role better suited to its splendid decor, but you can't see inside the building except as a guest of the Ambassador.

Oktyabrskaya, Leninskiy prospekt and Pavelets Station

Directly opposite stands the gaudily painted **Church of St John the Warrior** (*tserkov Ivana Voina*), one of the few buildings erected in Moscow under Peter the Great, who is said to have personally chosen its site and even sketched out a plan. Its construction (1709–13) was entrusted to Ivan Zarudny, whose design married the configuration of a Moscow Baroque church with new European decorative forms. The interior is obviously European in its lavish use of sculptural mouldings, but holds such native treasures as the *Icon of the Saviour* that once hung above the Saviour Gate of the Kremlin. St John's became the custodian of all kinds of relics, as it was one of the few churches in Moscow to escape closure in the 1920–30s. Its saint's feast day falls on August 12.

Leninskiy prospekt

Leninskiy prospekt is Moscow's longest avenue, running for 14km from Oktyabrskaya ploshchad to the outer Ring Road. The initial 2.8km stretch as far as ploshchad Gagarina is flanked on one side by Stalinist blocks, and on the other by Gorky Park and two eighteenth-century palatial buildings. The **Golitsyn Hospital** was a charitable bequest from Russia's ambassador to Vienna and now contains an orphanage run by nuns, while the Neskuchniy Palace was once the mansion of the mining magnate Demidov and now houses the **Russian Academy of Science**.

However, the main landmark is **ploshchad Gagarina**, where Leninskiy Prospekt metro exits behind a Stalinist apartment block that forms one half of a gigantic crescent defining the northern edge of the plaza, which used to be called Kaluga Gate Square. These flats for the elite were built by German POWs and Russian convicts – including Solzhenitsyn. Near the metro exit, the giant titanium **Gagarin Monument** resembles a muscular superhero braced to blast off on a column of energy. The square was renamed after tens of thousands of Muscovites turned out to welcome Gagarin as he arrived from Vnukovo Airport, following his sensational orbit around Earth in April 1961.

Around Pavelets Station

From Oktyabrskaya, the Circle line and trolleybus 6 run to **Pavelets Station** (*Paveletskiy vokzal*), designed in the nineteenth century to resemble a Loire Valley chateau and tastefully modernized in the 1980s. To visit the sights on either side of the traffic-choked square

Oktyabrskaya, Leninskiy prospekt and Pavelets Station

outside, use the long underpass that connects Pavelets Station to the northern exit of Paveletskaya metro.

Behind a cluster of kiosks to the east of the station is a small park harbouring a pavilion containing the **Lenin Funerary Train** (Mon–Fri 10am–6pm; free). Though now a car showroom, its glory is still the gleaming orange and black steam engine and wagon that brought Lenin's body to Moscow on January 23, 1924, for his funeral on Red Square. A giant bust of Lenin gazes blindly from a flame-shaped aperture at the back of the hall, and you can also see a model of a weird Lenin monument consisting of a pyramid of pumps and wheels symbolizing the dynamism of Communism. The inscription on the wall outside the pavilion asserts: "The name of V.I. Lenin is immortal, like his ideas and his deeds."

The Theatre Museum is open Mon–Fri 10am–6pm; free.

While Lenin's train is a surreal set piece, there's more to see in the **Theatre Museum** across the square on the corner of ulitsa Bakrushina, housed in a Neo-Gothic mansion once owned by the theatrical impresario Alexei Bakhrushin. Downstairs are opera set designs for *Boris Godunov* and *Ivan the Terrible*, and costumes worn by Chaliapin in the title role of Boris. Upstairs there's a gorgeous puppet theatre; Nijinsky's dancing shoes; decadent gouache designs by Michael Fokine; and stage-models for Constructivist dramas like *Zori*, which involved architects and painters. Though poorly laid out and only captioned in Russian, the museum should appeal to aficionados of theatre history or design.

The Museum of Wood is open Wed–Sun 10am–6pm; $2. ☎956 15 61.

By contrast, the **Museum of Wood** is superbly designed, with a genuine river flowing the length of its first floor in a granite riverbed, living trees and a mock-up forest complete with stuffed wildlife and realistic sound effects. A ship's bow and a nineteenth-century peasant *izba* (log cabin) are among the exhibits. The museum is sited at 3-y Monetchikovskiy pereulok 4, in the backstreets off Pyatnitskaya ulitsa, about ten minutes' walk from the Theatre Museum – but be sure to phone to check if it's open, as it doesn't always conform to schedule.

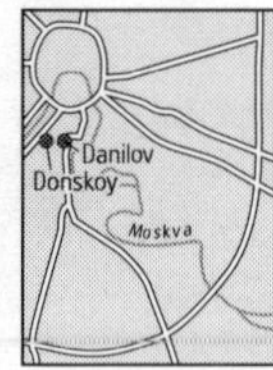

The Donskoy and Danilov monasteries

Indisputably the main attractions in this part of Moscow, the Donskoy and Danilov monasteries originally stood a mile or so beyond the city walls, playing a vital role as defensive outposts and sanctuaries. After decades of misuse, the monasteries once again draw believers who pray before their icons and relics, while tourists are enticed by the historical associations and architecture. While both monasteries are interesting, the Donskoy is far more atmospheric, with a beautiful cemetery. The Danilov's own cemetery lies further south, near the city's main Muslim burial ground.

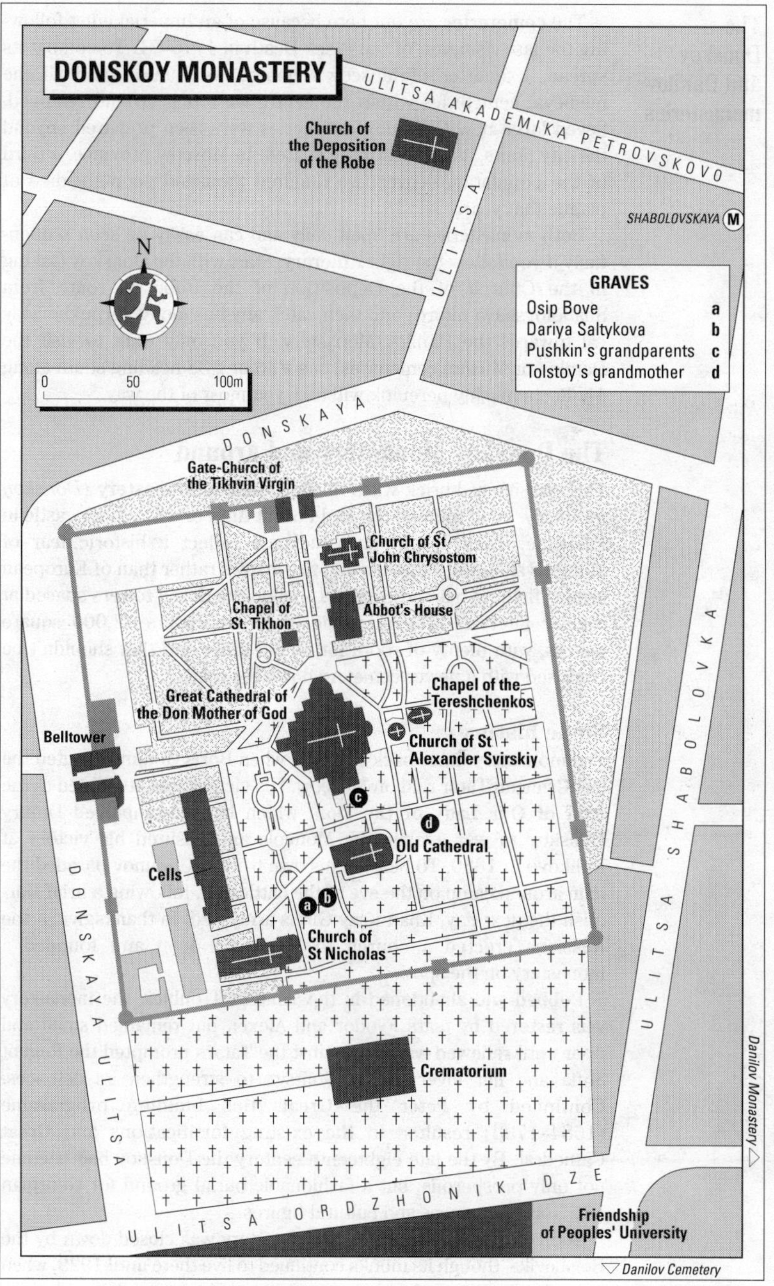
DONSKOY MONASTERY
ULITSA AKADEMIKA PETROVSKOVO
Church of the Deposition of the Robe
ULITSA
SHABOLOVSKAYA M
N
GRAVES
Osip Bove a
Dariya Saltykova b
Pushkin's grandparents c
Tolstoy's grandmother d
0 50 100m
DONSKAYA
Gate-Church of the Tikhvin Virgin
Church of St John Chrysostom
Chapel of St. Tikhon
Abbot's House
Great Cathedral of the Don Mother of God
Chapel of the Tereshchenkos
Belltower
Church of St Alexander Svirskiy
Old Cathedral
Cells
Church of St Nicholas
ULITSA SHABOLOVKA
DONSKAYA ULITSA
Crematorium
Danilov Monastery
ULITSA ORDZHONIKIDZE
Friendship of Peoples' University
Danilov Cemetery

The **cemeteries** are out here because of an Imperial edict following the last visitation of the Black Death in 1770–71. To combat its spread, a quarter of Moscow's houses were burnt and all the medieval cemeteries within the centre were dug up and removed. Seven large new Orthodox cemeteries were then prepared beyond the city limits, as the death toll soared. In Moscow province, a third of the population – over two hundred thousand people – died of plague that year.

Both monasteries are open daily and can easily be seen sequentially if you follow the right **itinerary**. Start with the Donskoy (taking in the Church of the Deposition of the Robe en route from Shabolovskaya metro) and then catch any bus along Serpukhovskiy val towards the Danilov Monastery. If you only want to visit the Danilov or Muslim cemeteries, bus #26 or #38 heading south along 1-y Roshchinskiy pereulok will take you most of the way.

The Donskoy Monastery and around

The massive red-brick walls of the **Donskoy Monastery** (*Donskoy monastyr*) call to mind the Red Fort at Agra or a Crusader castle in Palestine. Their height and thickness reflect a historic fear of Mongols shooting catapults and fire-arrows rather than of European armies fielding massed cannons – as do the dozen towers spaced at regular intervals. The monastic enclosure covers 42,000 square metres, with plenty of room for an old graveyard that shouldn't be confused with a newer cemetery down the road.

Some history

The monastery dates back to 1591, when Boris Godunov routed the last Crimean Tatar raid on Moscow. His victory was attributed to the **icon of Our Lady of the Don**, which had accompanied Dmitry Donskoy to war against the Mongols and ensured his victory at Kulikovo in 1380. To hearten his own troops, Godunov paraded the icon around camp on the eve of the battle and, following a brief skirmish the next day, Khan Kazy-Gire's army fled. In thanksgiving, the Russians erected a church to house the icon and founded a monastery on the spot.

Robbed and abandoned in the Time of Troubles, the monastery was restored by tsars Fyodor and Alexei, but remained small and poor until renewed warfare against the Tatars prompted the Regent Sofia and her lover Prince Golitsyn to strengthen its defences. Continued by Peter the Great, this building programme (1684–1733) resulted in the existing fortifications and Great Cathedral. By the late eighteenth century the Donskoy had become not only prosperous, but a fashionable burial ground for Georgian and Golitsyn princes and cultural figures.

Soon after the Revolution the monastery was closed down by the Bolsheviks, though its monks continued to live there until 1929, when they were evicted to make way for a **Museum of Atheism**. The monastery's hospital had by then been converted into Moscow's first **crematorium**, to promote secular funerals. During the mid-1930s it incinerated thousands of corpses – including Bukharin's – delivered at night from the Lubyanka or the Military Collegium, whose ashes were shovelled into pits and asphalted over. Meanwhile, the erstwhile monastery became a branch of the **Shchusev Architectural Museum**, collecting sculptures from demolished churches across Moscow.

Though services resumed at the Old Cathedral in 1946, it wasn't until 1992 that **Patriarch Tikhon**'s sanctified body was laid to rest there with due honours. Invested as Patriarch on the eve of the Revolution, he had been jailed by the Bolsheviks and buried in an unmarked grave within the monastery in 1925. Soon after his reburial a fire destroyed all the icons in the cathedral except *Our Lady of the Don*, and when restorers opened the tomb to check for damage they found his body to be uncorrupted. He was then canonized by the Orthodox Church. Today, the monastery has largely been restored and harbours a publishing house, a studio for restoring icons and an embroidery and icon-painting school for children, while the new cemetery now contains a **monument to the victims of the purges**.

The monastery

You enter the monastery from Donskaya ulitsa by a chunky **gateway** designed by Trezzini, surmounted by a three-tiered belltower added in the 1750s. Its medley of bells breaks a tranquil hush, as the noises of the city are muted by the monastery's high walls and drowned by crows cawing from the trees.

The Donskoy Monastery is open daily 7am–7pm; admission free.

At the exact centre of the complex rises the **Great Cathedral of the Don Mother of God** (*Bolshoy sobor Donskoy Bogomateri*), also known as the "New Cathedral" (*Noviy sobor*). Composed of four rotund tower bays grouped around a central drum beneath five bronze domes, this was one of the largest structures of its time, begun in 1684 under Golitsyn and finally finished in 1698. It is only open for major festivals, and services at weekends (Sat 5pm; Sun 8am). The interior features Apocryphal frescoes and images of the saints framed by fruity wreaths, and is dominated by a huge seven-tiered iconostasis that took four years to carve. During the plague, Archbishop Amvrosy hid behind it to escape an angry mob, but was found, dragged out and beaten to death.

Founded in tandem with the monastery, the small **Old Cathedral** (*Stariy sobor*) resembles a simple Moscow Baroque church, painted a soft russet, with tiers of green-and-white *kokoshniki* and a blue onion dome. The interior is low, white and vaulted, its floor polished by a stream of worshippers. All light a candle to the **icon** of *Our Lady of the Don* (a copy of the fourteenth-century original in the Tretyakov), and many prostrate themselves before **St Tikhon's relics**, in a gilded casket which is carried into the Great Cathedral on the Feast of the Annunciation (April 7). Other holy days marked at the Donskoy include the feast days of the Don Virgin (September 1) and St Fyodor Stratilites (February 21).

The cemetery

The monastery's two cathedrals are surrounded by a **cemetery** crammed with headstones and monuments. If you can read Cyrillic, each plot is identified by a map-board naming the famous Russians buried there – though the only ones likely to register with foreigners all have disappointingly plain graves. The architect Osip Bove rates a black granite slab next to one shaped like a bomb, while the serf-murdering Countess Dariya Saltykova is recalled by an obelisk without any inscription. Still more nondescript are the graves of Tolstoy's grandmother and Pushkin's grandparents.

The dark red **Church of St Nicholas** was built in 1806–09 as the private chapel of the Golitsyns. Nearby stands the tent-roofed Neo-Russian **Chapel of the Tereshchenkos**, decorated with Orthodox crosses and raised in 1899. Best of all is the Neo-Byzantine **Church of St John Chrysostom** (*tserkov Ioanna Zlatousta*), built by the Pervushins in 1891, past the Abbot's House and the recently built Chapel of St Tikhon (where his relics may be kept in the future).

Beyond it rises the **Gate-Church of the Tikhvin Virgin**, an imposing structure that is one of the last examples of Moscow Baroque. It was completed in 1713, the year after Peter the Great moved the capital to St Petersburg and forbade building in stone anywhere else in Russia, to spur the creation of his city on the Neva.

Other sights

Depending on which route you take from Shabolovskaya metro station, you may see a couple of other buildings that rate a mention. The **Church of the Deposition of the Robe** (*tserkov Ripolozheniya*), built in 1701, combines the traditional forms of a Moscow parish church with the attenuated drums and domes of the early medieval Yaroslavl style. Its ornamentation is similar to the gate-churches of Novodevichiy Convent, with white scalloped gables, double-crested *nalichniki* and engaged columns with acanthus-leaf capitals against a rose facade. The congregation are called to services by an amazingly deep bell, and a peal of smaller ones.

To the south of the Donskoy lies a gargantuan Stalin-style block housing several faculties of the **Friendship of Peoples University**, which was founded in 1960 to train students from the Third World. During Soviet times it bore the name of Patrice Lumumba, the murdered leader of the independence movement in the Belgian Congo, and was regarded by Western governments as a school for revolutionaries. Although Carlos "The Jackal" attended the university (and was expelled for rowdiness), the majority of its students bitched about the amount of time wasted studying Marxism-Leninism.

At the end of the road past the university, you can either cross the junction and head off along Serpukhovskiy val towards the Danilov Monastery, or catch bus #26 or #38 down 1-y Roshchinskiy pereulok to a pair of picturesque cemeteries.

The Donskoy and Danilov monasteries

The Danilov and Muslim cemeteries

Alighting at the 3-y Verkhniy Mikhailovskiy stop, before the bus turns off Roshchinskiy pereulok, a 200-metre walk will bring you to the **Danilov Cemetery** (*Danilovskoe kladbische*). Overgrown and archaic, its funerary monuments are as fine as those in the Donskoy's graveyard, owing to the numerous orthodox Metropolitans and nineteenth-century merchants buried here.

The **Muslim Cemetery** (*Musalmanskoe kladbishche*) lies 300m along a lane to the west. Established in 1771, its thousands of graves attest to a sizeable Muslim community in Moscow. Most of the headstones bear Tatar names, sometimes written in Arabic script. The most illustrious is that of **Imam Abdullah Shamsutdinov**, who was shot by the NKVD in the courtyard of his own mosque in 1937; his ashes were belatedly interred here in 1992. Normally frequented by a few amiable old Tatar ladies, the cemetery gets surprisingly busy on Islamic holidays.

Both cemeteries are open daily: summer 9am–7pm, winter 9am–6pm; admission free.

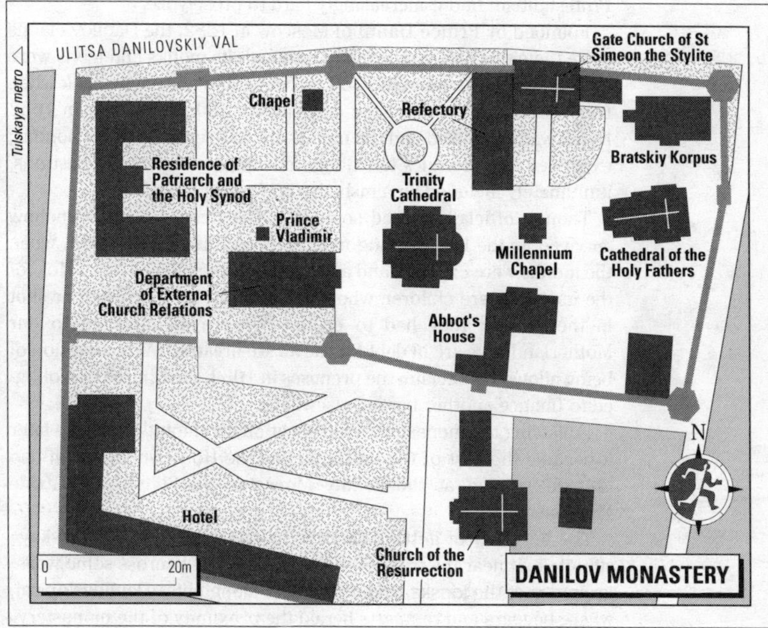

Serpukhovskiy val and the Danilov Market

There's little reason to walk 1km along **ulitsa Serpukhovskiy val** when you can ride a bus instead, though the avenue has a wooded central strip culminating in a Stalinesque flourish of giant urns and ornamental lamps. Like the Khamovnicheskiy val near Novodevichiy Convent, it once delineated the city's customs boundary, where goods entering or leaving Moscow were taxed. Despite being termed a *val* (rampart), it had no defensive purpose.

At the far end you can orientate yourself by the rusty domed **Danilov Market** (*Danilovskiy rynok*; daily 8am–7pm) on the corner of Mytnaya ulitsa, near Tulskaya metro. Pungent and colourful, the market is controlled by Cossack gangsters. Though it's fine to look around and taste the produce, taking photos could result in you being shown the exit by several beefy fellows. The Danilov Monastery is five minutes' walk from here.

The Danilov Monastery

As the official residence of the Russian Orthodox Patriarch, Alexei II, the **Danilov Monastery** (*Danilovskiy monastyr*) differs from Moscow's other monasteries in its modernity and businesslike air. While this might disappoint some visitors, it undeniably bespeaks the Orthodox Church's prestige and influence in the New Russia, which it wields to ensure that foreign religions such as Catholicism or Protestantism find it increasingly hard to proselytize.

Founded by **Prince Daniil** of Moscow in 1282, the Danilov claims to be the city's oldest monastery although its monks and icons were moved into the Kremlin in 1330 by Ivan I, and only came back when Ivan the Terrible revived the original site 230 years later. In 1652 Daniil was canonized and the monastery was renamed in his honour; expanded over decades behind a crenellated wall with ten bastions, it ultimately included an almshouse and a hospital.

Though officially closed soon after the Revolution, it somehow survived as the last working monastery in Russia until 1930, when the monks were expelled and a **borstal** was established here. Most of the inmates were children whose parents had been arrested or shot in the purges; they had to chant: "We are all indebted to our Motherland – we are in debt for the air we breathe." As a condition of being allowed to reclaim the premises in 1983, the Church was obliged to finance another borstal elsewhere.

Following the monastery's rededication ceremony, five years later it became the seat of the Patriarch and the Holy Synod, which had previously been at the Trinity Monastery of St Sergei, outside Moscow.

The best way of **getting there** is to catch the metro to Tulskaya station, exit near the front of the train, bear right across some waste ground past the kiosks, and walk 200m along ulitsa Danilovskiy val, where beggars and ramparts herald the proximity of the monastery.

The monastery

The Danilov Monastery is open daily 7am– 5pm; admission free, guided tour $4.

Visitors enter by the **Gate-Church of St Simeon the Stylite** (*Nadvodyashiy tserkov Simeonia Stolpnika*), which had to be entirely rebuilt since the original gate-tower was torn down in the 1920s and its bells sold to Harvard University. Painted a soft pink, with its archway framed by fat-bellied columns and an elaborate cornice, the gate is surmounted by a triple-tiered belltower inset with pictures of the saints, ending in a gold finial.

Inside the compound, you'll see some of the monastery's fifty monks putting the finishing touches to the administrative blocks and garden, while old women genuflect before the holy images on the walls of the churches – you may even spot a spurred and booted Cossack with a sabre, strutting across the yard. Straight ahead stands the gold-domed **Millennium Chapel**, with a quadruple arch erected to mark the millennial anniversary of Russian Orthodoxy in 1988.

A bronze **statue of Prince Vladimir** waves a crucifix near the turquoise building housing the **Department of External Church Relations**, while a huge gilded mosaic of the Saviour stares down from the modern **Residence of the Patriarch and the Holy Synod**, at the far end. The Patriarch is known to prefer living at the Trinity Monastery of Sergei or at his *dacha* in Peredelkino, outside Moscow, so is seldom in residence.

Relics of the canonized Prince Daniil are enshrined in two churches: the austerely Neoclassical **Trinity Cathedral** (*Troitskiy sobor*) built by Bove in the 1830s; and the seventeenth-century **Cathedral of the Holy Fathers** (*khram vo imya Svyatykh Ottsov*), with a deep porch and a refectory preceding two chapels, one dedicated to Daniil and the other to SS Boris and Gleb (feast day on August 6). Notice the sixteenth-century icons of *St Daniil* and *Our Lady of Vladimir*.

By passing through a gate in the rear wall, you'll find a large **hotel** for guests of the Patriarchate. Around the corner stands the **Church of the Resurrection**, a square-towered Neoclassical edifice.

Kolomenskoe

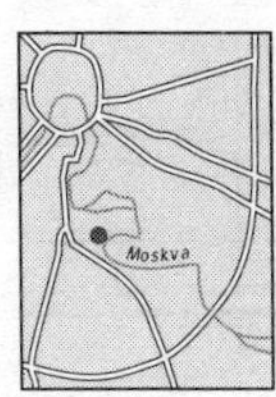

I have seen much in my life that I have admired and been astounded at, but the past, the ancient past of Russia which has left its imprint on this village, was for me something most miraculous . . . Here in the mysterious silence, amid the harmonious beauty of the finished form, I beheld an architecture of a new kind. I beheld man soaring on high. And I stood amazed.

Hector Berlioz, recalling Kolomenskoe in 1847

One of the most evocative sites in Moscow is the old royal estate of **Kolomenskoe**, on the steep west bank of the Moskva River, 10km southeast of the Kremlin. Though its legendary wooden palace no

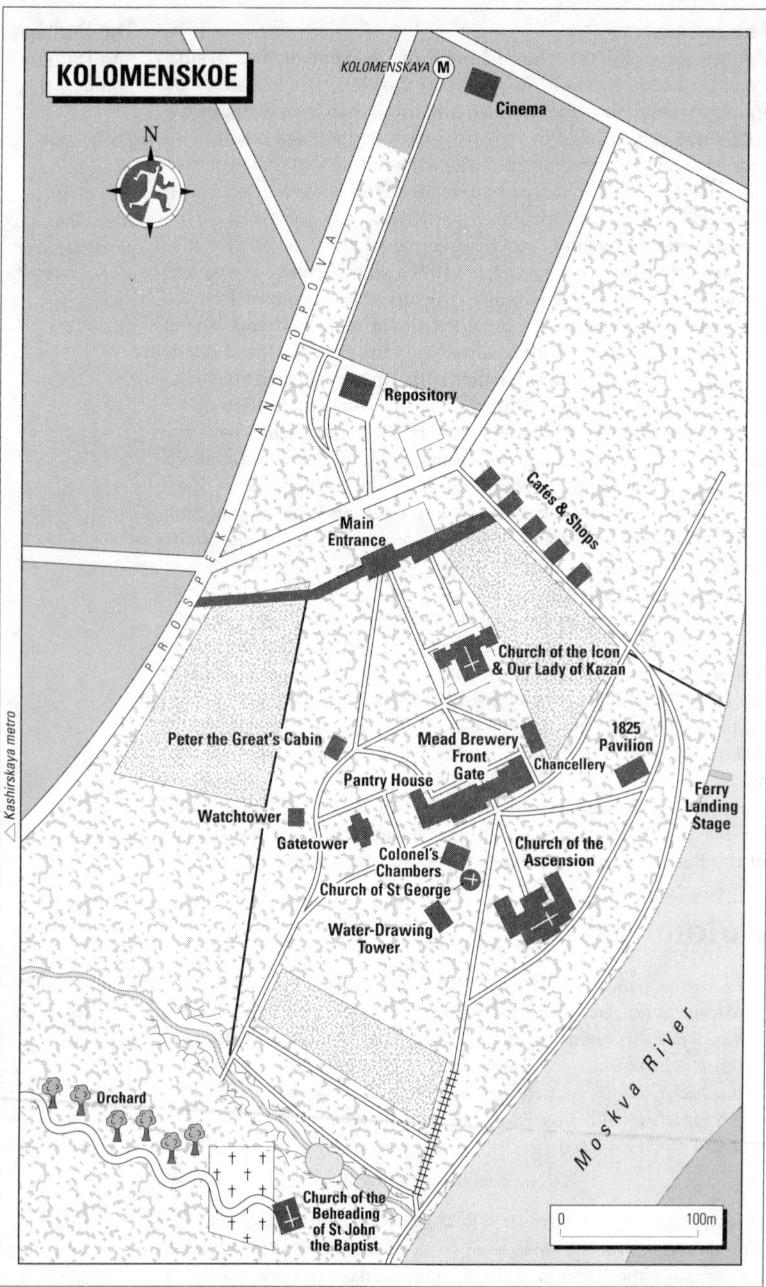
KOLOMENSKOE
N
KOLOMENSKAYA
M
Cinema
PROSPEKT ANDROPOVA
Repository
Cafés & Shops
Main Entrance
Church of the Icon & Our Lady of Kazan
Kashirskaya metro
Peter the Great's Cabin
Mead Brewery
Front Gate
Chancellery
1825 Pavilion
Pantry House
Ferry Landing Stage
Watchtower
Gatetower
Church of the Ascension
Colonel's Chambers
Church of St George
Water-Drawing Tower
Moskva River
Orchard
Church of the Beheading of St John the Baptist
0
100m

longer exists, Kolomenskoe still has one of the finest churches in the whole of Russia, and vintage wooden structures such as Peter the Great's cabin, set amid hoary oaks above a great bend in the river. In summer, Muscovites flock here for the fresh air and sunbathing; in winter, the eerie Church of the Ascension rises against a void of snow and mist as flocks of crows croak from the woods. If you make only one excursion to the edge of Moscow, it should be to Kolomenskoe.

While the earliest known settlement in the Moscow area existed nearby 2500 years ago, Kolomenskoe's **history** really begins in the thirteenth century, when a village was founded by refugees from Kolomna, a town destroyed by the Mongols. In the sixteenth century Kolomenskoe became a royal summer retreat, where Ivan the Terrible stayed as a child, and with his first wife, Anastasia. Though utterly destroyed by the Tatars in 1591, its palace was rebuilt by Mikhail Romanov, and superseded in 1667 by a wooden palace that Tsar Alexei's courtiers called the "eighth wonder of the world". As a child, Peter the Great took refuge there during the Streltsy revolt of 1682, and later held war games with his "toy" regiments on the estate.

Though Catherine the Great and Alexander I also built palaces, Kolomenskoe eventually reverted to being a mere village, whose fate was sealed after the Revolution. The cemetery was razed and the churches closed; then the village was destroyed by collectivization. It was only thanks to the architect Baranovsky that the churches were saved from ruin and a Museum of Wooden Architecture was established in the grounds in 1925, providing the justification to later declare it a conservation zone and spare 400 hectares of ancient woodland from the encroachment of flats. More recently it has been added to UNESCO's World Heritage List and amply funded by Mayor Luzhkov, so the site is now well cared for and its curators hope to create a village museum in the vicinity.

Practicalities, festivals and activities

Despite its distance from the centre, **getting there** is easy. From Teatralnaya metro, near the Bolshoy Theatre, it's only four stops to Kolomenskaya station. Take the exit near the front of the train; turn left in the underpass and then right at the end to surface at the correct spot. It's about ten minutes' walk along prospekt Andropova to the main entrance to the grounds of Kolomenskoe.

Opening hours and admission charges vary. You can wander around the grounds (daily: April–Aug 9am–10pm; Sept–March 9am–7pm) free of charge, but **tickets** are required to enter the Treasures of Kolomenskoe Museum (Tues–Sun 10.30am–7.30pm; $2), Peter's cabin (Tues–Sun 11am–5pm; $1), the 1825 Pavilion (same hours; $1) and the Church of the Ascension (same hours, May–Sept only; $1) – though admission to the church is free during services on Sundays (8–10am) and holy days. The museum *kassa*

Festivals at Kolomenskoe

As exact dates can vary from year to year, it's wise to confirm ahead by calling ☎112 81 74.

New Year (Jan 1–2)
A kids' festival round a Christmas tree, with Ded Moroz (Grandfather Frost), Leshy (wood sprites), the witch Baba Yaga, and other characters from Russian fairytales.

Christmas and Svyatki (Jan 7–19)
Following the all-night Orthodox Christmas service (Jan 6/7), the festival of *Syvatki* traditionally lasted until *Kreshenie*, or Epiphany (Jan 19), but at Kolomenskoe the masquerades, puppet theatre, songs, games and merry-making usually finish on the nearest Sunday to that date, with bell ringing and the blessing of the water.

Maslenitsa (Sat, one week before the beginning of Lent – usually in late Feb)
Based on the pagan spring festival that also marked the onset of Lent, it features performing bears, puppets, the building of snow forts and the burning of straw dolls, boxing matches, masquerades and giant swings. Everyone eats tons of pancakes, slathered in butter; the name *maslenitsa* comes from the Russian word for butter.

Easter Sunday (April 15, 2001)
Orthodoxy's chief holy day is marked by a ritual procession and a service in the Church of the Ascension.

My Moscow (May 1–2)
A May Day festival for residents of southern Moscow, with Orthodox music, and lots of handicrafts for sale.

Victory Day (May 9)
Military bands, a memorial service in the Church of the Icon of Our Lady of Kazan, and a fireworks display.

Peter the Great's Birthday (last Sun in May)
A pageant based on Peter's life and achievements, staged around his cabin.

Troitsa (first Sun in June)
Rituals surrounding the day of the dead, when families picnicked in cemeteries and girls wove garlands and told fortunes beside rivers or lakes.

Festival of Orthodox Spiritual Music (June–Sept)
A series of concerts in the Church of the Ascension; space is limited, so you must book tickets in advance.

Under St Andrew's Flag (last Sun in July).
A pageant in honour of Peter the Great's creation of the Russian Navy, with a regatta on the Moskva River.

Spasovki (Sat or Sun mid-Aug)
A traditional harvest festival, with folkloric displays and a big market selling honey, apples, nuts and pastries.

When Moscow thrives Russia is mighty (first Sat or Sun of Sept)
A pageant starring Ivan the Terrible, Alexei, Peter the Great and other figures from Kolomenskoe's history.

sells tickets for all of them except the 1825 Pavilion, where you buy them on the spot.

Almost uniquely among Moscow's tourist sites, Kolomenskoe hosts nearly a dozen **festivals** celebrating folk traditions, holy days or historical events, which can be enjoyed for free. Some are on fixed dates while others vary – the box overleaf gives further details. In addition, there are various **programmes** for groups of ten or more people (for which one pays), ranging from crafts workshops to banquets and operatic performances. For details and bookings, phone or fax ☎112 81 74. You can also arrange **private visits** to the Repository, which holds items that aren't displayed in the museum – the collection of Art Nouveau tiled stoves is especially remarkable.

On Saturdays and Sundays, visitors can enjoy a brief ride around parts of the estate on horseback (adults $3; children $2), while serious **horse-riding** can be arranged through the Karo Riding Club (☎313 02 41), which operates throughout the year. Another option is to take a two-hour **cruise** on the Moskva River, sailing downriver past Kolomenskoe and Dyakovo before heading upstream for a brief view of the isolated Nikolo–Perevenskiy Monastery. Cruises run from mid-April to the end of October, with departures every fifty minutes till as late as 2am in midsummer. You can buy tickets ($2) at the boat landing stage.

Into the grounds

Beyond the *kokoshniki*-topped **Main Entrance** (which was the rear gate in olden days, when visitors approached by river), you're confronted by the **Church of the Icon of Our Lady of Kazan** (*tserkov ikony Kazanskoy bogomateri*), whose azure domes spangled with gold stars glint alluringly. Its box-like refectory and covered stairway are typical of churches from the reign of Alexei, who erected it in 1644 in memory of the struggle against the Poles during the Time of Troubles. In modern times the church became famous for an **icon of the Virgin** known as *Derzhavnaya* (The Majestic), that was found in its attic on the day of Nicholas II's abdication, by a woman who dreamt of being told that the divine power vested in the tsars had now returned to the Mother of God. It shows the Virgin holding the Imperial orb and sceptre; an image regarded as subversive in Soviet times, when people were punished for possessing copies of the icon.

Originally, the church was connected by a covered walkway to the great wooden palace that sprawled to the west, till this was pulled down in the reign of Catherine the Great (see box overleaf). Today, you are drawn into the adjacent **oak woods**, where one of the trees is six hundred years old and others were planted by Peter when he was young. Sited in the vicinity is a trio of historic structures placed here when the Museum of Wooden Architecture was created. The best is **Peter the Great's cabin**, originally erected in 1702 on an island off Arkhangelsk, so that he could observe the construction of

> **The Wooden Palace and the death of Anastasia**
>
> Tsar Alexei's **Wooden Palace** was renowned as a marvel of Russian carpentry. Constructed without using saws, nails or hooks, it boasted 250 rooms and 3000 mica windows distributed around a maze of wings interspersed by bulbous domes and tent-roofed towers up to 50m high. "Its carved wooden ornamentation frothed like lace and its roofs were covered with multicoloured wooden tiles painted in delicate colours and gilded with gold" (Princess Shakhovskoe). Each member of the royal family had their own separate *terem*, or quarters, and the entire population of five villages and nine hamlets was enserfed to the estate. However, during Peter's reign the palace came to be regarded as an archaic liability, and fell into such disrepair that it had to be demolished later that century.
>
> In an earlier age on the same spot, Ivan the Terrible mourned the **death of Anastasia Romanova**, his first – and only beloved – wife, in 1560. As her demise occurred suddenly at a time when the boyars were trying to isolate him, Ivan decided that she had been poisoned (probably rightly, since modern forensics have found mercury in her hair). This revived his deep-rooted paranoia and liberated his darkest impulses, which Anastasia had restrained. Having buried her, he embarked on a debauch and a purge of his enemies with equal zeal. None of his other wives ever lasted for more than a few years – indeed, their life expectancy diminished as he grew older and crazier.

the Novodvinskaya fortress. Its four rooms have tiled stoves, log walls and mica windows; notice the huge wooden beer-scoop in the dining room, and the low ceilings that the six-foot-four-inch tsar accepted without a qualm. Further south you'll come upon a log **watchtower** from the Bratsk *ostrog*, a Cossack fort founded in 1652 on the Angara River in Siberia, which also served as a prison. Nearby stands an equally rough-hewn gate-tower from the St Nicholas Monastery in Karelia, whose hexagonal tower with its witch's-hat brim straddles an archway big enough to admit a wagon – all crafted to interlock without using any nails.

Around the Front Gate

The historic core of Kolomenskoe lies beyond the erstwhile **Front Gate** of the royal court, an impressive double-arched structure surmounted by a clocktower whose clock, salvaged from the Sukharev Tower in Moscow, strikes the hour with a tinkling of small bells, followed by a deep, brazen one. In Tsar Alexei's day the gate was guarded by two mechanical lions, which roared greetings; there are plans to replicate them in the future.

Flanking the gateway are buildings originally devoted to the administration and provisioning of the palace, which now house the **Treasures of Kolomenskoe Museum**. Tickets are sold in the two-storey **Pantry House** (*Sytniy dvor*), whose lower floor displays a splendid collection of icons and woodcarvings, including a superb altar canopy from the Solovetskiy Monastery in the White Sea.

Upstairs you'll find royal portraits, decorative stove-tiles, and a ceramic frieze by Vrubel depicting the legend of Volga and Mikula. Near the Pantry House are the recently restored **Frjazhsky Cellars**, once used for storing wine and nowadays for hosting banquets.

Once restoration work is finished visitors will also be able to enter the **Chancellery** (*Prikaznye Palaty*), to see a recreation of the room where royal scribes worked at a long table covered in red cloth, wanly illuminated by mica windows and flickering candles. Here too, you'll find a lovely 1:40 scale model of Alexei's palace, executed in 1868 from sketches, using wood salvaged from the building. It is also planned to re-create the interior of the **Guardhouse** and allow visitors to see the mechanism inside the clocktower.

In the vicinity of the Chancellery are two separate, unrelated buildings. The **Mead Brewery** (*Medovarnya*) dates from the twelfth century and was one of the few wooden buildings to survive the Great Fire of 1812. It originally stood in the village of Preobrazhenskoe where Peter the Great spent much of his youth, and now serves as a café, where you can buy mead (*medovukha*) and traditional Russian cookies. Downhill lies the **1825 Pavilion**, a small Neoclassical edifice which is all that remains of the palace that Alexander I built at Kolomenskoe; it's now used for temporary exhibitions.

The Church of the Ascension

Beyond the Front Gate the ground falls away towards the river and your eyes are drawn to the soaring **Church of the Ascension** (*tserkov Vozneseniya*), whose primeval grandeur rivals that of St Basil's Cathedral on Red Square. Though the two buildings look very different, they are related in that this church was commissioned by Vasily III in 1529 as a votive offering in the hope that he be granted an heir, who as Ivan the Terrible would later decree the creation of St Basil's; this feeling of ancestral kinship is almost palpable.

Aside from this, what makes the Ascension Church so remarkable is its stupendous **tent-roof**. Rising from an octagonal base culminating in tiers of *kokoshniki* resembling giant artichoke leaves, its facets are enhanced by limestone ribbing and rhomboid patterns, while a lantern, cupola and cross bring the total height to 70m. This was such a radical departure from the domed stone churches that then prevailed that architectural historians decided it must have sprung from the separate tradition of wooden tower churches, until new evidence that the Italian Petrok Maly had supervised its design led some to argue that it represented a late development of the Romanesque pyramid-roofed tower.

Like a rocket clamped to its launch-pad by gantries, the church is girdled at its base by an elevated **terrace** reached by three staircases, incorporating sharp turns that would have heightened the drama of ritual processions in olden days. When filming *Ivan the Terrible*, Eisenstein used this to frame the unforgettable scene in which Ivan watches a long column of people snaking over the snow-clad hills to beg him to return to rule them. On the river-facing side of the terrace are the remains of a stone throne, where Ivan used to sit and enjoy the view. The **interior** of the church is surprisingly light thanks to its double corner-windows, and remarkably small due to the thickness of the walls supporting the spire. The tsar and his family observed services from a gallery above the doorway; the original iconostasis hasn't survived, but services are once again held here on Sundays at 8pm.

On to Dyakovo

In the vicinity of the Ascension Church are two slender towers that form an integral part of the ensemble. The cylindrical **Church of St George** was designed to serve as Kolomenskoe's main belltower and dates from the mid-sixteenth century. In those days the courtyard was surrounded by huts and stables, while wagons rattled in through the gateway beneath the barrel-roofed **Water-Drawing Tower** (*Vodovzvodnaya bashnya*). Originally built as an eyrie for Alexei's hunting birds, it was adapted in 1675 by Bogdan Puchin, who constructed a mechanism to pump up water from the river and deliver it to the palace. The nearby **Colonel's Chambers** were once the residence of the commander of the palace guards, and stand on the site of a cemetery where casualties of the epic battle of Kulikovo were buried. However, as none of these buildings can be entered, there's no cause to linger.

The steps leading down towards the riverside bring you to two ponds formed by damming a stream flowing through the ravine that separates Kolomenskoe from what was once the village of Dyakovo. Although this area was inhabited as early as the first century BC, its only tangible relic is the hilltop **Church of the Beheading of St John the Baptist** (*tserkov useknoveniya chestnya glavy Ioanna Predtechi*), erected by Ivan the Terrible to celebrate his coronation in 1547, and to importune God to grant him an heir. Squatter and squarer than the Church of the Ascension, with four chapels around an octagonal core with a lofty onion dome, it was probably designed by the architect of St Basil's. The surrounding cemetery contains several **gravestones** from the sixteenth century, though most of the tombs are far more recent. Beyond the gate at the end of the path is an orchard where visitors gather apples in September, while the lovely view of the Moskva River attracts Sunday painters.

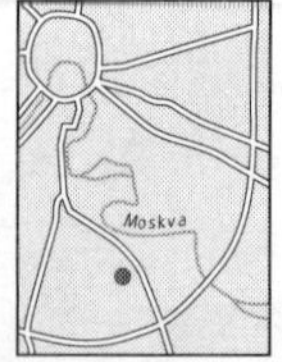

Tsaritsyno

The ruined palace of **Tsaritsyno** is an Imperial summer retreat that never was: a grandiose project that consumed resources for decades, only to be aborted as it neared fruition. The result is a haunting ruin

whose enigma is encoded in stone, though it must be said that some visitors have been left cold. One Oxford Fellow "grudged the labour and particularly the fine stone which has been thrown away in this motley and tasteless undertaking".

Its **history** goes back to the sixteenth century, when Irina, the wife of Tsar Fyodor, had an estate here, which passed eventually from Peter the Great to the Moldavian Prince Dimitrie Cantemir, whose writer son sold it back to Catherine the Great for 25,000 rubles in 1775. She changed its dismal name, "Black Mud" (*Chyornaya Gryaz*), to "Empress's Village", and envisaged an estate to match her glorious summer palaces outside St Petersburg.

Catherine entrusted the building task to Vasily Bazhenov, perhaps as recompense for cancelling a scheme to rebuild the Kremlin, on which he had worked for years. His brief specified a park with pavilions in the Moorish-Gothic style that was fashionable in Europe, and adjoining palaces for the Empress and her son Paul. Ten years later she returned to inspect the nearly completed buildings – only to order that the main palace be torn down and built anew by Bazhenov's young colleague, Matvei Kazakov.

Some believe this was because Catherine objected to the **Masonic symbols** used as ornamentation; others that she could no longer bear the idea of living with Paul, who had grown to loathe her. In the event, Kazakov devoted over a decade to the project until its abrupt termination in 1797, owing to the drain on the treasury caused by a war with Turkey, and the ageing Empress's waning desire for an estate outside Moscow.

A selection of contemporary works in Tsaritsyno's collection can be viewed on the Web site www.gif.ru /museum

Thereafter Tsaritsyno was abandoned to the elements, barring a brief interlude as a museum under Stalin, and various schemes to turn it into a barracks, a champagne factory or a diplomatic residential colony. In recent years some of the pavilions have been restored and there are ambitious plans for the main buildings should funds become available, but as Tsaritsyno comes under the auspices of the Federal rather than the Moscow government, Luzhkov has shown little interest. Somewhat surprisingly, however, Tsaritsyno owns a vast collection of antique tapestries, Russian and Central Asian folk art, contemporary glassware, ceramics and naive paintings, which are displayed in **temporary exhibitions** held in the buildings that have been restored so far.

Practicalities

Tsaritsyno is 3km south of Kolomenskoe and accessible by the same **metro** line. Alighting at Tsaritsyno station, use the exit at the front of the train, turn left and go on to the end of the underpass; bear right beneath two railway bridges and follow the road round to the right till you see the woods, then left along a road past two ponds. Alternatively, you can ride on to the next station, Orekhovo, exit near the rear of the train and turn left in the underpass, which brings you out directly opposite the far end of the avenue of lime trees on the eastern edge of Tsaritsyno park – a more attractive approach. As the grounds are open day and night year round, no tickets are required to explore them – just beware of slippery slopes and frozen ponds in winter, or thick mud in spring. Russians come here to picnic, fish, hunt for mushrooms or go sledging, depending on the season.

For those able to afford it, there are **troyka rides** in winter ($60 per hour; a *troyka* seats six) and **horse-riding** at weekends and on public holidays ($7 per hour). The stables are attached to the *Usadba* **restaurant** (daily noon–11pm), a posh establishment with a cheap *shashlyk* and beer tent outdoors, augumented by *bliny* and hot dog **stalls** on the lawn behind the Great Palace, where there may also be a **kids**' bouncy castle in the summer.

The ruins

Coming from Tsaritsyno station, you approach the estate by a causeway across the **Tsaritsyno Ponds** to pass beneath the **Patterned**

Bridge (*Figurniy most*), which spans a cleft in the hillside. Built of pinkish brick, it bristles with white stone pinnacles and Gothic arches, Rosicrucian blooms and Maltese Crosses – a combination that typifies all the buildings at Tsaritsyno.

The most imposing is the **Great Palace** (*Bolshoy dvorets*), whose twin wings stretch for 130 metres, replete with pilastered corner towers and rows of lofty pointed arches. In the nineteenth century its roof tiles and beams were purloined by a local factory, leaving a massive three-storey shell which is now signposted as too dangerous to enter, though rock-climbers are allowed to use it for training.

By following the palace back into the woods you'll reach the ornamental **Bread Gate** (*Khlebniy vorota*), leading into what was to have been the palace courtyard. Its name comes from the adjacent **Bread House** (*Khlebniy dom*), an enormous oval structure that was meant to be the palace kitchens. A Polish firm put a roof on the building before the money for its restoration ran out; the intention is to turn it into a museum of Tsaritsyno's art collection, which is currently stored in a suburban bunker.

The curators' policy is to exhibit a wide selection of antique and modern art in different mediums, as you can see from visiting the crenellated **Octahedron**. Admission tickets are sold at the kiosk outside, which also sells tickets for the Small Palace. In the vicinity stand the **First Kavalerskiy Korpus** housing Tsaritsyno's administration, the still-derelict **Third Kavalerskiy Korpus** and the nineteenth-century **Church of St Nicholas**, now restored as a working church. Except for the church, they are all Bazhenov's work, like the **Large Bridge** across the ravine beyond.

The Octahedron, the Small Palace and the Opera House are open Wed–Fri 11am–7pm, Sat & Sun 11am–6pm; closed the last Wed of each month; $0.15 each.

By heading in the opposite direction from the Patterned Bridge you'll come to the semicircular **Small Palace** (*Maliy dvorets*), another building designed by Bazhenov that briefly served as a coffee house. Its vaulted interior is wonderfully light and airy, and an ideal exhibition space for yet more artworks. Just beyond is the **Opera House** (*Operniy dom*), its pediment crowned by a Tsarist eagle. Intended for operatic performances but never finished by Bazhenov or Kazakov, its interior has now been completed using Bazhenov's plans. The beautifully proportioned hall is almost monastic in its simplicity, aside from four gold and red chandeliers; it now hosts concerts by chamber music ensembles. Temporary exhibitions are held on the upper floor; the stairway features lamp-brackets shaped like armoured fists.

For information on concerts ☎325 46 93 or 325 31 32.

Beyond the Opera House stands the **Grape Gate** (*Vinogradiy vorota*), named after the fruity pendant suspended from its archway. An avenue of lime trees continues southwards into the wooded, hilly park that surrounds Tsaritsyno, where you'll find a derelict **Belvedere** and an artificial **Ruin** such as was de rigueur for landscaped grounds in the late eighteenth century. The cryptically named **Nerastankino** is used by fantasy war gamers for **mock battles** at weekends, so don't

Tsaritsyno

be surprised to see teenagers whacking each other with fake battleaxes and swords, in the woods off the avenue of lime trees leading to the edge of the estate, near Orekhovo metro station.

Streets and squares

Chernigovskiy pereulok	Черниговский переулок
Bolshoy Kamenniy most	Большой Каменный мост
Donskaya ulitsa	Донская улица
1-y Kadashevskiy pereulok	1-й Кадашевский переулок
Krymskiy val	Крымский вал
Leninskiy prospekt	Ленинский проспект
Oktyabrskaya ploshchad	Октябрьская площадь
ploshchad Gagarina	площадь Гагарина
prospekt Andropova	проспект Андропова
Pyatnitskaya ulitsa	Пятницкая улица
1-y Roshchinskiy pereulok	1-й Рощинский переулок
Sofiyskaya naberezhnaya	Софийская набережная
ulitsa Bakhrushina	улица Бакрушина
ulitsa Bolshaya Ordynka	улица Большая Ордынка
ulitsa Bolshaya Polyanka	улица Большая Полянка
ulitsa Bolshaya Yakimanka	улица Большая Якиманка
ulitsa Danilovskiy val	улица Даниловский вал
ulitsa Serpukhovskiy val	улица Серпуховский вал

Metro stations

Kashirskaya	Каширская
Kolomenskaya	Коломенская
Novokuznetskaya	Новокузнецкая
Oktyabrskaya	Октябрьская
Park Kultury	Парк Культуры
Paveletskaya	Павелецская
Polyanka	Полянка
Shabolovskaya	Шаболовская
Tretyakovskaya	Третьяковская
Tsaritsyno	Царицыно
Tulskaya	Тульская

Museums

Central House of Artists	Центральный дом художника
Igor Talkov Museum	музей Игоря Талькова
Kolomenskoe	музей-усадьба Коломенское
Museum of Wood	музей Леса
Theatre Museum	театральный музей им. А.А. Бакрушина
Tretyakov Gallery	Третьяковская галерея
Tsaritsyno	музей-усадьба Царицыно

Chapter 8

Taganka and Zayauze

TAGANKA AND ZAYAUZE are the beachheads of Moscow's eastward expansion far beyond the Moskva and Yauza rivers, originally spearheaded by tsars and nobles who hunted in the forests and built country palaces that now stand marooned amid a tide of concrete. Eastern Moscow may be drab overall, but this area has enough sights and historical associations to justify a dozen forays into the hinterland.

Taganka, just east of the Yauza River, is the obvious starting point, with picturesque churches in the vicinity and a trio of monasteries further afield. The **Andronikov Monastery** is already known for its museum of icons, but the **Novospasskiy Monastery** has yet to be discovered by tourists, who might also be curious to see what's left of the **Simonov Monastery** after half of it was bulldozed to make room for a Constructivist Palace of Culture. The ecclesiastical roll call ends with the picturesque **Old Believers' Commune**, beyond the **Pet Market** a few miles east of Taganka. Further out lie the palatial **Kuskovo** estate of the Sheremetevs, and the neglected grounds of the **Kuzminki** mansion.

Zayauze's sights, further north, are more modest, and are only really worth a visit as part of a trip to somewhere else. The **Izmaylovo Art Market** attracts droves of tourists with a colourful glut of icons, handicrafts and Soviet kitsch, while in the vicinity is the royal estate where Peter the Great spent his childhood. Admirers of the tsar may also be interested in the ex-stamping grounds of his "toy" regiments, and the **Lefort Palace** where he roistered with the Drunken Synod. Last but not least, there's the **MVD Museum**, devoted to Russia's police forces, which is aptly located near the infamous Lefortovo Prison.

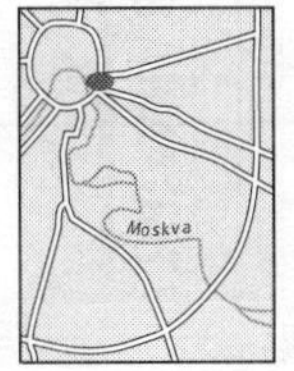

Taganka

The history of **Taganka** is as colourful as its main square and avenues are drab. Originally a quarter inhabited by smiths who made

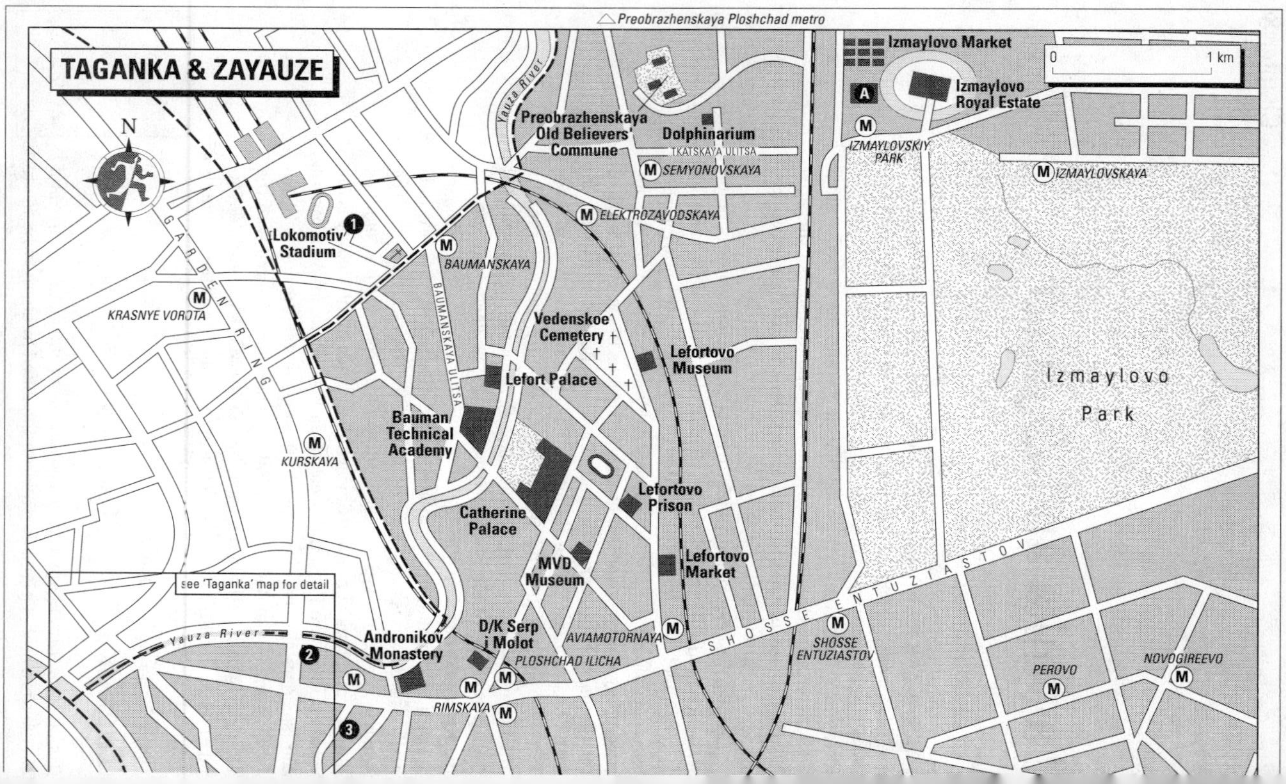

see 'Taganka' map for detail

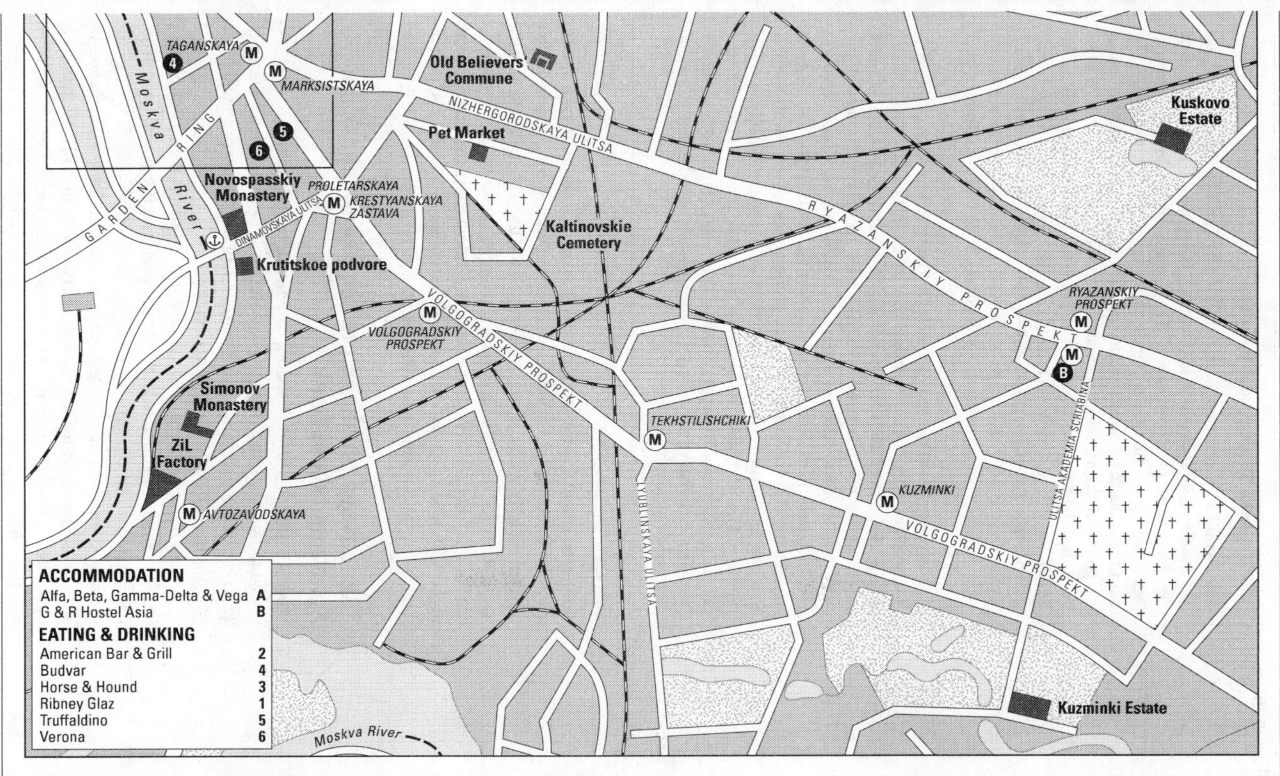

TAGANSKAYA
MARKSISTSKAYA
Old Believers' Commune
NIZHERGORODSKAYA ULITSA
Pet Market
Kuskovo Estate
Moskva
GARDEN RING
River
Novospasskiy Monastery
PROLETARSKAYA
KRESTYANSKAYA ZASTAVA
DINAMOVSKAYA ULITSA
Kaltinovskie Cemetery
Krutitskoe podvore
RYAZANSKIY PROSPEKT
RYAZANSKIY PROSPEKT
VOLGOGRADSKIY PROSPEKT
VOLGOGRADSKIY PROSPEKT
Simonov Monastery
ZiL Factory
TEKHSTILISHCHIKI
AVTOZAVODSKAYA
LYUBLINSKAYA ULITSA
KUZMINKI
ULITSA AKADEMIA SCRIABINA
VOLGOGRADSKIY PROSPEKT
Kuzminki Estate
Moskva River
ACCOMMODATION
Alfa, Beta, Gamma-Delta & Vega A
G & R Hostel Asia B
EATING & DRINKING
American Bar & Grill 2
Budvar 4
Horse & Hound 3
Ribney Glaz 1
Truffaldino 5
Verona 6

The Taganka Theatre and Vysotsky

The **Taganka Theatre** was founded in 1964 by **Yuri Lyubimov**, one of the generation of *Shestidesyatniki* (literally "Sixties people") whose hopes of freedom raised by Khrushchev's "Thaw" were dashed by the return to orthodoxy under Brezhnev. During those years, Lyubimov managed to skirt the limits of censorship with dynamic plays that were understood as allegories of Soviet life. Eventually, with the indulgence of KGB boss Andropov, he was able to present such explicitly political drama as *The House on the Embankment* and stage Bulgakov's *The Master and Margarita*. Exiled in 1983 for openly criticizing the authorities, Lyubimov was later allowed back and underwent a stormy new relationship with the company, which is still going strong under its octogenarian maestro.

The theatre is also synonymous with **Vladimir Vysotsky** (1938–80), whose black-jeaned, guitar-playing Hamlet electrified audiences in the 1970s. Actor, poet, balladeer and drunk, his songs of prison, low-life and disillusionment were spread by bootleg tape recordings throughout the USSR and known to everyone from truck drivers to intellectuals – even the KGB enjoyed them. Vysotsky's death during the Olympic Games went unannounced in the media, but tens of thousands turned out to line the route to the Vagankov Cemetery, where Lyubimov spoke for millions when he called him "Our bard, the keeper of the nation's spirit, of our pain and all our joys". A small **Vysotsky Museum** (Tues–Sat 11am–5.30pm; $0.30) has been established on Nizhniy Taganskiy tupik, near the theatre's modern, red-brick annexe.

cauldrons (*tagany*) for the Muscovite army, it later became a shelter area for thieves and various undesirables who were obliged to live beyond the city walls. It was well known for its prison, which was the inspiration for many ballads of the criminal underworld: "Taganka I am yours forever. My power and my talent perished inside your walls." This subculture profoundly influenced Vysotsky's performances at the famous Taganka Theatre.

Taganskaya ploshchad to the Kotelnicheskaya Apartments and back

Basically just a traffic junction, **Taganskaya ploshchad** is only traversable by the pedestrian subways that link its three metro stations. The Circle line station with its bas-reliefs of Soviet warriors will bring you out opposite the **Taganka Theatre**.

Across the street from the theatre, the **Church of St Nicholas by the Taganka Gate** (*tserkov Nikloy u Taganskikh vorot*) was originally hemmed in by the city walls. Its tall, narrow, dark red facade displays a panoply of engaged columns and *nalichniki*, crowned by slender domes and a tent-roofed belfry. Built in 1712, it has long been derelict but serves as a pointer towards the delightful **Church of the Assumption of the Potters** (*tserkov Uspeniya v*

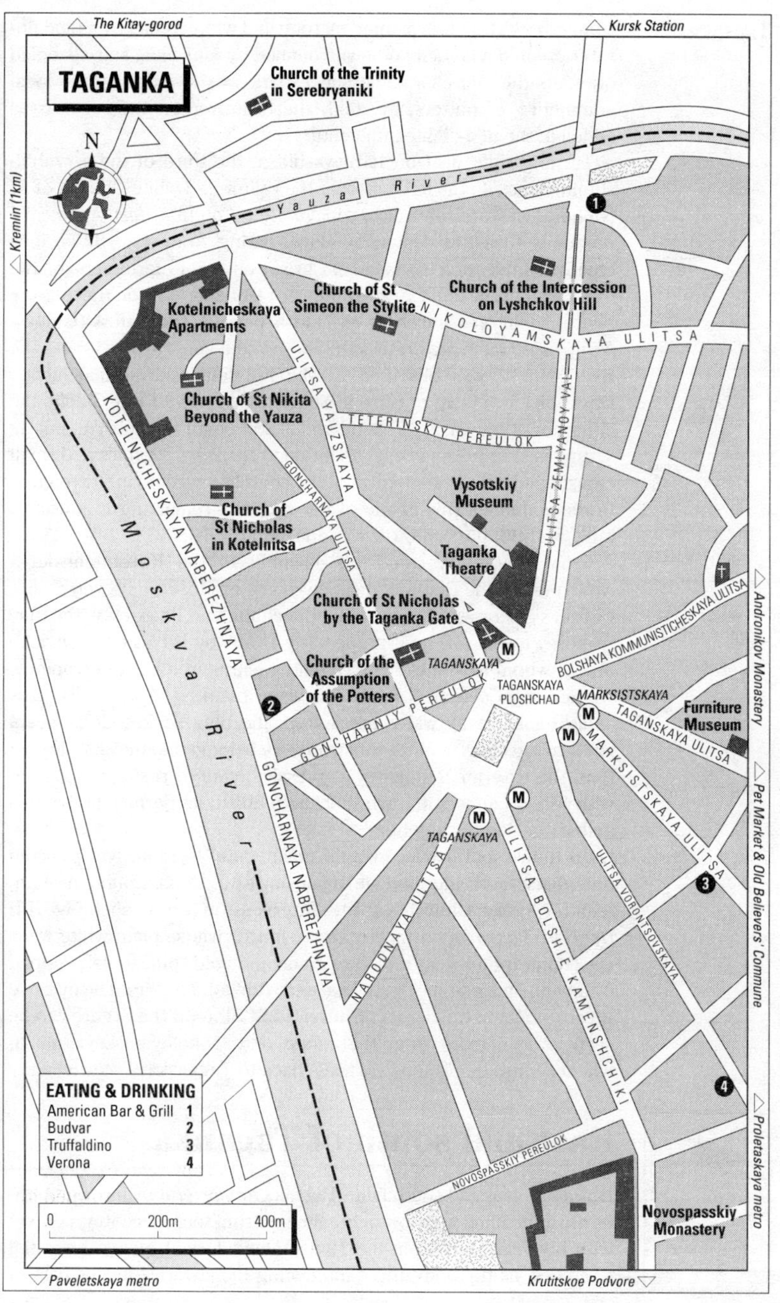

The Kitay-gorod
Kursk Station
TAGANKA
Church of the Trinity in Serebryaniki
N
Kremlin (1km)
Yauza River
Church of St Simeon the Stylite
Church of the Intercession on Lyshchkov Hill
Kotelnicheskaya Apartments
NIKOLOYAMSKAYA ULITSA
ULITSA YAUZSKAYA
Church of St Nikita Beyond the Yauza
TETERINSKIY PEREULOK
ULITSA ZEMLYANOY VAL
KOTELNICHESKAYA NABEREZHNAYA
GONCHARNAYA ULITSA
Vysotskiy Museum
Church of St Nicholas in Kotelnitsa
Moskva River
Taganka Theatre
Church of St Nicholas by the Taganka Gate
Church of the Assumption of the Potters
TAGANSKAYA
TAGANSKAYA PLOSHCHAD
BOLSHAYA KOMMUNISTICHESKAYA ULITSA
MARKSISTSKAYA
GONCHARNIY PEREULOK
TAGANSKAYA ULITSA
Furniture Museum
Andronikov Monastery
MARKSISTSKAYA ULITSA
Pet Market & Old Believers' Commune
GONCHARNAYA NABEREZHNAYA
NARODNAYA ULITSA
ULITSA BOLSHIE KAMENSHCHIKI
ULITSA VORONTSOVSKAYA
EATING & DRINKING
American Bar & Grill 1
Budvar 2
Truffaldino 3
Verona 4
NOVOSPASSKIY PEREULOK
Proletaskaya metro
Novospasskiy Monastery
0
200m
400m
Paveletskaya metro
Krutitskoe Podvore

Goncharakh). This is painted maroon and white, offset by a tiled floral frieze and a golden dome surrounded by four blue, star-spangled ones. As the church's name suggests, it was founded by the local community of potters, in 1654; the belltower on the corner was added in the mid-eighteenth century.

Turning right up Goncharnaya ulitsa, the third of the downhill-sloping lanes on the left harbours the yellow and white **Church of St Nicholas in Kotelnitsa** (*tserkov Nikoly v Kotelnikakh*). A typically pompous Classical design by Bove, dating from the 1820s, it is chiefly notable for a bas-relief of Christ's entry into Jerusalem, on the outer wall of the nave. At the far end of Goncharnaya on the left, the peaceful hilltop **Church of St Nikita beyond the Yauza** (*tserkov Nikity shto za Yauzoy*) used to command a superb view across the river until it was obscured by the Kotelnicheskaya Apartments. Described as a heap of ruins in Solzhenitsyn's *The First Circle*, the church was rebuilt in 1958–60 and is still being refurbished, but its setting is in any case lovely. Its rounded *zakomary* gables and small cap-shaped cupola are typical of the churches erected in the reign of Boris Godunov. This is one of the very few remaining in Moscow, built in 1595; the belltower was added in the 1680s.

From there you can head downhill to the **Kotelnicheskaya Apartments**, the first and most awesome of Moscow's seven Stalin-Gothic skyscrapers. Designed by Chechulin and Rostovsky, the thirty-storey tower was built in the early 1950s by POWs and convicts, one of whom is said to have emulated Icarus in a bid to escape, as workers who perished on the job were immured in the walls. This could explain why water oozes from the plug sockets forty years later, to the chagrin of tenants who once belonged to the elite. For all that, the exterior is mightily impressive, clad in rusticated granite with furled banners and wheatsheaves above its portals, and spires and statues on the heights.

To return to Taganka by a different route, head upriver past the humpback footbridge and into a housing estate built around the eighteenth-century **Church of the Intercession on Lyshchkov Hill** (*tserkov Pokrova na Lyshchkovoy gore*), whose plain white walls are counterpointed by a bizarre green and gold "pineapple", capped by an egg-shaped blue finial spangled with golden stars. The massive green cupola of the derelict **Church of St Simeon the Stylite** can be seen as one exits from the estate onto Nikoloyamskaya ulitsa, whence ulitsa Zemlyanoy val leads back to Taganskaya ploshchad.

East and south of Taganka

Radiating east and south from Taganka are several major thoroughfares, some lined with low ochre houses from the last century, others with high-rise flats from the 1970s. Don't be put off by the initial stretches, as there are three interesting monasteries in this part of

Moscow, not to mention the Pet Market and Old Believers' Commune, further out.

East and south of Taganka

The nearest sight, however, is the **Furniture Museum** at Taganskaya ulitsa 13, building 3 (Tues–Sun 11am–8pm; $0.30). Housed in the newly restored Arshenevsky mansion, it replicates a Russian aristocratic home, complete with living room, study and nursery, grandfather clocks and other period items. While Russian visitors want to see the armchair bearing the fingerprints of Alexander I – who sat in it before the varnish had dried – foreigners are more interested in the "Present to Clinton" – a chair in the form of a giant wooden zipper, located in the entranceway – or the stool shaped as Salvador Dali's ear, in the basement café. Also look out for the Nostradamus chair, with an elbow rest that resembles the soothsayer's hand holding a magic ball.

The Andronikov Monastery

The Andronikov Monastery is open Mon, Tues & Thurs–Sun 11am–6pm; closed Wed and the last Fri of each month; $3.

The **Andronikov Monastery** (*Spaso-Andronikov monastyr*) is situated on the steep east bank of the Yauza, just over a kilometre east of Taganskaya ploshchad. It was founded in 1360 by Metropolitan Alexei, who vowed that, should he survive the stormy return sea journey from Constantinople, he would found a monastery and dedicate it to the saint whose feast day coincided with his safe return to Moscow – which turned out to be Our Saviour (*Spas*). The monastery acquired its present name after Alexei was summoned to Crimea to treat the Khan's ailing wife and entrusted it to the monk Andronik, who became its first abbot. Its most famous monk was the great icon painter Andrei Rublev (see overleaf).

After the Revolution the monastery was turned into a prison camp, then into housing for workers at the nearby Hammer and Sickle Factory, and finally scheduled for demolition – but reprieved by the postwar upsurge of patriotism. In 1960 it was formally reopened as the Andrei Rublev Museum of Early Russian Art, in honour of the 600th anniversary of his birth. Though still designated as a museum, several of the buildings are once more occupied by Orthodox monks and institutions (including a choristers' school), and it may well revert to being a fully fledged monastery in the future.

To **get there** catch trolleybus #47 or #53 along Nikoloyamskaya ulitsa to Andronevskaya ploshchad. Another method is to travel by metro to Ploshchad Ilicha station, and then ride the same trolleybus in the other direction, to approach the monastery from the east. Alternatively, walk along Bolshaya Kommunisticheskaya ulitsa, lined with two-storey dwellings from the last century, where the prosperous Old Believers lived.

The monastery

The monastery is impressive from the outside but, except for the Refectory and the Archangel Michael church, is not nearly as romantic as the Donskoy or Novodevichiy monasteries. Enclosed by white stone ramparts with rounded crenellations and chunky towers at three corners, the complex is entered by a **Holy Gate** (*Svyatye vorota*). Flanked by turrets with conical wooden roofs, the gate was dominated by a Neoclassical belltower until it was demolished in the 1930s. To the left of the gate stands the seventeenth-century **Abbot's Residence** (*Nastoyatelskie Pokoi*), decorated with ceramic insets; the ticket office and an early nineteenth-century **Seminary** (*Dukhovnoe Uchilishche*) lie off to the right.

The elaborate structure near the west wall was created over several centuries, starting with the two-storey tent-roofed **Refectory** (*Trapeznaya palata*) in 1504–06. A saw-toothed cornice integrates this with the Moscow Baroque **Church of the Archangel Michael** (*tserkov Arkhangela Mikhaila*) that rises alongside in variegated tiers. The church was commissioned in 1694 as a private chapel and burial vault for the family of Yevdokiya Lopukhina, Peter the Great's first wife. Four years later he forced her into a convent and exiled the Lopukhins to Siberia, whereupon the pace of construction slackened so much that the church wasn't finished until 1731.

The smaller **Cathedral of the Saviour** (*Spasskiy sobor*), in the centre of the grounds, was built in 1425–27 and decorated by Rublev. Although traces of his frescoes remain, the cathedral is closed for restoration, so you can only see its weathered stone facade, whose perspective-arch is surmounted by a relief of the Saviour. The helmet-shaped dome and triple apses reflect the influence of early medieval Vladimir architecture, while the pyramid of *zakomary* and *kokoshniki* are characteristic of the early Moscow style. Much altered over the centuries, it was restored to its original

Andrei Rublev

The monk **Andrei Rublev** (pronounced "Rubl*yov*") is revered as the greatest painter of medieval Russia, whose work remained a beacon throughout the dark centuries of the Tatar invasions and the Time of Troubles. The place of his birth is unknown and its date uncertain (possibly 1360), but he probably served his apprenticeship in the icon workshop of the Trinity Monastery of St Sergei, outside Moscow. Having painted the icons for Zvenigorod Cathedral, 40km northwest of Moscow, in 1400 Rublev worked on the Cathedral of the Assumption in the Kremlin, and its namesake in Vladimir (with Daniil Cherny). He painted his masterpiece, the *Old Testament Trinity*, in about 1411 or 1422, for the monastery where he had served his novitiate, before retiring to the Andronikov Monastery, where he is said to have died in 1430.

The Soviets honoured him as an artist, but delayed the release of Tarkovsky's superb film, *Andrei Rublev*, with its scenes of Christian faith and pagan nudity, until the early 1980s. In 1989, he was canonized by the Russian Orthodox Church and a **statue of Rublev** was erected in the park outside the monastery, which hosts an annual **celebration** in his honour on July 17.

appearance during the 1950s. The feast day of Our Saviour falls on August 16.

The exhibitions

The **Rublev Museum**'s collection of icons is distributed around several buildings, some of which may be closed; your likeliest bets are the ground floor of the Refectory and the service block near the ticket office. Highlights include fifteenth-century icons by the school of Rublev (but none by the master himself), seventeenth-century icons from Novgorod, and an eighteenth-century *Our Lady of Tikhvin* from the Donskoy Monastery: the collection, however, doesn't compare with that of the Tretyakov Gallery. A separate exhibition of applied art contains jewellery, goblets, coins, vestments and other artefacts, from medieval times onwards, and there is also an exhibition devoted to church bells.

Novospasskiy Monastery and the Krutitskoe podvore

The high-rise sprawl to the south of Taganka harbours two unexpected treats near the river: the Novospasskiy Monastery and the Krutitskoe podvore. **Getting there** from Taganskaya ploshchad entails walking 1km down ulitsa Bolshie Kamenshchiki, or taking the metro to Proletarskaya station, which has several exits onto Krestyanskaya ploshchad, making it hard to get your bearings. Look out for a gilded dome peeping above the rooftops, or the start of Dinamovskaya ulitsa – either will lead you towards the monastery, whence it's an easy walk to the Krutitskoe podvore.

The Novospasskiy Monastery

The monastery is open for services (Mon–Sat 8–10am & 5–7pm, Sun 8am–8pm), and usually between times as well; admission free.

The **Novospasskiy Monastery** (*Novospasskiy monastyr*) claims to be the oldest in Moscow, tracing its foundation back to the twelfth-century reign of Yuri Dolguruky, who established a monastery dedicated to the Saviour on the site of the present-day Danilov Monastery. In 1300, Ivan I transferred this to the Kremlin, whence Ivan III relocated it to its present site in 1490 – hence the appellation, "New Monastery of the Saviour". Subsequently razed by the Tatars, most of the existing complex dates from the seventeenth century, when the monastery was surrounded by a thick wall with seven bastions, which preserved it through the Time of Troubles and determined its grim role in modern times, when it was used as a concentration camp by the Bolsheviks, who imprisoned and shot their victims in the almshouse and hospital alongside the northern wall. It then became an orphanage, an NKVD archive, a furniture factory, and finally a drunk-tank. Returned to the Church in 1991, the buildings are slowly being restored, but the ravages of its past are still evident.

The legend of Princess Tarakanova

The cathedral chapel contains the remains of Sister Inokinya Dosieeya, better known to Russians as **Princess Tarakanova**. As the illegitimate child of Empress Elizabeth and Count Razumovskiy, she was sent abroad to be educated, enabling a Polish adventuress to claim her identity and the right to inherit the throne of Russia. Though this impostor was swiftly incarcerated (and died in prison), Catherine the Great decided to lure Tarakanova back home and confine her to a nunnery "for the good of Russia". **Legend** has it that the task was entrusted to Catherine's lover, Count Orlov, who seduced Tarakanova aboard a ship before locking her in their nuptial cabin as they approached St Petersburg. Though one version maintains that she was imprisoned in an underground cell of the Peter and Paul fortress and drowned during a flood, Tarakanova was actually confined in Moscow's Ivanovskiy Convent, where she remained for 25 years until Catherine's death, by which time she had come to accept her fate and chose to remain a nun.

The **entrance** to the monastery is through an archway to the left of its gigantic four-tiered belltower, whose gold finial was once visible for miles around. A Cossack guard on the gate ensures that visitors are properly dressed; women must wear headscarves and long skirts. Inside you'll be confronted with a muddle of sheds and chapels, where the main cathedral stands out as the focus of attention for monks and pilgrims alike, while novices and kids lurk around the fringes where a publishing house and a Sunday school occupy the outbuildings.

The **Cathedral of the Transfiguration of the Saviour** (*sobor Spasa Preobrazheniya*) is a medieval-style edifice with huge arched gables and helmet-shaped domes, erected on the site of the original cathedral in 1645. An image of the Saviour watches over the portal to the (locked) crypt that served as the family vault of the Romanov boyars until Mikhail Romanov's ascension to the throne in 1613. The cathedral's lofty nave is dominated by a massive gilt-framed **iconostasis** that includes the icons of the *Image of Christ* and *Our Lady of Smolensk*, a gift from Tsar Mikhail's mother, who became a nun in later life. On either side are shrines containing relics from Kiev, including a piece of the Virgin's robe. The walls are covered in frescoes representing the genealogy of the sovereigns of Russia from St Olga to Tsar Alexei, and the descent of the kings of Israel, while the refectory stairway is flanked by images of ancient Greek philosophers.

The faded orange **Church of the Sign**, around the back of the cathedral, contains the tomb of Parasha Kovalyova, whose marriage to Count Sheremetev amazed Moscow society (see p.307). But the most curious story relates to the small tent-roofed chapel that stands in the yard to the north of the cathedral (see box above). Beyond the monastery's west wall lies a large pond that once supplied the monks with fish. During the mid-1930s, the NKVD used its steep bank as a burial ground for the bodies of foreign Communists secretly shot in the purges.

The landing-stage beside the river is the point of departure for riverboat cruises past the Kremlin and the Novodevichiy Convent – a scenic trip best made on a sunny day (see p.40).

The Krutitskoe podvore

The Krutitskoe podvore is open Mon–Fri 10am–6pm; admission free.

From the monastery, you can head downhill and across the main road to Krutitskaya ulitsa, leading uphill to the **Krutitskoe podvore**, a small complex or "yard" (*podvore*) of seventeenth-century buildings that gets its name from the steep (*krutoy*) bank of the nearby Moskva River. Established in the fourteenth century as the seat of the Metropolitan of the Christian minority among the Tatar Golden Horde, it originally covered a much larger area, until Catherine the Great turned part of it into a military prison that can still be seen around the back.

Architecturally, the *podvore* is remarkable for being devoid of any Western influences, its tent-roofed chapels and walkways arranged in a seemingly haphazard fashion that is purely Muscovite, an impression enhanced by the wooden houses in the yard dating from the 1920s, when the complex was turned into a workers' hostel. Its centrepiece is a **Cathedral of the Assumption** (*Uspenskiy sobor*) constructed entirely of brick – onion domes included – connected by an overhead arcade to the **Metropolitan's Palace** in the far corner of the yard. The arcade passes through an impressive arched structure called the **Teremok**, one wall of which is decorated with turquoise tiles in colourful floral designs and has beautiful window frames carved like grapevines.

While the cathedral's lower "winter" church is once again a place of worship, the upper "summer" church remains in the hands of a museum which uses it as a storeroom and refuses to hand it back. Otherwise, however, the *podvore* has been reclaimed by the Church, which has set up a printing house and holds meetings of Orthodox youth organizations here.

The Simonov Monastery

The grounds of the Simonov Monastery are open daily from 7am to dusk; admission free.

Founded in 1371 by the monk Fyodor, a nephew of Sergei of Radonezh, the **Simonov Monastery** (*Simonovskiy monastyr*) resisted many sieges until it was sacked by the Poles during the Time of Troubles, but was rebuilt with even thicker walls in the 1640s, and remained one of the city's mightiest defensive outposts – known as "Moscow's Sentinel" – for several hundred years. In Soviet times, however, its environs were considered an ideal site for a car factory, and much of the monastery was destroyed to make way for a football stadium and palace of culture. What remains attests both to its former strength and to the ravages that surpassed anything inflicted by foreign invaders; of all the city's monasteries, none is sadder-looking or more haunting.

Getting there involves catching the Zamoskvoretskaya line to Avtozavodskaya metro station and exiting by the front of the train; as you come up the steps, you'll see one of the monastery's towers, 400m ahead.

The ruins

The most impressive feature of the ruins is a 250-metre-long section of **fortified wall** (which once totalled 655m in length), guarded by three massive stone towers. Fyodor Kon, who designed the walls of the Beliy Gorod, is thought to have created the **Dulo Tower** on the corner by the river, with its tiers of windows at staggered intervals; the archers' gallery and tent-roofed spire were added in the seventeenth century, when the towers of the Kremlin received similar additions. Nearer the road, the **Solevaya** and **Kuznechnaya towers** resemble giant mushrooms, their white stalks capped by brown spires.

Entering the grounds by a gate in the fence near the palace of culture you're confronted by industrial debris where nineteenth-century visitors were delighted by "gardens of marigolds and dahlias, and bees humming in hedges of spiraea". Ahead looms the huge **Refectory-Church of Our Lady of Tikhvin**, where services are once again held in the uppermost part, reached by a stairway on the far side. There used to be six churches (the oldest built in 1405), but in 1934 five of them were blown up in a single day. Since the Church regained ownership in 1994 volunteers have cleared tons of rubbish, set up a factory to recycle scrap metal and planted sunflowers in the grounds, while religious life has revived in the form of a community for deaf people that's unique for holding services with signing – but there's still a long way to go before it becomes a fully fledged monastery again.

Other sights in the vicinity

In its medieval heyday the Simonov owned twelve thousand "souls" and a score of villages, while its walls encompassed three times the present area – a measure of how much was destroyed to create the Torpedo Football Stadium and the **ZiL Palace of Culture**, which was the largest and most lavishly appointed of the workers' clubs built in the 1930s. Designed by the Vsenin brothers, the foremost Constructivist architects of their day, the ZiL Palace, north of the monastery, is best viewed from the river-facing side, where an expansive curved gallery floods the interior with light. Otherwise, it has not aged well; like other Constructivist buildings of the time, its design required better materials than were available. As for the stadium, it has hardly been used since Torpedo decamped to Luzhniki (see p.223) after the club changed hands following the collapse of ZiL in the mid-1990s.

Previously, both the team and the Palace belonged to the **ZiL Motor Works** (*Avtozavod imeni Likhachova*), Russia's oldest car factory (founded in 1916), best known for producing the ZiL limousine used by Soviet Party leaders. In the 1990s ZiL barely averted bankruptcy by laying off thousands of workers and not paying others for months on end, before winning orders for a new model ZiL limousine. The half-moribund factory is a weird setting for the resurrected **Church of the Nativity of the Virgin in Old Simonov**, built in 1509. Previously used as a compressor shed, it now has a new iconostasis and a charming garden (services at 8am & 5pm). To have a look, enter the factory by the park gate facing the monastery's ramparts and follow the walkway – you can't go astray.

The Pet Market and the Old Believers' Commune

There are only two reasons for tourists to venture into the suburban hinterland 2–3km east of Taganskaya ploshchad: the Pet Market and the Old Believers' Commune. **Getting there** is easy. From the stand near the Taganskaya supermarket, catch trolleybus #16 or #63 out along Taganskaya ulitsa, counting each stop. To reach the market, alight at the fifth stop and cut through onto Bolshaya Kalitnikovskaya ulitsa, where it should lie straight ahead. For the commune, ride on to the next stop and look out for its belltower on the far side of Nizhergorodskaya ulitsa. A path skirting a car park and crossing the tracks should bring you to the site in under ten minutes.

The Pet Market

The outdoor **Pet Market** (*Ptichniy rynok*) off Bolshaya Kalitnikovskaya ulitsa – running parallel to Nizhergorodskaya – has no sign as such, but you can't miss the people clutching pets. Sellers can be found any day, but on Sunday (9am–5pm; $0.30 admission) the place is jam-packed with folk standing three deep, rickety stalls stocking everything from bird food to hunting gear and sections for talking birds (their vocabulary is noted on labels) and guard dogs. There are even people selling snakes and monkeys.

A grisly tale is attached to the **Kaltinovskie Cemetery** (*Kaltinovskoe kladbische*), off behind the market, which was used to dispose of victims during the Terror. So many were tipped into pits at night that dogs gathered from all over town to scavenge, leaving limbs strewn about – but residents were too frightened to complain.

The Old Believers' Commune

The **Old Believers' Commune** (*Staroobryadcheskaya Obshchina*) is a relic of an Orthodox sect that once loomed large in Tsarist Russia – especially in Moscow, where many of the merchants and coachmen were Old Believers (see box below). Their commune was founded in the 1770s after Catherine the Great granted them limited rights and

The Old Believers

During the 1650s, Patriarch Nikon's reforms of Orthodox ritual were rejected by thousands of Russians who felt that only their traditional rites offered salvation. Calling themselves **Old Believers** (*Staroobryadtsy*) – others termed them *Raskolniki* (Dissenters) – they held that crossing oneself with three fingers instead of two was an infamy, and shaving a beard "a sin that even the blood of martyrs could not expiate". Opposition intensified under Peter the Great, whom they saw as the Antichrist for promoting tobacco, ordering men to cut their beards (which believers kept to be buried with them, lest they be barred from paradise), and imposing the Julian Calendar and a chronology dating from the birth of Christ, rather than Creation – thus perverting time itself.

To escape forced conversions, the Old Believers fled into the wilds; if cornered, they burned themselves to death, singing hymns. During generations in exile, they became divided into the less stringent *Popovtsy*, who dealt with Orthodox priests and were willing to drink to the tsar's health; and the *Bezpopovtsy* (Priestless), who totally rejected both Church and state. The latter included wilder sub-sects like the *Skoptsy* or "Mutilated Ones", who castrated themselves, and the *Khlisty* (Flagellants), whose orgies and lashings expressed their belief in salvation through sin (Rasputin was said to have been one).

many returned from hiding in Siberia. Though Nicholas I reimposed discriminatory laws, the sect had become established enough to weather official disapproval until the onset of liberalization in 1905. After the Revolution, however, they were doubly suspect for their piety and wealth, and suffered even more severe repression, which forced the sect underground for decades. Today, the commune is coming back to life, but their strict ethics effectively disbar them from the cutthroat business world of the New Russia.

The commune's main landmark is its **belltower**, a soaring Neo-Byzantine structure with elaborate blind arcades and Moorish arches, which was built to celebrate the reopening of their churches in 1905. Soon after the Revolution, the Bolsheviks closed them down again and turned the **Cathedral of the Intercession** (*Pokrovskiy sobor*) into a cobblers' workshop. Built in 1792 by Kazakov, its Neoclassical facade doesn't prepare you for the vastness and magnificence of the interior, whose arches and pillars are outlined in gold and covered with frescoes of saints and biblical events. *Murray's Handbook* (1875) warned visitors that "the singing will be found very peculiar . . . especially that of the women, who perform Divine service in a chapel apart from the men". By turning up at 5pm, you can hear the liturgy and judge for yourself. Further north stands the attractive Neo-Russian **Church of St Nicholas** (*tserkov Nilolay*), whose white walls are jazzed up by red, white and blue *kokoshniki*, sage-green pendentives and turquoise shingled onion domes.

By passing through the church's tent-roofed archway – originally the entrance to the commune – you'll find the **Rogozhskoe**

Cemetery (Tues–Sun 9am–6pm), established in the plague year of 1771. Although less exotic than the Novodevichiy Cemetery, it does contain an odd mixture of Old Believers and Soviet functionaries. The main path leads uphill past the modest headstone of **Admiral Gorshkov** (who headed the Soviet Navy under Brezhnev) to the **Morozov family** plot, beneath a wrought-iron canopy. A thrifty serf couple who sold their homespun cloth on the streets of Moscow after the great fire, the Morozovs bought their freedom and within thirty years owned a cotton mill which their son **Timofey** developed into a textiles empire. (It was at the Morozov mills in Orekhovo Zuevo that football originated in Russia.) Alongside are buried Timofey's widow **Maria**, a fervent Old Believer who henceforth ran the show; their sons **Savva**, who sponsored the arts and left-wing causes before killing himself, and **Aseny**, who died of a stupid prank.

Kuskovo and Kuzminki

It's a measure of Moscow's growth that the southeastern suburbs now incorporate what were country estates in the eighteenth and nineteenth centuries. Kuskovo and Kuzminki once embodied a way of life that amounted to a credo: the pursuit of pleasure and elegant refinement by an aristocracy that was no longer obliged to serve the state (as Peter the Great had insisted). The fate of Kuskovo and Kuzminki since the Revolution illustrates the Soviets' Janus-like view of Russia's aristocratic heritage, with one estate being preserved as a museum and the other being allowed to moulder away.

Kuskovo is open summer Wed–Sun 10am–6pm, winter 10am–4pm; closed the last Wed of each month. The ticket office shuts 1hr earlier. One ticket ($2.50) covers the Palace, Grotto and Orangery; additional tickets ($0.40) are required for the Dutch and Italian cottages. The Palace is closed on very rainy days.

Kuskovo

The industrial suburb of **KUSKOVO** takes its name from the former Sheremetev estate – Moscow's finest example of an eighteenth-century nobleman's country palace. The **history** of the estate dates back as far as 1715, when Peter the Great awarded the village of Kuskovo to Boris Sheremetev, a general at the battle of Poltava, who built a summer residence there. Its present layout is owed to his son Pyotr, who devoted himself to managing the estate after inheriting some 200,000 serfs and marrying Varvara Cherkasskaya, whose dowry included the talented serf architects Fyodor Argunov and Alexei Mironov. In its heyday Kuskovo was known as the "Count's State" and included a zoo covering 230 acres, but after Pyotr's death it gradually fell into disuse as his son Nikolai preferred his own palace at Ostankino – so, barring some repairs after Kuskovo was looted by French troops in 1812, its mid-eighteenth-century decor remained unchanged until the estate was nationalized by the Bolsheviks in 1919.

Approaches – and festivals

Getting to Kuskovo is easier than it sounds. Take the metro to Ryazanskiy Prospekt station and leave by the exit near the front of

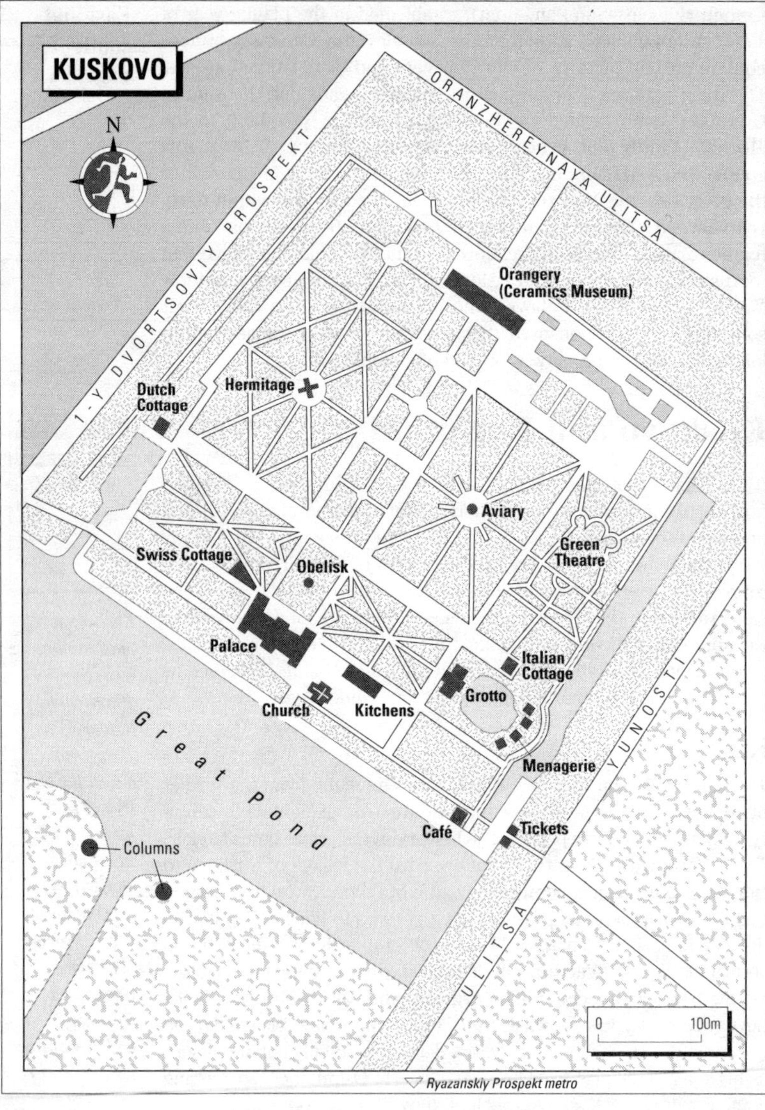

the train; then from the third bus stop on the right, ride bus #133 or #208 six stops to the main entrance, or alight one stop earlier to approach the palace through its extensive park. Though best visited in summer, when its formal gardens are in bloom, the grounds are also lovely in autumn, and the palace and the ceramics museum in the Orangery are worth seeing at any time.

Over summer there's the added bonus of **concerts** in the palace (☎370 01 60 for details), while on the Saturdays nearest to Independence Day (July 4) and Bastille Day (July 14) there are **festivals** organized by the US and French embassies, featuring bands, fashion shows, sports events and fireworks (tickets sold on the spot). At other times it's worth bringing a snack along, as the outdoor café only sells drinks and sweets.

On entering the main gate you'll pass alongside the **Great Pond**, where pleasure boats sailed in olden times. On the other side of the path you'll glimpse the Menagerie and Grotto (see below), and pass the ornate former **kitchens** and a grey-and-white **church** topped by a statue of the Archangel Michael (used for services twice a month). The adjacent golden-yellow **belfry** is modelled on the Admiralty in St Petersburg, as a compliment to its founder Peter the Great.

The palace

Made of wood and painted salmon-pink and white, the one-storey **palace** was built in 1769–77 by Argunov and Mironov, under the supervision of the professional architect Karl Blank. Ascending a ramp flanked by buxom sphinxes, visitors are obliged to put on *tapochki* before entering the Grecian Vestibule, replete with fake antique urns and marble.

The tour of the palace progresses through the silk-wallpapered **card room** and **billiard room** to the pink-and-white mirrored dining hall, and thence to the "informal" rooms in the west wing. These include a **tapestry room** hung with Flemish tapestries; a **mauve drawing room** upholstered in cerise and silver silk; a **state bedchamber** with an allegorical fresco, *Innocence Choosing Between Wisdom and Love*; and an oak-panelled **study**.

The highlight is the **ballroom**, dripping with gilt and chandeliers, whose fresco, *Apollo and the Muses*, glorifies the Sheremetevs. Relief panels on the walls depict the exploits of the ancient Roman hero Mucius Scaevola, who thrust his hand into fire to prove his indifference to pain, an image that resonated with the Russians at the time of the Napoleonic invasion.

The garden and pavilions

Behind the palace an obelisk introduces the **garden**, laid out in the geometrical French style; during winter its statues are encased in boxes to protect them from the cold. Off to the right you'll find the **Grotto** pavilion, with its prominent dome and ornate wrought-iron gates; the interior was decorated by the St Petersburg "Master of Grotto Work", Johannes Fokt, using shells, stones, textured stucco and porcelain. Nearby is the charming **Italian Cottage** (*Italyanskiy domik*), a miniature palace in its own right; if you're there on the hour, don't miss the melodious grandfather clock. The four cute little houses topped with urns, across the pond behind the **Grotto** once housed a **Menagerie** of birds and animals.

Further on, beyond the lattice-work **Aviary** and the open-air **Green Theatre**, the old **Orangery** houses a **Ceramics Museum** displaying a superb collection of eighteenth-, nineteenth- and twentieth-century porcelain, ranging from the Egyptian dinner service of Alexander I to plates and vases commemorating the construction of the Moscow metro. On the way back, cast an eye over Blank's Baroque **Hermitage** pavilion, topped by a statue of the goddess Flora, before visiting the steep-roofed **Dutch Cottage**, built in 1749, which contains three rooms entirely covered in Delft tiles. Nearby stands an elaborately gabled **Swiss Cottage**, created by the St Petersburg stage designer Nikolai Benois.

Kuzminki

A few miles to the south of Kuskovo lies another aristocratic estate of the same period, that of the Golitsyn family. **KUZMINKI**, however, has fared badly: its main house burned down in 1915, and during the Soviet era the other buildings were taken over or simply left to rot. While some are being repaired now, visitors shouldn't expect to find any palatial mansions or formal gardens; ruined follies and acres of birches, larch and spruce is what you'll get. In winter, especially, the isolation and solitude are Kuzminki's best features.

Getting there takes about an hour. Start by taking the metro to Kuzminki station. Cross the main road by an underpass and wait at the third stop on the right for bus #29, which eventually terminates near a café (daily 10am–10pm), 200m from the main entrance to the grounds.

Exploring the park

At the end of the avenue through the woods, a domed **Mausoleum** and a **Church of the Virgin** with a circular belltower presage what appears to be the mansion, but was in fact the estate's **Egyptian Pavilion**. Built by Voronikhin in 1811, the faded Neoclassical edifice is hardly redolent of Egypt, but is handsomely set back behind a fence guarded by statues of fierce gryphons and dozy lions, augmented by a statue of Lenin up the drive. Until a few years ago it served as a biological research centre (where chemical weapons were tested in the 1960s), but since the building was acquired by the Moscow History Museum, a modest **exhibition** on Kuzminki's past has been established, and the interior may be restored.

The Egyptian Pavilion is open Tues–Sun 11am–5pm, winter 10am–5pm; $1; ☎377 94 57.

Crossing the bridge over a weir between the **Upper and Lower Ponds**, you'll see the crumbling brick mass of the **Konniy dvor** (Stables) on the far bank. Actually a grandiose music pavilion built in

1793 by Rodion Kazakov, its name comes from the huge sculpted horses that rear beside the stairs to its entrance, which, though boarded up, are still visible through chinks in the planks.

Kuskovo and Kuzminki

Zayauze

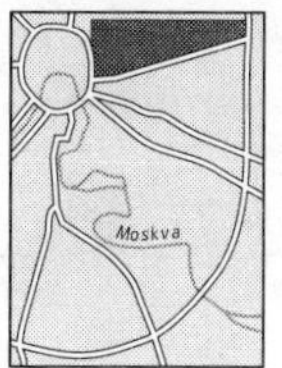

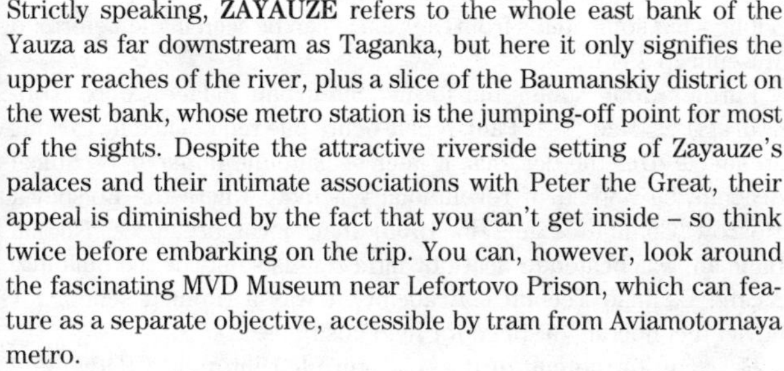

Strictly speaking, **ZAYAUZE** refers to the whole east bank of the Yauza as far downstream as Taganka, but here it only signifies the upper reaches of the river, plus a slice of the Baumanskiy district on the west bank, whose metro station is the jumping-off point for most of the sights. Despite the attractive riverside setting of Zayauze's palaces and their intimate associations with Peter the Great, their appeal is diminished by the fact that you can't get inside – so think twice before embarking on the trip. You can, however, look around the fascinating MVD Museum near Lefortovo Prison, which can feature as a separate objective, accessible by tram from Aviamotornaya metro.

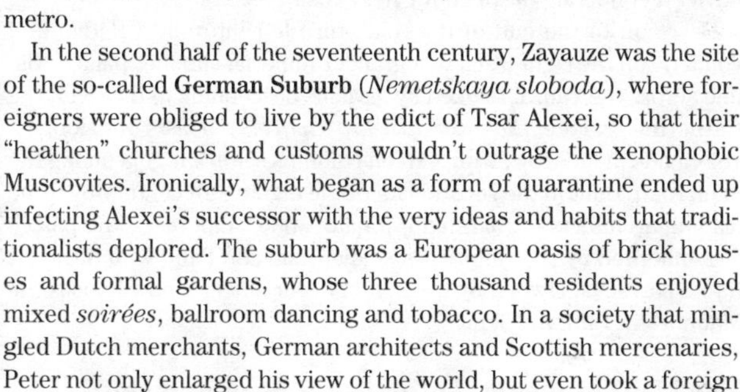

In the second half of the seventeenth century, Zayauze was the site of the so-called **German Suburb** (*Nemetskaya sloboda*), where foreigners were obliged to live by the edict of Tsar Alexei, so that their "heathen" churches and customs wouldn't outrage the xenophobic Muscovites. Ironically, what began as a form of quarantine ended up infecting Alexei's successor with the very ideas and habits that traditionalists deplored. The suburb was a European oasis of brick houses and formal gardens, whose three thousand residents enjoyed mixed *soirées*, ballroom dancing and tobacco. In a society that mingled Dutch merchants, German architects and Scottish mercenaries, Peter not only enlarged his view of the world, but even took a foreign mistress, Anna Mons.

From Baumanskaya to the Catherine Palace

Starting from Baumanskaya metro station on the Arbatsko-Pokrovskaya line, head south along Baumanskaya ulitsa until you reach the circular **Baumanskiy Market** hall, and turn right along Starokirochniy pereulok – the small house at no. 6 is where Peter visited **Anna Mons** at the start of their affair. The flaxen-haired daughter of a Westphalian wine merchant, Anna was encouraged to hope that she might become Empress because of Peter's lavish gifts and obvious disenchantment with his wife Yevdokiya. Although their relationship lasted for twelve years her ambition was ultimately fulfilled by her successor Catherine, whose origins were even humbler than Anna's.

The lane emerges onto 2-ya Baumanskaya ulitsa opposite the **Lefort Palace** (*Lefortovskiy dvorets*) that Peter built in 1697 to host parties for his "Jolly Company". From this evolved the famous "Drunken Synod", dedicated to mockery of Church rituals, whose

Zayauze

rule book stated that members were to "get drunk every day and never go to bed sober". The palace's nominal owner was the Swiss adventurer Franz Lefort, who had introduced Peter to Anna in 1690. It was in the Lefort Palace that the tsar's heir Peter II died of smallpox at the age of fourteen, on his wedding day. The palace's full size can only be appreciated by peering through the gateway; it now houses photographic and military archives, and isn't open to the public – but some items from the palace can be seen in the Lefortovo Museum (p.291).

Further along stands the former **Suburban Palace** (*Slobodskiy dvorets*) of "Mad" Tsar Paul. A pale ochre pile remodelled by various architects over the decades, it later became the Imperial Technical Academy, a hotbed of revolutionary activity where the Bolshevik Moscow Committee met in 1905; their local organizer, Nikolai Bauman, was beaten to death by ultra-rightists outside the building. As the Bauman Technical Academy, it was a training school for Soviet technocrats destined for high positions.

Carry on to the end of the road, turn left into ulitsa Radio, and you'll be on the right track to a grander Imperial summer palace, visible across the Yauza. Backed by gardens descending to the river, the **Catherine Palace** (*Yekaterininskiy dvorets*) boasts the longest colonnade in Moscow, with sixteen columns set in a loggia facing the main road. Built in the second half of the eighteenth century by three leading architects – Quarenghi, Rinaldi and Camporesi – the palace was inherited by the Empress's soldier-mad son Paul, who turned it into a barracks. Owned by the military ever since, it now houses the Malinovsky Tank Academy.

The MVD Museum, Lefortovo Prison and the Lefortovo Museum

The MVD Museum is open Mon–Fri 9am–6pm. ☎978 06 59 to book a tour in English; $3 per person (minimum five people or $15).

One place in this part of town that you can get inside is the **MVD Museum**, at Krasnokazarmennaya ul. 9a, 500m southeast of the Catherine Palace, which can also be reached by tram #24 or #37 from Aviamotornaya metro. The museum is devoted to the crime-fighting activities of the Ministry of the Interior (MVD), which in Tsarist times was also responsible for monitoring and repressing political dissent, tasks that the Soviets assigned to other agencies, but the MVD never fully relinquished. Beside the regular police, or Militia, it also controls the paramilitary OMON, which is heavily involved in the war in Chechnya.

It's worth booking a tour in English to make sense of the exhibits. One room is devoted to prisons and underworld subculture – with models of cells and pictures of criminals' tattoos – while another covers murder investigations, including horrific photos of the mutilated victims of the serial killer Andrei Chikatilo. There are drugs intercepted by border guards, and charmingly dated examples of "economic crimes" in the 1980s, like a counterfeit 25-ruble banknote and *matryoshka* dolls portraying Soviet leaders. You can also see an array of home-made weapons from the siege of the White House in 1993, and an exhibition on the war in Chechnya, which downplays the devastation wrought by the Russians and lauds the OMON's "struggle against banditry".

If you're curious about such things, it's possible to catch a glimpse of the notorious **Lefortovo Prison**, behind a row of houses on Energeticheskaya ulitsa, which can be reached by walking up ulitsa Lefortovskiy val. During the 1930s, "enemies of the people" like Yevgenia Ginzburg waited here to be transferred to camps in Siberia, as did Brezhnev-era dissidents such as Anatoly Sharansky and Father Gleb Yakunin. Under Gorbachev, the German flyer Matthias Rust spent eighteen months here for his escapade, while Yeltsin's foes were bundled into Lefortovo after the storming of the White House, only to be amnestied by parliament a few months later. As the FSB's holding prison and interrogation centre, it is often in the news for its high-profile prisoners. At the time of writing they included the Chechen commander Salman Raduev, the US businessman Edmond Pope (accused of spying), and the Olympic champion Alexander Tikhonov (charged with conspiracy to murder a provincial governor).

Further north lies the **Vedenskoe Cemetery**, where residents of the German Suburb were buried – an apt locality for the **Lefortovo Museum** at Kryukovskaya ulitsa 23. A branch of the Moscow History Museum, it contains engravings, uniforms and documents related to Peter's revels in the Lefortovo Palace (see above) and his reforms of Russian institutions and society. Though guided tours are available, nobody speaks any English so you might as well just drop in and look around if you're interested. The museum is about fifteen minutes' walk from the prison, or you can catch tram #32, #46 or #50 from Semyonovskaya metro to the "Ukhtomskaya" stop.

The Lefortovo Museum is open Tues–Sun 10am–6pm; $0.30. ☎360 01 47 for information.

Izmaylovo and Preobrazhenskoe

Further east lies the 300-hectare **Izmaylovo Park**, named after the royal estate where Peter the Great grew up, and nowadays known for its art market. The best way of getting there is to take the metro to Izmaylovskiy Park station (notice the Kalashnikov rifles used as decorative motifs). The **Izmaylovo Market** (*Izmaylovskiy rynok* or *Vernissazh*; Fri, Sat & Sun 10am–6pm; $0.50 admission) is one of Moscow's major tourist attractions, offering a vast range of souvenirs. Besides the inevitable *matryoshka* dolls and KGB sweatshirts, you can find prewar cameras, busts of Lenin, and all kinds of handicrafts. Prospective buyers should bear in mind that items predating 1960 are officially designated as antiques and need an export licence, while probably half of the icons on sale have been stolen from churches or private collections.

When the market palls, it's time to check out the **Izmaylovo Royal Estate**, on an island ten minutes' walk to the east. Owned by the

Streets and squares

Andronevskaya ploshchad	Андроньеская площадь
Baumanskaya ulitsa	Бауманская улица
Bolshaya Kalitnikovskaya ulitsa	Большая Калитниковская улица
Bolshaya Kommunisticheskaya ulitsa	Большая Коммунистическая улица
Energeticheskaya ulitsa	Энергеическая улица
Goncharnaya ulitsa	Гончарная улица
Krasnokazarmennaya ulitsa	Красноказарменная улица
Krutitskaya ulitsa	Крутитская улица
Kryukovskaya ulitsa	Крюковская улица
Nikoloyamskaya ulitsa	Николоямская улица
Nizhergorodskaya ulitsa	Нижергородская улица
Nizhniy Taganskiy tupik	Нижний Таганский тупик
Starokirochniy pereulok	Старокирочний переулок
Taganskaya ploshchad	Таганская площадь
Taganskaya ulitsa	Таганская улица
ulitsa Bolshie Kamenshchiki	улица Большие Каменщики
ulitsa Lefortovskiy val	улица Лефортовский вал
ulitsa Preobrazhenskiy val	улица Преображенский вал
ulitsa Radio	улица Радио
ulitsa Vostochnaya	улица Восточная
ulitsa Zemlyanoy val	улица Земляной вал

Metro stations

Aviamotornaya	Авиамоторная
Avtozavodskaya	Автозаводская
Baumanskaya	Бауманская
Izmaylovskiy Park	Измайловский парк
Kuskovo	Кусково
Kuzminki	Кузьминки
Marksistskaya	Марксистская
Preobrazhenskaya Ploshchad	Преображенская площадь
Proletarskaya	Пролетарская
Rimskaya	Римская
Ryazanskiy Prospekt	Рязанский проспект
Semyonovskaya	Семёновская
Taganskaya	Таганская

Museums

Andrei Rublev Museum of Early Russian Art	музей древне русской культуры им. Андрея Рублева
Ceramics Museum	музей керамики
Kuskovo	музей-усадьба Кусково
Lefortovo Museum	музей Лефортово
Museum of Furniture	музей Мебели
Museum of the MVD	музей МВД

Romanov boyars since the sixteenth century, Izmaylovo was the favourite country retreat of Tsar Alexei, whose son Peter spent much of his childhood here. In 1688 he discovered a small abandoned boat of Western design, and insisted on being taught how to sail by a Dutchman – the birth of his passion for the sea, which led to the creation of the Russian Navy and vistas of maritime power for what had previously been a landlocked nation.

Beyond a sports ground lies an enclosure of low whitewashed buildings; in the seventeenth century a wooden palace occupied the centre. Ahead stands the **Ceremonial Gate**, an impressive triple-arched structure with a tent-roof that brings you out opposite the **Cathedral of the Intercession** (*Pokrovskiy sobor*), overhung by five massive domes clustered so closely that they almost touch. Behind this stands the **Bridge Tower** that once guarded the approaches to the estate.

Preobrazhenskoe

Another stop on the Peter the Great trail is the old village of **Preobrazhenskoe**, immediately west of Izmaylovo market, where his childhood war games gradually evolved into serious manoeuvres using real weapons from the Kremlin Armoury. Playmates and servants were drilled by experts from the German Suburb; Peter insisted on being treated like a common soldier and on mastering every skill himself. Eventually, there were two companies, each 300 strong, which formed the nucleus of the first units of the Imperial Guard – the Preobrazhenskiy and Semyonovskiy regiments. Russians who mocked **Peter's "toy" regiments** were obliged to revise their opinion after the Guards crushed the Streltsy revolt of 1689, and subsequently won honours at Poltava and other battles.

Though nothing remains of their former stamping grounds, you might care to visit the **Preobrazhenskaya Old Believers' Commune**, founded in the late eighteenth century by *Bezpopovtsy* (Priestless) sectarians. Several of their churches and dormitories remain at no. 17 ulitsa Preobrazhenskiy val, which runs past the local cemetery, midway between Preobrazhenskaya Ploshchad and Semyonovskaya metro stations.

Chapter 9

The Northern Suburbs

Moscow's **NORTHERN SUBURBS** lack the eclectic charm of the inner city, and even if you wanted to wander about, the distances are too vast. Instead, they have a scattering of interesting museums and sights that call for a targeted approach, relying on the metro to get you within striking distance of each attraction.

Foremost among them is the **VVTs**, a huge exhibition park that has been likened to a Stalinist Disney World, juxtaposing extravagant pavilions and mothballed spaceships with foreign-made goods, and the beautiful **Ostankino Palace**. Moscow's **Botanical Gardens** and **TV Tower** are also in the vicinity.

Nearer to the centre of Moscow, an odd assortment of museums and theatres merits a few sorties beyond the Garden Ring. You'll find a superb collection of musical instruments at the **Museum of Musical Culture**; a weird **Animal Theatre**; the **Army Museum**; the fairytale **Vasnetsov House**; and a memorial museum in **Dostoyevsky's childhood home**. Travelling between these sights, you're likely to spot such Moscow landmarks as the **Olympic Sports Complex**.

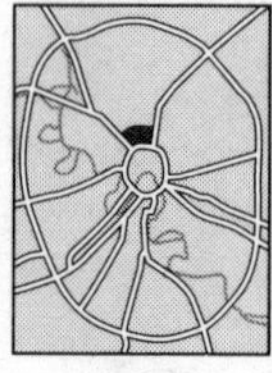

Near the Garden Ring

There are two fascinating museums **a few blocks beyond the Garden Ring**: one within ten minutes' walk of Triumfalnaya ploshchad (p.174); the other further away from Tsvetnoy Bulvar metro (p.192). To visit them both, it's best to start with the Museum of Musical Culture, and then catch a trolleybus б further round the Ring to Sadovaya-Samotyochnaya ploshchad, for the Vasnetsov House.

The Museum of Musical Culture

Two blocks north of Sadovaya-Triumfalnaya ulitsa, at ulitsa Fadeeva 4, the **Museum of Musical Culture**, named after the composer Glinka, exhibits all kinds of beautifully crafted instruments from around the world. You can hear recordings of some of them being played if you take the trouble to book a foreign-language tour beforehand. The museum also hosts concerts, lectures and temporary exhibitions.

The instruments are grouped according to their origins in colour-coded rooms, starting with pianos, guitars and zither-lyre hybrids in the red Western European section. Dragon-embossed Buryat horns and Shamen's skin drums from Yakutia are found in the green hall, along with a nineteenth-century 22-piece horn band from western Russia. The yellow room brings together Moldavian hurdy-gurdies, gorgeously inlaid Caucasian stringed instruments and a huge bowl-shaped contrabass from Khirgizia. Casting its net still wider, the blue hall displays Eastern European and Oriental instruments, such as Polish bagpipes, Chinese drums and a horse-headed Korean *morinkhuur*. There is also a small **memorial room** devoted to the Russian conductor and violinist David Ostrakh, whose Stradivarius viola was stolen from the museum in 1996, but recovered by the police in Sochi the following year.

Near the Garden Ring

The Museum of Musical Culture is open Tues–Sun 11am–7pm; closed the last day of each month; $0.30. ☎972 32 37 for details of concerts, or to book a tour ($2). The museum also has its own Web site: www.museum.ru/glinka.

The Vasnetsov House

Amid the towerblocks that rise across the Ring from Tsvetnoy bulvar, a lovely relic of *fin-de-siècle* culture exudes the spirit of its former owner, **Viktor Vasnetsov** (1848–1926), a key figure in the Russian revival style. Vasnetsov believed that "a true work of art expresses everything about a people . . . It conveys the past, the present and, perhaps, the future of the nation," and sought to express this in his own work. An architect as well as a painter, he designed the facade of the Tretyakov Gallery, a church for the artists colony at Abramtsevo, and the wooden house in Moscow where he lived for the last 32 years of his life.

To reach the **Vasnetsov House** from Tsvetnoy bulvar, cross the Ring beneath the flyover and head up the grass slope into a housing estate, turning left 50m later; the house is at the far end of pereulok Vasnetsova. Entirely built of wood, its ground floor comprises five rooms, all cosily furnished with tiled stoves, chairs and cabinets, designed by Vasnetsov himself. The pieces are massive but so delicately carved as to be fit for a boyar's palace. Echoes of medieval Russia abound, from pictures of processions to a chain-mail tunic, fixed to the spiral staircase leading to his studio.

The Vasnetsov House is open Wed–Sun 10am–5pm; closed the last Thurs of each month; $5.

Although you now have to use the backstairs, the studio's impact is undiminished, its cathedral-like space filled by Vasnetsov's huge paintings of warriors confronting monsters, and various Russian fairytales. One wall is dominated by *The Sleeping Princess*, whose realm lies under an evil spell, awaiting revival – painted in the last year of Vasnetsov's life, at a time when Stalin was tightening his grip on Russia. In the corner, *Baba Yaga* flies through the woods on her broomstick, clasping a terrified stolen child: while you'll also recognize *Princess Nesmeyana*, whose glumness led to the classic offer

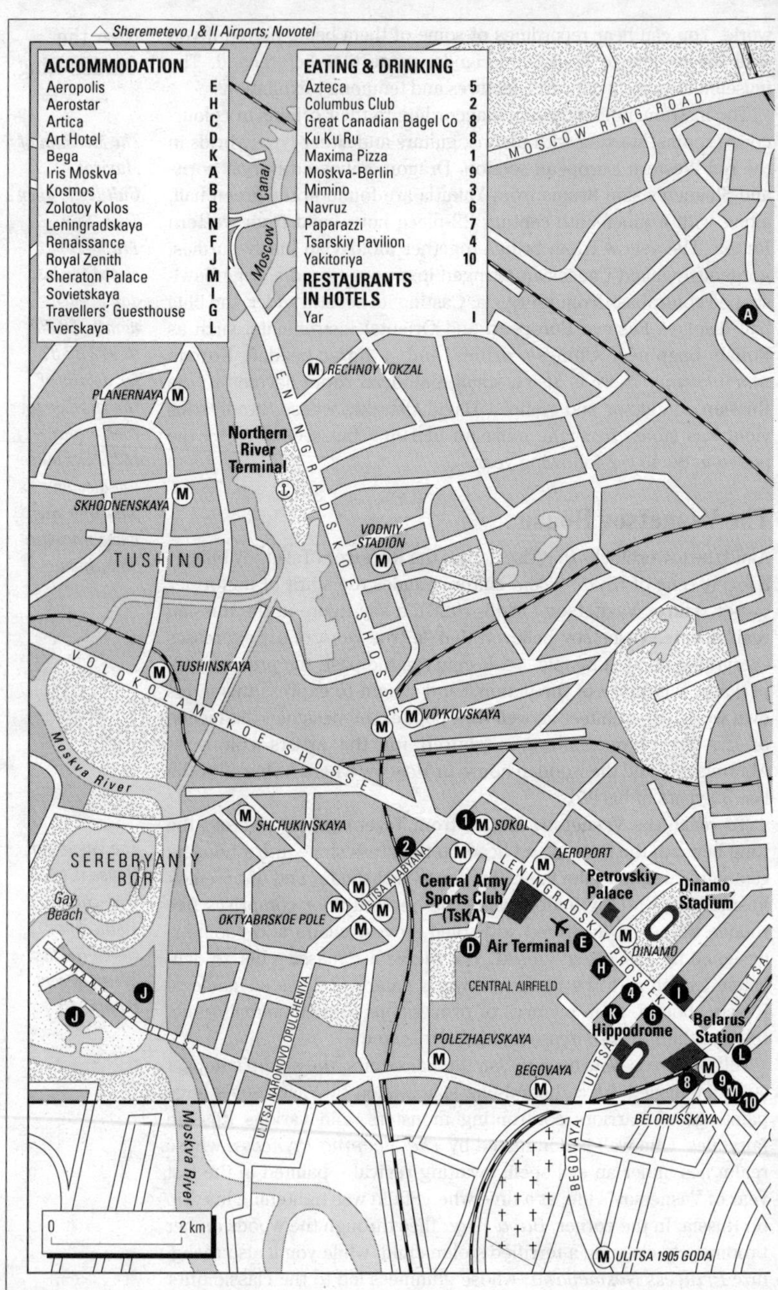
Sheremetevo I & II Airports; Novotel
ACCOMMODATION
Aeropolis E
Aerostar H
Artica C
Art Hotel D
Bega K
Iris Moskva A
Kosmos B
Zolotoy Kolos B
Leningradskaya N
Renaissance F
Royal Zenith J
Sheraton Palace M
Sovietskaya I
Travellers' Guesthouse G
Tverskaya L
EATING & DRINKING
Azteca 5
Columbus Club 2
Great Canadian Bagel Co 8
Ku Ku Ru 8
Maxima Pizza 1
Moskva-Berlin 9
Mimino 3
Navruz 6
Paparazzi 7
Tsarskiy Pavilion 4
Yakitoriya 10
RESTAURANTS IN HOTELS
Yar I
MOSCOW RING ROAD
Moscow Canal
LENINGRADSKOE SHOSSE
RECHNOY VOKZAL
PLANERNAYA
Northern River Terminal
SKHODNENSKAYA
VODNIY STADION
TUSHINO
TUSHINSKAYA
VOLOKOLAMSKOE SHOSSE
VOYKOVSKAYA
Moskva River
SHCHUKINSKAYA
SOKOL
AEROPORT
SEREBRYANIY BOR
ULITSA ALABYANA
LENINGRADSKIY PROSPEKT
Central Army Sports Club (TsKA)
Petrovskiy Palace
Dinamo Stadium
Gay Beach
OKTYABRSKOE POLE
Air Terminal
DINAMO
CENTRAL AIRFIELD
ULITSA
Hippodrome
Belarus Station
POLEZHAEVSKAYA
BEGOVAYA
ULITSA NARONOVO OPULCHENIYA
BELORUSSKAYA
BEGOVAYA
Moskva River
0
2 km
ULITSA 1905 GODA

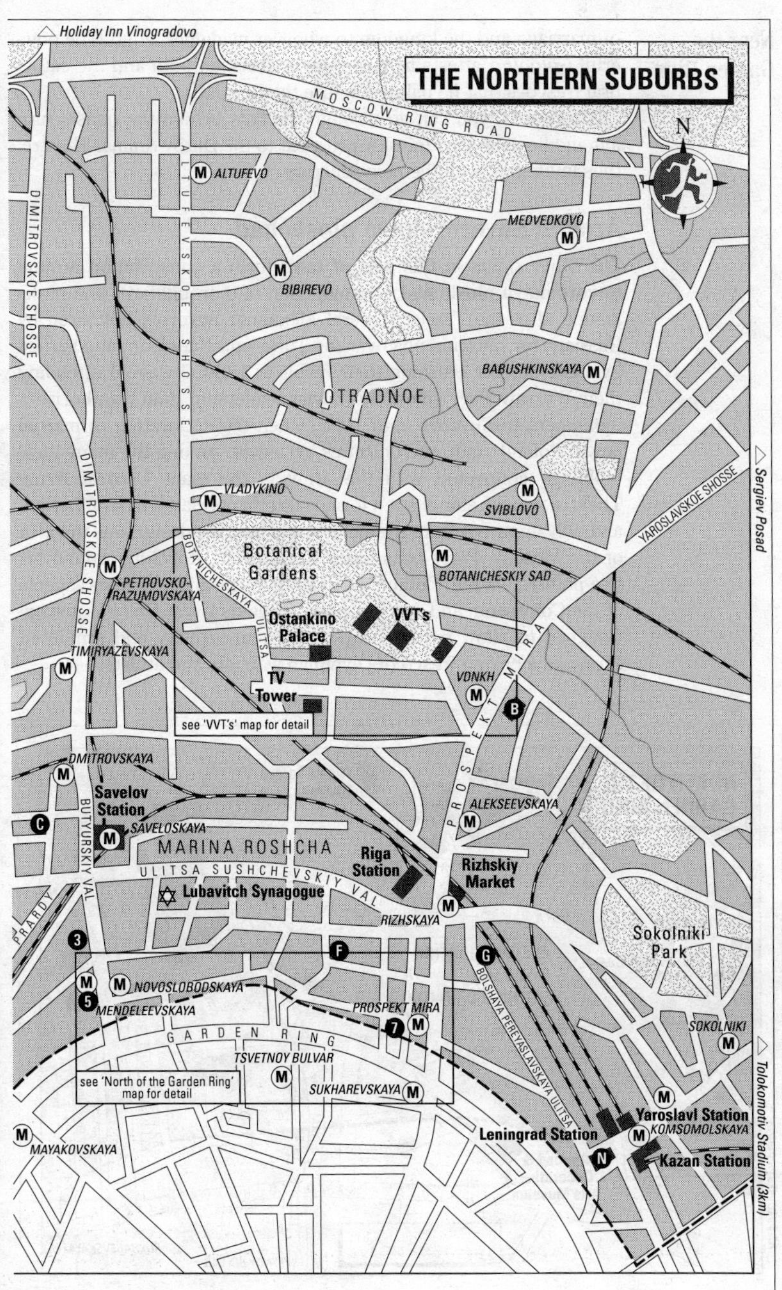

Holiday Inn Vinogradovo
THE NORTHERN SUBURBS
MOSCOW RING ROAD
N
ALTUFEVO
ALTUFEVSKOE SHOSSE
DIMITROVSKOE SHOSSE
MEDVEDKOVO
BIBIREVO
BABUSHKINSKAYA
OTRADNOE
VLADYKINO
SVIBLOVO
YAROSLAVSKOE SHOSSE
Sergiev Posad
Botanical Gardens
BOTANICHESKAYA ULITSA
BOTANICHESKIY SAD
PETROVSKO-RAZUMOVSKAYA
Ostankino Palace
VVT's
TIMIRYAZEVSKAYA
TV Tower
VDNKH
PROSPEKT MIRA
see 'VVT's' map for detail
DMITROVSKAYA
Savelov Station
BUTYURSKIY VAL
SAVELOSKAYA
MARINA ROSHCHA
ALEKSEEVSKAYA
Riga Station
Rizhskiy Market
ULITSA SUSHCHEVSKIY VAL
Lubavitch Synagogue
RIZHSKAYA
PRARDY
Sokolniki Park
NOVOSLOBODSKAYA
MENDELEEVSKAYA
BOLSHAYA PEREYASLAVSKAYA ULITSA
PROSPEKT MIRA
GARDEN RING
SOKOLNIKI
TSVETNOY BULVAR
Tolokomotiv Stadium (3km)
see 'North of the Garden Ring' map for detail
SUKHAREVSKAYA
Yaroslavl Station
Leningrad Station
KOMSOMOLSKAYA
MAYAKOVSKAYA
Kazan Station

of marriage and the kingdom to whoever made her laugh. The powerful *Golgotha* attests to Vasnetsov's Christian faith and the cathedral frescoes that he painted before the Revolution.

Afterwards, you can go through the flats behind the house, turn left and head up Olympiyskiy prospekt to the Durov Animal Theatre, thus linking up with the next itinerary.

Around Suvorovskaya ploshchad

The other sights in this part of town form a constellation around **Suvorovkaya ploshchad**, a conjunction of thoroughfares and parks named after the Tsarist General Alexander Suvorov, honoured by Russians for his triumphs over the Turks and Napoleon, and reviled by the Poles for crushing their revolt in 1830. To avoid offending their Warsaw Pact allies, the Soviet leadership didn't authorize a monument to Suvorov until 1982, when the declaration of martial law in Poland made such niceties irrelevant. Among the many local buildings connected with the army is the giant **Central Army Theatre**, whose star-shaped form is utterly unrelated to its function, and only apparent from the air. It's said that the design was the idea of the Moscow Party boss Lazar Kaganovich, doodling around his five-pointed ink pot. Completed in 1940, its facade combines aspects of the Colosseum and the Acropolis, while its Great Hall has a stage designed to allow battle scenes using real artillery and armoured cars, and a ceiling fresco of Olympian warriors and athletes.

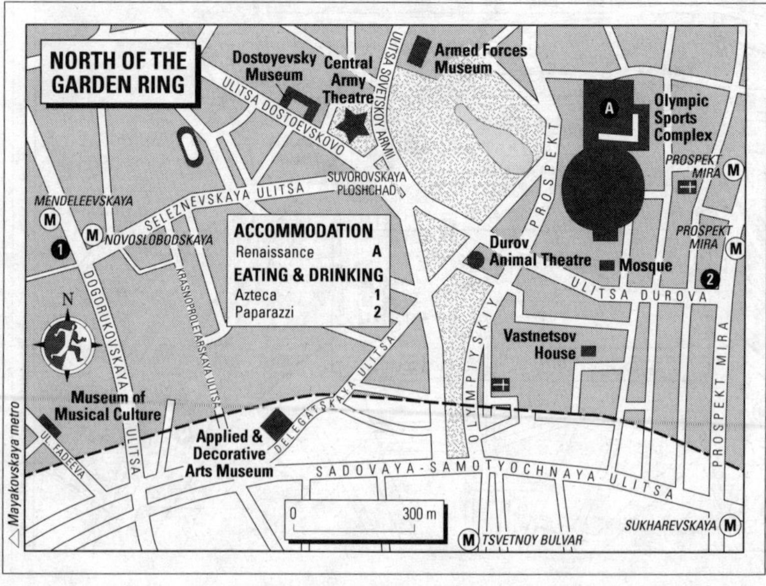

Until the completion of two new stations in the vicinity, getting there entails walking from Prospekt Mira or Novoslobodskaya metro station (worth seeing for its stained-glass panels) or the Vasnetsov House, which takes about fifteen minutes.

Near the Garden Ring

The Durov Animal Theatre

The most curious attraction is the bunker-like **Durov Animal Theatre** (*teatr Zvery imeni Durova*), a unique institution known to generations of Muscovites as "Dedushka (Grandpa) Durov". Its founder, Vladimir Durov (1863–1934), believed that circuses were cruel because they forced animals to perform tricks, rather than allowing their natural behaviour to be developed and shown on stage, accompanied by educational talks. His beliefs live on in this theatre, which still stages performances in which rabbits happily drum away, racoons wash their paws before meals, and monkeys appear to "read" a book while searching for seeds between the pages – Durov never used punishments, only rewards. His results impressed Pavlov, and the theatre's future was guaranteed after the Revolution by the Commissar of Public Enlightenment.

Durov once staged parodies of the Treaty of Versailles, and devised an act in which pigs and dogs boarded a train where a monkey punched their tickets, and a hen with a suitcase bustled up just as it departed "for Yalta". Sadly, this has now been relegated to the theatre's **museum** (Wed–Fri, Sat & Sun at 1pm, 2.15pm, 3pm; ☎971 40 37 to arrange a visit; $1) and is now performed by mice – as demonstrated by Durov's granddaughter, Natalya Durova, a vivacious octogenarian who regards the animals as her family. Though hard-pressed to feed the elephant, pelicans and (retired) lion, she still takes in abandoned animals, housing them willy-nilly, so that the parrots caged above cats have learned to miaow. Visitors should try to attend a full-blown show (see p.364 for details).

The Dostoyevsky Museum

The Dostoyevsky Museum is open Thurs, Sat & Sun 11am–6pm, Wed & Fri 2–9pm (2–6pm in winter); closed the last day of each month; $1. To arrange a guided tour ☎281 10 85.

The **Dostoyevsky Museum** occupies a small, gloomy house in the grounds of the Mariya Hospital for the Poor, granted to Dostoyevsky's physician father when he worked here. As his salary wasn't enough to maintain the standards expected of them, the family was dogged by financial worries, compounded by the doctor's alcoholism and violence (he was eventually murdered by his own serfs). After Dostoyevsky himself died in St Petersburg in 1881, his widow and brother preserved many of his possessions as the foundation of the memorial museum opened in 1928, which now features a reconstruction of his childhood home, based on Dostoyevsky's own diaries and descriptions of his youth.

He and his brother shared a tiny room filled by steel trunks and a tiled stove where they played with toy soldiers and a hobby horse, and had their lessons at the card table in the living room. A drawing room was so crucial to the family's social standing that their parents were prepared to sleep in a narrow bed behind a screen, jammed beside a washstand and a baby's crib. The museum also exhibits the parish ledger recording Dostoyevsky's birth in 1821, and his quill pen and signature preserved under glass.

The Armed Forces Museum

The Armed Forces Museum is open Wed–Sun 11am–5pm; $0.50.

Off in the other direction from Suvorovskaya ploshchad, the **Armed Forces Museum** is instantly recognizable by the T-34 tank and ballistic missile mounted out front, archetypal assertions of Soviet power that give no indication of how this bastion of ideological rectitude was shaken by glasnost and the fall of Communism. One result is a sympathetic exhibition on the White Army, centred on a diorama of trench warfare in Eastern Siberia. Upstairs is devoted to the Great Patriotic War and features such emotive juxtapositions as a replica partisan hide-out, human hair and tattooed skin from Maidenjak concentration camp, and a poster of a woman prisoner entitled *All hopes are on you, Red forces*. Victory is represented by a shattered bronze eagle from the Reichstag and the Nazi banners that were cast down before the Lenin Mausoleum in 1945 – as depicted in a huge painting.

The upbeat postwar section proudly displays the wreckage of an American U-2 spy-plane shot down over the Urals in 1960 (hall 20), and barely mentions the invasions of Hungary and Czechoslovakia. In the two rooms on Afghanistan, evidence of casualties and atrocities is confined to photo albums, easily overlooked beside the huge booster-stage of an SS-16 missile, which the Soviets agreed to scrap under SALT II. Don't miss the gleeful picture of the burning of Hitler's corpse, at the top of the stairs.

Parked around the sides and back of the museum is an array of hardware that includes an **armoured train** such as carried Trotsky into battle during the Civil War, and a **helicopter gunship** and a **MiG-25** of the type used to slaughter Afghans in the name of Internationalism. As yet, there is no hardware from the Chechen wars.

The Olympic Sports Complex and beyond

Across the highway from the Durov Theatre looms the **Olympic Sports Complex** (*Sportkompleks Olympiyskiy*), the largest of the facilities created for the 1980 Moscow Olympics. This prestige project was headed by Mikhail Posokhin, a fervent advocate of the international modern style, and Moscow's Chief Architect under Brezhnev. Its vast enclosed stadium seats up to thirty-five thousand, and is capable of being converted from a football ground into an athletics track or a skating rink. Dynamic murals of skaters and gymnasts decorate the adjacent training rink and gymnasium, while the smaller block to the north contains an Olympic-sized pool.

In the shadow of the stadium stands a Neo-Russian edifice that's only recognizable as a **mosque** (*mechet*) by the Islamic crescents atop its domes. Such discretion is understandable given the fate of another mosque in Moscow whose Imam was shot on the premises by the NKVD, though this one was cynically permitted to continue working as "proof" that religious freedom existed in the USSR. Today, its Imam is spiritual head of the (mainly Sunni) Muslim communities of Moscow, Yaroslavl and Tver.

Prospekt Mira and Marina Roshcha

To the east of the stadium, Moscow's main northbound thoroughfare, **prospekt Mira**, follows the medieval road to the Trinity Monastery and Yaroslavl, which from the sixteenth century also led to Russia's northern port at Arkhangelsk. Its present name – Peace Avenue – commemorates the 6th World Festival of Youth, in 1957, which had peace as one of its major themes. Ten kilometres long and groaning with traffic, prospekt Mira is really only of interest at two points – Rizhskiy Market and the surreal VVTs. Though both are best reached by the Kaluzhsko-Rizhskaya metro line, it's also possible to catch bus #85, from one block north of Sukharevskaya ploshchad (p.193), all the way to the VVTs.

Two kilometres beyond the Ring, the first major intersection is named after **Riga Station** (*Rizhskiy vokzal*), the terminus for the Baltic states; as is **Rizhskiy Market** (Mon–Sat 7.30am–7.30pm, Sun 7.30am–5pm), across the avenue. Moscow's largest food market

Tales of old Marina Roshcha and the Butyurka

Before it was redeveloped in the 1960s, old **Marina Roshcha** was a labyrinth of shacks where only the locals knew their way around and the police seldom ventured; where pious Jews rubbed shoulders with denizens of the *Blatnoi mir* (Thieves' World). A tale is attached to every grave in the local cemetery, such as the one that belonged to a youth who unknowingly impregnated his own mother and then married his daughter (whom he believed to be his adopted sister), inscribed: "Here lies father and daughter, brother and sister, husband and wife".

Equally renowned in folklore but still very much in existence is the **Butyurka Prison** near Savelov Station. Founded by Catherine the Great, it was the point of departure for Tsarist convoys of prisoners bound for Siberia, who walked there in fetters. Muscovites always came to give them food and clothing and distribute alms at Easter. Political prisoners were so unusual that the staff apologized to a Bolshevik who disliked the food. Conditions worsened after the Revolution, when Butyurka became a transit-prison handling over 100,000 people a year. This was achieved by cramming 140 into a cell meant for 25, and 2000 extra men (including Solzhenitsyn) into the prison church. More recently, the media mogul **Vladimir Gusinsky** spent three days in Butyurka as a warning to other oligarchs that the immunity they enjoyed in the Yeltsin era could no longer be taken for granted under Putin.

offers a feast of sights, smells and free nibbles to tempt buyers, while vendors outside purvey everything from sex aids to sheepskins. Like most other markets here, the Rizhskiy is controlled by gangsters, – in this case the Lyubertsky, named after a grim Moscow satellite town whose illegal body-building clubs spawned a generation of thugs in the 1980s.

To the west of Riga Station lies the Marina Roshcha district, which rates a mention for its past (see box on p.301) though the only "sight" is the **Lubavitch Synagogue** on 2-y Vysheslavtsev pereulok. The only synagogue in the country built during the Soviet era (in 1926), the original wooden building was destroyed by arsonists in 1993 and the brick one that replaced it was bombed in 1996, but it continues to function as a place of worship (Mon–Thurs 9am–6pm, Fri & Sun 9am–4pm).

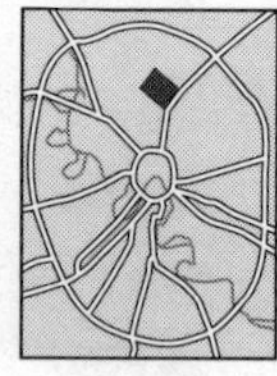

The VVTs (VDNKh) and around

The main reason for venturing this far north is the **All-Russia Exhibition Centre** or **VVTs**, still better known by its Soviet title, the **Exhibition of Economic Achievements** or **VDNKh** ("Vay-den-ha") – a permanent trade fair-cum-shopping centre for Russian consumers, which reflects the state of the national economy more faithfully than its founders intended. Grandiose architecture mocks the denuded halls where imported cars and TVs have ousted Russian products, while crowds of shoppers ignore the gilded fountains and livestock pavilions, and Indian merchants tout their wares as if in a Delhi bazaar. The surreality of the scene is enhanced by the two amazing monuments near the entrance, which are worth the trip in themselves.

Two great Soviet monuments

One of the best ever Soviet monuments, the **Space Obelisk** consists of a rocket blasting nearly 100m into the sky on a stylized plume of energy clad in shining titanium. It was unveiled in 1964, three years after Gagarin orbited the earth, an unabashed expression of pride in this unique feat. Tableaux on either side of the obelisk's base show engineers and scientists striving to put a cosmonaut into his rocket, and Lenin leading the masses into space, as a woman offers her baby to the sun. In summertime, Moscow hippies gather here to strum guitars.

The Museum of Cosmonautics is open Tues–Sun 10am–7pm; closed the last Fri of each month; $0.30.

Beneath the monument is a **Memorial Museum of Cosmonautics**, tracing the history of rocketry and space exploration from the 1920s till the present day. Exhibits include the first rocket engine, created by Tsander and tested in 1931; models of missiles, satellites and moon-walkers; genuine spacesuits (for $2, you can have your picture taken wearing Gagarin's suit) and space food; and photos from Star City, showing cosmonauts learning the art of working and eating in zero gravity. Beyond the obelisk, a **statue of Konstantin Tsiolkovsky** (1837–1935), the "father of rocketry", gazes over the

Alley of Cosmonauts, flanked by bronze busts of intrepid space voyagers.

Off in the other direction, past the main entrance to the VVTs, stands an even more celebrated monument, the **Worker and Collective Farm Girl**. Designed by Vera Mukhina for the Soviet pavilion at the 1937 Paris Expo, its colossal twin figures stride forward in unison, raising the hammer and sickle. Weighing thirty tons apiece and fashioned from stainless steel blocks, they were hailed as the embodiment of Soviet industrial progress, though in fact each block had been hand-made on a wooden template, and the finished monument was rigorously scrutinized due to a rumour that Trotsky's profile could be seen in the folds of the drapery. Once it had been erected outside the VDNKh, Stalin was taken to view it at night, and loved it. Should you risk darting across the busy road for a closer look, notice the large service hatch visible beneath the Farm Girl's billowing skirts. Homeless people regularly sleep within her figure, like the student who installed himself inside El Lissitsky's street monument *The Red Wedge Invades the White Square*, in the winter of 1918.

Visiting the VVTs

The VVTs is within walking distance of VDNKh metro station (as it's still called), just beyond the Space Obelisk – though neither are initially visible due to the shopping arcade beside the metro exit. Although the VVTs is best explored on foot if you're interested in its architecture, the miniature "trains" that run from just inside the main entrance to the Space Pavilion at the far end of the grounds can provide a quick overall tour for the equivalent of $1. Try to avoid sale days (advertised in the press), when crowds of buyers jam the pavilions and bring mayhem to the parking lots for half a mile around. In winter, when the fountains are turned off and its icy paths are hazardous, the VVTs hosts a **Russian Winter Festival** (Dec 25–Jan 5) featuring *troyka* rides and folk dancing.

The VVTs is open daily 10am–9pm; free. Most of the pavilions are open 10am–6pm. Except for a few that have become "exclusive" showrooms, free admission is the rule.

To fully appreciate the park, you need to know something of the **history of the VDNKh**. Its genesis was the All-Union Agricultural Exhibition of 1939, a display of the fruits of Socialism and a showpiece of Stalinist monumental art that was intended to open two years earlier, but was delayed by the purging of many of its leading participants. Scores of pavilions trumpeted the achievements of the Soviet republics and the planned economy; there was even one devoted to the construction projects of the Gulag. While propaganda belied the fact that the USSR had been harrowed by collectivization and was still gripped by the Great Terror, paranoia was so rampant that the statue of Stalin that dominated the show was searched for bombs, as if any harm to the idol might endanger the state.

In the event, the exhibition was so successful that it was revived on a permanent basis in 1954, with some eighty pavilions spread over

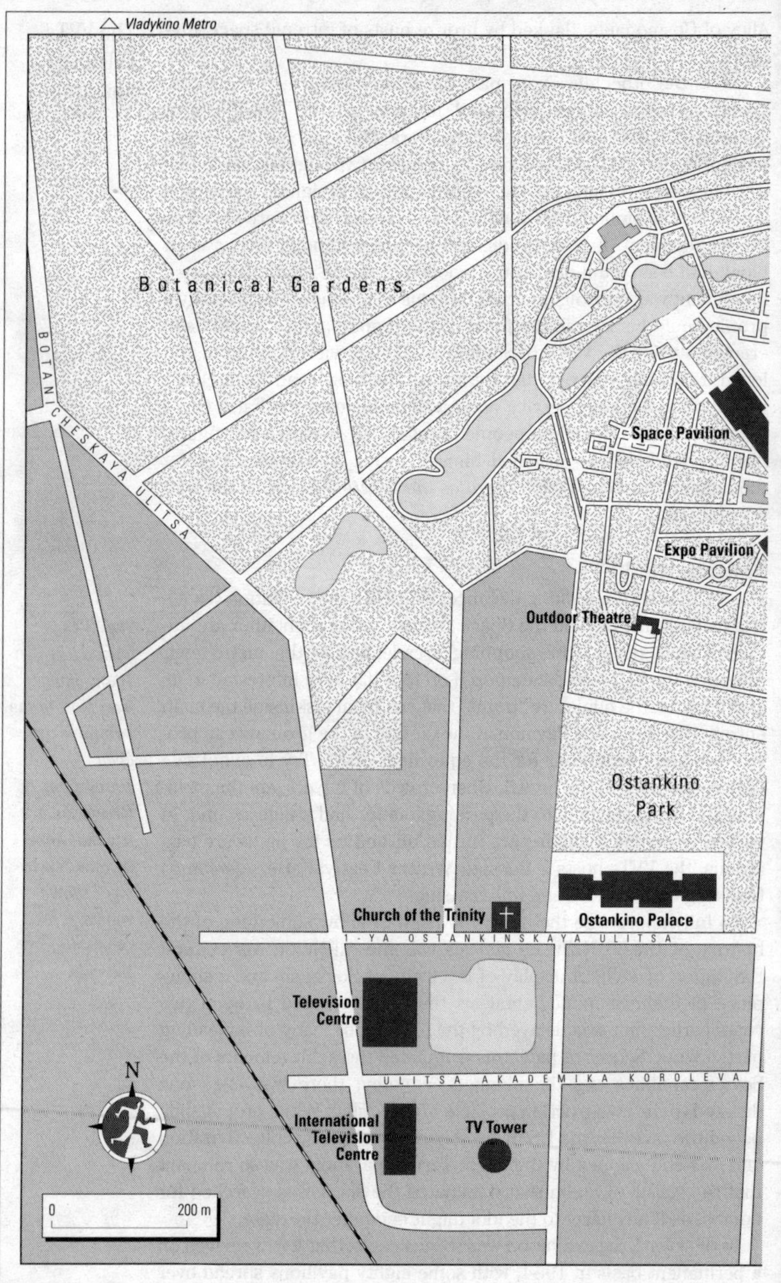
Vladykino Metro
Botanical Gardens
BOTANICHESKAYA ULITSA
Space Pavilion
Expo Pavilion
Outdoor Theatre
Ostankino Park
Church of the Trinity
Ostankino Palace
1-YA OSTANKINSKAYA ULITSA
Television Centre
ULITSA AKADEMIKA KOROLEVA
International Television Centre
TV Tower
N
0
200 m

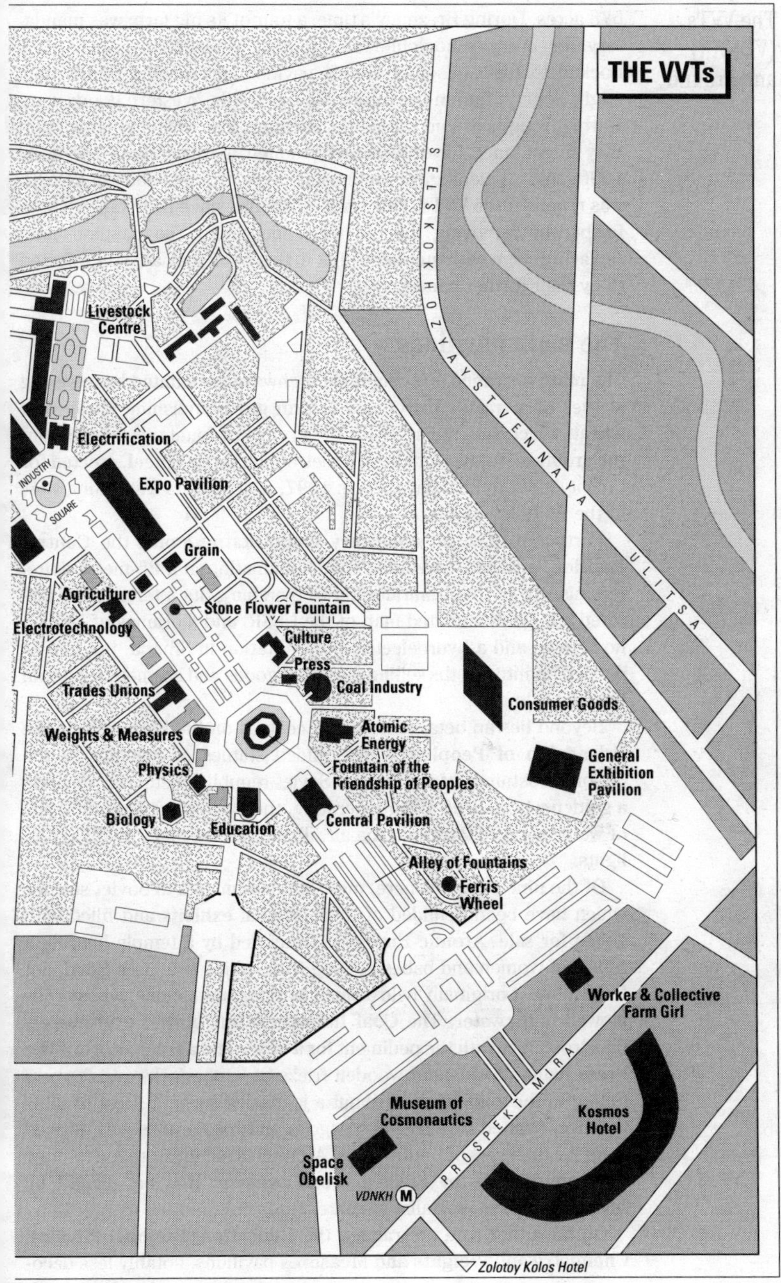
THE VVTs
SELSKOKHOZYAYSTVENNAYA ULITSA
Livestock Centre
Electrification
INDUSTRY SQUARE
Expo Pavilion
Grain
Agriculture
Stone Flower Fountain
Electrotechnology
Culture
Press
Coal Industry
Trades Unions
Consumer Goods
Weights & Measures
Atomic Energy
General Exhibition Pavilion
Fountain of the Friendship of Peoples
Physics
Biology
Education
Central Pavilion
Alley of Fountains
Ferris Wheel
Worker & Collective Farm Girl
PROSPEKT MIRA
Museum of Cosmonautics
Kosmos Hotel
Space Obelisk
VDNKH
M
Zolotoy Kolos Hotel

578 acres. During Brezhnev's time, a tour of its pig farm was mandatory for every schoolchild and tourist, while canny Muscovites flocked to the Consumer Goods pavilion, previewing things they might hope to find in the future. By the 1980s, Western goods were starting to appear and the Soviet pavilions lost whatever conviction they might once have possessed, though it wasn't until the early 1990s that all ideological pretensions were dropped and the VDNKh was renamed the VVTs. This revisionism has since been taken a step further by removing the old signs identifying the pavilions and replacing them with numbers – but in this book they are still referred to by their former names.

The main pavilions

The **main entrance** is a triumphal archway surmounted by towering statues of a tractor driver and a farm girl brandishing sheaves of wheat, which sets the scale for the avenue of fountains leading into the grounds. To the right is a 75-metre-high **ferris wheel**, erected for the city's 850th birthday bash in 1997, which offers a stunning view of the VVTs for $1.50.

Further in past an obligatory **Lenin statue** looms the **Central Pavilion**, a Stalinist wedding-cake culminating in a 35-metre spire, reminiscent of the Admiralty in St Petersburg. Its interior once featured a huge illuminated map of the USSR, and dioramas of Lenin's hometown and a hydroelectric power station in Siberia, but is now divided up into booths selling electrical goods and cosmetics, plus an Internet salon.

Beyond lies an octagonal square centred on the **Fountain of the Friendship of Peoples**, whose gilded statues of maidens in the national costumes of the sixteen Soviet republics demurely encircle a golden wheatsheaf. When operating, the basin erupts into 800 jets of water sprayed 24m into the air, illuminated at night by 525 spotlights.

Of the nine pavilions here, most are monuments to Soviet science which have been denuded of their original exhibits and filled with goods for sale. **Atomic Energy** is sanctified by a temple bearing a fresco of women and babes picking fruit, which promises Eden, not Chernobyl. It originally held a small working atomic pile, whose rods glowed underwater. The **Coal Industry**'s fruit-laden facade barely finds room beneath the pediment for a miner and a teacher, while **the Press** flaunts a splendid wooden frieze of lumberjacks and farmers toiling in the wilderness, without a journalist in sight. Best of all is **Culture**, fronted by a star-like pagoda and tiled arabesques derived from the mosques of Central Asia. Architects felt encouraged to draw on ethnic motifs by Stalin's pronouncement that art should be "national in form, socialist in content".

On the other side are ranged the **Education**, **Biology**, **Physics**, **Chemistry** and **Weights and Measures** pavilions, notably less decorative but not as dull as the post-Stalinist ones off the square. Unless you want to discover what's being sold inside, most of the other pavilions can be ignored, but the silvery clouds in the lobby of the **Trade Unions** building deserve a look.

The Soviet taste for mineral extravagance runs riot with the mosaic-encrusted **Stone Fountain**, flanked by spouting geese and fish, like a fountain at one of the Imperial palaces outside St Petersburg. Even wilder are the pavilions beyond, dedicated to **Electrotechnology**, **Agriculture** and **Grain**. The columns of the first are wreathed in mosaic ribbons, while Agriculture is crowned by a florid rotunda and a gilded spire, and crenellated with ears of corn. When opened as the Ukrainian pavilion in 1939, it boasted of abundance when Ukraine was still depopulated and half-starved after collectivization. On either side of its fruit-heavy portal, statues of husky peasants enthuse over the harvest and Stalin's wisdom, while the entrance to the Grain pavilion is similarly adorned.

At the far end of the avenue, a **Vostok rocket** of the type that carried Gagarin into orbit is suspended from an enormous gantry outside the **Space Pavilion**, once the VDNKh's crowning glory. Although a giant portrait of Gagarin still gazes down on its hanger-like interior, virtually all of the once vast array of space hardware has been auctioned off, and the hall is now full of Indians pushing trolleys laden with TV sets, unloaded in an endless stream from trucks outside.

If from here you're planning to visit the Ostankino Palace, the quickest way of getting there is to leave the VVTs via the gates near the Outdoor Theatre, and cut through the park across the road. Alternatively, you can head northwards from the Space Pavilion to reach the Botanical Gardens – for details of both, see the following sections.

Ostankino Palace

The pink and white Neoclassical **Ostankino Palace** (*Ostankinskiy dvorets*) is inseparably linked to the story of Count Nikolai Sheremetev, his love of the theatre and Parasha Kovalyova, a serf girl on his Kuskovo estate (see p.285) whom he is said to have first set eyes on as she was leading a cow home from the woods. Tutored in the dramatic arts, she became a gifted opera singer with the stage name of "Zhemchugova" (from the Russian word for "pearl"), and the prima donna at Ostankino, a palace specially built for staging performances. Its grandeur and theatricality were epitomized by a reception staged for Tsar Paul in 1795. As he rode through the woods, dozens of pre-sawn trees suddenly fell aside to reveal the palace in all its glory. Remarkably, the whole palace is made of wood, disguised beneath a thin layer of stucco; for fear of fire, the building is unheated and has never been electrified.

The first room on the **guided tour** contains an exhibition on the Sheremetev family, which owned three million acres and 300,000

The palace is open late May–Sept Wed–Sun 10am–5pm, except on very rainy days; $1 ($0.30 on Sun). Tours every 30min. From June to Aug concerts are held three times a week; ☎283 46 45 or 286 62 88 for details. To get there from VDNKh metro, take trolleybus #11.

serfs and preserved its fortune by bequeathing the lot to the eldest son instead of dividing it between several heirs – a custom maintained until Nikolai's grandsons agreed to take equal shares. On the left of the columned hall beyond is a portrait of Parasha, visibly pregnant with Count Nikolai's child; she died twenty days after giving birth, whereupon he revealed that they had secretly married three years earlier, after fourteen years of living together out of wedlock.

Beyond the hall lies the **Italian Pavilion**, a large room sumptuously decorated with Classical motifs made from tiny pieces of paper glued together, with fake marble columns and bronze sconces, and a superb parquet floor of mahogany, birch and ebony. A vaulted **Gallery** awash with fake malachite and gilded sphinxes provides a suitably dramatic approach to Ostankino's *pièce de résistance* – the **Theatre** where the Count staged performances by 200 serf actors, trained since the age of seven. As it stands today the hall is configured as a ballroom, but was designed so that the floor could be lowered and the chandelier lifted into the ceiling, where a copper sheet reflected its light onto the stage; the columns could be moved around, and there were ingenious devices for simulating the sound of rain and thunder (which still work) and lightning flashes. It is now used for concerts of classical music.

Visitors may also see the **Egyptian Pavilion**, with its pseudo-Pharaonic statues, but the rest of the upper floor is still being restored, having been occupied and looted by one of Napoleon's generals in 1812, and last inhabited in 1856. The palace was subsequently allowed to decay until Soviet times, when it was opened as a Museum of Serf Art in recognition of the fact that it was designed and built by serf artisans. Finally, you can roam the formal gardens behind the palace, featuring a Hill of Parnassus and numerous copies of antique statues.

Beside the road in front of the palace stands the **Church of the Trinity** (*tserkov Troitskiy*), whose elaborate *nalichniki*, *kokoshniki*, and blue-and-gold ceramic insets are typical of the Moscow Baroque style of the 1680s. Commissioned by the Cherkassky family which owned this land before the Sheremetevs, the church was at one time connected to the palace by a covered walkway, and served as its private chapel.

The TV Centre and Tower

Across the road from the Church of the Trinity, a large ornamental pond and vistas of concrete surround the glassy **Ostankino Television Centre**, a complex of studios at the base of a **TV Tower** (*Telibashnya*) whose 35,000 tons of ferroconcrete taper from 50m in diameter at the base, to a needle-like shaft 540m high – making it the tallest freestanding structure in Europe. Heralded as proof of Soviet technological prowess when it was constructed in 1967, the TV Tower became yet another symbol of Russia's decline when it caught fire on August 27, 2000 – due to a short-circuit in the power cables. Fire-fighting efforts were hindered by the fact that Ostankino's management refused to turn off the electricity, and the discovery that the central part of the tower was not linked to the automatic fire extinguisher system, as the architects' plans had specified. As a result, Russia was briefly without a national television system, and the choice of channels for Muscovites was severely restricted for months – while repairs were estimated to take a year and cost $3.6 billion. It also deprived tourists of the bird's-eye view of the VVTs and Moscow from 337 metres up, that was formerly provided by an **observation deck** and the **revolving restaurant** "Seventh Heaven". Prior to its "towering inferno" notoriety, Ostankino had been best known abroad for its role in the battle between Yeltsin and parliament in 1993 (see box below).

The Botanical Gardens

Founded in 1945, Moscow's **Botanical Gardens** (*Botanicheskiy sad*) contain the finest collection of flora in Russia, including such exotica as giant water lilies in greenhouses, and a Japanese rock garden. From nearer home, at the centre of the 860-acre park, there are groves of birches and 200-year-old oaks to delight the Russian soul, and rose gardens planted with sixteen thousand varieties of blooms. The gardens are open Wednesday to Sunday from 10am to 4pm (8pm in summer), except during April and October; separate tickets ($0.30) are required for the dendrarium, the Japanese garden and the orangerie.

What really happened at Ostankino?

Nobody who was in Moscow at the time can forget the **battle of Ostankino** on the night of October 3, 1993, when a mob of 4000 parliamentary supporters tried to capture the TV Centre. The national news channel announced "We're under attack" and then went off the air, leaving millions of Russians convinced that it had fallen to Yeltsin's enemies in a *coup d'état*. Only those with access to CNN were aware that it remained in government hands despite an eight-hour battle in which over sixty people died, till the army moved in to crush the rebels in the White House next day – an action justified as a legitimate response to the attack on Ostankino.

Though this scenario was widely accepted at the time, a more sinister interpretation has been advanced. Contrary to initial reports, the TV Centre was strongly defended by troops and the cessation of transmissions was ordered by the Kremlin rather than Ostankino's directors, suggesting that the government wished to heighten the sense of crisis and hide the fact that virtually all those killed were outside, rather than inside, the building. When one also considers the mysterious lack of OMON on the streets, and how easily the rebels seized a fleet of trucks (complete with ignition keys) that they used to reach Ostankino, it's hard to resist the conclusion that they were lured into a trap, which gave Yeltsin the pretext to use force against parliament whilst posing as a champion of democracy.

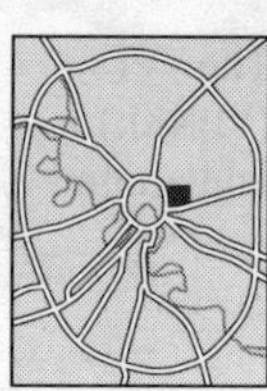

Komsomolskaya ploshchad, Sokolniki Park and Lokomotiv Stadium

Nearer the centre of town, the Sokolnicheskaya metro line provides rapid access to Komsomolskaya ploshchad and Sokolniki Park, two disparate expanses that reflect Moscow's Janus-like profile. Though hardly high on most visitors' list of priorities, anyone with an hour or two to spare might consider checking them out. Football fans, however, have good reason to ride on to Cherkizovskaya, to see Spartak or Lokomotiv play at the Lokomotiv Stadium, once the ground's refurbishment has been completed.

Komsomolskaya ploshchad

Notwithstanding its earnest name, **Komsomolskaya ploshchad** (Young Communists Square) is one of Moscow's grungiest localities, dominated by three main-line stations swarming with provincial visitors, hustlers and homeless drunks. From being merely disreputable in Soviet times, it has sunk to a level of squalor akin to the notorious pre-Revolutionary Kalchanovka Market that used to stand here, on what was then called "Three Stations Square". In an effort to maintain order, access to the station waiting rooms is restricted to ticket holders.

The two stations on the north side are separated by the columned pavilion of Komsomolskaya metro. **Yaroslavl Station** (*Yaroslavskiy vokzal*), built in 1902–04, is a bizarre Style Moderne structure with Tatar echoes, whose hooded arch sags with reliefs of Arctic fishermen and Soviet crests. In 1994, it was here that Solzhenitsyn arrived back in Moscow twenty years after his deportation from the USSR, and promptly denounced the post-Soviet Babylon outside. Further west is **Leningrad Station** (*Leningradskiy vokzal*), a yellow and white Neoclassical edifice with a modern annexe around the back.

Directly opposite, the spectacular **Kazan Station** (*Kazanskiy vokzal*) was designed by Shchusev in 1912 but only completed in 1926. Its seventy-metre spired tower (based on the citadel in the old Tatar capital of Kazan), faceted facade and blue-and-gold astrological clock have led many a yokel stumbling off the train to ask if this was the Kremlin. At the end of the square nearest the Garden Ring looms the Gothic-spired **Leningradskaya Hotel**, a pocket-sized Stalin skyscraper that represents the functional nadir of Soviet architecture, utilizing only 22 percent of its space. After Stalin's death, architectural excess came in for criticism, and in 1955 the architects of the hotel were deprived of their Stalin Prizes.

Sokolniki Park

After Komsomolskaya ploshchad, **Sokolniki Park**, several miles to the north, comes as light relief. Laid out in 1930–31, as Moscow's second "Park of Culture and Rest", it used to welcome citizens with martial music blaring from loudspeakers at the entrance, but was nevertheless cherished for its "emerald paths" through the old Sokolniki Woods, named after the royal falconers (*sokolniki*) who lived here in the seventeenth century. Nowadays the park swarms with Muscovites bound for the cash-and-carry warehouses at one end, but people also come to go jogging or enjoy more traditional pleasures. Off behind the cafés facing the *étoile*, pensioners meet in a glade for outdoor ballroom dancing on Sunday afternoons (weather permitting); while in the woods near the central pavilions is a special chess corner, where matches are played against the clock. The Exhibition Pavilions are used for international trade fairs; at the first US–Soviet exhibition in 1959, Khrushchev and the then Vice-President Nixon had a famous, impromptu "washing machine debate" over the superiority of their respective systems.

Komsomolskaya ploshchad, Sokolniki Park and Lokomotiv Stadium

Lokomotiv Stadium

Around the corner from Cherkizovskaya metro, the **Lokomotiv Stadium** is a superbly kitsch example of Stalinist architecture encrusted with motifs related to trains, befitting the railway workers' team, **Lokomotiv**. Though lame in Soviet times, the club showed an eye for talent in the 1990s, signing on such future internationals as Andrei Salomatin and Sergei Ovchinnikov, who helped beat Bayern Munich in the UEFA Cup tie and won the Russian cup in 1996. In recent years the stadium has also been used by **Spartak**, Moscow's most popular team, founded by Nikolai Starostin, who paid for his vision of a club to represent Moscow that wasn't in thrall to authority by ten years in the Gulag, till his release was secured by Stalin's son Vasily. In the post-Soviet era, Spartak won the Russian cup three years in succession with the support of Gazprom and retained it in 1996 thanks to a tax break by Mayor Luzhkov. Despite such powerful patrons, however, the club's director-general was murdered at her *dacha* the following year.

With the stadium scheduled to close for modernization in 2001, both teams are likely to play at Luzhniki Stadium until their own ground is ready. For up-to-date details, see p.380.

Leningradskiy prospekt and Serebryaniy bor

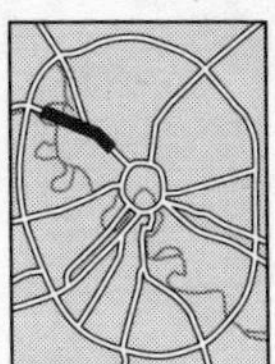

Leningradskiy prospekt is the main artery of the northwestern suburbs, running from Belarus Station out to Sheremetevo Airport. Before the Revolution it was the road from Moscow to the Imperial capital of St Petersburg. After World War II, the avenue was transformed into an eight-lane motorway flanked by monumental apartment blocks, superseded by humbler "*Khrushchoby*" flats and

Leningradskiy prospekt and Serebryaniy bor

newer, high-rise estates further out. For all that, it does have several points of interest – notably the Hippodrome and the Petrovskiy Palace – and leads to Moscow's favourite summer bathing spot, **Serebryaniy bor**.

While most are within walking distance of a metro station on the Zamoskvoretskaya line, a few sights are better reached by trolleybus (#12, #70) or tram (#23) along the prospekt, which begins at ploshchad Belorusskovo Vokzala, named after **Belarus Station** (*Belorusskiy vokzal*) on the western side of the square. If you happen to be in the area, it's worth crossing the square to take a look at the **Armenian Church** on the corner of Butyurskiy val. Its golden dome and giant mosaic *Image of the Saviour not Made by Human Hands* are offset by white walls and severe lines reminiscent of Pskovian architecture, while the murals and icons inside are Armenian in spirit, reflecting the fact that the church was built for Old Believers in 1914, but never used as such due to war and revolution, till Moscow's Armenian community made it their own in the 1990s. There was also traditionally a Polish quarter, inhabited by skilled railway workers, in the backstreets to the south of the station.

The Hippodrome

Well over a kilometre out along Leningradskiy prospekt, Moscow's **Hippodrome** (*Ippodrom*) racecourse is a world unto itself, its fans hooked on *troyka* races that seem lame compared with Western flat racing. They are also indifferent to the crumbling premises, reconstructed in a monumental Neoclassical style in the 1950s, and now containing a plush casino that cold-shoulders the plebeian **grandstand**, patrolled by gun-toting OMON. Everyone is drunk and into betting, often with illegal bookies who take wagers over the limit in the betting office beneath the stands. You don't have to enjoy racing to find it interesting; anyone studying Russian can vastly improve their knowledge of *mat* (obscenities) by spending an hour here. To get into the spirit, buy a cup of vodka before heading up the backstairs to the highest tier of the stands.

See p.378 for more about visiting the races.

The hippodrome is located 500m down **Begovaya ulitsa** (Running Street), which turns off the prospekt just after another side street, flanked by twin statues of horses. To avoid trudging 1km from Dinamo metro, ride overground to Begovaya and switch to any vehicle heading in the right direction. Some turn off shortly before the Hippodrome, near the **Botkin Hospital**, where Lenin underwent an operation in 1922 to remove a bullet that had remained in his body since an assassination attempt in 1918.

Between Dinamo and Aeroport metro

There are several places worth a visit along the 1500m stretch of the Leningradskiy prospekt between Dinamo and Aeroport metro stations. The **Dinamo Stadium** is home to Russia's oldest football club (founded in 1887), which was renamed Dinamo by Dzerzhinsky and later patronized by Beria, becoming the model for postwar secret police teams throughout the Eastern bloc. To learn more about the club, visit the **Dinamo Museum** (Mon–Thurs 10am–1pm & 2-6pm; $0.30) in front of the north stand, which has some Dzerzhinsky exhibits on the first floor and a display about the great Sixties goalie Lev Yashin upstairs. There is also a shop, selling memorabilia.

Leningradskiy prospekt and Serebryaniy bor

A bit further from Dinamo metro stands the romantic **Petrovskiy Palace**. Founded as a rest house for travelling royalty by Catherine the Great, the palace served as a refuge for Napoleon at the height of the fire of 1812. An early work by Kazakov, the palace is sheltered by crenellated walls and outbuildings; its red brick and white masonry prefigure his design for Catherine's Gothic summer palace at Tsaritsyno. During the nineteenth century it was fashionable for the rich to show off their carriages or *troykas* here, while bourgeois families picnicked on the grass with samovars. In 1923 the palace became the Zhukovskiy Air Academy, whose alumni include the aircraft designers Mikoyan and Ilyushin and the cosmonauts Gagarin and Tereshkova.

See p.379 for more about football matches.

Nicholas II was the last monarch to stay at the palace for his ill-fated coronation in May 1896, when disaster struck on the **Khodynka Field** across the road, which had been chosen as the site for the traditional distribution of gifts. The arrival of the beer wagons coincided with a rumour that the souvenir mugs were running out, causing a stampede in which more than 1500 people were trampled to death. In Soviet times, Khodynka Field became Moscow's first civilian airport, the **Central Airfield**, which is nowadays used by sports flyers.

Closer to the highway, a pair of sea-green blocks identify the **Air Terminal** (*Aerovokzal*), from which buses depart for the five airports outside Moscow; while further on towards Aeroport metro, the grounds of the **Central Army Sports Club** – or **TsKA** – are packed with shoppers, as the site of one of Moscow's largest "Things markets" (see p.370).

Airport buses are detailed on p.32.

Further out: the Moscow Canal and Serebryaniy bor

Further northwest, the prospekt runs past the Khimkinskoe Reservoir, where the **Northern River Terminal** (*Severniy rechnoy vokzal*) is the point of departure for ships to St Petersburg and the Volga cities. A grand, spired edifice near Rechnoy Vokzal metro, the terminal was inaugurated with great pomp upon the completion of a 128-kilometre-long canal joining the Moskva and Okha rivers to the Volga. One of the "hero projects" of the second Five Year Plan, the **Moscow Canal** was constructed (1932–37) by forced labour. Mostly peasants convicted of being *kulaks*, or rich exploiters, they toiled all winter in thin jackets, using only hand tools and wheelbarrows, with up to five hundred thousand perishing from cold and exhaustion.

Leningradskiy prospekt and Serebryaniy bor

Needless to say, the two colossal **statues of workers** that ennoble the canal banks near Vodniy Stadion metro look well fed and pleased with themselves.

The final leg of the Moscow Canal descends through two locks to join the Moskva River just upstream of **Serebryaniy bor**, a popular recreation area named after its giant silver pines, some of which are more than two hundred years old. Aside from its beautiful trees, the resort is noted for its colonies of wooden *dachas* and various bathing and fishing lakes – there is even a semi-official **nudist beach** and a more discreet one for **gays** at the end of a peninsula. Over summer Serebryaniy bor is inundated by visitors at weekends, and in

Streets and squares

Begovaya ulitsa	Беговая улица
Komsomolskaya ploshchad	Комсомольская площадь
Leningradskiy prospekt	Ленинградский проспект
pereulok Vasnetsova	переулок Васнецова
prospekt Mira	проспект Мира
Sadovaya–Triumfalnaya ulitsa	Садовая-Триумфальная улица
Seleznevskaya ulitsa	Селезневская улица
Suvorovskaya ploshchad	Суворовская площадь
ulitsa Fadeeva	улица Фадеева
2-y Vysheslavtsev pereulok	2-й Вышеславцев переулок

Metro stations

Belorusskaya	Белорусская
Cherkizovskaya	Черкизовская
Dinamo	Динамо
Komsomolskaya	Комсомольская
Novoslobodskaya	Новослободская
Polezhaevskaya	Полежаевская
Prospekt Mira	Проспект Мира
Rechnoy Vokzal	Речной вокзал
Rizhskaya	Рижская
Shchukinskaya	Щукинская
Sokolniki	Сокольники
Tsvetnoy Bulvar	Цетной бульвар
Tushinskaya	Тушинская
VDNKh	ВДНХ

Museums

Armed Forces Museum	музей Вооруженных Сил
Dinamo Museum	музей Динамо
Dostoyevsky Museum	музей-квартира Ф.М. Достоевского
Memorial Museum of Cosmonautics	Мемориальный музей космонавтики
Museum of Musical Culture	музей музыкальной культуры им. М.И. Глинки
Ostankino Palace	Останкирский дворец
Viktor Vasnetsov House	дом-музей В.М. Васнецова

June, when it stays light till 11pm, there are daily beach parties and discos. From May to October **motorboats** ply the river between the Strogino and Serebraniy bor-4 landing stages, calling at several points en route, including the village of Troitse-Lykovo, where Solzhenitsyn has lived since returning to Russia in 1994.

The simplest way of **getting there** is to catch trolleybus #20 all the way from Okhotniy ryad in downtown Moscow, which terminates near Serebryaniy bor-4. However, it's faster to travel to a metro station in the northwestern suburbs and then switch transport; trolleybus #65 from Sokol metro terminates at Serebryaniy bor-2, while #21 from Polezhaevskaya runs on to the banks of the Moskva River, further upstream. If you're aiming for the gay beach, take any bus from Shchukinskaya metro as far as the bridge; descend the steps and walk south, bearing right where the peninsula forks to reach the correct headland – it's about fifteen minutes' walk.

7
ROW K SEAT 15

Part 3

Moscow: Listings

Chapter 10

Accommodation

Accommodation

Anyone travelling on a tourist visa to Russia must have **accommodation** arranged before arriving in Moscow (see p.23 for details). However, now that it is easier to obtain business visas – which don't oblige you to pre-book lodgings – independent travellers may be faced with the challenge of finding somewhere to stay on arrival. Having been spoon-fed with guests for years by Intourist, many hotels are still unused to coping with people just turning up. That's not to say that they won't have a room for you, but the price will in all likelihood be far above the rate charged to package tourists.

One way of getting around this is to book through a **travel firm**, in Russia or abroad. Many of the specialist tour operators listed in "Basics" get reduced rates for their clients, as do numerous firms in Moscow. Or you can compare the hotels's own quote with the rates and special deals on the All Hotels Russia site (*www.all-hotels.ru*) and other similar **online booking** systems.

However, the fact remains that most **hotels** in Moscow are expensive, so budget-travellers are limited to a handful of places and might do better by opting for a **hostel** or **private accommodation** instead. Forget about **campsites**, which are miles outside the city, have poor facilities and security, and only function over the summer (if at all).

Hostels

While Moscow's two Russian-managed **hostels** are among the cheapest accommodation in town, it's worth bearing in mind that a handful of hotels actually charge the same, or less, for private rooms with bathrooms, and have other advantages such as being dead central or in a fresh-air zone, which the hostels lack – so read what the *Tsentralnaya* (p.324), *Sputnik* (p.326), *Tsentralniy Dom Turista*, or *Alfa* and *Beta* (p.326) have to offer before making up your mind. On the other hand, hostels can provide visa support, and their staff can help out with many of the problems that face low-budget travellers in Russia, while the *Travellers Guesthouse* is a sure-fire place to meet other foreigners.

Booking ahead is definitely advisable, especially over summer. Both hostels keep a low profile, with no prominent identifying signs on the buildings in which they're located.

G&R Hostel Asia, Zelenodolskaya ul. 3/2 ☎378 00 01, fax 378 28 66, *hostel-asia@mtu.net.ru*; *www.hostels-trains.ru*; near Ryazanskiy Prospekt metro (see map on p.272). Moscow's latest hostel is on the top three floors of a fifteen-storey block (reception on the 14th floor), offering dorm beds with shared facilities ($16), and singles ($20) or doubles ($35) with bathrooms. You can reach the centre by metro in 15–20 minutes, while Kuskovo Palace (see p.285) is a short bus ride away. Run by G&R Travel, which can provide visa support ($25) and meet guests at the airport ($25).

Travellers Guest House, Bolshaya Pereslavskaya ul. 50, 10th floor ☎971

Accommodation

40 59, fax 280 76 86, *tgh@startravel.ru*; 10min from Prospekt Mira metro (see map on p.305). Though standards have fluctuated under different managers, this is still the best-known and most popular hostel with backpackers. Doubles and singles with showers ($54); singles ($36), doubles ($48) and 4–5 bed dorms ($18 per person) with shared bathrooms; 5 percent discount for ISIC and IYHF card-holders; breakfast included. Internet access ($6.50 per hour), kitchen, laundry; awful café. Their in-house agency, STAR Travel, is affiliated to STA abroad, and can provide visa support ($40; $20 for hostel guests). Visa, MC.

Private accommodation – and renting a flat

Private accommodation for tourists is slowly catching on in Moscow, but there is still no booking office where you can just turn up and find a room: it has to be arranged in advance, from abroad. Some agencies provide self-contained flats, but most offer bed and breakfast in Moscow households. **Staying with a Russian family**, you will be well looked after and experience the cosy domesticity and tasty home cooking that is the obverse of the scornful indifference and iffy meals you may experience in public. Your introduction to this homely world will be a pair of *tapochki* – the slippers which Russians wear indoors to avoid tramping in mud – followed by a cup of tea or a shot of vodka. Your room will be clean and comfortable, though it can be disconcerting to discover, particularly in small apartments, that it belongs to one of the family, who will sleep elsewhere for the duration of your stay. Another, more disagreeable surprise might be that the **hot water** has been cut off, as happens for up to two weeks during the summer, so that the municipal water company can clean the water mains. Don't blame your hosts should this happen – it's not their fault. All you can do is put up with it, or move to another district of the city that isn't affected at the time.

Your hosts may volunteer to act as guides or drivers, and are often keen to offer insights into Russian life. Most people in the habit of renting rooms to foreigners speak some English or another foreign language. The cost varies from $30 to $100 per person per night, depending on factors such as the location of the flat and whether you opt for B&B or full board, so it definitely pays to shop around the **foreign operators** offering homestay accommodation (see box for details). If possible, you should try to get the address of the flat and check how far it is from the centre, and the nearest metro station.

Since visas and accommodation are interrelated (see p.23), you'll need to obtain a tourist or business visa before leaving home. Most foreign agencies that supply private rooms in Moscow can also provide visa support; there's no point in doing business with them if they can't. They also need to be able to register you in Moscow.

Renting a flat

If you're planning to stay over a month in Moscow, **renting a flat** will probably prove the most economical option – although real bargains are few. A nice two- or three-bedroom flat within the Garden Ring is likely to cost more than $2000 per month, though if you're prepared to stay in the suburbs a decent two-bedroom flat within walking distance of a metro station can be had for $400–500. If you don't speak Russian or have Muscovite friends to make enquiries on your behalf, the obvious place to start looking is the classified ads in the back of the *Moscow Times* and *Russia Journal*. If you do understand Russian, there are scores of flat agencies and offers in local trade papers like *Iz Ruk v Ruki* (From Hand to Hand) and *Tovary i Tseny* (Goods and Prices). If you go through an agency expect to pay commission, which is often equivalent to one month's rent.

Without going too deeply into the intricacies of **living in Moscow**, a few points should be kept in mind. Proximity

Accommodation

Homestay booking agencies

Croydon Travel, 34 Main St, Croydon, Vic, Australia ☎ 03/9725 8555.

Eastern European Travel Bureau-Russian Travel Centre, 5/75 King St, Sydney ☎ 02/9262 1144, *eetb@ozimail.com.au*. Branches in Melbourne, Brisbane and Perth.

Elderhostel USA ☎ 1-877/426-8056; *www.elderhostel.org*.

Findhorn EcoTravels, The Park, Forres, Morayshire, Scotland IV36 OTZ ☎ 01309/690995, *ecoliza@rmplc.co.uk*; *www.rmplc.co.uk/eduweb/sites/ecoliza*

Gateway Travel, 48 The Boulevard, Strathfield, Sydney ☎ 02/9745 3333, *agent@russian-gateway.com.au*; *www.russian-gateway.com.au*

Host Families Association (HOFA) USA ☎ 202/333-9343; *www.webcenter.re/~hofa*

IBV Bed and Breakfast Systems USA ☎ 301/942-3770, fax 933-0024.

Interchange, Interchange House, 27 Stafford Rd, Croydon CR0 4NG, England ☎ 020/8681 3612, fax 020/8760 0031, *interchange@interchange.uk.com*

Mir Corporation USA ☎ 1-800/424-7289; *www.mircorp.com*

Passport Travel Services, Suite 11a, 401 St. Kilda Rd, Melbourne ☎ 03/9867 3888 or ☎ 1800 337031; *www.travelcentre.com.au*

Pioneer Tours and Travel USA ☎ 1-800/369-1322 or 617/547-1127; *www.pioneerrussia.com*

Russia and Beyond, 191 Clarence St, Sydney ☎ 02/9299 5799.

Russian Travel Service USA ☎ & fax 603/585-6534, *jkates@top.monad.net*

Sundowners Adventure Travel, Ste 15, 600 Lonsdale St, Melbourne ☎ 03/9600 1934 & 1800/337 089; *www.sundowners.com.au*

The Russia Experience, Research House, Fraser Rd, Perivale, Middx UB6 7AQ, ☎ 020/8566 8846, *info@trans-siberian.co.uk*; *www.trans-siberian.co.uk*

to a metro station is crucial, as are decent shops or a market in the vicinity. Security is also vital: look for a flat with a steel door; keep as low a profile as possible, and don't let strangers or casual acquaintances know where you live. Check that the hot water works and the phone bill has been paid before committing yourself. Flats with their own **boiler** (*kolkonka*) are comparatively rare, but ensure that you wouldn't lack hot water if the district heating system is shut down in the summer.

There are almost no private houses, so apartment blocks are the norm throughout Moscow. It's preferable to live in one with a sturdy outer door, locked by a device which requires you to punch in a code. **Door codes** usually consist of three digits; you have to push all three buttons simultaneously to make it work. Some involve inserting a plastic or metallic rod, as well.

Hotels

Moscow's **hotels** run the gamut from opulent citadels run as joint ventures with foreign firms – which can be relied upon to deliver the goods at a price that warps your credit card – to seedy pits inhabited by mobsters, where strangers risk more than their property. In between fall numerous hotels that are far from perfect but might be tolerable. The buildings themselves range from Art Nouveau edifices to stupendous Stalin skyscrapers or ugly, low-rise blocks. Some are in prime locations but others are in dreary suburbs. Given all this, it definitely pays to shop around (or, in the case of package tourists, check in advance where you'll be accommodated).

While joint-venture hotels are comparable to their Western four- and five-star counterparts, wholly Russian places tend to have lower **standards** than suggested

Accommodation

Hotel prices

All the hotels below are listed in alphabetical order under area headings, according to their location in the city. After each entry you'll find a symbol that corresponds to one of eight **price categories**:

① under $20	⑤ $100–150
② $20–40	⑥ $150–200
③ $40–70	⑦ $200–300
④ $70–100	⑧ over $300

All prices are for the lowest priced double room available, which may mean without a private bathroom or shower in the cheapest places. For a single room, expect to pay around two-thirds the price of a double. Some hotels also offer "lux" or "half-lux" rooms with a lounge and/or kitchen, suited to several people self-catering.

Note that these prices include 20 percent **VAT** (НДС in Cyrillic) and four percent **city tax**. The acceptability of **credit cards** (CC) is specified in the hotel listings below.

by the Intourist system of two to four stars, which should be taken with a pinch of salt – for example, air-conditioning (A/C) is a comparative rarity. Two-star hotels mostly consist of 1950s low-rises with matchbox-sized rooms, while three-star hotels are typical 1960s and 1970s towerblocks, equipped with several restaurants, bars and nightclubs. Four-star hotels tend to date from the 1980s or 1990s and come closest to matching the standards (and prices) of their Western counterparts. Conversely, the older, low-rate places are generally shabby, with erratic water supplies and surly staff – although there's a new breed of two-star hotels, often located on one or two floors of a residential block, where the rooms are better than you'd expect from the public areas or the locality.

Wherever you're hoping to stay, it's obviously safer to book a room before you arrive; **reservations** from abroad are best made by fax, email or the Internet (if possible), or through a travel agent or booking system. In Moscow, there's a hotel reservations desk at Sheremetevo-2 airport. It's best to pay for one night only, in case you decide to move somewhere else the next day.

Without being alarmist, there's a real risk of break-ins or muggings at hotels that don't maintain adequate **security**; or in places where all the other guests are from the former Soviet republics, so that you stick out a mile (staying there is only advisable if you speak Russian and know the score). Don't leave valuables in your room (or put all your money in the hotel safe); stash most other items in a locked suitcase out of view; and lock the door before going to sleep. Hotels geared towards businessmen tend to have lots of **prostitutes** whose late-night phone calls (or surprise visits with the use of a passkey) are disturbing, to say the least.

When checking in, you should receive a *propusk* or **guest card** that enables you to get past the doorman and claim your room key – don't lose it. Most hotels have a service bureau, which can obtain theatre tickets and arrange tours, rental cars and the like. Each floor is monitored by a **dezhurnaya** or concierge, who will keep your key while you are away and can arrange to have your laundry done. A small gift to her upon arrival should help any ensuing problems to be resolved, but her presence is no guarantee of security. Though relatively few hotels still include breakfast in the price, it does no harm to ask; indeed, in low-rated places it's wise to check if there's anywhere to eat at all.

You can make **online bookings** at most hotels listed below via the Web site *www.all-hotels.ru.*

Accommodation

Central Moscow

We've taken this to mean anywhere within fifteen minutes' walk of Red Square, Pushkinskaya ploshchad or the Arbat, thus including the whole area within the Garden Ring, plus a few places just outside it or across the river from the Kremlin. High prices are the rule for everywhere with excellent facilities and security, but if you're not bothered, it's worth investigating cheaper hotels in prime locations. Each hotel is marked on the chapter map of the area where it's located (as specified below).

Arbat, Plotnikov per. 12 ☎244 76 53. Comfy, discreet three-star hotel above the *Vostochniy kvartal* restaurant, just off the Arbat. Popular with Russian and Trans-Caucasian businessmen. Amex, Visa, DC, EC, MC. Discounts on bookings through All Hotels Russia. See map p.170. ④–⑥.

Baltschug Kempinski, ul. Balchug 1 ☎230 65 00, fax 230 65 02; 15min from Kitay-Gorod or Novokuznetskaya metro. Across the river from Red Square, with an amazing view from its corner rooms, this stylishly modernized 1900s establishment is all you'd expect from a top-class hotel under German management, and boasts such celebrity guests as David Bowie, Michael Jackson and Chuck Norris. Amex, Visa, MC, DC, JCB. See map p.77. ⑧.

Belgrad, Smolenskaya ul. 8 ☎248 16 43, fax 230 21 29; near Smolenskaya metro. Situated just across the Garden Ring from the Arbat, this 1970s three-star block has yet to be refurbished, unlike its twin, the *Zolotoe Koltso* (see below). Slightly shabby, but not a bad deal given its location and amenities. Breakfast included. Visa, EC, MC, Maestro. See map p.170. ④.

Budapest, Petrovskie Linii 2/18 ☎923 23 56, fax 921 12 66; 10min from Teatralnaya or Kuznetskiy Most metro. Just off ul. Petrovka, between the Bolshoy Theatre and the Sandunovskiy Baths. Pleasantly old-fashioned but comfy; rooms are thirty percent cheaper Fri–Mon nights and over New Year. Breakfast included. Amex, Visa, MC, DC, JCB. See map p.129. ⑤.

Club 27, ul. Malaya Nikitskaya 27 ☎202 56 50, fax 202 12 13; 5min from Barrikadnaya metro. Small, discreet four-star hotel on the edge of the Garden Ring, catering to Russian businessmen and their mistresses. Banqueting hall and satellite communications. Amex, Visa, DC, EC, MC, JCB. See map p.170. ⑥.

East-West, Tverskoy bul. 14, str. 4 ☎290 04 04, fax 956 30 27, *east-west@col.ru*; 10min from Tverskaya/Pushkinskaya metro. A tastefully modernized nineteenth-century mansion on the Boulevard Ring; its individually styled rooms range from minimalist chic to Madame de Pompadour, via everything in between. Very popular, so you need to reserve months ahead. No CC. See map p.128. ⑤.

Intourist, Tverskaya ul. 3/5 ☎956 83 04, fax 956 84 50; near Okhotniy Ryad metro. Located just off Manezhnaya ploshchad, within sight of Red Square, this 1970s block is overrated as a four-star hotel and charges like the three-star place it is. See map p.128. Visa, MC, DC, JCB. ⑤.

Marco Polo Presnya, Spiridonovskiy per. 9 ☎244 36 31, fax 926 54 02; 10min from Mayakovskaya or Pushkinskaya metro. Modern, A/C four-star hotel, in a side street near the Patriarch's Ponds. Solarium, satellite TV and other amenities. Breakfast included. Amex, Visa, DC, EC, MC. See map p.170. ⑦.

Marriott Aurora (or Royal), ul. Petrovka 11/20 ☎937 00 55, fax 937 08 01, *www.marriott.com* or *www.visitmoscow.com*; 10min from Teatralnaya or Tverskaya metro. The latest addition to the Marriott chain, with all the facilities you'd expect. Guests have free access to the health club. All major CC. See map p.128. ⑧.

Marriott Grand, Tverskaya ul. 26 ☎935 85 00, fax 937 00 01; 10min from Tverskaya, Pushkinskaya or Mayakovskaya metro. The five-star flagship of the Marriott's fleet, featuring

Accommodation

modems in every room and a suite on each floor designed for wheelchair users. Amex, Visa, DC, MC. See map p.170. ⑧.

Metropol, Teatralniy proezd 1/4 ☎927 60 40, fax 927 60 10, *moscow @interconti.com*; near Teatralnaya, Ploshchad Revolyutsii and Okhotniy Ryad metros. Luxuriantly Art Nouveau building with five-star facilities, including a pool and gym, it is acknowledged by most as Moscow's finest hotel. Amex, Visa, DC, MC, JCB. See map p.115. ⑧.

Minsk, Tverskaya ul. 22 ☎229 12 13, fax 229 03 62, *minck@chat.ru*; 5min from Mayakovskaya or Pushkinskaya metro. Anonymous grey 1970s block with matchbox rooms; those at the back are quieter and dearer. The cheapest hotel in the centre after the *Tsentralnaya* (see below); mainly used by Caucasians. Breakfast included. Amex, Visa, DC, MC. See map p.170. ③.

Moskva, Okhotniy ryad 2 ☎960 20 20, fax 292 92 14, *root@hotel-moskva .aha.ru*; near Okhotniy Ryad and Teatralnaya metros. Sombre Stalinist warren whose west-facing rooms overlook the Kremlin, while the other side is impinged on by the street-walkers of Teatralnaya ploshchad. Facilities include a sauna. Amex, Visa, MC. See map p.115. ⑤.

National, Okhotniy ryad 14/1 ☎258 70 00, fax 258 71 00, *hotel@national.ru*; near Okhotniy Ryad and Teatralnaya metros. An Art Nouveau pile, rivalling the *Metropol* for splendour and high standards, and surpassing its prices. Gym, pool and sauna. See map p.128. Amex, Visa, DC, MC, JCB. ⑧.

Pekin, ul. Bolshaya-Sadovaya 5/1 ☎209 24 42, fax 200 14 20, *bc-pekin@mtu-net .ru*; near Mayakovskaya metro. Built in the era of Sino-Soviet friendship and refurbished in the 1990s, this Stalin-Gothic edifice on the Garden Ring has spacious rooms, a dubious Chinese restaurant, and a nightclub full of goons and hookers. Amex, Visa, EC, MC. See map p.170. ④–⑤.

Rossiya, ul. Varvarka 6 ☎232 62 54, fax 232 62 48, *h-russia@col.ru*; 5min from Kitay-Gorod or Ploshchad Revolyutsii metro. Colossal mice- and cockroach-infested labyrinth with 3070 rooms and poor security, redeemed by its lowish prices and great location, just off Red Square. Though its pool is out of action, it still boasts the Manhattan Express nightclub. DC, MC, Visa. See map p.115. ④.

Savoy, ul. Rozhdestvenka 3 ☎929 85 00, fax 230 21 86, *infa-hotel@mtu-net.ru*; near Kuznetskiy Most metro. Small four-star hotel with splendid Art Nouveau/Baroque decor, rivalling the *Metropol* or the *National* for grandeur. Business centre, sauna and art gallery on the premises. Amex, Visa, DC, MC. See map p.129. ⑧.

Tsentralnaya, Tverskaya ul. 10 ☎229 89 57; near Tverskaya, Pushkinskaya and Chekhovskaya metros. Old-fashioned and with an infamous past (see p.134) but as cheap as you'll get right in the centre of town. Rooms with basins, TV and phone; most lack bathrooms but the shared facilities are clean. Bar, email and laundry services. Reserve through TourService International (*alexpov@cyberax.ru*). No CC. See map p.128. ②.

Zolotoe Koltso, Smolenskaya ul. 5 ☎725 01 00, fax 725 01 01; near Smolenskaya metro. Newly renovated, Swiss-affiliated towerblock just beyond the Garden Ring and the Arbat, whose amenities include a gym and sauna. Amex, Visa, DC, JCB. See map p.170. ⑥.

Zamoskvareche and the south

This corresponds to the area covered by Chapter 7, minus the island opposite the Kremlin. Hotels within Zamoskvareche (see map on p.233) are predictably more expensive than those further out (see map on p.230).

Akademicheskaya, Donskaya ul. 1 ☎230 05 14, fax 237 31 77; near Oktyabrskaya metro. Once reserved for guests of the Academy of Sciences, this Spartan block just off Oktyabrskaya ploshchad now takes anyone, but is way overpriced given that most of the rooms lack bathrooms and the only amenity is a café. No CC. Breakfast included. ③.

Accommodation

Alrosa, 1-iy Kazachiy per. 4 ☎745 21 90, fax 745 77 63, *hotel@alrosa-msk.ru*; 10min from Tretyakovskaya metro. A small new three-star hotel in the atmospheric backstreets near the Tretyakov Gallery, whose rooms are pleasant and comfortable, but don't merit the absurdly high price – especially when you could stay at the *Danilovskiy* or the *President* for less. ⑥.

Danilovskiy, Bolshoy Stariy Danilovskiy per. 5 ☎954 05 03, fax 954 07 50; 10min from Tulskaya metro. Built alongside the Danilov Monastery to lodge Patriarchal guests, but open to anyone if they book ahead. Its facilities include a pool with a waterfall, a banya and laundry. Amex, Visa, DC, EC, MC. ⑦.

President, ul. Bolshaya Yakimanka 24 ☎239 38 00, fax 230 78 13; 10min from Polyanka metro. Grandly kitsch four-star hotel, once reserved for foreign Communist leaders and still owned by the Kremlin. Swimming pool, billiards and sauna. Breakfast included. Amex, Visa, DC, EC, MC. ⑥.

Tsaritsyno, Shipilovskiy proezd 47, korpus 1 ☎343 43 43, fax 343 43 63; 10min from Orekhovo metro (30min ride from the centre). This high-rise block in a fresh air zone near Tsaritsyno has 1–4 room flats with TV, phone and kitchenette, furnished to Russian or "Euro" standard. Washing machine, gym and sauna on the premises. ③–④.

Krasnaya Presnya, Fili and the southwest

Muscovites and expats rate Krasnaya Presnya and Fili as good areas to live, due to their amenities. However, less expensive accommodation is generally located miles out along Leninskiy prospekt or in the Sparrow Hills, so the number of metro stops from the centre and the walking distance to the hotel are crucial. All hotels are marked on the map on p.200–201.

Kievskaya, Kievskaya ul. 2 ☎240 12 34; near Kievskaya metro. An unsavoury dump used by traders passing through Kiev Station. Though its staff discourage Westerners from staying, travellers on a tight budget with no valuables to lose might be swayed by the low prices and proximity to the Circle line. Singles with shared facilities, doubles with showers. No CC. ②–③.

Mezhdunarodnaya, Krasnopresnenskaya nab. 12 ☎253 22 87, fax 258 19 31, *interhot@wtc.msk.ru*; *www.wtcmo.ru*; 20min from Krasnopresnenskaya metro. The "Mezh" is a five-star corporate haven with an atrium, a mall, a pool, gym and solarium, and smallish, sterile rooms. Located upriver from the White House and hard to reach except by taxi. Amex, Visa, DC, MC. ⑦.

Orlyonok, ul. Kosygina 15 ☎939 88 74, fax 938 84 54; Leninskiy Prospekt metro, then trolleybus #7. On the edge of the Sparrow Hills, with fine views of Moscow, it once catered to youth groups but now features an erotic massage parlour on the eighteenth floor. Other amenities include satellite TV and a sauna. No CC. ④.

Pallada, ul. Ostrovityanova 14 ☎336 05 45, fax 336 96 02, *pallada@cityline.ru*; *www.pallada.ct.ru*; near Konkovo metro (20min from the centre). Two dozen rooms with bath, fridge and TV; 20 percent surcharge on the first night. Sauna, pool and hydro-massage. Amex, Visa, DC, EC, MC, JCB. ⑤.

Radisson Slavjanskaya, Berezhovskaya nab. 2 ☎941 80 20, fax 941 80 00; *www.radisson.com/rr*; near Kievskaya metro. Moscow's only US-managed four-star chain hotel contains the Americom House of Cinema, several TV news agencies, a gym, pool and sauna. Bill Clinton and the Smashing Pumpkins have stayed here. Amex, Visa, DC, MC, JCB. ⑦.

7th Floor, pr. Vernadskovo 1b-88 ☎ & fax 956 60 38 or 437 99 97, *sev.floor@mtu.net.ru*; *www.mtu-net/sev.floor/*; 10min from Yugo-Zapadnaya metro (20min from the centre). A fairly comfy, business-like retreat equipped with Internet-dedicated lines in every room, located on one floor of a tower block off Troparevskaya ulitsa, near the Pedagogical University. ③.

Accommodation

Sputnik, Leninskiy pr. 38 ☎930 22 87, fax 930 63 83, *hsputnik@dol.ru*; 10min from Leninskiy Prospekt metro. Despite being ugly and dowdy, this 1970s youth hotel has a great Indian restaurant, easy access to the centre, and low prices; a private room with a shower costs less than one at the *Travellers Guesthouse*. Visa, MC, Maestro. ②.

Tsentralniy Dom Turista, Leninskiy pr. 146 ☎434 37 19, fax 434 31 97, *cthouse@cityline.ru*; *www.acase.ru* or *http://moscow.in-europe.org/cdt.htm*; trolleybus #62 or #84 from Yugo-Zapadnaya metro. Further out than the *Sputnik*, but cleaner, safer and friendlier, this 34-storey block's facilities include bowling, a swimming pool and sauna. Visa, MC. ②.

Ukrainiya, Kutuzovskiy pr. 2/1 ☎243 25 96, fax 956 20 78, *UKRASU@elnet.msk.ru*; 10min from Kievskaya metro. A Stalinesque behemoth across the river from the White House, whose spacious rooms and period décor make it the best of the old Soviet-style hotels. Cable TV, sauna, business centre. Breakfast included. Amex, Visa, DC, MC. ⑤.

Taganka and Zayauze

Happily, the area of Moscow covered by Chapter 8 (see map on p.273) contains several cheap hotels in a desirable location only 20 minutes from the centre by metro – Izmaylovo, near souvenir market and park of the same name (see p.291). Here, a massive complex of six 28-storey blocks built for the 1980 Olympics now functions as four hotels occupying five of the blocks (the sixth is an entertainments and service wing), whose standards, décor and prices vary.

Alfa, Izmaylovskoe shosse 71 ☎166 01 63, fax 166 00 60, *asu@alfa.lvl.ru*; *http://alfa-hotel.ru*; near Izmalovskiy Park metro. Its simply furnished boxlike rooms with private bathrooms are good value by Moscow standards, though the hotel has few facilities beyond a bar, restaurant and sauna. ②.

Beta, Izmaylovskoe shosse 71 ☎792 98 98, fax 166 21 84. Facilities and prices are virtually identical to the neighbouring *Alfa* block, though the rooms also have cable TV. ②.

Gamma-Delta, Izmaylovskoe shosse 71 ☎737 70 70, fax 166 74 86, *hotel@Izmailovo.ru*; *www.izmailovo.ru*. Two blocks, refurbished to a higher standard than the others, *Gamma-Delta* would be okay if they charged for the three-star hotel that it is, instead of imagining that it's the *Metropol*. ⑧.

Vega, Izmaylovskoe shosse 71 ☎956 05 06, fax 956 06 47, *vega@lvl.ru*; *http://hotel-vega.ru*. A bit fancier than *Alfa* and *Beta*, and far more affordable than *Gamma-Delta*. Rooms with phone, fridge and TV; Internet facilities and business centre. ③.

Northern Suburbs

The area covered by Chapter 9 (see map on p.296) ranges from the Garden Ring out as far as Sheremetevo airport. Although Serebryaniy bor is the only truly pleasant location, some hotels in other areas have parks or sports facilities nearby. Unless your hotel provides a bus into the centre, proximity to a metro station is as vital as good security.

Aeropolis, Leningradskiy pr. 37, korpus 5 ☎151 04 42, fax 151 75 43, *aeropolis@deol*; 15min from Dinamo or Aeroport metro. An ex-Aeroflot staff hotel beside the busy Air Terminal. Its institutional décor and unfriendly staff would be tolerable if its rates were lower, but as it is, you can find better deals elsewhere. Visa, Amex, MC, JCB. ④.

Aerostar, Leningradskiy pr. 37 ☎213 90 00, fax 213 90 01, *booking@aerostar.ru*; *www.aerostar.ru*; 15min from Dinamo or Aeroport metro. Sited near the *Aeropolis*, this soulless but comfy Canadian-managed four-star hotel has disabled access, a free gym and shuttle-bus for guests, and some rooms overlooking the Petrovskiy Palace. Amex, Visa, DC, MC, JCB. ⑦.

Arctica, Butyurskaya ul. 79-V ☎210 11 18, fax 979 98 55, *arctica@orc.ru*; *www.arctica.newmail.ru*; 5min from

Dmitrovskaya metro. Despite its grim public spaces and the 25 percent surcharge on the first night, this two-star hotel in a residential block is a good deal, since a double room with a shared bathroom costs less than a dorm bed in the *Travellers Guesthouse* – though you won't meet any Westerners here. It also has "lux" apartments with kitchenettes. Visa, MC. ①.

Art Hotel, 3-ya Peschanaya ul. 2 ☎725 09 05, fax 725 09 04, *artsport@glasnet.ru*; 15–20min from Sokol or Polezhaevskaya metro. A humdrum new hotel in a quiet neighbourhood on the edge of the TsKA complex, with excellent tennis courts nearby. Facilities include satellite TV and accommodation for pets. Reductions at weekends. Visa, DC, EC, MC. ⑦.

Bega, Begovaya alleya 11 ☎945 52 13, fax 946 15 37, *bega@mccinet.ru*; 15min from Dinamo or Begovaya metro. Sited opposite the Hippodrome, this three-star hotel has large, plain MFI-style rooms, a sauna and laundry. Amex, Visa, EC, MC. ④.

Holiday Inn Vinogradovo, Dmitrovskoe shosse 171 ☎937 06 70, fax 937 06 71, *hinnv@geocities.com*; *www.holiday-inn.com*; bus shuttle to Sheremetevo-2 and the centre. Aimed at those who crave a respite from Moscow, this upscale Holiday Inn has a pool, gym, sauna and full business facilities, by a lake just beyond the outer ring road. Amex, Visa, DC, MC. ⑤.

Iris Moskva, Korovinskoe shosse 10 ☎488 80 00, fax 488 88 44. Bland four-star hotel in a park with sports grounds, not near any metro station, but connected by shuttle-bus to the centre (7.30am–midnight). Pool, gym, sauna and launderette. ⑦.

Kosmos, pr. Mira 150 ☎234 12 12, fax 215 79 91, *hcosmos@dol.ru*; 5min from VDNKh metro. Sited opposite the Space Obelisk and the Worker and Collective Farm Girl monument, this vast 1970s hotel teems with whores and mobsters. Amenities include eight bars, a casino and a bowling alley; the rooms have cable TV and minibar. Amex, Visa, MC. ⑤.

Leningradskaya, Kalanchovskaya ul. 21/40 ☎975 18 15, fax 975 18 02; near Komsomolskaya metro. Pint-sized Stalin skyscraper at the end of the busy, lowlife Komsomolskaya ploshchad (see p.310), with a grandiose lobby and varying sized rooms with en-suite facilities, fridge and minibar. Its main drawback is the dodgy clientele and locality. Amex, Visa, MC. ④.

Novotel, near Sheremetevo-2 airport ☎926 59 00, fax 926 59 03, *novotel.reservations@co.ru*; *www.novotel-moscow.ru*. A soulless four-star hotel miles outside the city, connected by a free shuttle-bus to the airport and the centre. Good for a quick getaway, but its only other attraction is a Mexican restaurant. Amex, Visa, DC, MC. ⑦.

Renaissance, Olympiyskiy pr. 18/1 ☎931 90 00, fax 931 90 76; 15min from Prospekt Mira metro. This four-star block near the Olympic Sports Complex is as costly as the *Savoy*, but more like the *Radisson Slavjanskaya* in character. Pool; business centre; Dome Theatre English-language cinema. Amex, Visa, DC, MC, JCB. ⑧.

Royal Zenith, Tamanskaya ul. 49b ☎199 80 01, fax 199 81 01, *4545.g23@23.relcom.ru*; and 1-ya liniyia Serebryanaya bora 7 ☎199 58 25, fax 199 14 36; trolleybus #20k or #65 to the end of the line and then 10min walk. Two cosy hotels under one management, amid the pines and dacha colonies of Serebryaniy bor. All rooms en suite with TV; sauna and small pool on the premises. Free car to Sheremetevo airport or the centre. Reservations must be confirmed by 6pm. ⑥.

Sheraton Palace, 1-ya Tverskaya Yamskaya ul. 19 ☎931 97 00, fax 931 97 04, *palacehotel.admin@ns.co.ru*; 10min from Mayakovskaya metro. Modern A/C five-star hotel only 500m beyond the Garden Ring, with rooms for non-smoking and disabled guests; gym, Jacuzzi and sauna, and the best seafood

Accommodation

Accommodation

restaurant in Moscow. Amex, Visa, DC, MC, JCB. ⑧.

Sovietskaya, Leningradskiy pr. 32/2 ☎960 20 00, fax 250 80 03, *hotelsov@cnt.ru*; 5min from Dinamo metro. A tastefully refurbished Stalinist pile where Margaret Thatcher, King Juan Carlos, Indira Gandhi and Arnold Schwarzenegger have stayed. Its *Yar* restaurant is named after a famous pre-revolutionary citadel of Russian cuisine, frequented by Tolstoy, Chekhov and Rasputin. Though less grand than its predecessor, the food is still excellent. Amex, Visa, MC. ⑥.

Tverskaya, 1-ya Tverskaya Yamskaya ul. 34 ☎290 99 00, fax 290 99 99; 10min from Belorusskaya metro. Another four-star hotel in the *Marriott* chain, on the busy avenue between the Garden Ring and Belarus Station. Business centre; free gym and sauna. Amex, Visa, DC, EC, MC. ⑧.

Zolotoy Kolos, Yaroslavskaya ul. 15 ☎217 43 55, fax 217 43 56; 10min from VDNKh metro. A typically charmless 1970s two-star hotel in the vicinity of the *Kosmos*, redeemed by good management, a friendly atmosphere and low prices for rooms with or without bathrooms, equipped with TV and phone; laundry, bar and billiards on the premises. ①–②.

Chapter 11

Eating and drinking

Eating and drinking

When I eat pork at a meal, give me the whole pig; when mutton, give the whole sheep; when goose, the whole bird. Two dishes are better than a thousand provided a fellow can devour as much of them as he wants.

Dead Souls, Gogol

As the above quotation suggests, quantity rather than variety has long characterized the Russian appetite – especially under Communism, when citizens made a virtue of the slow service that was the norm in Soviet restaurants, by drinking, talking and dancing for hours. The modern Western notion of a quick meal was unthinkable.

Nowadays, the gastronomic scene has improved enormously, with hundreds of new **cafés** and **restaurants** offering all kinds of cuisines and surroundings, aimed at anyone with a disposable income – from mega-rich New Russians and expense-account expatriates to fashion-conscious but not so wealthy teenagers. While some places at the top end of the market can rightfully boast of their haute cuisine, there are lots whose decor and pretensions surpass their cooking, and where the clientele's main aim seems to be to flash their money around.

Unlike in the early 1990s, all bars, cafés and restaurants now take **payment** in rubles only – though more tourist-oriented places may list prices on their menus in dollars or so-called "Conditional Units" (using the Cyrillic abbreviation УЕ), which amounts to the same thing. In that case, the total is converted into rubles at the current central bank rate or the rate of exchange advertised on the premises (which may be less favourable). It's often (though not invariably) true that a menu in dollars is an indication that the establishment is overpriced by local standards.

Credit cards (CCs) are accepted by most top-range or foreign-managed restaurants, as indicated in our listings by the relevant abbreviations (Amex=American Express, DC=Diners Club, EC=Eurocard, MC=Mastercard, JCB=Japanese Credit Bank) – but you shouldn't take it for granted. As for paying with travellers' cheques, forget it.

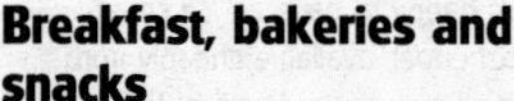

Breakfast, bakeries and snacks

At home, most Russians take **breakfast** (*zaftrak*) seriously, tucking into calorific dishes like buckwheat pancakes (*bliny*) or porridge (*kasha*), with curd cheese (*tvorog*) and sour cream (*smetana*) – though some simply settle for a cup of tea and a slice of bread. Hotels usually serve an approximation of the "Continental" breakfast – probably just a fried egg, bread, butter and jam – though ritzier hotels may provide a buffet (sometimes a *smörgasbord*-style *Shvedskiy stol*, or "Swedish table"), and offer a Western-style brunch on Sundays.

Eating and drinking

Pastries (*pirozhnoe*) are available from cake shops (*konditerskaya*) and some grocers (*gastronom*). Savoury pies (*pirozhki*) are often sold on the streets from late morning – the best are filled with cabbage, curd cheese or rice. It's advisable to steer clear of the meat ones unless you're buying from a reputable café.

Bread (*khleb*), available from bakeries (*bulochnaya*), is one of the country's culinary strong points. "Black" bread (known as *chorniy* or *rzhanoy*) is the traditional variety: a dense, rye bread with a distinctive sourdough flavour and amazing longevity. *Karelskiy* is similar but with fruit; *surozhniy* is a lighter version, made with a mixture of wheat and rye. French-style baguettes (*baton*) – white, mixed-grain or plaited with poppy seeds – are also popular. Unfortunately the old custom whereby shoppers could test a loaf's freshness with long forks has gone (people started stealing the forks), but the system of queuing at the *kassa* before queuing for the bread remains.

As in most of eastern Europe, the Russians are very fond of **cakes** (*tort*). There are over sixty varieties, but the main ingredients are fairly standard: a sponge dough, a good deal of honey and a distinctive spice like cinnamon or ginger or lots of buttery cream and jam. Whatever the season, Russians are always happy to have an ice cream (*morozhenoe*), available cheaply from kiosks all over town. Much of the locally produced ice cream is cheaper and of better quality than the imported brands; try the popular crème-brulée flavour, or eskimo, a sort of choc-ice. Alternatively, there are a few *Baskin Robbins* and *Italian Geletaria* outlets dotted around town.

Western-style **fast food** is now common in Moscow, with numerous branches of *McDonald's*, *Rostik's* and various Russian chains that sell traditional pies and pancakes in a fast-food setting. Alternatively, some department stores feature a stand-up buffet, offering open sandwiches with salami, caviar or boiled egg, as well as other nibbles. Less appealing buffets can be found in train and bus stations, and around metro stations and markets.

Zakuski

Despite the increasing popularity of fast food and foreign cuisine, most Russians remain loyal to their culinary heritage – above all, to **zakuski**. The Russian equivalent of Spanish tapas, these small dishes are either consumed before a big meal, nibbled as an accompaniment to vodka, or eaten as a light snack at any time of the day. They can also constitute a meal in themselves.

Zakuski form the basis of the famous *Russkiy stol*, or "Russian table", a feast of awesome proportions in which the table groans under numerous dishes while the samovar steams away – in Tsarist times, among the upper classes, this was merely the prelude to the main meal, as foreign guests would discover to their embarrassment after gorging themselves. Salted fish, like sprats or herrings, are a firm favourite, as are gherkins, assorted cold meats and salads. Hard-boiled eggs or *bliny*, both served with caviar (*ikra*), are also available. Caviar is no longer as cheap as during the Brezhnev era, when people tired of eating so much of it, but it's still cheaper than in the West. It comes in two basic varieties: red (*krasnaya*) or black (*chornaya*); the latter consists of smaller eggs and is more expensive.

Meals

Russians usually eat their main meal of the day at lunchtime (*obed*), between 1pm and 4pm, and traditionally only have *zakuski* and tea for supper (*uzhin*). Restaurants, on the other hand, make much more of the evening, and may often close for a couple of hours in the afternoon – although many now offer a set-price business lunch to attract extra customers.

Menus are usually written in Russian only, though some places offer a shorter

Eating and drinking

version in English; the Russian menu is typed up every day, whereas the English version may give only a general idea of what's actually available. In such cases, you're probably better off asking what they recommend (*shto-by vy po rekomendovali?*), which can elicit some surprisingly frank replies.

If your main concern is price, you'll need to stick to **fast-food** outlets or **cafés**, or take advantage of the business lunches and other special deals offered by a fair number of cafés and restaurants, as advertised in the *Moscow Times* and *eXile*, and noted in our listings. Many deals feature ethnic food, including Armenian (*Armyanskiy*), Georgian (*Gruzinskiy*) and Korean (*Koreyskiy*), not to mention Tex-Mex and US chow like nachos, burritos and burgers.

Russian cuisine owes many debts to Jewish, Caucasian and Ukrainian cooking, but remains firmly rooted in its peasant origins. In former times, the staple diet of black bread, potatoes, cabbages, cucumber and onions made for bland eating – *Shchi da kasha, pishcha nasha* ("cabbage soup and porridge are our food"), as one saying goes – with flavourings limited to sour cream, garlic, vinegar, dill and a few other fresh herbs. These strong tastes and textures – salty, sweet, sour, pickled – remained the norm, even among the aristocracy, until Peter the Great introduced French chefs to his court in the early eighteenth century.

Most menus start with a choice of soup or *zakuski* (see p.330). **Soup** (*sup*) has long played an important role in Russian cuisine (the spoon appeared on the Russian table over 400 years before the fork). Cabbage soup, or *shchi*, has been the principal Russian dish for the last thousand years, served with a generous dollop of sour cream. Beetroot soup, or *borshch*, originally from Ukraine, is equally ubiquitous. Soups, however, are often only available at lunchtime, and Russians do not consider that even the large meaty soups constitute a main meal; you'll be expected to have a main course afterwards. Chilled soups (*okroshki*) are popular during the summer, made from whatever's available.

Main courses are overwhelmingly based on **meat** (*myaso*), usually beef, mutton or pork, sometimes accompanied by a simple sauce (mushroom, sour cream or cheese). Meat may also make its way into *pelmeni*, a Russian version of ravioli, often served in a broth. As far as ethnic meat dishes go, the most common are Georgian kebabs (*shashlyk*) or pilau-style Uzbek rice dishes called *plov*.

A wide variety of fish and seafood is available in Moscow. Pickled fish is a popular starter (try *selyotka pod shuboy*, herring in a "fur coat" of beetroot, carrot, egg and mayonnaise), while fresh fish occasionally appears as a main course – usually salmon, sturgeon or cod. Lobster and prawns feature in deluxe restaurants, which boast of flying them in from America. However, if you're cooking for yourself, a vast range of fresh and frozen seafood can be found in local shops.

In cafés, most main courses are served with boiled potatoes and/or sliced fresh tomatoes, but more expensive restaurants will serve a selection of accompanying vegetables. These are called *garnir* and occasionally have to be ordered and paid for separately. Where the meat is accompanied by vegetables, you may see an entry on the menu along the lines of 100/25/100g, which refers to the respective weight in grams of the meat (or fish) portion, and its accompanying rice or potatoes and *garnir*. In ethnic restaurants, meat is almost always served on its own.

Desserts (*sladkoe*) are not a strong feature of Russian cuisine. Ice cream, fruit, apple pie (*yablochniy pirog*) and jam pancakes (*blinchikiy s varenem*) are restaurant perennials, while in Caucasian restaurants you may get *pakhlava* (like Greek/Turkish *bakhlava*).

Ethnic food

The former Soviet Union incorporated a vast number of different ethnic groups, each with their own popular and widely disseminated national dishes – many Georgian or Armenian dishes, for exam-

Eating and drinking

> **Vegetarian phrases**
>
> The concept of vegetarianism is a hazy one for most Russians, so simply saying you're a vegetarian may instil panic and/or confusion in the waiter – it's often better to ask what's in a particular dish you think looks promising.
>
> The phrases to remember are *ya vegetarianets/vegetarianka* (masculine/feminine). *Kakiye u vas yest blyuda bez myasa ili ryby?* ("I'm a vegetarian. Is there anything without meat or fish?"). For emphasis you could add *ya ne yem myasnovo ili rybnovo* ("I don't eat meat or fish").

ple, are now standard elements of Russian cooking, and there are few restaurants which do not offer *shashlyk*, the Georgian kebab, or *tolma*, Armenian stuffed vine leaves. **Georgian** is the most easily found ethnic food and has good vegetarian options, such as *lobio* (spiced beans), or aubergine stuffed with ground walnuts. Carnivores can try the *kharcho*, a spicy meat soup, or *tsatsivi*, a cold dish of chicken in walnut sauce. **Armenian** and **Azeri** cuisine is closer to Middle Eastern cooking (with the addition of dried fruits, saffron and ginger), while **Uzbek** features *khinkali* (a spicier kind of *pelmeni*) and sausages made from pony meat. Perhaps the best treat in store is **Korean** food, originally introduced by Koreans exiled to Kazakhstan in the 1930s. Marinaded beef dishes like *bulkogi* are fried at your table, accompanied by raw vegetables and hot pickled garlic relish (*kimichi*). One Korean dish often found even in non-Korean eateries is spicy carrot salad (*morkov po-koreyskiy*). **Indian** and **Chinese** cuisine tends to be rather a disappointment for anyone used to the dishes served in such restaurants in the West; either the chefs find it hard to get hold of the right ingredients, or the dishes are toned down a lot to suit Russian tastes.

Among the other cuisines represented by at least one restaurant in Moscow are American, Jewish, Italian, French, German, Spanish, Mexican, Japanese, Thai, Vietnamese and Filipino.

Vegetarian food

Russia is not a good place for **vegetarians**; meat takes pride of place in the country's cuisine, and the idea of forgoing it voluntarily strikes Russians as absurd. The various non-Russian dishes that find their way onto the menu offer some solace, and if you eat fish you will usually find something. Bliny are sometimes a good fall-back; ask for them with sour cream, or fish if you eat it. If you're not too fussy about picking out fragments of meat, *plov* is a possibility, as are *borshch* and *shchi*, but the best dishes to look out for are mushrooms cooked with onions and sour cream, and *okroshka*, the cold summer soup.

Lobio, a widely available Georgian bean dish (served hot or cold), is also recommended. In general, ethnic restaurants (Georgian, Armenian, Indian, Chinese or Tex-Mex) are better for vegetarians. Some pizzerias have vegetarian choices and salad bars. The outlook is a lot better if you are **self-catering**, as fresh vegetables, nuts and pulses are widely available in markets and on the streets (near metro stations in the suburbs). Note that locally produced fruit and vegetables are available only from June to October; at other times of the year everything is imported and therefore pricier.

Drinking

The story goes that the tenth-century Russian prince Vladimir pondered which religion to adopt for his state. He rejected Judaism because its adherents were seen as weak and scattered; Catholicism because the pope claimed precedence over sovereigns; and Islam because his subjects would never tolerate renouncing alcohol, due to the fact that "Drinking is the joy of the Russians. We cannot live without it." A thousand years on, alcohol remains a central part of Russian life, and the main cause of the soaring mortality rate among males, who statisticians claim are drinking themselves to death at a rate rarely seen in any society.

As more and more private **cafés** and **bars** open, the choice of drinks and surroundings in which to enjoy them has increased enormously, so that the old spit-and-sawdust Soviet beer halls are now a thing of the past. However, as the price of drinks in these new establishments is at least double that charged by **shops** or **kiosks**, many Russians still prefer to buy booze from them and drink it at home, or on the nearest bench. Partly due to the prevalence of bootlegging (see below), the city council prohibits the sale of spirits from kiosks, though many continue to sell vodka under the counter. If you're drinking spirits in a bar, the usual measures are 50g or 100g (*pyatdesyat/sto gram*), which for those used to British pub measures seem extremely generous.

Eating and drinking

Vodka and other spirits

Vodka (*vódka*) is the national drink – its name means something like "a little drop of water". Normally served chilled, vodka is drunk neat in one gulp, followed by a mouthful of food, traditionally pickled herring, cucumber or mushrooms; many people inhale deeply before tossing the liquor down their throats. Drinking small amounts at a time, and eating as you go, it's possible to consume an awful lot without passing

Vodka folklore

Russians have a wealth of phrases and gestures to signify drinking vodka, the most common one being to tap the side of your chin or windpipe. The story goes that there was once a peasant who saved the life of Peter the Great and was rewarded with the right to drink as much vodka as he liked from any distillery. Fearing that a written *ukaz* would be stolen while he was drunk, the man begged the Tsar to stamp the Imperial seal on his throat – the origin of the gesture.

Fittingly, the Russian word for drunk – *pyany* – comes from an incident where two columns of drunken soldiers advancing on either side of the Pyany River mistook each other for the enemy and opened fire. Given its long and disreputable role in Russian warfare, it's ironic that the Tsarist government's prohibition of vodka for the duration of World War I did more harm than good, by depriving the state of a third of its revenue and stoking class hatred of the aristocracy, whose consumption of cognac and champagne continued unabated. Stalin knew better during World War II, when soldiers received a large shot of vodka before going into battle.

In Soviet society, vodka was the preferred form of payment for any kind of work outside the official economy and the nexus for encounters between strangers needing to "go three" on a bottle – a half-litre bottle shared between three people was reckoned to be the cheapest and most companionable way to get a bit drunk. Whereas rationing vodka was the most unpopular thing that Gorbachev ever did, Yeltsin's budgets categorized it as an essential commodity like bread or milk. Yet despite Yeltsin's notorious fondness for vodka, one would rather not believe Shevardnadze's claim to have found him lying dead drunk in the White House during the 1991 putsch, though at the time Shevardnadze told the crowd outside that "I have met the President and he is standing firm in defence of democracy." At least Yeltsin never lent his name and face to his own brand of vodka – unlike Zhirinovsky (who professes not to drink the stuff).

A FOOD GLOSSARY

Useful words		
завтрак	*zavtrak*	breakfast
обед	*obéd*	main meal/lunch
ужин	*úzhin*	supper
нож	*nozh*	knife
вилка	*vílka*	fork
ложка	*lózhka*	spoon
тарелка	*tarélka*	plate
чашка	*cháshka*	cup
стакан	*stakán*	glass
десерт	*desért*	dessert

Basics		
хлеб	*khleb*	bread
масло	*máslo*	butter/oil
мёд	*myod*	honey
молоко	*molokó*	milk
сметана	*smetána*	sour cream
яйца	*yáytsa*	eggs
яичница	*yaichnitsa*	fried egg
мясо	*myáso*	meat (beef)
рыба	*ryba*	fish
фрукты	*frúkty*	fruit
овощи	*ovoshehi*	vegetables
зелень	*zélen*	green herbs
рис	*ris*	rice
плов	*plov*	rice dish
овощной плов	*ovoshchoy plov*	vegetable plov
пирог	*piróg*	pie
хачапури	*khachapuri*	nan-style bread, stuffed with meat or melted cheese
сахар	*sákhar*	sugar
соль	*sol*	salt
перец	*pérets*	pepper
горчица	*gorchítsa*	mustard

Soups – супы		
борщ	*borsch*	beetroot soup
постный болщ	*póstny borsch*	borsch without meat
хаш	*khásh*	tripe soup, traditionally drunk with a shot of vodka as a hang-over cure
клёцки	*klyotski*	Belorussian soup with dumplings
бульон	*bulón*	consommé
рассольник	*rassólnik*	brine and cucumber soup
окрошка	*okróshka*	cold vegetable soup
щи	*shchi*	cabbage soup
солянка	*solyánka*	spicy, meaty soup flavoured with lemon and olives
уха	*ukhá*	fish soup

Vegetables – овощи		
лук	*luk*	onions
редиска	*redíska*	radishes
картофель	*kartófel*	potatoes
огурцы	*ogurtsy*	cucumbers
горох	*gorókh*	peas
помидор	*pomidóry*	tomatoes
морковь	*morkóv*	carrots
салат	*salát*	lettuce
капуста	*kapústa*	cabbage
свёкла	*svyokla*	beetroot
лобио	*lóbio*	red or green bean stew

Fruit – фрукты		
яблоки	*yábloki*	apples
абрикосы	*abrikósy*	apricots
ягоды	*yágody*	berries
вишня	*víshnya*	cherries
финики	*finiki*	dates
инжир	*inzhír*	figs
чернослив	*chernoslív*	prunes
груши	*grushi*	pears
сливы	*slivy*	plums
виноград	*vinográd*	grapes
лимон	*limón*	lemon
апельсины	*apelsíny*	oranges
арбуз	*arbúz*	watermelon
дыня	*dynya*	melon

Fish – рыба		
карп	*karp*	carp
лещ	*leshch*	bream
скумбрия	*skúmbriya*	mackerel
треска	*treská*	chub
щука	*shchúka*	pike
лососина /сёмга	*lososína/ syomga*	salmon

Some terms

Note: all adjectives appear in their plural form

отварные	*otvarnye*	boiled
варёные	*varyonye*	boiled
на вертеле	*na vertele*	grilled on a skewer
жареные	*zhárenye*	roast/grilled /fried
тушёные	*tushonye*	stewed
печёные	*pechonye*	baked
паровые	*parovye*	steamed
копчёные	*kopchonye*	smoked
фри	*fri*	fried
со сметаной	*so smetánoy*	with sour cream
маринованные	*marinóvannye*	pickled
солёные	*solyonye*	salted
фаршированные	*farshiróvannye*	stuffed

Zakúski – закуски

ассорти мясное	*assortí myasnóe*	assorted meats
ассорти рыбное	*assortí rybnoe*	assorted fish
ветчина	*vetchiná*	ham
винегрет	*vinegrét*	"Russian salad"
блины	*bliny*	pancakes
грибы	*griby*	mushrooms
икра баклажанная	*ikrá baklazhánnaya*	aubergine (eggplant) purée
икра красная	*ikrá krásnaya*	red caviar
икра чёрная	*ikrá chornaya*	black caviar
шпроты	*shpróty*	sprats (like a herring)
колбаса копчёная	*kolbasá kopchonaya*	smoked sausage
маслины	*maslíny*	olives
огурцы	*ogurtsy*	gherkins
осетрина с майонезом	*osetrína s mayonézom*	sturgeon mayonnaise
салат из огурцов	*salat iz ogurtsóv*	cucumber salad
салат из помидоров	*salát iz pomidórov*	tomato salad
сардины с лимоном	*sardíny s limónom*	sardines with lemon
сельдь	*seld*	herring
столичный салат	*stolíchniy salát*	meat and vegetable salad
сыр	*syr*	cheese
брынза	*brynza*	salty white cheese
язык с гарниром	*yazyk s garnírom*	tongue with garnish

Meat and poultry – мясные блюда

азу из говядины	*azú iz govyádiny*	beef stew
антрекот	*antrekot*	entrecôte steak
бифстроганов	*bifstróganov*	beef stroganoff
биточки	*bitóchki*	meatballs
бифштекс	*bifshtéks*	beef steak
шашлык	*shashlyk*	kebab
свинина	*svinína*	pork
котлеты по-киевски	*kotléty po-kíevski*	chicken Kiev
кролик	*królik*	rabbit
курица	*kúritsa*	chicken
рагу	*ragú*	stew
телятина	*telyátina*	veal
сосиски	*sosíski*	sausages
баранина	*baránina*	mutton/lamb
котлета	*kotlet*	fried meatball

Eating and drinking

out – though you soon reach a plateau of inebriated exhilaration.

Taste isn't a prime consideration; what counts is that the vodka isn't **bootleg liquor** (*podelnaya, falshivaya* or *levnaya*). At best, this means that customers find themselves drinking something weaker than they bargained for; at worst, they're imbibing diluted methanol, which can cause blindness or even death. To minimize the risk, familiarize yourself with the price of a few brands in the shops; if you see a bottle at well below the usual price, it's almost certainly bootleg stuff. Among the hundreds of native brands on the market, Smirnov and the varieties produced under the Liviz and Dovgan labels are probably the best, though many drinkers regard imported vodkas such as Absolut, Finlandia or Smirnoff as more prestigious. Always check that the bottle's seal and tax label are intact, and don't hesitate to pour its contents away if it smells or tastes strange. A litre of decent vodka costs about $4 in the shops.

In addition to standard vodka you'll also see **flavoured vodkas** such as *pertsovka* (hot pepper vodka), *limonaya* (lemon vodka), *okhotnichaya* (hunter's vodka with juniper berries, ginger and cloves), *starka* (apple and pear-leaf vodka) and *zubrovka* (bison-grass vodka). Many Russians make these and other variants at home, by infusing the berries or herbs in regular vodka. Other domestic liquors include **cognac** (*konyak*), which is pretty rough compared to French brandy, but easy enough to acquire a taste for. Traditionally, the best brands hail from Armenia (Ararat) and Moldova (Beliy Aist), but as both states now export their production for hard currency, bottles sold in Russia are almost certainly fakes. More commonly, you'll find Georgian or Dagestani versions, which are all right if they're the genuine article, but extremely rough if they're not. Otherwise, you can find imported spirits such as whisky, gin and tequila in many bars and shops, along with Irish Cream, Amaretto and sickly Austrian fruit brandies. Though kiosks are forbidden to sell neat spirits, most of them stock ready-mixed cans of gin and grapefruit or vodka and cranberry juice.

Beer, wine and champagne

Most of the bestselling **beers** in Russia come from two St Petersburg breweries, Baltika and Vena. **Baltika** beers come in

Drinks

чай	*chay*	tea
кофе	*kófe*	coffee
с/без сахаром/сахар	*s/bez sákharom/sákhara*	with/without sugar
сок	*sok*	fruit juice
пиво	*pívo*	beer
вино	*vinó*	wine
красное	*krásnoe*	red
белое	*béloe*	white
бутылка	*butylka*	bottle
лёд	*lyod*	ice
минеральная вода	*minerálnaya vodá*	mineral water
водка	*vódka*	vodka
вода	*vodá*	water
шампанское	*shampánskoe*	champagne
брют/сухое	*bryut/sukhoe*	extra dry/dry
полусухое/сладкое	*polsukhóe/sládkoe*	medium dry/sweet
коньяк	*konyák*	cognac
на здоровье	*za zdaróve*	cheers!

50cl bottles, numbered from 1 to 9 according to their strength. The most popular are #3 "Classic" lager (ask for *Troika*), #4 "Original" brown ale and #5 "Porter" stout; #6 and #7 are often found on tap in seedy pool bars; while it doesn't take much #9 to get you slaughtered. **Vena** does two lager-type beers in 30cl bottles or cans: Nevskoe – which many rate as the finest beer in Russia – and Petergof. Other lagers include Stariy Melnik from Moscow, Sibirskaya Korona from Siberia and Zolotaya Bochka from Kaluga, while Afanasy is a mild ale brewed in Nizhniy Novgorod. You're bound to find one or more of these on tap (*razlivnoe*) in bars, together with foreign imports such as Tuborg, Carlsberg, Holsten, or Guinness, which may also come in bottles or cans in shops. Beer is rarely, if ever, counterfeited, so you needn't worry about drinking it.

The **wine** (*vino*) on sale in Moscow comes mostly from the vineyards of Moldova, Georgia and the Crimea, although European imports are increasingly common. **Moldovan** wine tends to come in tall, slender bottles labelled in Roman rather than Cyrillic script: *sec* means dry and *dulce* sweet. **Georgian** wines are made from varieties of grapes that are almost unknown abroad, so it would be a shame not to sample them, but since the cheapest generic brands in shops and kiosks are either bootlegs or simply disgusting, you should stick to the more expensive versions ($5 upwards). The ones to look out for are the dry reds Mukuzani and Saperavi, or the sweeter full-bodied reds Kindzmarauli and Hvanchkara, drunk by Stalin. Georgia also produces some fine white wines, like the dry Gurdzhani and Tsinandali (traditionally served at room temperature), as well as the **fortified wines** Portvini (port) and Masala, which are also produced in the Crimea and known in Russian as *baramatukha* or "babbling juice", the equivalent of Thunderbird in the US.

Finally, there's what is still called "Soviet" champagne (*Sovetskoe shampanskoe*), some of which is really pretty good if served chilled, and far cheaper than the French variety. The two types to go for are *sukhoe* and *bryut* which are both reasonably dry; *polusukhoe* or "medium dry" is actually very sweet, and *sladkoe* is like connecting yourself to a glucose drip – it's indicative of Russian taste that the last two are the most popular of the lot. Like beer, *shampanskoe* is safe to drink as it's difficult to counterfeit.

Tea, coffee and soft drinks

Tea (*chay*) is brewed and stewed for hours, and traditionally topped up with boiling water from an ornate tea urn, or samovar, but even the more run-of-the-mill cafés now tend to use tea bags. If you're offered tea in someone's home, it may well be *travyanoy*, a tisane made of herbs and leaves. Russians drink tea without milk; if you ask for milk it is likely to be condensed. Milk (*molokó*) itself is sold in shops and on the streets, along with *kefir*, a sour milk drink.

Coffee (*kófe*) is readily available and of reasonable quality if imported espresso brands like Lavazza or Tchibo are used, though anything called "Nescafé" is likely to be vile. Occasionally you will be served an approximation of an espresso or, better still, a Turkish coffee. Another favourite drink is weak, milky cocoa, known as *kakao*, poured ready-mixed from a boiling urn.

Pepsi and Coca-Cola predictably enough lead the market in **soft drinks**, although they are being challenged by cheaper brands from Eastern Europe. Russian lemonades have all but disappeared, though **kvas**, an unusual but delicious thirst-quencher made from fermented rye bread, has staged a comeback – draught *kvas* is generally superior to the bottled stuff. Imported **mineral waters** are now as widely available as the traditional Soviet brands, Narzan and Borzhomi, from the Caucasus, which may be a bit too salty and sulphurous for most Westerners, though they seem to have been toned down in recent years with a view to their being launched on foreign markets. Russians who can afford to also drink bottled spring water from ecologically pure sources in Russia – the

Brunches

Many top hotels feature all-you-can-eat **Sunday brunches** aimed at Moscow's expat executives and their families, with music for the adults and entertainments for the kids. Though prohibitively dear for budget travellers, the charge per person isn't so costly when you reckon what you'd pay for a slap-up feed at any of the city's better restaurants, especially if drinks are included. If this sounds tempting, reserve in advance and come fairly smartly dressed – scruffy types may not get past the doormen.

Baltschug, *Baltschug-Kempinski Hotel*, ul. Baltschug 1 ☎230 65 00; 15min from Kitay-Gorod or Novokuznetskaya metro. Smoked fish, veal, spaghetti and all kinds of salads and pastries for the corporate crowd, with some diversions for kids. About $55 (under-12s half price). Noon–4pm.

Café Taiga, *Aerostar Hotel*, Leningradskiy pr. 37 ☎213 90 00; 15min from Dinamo or Aeroport metro. The worst of the brunches on offer – you have been warned 7–11am, noon–5.30pm & 6–11pm.

Iris, *Iris Moskva*, Korvinskoe shosse 10 ☎488 81 31; accessible by shuttle-bus from the centre. A decent spread with free French wine and discretionary champagne, plus a clown show and magicians. $45 (under-5s free, under-12s half price). Noon–4pm.

Lomonosov, *Palace Hotel*, 1-ya Tverskaya-Yamskaya ul. 19 ☎931 97 00. Moscow's best spread of fish, caviar and meats, with a few champagne cocktails for good measure. Tasteful music and stage show; clowns and magician for kids. $47 (under-6s free, under-12s half price). Noon–1am.

Metropol, *Metropol Hotel*, Teatralniy proezd 1/4 ☎927 60 61; near Teatralnaya, Ploshchad Revolyutsii and Okhotniy Ryad metros. Fabulous buffet in a lovely hall, with a jazz or Dixie band and plenty of room for private conversation. $52 (children half price). 7–10.30am, noon–3pm & 6–11pm.

Radisson Slavjanskaya, *Radisson Slavjanskaya Hotel*, Berezhovskaya nab. 2 ☎941 80 20 ext 3236; near Kievskaya metro. Swedish *smörgasbord* buffet, with lots of smoked meats and marinated fish – the cheapest brunch in town. $35 (under-8s free, 9–12 years $10). Noon–3pm.

Svyati Istochik (Sacred Spring) brand even comes with a blessing from the Orthodox Patriarch. Lastly, if you're staying with Russians, you may be offered some **gryb**, a muddy-coloured, mildly flavoured infusion of a giant fungus known as a "tea mushroom".

Fast-food chains

Over the last decade, **fast-food chains** have become hugely popular in Moscow, offering a variety of food and standards of hygiene and service infinitely superior to the grimy *stolovaya* (canteens) that were the lot of generations of citizens during Soviet times, but which younger Russians now take for granted. Besides such worldwide giants as *McDonald's* and *Pizza Express*, there are homegrown chains such as *Russkoe Bistro*, *Russkiy Bliny* and *Koshka Kartoshka* – details can be found in the box opposite.

Cafés and bars

Cafés and **bars** in Moscow run the gamut from humble eateries to slick establishments, and since most places serve alcohol (or beer, at any rate) the distinction between them is often a fine one. Except for establishments in top-class hotels, cafés are generally cheaper than fully fledged restaurants, making them popular with Russians who have some disposable income, but don't ride around in a Mercedes.

Though almost all cafes are private ventures nowadays, some retain the surly habits of Soviet days, when customers counted themselves lucky if they got served at all, and even where they aim to please you sometimes find inex-

Eating and drinking

The chain gang

Koshka Kartoshka *Outdoor kiosks selling filled jacket potatoes and salads. No CCs.* Pl. Revolyutsii, Ploshchad Revolyutsii or Teatralnaya metro; corner of ul. Petrovka & Stoleshnikov per., Teatralnaya or Kuznetskiy Most metro; and many other locations; all daily 9am–11pm.

McDonald's *The cleanest toilets in Moscow.* ul. Arbat 50, Smolenskaya metro (daily 8am–midnight); Bolshaya Bronnaya ul. 29/corner of Tverskaya ul., Tverskaya metro (daily 8am–11.30pm); Bolshaya Dorogomilovskaya ul. 8, Kievskaya metro (daily 8am–midnight); ul. Bolshaya Ordynka 16, Tretyakovskaya metro (daily 8am–midnight); Bolshaya Serpukhovskaya ul. 4, Tulskaya metro (daily 24hr); Gazetniy per. 17/corner of Tverskaya ul., Okhotniy Ryad metro (daily 8am–midnight); Krasnaya Presnya ul. 31, Ulitsa 1905 Goda metro (daily 8am–midnight); ul. Maroseyka 9, Kitay-Gorod metro (daily 8am–midnight); Zelenonodolskaya ul. 38, Ryazanskiy Prospekt metro (daily 8am–midnight).

Patio Pizza *Thin-crust wood-oven pizzas, salad bar ($7), alcohol. Child-friendly. Visa, MC, JCB.* ul. Volkhonka 13a ☎201 56 26, Kropotkinskaya metro; 1-ya Tverskaya-Yamskaya ul. 2, Mayakovskaya metro; Leninskiy pr. 68/10, Universitet metro; pr. Mira 33/1, Prospekt Mira metro (all daily noon until the last person leaves); Tverskaya ul. 3, *Intourist Hotel*, Okhotniy Ryad metro (Sun–Thurs 10am–midnight); Smolenskaya ul. 3, Smolenskaya metro (daily noon–11pm).

Pizza Express *Live jazz Mon–Fri 7–11pm, Sat & Sun 2pm. Amex, Visa, MC, EC, DC, JCB, Unioncard.* Smolenskiy Passazh shopping centre, Smolenskaya pl. ☎937 81 00, Smolenskaya metro (daily noon–midnight).

Rostiks *Chicken, fries, doughnuts, milkshakes. No CCs.* GUM, Nikolskaya ul., Ploshchad Revolyutsii metro; Okhotniy Ryad mall, Manezhnaya pl., Okhotniy Ryad metro; Leninskiy pr. 68, Akademicheskaya metro; pr. Mira 92, Rizhskaya metro; all daily 8am–8pm.

Russkiy Bliny *Freshly made bliny (pancakes) with sweet or savoury fillings, including caviar. No CCs.* Okhotniy Ryad mall, Manezhnaya pl., Okhotniy Ryad metro; ul. Petrovka, behind the TsUM, Kuznetskiy Most or Teatralnaya metro; corner of ul. Petrovka & Stoleshnikov per., Teatralnaya or Kuznetskiy Most metro; and many other locations; all daily 9am–11pm.

Russkoe Bistro *Savoury pirozhki (pies), bliny, herbal teas and kvas; some branches sell vodka. No CCs.* Bolshaya Gruzinskaya ul. 50, Belorusskaya metro (Mon–Sat 11am–9pm, Sun noon–10pm); Bolshoy Tolmachevskiy per. 4, Tretyakovskaya metro (daily noon–8pm); Energeticheskaya ul. 18, Aviamotornaya metro (24hr); pl. Kurskovo vokzala, Kurskaya metro (daily 24hr); Myasnitskaya ul. 42, Turgenevskaya/Chistye Prudy metro (daily 24hr); Nikolskaya ul. 15, Ploshchad Revolyutsii or Lubyanka metro (Mon–Sat 11am–9pm, Sun noon–10pm); ul. Noviy Arbat 21, Arbatskaya metro (Mon–Sat 11am–9pm, Sun noon–10pm); Tverskaya ul. 16, Tverskaya/Pushkinskaya/Chekhovskaya metro (Mon–Sat 11am–9pm, Sun noon–10pm); Tverskaya ul. 23, Tverskaya/Pushkinskaya metro (daily 10am–11pm).

Eating and drinking

Price categories

We have graded all the cafés and restaurants in this chapter into **price categories**. In the **café** listings, these relate to the approximate per-person cost of a snack or light meal plus a non-alcoholic drink (although in many cafés you can have a full meal). For **restaurants**, the categories refer to the rough cost of a starter, main course and dessert – but no alcohol, which in many restaurants can easily double your bill.

Cheap	Less than $15
Inexpensive	$15–30
Moderate	$30–50
Expensive	$50–100
Very expensive	Over $100

plicable lapses in standards or decorum. However, you can also find some delicious meals and friendly watering holes if you know where to look, and the number of acceptable places is rising all the time.

The following selection is listed in alphabetical order under area headings corresponding to the chapters in the guide section. Where we have provided phone numbers for bars and cafés, it's advisable to phone ahead and reserve a table, particularly if you are planning to eat in the evening.

Red Square and the Kitay-gorod

The listings in this section are marked on the map on pp.76–77.

Apollo, Okhotniy Ryad mall, 3rd level, Manezhnaya pl.; Okhotniy Ryad metro. One of the best of the options in the mall, with all-you-can-eat buffets ($10) from a choice of three cuisines – Russian, Georgian or Japanese – each represented by 25 dishes. Amex, Visa, DC, EC, MC. Daily 11am–10pm. Cheap.

Café Maner, Okhotniy Ryad mall, 3rd level, Manezhnaya pl.; Okhotniy Ryad metro. A classy air-conditioned coffee house serving Viennese- and Italian-style coffee and desserts at Viennese prices. All major CCs. Daily 11am–midnight.

Copacabana, on the second floor of GUM, at the ul. Ilinka end of the second line. Café serving espresso, ice cream, pastries and toasted sandwiches. No smoking. No CCs. Mon–Sat 9am–8pm. Cheap.

Sbarro, Okhotniy Ryad mall, beside the Alexander Garden; Okhotniy Ryad metro. A tempting array of pizzas and salads, though they're not as tasty as they look, and you may have to queue so long that they hardly count as fast-food. Amex, Visa, EC, DC, MC. Daily 10am–midnight. Cheap.

Suliko, Okhotniy Ryad mall, 3rd level, Manezhnaya pl.; Okhotniy Ryad metro. Georgian bistro with a stupendous buffet ($30), a good-value business lunch ($10) and *a la carte* dishes. They also do takeouts and deliveries (☎737 84 69). All major CCs. Daily 11am–10pm. Cheap.

Yunikon, Nikolskaya ul. 13; Ploshchad Revolyutsii metro. A cosy student café with hot drinks and simple food, within the Russian State Humanitarian University. No CCs. Daily noon–midnight. Extremely cheap.

Zolotoy Drakon, on the second floor of GUM, at the ul. Ilinka end of the third line. A nice spot for a coffee or fruit salad, or a stiff drink. No CC. Mon–Sat 9am–8pm. Cheap.

Beliy Gorod

The listings in this section are marked on the map on pp.128–129.

Bubliki, ul. Petrovka 24/1; 5min from Kuznetskiy Most metro. A cavernous haunt of workers in the financial district that's only busy at lunchtime, when bagels, soups, salads and vaguely nouvelle dishes are on the menu, and after

5pm, when cocktails flow. Don't be deterred by the "Erotic Club" upstairs. Daily noon–midnight. Cheap–inexpensive.

Chevignon Café, Stoleshnikov per. 14 (in the Baza 14 fashion mall); Teatralnaya metro. Equally good for breakfast, lunch or dinner, with tables outside in fine weather. Delicious soups, foie gras, fillet de boeuf and profiteroles. Business lunches ($10–20) are served noon–5pm, and wine- and cheese-tasting sessions are held every third Thursday of the month. There's also English-language Internet access ($4 per hour). Visa, MC, Unioncard. Daily noon–11pm. Inexpensive.

Coffee Bean, branches at ul. Pokrovka 18, Kitay-Gorod or Chistye Prudy metro; and beneath the arch from Kuznetskiy Most metro to ul. Bolshaya Lubyanka. Seattle meets Moscow at the flagship branch on Pokrovka, which does wine by the glass as well as great coffee and cakes. The hole-in-the-wall Kuznetskiy branch is more Haight-Ashbury, but likewise brews and sells the best coffee and coffee beans in Moscow. Non-smoking. No CCs. Pokrovka branch: daily 8am–10pm; Kuznetskiy branch: daily 8am–8pm. Cheap.

Drova, Myasnitskaya ul. 24; Chistye Prudy/Turgenevskaya metro. One of the best deals in town: a delicious all-you-can-eat buffet of soups, sushi, salads and desserts for $9; lunch specials $4; and buffet with entrée $6. Faux rustic ambience, with candles and recorded birdsongs, replaced by cable TV and music during the small hours. No CCs. Daily 24hr. Cheap.

Johnny-Tolstyak, Myasnitskaya ul. 22; 5min from Chistye Prudy/ Turgenevskaya metro. Down the road from *Drova*, this long-established American café with jukebox offers burgers, burritos, pizzas and Moscow's cheapest egg, bacon and toast breakfast ($2.50) – and also delivers pizzas (☎755 95 54). Daily 8am–midnight. Visa, DC, MC. Cheap.

La Cantina, Tverskaya ul. 5; 5min from Okhotniy Ryad metro. A popular pick-up spot and watering hole for foreigners and hookers, featuring live music some evenings. OK for a beer or a cocktail, but you'd do better eating at *Azteca*, next door, or *Hola! Mexico* (see p.344). No CCs. Daily noon–11pm. Inexpensive.

Galereya, ul. Bolshaya Lubyanka 15; Lubyanka metro. Up the road from the secret police club, this cosy café serves fabulous cakes, ice cream, tiramisu and freshly squeezed juices, and features an ever-changing exhibition of avant-garde art. No CCs. Daily 10am–midnight. Cheap.

Rosie O'Grady's, ul. Znamenka 9/12; 5min from Borovitskaya metro. Moscow's best-known "Irish" pub is quieter than it was, but still popular with homesick expats and young Russians. Darts, pub grub and Sunday brunch, plus business lunches ($5) till 5pm. Live music from 6pm. Amex, Visa, DC, EC, MC, JCB. Open daily noon till the last person leaves. Inexpensive.

Sbarro, Tverskaya ul. 10; Tverskaya metro. Another branch of the Italian fast-food chain, whose pizzas look better than they taste but hit the spot when you feel like comfort food. Amex, Visa, DC, EC, MC. Daily noon–midnight. Cheap.

Shashlychnitsa u Nikitskie vorot, Kalashniy per. 9; 5min from Arbatskaya metro. A good low-budget option off Nikitskie vorota, where you can tuck into tasty *shashlyk*, *khachapuri* and other Georgian dishes, washed down with beer. Not to be confused with the restaurant of the same name just around the corner. No CCs. Daily 10am–9pm. Cheap.

Varcha Traktir, ul. Bolshaya Lubyanka 13; Lubyanka metro. Another good place to try Georgian cuisine, with a wider choice than at *Shashlychnitsa u Nikitskie vorot*. For dessert, drop into *Galereya*, a few doors along. No CCs. Daily 11am–11pm. Cheap.

Yolki Palki (Fiddlesticks), branches at ul. Kuznetskiy most/corner of ul. Neglinnaya, Kuznetskiy Most or Teatralnaya metro; and Bolshaya Dmitrovka ul. 28, 5min

Eating and drinking

from Chekhovskaya metro. Two popular cafés styled like nineteenth-century inns, serving Russian cuisine. Vegetarians should try the *zakuski* buffet (*telega*), a meal in itself ($5), washed down with a large glass of *kvas* or a vodka. No CCs. Kuznetskiy branch: daily 11am–1am; Bolshaya Dmitrovka branch: daily 11am–11pm. Cheap.

Zemlyanoy Gorod

The listings in this section are marked on the map on pp.170–171.

American Bar & Grill, Tverskaya-Yamskaya ul. 32/1 ☎251 79 99; near Mayakovskaya metro. Slightly pretentious and overpriced diner for shy expats and aspiring Russians, with burgers, pizzas, baked potatoes and ribs, plus hash browns for breakfast. Daily 24hr. All major CCs. Inexpensive.

DéliFrance, Triumfalnaya pl. 4; next to Mayakovskaya metro. Upscale self-service café selling filled croissants, mushroom savouries, pastries, French wine and Russian beer; there are outside tables too. Access is via the lobby of the Tchaikovsky Concert Hall. No CCs. Daily 10am–10pm. Cheap.

Fox Pub, Daev per. 2; 10min from Sukharevskaya metro. Lurking in the blighted backstreets off ul. Sretenka, this hip modern pub serves big portions of tasty bar food and yummy desserts. No CCs. Daily 11am–midnight (or later). Inexpensive.

It's Sushi, Triumfalnaya pl. 4; next to Mayakovskaya metro. Excellent, affordable sushi bar in the lobby of the Tchaikovsky Concert Hall, with a few veggie options such as egg and black mushroom sushi. No CCs. Daily 10am–10pm. Cheap.

Soleil Express, ul. Sadovaya-Samotochnaya 24/27; 5min from Tsvetnoy Bulvar metro. Pleasant bistro, very popular with office workers, with lots of grilled vegetables, sandwiches, salads, and delicious desserts (try the "soleil express"). Pastries are two-thirds cheaper after 9pm. Visa, DC, MC, JCB. Mon–Fri 8.30am–11pm, Sat & Sun 10am–11pm. Cheap.

Spartak ul. Zemlyanoy val 50; Kurskaya or Taganskaya metro. Large Garden Ring sports bar-cum-restaurant with TVs showing soccer and tennis, and live strippers. No CCs. Mon–Wed noon–11.30pm, Thurs–Sun noon–5am. Inexpensive.

Sports Bar, ul. Noviy Arbat 10; Arbatskaya metro. Decent bar food and affordable sushi in an atrium with lots of TVs showing Eurosports, NFL and NBA, plus pool tables. At night, strippers and drunk, libidinous revellers set the tone. Drinks are overpriced, and the security guards mean. No CCs. $3 entry at night. Inexpensive.

Starlite Diner 1, Bolshaya Sadovaya ul. 16; Mayakovskaya metro. Ever-popular American eatery, with a good breakfast special (till 11am), chilli cheese fries and spicy Thai wraps. Amex, Visa, MC. Daily 24hr. Cheap–inexpensive.

Taras Bulba Korchma, ul. Petrovka 30/7, str. 1; Chekhovskaya metro. Named after the legendary Cossack warrior and decorated like a rural inn, *Taras Bulba* does tasty Ukrainian *borshch* and *vareniki* (dumplings) for a fraction of what you'd pay at *Shinok* (see p.348). No CCs. Daily noon–11pm. Cheap.

T.G.I. Friday's, Tverskaya ul. 18 ☎209 36 01; near Pushkinskaya/Tverskaya metro. Located above the Art Nouveau Sytin dom, but otherwise like *T.G.I. Friday's* everywhere, complete with juggling barmen and Tiffany lampshades. Filet mignon ($10), burgers, cajun chicken, Caesar salad, ribs – try the Jack Daniels salmon for something different. Amex, Visa, DC, MC. Daily 10am–1.30am. Inexpensive.

Krasnaya Presnya, Fili and the southwest

The listing in this section is marked on the map on pp.200–201.

Planet Hollywood, Krasnaya Presnaya ul. 23b; 5min from Ulitsa 1905 Goda metro. A mecca for Russian yuppies and wannabes, where lap dancing is regarded as wholesome family entertainment. Decent cocktails, burgers and fried chicken, but the service and videos suck. Frequent happy hours, free hors d'oeuvres Wed 7–9pm, and male striptease on ladies' night (Thurs). Amex, Visa, MC. Daily 11am–1am. Moderate.

Zamoskvareche and the south

The listings in this section are marked on the map on pp.230–231. Some also appear on the large-scale map of Zamoskvareche (p.233).

Moosehead, ul. Bolshaya Polyanka 54; 5min from Dobryninskaya metro. Expat watering hole that offers a tasty $10 lunch (11am–5pm), $5 burritos on Wed and $1 buffalo wings on Tues; give the salad bar (or anything else) a miss. In the evening *Moosehead* is strictly for partying. Amex, Visa, DC, MC. Daily noon–5am (10am at weekends). Cheap.

Sally O'Brien's, ul. Bolshaya Polyanka 1/3; 10min from Polyanka or Tretyakovskaya metro. A quieter and cheaper alternative to *Rosie O'Grady's* (see p.341), likewise serving pub grub, draught beers, Irish coffee and cocktails. Visa, MC, EC, DC. Daily noon–1am or later. Inexpensive.

Starlite Diner 2, ul. Koroviy val 9; 5min from Oktyabryskaya/Dobryninskaya metro. Good-value American food day or night; the weekday breakfast special, chilli cheese fries and the broccoli and cheese omelettes are the best in Moscow. Amex, Visa, MC. Daily 24hr. Cheap–inexpensive.

Taganka and Zazauze

The listings in this section are marked on the map on pp.272–273.

American Bar & Grill, ul. Zemlyanoy val 59; 10min from Taganskaya metro. Another branch of the US diner, with a patio for BBQs. Pizzas, baked potatoes, ribs and "kickin' chicken", plus a big choice of $6–10 combos (11am–3pm). Amex, Visa, MC. Daily noon–2am. Inexpensive.

Horse and Hound, ul. Malaya Kommunisticheskaya 16/27; 10min from Taganskaya/Marksistskaya metro. A comfy "British" pub serving hearty meals of fish 'n' chips, steak or chicken, a few veggie options and a $10 lunch. Punters can bet on the horse and dog races that are shown on TV (Mon–Sat). Amex, Visa, MC. Daily noon–midnight. Inexpensive.

Northern Suburbs

The listings in this section are marked on the map on pp.296–297.

Great Canadian Bagel Co./Ku Ku Ru, ul. Gruzinskiy val 31; near Belorusskaya metro. Two foreign chains sharing the same premises. One features live jazz as well as twelve kinds of bagel (pay before ordering); the other does fries, pizzas and chicken combos. No CCs. Daily 10am–10pm. Cheap.

Moskva-Berlin pl. Tverskaya Zastava 52/2; near Belorusskaya metro. Across the square from Belarus Station, this stylish, comfy and popular hangout plays trip-hop, ambient, house and techno in the evening. Its VIP room features such delights as banana toast with cheese and onion omelette, while the bar offers ice cream with fruit and liquor. No CCs. Daily 24hr. Cheap.

Restaurants

Moscow's **restaurants** reflect the social revolution of the last decade, as ever more exotic places pander to the *novie bogatie* (new rich). At the top end of the scale, you'll probably feel uncomfortable if you're not dressed to the hilt – though relatively few places impose a formal dress code (a jacket and tie for men, a skirt or dress for women). At most restaurants it's customary to consign your coat to the *garderob* on arrival; if helped to put it back on later, a small tip is warranted.

More and more places offer **business lunches** at lower prices than you'd pay dining *a la carte* – they're advertised by signboards outside with the words бизнес ланьч in Cyrillic and in the city's

Eating and drinking

Eating and drinking

foreign-language press, where you may also find details of **food festivals** being held at hotels. At present, relatively few places include a **service charge** in the bill, so you can tip (or not) as you like. Some places feature **floorshows** consisting of "folk music" and maybe some kind of striptease act (which Russians regard with equanimity), for which there may or may not be a surcharge.

We've provided **telephone numbers** for all the restaurants listed, as reserving in advance is always a good idea, particularly if you want to eat after 9pm. Most places now have at least one member of staff with a rudimentary grasp of English. If not, a useful phrase to get your tongue around is *Ya khochu zakazat stol na . . . cheloveka sevodnya na . . . chasov* (I want to reserve a table for . . . people for . . . o'clock today). Restaurants below are listed in alphabetical order under area headings corresponding to the chapters in the guide section.

Red Square and the Kitay-gorod

The following listings appear on the map on p.115, except *Krasnaya Ploshchad*, which is shown on the map on p.76.

Boyarskiy Zal (Boyar's Hall), *Metropol Hotel*, fourth floor ☎927 60 00; near Ploshchad Revolyutsii, Okhotniy Ryad and Teatralnaya metros. Princely Russian cuisine and folk music (from 8pm) in a room decorated in the style of a sixteenth-century boyar's palace. Amex, Visa, DC, EC, MC. Mon–Sat 7pm–midnight. Expensive.

Krasnaya Ploshchad (Red Square), in the Historical Museum ☎925 36 00; Ploshchad Revolyutsii/Okhotniy Ryad metro. As central as you can get, with excellent Tsarist-era dishes served in a cosy setting. There's a business lunch (noon–4pm; $15), and nightly live jazz or music from a trio of psaltery, flute and zither (from 7pm). Amex, Visa, MC, DC, EC, Unioncard. Daily noon–midnight. Moderate.

Lobster Grill, *Metropol Hotel* ☎927 60 69. Delicious lobster, shrimp, tiger prawns and other imported seafood, personally selected from the aquarium. Daily 11am–2am. Most CCs. Very expensive.

Beliy Gorod

The listings in this section are marked on the map on pp.128–129.

Amarcord, ul. Pokrovka 6 ☎923 09 32; Chistye Prudy metro. Steadily supplanting *Il Pomodoro* as the "in" Italian place, with superb pasta and salmon carpaccio, and cheap thin-crust pizzas ($5) – although the desserts and Chianti are rather overpriced. Amex, Visa, MC, DC. Daily 11am until the last person leaves. Inexpensive–moderate.

Azteca, *Intourist Hotel*, Tverskaya ul. 3/5 ☎956 84 67; near Okhotniy Ryad metro. Moscow's first Mexican eatery is still going strong. Friendly service but slow at lunchtime, due to demand for their $15 lunch (noon–4pm). Check out the fantastic view of the Kremlin from the top floor of the hotel. Daily noon–midnight. Visa, MC. Moderate.

Dzhonka (The Junk), Tverskoy bul. 22 (around the side of MKhAT) ☎203 94 30; 5min from Tverskaya metro. Relaxed, uncrowded Chinese restaurant styled like a junk. Try the sweet and sour carp or Gonbo chicken, but give the dim sum a miss. There's a lunch menu (noon–4pm; $10) and a 20 percent reduction for takeouts. Billiards. Daily noon–midnight. Visa, DC, MC, JCB. Moderate.

Emerald Buddha, ul. Sretenka 1 ☎925 94 82; Turgenevskaya/Chistye Prudy metro. Currently the top Thai restaurant in Moscow – though Thai chefs move around so often that it may not stay that way for long. Try the spicy grilled pork salad or sweet-and-sour fried beef with veg, spiced to taste. All major CCs. Daily noon–midnight. Moderate–expensive.

Hola Mexico!, Pushchennaya ul. 7/5 ☎925 82 51; near Kuznetskiy Most metro. Moscow's best Cali-Mex eatery, serving wonderful pork enchiladas and fajitas – finish up with a banana split. Special deals include a business lunch (noon–4pm; $5.50) and happy hour

(4–6pm), with two cocktails for the price of one, plus a Mexican band and dancing at night. Daily noon–5am. Inexpensive.

Limpopo, Varsonofievskiy per. 1 ☎925 69 90; *www.limpopo.ru*; Kuznetskiy Most metro. Shamelessly pandering to stereotypes, this tribal hut-style African restaurant serves grilled crocodile, baked tortoise, kangaroo and impala steaks, plus South African wine and beer, and cocktails with zoomorphic swizzle-sticks. Visa, MC. Daily noon–midnight. Moderate–expensive.

Marharaja, ul. Pokrovka 21 ☎921 98 44; Kitay-Gorod metro. Sadly, the classy service and presentation aren't matched by the quality of the food, and prices are higher than at *Mos-Bombay* (see below) – though all dishes can be served without spices if required, and they do take-outs. Amex, Visa, DC, EC, MC. Daily noon–10.30pm. Moderate.

Mos-Bombay, Glinishchevskiy per. 3 ☎292 97 31; 5min from Pushkinskaya metro. Spicy Indian and less authentic Chinese cuisine, with lots of vegetarian options and a business lunch ($4.50) till 3pm – good service, too. There's also live music (Thurs & Fri 8.30–10.30pm) and oriental dancing (Fri 8.30–9.30pm). Daily 11am–11pm. Amex, Visa, DC, MC. Inexpensive.

Noev Kovcheg (Noah's Ark), Maliy Ivanovskiy per. 9 ☎917 07 17; *www.noevkovcheg.ru*; 10min from Kitay-Gorod metro. Spacious, upmarket Armenian restaurant whose reasonably priced *lobio*, cheese plates, *basturma* with peppers and diverse *shashlyks* encourage rash splurging on their fine wines and brandies. All major CCs. Daily noon–midnight. Moderate.

Samovar, Myasnitskaya ul. 13 ☎924 46 88; 5min from Turgenevskaya/Chistye Prudy metro. Discreet, smart Russian restaurant with good service, tasteful music and atmosphere, plus ten sorts of *bliny* and twenty types of *pelmeni*. All major CCs. Daily noon–11pm. Moderate.

Savoy, *Savoy Hotel*, ul. Rozhdestvenka 3 ☎929 86 00; near Kuznetskiy Most metro. One of the best restaurants in Moscow, with magnificent Rococo decor, superb French, Russian and Scandinavian cuisine, and top-class service – enjoy it on the cheap with a $23 business lunch (noon–4pm). Also has a buffet breakfast (7.30–11am) and live jazz or "romantic" music (from 7.30pm). Amex, Visa, DC, EC, MC. Daily 7.30–11am & noon–11pm. Expensive.

Spago, Bolshoy Zlatoustinskiy per. 1/1 ☎921 37 97; near Kitay-Gorod/Lubyanka metro. No relation to the Belgian *moules* chain, but a welcome source of fresh Mediterranean seafood, homemade pasta and tiramisu, accompanied by Italian wines and free bruschetta, if you ask for it. Amex, Visa, DC, EC, MC. Daily noon until the last client leaves. Moderate–expensive.

Tibet Himalaya, ul. Pokrovka 19 ☎917 39 85; 10min from Kitay-Gorod or Chistye Prudy/Turgenevskaya metro. Laidback haunt of ethnic food lovers, with hookahs for chilling out. The house speciality is meat with bamboo, but you can't go wrong with the *momo* dumplings, egg fried noodles or aubergine with spicy garlic sauce either. Business lunch $4.50. Amex, Visa, MC, DC. Daily noon–midnight. Inexpensive.

Tibet Kitchen, Kamergerskiy per. 5/6 ☎923 24 22, 961 34 41; 5min from Okhotniy Ryad metro. Arguably superior to its older rival above on the culinary front, with great vegetable or chicken spring rolls and garlic noodles, though the ambience is marred by the TV monitors playing an endless loop of *Seven Years in Tibet*. No CCs. Daily noon–11pm. Inexpensive.

Yakitoriya, Tverskaya ul. 18a, Pushkinskaya/Tverskaya metro; ul. Petrovka 16, 10min from Teatralnaya or Kuznetskiy Most metro. One of several Moscow branches of this affordable chain, serving fine sushi, seaweed salads, miso and kento soups, with Fuji cake or bean pastila for dessert. All major CCs. Daily 11am–6am. Cheap–inexpensive.

Zemlyanoy Gorod

The listings in this section are marked on the map on pp.170–171.

011, Sadovaya-Triumfulnaya ul. 10 ☎209 09 63; near Mayakovskaya metro. A Serbian restaurant that started off as a nightclub and retains an air of intrigue. Good for a candlelit tête-à-tête or a raucous meal with a bunch of friends. Fish dominates the menu. No CCs. Daily 10am–11pm. Moderate.

Barracuda, Sadovaya-Kudrinskaya ul. 24/27 ☎203 62 66; near Barrikadnaya metro. One of Moscow's best seafood restaurants, despite the kitsch *20,000 Leagues Under the Sea* décor and waiters in Bavarian costumes. All major CCs. Daily noon–midnight. Moderate.

B.B. King, Sadovaya-Samotyochnaya ul. 4/2 ☎299 80 26; 10min from Tvestnoy Bulvar metro. Cajun/soul dishes including seafood okra gumbo, jambalaya and fried chicken salad, with a set lunch for $10 (noon–4pm). There's a rock and blues jukebox, and live blues or jazz most evenings. No CCs. Mon–Thurs & Sun noon–2am, Fri & Sat noon–5am. Inexpensive.

Bosfor (Bosporus), ul. Arbat 47/23 ☎241 93 20; near Arbatskaya/Smolenskaya metro. Turkish-Caucasian restaurant just off the Arbat, serving the usual starters and *shashlyks*, plus a few fancier dishes like baked trout in wine sauce, with Georgian, Italian or Spanish wines. The outdoor bit is good for watching life on the Arbat. Visa, MC. Daily 11am–midnight. Moderate.

Bungalo Bar, ul. Zemlyanoy val 6 ☎916 24 32; 10min from Kurskaya metro. An authentic, funky Ethiopian restaurant serving huge portions of delicious spicy dishes, with veggie choices galore. Very friendly service, cheap beer and great coffee. Puts *Limpopo* (see p.345) to shame. No CCs. Daily noon–midnight. Inexpensive.

Dioscuria, Nikitskiy bul. 5, str. 1 (through the post office arch off Noviy Arbat) ☎291 37 59; near Arbatskaya metro. Some of the finest Georgian food in town, especially the *khachapuri* and sturgeon *shashlyk* with pomegranate sauce – but the choice gets more limited as evening wears on, and they hate people arriving after 10.30pm. No CCs. Daily 11am–midnight.

El Gaucho, Bolshoy Kozlovskiy per. 2 ☎923 10 98; near Krasnye Vorota metro. Top-quality grills prepared by an Argentine chef. Cholesterol-watchers and vegetarians needn't bother. No CCs. Daily noon–midnight. Moderate.

El Rancho, ul. Prichistenka 23 ☎201 56 62; 10min from Kropotkinskaya or Park Kultury metro. A Spanish restaurant with lots of tasty Latin dishes, loud Mexican pop music and cosy decor. $13 lunch (noon–3pm). Daily 11am–midnight. Moderate.

Genatsvale ul. Ostozhenka 12/1 ☎202 04 45; 5min from Kropotkinskaya metro. Excellent, low-priced Georgian food and wine – the *shashlyks* are especially good value, or try the *matsoni* (*kefir* with honey and nuts). Eat during the day to avoid the loud band and toasting in the evenings. No CCs. Daily 11am–midnight. Cheap.

Il Pomodoro, Bolshoy Golovin per. 5 ☎924 29 31; 5min from Sukharevskaya/Tsvetnoy Bulvar metro. Moscow's top Italian restaurant before *Amarcord* (see p.344) and *Dorian Gray* (see p.348) came along, and still full of Italian businessmen and their escorts sampling the zesty appetizers and fresh vegetables. Daily noon–11pm. Amex, Visa, DC, MC. Moderate.

Mama Zoya, Sechenovskiy per. 8 ☎201 77 43; 10min from Kropotkinskaya metro. Popular Georgian restaurant with engagingly kitsch decor, fine food and schmaltzy music. Best by day, when it's not packed with expats and you're not hassled to eat up and go. Children welcome if it's not too crowded. No CCs. Daily noon–11pm. Inexpensive.

Mehana Bansko, Smolenskaya pl. 9/1 ☎244 73 87 or 241 31 32; Smolenskaya metro. Agreeable taverna-style Bulgarian restaurant with staff in national costume and live folk music after 6pm. Ask for the lamb dish that arrives on fire. No CCs. Mon–Thurs & Sun noon–midnight, Fri & Sat noon–2am. Inexpensive–moderate.

Pancho Villa, ul. Arbat 44/1 ☎241 98 53; near Arbatskaya/Smolenskaya metro. Decent Mexican eatery overlooking the Arbat, serving meatball soup ($5), burritos ($9.50) and nachos ($5–7). Deals include the "Huevos Rancheros" breakfast (5am–11am), business lunch (noon–4pm; $6) and happy hour (6–8pm & midnight–11am), and there's live music too (Wed–Sun 8am–midnight). Amex, Visa, EC, MC, JCB, Maestro. Daily 24hr. Cheap.

Patio Pasta, 1-ya Tverskaya-Yamskaya ul. 1/3 ☎251 56 26; Mayakovskaya metro. A spin-off of the *Patio Pizza* chain, more focused on pasta than pizzas, and offering business lunches ($9) and unlimited salad bar ($7). Visa, MC, JCB. Daily noon–midnight. Cheap–inexpensive.

Pyat Spetsii (Five Spices), per. Sivtsev Vrazhek 3/18 (corner of Gogolevskiy bul.) ☎203 12 83; 5min from Kroptokinskaya metro. One of those Moscow hybrids: an Indian-run Chinese restaurant serving yummy Thai prawn soup, vegetable spring rolls, honey-glazed ribs, stir-fry noodles, king prawns in oyster sauce, and barbecue chicken in hot black bean sauce. Business lunch ($10) noon–4pm. Amex, Visa, MC, JCB. Daily noon–4pm. Moderate.

San Marco, ul. Arbat 25 ☎291 70 89; 5min from Arbatskaya metro. Probably the best choice on the Arbat if you don't fancy Caucasian cuisine. Fine carbonara, duck-and-mushroom risotto, carpaccio with pesto, and spicy sausage pizzas. No CCs. Daily noon–11pm. Inexpensive.

Tandoor, Tverskaya ul. 30/2 ☎299 59 25; near Mayakovskaya metro. Variable Indian food, dearer than *Mos-Bombay* (see p.345), and poor value compared to *Darbar* (see below). Daily noon–11pm. Amex, Visa. Moderate.

TRAM, ul. Malaya Dmitrovka 6 ☎299 07 70; near Chekhovskaya metro. A basement hang-out beside the Lenkom Theatre: the interior is smoky and intimate; tables on the street are less glamorous. Russian, European and vaguely Asian dishes are named after plays or theatrical genres – try the Kabuki. Business lunches are only $3–4, and there are Chaplin movies and live piano music in the evenings. No CCs. Daily 24hr. Inexpensive.

Krasnaya Presnya, Fili and the southwest

The listings in this section are marked on the map on pp.200–201.

Baan Thai, Bolshaya Dorogomilovskaya ul. 11 ☎240 05 97; 5min from Kievskaya metro. If you can't afford the *Emerald Buddha* (see p.344) this is the next best Thai place in Moscow. The satay, spicy noodle soups and duck curry are perfect, and the service attentive. No CCs. Daily noon–midnight. Moderate.

Bali ul. Timura Frunze 11 ☎246 45 03; 5min from Park Kultury metro. Indonesian restaurant, decked out with a waterfall, fountain and wicker chairs, and serving delicious satay and shellfish soups, with draught Czech beer. Business lunches (12.30–5pm; $5), live music and karaoke (from 8pm) and free secure parking. No CCs. Daily noon–midnight. Moderate.

Bochka ul. 1905 goda 2 ☎252 30 41; 10min from Ulitsa 1905 Goda metro. Opposite the Mezh, this rustic-style place does wonderful Russian food with a Caucasian twist; try the *golubtsy* (stuffed cabbage) with sour cream. Full of New Russians jabbering into their mobiles. Amex, Visa, MC. Daily 24hr. Moderate.

Darbar, *Sputnik Hotel*, Leninskiy pr. 38 ☎930 29 25; 5min from Leninskiy Prospekt metro. Worth the trip to eat the best Indian food in Moscow, but be sure to reserve a table. Set lunch (noon–4pm; $10) and live Indian music nightly. Visa, MC. Daily 11am–midnight. Inexpensive–moderate.

Guriya, Komsomolskiy pr. 7/3 ☎246 03 78; near Park Kultury metro. On the ground floor of a block of flats set back

Eating and drinking

Eating and drinking

from the road, the older sister restaurant to *Mama Zoya* (see p.346) serves fine Georgian food, with a dash of sleaze. Popular with expats and backpackers, so you may have to queue. No CCs. Daily 7am–11pm, noon–2.30pm & 5.30–10.30pm. Inexpensive.

Little India, ul. Krizhizhanovskovo 18/3 ☎125 81 49; 5min from Profsoyuznaya metro. Another great Indian restaurant on the Kaluzhsko-Rizhskaya metro line – try the chicken with tomato and plums with lemon rice. There's even a shop selling Indian sweets. No CCs. Daily noon–11pm. Inexpensive.

Mao, ul. 1905 goda 2a ☎255 59 55; 10min from Ulitsa 1905 Goda metro. *Mao* boasts of serving the best of Chinese, Japanese, Thai, Indonesian and Filipino cuisine, but fails to deliver. Business lunches (noon–5pm; $5.50) and secure parking. Amex, Visa, DC, MC. Daily noon till the last person leaves. Inexpensive–moderate.

San Carlo, pl. Pobedy 2/1; 5min from Kutuzovskaya metro. Classy Italian restaurant near the Triumphal Arch. Try the salmon carpaccio or shrimp with avocado, followed by the spaghetti vongole. Visa. Daily noon–1pm. Moderate.

Shinok, ul. 1905 goda 2 ☎255 59 63; 10min from Ulitsa 1905 Goda metro. Faux-Ukrainian tavern with a captive cow and milkmaid for diners to gawp at. The menu lists two kinds of *borshch*, four varieties of *vareniki* (dumplings) and five types of *salo* (lard) as starters, with suckling pig, chicken or rabbit to follow, accompanied by *gorilka* (Ukranian vodka) and folk music after 7pm. Amex, Visa, MC. Daily noon–midnight. Moderate.

Talk of the Town, *Park Place Hotel*, Leninskiy pr. 113 ☎956 59 99; bus #144, #261, #699 or #720 from Yugo-Zapadnaya metro. Though the hotel looks rather intimidating, this Chinese-Indian restaurant is fine once you're inside. Free secure parking. Amex, Visa, MC, DC. Daily 12.30am–11.30pm. Moderate.

Uley, ul. Gadeshka 7 ☎797 30 90; 10min from Mayakovskaya metro. Superb fusion cuisine: try the monkfish with absinthe pork, the smoked duck or the red pepper bisque, followed by a slice of super-rich chocolate cake. They also sell absinthe and even distil grappa at your table. Mon–Thurs 5pm–2am, Fri–Sun 5pm–5am. No CCs. Moderate-expensive.

U Pirosmani (At Pirosmani's), Novodevichiy proezd 4 ☎247 19 26; 15min from Sportivnaya metro. Moscow's best-known Georgian restaurant (Bill Clinton ate here in 1995), named after the country's national painter. There's violin music at night, and a superb view of the floodlit Novodevichiy Convent, though the food is less to rave about. Daily 2–11pm. Moderate.

Zamoskvareche and the south

The listings in this section are marked on the map on pp.230–231.

Bangkok, Bolshoy Strochenovskiy per. 10; 5min from Serpukhovskaya metro. Another Thai restaurant that's almost as good as the *Emerald Buddha* or *Baan Thai*, with relaxing couches and layout and great entrées, though their soups and salads could be improved. No CCs. Daily 2–11pm (Fri & Sat till 1am). Moderate.

Cabana, Raushskaya nab. 4 ☎239 30 45; 15min from Novokuznetskaya metro. Conveniently close if you're staying at the *Hotel Baltschug*, the eclectic menu includes plentiful salads, black bean soup, chicken dishes and lunchtime special deals. No CCs. Daily 6pm–6am. Moderate.

Dorian Gray, Kadashevskaya nab. 6/1 ☎237 63 42; 10min from Tretyakovskaya or Polyanka metro. Wonderful Italian restaurant beloved of Russian film moguls. Try the shrimp salad with rucola, the veal fillet with mushroom sauce or the sautéed seafood, followed by a divine tiramisu. Free secure parking. Amex, Visa, DC, EC, MC, JCB. Daily noon–midnight. Expensive.

El Gaucho, ul. Zatsepskiy val 6/13 ☎953 28 76; Paveletskaya metro. Another branch of the top-quality Argentine grill restaurant that's strictly for meat-lovers. No CCs. Daily noon–midnight. Moderate.

Louisiana, Pyatnitskaya ul. 30, str. 4 ☎951 42 44. American steak house with southern flavour. If you're not up for the gigantic Finnish T-bone steaks ($23–40), go for the chicken and seafood jambalaya ($12). There's also a children's menu, Californian wines, cheap drinks for women (7–8pm), and family discounts on Sun. Amex, Visa, DC, EC, JCB, Maestro. Daily 11am–11pm. Moderate.

Suliko, ul. Bolshaya Polyanka 42/2 ☎238 25 86; Polyanka metro. Relaxed and agreeable Georgian restaurant offering the same buffet ($30), business lunch ($10) and *a la carte* dishes as their bistro in the mall on Manezhnaya ploshchad. VIP rooms available. All major CCs. Daily noon–6am. Cheap–inexpensive.

U Babushki, ul. Bolshaya Ordynka 42, in the basement ☎230 27 97; 10min from Tretyakovskaya or Polyanka metro. Friendly ambience and fine Russian food. Tastefully decorated with theatrical memorabilia – the owner is a former actress. Daily noon–11pm. Visa, MC. Moderate.

Taganka and Zayauze

The listings in this section are marked on the map on pp.272–273.

Budvar, Kotelnicheskaya nab. 33 ☎915 15 98; 10min from Tanganskaya metro. Huge portions of rich Central European food washed down with draught Czech beer or Russian *kvas*. Try the crackled duck, smoked venison or crawfish. Visa, MC, EC. Daily noon–midnight. Moderate.

Ribniy Glaz (Fish Eye), ul. Novoryazanskaya 29, str. 3 ☎261 11 48; 5min walk from Baumanskaya metro. Worth the effort to find it at the back of a courtyard if you fancy fish 'n' chips, salmon mousse, sturgeon or *pelmeni*. The business lunch with beer is only $3, and there's a wide range of drinks. No CCs. Daily noon–11pm. Cheap.

Truffaldino, Marksistskaya ul. 20/1 ☎270 52 02; 5min from Marksistskaya metro. One of two inexpensive Italian places in this neck of the woods – the prosciutto with melon, pizzas and coffee are all top-rate, though the *Verona* (see below) offers a wider choice of pasta dishes. No CCs. Daily 11am–11pm. Cheap–inexpensive.

Verona, Vorontsovskaya ul. 32/36 ☎912 06 32; 10min from Proletarskaya metro. The original model for *Truffaldino*, just a couple of blocks away, with the same fabulous prosciutto and a wonderful *penne arrabbiata* for only $3. No CCs. Daily 11am–11pm. Cheap–inexpensive.

Northern Suburbs

The listings in this section are marked on the map on pp.296–297.

Azteca, Novoslobodskaya ul. 11, str. 1 ☎972 05 11; opposite Novoslobodskaya metro. An offshoot of *Azteca* on Tverskaya that's more fun than the original, with Cuban students dancing to mariachi music and tables outside during summer. Try the crab tostadas or chicken mole enchilada. Visa, MC. Daily noon–5am. Moderate.

Columbus Club, ul. Alabyana 10/1 ☎943 60 29; 15min from Sokol metro. Relaxed Spanish place with tapas, tangy Creole soup and tequila-marinated steak; only the quesadillas suck. Cheap house wine by the glass. No CCs. Daily 24hr. Inexpensive.

Maxima Pizza, Leningradskiy pr. 78 ☎152 08 37; 5min from Sokol metro. Decent, unpretentious pizza house with an all-you-can-eat salad bar and inexpensive drinks – though you'd best avoid the lasagne. No CCs. Daily noon–11pm. Inexpensive.

Mimino, Novoslobodskaya ul. 46 ☎972 44 12; 10min from Mendeleevskaya/Novoslobodskaya metro. Over 250 Georgian dishes, including roast beef with apples, chicken fillet with apples, nuts and honey, pork with

Eating and drinking

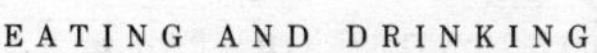

Eating and drinking

mushrooms and champagne sauce, and the house speciality *aureli* (marinated beef with mushrooms and spices). Daily noon–midnight. Inexpensive.

Navruz, Begovaya ul. 36 ☎945 04 51; 10min from Dinamo metro. The place to try authentic Uzbek cooking – though vegetarians needn't bother as the body count escalates from *plov* to *lagman*, *shashlyk*, and pony sausages. Funky decor with floor cushions and hookahs, plus floorshow from 9pm. Secure parking. Amex, Visa, MC, EC. Daily noon–midnight. Moderate.

Paparazzi, pr. Mira 21 (Zaitsev House of Fashion) ☎971 09 84; near Prospekt Mira metro. Set up by defectors from *Il Pomodoro* and serving superb pasta with pesto dishes, though the seafood isn't so hot. Live jazz or blues some evenings. Daily noon–midnight. No CCs. Inexpensive.

Tsarskiy Pavilion, Leningradskiy pr. 27 (Young Pioneers stadium complex) ☎212 22 73 or 213 78 66; 10min from Dinamo metro. Tsarist-style establishment noted for its Russian cuisine – particularly the soups and richly sauced entrées. Probably better by day, when you don't have to hear the crooning duo. No CCs. Daily noon–midnight. Inexpensive.

Yakitoriya, 1-ya Tverskaya-Yamskaya ul. 29, str. 1 ☎250 53 85; Belorusskaya metro. Another branch of the highly regarded sushi restaurant chain. All major CCs. Daily 11am–6am. Cheap–inexpensive.

Yar, *Hotel Sovetskaya*, Leningradskiy pr. 32/2 ☎960 20 04; 5min from Dinamo metro. A recreation of the famous pre-revolutionary restaurant where Rasputin once caused a scandal by exposing himself, the *Yar* is an ideal place to try aristocratic dishes like Tsar's sterlet, venison steak or stuffed quail. Buffet breakfast ($10) till noon. Gypsy programme 8.30–11pm. Amex, Visa, EC, MC, JCB. Daily 7.30am till the last guest leaves. Moderate–expensive.

Chapter 12

Nightlife

Nightlife

During the mid-1990s, Moscow's nightlife became synonymous with every kind of excess, from over-the-top decor to wall-to-wall hookers; prices that made foreigners reel, and cloakrooms where patrons checked in their Uzis. While the crash of '98 saw many places bite the dust or slash their prices, such manifestations are still common enough to raise no eyebrows – even though the trend nowadays is towards more relaxed, low-key places.

Though Moscow's clubs change constantly, they invariably pander to the tastes of particular groups of people, from pop- and porn-loving Mafiosi to cool bohemian types; punks to rockabillies. The atmosphere can be anything from intellectual to brash and decadent, with theme nights, spectacular lighting and raunchy floorshows. There are also more mainstream discos – mostly the province of teenagers – several blues clubs and a discreet but thriving gay scene.

Besides the many clubs that double as live music venues, one-off live concerts and/or parties are held in cinemas, palaces of culture, etc; you'll see flyers advertising them all over town.

Clubs

The term *klub* can cover anything from an arthouse café featuring the odd spot of music to a full-blown nightclub with restaurant and casino attached. Due to licensing laws, some clubs function only at weekends, or close early – though the majority stay open until dawn. For ritzy places aimed at the new rich, exclusivity is crucial, so foreigners who don't look rich are treated with the same disdain as ordinary Russians. Being sized up by a uniformed thug acting as the arbiter of style and wealth can be a demeaning experience: women are expected to **dress** like hookers, and a jacket and tie are de rigueur for men. Elsewhere, however, smart casual dress should fit the bill – except at punk clubs, where the grungier you look the better.

The other factor to consider is **safety**, as many places are frequented by mobsters ("flatheads", in expat parlance) and can be dangerous if you don't know the score. We've warned of some trouble spots, but there's no guarantee that once-safe places won't turn risky. If you're going to visit such clubs, only take as much money as you want to spend, and be extremely wary of trouble (without appearing to be too nervous, of course). Some will also be deterred by the floorshows: **striptease** (or raunchier) acts are often the main entertainment besides the disco. Men should also be aware that many clubs are full of **prostitutes**, for whom dancing with guys is just a prelude to business (see p.66).

To find out the latest on up-and-coming events, check the listings sections in the *Moscow Times* (Sat edition) and *Russia Journal*, and the club reviews in the *Russia Journal* and the *eXile*, which grade them by such user-friendly criteria

Nightlife

as the price of drinks and the likelihood of you going home with somebody. Note that although admission prices are given in dollars below, you pay in rubles. Unless stated otherwise, credit cards are not accepted.

A-Club, Delegatskaya ul. 1 ☎972 11 32; near Mayakovskaya metro. More mainstream than arty nowadays, with "democratic" face control, the *A-Club* has house music on the dance floor and rock, pop or punk bands most nights; pool tables and a chill-out room with monitors. Visa, DC, MC. Daily noon until the last customer leaves; $2–5.

Art Garbage, Starosadskiy per. 5 ☎928 87 45; 10min from Kitay-Gorod metro. More of a restaurant-hangout than a club, its dance hall comes to life on Friday nights, or whenever bands play, but otherwise there's just a crowd chilling out in the sitting rooms or dining on the patio. Daily 6pm–6am; $3 on concert nights

Bells, ul. Bolshaya Polyanka 51a ☎951 49 00; 5min from Dobryninskaya metro. A singles' bar and techno club full of flatheads, slappers and hookers at the weekends. Misunderstandings and/or fights virtually guaranteed. Daily noon–6am; $3 (free for Americans with passports).

Bunker, Tverskaya ul. 12 ☎200 15 06; near Tverskaya/Pushkinskaya metro. Popular, friendly live music bar with nightly concerts; DJs play techno and pop at other times, and there's also a (crap) karaoke bar. The drinks are cheap and the food delicious. Tues–Sun 24hr; $2–7 after 9pm.

Cabana, Raushskaya nab. 4 ☎238 50 06; 15min from Novokuznetskaya metro. Famed for its black male stripper, Dillon, who once outraged some Duma deputies with his "livened up" dance to the Soviet anthem. He performs on Tues & Fri, when women are plied with free champagne and vodka to fuel a near-orgy. Pricey cocktails, offset by a prolonged happy hour (daily 6–10pm). If you don't like the scene, *Vermel* (see below) is just nearby. Daily 6pm–6am; $5–9.

Diamond, Stromynskiy per. 5 ☎269 96 15; 15min from Sokolniki metro. No-frills venue for new rock, punk and grunge bands, that occasionally features celebs like Va-Bank. The crowd is entirely Russian – punks, *metalisti*, rockabillies and bikers – but far less threatening than at the *R-Club* (see below). Cheap drinks and hot snacks. Tues–Sun 6pm–1am; $2–3.

Dirty Dancing, ul. Gruzinskiy val 31 (upstairs in the *Great Canadian Bagel Co.*) ☎250 04 79; near Belorusskaya metro. What its name suggests – a wannabe Latin club where going home with somebody is the main idea. Drinks are so cheap that anyone can afford to join the party – and does. Daily 10pm–6am; $3.

D/K Gorbunova, ul. Novozavodskaya 27 ☎145 88 43; 15min from Bagrationovskaya metro. Moscow's main "alternative" venue for rock and punk bands, in an ex-Soviet House of Culture that's also the site of the Gorbunov market (see p.212). Nick Cave and the Smashing Pumpkins played here. Gigs as advertised – don't bother coming if they're not. $5–10.

Doug and Marty's Boar House, ul. Zemlyanoy val 26 ☎917 01 50; near Kurskaya metro. The old-time expats' bar *Chesterfield's* has now become a certified pick-up spot with hot Latin nights (Tues), swinging weekends and working girls; regular live music and sports, including British soccer and rugby and NFL matches. Mon–Fri noon–6am, Sat & Sun noon–9am; $2.50.

Hippopotamus, ul. Mantulinskaya 5/1, str. 6 (behind the *Sante Fe* restaurant) ☎256 23 46, 256 23 27; 15min from Ulitsa 1905 Goda metro. Cavernous meat-market with lick-this-stranger's-stomach contests and lots of stripping-off. Wed, male strippers; Thurs, Latin American night; Fri, funky concerts; Sat, female strippers; Sun, soul & hip-hop. Cheap drinks and snacks. Free guarded parking. Amex, Visa, DC, EC, MC, Maestro, JCB. Wed–Sun 10pm–6am; men $3, women $1.50.

Kitayskiy Lyotchik Dzhao Da, Lubyanskiy proezd 25, str. 1 ☎924 56 11; near Kitay-Gorod metro. Set up by Irina Papernaya, the doyenne of the Boho club scene, this basement club/restaurant themed around the mythical Chinese pilot Dzhao Se is packed at night, when you can expect in-house band TAM or the likes of Markschneider Kunst or Prepinaki to play – plus a disco or concerts of Tuvan throat-singing. Cheap drinks; tasty Russian food. Daily 24hr; $2–3 on gig nights.

Krai, Spartakovskaya ul. 14 ☎267 03 90; 5min from Baumanskaya metro. Another artsy basement club with live performances and diverse theme nights (seldom raunchy) that either pack audiences in or drive them away. Entered via an anonymous door in the yard. Mon–Thurs & Sun 6.30pm 12.30am, Sat & Sun 9pm–5am; $2.

Krisis Zhanra, Prechistenskiy per. 22/4 ☎241 19 28; 10min from Kropotkinskaya metro. An earlier venture by Papernaya and her husband, it's now less trendy than *Kitayskiy Lyotchik* but remains popular with students, not least for its tasty cheap *solyanka* and *khatchapuri*. Concerts start at 8.30pm on weekdays, 9pm on Fri & Sat. Good for meeting people, but hardly a rave spot. Daily 11am–11pm; $1–3 on gig nights.

Letuchaya Mysh, Povarskaya ul. 33 ☎290 44 89; 5min from Barrikadnaya metro. Hip-hop rules at "The Bat", currently the club of choice for Africans living in Moscow and the city's growing subculture of young Russian Wiggers. Cheap drinks; fights quite common. Thurs–Sun 11pm–6am; $2.50.

Luch, 5-y Monetchikovskiy per. 5/3 ☎231 94 63; 5min from Paveletskaya metro. Moscow's coolest rave club, in a bomb shelter beside a church, features Fonar, Solar X and other top DJs, and occasional shamanistic dancing from Tuva. Low on flatheads due to its strict face control. Visa, DC, MC. Daily 10pm–4am (no entry after 12.30am); $7–14.

Manhattan Express, on the Red Square side of the *Rossiya Hotel* ☎298 53 5; 5min from Kitay-Gorod metro. Years past its sell-by date with the discerning, but it still attracts minor Mafiosi and the occasional genuine Russian pop celeb. Male and female strippers on Thurs. Discount of 10–30 percent on restaurant prices until 9pm. Daily 6pm–4am (restaurant); 10pm–6am (club); $7–9 (foreigners with ID free on Thurs, otherwise half-price).

Mesto Vstrechi, Maliy Gnezdnikovskiy per. 9/8, str. 7 ☎229 23 73; Tverskaya/.Pushkinskaya metro. The "Meeting Place" is a roomy cellar-club featuring British DJs (Sat), jazz (Thurs), regular theme nights and special events (by invitation only). Moderately priced drinks, including cider (a rarity in Moscow). Amex, Visa, MC. Daily noon–5am; $2.

Metelitsa, ul. Noviy Arbat 21 ☎291 11 70; 10min from Arbatskaya metro. The club that epitomizes Moscow's nouveaux-riches nightlife, where the swankiest casino and classiest whores in town relieve the biggest big-shots and flattest flatheads of their surplus cash. Worth trying once, if you've got the money. Live entertainment; Western-style kitchen. Formal dress. Visa, DC, MC. Daily 9pm–5am; $25.

Moosehead, ul. Bolshaya Polyanka 54 ☎230 73 33; 5min from Dobryninskaya metro. More of a pub than a club, with a range of cheap food deals (Mon–Thurs nights), $1 drinks for women (Tues), and live music from Thurs–Sun (10pm–2am). There's singles' action for those who want it, but it's not in your face. Popular with expats. All major CC. Daily noon–5am; free.

Na Bei Kopytom, ul. Ramenky 5 ☎932 01 01; *www.nbk.orc.ru* (in Russian); get a taxi from Universitet or Prospekt Vernadskovo metro. An out-of-the-way location for a popular studenty club with live indie music. Come early rather than late. Cheap drinks. Trouble-free. Fri & Sat 7pm–6am; $7–8.

Night Flight, Tverskaya ul. 17 ☎229 41 65; *www.nightflight.ru*; 5min from Tverskaya metro. Split-level bar with a tiny dance floor full of deluxe hookers

Nightlife

Nightlife

and foreign businessmen, and an expensive restaurant upstairs. Don't bother to come unless for paying sex ($200). Disco from 11pm. Visa, Amex, DC, EC, MC. Daily restaurant noon–4am; club 9pm–5am; $20.

Oranzhevyi Galstuk, Kamergerskiy per. 5 ☎299 19 52; 5min from Okhotniy Ryad metro. A retro Sixties club near the Moscow Art Theatre, the "Orange Tie" features seats styled like cars, and photos of Monroe, Elvis and Gagarin (in case anyone forgets it's in Russia). Sometimes hosts Elvis nights or other themed events. $2–3.

Papa John's, Myasnitskaya ul. 22 (below *Johnny-Tolstyak*) ☎755 95 54; 5min from Chistye Prudy/Turgenevskaya metro. Alcoholism and lechery rule at this successor to the infamous *Hungry Duck* (see *Utka*, below). Wet T-shirt contests, audience strips, cockfights, turtle races and brawls to amuse drunken US Marines. Cuban bartenders in nappies serve a wide range of pricey drinks (happy hour 6–8pm). Daily 6pm–5am; $5 at weekends.

Parizhskaya Zhizn, ul. Karetniy ryad 3 (in the Hermitage Gardens) ☎209 45 24; 10min from Tsvetnoy Bulvar metro. Though bands playing upstairs are the main attraction, many come to "Parisian Life" just to chill out in the cosy café with pool tables, before moving on to somewhere else. Visa, EC, MC. Daily 11am–7am; $3 on Sat & Sun.

Planet Hollywood, ul. Krasnaya Presnya 23b ☎255 05 39; 5min from Ulitsa 1905 Goda metro. A fairly respectable family place by day, *Planet Hollywood* shows its true colours at night, when lap-dancers and bargirls emerge. Its basement *Millennium Club* has cheaper drinks (happy hour till 2am) and hipper music, but only cooks with "Muddy's Freestyle Parties" (Sat). Both 10pm till the last customer leaves; free entry to *Planet Hollywood*; *Millennium Club* men $4, women $2.

Project O.G.I., Potapovskiy per. 8/12, str. 2 (via the courtyard) ☎927 56 09, *proekt-ogi@mail.ru*; 10min from Chistye Prudy metro. An evolving culture club offering good food at bargain prices, an all-night bookshop (upstairs) and energetic dancing to recorded music after midnight. They also host live concerts, poetry readings, and kids' events (Sun). Daily 9am–6am; free.

Propaganda, Bolshoy Zlatoustinskiy per. 7 ☎924 57 32; near Kitay-Gorod or Lubyanka metro. Relaxed bar-club with a mix of cool students, models and expats, grooving to garage, house and jungle music, spun by Zad and Sanches, or visiting Brit DJs on Thurs – the busiest night. Mon–Fri noon–6am, Sat & Sun 3pm–6am; $2.50–5.

R-Club, 4-y Roshchinskiy proezd 19/21 ☎928 04 78; 10min from Tulskaya metro. A seriously hardcore punk club with wire mesh around the stage to deflect missiles. Don't come unless you can handle trouble. Dirt-cheap booze. Daily 6pm–3am; $2.

Respublica Beefeater, Nikolskaya ul. 17 ☎928 46 92; near Kitay-Gorod metro. Weirdly named maze-like basement club whose central location and funky ambience draws a lively crowd of regulars. Plays all kinds of music on the dance floor and often stages fashion shows and entertainments. MC. Daily 11am–6am; free.

Sixteen Tons, ul. Presnenskiy val 6 ☎253 53 00; near Ulitsa 1905 Goda metro. An English-style pub with a microbrewery, and a disco that often features live bands upstairs. Lots of singles action, but it's not obligatory. Avoid the so-called "mozzarella" snacks. All major CC. Daily 11am–6am; Thurs–Sat $3–6.

Sports Bar, ul. Noviy Arbat 10 ☎290 43 11; 5min from Arbatskaya metro. Despite its name and televised Eurosports, evenings are really about dancing and lechery, with nightly female strippers and guys for the gals at weekends, plus regular concerts or themed events. Daily noon–6am; Mon & Tues free; Wed–Sun men $7, women $5 on strip or concert nights.

Studio, Tverskaya ul. 10 (entrance on Glinishchevskiy per.) ☎292 50 80; near

Nightlife

Tverskaya metro. Originally a gay club but now quite mainstream, it features a restaurant and chill-out room on the second floor, and a dance floor, karaoke and striptease bar on the floor above, plus a private sauna and VIP rooms for intimate encounters. Packed out at weekends, when the security is extremely heavy. Visa, MC. Daily 24hr; $3 (Fri & Sat $6).

Svalka, ul. Profsoyuznaya 27/1 ☎128 78 23; Profsoyuznaya metro. Designer-grunge dance club for middle-class Russians pretending to be bikers, featuring techno and, sometimes, live music. Its name means "Rubbish Dump". Daily 6pm–6am; $1–2 (includes one free beer Sun–Tues, and a glass of *shampanskoe* for women on Thurs).

Tabula Rasa, Berezhkovskaya nab. 28 ☎240 92 89; four stops by trolleybus #17 or #34 from Kievskaya metro. A venue for cool bands like Dva Samoloty, that otherwise spins Eurotrash and Russian pop for an expat-heavy crowd. Daily 7pm–6am; Mon–Wed $7, Thurs & Sun $12, Fri & Sat $15; students $3 except at weekends.

Taxman, ul. Krymskiy val 6 (on the same side as the New Tretyakov Gallery) ☎238 08 64; 5–10min from Oktyabrskaya or Park Kultury metro. Crowded meat-market with strippers and arm-wrestling contests, which sometimes hosts bands. Depending on how things pan out, you risk being punched or catching something nasty. Daily noon–6am; $2–3 on gig nights.

Titanik, Leningradskiy pr. 31, inside the Young Pioneers Stadium ☎213 60 95; 5min from Dinamo metro. Archetypal New Russian club with awesome decor and deafening techno. Seething with Mafiosi; it's a quiet night when nobody gets shot. Thurs–Sun 10pm–6am; $30.

Tochka, Zvenigorodskoe shosse 4 ☎495 89 21; near Ulitsa 1905 Goda metro. Sited in a deserted factory, "Dot" is a large room with two bars, pool tables, a restaurant, a decent-sized dance floor and a stage for live music at weekends, also sometimes used by Celtic/Sword 'n' Sorcery troupes for sword battles. Face control. Visa, DC, MC. Daily noon–6am; free.

Trety Put, ul. Pyatnitskaya 4 ☎951 87 34; 5min from Novokuznetskaya metro. Far from being a nightclub for aspiring Blairites, "Third Way" is a cosy bohemian dive in a former *kommunalka*, featuring chess tables, cheap beer, penurious regulars and occasional gigs. Fri & Sat 10pm–5am; $2.

Utka (aka Duck), ul. Pushechnaya 9; beside the tunnel from Kuznetskiy Most metro. Formerly the *Hungry Duck*, and famed for offering women free entry and drinks, inflaming them with strippers, and then admitting hordes of guys bent on sex. Rather tamer nowadays, with no free drinks, but still the kind of place where groping somebody counts as an introduction, especially on ladies' nights (Tues & Sun). Daily 7pm–6am; women free or $2; men $4-6.

Vermel, Raushkaya nab. 4/5 ☎959 33 03; 15min from Novokuznetskaya metro. From the same stable as *Krisis Zhanra* and *Kitayskiy Lyotchik Dzao Da*, with a young, fashionable Russian crowd dancing to diverse sounds – even *Zorba the Greek* – and live music till midnight on Sat. Affordable drinks. Beware of the low doorways. Daily noon–5am; $2.

Voodoo Lounge, Sredniy Tishinskiy per. 5/7 ☎253 23 23; 10min from Belorusskaya metro. One of Moscow's better pick-up spots, with a popular summer patio, Latin music and a quiet Mexican restaurant where you can get to know each other, thanks to the slow service and inaccessible bar. Try the Macchiato cocktail with mint leaves, rum and sugar. Daily 6pm–6am; men $5, women $2.

Gay and lesbian nightlife

Though some of the clubs listed above are popular with gays and lesbians, overt displays of affection can be safely indulged in only at specifically gay and lesbian clubs. For information on gay and lesbian life in Russia, including

Nightlife

saunas and bathhouses in Moscow (not covered below), visit the Web site *www.gay.ru*.

Chameleon, ul. Presnenskiy val 14 ☎253 63 43; Ulitsa 1905 Goda metro. An alternative to the long-established *Chance* that risks succumbing to flat-heads unless it tightens up on the face control, especially on students nights (Wed & Sun). Two dance floors playing Russian pop or house, and a "Maze of Lust". Daily 6pm–6am; men $1.50, women $2.50.

Chance, D/K Serp i Molot, ul. Volochaevskaya 11/15 ☎267 45 04 or 956 71 02, *www.gay.ru/chance* (in Russian only); near Ploshchad Ilicha metro. Moscow's best-known gay club, with naked mer-youths swimming in a tank, soft porn and striptease acts on stage. Often busted by the OMON, who sometimes plant drugs on clubbers. Daily 11.15pm–6am; men $2, women $3.50.

Imperia Kino, Povarskaya ul. 33 ☎290 44 89; 5min from Barrikadnaya metro. On good nights you find a relaxed mix of young dykes, TVs and straights, dancing to anything from ambient techno to tacky Russian pop. On bad nights it's a graveyard. Cheap drinks. Thurs–Sun 11pm–6am; $2–3.

Kazarma, ul. Presnenskiy val 14 ☎253 63 43; Ulitsa 1905 Goda metro. Located within the larger *Chameleon* club, the "Barracks" features non-stop male strippers and erotic videos, dark corners with sofas, and walls with spy holes and apertures for gratification. Women only on Tuesdays. Daily 10pm–8am; $3.

Nochnaya Sava, Golovinskoe shosse 8 ☎452 71 75; 5min from Vodniy Stadion metro. Far from the centre so only used by locals, the "Night Owl" features two dance floors, a sauna and rooms that can be rented for the night. Tues–Sun 8pm–7am; $2–4.

Three Monkeys, Sadovicheskaya ul. 71, str. 2 ☎953 09 09, *www.gau.ru /3monkeys* (in Russian only); 15min from Paveletskaya metro. Located on the island between Zamoskvareche and Taganka, this small, fun club is the only place in Moscow with dyke nights (Sat), though you need to beware of hustlers other nights of the week. Daily 6pm–9am; free.

Tsentralnaya Stantsiya, Bolshaya Tatarskaya ul. 16/2, str. 2 ☎959 46 43; 5min from Novokuznetskaya metro. Another, more upmarket alternative to *Chance*, "Central Station" features a restaurant and summer patio, two dance floors, and drag and striptease shows from 2am. Daily 7pm–7am; men $5, women $10.

Jazz and blues

The serious **jazz and blues** scene revolves around four venues, although other places will also play them some nights (see "Clubs"). The **International Jazz Festival** (spring or autumn) is the main event in the calendar and takes place at the Tchaikovsky Concert Hall and the Union of Composers hall (contact Vladimir Kaushansky ☎941 22 86, *mcla@cea.ru*); the others are **Jazz at the Hermitage Garden** in late August (Mikhail Green ☎236 33 63, *mgreen@home.relline.ru*); **Jazz Voices** at the Jazz Art Club (see below) in December; and the **Boheme festival**, sponsored by Russia's only jazz label (Olga Golovina ☎973 71 01, *O_Golovina@boheme.ru*).

B.B. King, ul. Sadovaya Samotyochnaya 4/2 ☎299 82 06; 10min from Tsvetnoy Bulvar metro. Cookin' blues/jazz hang-out known for its after-gig jam sessions by Michael Nyman, Marc Almond, Sting, and B.B. King himself. Tasty Cajun food, a big choice of beers (happy hour Mon–Fri 4–7pm) and live music from 9.30pm: Thurs, jazz; Fri, club parties; Sat, blues and rock. Mon–Thurs & Sun noon–2am, Fri & Sat noon until the last person leaves; $3 for gigs, otherwise free.

Jazz Art Club, Vernisazh Theatre, Begovaya ul. 5 ☎191 83 20; near Begovaya metro. Friendly one-night venue for jam sessions and art exhibitions, that closes in June and hosts the Jazz Voices festival in December. Live music till 11pm. Cheap drinks and snacks. Fri 7.30–1am; $3, students half price.

M-Bar, ul. Petrovka 28 ☎200 27 66; 10min from Chekhovskaya metro. A cosy bar in the grounds of the Upper Monastery of St Peter, with tables outside, a sub-level with a piranha-filled aquarium and a stage featuring new talent on the Moscow, Petersburg, Kiev and Saratov jazz scenes. Concerts start at 8pm (Sun 8.30pm). All major CC. Daily noon–11pm.

Sinaya Pititsa, Malaya Dmitrovka ul. 23/15 ☎209 30 27; 10min from Mayakovskaya or Chekhovskaya metro. Jazz restaurant (from $25 per head) with live music 7.30–11.30pm: Sun, Mon & Wed jazz trio; Tues & Sat music of the 1920s and '30s, and jazz improvisations; Fri, Sergei Manukyan's jazz ensemble. Also karaoke, pool tables, bar and videos, lest anyone get bored. Amex, Visa, EC, MC, Unioncard. Daily 24hr; free.

Bard music

Russian **Bard music** is associated with the *shestdesyatniki* or "Sixties people" who came of age under Khrushchev and Brezhnev, when Bulat Okhudzhava, Alexander Gallich and the gravel-voiced Vladimir Vysotsky (see p.274) moved millions with their bitter-sweet, satirical or savage ballads, skirting or straying well over the edges of what was officially permissible. Thirty years on, Vysotsky remains almost as popular as ever and new generations of Bards have attracted a devoted following, even if it's not on the scale of their predecessors' appeal. If you're interested in hearing how the genre has developed, visit the Web site *http://Bard-Cafe.komkon.org/*, or reserve a table at the *Gnezdo Glukharya*.

Gnezdo Glukhanya, Bolshaya Nikitskaya ul. 22 ☎291 93 88; *www.mtu.net/gnezdo_gluharya*; 10–15min from Arbatskaya, Pushkinskaya or Okhotniy Ryad metro. The "Widgeon's Nest" is packed on concert nights, when two or three Bards play from 7pm (table reservations essential), but otherwise empty except on weekdays, when its $2 lunch is irresistible. The Russian food is only average, but at that price you can't complain. Daily noon–11pm; $3 for concerts.

Occasional live music venues

The following places occasionally host rock or pop concerts by Russian or foreign bands, as advertised in the *Moscow Times*, the *eXile* and the *Russia Journal*, and by posters around the city.

Luzhniki Stadium, Luzhnetskaya nab. 24 ☎201 18 06; 10min walk from Sportivnaya metro, or trolleybus #28 from Park Kultury metro. Moscow's largest stadium is used for concerts by such foreign acts as Michael Jackson, Whitesnake and Motorhead. Tickets from any theatre booking office (see "The Arts").

Rossiya Concert Hall, Moskvaretskaya nab. 1 ☎298 11 24; 10min from Kitay-Gorod metro, on the embankment side of the *Rossiya Hotel*. No regular programme, but often used for gala concerts by the likes of Alla Pugachova and other Russian stars, with rare visitations by the likes of Prodigy, Elton John and Cliff Richard. Tickets as above, or on the spot.

State Kremlin Palace, in the Kremlin ☎299 76 92; near Biblioteka Imeni Lenina and Aleksandrovskiy Sad metros. Though usually a venue for ballet, the hall that once hosted Party congresses has also been used for concerts by David Bowie, Sting, Tina Turner and Diana Ross. The booking office is beside one of the exits from Aleksandrovskiy Sad metro.

Chapter 13

The Arts

The Arts

Alongside the city's restaurants and clubs, there's a rich cultural life in Moscow. **Classical music**, **opera** and **ballet** are strongly represented with a busy schedule of concerts and performances throughout the year, sometimes held in the city's palaces, churches or – in summer – parks and gardens. Rock, pop and jazz gigs have been covered in the "Nightlife" section. Russian **theatre** has done better than **film** in coming to terms with the loss of state subsidies, if only because it doesn't face competition from Hollywood. Even if you don't speak Russian, **puppetry** and the **circus** transcend language barriers, while several **cinemas** show films in their original language. At any one time, there are dozens of exhibitions in Moscow's **galleries**.

Tickets and information

For most concert and theatrical performances, you can buy tickets from the venue box office (*kassa*), or one of the many licensed ticket kiosks (*Teatralno-Konsertnaya kassa*, Театрально-Концертная касса) on the streets and in the metro – or if not, possibly from another concertgoer, outside the venue. The chief exceptions to this rule are gala concerts and the Bolshoy Theatre, tickets for which are seldom available except from touts outside the venue, hotel service bureaux or booking agencies such as IPS in the Metropol Hotel (☎927 67 28; Mon–Fri 10am–6pm, Sat & Sun 10am–3pm).

The *Russia Journal* and the Friday edition of the *Moscow Times* carry extensive arts listings, while the monthly magazine *Where Moscow* highlights events for the weeks ahead. Alternatively, look out for posters around town, or ask about current events at a hotel service bureau. Finally, there's the Web, where a compendium of links to all kinds of Russian music sites (classical, opera, pop, rock, blues) can be found at *http://users.aimnet.com/ksyrah/ekskurs/music.htm/*.

Classical music, opera and ballet

Russians are justifiably proud of their classical music tradition, and the composers, conductors, musicians, opera singers, ballet dancers and choreographers who have made their name in Moscow are legion. Moscow audiences are among the world's most discerning; unsparing in their criticism, but ready to embrace artists with a passion. Only a few years ago, concertgoers complained that the removal of two urns spoiled a hall's acoustics; while fans' devotion was epitomized by the thousands who attended the funeral of the ballerina Ulanova, forty years after she left the stage where she had captivated the public during Stalin's time.

Classical concerts take place throughout the year, but especially during **festivals**. Over the Russian Winter or *Russkaya Zima* festival (Dec 20–Jan 13),

The Arts

the main venues are the Conservatory, the Tchaikovsky Concert Hall and the Pushkin Museum, which has its own prestigious "December Evenings". Events in the *Moskovskiy Zvyodiy* (Moscow Stars) festival in May (aka the "May Stars" or *Mayskiy Zvyodiy*) are held in the Tchaikovsky or Rossiya concert halls; and the last two venues are also used for the *Talanty Rossii* (Talents of Russia) festival in the first half of October. The Tchaikovsky Hall also hosts the one-night Tchaikovsky Festival, a concert to pick the winner of the Slava Gloria awards sponsored by Uneximbank, whose lavish prizes guarantee stellar performers and publicity. Other festivals are harder to predict and scarcely publicized ahead of time, so all you can do is scan the local English-language press when you're there. In particular, watch out for events organized by the Musica Viva Orchestra or the Ensemble XXI (*www.paqo.demon.co.uk/enshome.htm*).

The Bolshoy

Bolshoy Theatre (*Bolshoy teatr*), Teatralnaya pl. 1 ☎292 99 86; *www.bolshoi.ru*; near Teatralnaya metro. With the historic theatre undergoing major repairs, the company currently performs at the State Kremlin Palace (☎917 23 36; see below) or other venues (as advertised), and may well scale down its uniquely large repertoire (22 ballets and 3 operas with balletic scenes). As interpretation is crucial, it's worth noting who's dancing in what ballet. Nina Aniashevilli, Alexei Fadeechev, Ina Petrova and Nina Semizorova are great in almost anything; Nadya Gracheva and Galya Stepanenko shine in *La Bayadère*, while Masha Bylova is best in *Spartacus, The Stone Flower* and *Ivan the Terrible*. During summer the company is usually abroad, leaving the junior corps de ballet to entertain visitors. In season, there are performances at 7pm, and sometimes a noon matinee on Sunday.

The Bolshoy's official sales agent (☎299 53 25, *tickets@bolshoi.ru*) charges $3 to deliver tickets. Otherwise, try the theatre ticket booths in the underpass of Teatralnaya metro station (immediately as you exit the barriers); the booth in the underpass leading from the Dostoyevsky Library to the Alexander Gardens; or the Kremlin Palace bookings office near the Alexander Gardens – which all only sell legit tickets. It's best to eschew street touts, as many sell fake or out-of-date tickets. All tickets are marked "unfixed prices", which means that their face value is whatever you pay for it. Buying through an agency you're likely to pay $10–15 for a seat in the fourth- or fifth-tier balcony (bring binoculars); $15–40 for the second or first tier (*beletazh*) balcony; and $40–60 for a seat in the stalls (*parter*). As a rule, tickets for the opera are cheaper than tickets for the ballet.

Other ballet companies

Academic Theatre of Classical Ballet, Skakovaya ul. 3 ☎924 55 24; near Belorusskaya metro. Directed and choreographed by former Bolshoy stars Natalya Kasatkina and Vladimir Vasilev, it has 23 classical and modern ballets in repertory. During July and August it may perform at the concert hall in the *Kosmos Hotel*, pr. Mira 150 ☎215 65 91; near VDNKh metro.

Moscow Musical Theatre of Plastique Arts, Novaya Basmannaya ul. 25/2, str. 2 ☎261 76 03; 5min from Krasnye Vorota metro. Modern dance company directed by Aida Chernova, whose repertoire includes *Man and Woman, or Concerto for Viola with Orchestra* to music by Alfred Schnittke, and *Elan Vital* to the music of Jean Michel Jarre.

Russian Chamber Ballet "Moskva" Small experimental group founded in 1991, that fuses traditional ballet with modern dance in such classics as *Giselle* and *Les Sylphides*, and contemporary works like *Where From and Where To?* It performs at the Pushkin Theatre, Tverskoy bul. 23 (5min from Pushkinskaya/Tverskaya metro), and the Russian Academic Youth Theatre, Teatralnaya pl. 2 (near Teatralnaya/Okhotniy Ryad metro). For information and tickets ☎261 65 34, 207 70 97.

The Arts

Permanent venues

Helikon-Opera, Bolshaya Nikitskaya ul. 19 ☎290 09 71; 10min from Arbatskaya metro. Under Dmitry Bertman, the Helikon's bold and bawdy productions of *La Traviata*, *Yevgeny Onegin* and other operas have delighted and outraged spectators (some have an "adults only" restriction). As a full-sized orchestra plays in a venue meant for chamber music, it's best to sit near the back or you might get a violin bow up your nose. Tickets are dear by local standards ($11–17) but worth every last kopek to see Moscow's most stunning and controversial ensemble.

Kamerniy Musical Theatre, Leningradskiy pr. 71 ☎157 47 07; near Sokol metro; Nikolskaya ul. 17 ☎929 13 20; near Ploshchad Revolyutsii metro. The company's "old" and "new" stages feature chamber operas and philharmonic concerts. Its repertoire includes *Cosi fan Tutte*, *The Barber of Seville* and several Russian/Soviet classics rarely seen outside the country – notably a sparky rendition of Shostakovich's *The Nose* (based on Gogol's story of the same name).

Moscow Conservatory, Bolshaya Nikitskaya ul. 13 ☎299 74 12 or 229 94 36; 10min from Okhotniy Ryad, Aleksandrovskiy Sad/Biblioteka Imeni Lenina or Arbatskaya metros. Box office noon–3pm & 4–7pm. Varied programmes of top-quality concerts in the Great Hall (venue for the Tchaikovsky Competition, see p.136), the Small Hall, and the Rachmaninov Hall next door at no. 11 (where purists complained that the removal of two urns from the hall's niches spoilt its acoustics). The Small and Rachmaninov halls have a separate box office (4pm–7pm; closed Tues ☎229 77 95 or 229 36 81).

Moscow Operetta Theatre, Bolshaya Dmitrovka ul. 6 ☎292 63 77; near Teatralnaya metro. Performs Strauss's *Die Fledermaus*, Lehar's *The Merry Widow*, Offenbach's *Prima Donna* and Kalman's *The Queen of Csardas* in a slightly "over-milked" style, for a doting audience of fans. They also sometimes do short runs of musicals.

New Opera (*Novaya Opera*), Hermitage Gardens, ul. Karetniy Ryad 3 ☎200 18 30 or 200 08 68; 10min from Mayakovskaya or Tsvetnoy Bulvar metro. Popular company directed by Yevgeny Kolobov, that performs Mussorgsky's *Boris Godunov*, Tchaikovsky's *Yevgeny Onegin*, Rubinstein's *Demon* and a potpourri of Mozart, Salieri and Rimsky-Korsakov, entitled *Oh, Mozart! Mozart!* They also do some "performance art" productions mixing poetry and drama.

Rossiya Concert Hall, Moskvaretskaya nab. 1 ☎298 11 24; 10min from Kitay-Gorod metro, on the embankment side of the *Rossiya Hotel*. No regular programme, but often used for gala concerts (rock and pop as well as classical music).

Russian Academy of Music, ul. Paliashvilli 1 ☎290 67 37; 10min from Arbatskaya metro. The concert hall is behind the Academy building on Povarskaya ulitsa.

Stanislavsky & Nemirovich-Danchenko Musical Theatre, Bolshaya Dmitrovka ul. 17 ☎229 28 35 or 229 83 88; 5min from Chekhovskaya metro. Maestro Wolf Gerelik elicits fine performances across an enormous repertoire of ballet, opera and musicals, including Tchaikovsky's *Swan Lake* and *The Nutcracker*, Rimsky-Korsakov's *Tale of Tsar Sultan*, Rossini's *Barber of Seville* and Bizet's *Carmen*; their 1999 production of *La Bohème* rightly scooped awards. Tickets $1–8.

State Kremlin Palace (*Kremlevskiy Dvorets*), in the Kremlin ☎299 76 92; *www.kremlin-gkd.ru*; near Biblioteka Imeni Lenina and Aleksandrovskiy Sad metros; the booking office (☎917 23 36) is beside the latter. Currently used by the Bolshoy while its own theatre is

Summer concerts

Summer concerts are held in the Gorky, Izmaylovo and Sokolniki parks, as advertised. The nearest metros are Park Kultury, Izmaylovskiy Park and Sokolniki.

The Arts

being rebuilt, as well as by the Kremlin Ballet Company that traditionally performs here. Built for Party congresses (see p.94), the 6000-seat hall allows a fine view of the stage but suffers from poor acoustics.

Tchaikovsky Concert Hall (*Konsertniy Zal Chaykovskovo*), Triumfalnaya pl. 4/31 ☎299 39 57; near Mayakovskaya metro. The home of the Academic Orchestra of the Moscow Philharmonic also hosts concerts by the Moscow Symphony Orchestra, choral and instrumental ensembles, and is one of the main venues during Moscow's music festivals.

Other venues

The following is a selection of churches, museums and mansions that regularly hold concerts. Phone to enquire about concerts, and when you can buy tickets; these may also be available from kiosks. Tickets usually cost $2–3.

Arkhangelskoe, outside Moscow ☎560 22 31; minibus #T-151 or #T-549 from Tushinskaya metro. Concerts may be held in the "Colonnade" in the palace grounds (see p.398) during June, July and August.

Chaliapin House-Museum, Novinskiy bul. 25 ☎205 62 36; 5min from Barrikadnaya metro. Solo operatic renditions in the White Hall of the maestro's mansion (p.181).

Church of the Intercession in Fili, Novozavodskaya ul. 6 ☎148 45 52; 10min from Fili metro. Choral and chamber music in one of Moscow's finest Naryshkin Baroque monuments (see p.212).

Dostoyevsky Library, ul. Vodvizhenka 3, entrance #3 ☎488 88 92; near Biblioteka Imeni Lenina/Aleksandrovskiy Sad metro. An occasional venue for piano recitals.

English Court, ul. Varvarka 4a ☎298 39 61; 10min from Kitay-Gorod metro. Monthly concerts of medieval English and Russian music in the vaulted hall of this sixteenth-century embassy (see p.120).

Hall of Columns, in the House of Unions, Bolshaya Dmitrovka ul. 1 ☎292 48 64; near Teatralnaya metro. Splendid, historic hall (p.131) sometimes used for concerts or political meetings.

Museum of Musical Culture, ul. Fadeeva 4 ☎972 32 37 or 251 10 66; 10min from Mayakovskaya metro. Interesting programmes of classical, avant-garde and ethnic music. For details of the museum, see p.294.

Ostankino Palace, 1-ya Ostankinskaya ul. 5a ☎283 46 45 or 286 62 88; trolleybus #11 from VDNKh metro. Box office Wed–Sun 10am–5pm. Classical concerts three times a week over summer, in Count Sheremetev's private theatre (see p.303).

Pushkin Museum of Fine Arts, ul. Volkhonka 12 ☎203 95 78 or 203 79 98; near Kropotkinskaya metro. Hosts concerts during the "December Evenings". Mostly classics, but sometimes also modern composers. See p.143.

Stanislavsky House-Museum, Leontevskiy per. 6 ☎229 28 55 or 229 11 92; 10min from Arbatskaya metro. The Onegin Hall in Stanislavsky's former residence (see p.137) is used for piano recitals. Tickets sold one hour before the concerts begin (usually at 7pm).

Tsaritsyno, Dolskaya ul. 1 ☎325 46 63 or 325 31 32; 10–15min from Orekhovo or Tsaritsyno metros. Box office Wed–Sun 11am–4.30pm. The Opera House at Tsaritsyno palace (see p.269) makes a fine venue for chamber music ensembles.

Theatre

Traditionally, **theatre** (*teatr*) has had a special place in Russian culture as an outlet for veiled criticism under autocratic regimes. In Soviet times it was both nurtured and controlled, so that audiences came to expect top-class acting (due to extensive training based on Stanislavsky's "Method") in conservatively staged, often mediocre plays – the few theatres that dared stage bold dramas attracted queues stretching round the

The Arts

block. Nowadays there are no taboos, and most theatres have learned to woo audiences by offering popular favourites or carving a niche for themselves with controversial productions. If you understand some Russian, Moscow has as much to offer drama-lovers as London or New York does – at far lower prices.

Directors and companies to watch out for include Pyotr Fomenko (the Fomenko Workshop Theatre), Konstantin Raykin (the Satirikon Theatre), Vladimir Miroev (the Stanislavsky Drama Theatre), Genrietta Yanovskaya and Kama Glinkas (at the Theatre of Young Spectators) and Valery Fokin (as guest director) – nearly all of whom made their names in the Sixties or Seventies. New playwrights and directors are most often seen at the Debut Centre.

The main events in the theatrical calendar are the **Chekhov International Theatre Festival** (some time between April and June, every three years; next in 2001) – where troupes from around the world perform Chekhov's plays at venues all over town – and the annual **Golden Mask Festival** (late February–early March), honouring the best of the previous year's drama, dance, opera and puppetry in Russia, with dozens of shows over two weeks, culminating in a gala awards ceremony (for information ☎209 21 93, *maska@theatre.ru*).

Debut Centre, House of Actors, ul. Arbat 35 ☎248 91 06; near Arbatskaya/Smolenskaya metro. Moscow's main showcase for new talent has garnered mixed reviews since its foundation in 1996, but remains committed to taking chances. Located in the actors' residential block opposite the Vakhtangov Theatre, it's reached via Kaloshin pereulok. Tickets $1.50–6.

Fomenko Workshop Theatre, Kutuzovskiy pr. 30/32 ☎249 17 03, *formenko@theatre.ru*; *www.theatre.ru/formenko/*; near Kutuzovskaya metro. This troupe of young actors under the veteran director Pyotr Fomenko has sparkled in recent years, and is definitely worth checking out. Formenko often directs at other venues, with or without his protégés (all of whom he once taught at the Russian Academy of Theatre Arts). Tickets $1–9.

Lenkom Theatre, Malaya Dmitrovka ul. 6 ☎299 96 68; near Chekhovskaya metro. Colourful drama and musicals directed by Mark Zakharov, who introduced lasers and rock to the Soviet stage. Many of the productions can be enjoyed without much knowledge of Russian – though not Chekhov's *The Seagull* or Turgenev's *Two Women*. Tickets $3–9.

Malaya Bronnaya Theatre (*teatr na Maloy Bronnoy*), Malaya Bronnaya ul. 4 ☎290 40 93; 15min from Tverskaya or Arbatskaya metro. Good actors and a fine tradition, but it hasn't made waves for many years. Its repertoire includes Molière's *Georges Dandin* and Coward's *Blithe Spirit*.

Maly Theatre, Teatralnaya pl. 1/6 ☎925 98 68 or 921 03 50; near Teatralnaya metro. Old-fashioned productions of mostly nineteenth-century Russian plays (many of which were premiered here), plus new historical dramas such as AK Tolstoy's *Tsar Boris*. They also have an affiliate stage at ul. Bolshaya Ordynka 69 (☎237 31 81). Tickets $1–4.

Moscow Art Theatre (*MKhAT imeni Chekhova*), Kamergerskiy per. 3 ☎229 87 60; *www.theatre.ru/mhat/*; 5min from Okhotniy Ryad or Teatralnaya metros. The old MKhAT (named after Chekhov) was the birthplace of modern drama and the Method, but isn't rated so highly nowadays, despite the efforts of director Oleg Yefremov. Its repertoire includes works by Chekhov, Gogol and Dostoevsky, *A Midsummer Night's Dream* and Tennessee Williams's *The Rose Tattoo*.

Moscow Art Theatre (*MKhAT imeni Gorkovo*), Tverskoy bul. 22 ☎203 62 22 or 203 73 99; 5min from Tverskaya/Pushkinskaya metro. Box office noon–3pm & 4–7pm. The new MKhAT (named after Gorky) specializes in plays by its namesake, and has two stages. Tickets $0.30–3.

The Arts

Mossovet Theatre, Aquarium Garden, Bolshaya Sadovaya ul. 16 ☎200 59 43 or 299 33 77; near Mayakovskaya metro. Box office noon–3pm & 4–7pm. Farces, popular classics and musicals, including Molière, Bulgakov's *The White Guard* and a Russian interpretation of *Jesus Christ Superstar*. Tickets $1–5.

Satirikon Theatre, Sheremetevskaya ul. 8 ☎218 10 19; trolleybus #18 or #42 from Rizhskaya metro. Besides directing *Romeo and Juliet* and *The Three-penny Opera*, Konstantin Raykin plays the lead role in scintillating productions by guest directors – Fokin's *Metamorphosis*, Fomenko's *The Magnificent Cuckold* and Robert Sturua's *Hamlet* – which are keenly awaited by theatre lovers.

Shalom, Varshovskoe shosse 71 ☎113 27 53; bus #147 from Varshavskaya metro. Russia's only professional Jewish theatre, staging plays about topical issues, and musicals for children or adults, in Russian and Yiddish with simultaneous translation into English.

Sovremennik Theatre, Chistoprudniy bul. 19 ☎921 64 73; near Chistye Prudy metro. Box office noon–3pm & 4–7pm. Famous 1960s theatre, enjoying a new lease of life under director Galina Volchek. Productions include Shakespeare's *The Merry Wives of Windsor*, Shaw's *Pygmalion* and Chekhov's *The Cherry Orchard*. Tickets $1–18.

Sphere Drama Theatre, Hermitage Garden, ul. Karetniy ryad 3 ☎299 07 08; 10min from Chekhovskaya or Tsvetnoy Bulvar metro. Named after its round stage, the theatre's repertoire includes plays based on Nabokov stories, such as *Lolita* and *Laughter in the Dark*, and the musical *West Side Story*.

Stanislavsky Drama Theatre, Tverskaya ul. 23 299 72 24; near Okhotniy Ryad metro. Director Vladimir Miroev's avant-garde productions of *The Government Inspector*, *Twelfth Night* and *Amphitryon* arouse strong feelings among theatregoers and critics. Not to be confused with the Stanislavsky & Nemirovich-Danchenko Musical Theatre. Tickets $1–10.

Tabakov Theatre, ul. Chaplygina 1a ☎928 96 85; 10min from Chistye Prudy/Turgenevskaya metro. Crowd-pleasing playhouse under actor-director Oleg Tabakov, whose repertoire includes Gorky's *The Lower Depths* and Thomas Mann's *The Confessions of Felix Krull, Confidence Man*. Tickets $2–13.

Theatre at Nikitskie Vorota (*teatr u Nikitskikh vorot*), Bolshaya Nikitskaya ul. 23/9 ☎202 82 19, *nikitski@glasnet.ru*; 10min from Arbatskaya metro. A vehicle for the talents and ego of director, playwright, actor and designer Mark Rozovsky. Repertoire includes Chekhov's *Uncle Vanya*.

Theatre of Young Spectators (*MTYuZ*), Mamonovskiy per. 10 ☎299 53 60, *mtyuz@online.ru*; *www.theatre.ru/mtuz*; Pushkinskaya/Tverskaya metro. MTYuz owes its reputation for bold, innovative drama to Genrietta Yanovskaya's productions of *The Heart of a Dog* and *The Storm*, her husband Kama Glinkas's internationally renowned *KI from Crime* (based on the story of Katerina Ivanovna in *Crime and Punishment*), and guest directors such as Mirzoev, whose zany *Amphitryon* was premiered here.

Theatre on Yugo-Zapade (*teatr na Yugo-Zapade*), pr. Vernadskovo 125 ☎433 11 91; 5min from Yugo-Zapadnaya metro. Intense amateurs (its star, Avilov, used to be a truck driver) in a tiny theatre beneath a towerblock. Repertoire includes Chekhov, Gogol, *Hamlet*, Ionesco's *Rhinoceros* and a five-hour-long adaptation of Bulgakov's *The Master and Margarita*.

Taganka Theatre (*teatr na Taganke*), ul. Zemlyanoy val 76/21 ☎915 12 17; near Taganskaya metro. Box office 1–7pm. A breath of fresh air during the Era of Stagnation (see p.274), this famous theatre's productions include *The Master and Margarita*, Pushkin's *Yevgeny Onegin* and a dramatization of Solzhenitsyn's *The First Circle*. Tickets $1–18.

Vakhtangov Theatre, ul. Arbat 26 ☎241 07 28; 5min from Smolenskaya metro. One of the old heavyweights of Soviet

drama, which last wowed audiences with Olga Mukhina's acclaimed *Tanya-Tanya*.

Puppetry, circus and children's theatre

Puppet theatre (*Kukolniy teatr*) has a long tradition in Russia, and there are two theatres devoted to the art in Moscow. Other performing arts for which a knowledge of Russian isn't necessary may deter some visitors by their use of trained animals, namely the Circus – acclaimed as one of the best in the world – the House of Cats, the Durov Animal Theatre and the Dolphinarium. Shows at the Children's Musical Theatre present no such dilemmas, and should appeal to younger kids. Tickets for all these events can be purchased from vendors in the Barrikadnaya and Tverskaya metro underpasses, or from any theatre bookings kiosk.

Children's Musical Theatre, pr. Vernadskovo 5 ☎930 70 21 or 930 63 64; 5min from Universitet metro. A wonderful playhouse (see p.225) whose repertoire includes Prokofiev's *Peter and the Wolf* and *Cinderella*, Ravel's *Bolero*, *Snow White*, *The Little Match Girl*, *Winnie the Pooh* and *The Wizard of Oz*. Its charm is enhanced by the costumed actors mingling with the audience before performances (Mon–Fri 3pm & 6pm; Sat & Sun noon, 4pm & 6pm).

Circus on prospekt Vernadskovo, pr. Vernadskovo 7 ☎930 28 15 or 930 02 72; near Universitet metro. One half of the world-renowned Moscow State Circus (the other being the Nikulin Circus, see below). Animal acts and clowns are its forte. Box office daily 10am–7pm. Performances Wed & Fri at 7pm, Sat & Sun 11.30a, 3pm & 7pm; free for children up to 6.

Dolphinarium, Mironovskaya ul. 27 ☎369 79 66; 15min from Semyonovskaya metro. A 50-minute show by cetaceans and sea lions (with which kids can be photographed). Adults may be dismayed by the conditions. Box office daily 11am–6pm. Performances Wed noon, 4pm & 6pm, Thurs 4pm & 6pm, Fri noon & 4pm, Sat & Sun noon, 2pm & 4pm.

Durov Animal Theatre, ul. Durova 4 ☎971 30 47 or 971 37 87; 15min from Novoslobodskaya or Tsvetnoy Bulvar metro. A unique institution loved by generations of kids, with some surreal acts (see p.299). Not recommended for anyone with allergies. Book as far ahead as possible. Performances Wed–Fri at 4pm, Sat & Sun at noon, 2pm & 5.30pm.

Entrée Circus, near the Stone Fountain in the VVTs (see p.307) ☎216 12 20; 10min from VDNKh metro. A small circus with acrobats, clowns, monkeys, a python and an elephant. Its tent also serves for a children's disco on Sat & Sun (after 7pm). Performances Fri at 4pm, Sat & Sun at 2pm & 4pm.

House of Cats, Kutuzovskiy pr. 25 ☎249 29 07; bus #174 from Kievskaya metro. An exclusively feline version of the Durov, in a small hall with a family ambience. The theatre is named after the animal trainer and clown, Yuri Kuklachev. During the summer they also do shows at the Zoopark. Performances Wed–Fri at 4pm, Sat & Sun at 11am, 2pm & 5pm.

Merry Arena Circus, Gorky Park, in the children's area of the Neskuchniy Gardens ☎954 72 75; 15min from Oktyabrskaya metro. A summer circus whose two-and-a-half-hour show features acrobats, clowns, bears, dogs, monkeys and horses. Performances Fri at 7pm, Sat at 2pm & 6pm, Sun at 1pm & 5pm.

Nikulin Circus, Tsvetnoy bul. 13 ☎200 06 68 (recorded information), 200 19 01, *info@cricusnikulin.ru*; *www.circusnikulin.ru*; near Tsvetnoy Bulvar metro. The "Old" Moscow State Circus has more of a "big top" feel than the "New" Circus on pr. Vernadskovo. Acrobats, jugglers, bears, monkeys, sea lions and a pas-de-deux on camels. Box office Mon–Fri 11am–2pm & 3–7pm, Sat & Sun 12.30–1.30pm. No performances on Tues or Wed; schedules vary other days, but there are usually shows at 6pm.

The Arts

Obraztsov Puppet Theatre, Sadovaya-Samotyochnaya ul. 3 ☎299 59 79 or 299 33 10; 10min from Tsvetnoy Bulvar metro. One of the world's oldest and best puppet theatres – founded by Sergei Obraztsov in 1931 – it still features some of his own productions, such as *The Divine Comedy*, which were once innovative for injecting adult themes into an art form regarded as children's entertainment. The matinees are funny for children of all ages, and include puppet versions of *Aladdin*, *Hercules* and *The Jungle Book*; evening performances are more adult-oriented. The theatre contains a winter garden and aquariums.

Shadow Theatre, Oktyabrskaya ul. 5 ☎281 15 16 or 281 35 90; 15min from Novoslobodskaya metro. Phone ahead to confirm that this family theatre is at home before trying to find it in the back streets behind the Central Army Theatre (see p.298). Ilya Epelbaum and Maya Krasnopolskaya are often abroad, presenting their acclaimed miniature *Swan Lake: The Opera* and *The Tour*.

Cinema

Since Russian **cinema** (*kino*) imploded in the early 1990s, a handful of directors have managed to produce box-office hits to challenge Hollywood on the home market, that have also been praised abroad. Andrei Balabanov's *Brother* and *Of Beasts and Men*, Sergei Bodrov's *Prisoner of the Mountains*, Pavel Chukrai's *Thief* and Kira Muratova's *Three Stories* all augur well for the future – but alas, the biggest recipient of state and private funding has been Nikita Mikhalkov, whose epic *The Barber of Siberia* provoked mass walkouts at Cannes but won its director the place of honour at the Moscow 2000 Film Festival, attended by Putin (who went on to restore the Soviet anthem, whose words had been written by Mikhalkov's father).

Meanwhile the public remain in love with Hollywood, whose films account for ninety percent of what's on in Moscow's cinemas. Though many have now been modernized to Western standards, none of them accept credit card bookings. Aside from a handful of places that show films in their original language, most foreign movies are dubbed into Russian – hopefully by several people doing the speaking parts, rather than just one or two people.

The *Russia Journal* and the Friday edition of the *Moscow Times* list films in English and Russian currently showing. As you'd expect, the widest choice of Russian and (subtitled) foreign films is during the **International Film Festival**, for two weeks in July. Fans surround the Pushkin cinema to watch the stars arrive each night, and many other cinemas host their own events. Depending on funding, there may also be a two-week **Experimental Film Festival** in early June.

Americom House of Cinema, *Radisson Slavjanskaya Hotel*, Berezhkovskaya nab. 2 ☎941 87 47; near Kievskaya metro. Comfy seats and digital sound adds to the enjoyment of their regular programme of (mostly new US) movies in English, with Russian translations by headphone. Tickets $6 (matinees $3).

Cinema Centre on Krasnaya Presnyna (*Kinotsentr na Krasnoy Presne*), Druzhinnikovskaya ul. 15 ☎255 92 37 or 205 73 06; near Barrikadnaya metro. The Muscovite film buff's mecca, with two halls screening classic and new Russian and (dubbed) foreign films; also holds lectures.

Dome, *Renaissance Hotel*, Olympiyskiy pr. 18/1 ☎931 98 73; 10min from Prospekt Mira metro. Located in a small building outside the hotel, this 300-seat hall with a Dolby Surround system screens US movies with Russian translation by headphone.

Illusion, Kotelnicheskaya nab. 1/15 ☎915 43 39; in a wing of the Kotelnicheskaya Apartments, 15min from Kitay-Gorod or Tanganskaya metro. Located in a Stalin skyscraper, this well-loved art house cinema shows Soviet classics, and foreign films in the original language (English, Thurs; French, Mon), starting at 7pm. Dolby sound. Tickets $0.30–$2.

Karo Film, Sheremetevskaya ul. 60a ☎937 26 116; trolleybus #18 or #42 from Rizhskaya metro. Moscow's first purpose-built multiplex, with four screens and Dolby Digital sound, heralds the delivery of high-quality facilities to suburban neighbourhoods – but it's a hassle to reach if you don't live there. Tickets $2–8.

Kodak Cinema World, Nastasinskiy per. 2 ☎209 43 59; near Pushkinskaya/Tverskaya metro. Popular US-style movie theatre just off Tverskaya, complete with popcorn, a video shop, bar and café. Tickets $2–7 on weekdays, $3–9 at weekends.

Mir, Tsvetnoy bul. 11, str. 2 ☎424 46 47; near Tsvetnoy Bulvar metro. Wide-screen cinema with 1050 seats and Dolby Surround, that sometimes shows foreign art movies. Tickets $2–3.

Pushkin, Pushkinskaya pl. 2 ☎299 21 11; near Puskinskaya metro. Moscow's largest cinema (2350 seats) is regularly used for glitzy premieres of new Russian films and foreign blockbusters, and is the venue for the annual International Film Festival. Dolby sound. Tickets $2–8.

35 MM, ul. Pokrovka 47/24 ☎917 54 92 or 917 18 83; 10min from Kurskaya or Krasnye Vorota metro. Only in Moscow would you find a cinema with double-sized divans instead of seats, showing one or two movies around the clock – thrillers or art-house erotica, usually. Tickets $8.

The visual arts

Moscow has dozens of art galleries and exhibition halls, in addition to the temporary displays on show in its museums and major galleries. Listed below are some of the best-known galleries, where you can be fairly sure of finding something interesting at most times of the year. Most of them have works for sale; some levy a small admission charge.

Manège Exhibition Hall, Manezhnaya pl. 1 ☎202 89 76 or 202 82 52; near Okhotniy Ryad, Biblioteka Imeni Lenina and Aleksandrovskiy Sad metros. Large art exhibitions and trade fairs. Wed–Sat noon–7pm, Sun noon–5pm; free.

Central House of Artists, ul. Krymskiy val 10 ☎238 98 34 or 238 98 43; 10min from Park Kultury metro. Huge exhibition complex with over a dozen halls; some items for sale, others not. Tues–Sun 11am–8pm; $0.20.

Dar, ul. Malaya Polyanka 7/7, str. 5 ☎238 66 54; 10min from Oktyabrskaya metro. Specializes in naive art. Sat & Sun 2–5pm, Wed–Fri by appointment only; free.

Design Club, Bolshoy Kiselniy per. 5, str. 1–2 ☎200 60 10; 10min from Kuznetskiy Most metro. Showcase for contemporary furniture, interiors, fashion and jewellery by Russian designers. Mon–Fri 10am–5pm; free.

Gertsev Gallery, ul. Karetniy ryad 5/10/corner of Sadovaya-Karetnaya ul. ☎209 66 65; 15min from Tsvetnoy Bulvar or Mayakovskaya metro. Abstract, primitivist and postmodernist paintings. Mon–Fri 11am–8pm, Sat & Sun 11am–6pm; free.

M'ARS, Malaya Filyovskaya ul. 32 ☎146 20 29; 5min from Pionerskaya metro. The city's first private art gallery, organized by previously underground artists like the Mytiki. Tues–Sat noon–8pm, Sun noon–6pm; free.

House of Artists on Kuznetskiy most, ul. Kuznetskiy most 11 ☎924 24 50; near Kuznetskiy Most metro. Officially a showcase for graphics, paintings, sculpture and decorative art by Moscow artists, but stalls selling posters, jewellery and joss-sticks take up much of the space. Mon–Sat noon–7pm; $0.20.

Irida, pr. Mira 68 ☎971 03 28; 5min from Prospekt Mira or Rizhskaya metro. Exclusively devoted to Russian women artists. Paintings, graphics, batiks, shawls, jewellery, ceramics and dolls. Daily 11am–7pm; free.

Moscow Centre of Arts, Neglinnaya ul. 14 ☎924 88 72; 10min from Tsvetnoy Bulvar metro. Paintings and graphics by Soviet and contemporary artists, plus a photographic gallery that's one of several venues during the Photo-Biennial (in May, every even-numbered year). Daily 11am–7pm; free.

Moscow Fine Art, Bolshaya Sadovaya ul. 3 ☎251 76 49; near Mayakovskaya metro. Mostly exhibits oil paintings and watercolours. Mon–Sat 11am–6pm; free.

Moscow House of Sculptors, 1-y Spasonalivkovskiy per. 4 ☎238 02 77; 5min from Oktyabrskaya metro. All kinds of sculpture, from bronze busts to installation art, plus some graphics, too. Tues–Sat noon–7pm.

Photo Centre, Gogolevskiy bul. 8 ☎291 56 85; near Kropotkinskaya metro. Moscow's leading photographic gallery has ever-changing exhibitions and an archive of prints for sale. Tues–Sun noon–8pm; $0.20.

Roza Azora Gallery, Nikitskiy bul. 12a ☎291 45 79; 5min from Arbatskaya metro. Contemporary work, from multi-media installations to portraits. Mon–Fri 11am–7pm, Sat 11am–1pm & 2–6pm; free.

Shishkin Gallery, Neglinnaya ul. 29/14, str. 1 ☎200 35 10, *uart@ropnet.ru*; 10min from Tsvetnoy Bulvar metro. Specializes in nineteenth- and twentieth-century Russian art, especially postwar Soviet painting. Mon–Sat 10am–7pm; free.

XL Gallery, Bolshaya Sadovaya ul. 6 ☎299 37 24; near Mayakovskaya metro. Contemporary avant-garde art, particularly video art and installations. Mon–Fri 4–8pm; free.

Zoo, in the Monkey House at the Zoopark ☎255 95 41; near Barrikadnaya/Krasnopresnenskaya metro. Entirely devoted to "animalistic art" – paintings, drawings, sculptures and photos of animals. Tues–Sun 11am–7pm; free.

The Arts

Chapter 14

Shops and markets

Shops and markets

Shopping in Moscow brings home all you've ever heard about the "wild capitalism" of New Russia. Between the extremes of marbled malls of designer-label stores and pensioners selling cigarettes on street corners, the shops and kiosks that have sprung up on every vacant plot offer a bewildering choice of genuine, counterfeit and dubious goods. While shopping has become infinitely more rewarding in recent years and the truly wealthy can now shop as blithely as they do abroad, for the average citizen or visitor Moscow is still a jungle rather than a playground for consumers. Try to be flexible about what you want – and always carry a shopping bag with you.

Some former state stores still insist on the infuriating system where customers pay at the *kassa* before collecting their goods, which entails **queuing** at least twice, but most new shops use the one-stop system.

Antiques and souvenirs

Antiques cannot be exported without special permission, although some smaller items may be allowed through. If you buy anything of value and want to take it out of the country, make sure you get an export licence from the Ministry of Culture (see p.26). Though much is smuggled out via Belarus or Ukraine, where customs are laxer, samovars and icons will definitely be detected by the X-ray scanners at Moscow's airports.

Souvenirs are safer buys, and widely available. Favourites include the matryoshka doll, which also comes in versions depicting Putin, Yeltsin, Gorby et al; lacquered Palekh boxes painted with fairytale scenes; colourful wooden spoons and bowls from Khokloma; banners, fur hats, army gear and mock KGB sweatshirts. Any of these can be taken abroad without difficulty.

Antiques

Aktsiya, Bolshaya Nikitsaya ul. 21/18 ☎291 75 09 (Pushkinskaya or Arbatskaya metro); Bryusov per. 2/14 ☎229 06 10 (Okhotniy Ryad/Teatralnaya metro). Two shops offering a mixture of pre-Revolutionary

Opening times

These vary widely, but you can usually count on shops opening from Monday to Saturday at around 10am (9am for food stores), closing for an hour or so between 1 and 3pm and staying open until around 7pm. Some department stores stay open until 8 or 9pm and also open on Sundays (11am–6pm), though this tends to be rather erratic. Many neighbourhood food stores and kiosks function 24 hours a day.

objets and Soviet kitsch; paintings, china and bronzes. Fun to browse. The Bolshaya Nikitskaya branch holds regular auctions. Both Mon–Sat 11am–7pm.

Antikvar na Myasnitskoy, Myasnitskaya ul. 13 ☎925 76 08; 5min from Turgenevskaya metro. Timepieces, silver, porcelain, coins, icons and samovars. Mon–Fri 10am–7pm, Sat 10am–6pm.

Bukinist, ul. Sretenka 9 ☎928 96 36 (Sukharevskaya/Turgenevskaya metro); Trubnaya ul. 23 ☎925 37 72 (Tsvetnoy Bulvar/Sukharevskaya metro). The former (Mon–Fri 10am–2pm & 3–7pm) specializes in antique books, art magazines, haberdashery and chess sets; the latter (Mon–Fri 10am–7pm, Sat 10am–6pm) in prints, paintings, porcelain, watches and collectibles.

Knizhnaya lavka pisateley, ul. Kuznetskiy most 18 ☎921 22 98; near Kuznetskiy Most metro. First editions, antique books, engravings and porcelain. Tues–Sat 10am–2pm & 3–7pm.

Kupina, ul. Arbat 18 ☎202 44 62; 5min from Arbatskaya metro. All kinds of Russian antiques, sometimes sold at auctions. They have a specialist department for bronzes, pictures and porcelain. Mon–Fri 10am–6pm.

Kuznetsov's, Myasnitskaya ul. 8; 5min from Lubyanka metro. Pre-Revolutionary emporium for porcelain, crystal and bronzes, both antique and contemporary, Russian and foreign. Mon–Fri 10am–7pm, Sat 10am–6pm.

Mir iskusstva, Petrovskiy Passazh 1st floor ☎923 27 82 (Teatralnaya or Kuznetskiy Most metro); ul. Prichistenka 26 ☎201 43 95 (Kropotkinskaya metro). The Petrovskiy outlet sells paintings and frames; the Prichistenka branch pictures and furniture. Both Mon–Sat 10am–8pm.

Souvenirs

Church of St George, ul. Varvarka; 5min from Kitay-Gorod metro. The best of the souvenir shops in the Zaryade churches, with charming gifts and toys by local craftspeople. Mon–Sat 9am–6pm.

Gorbunov Collectors' Fair (aka the *Gorbushka*), Filyovskiy Park; 10min from Bagrationovskaya metro. All kinds of new and second-hand records, CDs, tapes, videos, cameras and audio equipment. Often busted by the OMON, cracking down on pirate CDs and software. Sat & Sun 11am–2pm.

GUM (see "Department Stores") has several souvenir shops on the second line of the first floor. You might also find people selling embroidered cushion covers and tea cosies, made by schoolchildren.

Izmaylovo Art Market (aka the *Vernisazh*); 5min from Izmaylovskiy Park metro. Dozens of stalls selling handicrafts, icons, Soviet kitsch, vintage cameras and watches. The biggest choice of souvenirs, if not the lowest prices. Beware of pickpockets. Fri, Sat & Sun 10am–6pm. $0.20 admission charge.

Museum, in the Museum of Modern History, Tverskaya ul. 21; near Tverskaya/Pushkinskaya metro. Stocks posters, postcards, badges and other memorabilia from the Soviet era. For enquiries email *kwardra@dol.ru*. Tues & Thurs–Sun 10am–6pm, Wed 11am–7pm.

Yantar, in the Culture Pavilion (#66) at the WTs; near VDNKh metro. Necklaces, earrings, rings, caskets, chessboards and mosaics made of Kaliningrad amber, ranging from $2 to 500. Another shop in the same pavilion sells inexpensive Latvian ceramics and kitchenware. Both Mon–Fri 10am–6pm, Sat & Sun 10am–7pm.

Department stores and "things markets"

The last decade has seen the habit of shopping (or at least window-shopping) for pleasure firmly established in Moscow, as **department stores** and **malls** have burgeoned. On a humbler level, there are several large markets for clothing, appliances and cosmetics, held inside sports stadiums and known as "**things markets**" (*Veshchevye rynok*). As the goods are generally poor-quality imitations of international brand-products,

Shops and markets

made in China, Turkey or Poland, the scene is closer to a warehouse sale than a flea market. There's a small admission charge.

Department stores and malls

Arbat Irish House, ul. Noviy Arbat 13; 5min from Arbatskaya metro. Good selection of imported appliances and clothing, above an enormous food store with an excellent bakery. Amex, Visa, MC. Mon–Sat 9am–10pm, Sun 9am–8pm.

Detskiy Mir, Teatralniy proezd 5; near Lubyanka metro. The largest, if not the best toy shop in Moscow, with a carousel in the main hall, and scores of shops on three levels. No CC. Mon–Sat 9am–9pm, Sun 11am–7pm.

Dom Igrushki, ul. Bolshaya Yakimanka 26; 10min from Polyanka metro. A one-floor version of Detskiy mir, stocking a big range of Russian and imported toys for kids of all ages. No CC. Mon–Sat 8am–8pm.

Galereya Aktyor, Tverskaya ul. 16; near Pushkinskaya/Tverskaya metro. Discreetly located on the corner of Tverskaya and Strastnoy bulvar, this black marble and chromed mall with a central fountain contains a score of designer outlets, of which the least expensive are Naf Naf and Levi's. Some take CC. Daily 10am–9pm.

Global USA, Tverskaya ul. 6 (Teatralnaya metro); ul. Simonovskiy val 12 (trolleybus #12, #20, #43 or #46 from Proletarskaya metro). Two branches of the US chain, selling computers, home appliances, clothing, toys and sports goods. Daily 10am–10pm.

GUM, Krasnaya pl. 3; near Ploshchad Revolyutsii metro. Although Benetton and their ilk have colonized the lower floor, a few Soviet-style shops can still be found upstairs. There's also a small branch at Tverskaya ul. 15, selling designer clothes and cosmetics. Some of the outlets take CC. Both Mon–Sat 8am–9pm, Sun 11am–6pm.

Kalinka-Stockmann, Smolenskiy Passazh, Smolenskaya pl.; near Smolenskaya metro. A huge department store with imported clothes and household goods, a supermarket and deli, marking the apotheosis of Stockmann's presence in Moscow, which dates back to the 1970s. Visa, MC. Daily 10am–10pm.

Okhotniy Ryad, Manezhnaya pl.; near Okhotniy Ryad/Ploshchad Revolyutsii metro. 10, *uart@ropnet.ru*; 10min from Tsvetnoy Bulvar metro. Mayor Luzhkov's apotheosis – a triple-level subterranean mall decorated by his court artist, Tsereteli, featuring Benetton, Calvin Klein, Estee Lauder, Geiger, Mothercare and Speedo, with fast-food outlets opening onto the Alexander Gardens that keep it busy until the small hours. Check out the "updated" Palekh boxes and Gizhel porcelain featuring New Russians in Landcruisers or saunas instead of the traditional fairytale themes, sold in Noviy Russkiy Mir. Some shops take CC. Daily 11am–10pm.

Petrovskiy Passazh, ul. Petrovka 10; 5min from Okhotniy Ryad metro. Chic arcade popular with the nouveau riche; mostly French, Italian and German designer clothing, household furnishings and appliances. Some shops take CC. Mon–Sat 9am–8pm, Sun 9am–6pm.

TsUM, ul. Petrovka 2; near Teatralnaya metro. Moscow's oldest-established department store, stocking Russian and imported clothing, household goods and toys. Visa, MC. Mon–Sat 9am–9pm, Sun 11am–8pm.

"Things markets"

Cherkizovskiy, near Lokomotiv Stadium, Bolshaya Cherkizovskaya ul. 125; near Cherkizovskaya metro. Tues–Sun 7am–7pm.

Dinamo, in the Manezh near the stadium; near Dinamo metro. Daily 10am–6pm.

Luzhniki sports complex; 10min from Sportivnaya metro. Clothing and audio-visual equipment. Daily 10am–6pm.

TsKA sports complex; trolleybus #12 or #70 from Dinamo metro. Daily 8am–6pm.

Shops and markets

Kiosks

In the early years of "wild capitalism", street kiosks and vendors sold everything from bootleg scotch to videos to frozen chickens. Now there are fewer than before, as the shops contain far more goods and the Council has cracked down on unlicensed traders, but kiosks still purvey cigarettes, booze, flowers and cosmetics in residential areas, and snacks around metro stations. Aside from the risk of counterfeit liquor (see p.336), food should be treated with caution: ice cream and fruit are usually OK, but sausages and pies should be avoided, particularly from stalls at train stations.

Food and drink

Imported goods are available in all shops and department stores, alongside **Russian products** that regained a slice of the market after the crash of 1998. So far as food products are concerned it can be hard to tell them apart, as many foreign brands are now made under licence or counterfeited in Russia – so it pays to examine items before buying. Alternatively, you could stick to one of the expensive foreign stores such as Kalinka-Stockmann, where everything is imported.

While food shops are far better stocked than in Soviet times, it's still true that the widest selection of fresh produce is to be found in **markets** (*rynok*), where vendors tempt buyers with nibbles of fruit, cheese, ham, pickles and other homemade delights. You need to bring cash, as credit cards are useless and there are rarely any ATMs in the vicinity.

Delis and liquor shops

Armeniya, Tverskaya ul. 17; near Tverskaya metro. Well stocked with foreign and Russian foodstuffs and delicacies, including paper-thin *lavash* bread and vintage Georgian and Armenian wines and cognacs. Visa, MC. Daily 9am–11pm.

Diabet Dieta, Leontevskiy per. 14; 10min from Tverskaya metro. Sells food and drink formulated for diabetics. No CC. Mon–Fri 9am–9pm, Sat 9am–5pm, Sun 10am–6pm.

Kristall, GUM, Krasnaya pl 3; near Ploshchad Revolyutsii metro. Outlet for Moscow's Kristall distillery, selling all kinds of vodka including "celebrity" labels bearing the face of the director Mikhalkov and the ultra-nationalist Zhirinovsky, and bottles in the form of bears or matryoshka dolls. No CC. Mon–Sat 8.30am–8.30pm, Sun 11am–7pm.

Novoarbatskiy, ul. Noviy Arbat 13; 10min from Arbatskaya or Smolenskaya metro. Well-stocked Russian supermarket with an excellent bakery, a deli, coffee shop and snack bar. No CC. Daily 24 hours.

Put k sebe, Leningradskiy pr. 10; 10min from Belorusskaya metro. Sells health food and a wide range of teas; its name means "Way to Yourself". No CC. Mon–Sat 10am–6pm.

Yeliseev's, Tverskaya ul. 14; near Pushkinskaya metro. Worth a visit purely for its fabulous decor (see p.135), but it also stocks a good range of gourmet foods. No CC. Mon–Sat 8am–9pm, Sun 8am–7pm.

Food markets

Cheremushinskiy, Lomonosovskiy pr. 1; 10min from Universitet or Profsoyuznaya metro. The largest and most expensive in Moscow. Mon–Sat 7am–7pm, Sun 7am–6pm.

Danilovskiy, ul. Mytnaya 74; near Tulskaya metro. Daily 7am–7pm.

Palashevskiy, Sytninskiy tupik 3a; 5min from Pushkinskaya metro. Tucked away in a cul-de-sac off Tverskoy bulvar, this market only sells fish (live and frozen), and Moscow's chefs do their buying here. Mon–Sat 7am–5pm.

Shops and markets

Rizhskiy, pr. Mira 88; near Rizhskaya metro. Daily 7am–7pm.

Newspapers, books and video rental

Foreign newspapers are sold in all the big hotels and most of the supermarkets used by foreigners, but prices are steep and the selection is often limited. The *Vesti* kiosks in or outside the *Intourist, National, Kosmos* and *Radisson Slavjanskaya* hotels have the best choice.

Books in foreign languages also fetch a high price, whether they're pictorial guides, textbooks or secondhand thrillers. All the hottest items are snapped up by traders for resale on the streets, often right outside the bookstore. Beware, however, that the restrictions on exporting Russian books are as strict as on antiques. In theory, you must submit a form listing all the details of every book; reference books are liable to be taxed, and nothing printed before 1960 can be exported.

Whereas **videos** of Western films dubbed into Russian can be rented from kiosks all over town, for recordings in English you need to go to *Storm*, whose branches at ul. Krasnoarmeyskaya 24 (☎155 93 48), Lobenskaya ul. 6 (☎483 59 92) and Yartsevevskaya ul. 4 (☎140 22 94) each stock around ninety titles in English.

Bookshops

Anglia, Khlebniy per. 2/3 ☎209 36 66, *dint@glasnet.ru*; Arbatskaya metro. Moscow's largest British bookshop sells everything from *Rough Guides* to romances, and hosts literary evenings. Amex, Visa, MC. Mon–Wed & Fri 10am–7pm, Thurs 10am-8pm, Sat 10am–6pm.

Angliyskaya kniga, ul. Kuznetskiy most 18 ☎928 20 21; near Kuznetskiy Most metro. Stocks a wide range of US and British books. Amex, Visa, MC. Mon–Fri 10am–7pm, Sat 10am–6pm; closed for lunch 2–3pm.

Biblio-Globus, ul. Myasnitskaya 6 ☎921 81 52; *www.biblio-globus.ru*; near Lubyanka metro. A huge range of Russian books plus some foreign-language art books and pulp fiction, spread around two floors beneath the secret service's computer centre. No CC. Mon–Sat 10am–8pm, Sun 11am–5pm.

Book Fest, Leninskiy pr. 113 ☎956 53 51; trolleybus #62 from Yugo-Zapade metro. Novels, dictionaries and albums in English. No CC. Mon–Sat 9am–5pm.

Evrolingua, Volgogradskiy pr. 4 ☎274 90 28; near Proletarskaya metro. All kinds of books in different European languages. No CC. Mon–Sat 10am–6pm.

Pangloss, Bolshoy Palashevskiy per. 9 ☎926 45 38; *www.aha.ru/~pangloss*; Pushkinskaya/Tverskaya metro. Books on the liberal arts, music and architecture, in English, French, German and Italian. They also show foreign films in those languages. No CC. Mon–Fri 10am–6pm, Sat 10am–5pm.

Shakespeare & Co., 1-y Novokuznetsiy per. 5/7 ☎951 93 60; 5min from Novokuznetskaya metro. Small, friendly English-language bookshop with a secondhand book exchange, coffee, and occasional literary evenings. Visa, MC. Mon–Sat 10am–2pm & 3–7pm.

Chapter 15

Children's Moscow

Children's Moscow

Although Russians dote on **children**, Moscow is not a child-friendly environment, especially for toddlers: parks and playgrounds are littered with broken glass and dogshit, and the slides and swings are often unsafe. However, in compensation, there are many things for kids to see and enjoy. Many have already been covered in the text, so you can get more information by turning to the relevant page. For sporting activities or a trip to the steam baths, see the next section.

Children's Musical Theatre Wonderful drama and ballet, including *Peter and the Wolf* and Russian fairytales that can be enjoyed by young children without understanding the language. See p.364 for details, and p.225 for more about the theatre and its history.

Circus Outstanding performances with lots of clowns and animals, at several venues; see "The Arts" (p.364) for details.

Cinemas Places that screen films in foreign languages are listed under "The Arts". Many other cinemas show cartoons (*multiki*) in the afternoons; look out for Kot Leopold, Karlson and Vinni Pukh (Winnie the Pooh).

Durov Animal Theatre and the **House of Cats**. Two uniquely Muscovite institutions whose shows are sure to charm younger children, and adults too (assuming they're not into animal lib). Details appear under "The Arts".

Eating out Options include *McDonald's* and *Rostik's* (especially the branch opposite Mayakovskaya metro, which has a play area); *Patio Pizza* opposite the Pushkin Museum of Fine Arts, which supplies crayons and high chairs and is conveniently near the Cathedral of Christ the Saviour if your critters suddenly want to dash around; and the Georgian restaurant *Mama Zoya*, where the staff make a fuss of kids and the accordionists want to sit them on their knee. See "Eating and drinking" for details.

Funfairs Moscow's principal funfairs are located in Gorky Park (p.248), the VVTs (p.302) and Sokolniki Park (p.310). In Gorky Park, children can ride for free on the attractions beside the river for the first hour after opening on weekdays.

Kolomenskoe Magical buildings and festivals to capture your children's imagination, in a wooded park that's also great for riding all year and sledging in wintertime (see p.263).

Metro rides Can be fun providing you avoid travelling at rush hour, and on the Circle line. See the "Sightseers Guide to the Metro" on p.36 for a list of decorative stations.

Moscow Marathon Best viewed from Gorky Park, where the race starts and finishes, or the Sparrow Hills, overlooking the route (p.378).

Museums Some that might be of particular interest to children include the Kremlin Armoury (p.106); the Palace of the Romanov Boyars in Zaryade (p.121); the Vasnetsov House (p.295); the

Children's Moscow

Museum of Cosmonautics (p.302); the Armed Forces Museum (p.300) or Central Museum of the Great Patriotic War (p.211); and the Museum of Unique Dolls (p.173).

Pet markets If you don't feel up to visiting the big Sunday Pet Market out beyond Taganka (p.283), children can stroke puppies and kittens on the steps of the Arbatskaya pl. underpass any day of the week (p.139).

Police Relay-Race Fun to watch if you pick the right vantage point on the Garden Ring; the most exciting stages are the motorcycle and patrol car races. Described on p.379.

Puppet theatre See "The Arts" section for details of where to find puppet theatre for children in Moscow.

Streetlife Except in the foulest weather, the Arbat is always busy with buskers, performing artists and street photographers (whose props include giant cuddly toys). Kids can also get their picture taken with people dressed in medieval costumes, on Red Square and at Kolomenskoe.

TV programmes To prepare young children for bed, try *Spokoini Nochi, Malyshi* (Goodnight, Kids), a fifteen-minute puppet and cartoon show shown on ORT. Russian pop music and game shows are less likely to prove a hit with older kids.

Toys Barbie is all the rage, while Russian-made toys have all but vanished from the shelves, but you can still find charming wooden toys from Novgorod at reasonably low prices in souvenir shops. To pig out on Barbie and My Little Pony visit the *Dom Igrushki* or *Detskiy Mir* (see "Department Stores", p.370).

Tsaritsyno Romantic ruins to scramble over and woods to play in. The stables attached to the *Usadba* restaurant can arrange horse-riding all year round, and *troyka* rides in winter. See p.266 for details.

VVTs Stalinesque Disney World with some attractions for kids: a ferris wheel, a real space rocket, and *troyka* rides over winter. Described on p.302.

Zoopark The children's zoo on the other side of Bolshaya Gruzinskaya ul. from the main entrance is accessible by an overhead bridge. See p.202 for details.

Chapter 16

Sports, outdoor activities and bathhouses

In Soviet times, **sport** was accorded high status: a carefully nurtured elite of Olympic medal-winning sportsmen and women were heralded as proof of Communism's superiority, while ordinary citizens were exhorted to pursue sporting activities to make them "ready for labour and defence". Consequently, there's no shortage of sports facilities in Moscow, though most are for club members only; visitors can try striking some kind of deal with the staff, or settle for paying higher rates to use hotel facilities.

For the slothful majority of Muscovites, however, the most popular activity remains visiting the **bathhouse**, or *banya*. Russian bathhouses are a world unto themselves, and are the preferred cure for the complaint known locally as "feeling heavy" – which encompasses everything from having flu to feeling depressed. For a truly Russian experience, a visit to the *banya* is a must.

Baseball

It's widely believed in Russia that **baseball** (*beysbol*) derives from the ancient Russian game of *lapta* – which might explain the success of the national team on the European circuit, and the excellence of local teams such as MGU-Tornado, Moskvich and RusStar. The majority of matches are played in the thousand-seat SKA Stadium (☎725 45 24; bus #322 from Izmaylovskiy Park metro to the "Lesnaya" stop). The season runs from April to October, with the Russian Championship in July. Admission is usually free.

Bathhouses

The Russian ***banya*** is as much a national institution as the sauna is in Scandinavia. Traditionally, peasants stoked up the village bathhouse and washed away the week's grime on Fridays; Saturdays were for drinking and Sundays for church – a "*banya* for the soul". Townspeople were equally devoted to the *banya*: the wealthy had private ones, while others visited public bathhouses, favoured as much for their ambience as the quality of their hot room. Today, these bathhouses are classless institutions, where all ages and professions are united in sweaty conviviality. Moscow's gangsters tend to make a day of it on Thursday, so the fainthearted are advised to come another day.

Before you set off, it's as well to know the procedure when **visiting a *banya***. Most bathhouses have separate wings or floors for men and women, though a few operate on different days for either sex, but whatever the setup there's no mixed bathing, except in spe-

Sports, outdoor activities and bathhouses

Sports, outdoor activities and bathhouses

cial deluxe saunas (available for private rental). At most places you can rent a sheet to wrap yourself in, plastic sandals and a comical felt hat to protect your head, though dedicated *banya*-goers come equipped with all these items, plus shampoo, soap and a towel. At the entrance you can buy a *venik* – a leafy bunch of birch twigs – with which bathers flail themselves (and each other) in the steam room, to open up the skin's pores and enhance circulation. This isn't compulsory.

Hand your valuables to the cloakroom attendant before going into the changing rooms. Beyond these lies a washroom with a cold plunge pool or bath; the basins are for soaking your *venik* to make it supple. Finally you enter the hot room (*parilka*), with its tiers of benches – it gets hotter the higher you go. It's a dry heat, although from time to time water is thrown onto the stove to produce steam. Five minutes is as long as a novice should attempt in the *parilka*. After a dunk in the cold bath and a rest, you can return to the *parilka* for more heat torture, before cooling off again – a process repeated several times, with breaks for tea and conversation.

Many *banya*-goers cover their hair (the heat can make it go frizzy), while others go in for traditional health cures and beauty treatments: men rub salt over their bodies to promote sweating, and women may coat themselves with honey to make their skin softer. As *banya*-going is a dehydrating experience, it's inadvisable to go drunk, with a bad hangover or on a full stomach. The traditional farewell salutation to fellow *banya*-goers is "*S lyogkim parom*" – "May the steam be with you".

There are inconspicuous *banyas* in every district of Moscow; those listed below are two of the best known. Both include private *banyas*, which can be rented by groups. The prices cited here refer to the cost of a two-hour session in the public section, unless stated otherwise.

Krasnopresnenskiy, Stolyarniy per. 7 ☎253 86 90; 10min from Ulitsa 1905 Goda metro. Archetypal Soviet-style *banya* with above-average amenities, including a pool, gym and solarium. The women's section has a lively atmosphere, while the men's wing is patronized by gangsters, who hold lascivious parties in its private section. Admission to the regular wings costs $9 on weekdays, $11 at weekends; private baths for up to six ($49) or twelve ($54) people rented by the hour. Mon 2–9pm, Tues–Sun 8am–10pm. The only *banya* in Moscow (and probably in Russia) to take credit cards (Amex, DC, MC, Visa).

Sandunovskiy, Neglinnaya ul. 14 ☎925 46 31; 10min from Kuznetskiy Most metro. Historic *banya*, restored to its original grandeur. If you can afford it, go for the *lux* section on the top floor, with its columned swimming pool ($19); the regular section ($11) on the floor below is well appointed, but not as spectacular. The wing behind (☎928 46 33) contains private baths for up to six ($36) or twelve ($125) people, rented by the hour. Open 8am–10pm; closed Tues.

Boating and yachting

In fine weather, **riverboat cruises** are an enjoyable way to see Moscow while getting some sun and fresh air. The Moskva River is navigable from the last week in April until the end of September or later (weather permitting). Sightseeing boats depart every 20–30 minutes (daily noon–8pm) **from the Novospasskiy Bridge** (10min from Proletarskaya metro), calling at piers near the Kremlin, Gorky Park and the Novodevichiy Convent, before terminating near Kiev Station (1hr 45min). Another cruise (50min), offering a view of the Nikolo-Perevenskiy Monastery and the Church of St John the Baptist, leaves **from Kolomenskoe**, sailing till late at night over summer (see p.263). At weekends over summer and on national holidays, you can also catch a hydrofoil **from Gorky Park**, downriver past the Novodevichiy Convent and the Kremlin, to the Novospasskiy Bridge (30min). And from late April to August smaller motorboats ply the beaches of

Serebryaniy bor (see p.315); you can reach one of the piers by trolleybus #21 from Polezhaevskaya metro.

Cruises on the Moscow Canal **beyond the city limits** start from the **Northern River Terminal** (*Severniy rechnoy vokzal*), Leningradskoe shosse 51; 15min from Rechnoy Vokzal metro. From May to August, *raketa* **hydrofoils** (daily 7am–9pm) cruise the reservoirs along the canal, which are surrounded by woods with abundant bird life and fishing. Most services run as far as Klyazma. The terminal is also the point of departure for **longer cruises** to Uglich and Kostroma, St Petersburg or Astrakhan; for details, contact the tourist agency on the spot (☎459 74 76).

Chartering a **yacht** is a popular way for rich Russians to enjoy themselves, but their interest in sailing is summed up by the club that boasts of its "girls, sauna, bar and yachts". If that seems a winning combination, the *Savoy Hotel* can put enquirers in touch with several clubs, but warns "If you need to ask the price, you can't afford it."

Alternatively, you can rent **skiffs** in Gorky Park or **rowing boats** at Serebryaniy bor for just a few dollars an hour.

Bowling

Ten-pin **bowling** (often known by its German name, *Kegelbahn*) is a popular activity; new bowling alleys are opening all the time, bringing prices down to a more reasonable level ($15–20 an hour) than a few years ago. Options include Kegelbahn in the basement of the *Kosmos Hotel*, pr. Mira 150 (☎217 01 96; daily noon–6am), 5min from VDNKh metro; the Bowling Club in the *Beta Hotel*, Izmaylovskie shosse 71 (☎792 98 98; daily noon–11pm), near Izmaylovskaya metro; Zvera in the Palace of Youth, Komsomolskiy pr. 28 (☎245 02 21; daily noon–5am), near Frunzenskaya metro; 480 BC in the *Orlyonok Hotel*, ul. Kosygina 15 (☎939 81 29; daily 24hr), trolleybus #7 from Leninskiy Prospekt metro; and Cosmik, ul. Lva Tolstovo 18 (☎246 36 66; Mon–Fri noon–5am, Sat & Sun 11am–5pm), 10min from Park Kultury metro. Most of these places have billiards tables, pool and slot machines, restaurants and bars (with happy hours) as well.

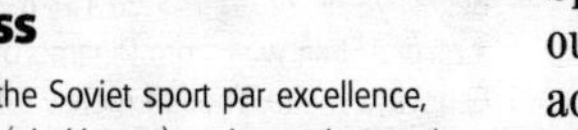

Chess

Once the Soviet sport par excellence, **chess** (*shakhmaty*) no longer has such a high profile in Russia, but amateur chess still thrives, with games in every courtyard and park over summer (Sokolniki, Izmaylovskiy and Gorky parks have special "chess corners"), where a foreign challenger will always be welcomed. Serious players could also contact the Central Chess Club, Gogolevskiy bulvar 14 ☎291 86 27 (Mon–Thurs 5–10pm, Sun 11am–4pm), 10min from Arbatskaya metro.

Horse-riding and racing

There are several places in the city where you can go **horse-riding** throughout the year. While the Karo Riding Club at **Kolomenskoe** (☎210 02 94) and the Usadba stables at **Tsaritsyno** (☎343 15 10) are both nearby historic sites that are attractions in themselves (see Chapter 7 for details), the best location is the **Bittsa Forest Park** (*Bittsevskiy Lesopark*) bordering the Moscow Ring Road. Book through the Bittsa Horseback Riding Complex, Balaklavskiy pr. 33 (☎318 57 44; daily 9am–8pm), bus #28, #163, #624 or #671 from Kaluzhskaya metro. The complex has indoor and outdoor facilities, including a pool, gym and shooting galleries, and is beside a forest park with baseball, volleyball and badminton on offer too. Their rates per hour are fairly standard: group tuition $7, individual lessons $14, and kids' ponies $5; adults can get four sessions for $23, and there's a school for teenagers for $18 per month (two sessions per week). The Matador Riding Club at the Hippodrome (see below) offers group (Mon–Fri 8am–noon) and individual (Mon–Fri 2–10pm, Sat & Sun

8am–10pm) lessons at similar rates, and a five-session pass for $36 (children $30). At all these clubs it's essential to reserve lessons at least one day in advance.

For a seedier equestrian encounter, attend **horse races** at the **Hippodrome**, Begovaya ul. 22 (☎945 66 11), tram #23 or 15min walk from Dinamo or Begovaya metro. Though merely trotting races, the drunken crowd takes it as seriously as the Kentucky Derby. The racetrack is a grand structure gone to pot, with a bar and betting office beneath the stands. Bets (*stavki*) are placed on pairs (*parniy*) or combinations (*kombinatsiya*) of winners in each race (*zaezd*). From May to September races start at 6pm on Wednesday and 1pm on Saturday and Sunday; in wintertime on Saturday and Sunday at noon.

Alternatively, you can watch flat races on satellite TV and make wagers in comfort at one of Moscow's **betting pubs**, such as the *Horse and Hound* (see p.343).

Ice hockey

Ice hockey is Russia's second most popular sport and Moscow is a major venue on the national and international circuit. Though the season runs from September to April, the highlights of the calendar for many fans are the Spartak Cup in August – a pre-season tournament featuring the Russian All-Stars – and the World Championship in July. The latter is unlikely to be in Russia again for some years as St Petersburg hosted the event in 2000 – when Russia came eleventh. Its poor showing internationally has been matched by the decline of Moscow's hegemony back home. Since the legendary TsKA team split into two clubs in 1997, the RHL "pro" league has been dominated by provincial hotshots Torpedo Yaroslavl and AK Bars of Kazan, and Muscovites' hopes of victory have depended on TsKA's old rivals, Spartak and Dinamo. For a real grudge match, watch TsKA versus its sibling offshoot, HC (Hockey Club) TsKA.

Besides the sports pages of the Moscow Times, you can find details of matches on *www.hockey2000.8k.com*. Other sites include *www.nhl.ru* and *www.eurohockey.com/Russia/* (for general information); the Russian Hockey Federation site *www.fhr.ru* (in Russian only); and the homepages of Dinamo (*www.dynamo.ru*), Spartak (*www.spartak.ru*) and TsKA (*www.cska.ru*).

Dinamo Ice Palace, Leningradskiy pr. 36 ☎221 31 45; near Dinamo metro. Although the team more often plays at Luzhniki, this remains the official home ground of the "blue-and-whites", who are reckoned by many to be Moscow's strongest team.

Krilya Sovetov Ice Palace, ul. Tolbukhina 10/3 ☎448 04 07; train from Belarus Station to the "Setun" stop. Far-flung home ground of the Krilya Sovetov (Soviet Wings) club, which nips at the heels of Spartak and Dinamo.

Luzhniki Sports Palace, Luzhnetskaya nab. 24 ☎213 71 63; 10min walk from Sportivnaya metro, or trolleybus #28 from Park Kultury metro. The home of Spartak (whose fan club is based at Maliy Oleyniy per. 23 ☎964 15 10), also used by Dinamo.

Sokolniki Ice Palace, ul. Sokolnicheskiy val 1b ☎268 69 58; 10min from Sokolniki metro. A frequent venue for outsiders.

TsKA Ice Palace, Leningradskiy pr. 39 ☎213 71 63; 15min from Aeroport or Dinamo metro. Used by both TsKAs, and for major league games and international events.

Marathons and the Relay-Race

Victory Day (May 9) and City Day (last Sun in Sept) both occasion **marathons** which start and finish at Gorky Park, following the Moskva embankment around to the Sparrow Hills before doubling back; the full marathon entails two laps of this circuit. The hills afford the best view of the course, and soon separate the well-trained from the dilettantes. The nearest metro station is Park Kultury.

A more amusing event for spectators is the annual **Police Relay-Race**, when Moscow's Militia, traffic cops and fire brigade field teams which race around the Garden Ring. Starting from Triumfalnaya ploshchad at noon, runners, skiers and dogs carry the baton as far as Krasnye vorota; bikers take over at Pavelets Station; firemen drag hoses over an obstacle course near Park Kultury; policewomen sprint up Zubovskiy bulvar; squad cars manoeuvre outside the US Embassy; and cops in parade uniforms race to the finishing line. The event is usually scheduled for the Sunday nearest Police Day (Oct 24), but may be moved if the weather is bad.

Rollerblading and skateboarding

Rollerblading are **skateboarding** are big among Moscow teens. Favourite spots include Victory Park, Gorky Park, the Sparrow Hills and Dinamo sports complex. The steps of the Lenin statue on Oktyabrskaya pl. are ideal for spins and crashes, while experts risk their necks on the steps leading to the MGU building. You can buy Western and (cheaper) Chinese rollerblades and skateboards in the first-floor sports department of Detskiy Mir (see p.370)

Skating, sledging, skiing and troyka rides

During winter, Russians dig out their ice skates or skis and revel in the snow. There are outdoor **ice-skating** rinks at Gorky, Sokolniki and Izmaylovo parks, and there's a temporary rink on Red Square for a few days either side of New Year. You can rent skates at Gorky Park or Sokolniki for about $1.50 an hour (plus deposit); Sokolniki has the best gear. The ideal temperature for outdoor skating is between −1°C and −8°C.

The steepest hills for **sledging** are at Kolomenskoe (see p.259) and near the ski runs at Krylatskoe, but you needn't go further than the Alexander Gardens beside the Kremlin to find shorter slopes where young children can enjoy themselves.

Although Russia's terrain dictates that cross-country rather than downhill **skiing** is the norm, experts can risk their necks on two ski jumps in the Sparrow Hills (p.224) or make for the popular slopes at Krylatskoe (Krylatskaya metro). The best place for cross-country skiing is **Losiniy Ostrov**, in northeast Moscow, which is named after the elks (*los*) that roam its 110 square kilometres of deciduous and evergreen forest. You can get there from Shcholkovskaya metro, or the Yauza Station on the suburban train line from Yaroslavl Station.

When the snow is deep, riding in a horse-drawn sleigh or ***troyka*** is a romantic option. To experience the thrill of speeding across a snowy wilderness, lash out $60 for an hour's ride at Tsaritsyno (☎343 15 10; see p.268) or Kolomenskoe (☎210 02 94; see p.263). A *troyka* seats four to six adults; bring a bottle.

Soccer

Russia's poor performance abroad in recent years shouldn't deter you from attending a **soccer** match. Moscow's teams embody the best and worst of Russian football, with a history as colourful as any in Europe. Dinamo is Russia's oldest club (founded by British factory managers in 1887) and was sponsored by the secret police in Soviet times – though fans prefer to recall its legendary goalie, Lev Yashin, the hero of postwar Soviet soccer. Their chief rival, TsKA (known abroad as CSKA), was founded as the Red Army team, giving both clubs first call on young players by conscripting them, while Lokomotiv and Torpedo were affiliated to the railway workers and the ZiL auto factory. By contrast, Spartak lacked a powerful institutional base, but was widely popular with Muscovites as a maverick challenger.

In the post-Soviet era, financial crises and organized crime have taken their toll – with schisms in TsKA and the murder of Spartak's director – but there's hope that Russian football has finally turned

Sports, outdoor activities and bathhouses

the corner. Moscow's fans and soccer-mad mayor are certainly happy: in the 2000 championship, not only did Moscow triumph for the fifth time in a row thanks to Spartak, but the capital's supremacy was confirmed by Lokomotiv and Torpedo taking the silver and bronze prizes, while Dinamo and TsKA came fifth and eighth in the league respectively.

Their changing fortunes have been echoed by disruptions in their stadia – with rising violence and an ongoing process of **refurbishment** that has closed one stadium after another, obliging rivals to share the same grounds. The Luzhniki (formerly Lenin) stadium got to host the 1999 UEFA Cup finals following its $200 million refit; TsKA was the next to benefit; and Lokomotiv stadium is now set to be modernized. This makes it difficult to predict where teams will end up playing. Spartak, for instance, is currently playing at Luzhniki and Lokomotiv while its own new stadium is constructed, but the impending closure of Lokomotiv stadium will displace both Spartak and Lokomotiv, putting pressure on other club grounds.

While *Sport Express* has supplanted stodgy old *Sovetskiy Sport* as the paper of choice for Russian fans, foreigners who don't speak the language will find the Internet a better source of **information**. For starters, access the official Russian Football Union site *www.rfs.ru*, or *www.russianfootball.com*, which features a schedule of matches for the year. Club homepages offer more partial coverage: Lokomotiv's (*www.lokomotiv.ru*) and Torpedo's (*www.torpedo.ru*) in Russian; TsKA's (*www.cska.ru*) and Spartak's (*www.spartak.com*) in English. Nearer the time, details may also appear in the *Moscow Times* or *Russia Journal*.

There are two national tournaments, running concurrently. The **Russian Championship** starts in March and ends in November, while the **Russian Cup** starts in the summer and ends in the summer of the following year. Due to the number of teams participating, preliminary rounds for the Russian Cup occur just before the previous year's cup final in May. A third major competition is the indoor **CIS Cup** in January, featuring teams from all the former Soviet republics.

Matches usually begin at 6.30pm. **Tickets** are easy to obtain on the spot and cost between $1 and $10.

Dinamo Stadium, Leningradskiy pr. 36 ☎212 70 92; near Dinamo metro. Dinamo's 12,000-seat home ground is also used for Russian Championship and Cup matches, and features a Dinamo Museum (see p.313).

Luzhniki Stadium, Luzhnetskaya nab. 24 ☎201 03 76 or 201 03 21; 10min walk from Sportivnaya metro, or trolleybus #28 from Park Kultury metro. Moscow's largest stadium (80,000 seats), refurbished to UEFA standards, it hosts Russian Cup and Championship and international matches, and is the home ground of Torpedo, the "black-and-whites".

Lokomotiv Stadium, Bolshaya Cherkizovskaya ul. 125a ☎161 97 04; near Cherkizovskaya metro. This Stalinist stadium decorated with train motifs is set for refurbishment, so Lokomotiv will soon be playing elsewhere. For the latest info check out their Web site in Russian (see above), or enquire by email: *fclm@mail.ru*.

TsKA Stadium, Leningradskiy pr. 39 ☎213 22 88 or 213 65 92; tram #6, #23 or #28 from Dinamo metro. Covered arena used for Russian and CIS Cup and international matches, plus athletics and basketball, sometimes. Home of TsKA, the "red-and-blues".

Sunbathing, swimming and working out

After the long dark winter, Muscovites are keen to go **sunbathing** as soon as the weather allows, stripping down to their underwear on any available patch of grass. The most popular bathing spot is **Serebryaniy bor**, a series of beaches on a bend in the upper reaches of the Moskva River, with the cleanest water within the city limits (which isn't saying that much). See p.314 for details of its amenities (which include nudist and gay beaches) and how to get there.

To go **swimming** in really pure water entails travelling 35km outside Moscow to the **Pirogovskoe Reservoir**, amid a forest. The reservoir can be reached by suburban trains from Leningrad Station to the Pirogovskiy halt; by driving along the M8 and turning left at Mytishchi; or by hydrofoil from the Northern River Terminal (see "Boating") during summer. At other times of the year, **indoor pools** come into their own. All the ones listed below are coupled with **gyms**; the majority can be used by anyone willing to pay a fee, but some require membership. Oddly, it's harder for visitors to use public pools, which insist that bathers show a doctor's letter (*spravka*) certifying that they're in good health.

Pools and gyms

Atlantis Fitness Club, *Mezhdunarodnaya-1 Hotel*, Krasnopresnenskaya nab. 12 ☎937 03 73. Non-residents can use the gym, pool and jacuzzi for $16/$20 on weekdays (before/after 2pm) and $32 at weekends; season tickets from $107; solarium and sauna cost extra; under-12s half-price. Daily 7am–2am (last entry at midnight).

Beach Club, Lenkom Theatre, ul. Malaya Dmitrovka 6 ☎299 73 53; 5min from Chekhovskaya metro. A private gym with solarium and aerobics classes that offers various medium- and long-term membership deals. Mon–Fri 7am–10pm, Sat & Sun 10am–4pm.

Fit & Fun, Chistoprudniy bul. 12, str.1 ☎924 43 15; near Chistye Prudy metro. Private club with several categories of membership. Gym, pool, saunas, jacuzzis, aerobics and aqua-aerobics. Mon–Fri 7am–11pm, Sat & Sun 9am–10pm.

Marco Polo Health Club, *Marco Polo Hotel*, Spiridonevskiy per. 9 ☎202 03 81; 10min from Pushkinskaya metro. Gym $20 an hour; 2hr $38; season ticket $120. Jacuzzi and solarium cost extra. All these facilities are free for hotel guests. Daily noon–midnight.

Olympic Sports Complex, Olimpiyskiy pr. 16 ☎288 15 33; 10min from Prospekt Mira metro. Features an Olympic-sized pool ($8 per hour; $40 per month, in which case a *spravka* is needed), down the road from a gym ($5 per hour) bedecked with Soviet murals. Daily 7am–9pm.

Savoy Health Club, *Savoy Hotel*, ul. Rozhdestvenka 3 ☎929 85 00; near Kuznetskiy Most metro. Small gym and sauna, due to be upgraded soon; massage from $12, depending on which bit you want rubbed. Open daily.

Sports, outdoor activities and bathhouses

Tennis

As a keen **tennis** player, Yeltsin did much to promote the sport in Russia, which became chic in a way that would have been inconceivable in Soviet times – while the photogenic Anna Kournikova raised the country's sporting profile abroad. Although Mayor Luzhkov is also a keen player, it remains to be seen whether the international **Kremlin Cup** tournament will continue to attract top players now that it no longer offers over $1 million in prize money. The ladies' event is held in October and the men's in November, at the indoor Olympic Stadium on Olimpiyskiy prospekt. Tickets cost $2–40. ☎956 33 60; *www.kremlincup.ru* for information.

Unfortunately for visitors who might want to play, many former public courts have become private clubs, and rates have rocketed – not that this bothers its nouveau riche devotees.

Chaika Tennis Courts, Korobeynikov per. 1/2 ☎202 04 74; 10min from Park Kultury metro. Indoor courts, rented by the hour ($29). Daily 7am–11pm.

Dinamo Stadium, Leningradskiy pr. 36 ☎212 73 92; near Dinamo metro. One grass court and eight gravel ones, at around $30 an hour. Daily 6am–midnight.

Druzhba Tennis Courts, Luzhniki Sports Complex ☎201 17 80; Park Kultury metro, then trolleybus #28. Indoor and outdoor courts for rent by the hour, Mon–Fri 8–11am $30, 11am–5pm $27, 5–11pm & Sat & Sun $32. Daily 8am–11pm.

Part 4

Out of the city

Chapter 17

Introduction

Beyond Moscow's outer Ring Road, forests of birch trees or conifers are interspersed by colonies of gaily painted *dachas* – the clapboard cottages where Muscovites relax at weekends or rusticate over summer – juxtaposed with the pretentious villas of the nouveaux riches, and run-down villages where cows roam the

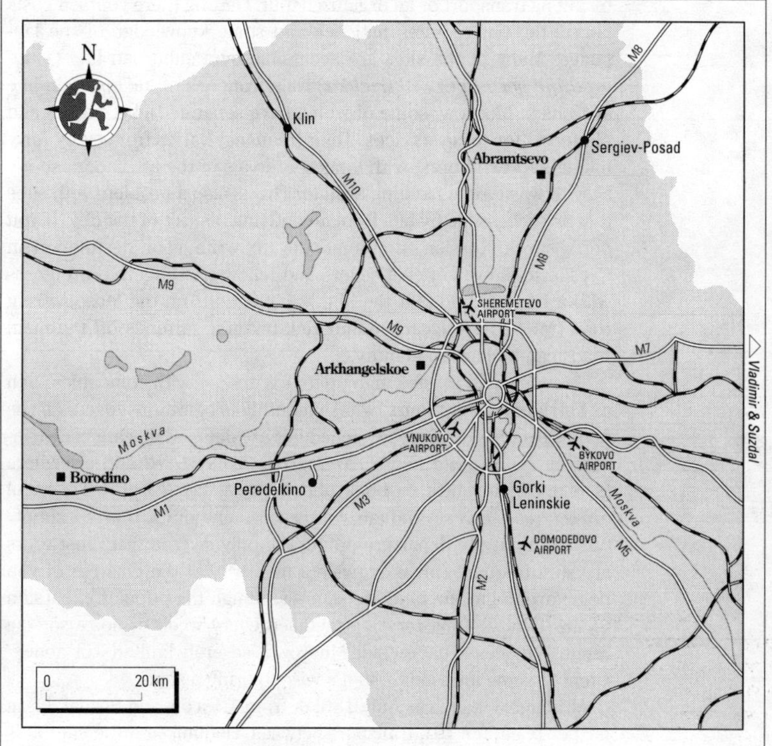

muddy lanes. By venturing **OUT OF THE CITY**, you'll glimpse the vast gulf between Moscow and its ramshackle hinterland, a disparity that underlies the duality of life in Russia and the national psyche – without which, neither can be understood.

Less metaphysically, there's much to enjoy within the city's environs, starting with the magnificent **Trinity Monastery of St Sergei** and the delightful artists' colony of **Abramtsevo**, to the northeast of Moscow. For lovers of Russian music or literature, a visit to Tchaikovsky's home in **Klin** or Pasternak's *dacha* at **Peredelkino** should prove irresistible, while history buffs will be drawn to Lenin's retreat at **Gorki Leninskie**, the former Yusupov estate at **Arkhangelskoe**, or the famous battlefield of **Borodino**, immortalized in Tolstoy's *War and Peace*. Travelling further afield and back in time, there is the enchanting medieval town of **Suzdal** and the neighbouring city of **Vladimir**, which once surpassed Moscow in wealth and power.

Practicalities

It's possible to visit all the places in Chapter 18 as **day-trips**, reached by public transport or an organized tour. Getting there yourself costs very little, but requires patience and some knowledge of the language. Many of the sites are accessible by a suburban line (*prigorodnye poezda* or *elektrichka*) train from one of the big main-line stations in Moscow, some of which have separate ticket offices and platforms for these services. Their frequency varies from every forty minutes to two hours, with longer intervals in the afternoon, so it's easy to waste time hanging around. This is also a problem with sites that are accessible by bus from an outlying district of the city. If you don't speak Russian, get somebody to write your destination in Cyrillic to show to ticket-sellers and fellow passengers. Foreigners with a car will find that the highway junctions on the Moscow ring road (MKAD) are clearly numbered, but side turnings off the main roads can be hard to identify.

To avoid such hassles, sign up for excursions with companies such as Patriarshy Dom Tours, whose monthly programme covers all the main sites outside Moscow. Schedules are detailed in leaflets distributed at the *Starlite Diner*, *American Bar & Grill* and elsewhere (see p.43); it's best to book ahead (☎ & fax 795 09 27; email *alanskaya@co.ru*), though you can usually join a tour by simply turning up at the departure point. The only snag is that most tours are so infrequent (once or twice a month) that the chances of you being around at the time are slim – although the popular excursion to the Trinity Monastery is scheduled every week or so. Also, the range of places to eat outside Moscow is severely limited – or nonexistent at some locations – so it's wise to bring a snack.

Although Vladimir is only 180km from Moscow and Suzdal 35km farther (Chapter 19), transport between Vladimir and the capital is slow enough to make it hard to visit Suzdal as a day-trip unless you hire a car or take an Intourist or Patriarshy Dom excursion, which is unlikely to allow more than a couple of hours sightseeing. If you've got time it's far better to stay **overnight** in Suzdal and imbibe its charms at leisure, sparing an hour or so for the sights of Vladimir as well.

Chapter 18

Day-trips from Moscow

The chief reason to venture to the city's outer reaches is the glorious **Trinity Monastery of St Sergei**, a Kremlin-like citadel better known in the West as "Zagorsk", after the Soviet-era name of the town in which it is located, 75km northeast of Moscow. A bit closer to the capital is the former artists' colony of **Abramtsevo**, a lovely estate, where most of the big names of late nineteenth-century Russian art painted the local landscape and created fairytale buildings that still stand. While both can be enjoyed by anyone, the appeal of the other sites is more particular. If stately homes and parks are your thing, there is the romantic, half-ruinous **Arkhangelskoe** estate, and Lenin's country retreat at **Gorki Leninskie**. Lovers of the arts will be drawn to Tchaikovsky's home in **Klin** or Pasternak's *dacha* in **Peredelkino**; while those into military history can tread the famous battlefield of **Borodino**, and even see the battle re-enacted in September.

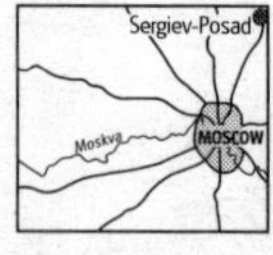

The Trinity Monastery of St Sergei

Of all the monasteries in Russia, none is holier than the **TRINITY MONASTERY OF ST SERGEI** (*Troitse-Sergeeva lavra*), a bastion of Orthodoxy that was a place of pilgrimage for tsars and peasants alike. Even Stalin recognized its spiritual potency by allowing the monastery to reopen in 1946 as a reward for the Church's support in wartime; for decades afterwards it was one of the few surviving vestiges of Holy Russia in an avowedly atheist state.

The monastery is named after **St Sergei of Radonezh** (c.1321–91), who is said to have cried from his mother's womb while in church, refused to consume milk on Wednesdays or meat on Fridays as a baby, and had a vision of a hooded figure who explained the Bible to him as a child. Forsaking a diplomatic career to become a hermit in the forest with his brother, he later urged Prince Dmitry Donskoy to fight the Tatars at Kulikovo, blessing his army as it left

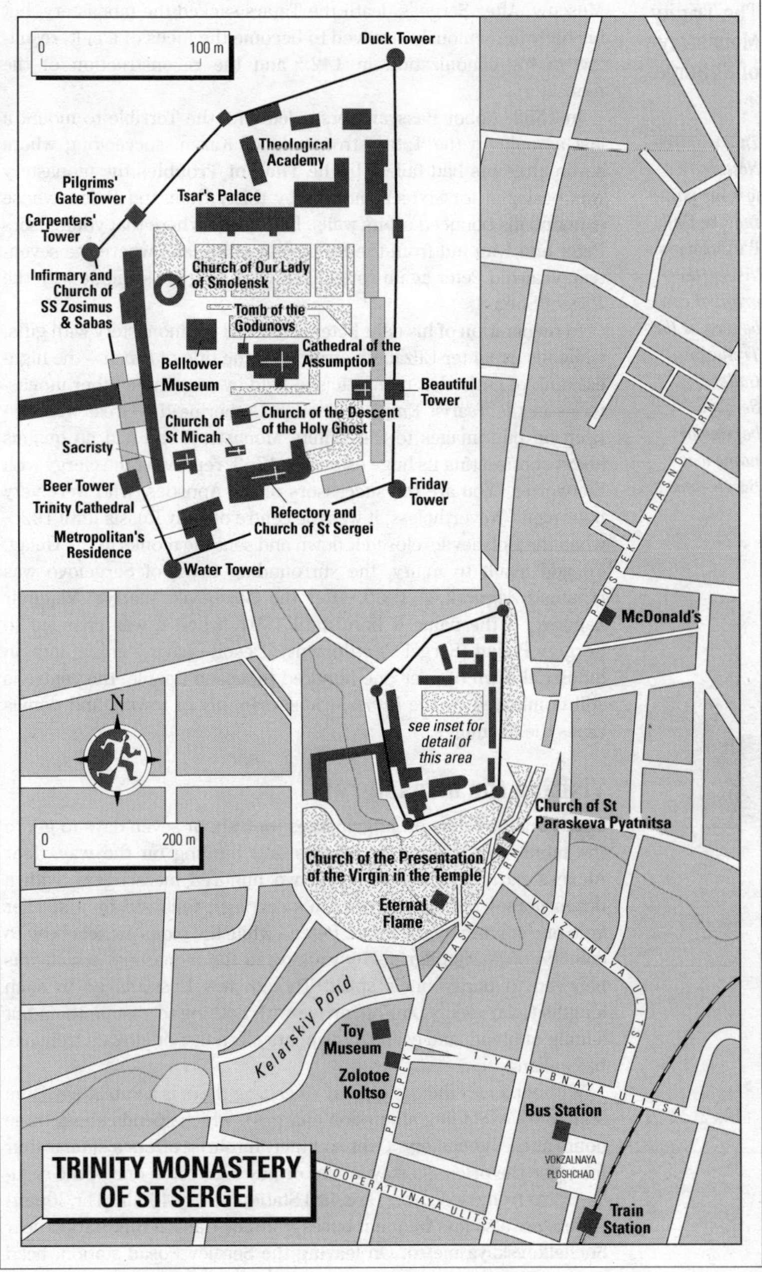
TRINITY MONASTERY
OF ST SERGEI
0
100 m
Duck Tower
Theological
Academy
Pilgrims'
Gate Tower
Tsar's Palace
Carpenters'
Tower
Infirmary and
Church of
SS Zosimus
& Sabas
Church of Our Lady
of Smolensk
Tomb of the
Godunovs
Cathedral of the
Assumption
Belltower
Museum
Beautiful
Tower
Church of
St Micah
Church of the Descent
of the Holy Ghost
Sacristy
Beer Tower
Friday
Tower
Trinity Cathedral
Refectory and
Church of St Sergei
Metropolitan's
Residence
Water Tower
McDonald's
PROSPEKT KRASNOY ARMII
N
see inset for
detail of
this area
0
200 m
Church of St
Paraskeva Pyatnitsa
Church of the Presentation
of the Virgin in the Temple
Eternal
Flame
VOKZALNAYA ULITSA
Kelarskiy Pond
Toy
Museum
Zolotoe
Koltso
1-YA RYBNAYA ULITSA
Bus Station
VOKZALNAYA
PLOSHCHAD
KOOPERATIVNAYA ULITSA
Train
Station

The Trinity Monastery of St Sergei

This inspired Nesterov's famous painting The Child Bartholomew's Vision *(the original can be seen at the Tretyakov Gallery). Sergei's baptismal name was Bartholomew.*

Moscow. After Sergei's death the Tatars sacked the monastery, but his body miraculously survived to become the focus of a cult, resulting in his canonization in 1422 and the reconstruction of the monastery.

In 1552, Abbot Bassyan persuaded Ivan the Terrible to mount a last assault on the Tatar stronghold of Kazan, succeeding where seven attempts had failed. In the **Time of Troubles** the monastery was besieged for sixteen months by thirty thousand Poles, whose cannonballs bounced off its walls. Later, it was here that young tsars Peter and Ivan hid from the Streltsy in 1685; and where the seventeen-year-old Peter again sought refuge during his struggle with the Regent Sofia.

In recognition of his debt Peter showered the monastery with gifts, while his daughter Elizabeth awarded it the title of *lavra* – the highest rank of Orthodox monasticism, held by only three other monasteries in the Tsarist Empire. Though Catherine the Great was also keen on pilgrimages to the Trinity Monastery, she had no qualms about confiscating its huge estates in 1763, reproving the clergy with the words: "You are the successors of the Apostles, who were very poor men." Nevertheless, it was the centre of Holy Russia until 1920, when the Bolsheviks closed it down and sent the monks to the Gulag. To add insult to injury, the surrounding **town** of Sergeiovo was renamed **Zagorsk** in 1930, after the Bolshevik "martyr" Vladimir Zagorsky – the name it bore until 1991, when it was changed to **Sergiev Posad** (Sergei's Settlement). Despite having grown into an industrial town of over one hundred thousand people, the centre is still dominated by the *lavra*, whose panoply of towers and domes rivals the Kremlin's.

Visiting the monastery

Traditionally, rulers on **pilgrimages** took six or seven days to get to the monastery, resting at palaces and hunting on the way. Tsar Alexei's party was preceded by two hundred messengers, with a dozen horses pulling the tsaritsa's carriage, followed by a smaller gold one containing the infant Peter – while the pious Alexei chose to emulate ordinary pilgrims by walking to the monastery, which was believed to purify one's spirit. Though few Russians go to such lengths today, many old folk arrive with nothing to sustain them but a hunk of bread, and even day-trippers often fast or abstain from sex beforehand.

Without a car, the easiest way of getting there is a Patriarshy Dom tour ($30, excluding admission charges), which spends about three hours at the monastery. Over summer, Intourist offers a similar tour for twice the price. To stay longer or pay less, catch one of the regular trains from Moscow's Yaroslavl Station (every 40min; 1hr 30min) – there are also less frequent buses from the Central Bus Station near Shchelkovskaya metro. On leaving the Sergiev Posad station, head

The Trinity Monastery of St Sergei

right across the square and along Vokzalnaya ulitsa to reach the *lavra*.

The monastery is open daily from 8am to 6pm, though its churches are closed to the public at weekends, and the museum and sacristy are closed on Monday. Inside the gate is a kiosk selling photo permits, where tourists with a guide are charged the ruble equivalent of $8; other visitors enter free of charge. You'll need separate tickets to visit the museum and sacristy, and these are sold on the spot; don't feel obliged to do so, however, as neither compares with the monastery itself. Visitors must dress decorously (no shorts), and are forbidden to take photos inside the museums and churches, or smoke in the grounds.

The monastery complex

The monastery is enclosed by brick **walls** a mile in circumference, which replaced the original wooden ramparts in 1540–50 and were doubled in height a century later, when tent-roofed spires were added to six of the twelve towers (as happened to the Kremlin around the same time). A gate in the bronze-mantled **Beautiful Tower** and a tunnel painted with scenes of Sergei creating his hermitage in the wilderness bring you out below the **Gate-Church of St John the Baptist**. Built by the Stroganov boyars in 1693, its terracotta walls, Venetian scallops and gilded domes pale before the glorious buildings ahead, whose harmony belies their "picturesque carelessness of arrangement".

The **Refectory** (*Trapeznaya*), just inside the gates, resembles a gaudy version of the Faceted Palace in the Kremlin, with painted red, orange, pistachio and grey facets, and slender columns entwined in carved vines. Late last century, the British traveller Augustus Hare found four hundred monks dining in its vaulted hall, glittering with gold and "smelling terribly of the cabbage they adore". These days the hall is only used for ceremonies and is often locked.

The cathedrals

Across from the Refectory looms the majestic **Cathedral of the Assumption** (*Uspenskiy sobor*), similar in shape to its namesake in the Kremlin, but with four azure onion domes clustered around a huge gilded one. Begun by Ivan the Terrible to honour the fall of Kazan, it was completed in 1585 by his imbecile son Fyodor – a cat's paw of the regent, Boris Godunov, who succeeded him as tsar. It's indicative of their bad name that the **tomb of the Godunovs** is half-sunk into the ground outside the church, while dozens of Golitsyns, Trubetskoys and other nobles are entombed inside.

Boris Godunov's story is related on p.422.

In the nave, a Tsarist eagle commemorates the moment in 1685 when the Streltsy found Peter's mother and her two sons hiding behind the iconostasis, and were about to kill them when a mutineer shouted "Comrades, not before the altar!", and loyal cavalry arrived to rescue them.

Downhill stands the **Church of the Descent of the Holy Ghost** (*Dykhovskaya tserkov*), whose walls are girdled by a band of intricate fretwork, tapering into a belltower with a blue-and-gold, star-spangled dome. Built by craftsmen from Pskov in 1476–77, it is unusual for having its bells in the base of the tower, which was used as a lookout post in the days when the monastery walls were much lower.

Before the walls were raised in the sixteenth century, the white stone **Trinity Cathedral** (*Troitskiy sobor*), near the southwest corner, was the tallest structure in the monastery. Erected in 1422–23, it pioneered the use of *kokoshniki* – the leitmotif of Muscovite church architecture – and inspired the "gold-topped" Cathedral of the Assumption in the Kremlin. The nave is astir with believers queuing up to kiss a silver shrine containing the **relics of St Sergei**, and tourists jostling to see the **iconostasis**, three rows of which were painted by Andrei Rublev, Daniil Cherny and their artel. The copy of the *Old Testament Trinity* that replaces the original (now in the Tretyakov Gallery) was donated to the monastery by Ivan the Terrible. In the southeast corner is the Chapel of St Nikon, built over the tomb of Sergei's successor, Nikon of Radonezh.

Behind the cathedral is an eighteenth-century Metropolitan's Residence that served as the home of the Patriarch of All Russia from 1946 until 1988, when the Danilov Monastery (p.258) became the Patriarchal seat.

Chapels, towers and museums

Between the cathedrals, you can't miss the small octagonal **Chapel over the Well** (*Nakladeznaya chasovnya*), whose pillars and *nalichniki* are carved with flowers and vines, offset by blue arabesques and white seraphim. The chapel was built over a spring discovered by the monks in 1644, and today its interior (daily 8.30am–5pm) is packed with people filling bottles with holy water, and murals of divine miracles. You can also drink from a fountain beneath a pillared **pavilion**, outside.

Building continued into the late eighteenth century, when Prince Ukhtomsky erected an 88-metre **Belltower** (*Kolokolnitsa*), whose five turquoise-and-white tiers are equal in height to the surrounding churches, and which once boasted fifty bells. Ukhtomsky also built the rounded Baroque **Church of Our Lady of Smolensk**, with its pilastered facade and gold finial, to house an icon of the same name. Off to the left stand the former **Infirmary** and **Church of SS Zosimus and Sabas**, dating from the 1630s; this church is the only one in the monastery with a tent-roofed spire.

En route to SS Zosimus and Sabas you'll pass the ticket office for the **History Museum** (Tues–Thurs, Sat & Sun 10am–6pm; closed the last Tues of each month; $5). The best of the many icons on the ground floor is Simon Ushakov's *Venerable Nikon of Radonezh*, painted in the 1670s. Upstairs is more interesting, with two English coaches belonging to former metropolitans; some arresting royal portraits (notice Peter's first wife Yevdokiya to the right as you enter); and a surfeit of gold plate, pearl-encrusted mitres and robes. More of the same can be seen in the monastery's **sacristy** (*riznitsa*), now described as an **Art Museum** (Tues–Sun 10am–6pm; closed the last Wed of each month; $5).

From June to August, visitors can enjoy exploring the **ramparts** between the **Beer Tower** and the **Carpenters' Tower** – except on Tuesdays and Wednesdays. Otherwise, bear right at the green-spired **Pilgrims' Gate Tower** to reach the former **Tsar's Palace** (*Tsarskie Chertogi*). Constructed in the late seventeenth century for Tsar Alexei and his entourage of 500, its elongated facade is patterned with red-and-mauve facets and crested *nalichniki*. It is now a seminary, which includes an offshoot for young women bent on marrying priests, where they're taught housekeeping. The ceiling of the main hall bears a fresco of the triumphs of Peter the Great, who, while sheltering here in 1685, relaxed by shooting fowl from what was henceforth called the **Duck Tower**, and decorated with a bronze duck.

Other sights

The square outside the monastery hosts a lively market in religious artefacts and handicrafts. Off to the right downhill are the gold-domed **Church of St Paraskeva Pyatnitsa** – dedicated to the "Friday Saint" revered in Orthodox countries – and the **Church of the Presentation of the Virgin in the Temple**, likewise built in 1547. Further along, past an **Eternal Flame** to the dead of World War II, the **Kelarskiy Pond** is rimmed by garden walls, offering splendid views of the monastery, and frequented by artists in summer. On the far side of the pond, in a red-brick edifice at pr. Krasnoy Armii 15, the **Toy Museum** (Wed–Sun 10am–5pm; closed the last Fri of each month; $0.30) boasts a fine collection of historic toys. It was a local artist who invented the ubiquitous matyroshka doll, and there's still a tradition of toy making in the town. You can buy all kinds in the market or the souvenir section of the museum.

If you're feeling hungry at this point, there's the seedy *Zolotoe Koltso* **restaurant** near the Toy Museum, or a *McDonald's* at prospekt Krasnoy Armii 194.

Abramtsevo

If the Trinity Monastery redeemed Russia's soul in medieval times, the **ABRAMTSEVO** estate helped define it during the nineteenth century, when disputes between Slavophiles and Westernizers dominated cultural life. Indeed, Abramtsevo was acquired by the devout Slavophile writer Aksakov because of its proximity to the *lavra*, which made it an apt meeting place for like-minded, devoutly Orthodox intellectuals. The estate's next owner, the millionaire Mamontov, was equally passionate about Russian culture, supporting an **artists' colony** that gave rise to Russia's modern art movement. Many of the works in the Tretyakov Gallery – by Repin, Serov, Vrubel and the Vasnetsov brothers – reflect their shared interest in medieval architecture, folk art and mythology – as do the fairytale buildings on the Abramtsevo estate, whose rolling woodlands have been depicted on canvas more than any other landscape in Russia. And on a humbler but more pervasive note, it was at their Children's Education Workshop that Sergei Malyutin produced the first matryoshka doll, in 1890.

Practicalities

Abramtsevo lies about 6km south of Sergiev Posad; the turn-off is clearly signposted. By **car**, follow the road to Khotkovo and bear left before a half-derelict convent. En route to the estate you'll pass a big pond; the entrance to the grounds is further uphill. Not all of the **trains** from Yaroslavl Station to Sergiev Posad stop at Abramtsevo en route, so be sure to ask; from the station, it's a pleasant twenty-minute country walk to the estate. Alternatively, you might be lucky enough to be around when Patriarshy Dom schedules a **tour** to Abramtsevo in conjunction with the Trinity Monastery ($30, excluding admission charges to both sites).

To avoid a wasted journey, phone ahead (☎8/254 32470) to verify the **opening hours** (Wed & Thurs 10am–7pm). **Guided tours** in English ($6) can be arranged in advance. Individual **tickets** are required for the main house ($0.50) and each of the outbuildings ($0.20). The charm of the **estate** is best appreciated by wandering around the outbuildings constructed by the artists, which lead you away from the main house. Summer or autumn are the best times to visit.

The main house

Knowing that Chekhov used the main **house** as a model for the manor in his play *The Cherry Orchard* raises your expectations of the plain, grey-and-white clapboard building. The interior (which can still be visited) is a vivid reflection of its former owners: **Sergei Aksakov** (1791–1859) was a friend of Gogol (who wrote part of *Dead Souls* here) and a foe of Westernizers such as Herzen, who mocked him for wearing "a dress so national that people in the street took him for a Persian". In 1870, the house was bought by the railroad tycoon **Savva Mamontov** (1841–1918) and his wife Elizabeth, who vowed to continue its traditions and preserved half of the house as Aksakov had left it – hence the different decors in each wing. While the Slavophile Aksakov shared the mid-nineteenth-century gentry's taste for French Empire, the worldlier Mamontovs preferred Neo-Russian and Style Moderne.

Across the way is a larger white building housing an **exhibition** of modernist paintings by Aristakh Lentulov, Robert Falk and other artists of the Soviet era who also worked at Abramtsevo, with graphics such as Alimov's illustrations for *Dead Souls* and *The Master and Margarita* upstairs.

The outbuildings

More alluring is the tiny wooden **studio**, with its fretwork roof, where the painters Serov and Vrubel tried their hands at ceramics. The small Egyptian and Russian figures on display here presage Vrubel's bas-relief for the *Metropol Hotel* in Moscow, while the tiled stove epitomizes the colony's interest in old Russian applied arts. Peasant crafts were a major source of inspiration: the kitchen now displays part of their collection of artefacts (including cake moulds and ironing boards) as a **Museum of Folk Art**.

Their vision of an ideal cottage was realized in the **Teremok**, or guest house, whose steep roof and gable call to mind the *podvore* of medieval Muscovy. It is furnished with heavy, carved furniture, like the Mamontovs' section of the main house. Further into the woods you'll come upon the **House on Chicken Legs**, built by the Vasnetsov brothers for the estate's children to play in. A tiny hut on chunky stilts, the house is based on the fairytale cottage of Baba Yaga, which shuffled around to face trespassing kids who uttered the words "*Izbushka, izbushka, povernis k mne peredom, a k lesy zadom*" ("Little House, Little House, turn around to face me with your back to the woods") – just before she flew out and threatened to eat them.

The whole colony collaborated on the **Church of the Saviour Not Made by Human Hand**, a diminutive structure based on medieval churches at Novgorod, whose strong lines and whitewashed walls are softened by curvaceous ogees and tiled friezes. The icons were painted by Repin, Polonev, Nesterov and Apollinarius Vasnetsov, whose brother Viktor designed and laid the mosaic floor in the form of a spreading flower, while Vrubel made the tiled stove, and the pulpit was painted by Andrei Mamontov, who died as a child and was buried in a vault to the left of the nave.

The woods beyond are a quintessentially Russian mixture of birch, fir, oak, larch, elder and hazel, with sedge creeks and ponds marking the course of the Vorya River.

Arkhangelskoe

During the heyday of the Russian aristocracy in the late eighteenth and early nineteenth centuries, the epicurean ideal of enjoying life to the hilt reached its apotheosis at **ARKHANGELSKOE**, the suburban estate of **Prince Nikolai Yusupov** (1751–1831). So rich that he was unable to count all his properties without the aid of a notebook,

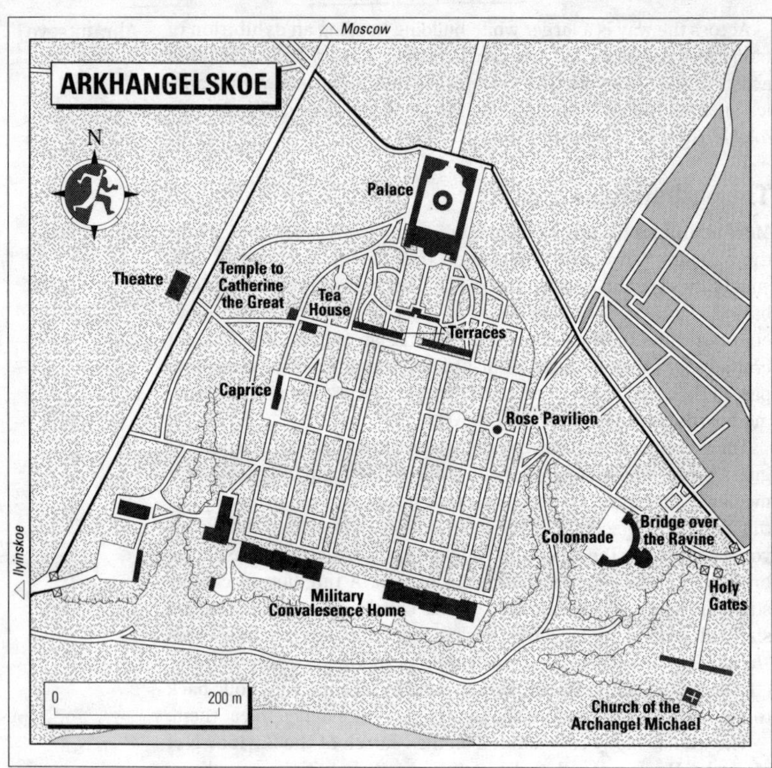

Yusupov collected art, dabbled in science, discussed philosophy with Voltaire and poetry with Pushkin, and kept a harem at Arkhangelsoe. Herzen recalls the 80-year-old Prince "sitting in splendour, surrounded by beauty in marble and colour, and also in flesh and blood". He opened his art collection and grounds to the public, but his private theatrical performances reputedly included nude dancing.

Arkhangelskoe's allure for visitors has waned since the palace was closed for repairs in 1989, and its appeal now lies mainly in the beauty of the park, dotted with pavilions and statues – best seen in summer, when its roses are blooming; in winter, the statues are encased in boxes to prevent them from cracking in the cold. However, the museum's new director is determined to advance Arkhangelskoe's restoration and display some of its art collection once again – so don't be surprised to find changes in the future.

Practicalities

There are no organized excursions to Arkhangelskoe, so you'll need to take the metro to Tushkinskaya station, then find the stop for

#549 buses (at roughly five past, half-past and a quarter to each hour), or #T-151 or #T-159 minibuses, which take thirty minutes to reach the "Sanatorium" stop. To get there by car, drive out along the Volokolamskoe shosse (M9) and turn left onto the Ilyinskoe shosse, a few miles past the Moscow ring road.

Arkhangel-skoe

Official **opening hours** (Tues–Sun 10am–5pm; closed the last Fri of each month; $1) seem to be honoured more in the breach than the observance – in practice you can slip through a hole in the fence and wander around any day of the week.

Around the estate

Although the estate dates back to the 1670s, its features recall the era of Catherine the Great, who put Prince Nikolai Golitsyn in charge of the building project. When Golitsyn died in 1809, his heirs sold the estate to Yusupov, who continued with the project undaunted by a serf riot in 1812 and a fire in 1820. Embodying five decades of Neoclassical architecture and interior design, the palace and pavilions were near to completion when Yusupov himself died in 1831, whereupon the estate was neglected until the early years of this century, when it had a brief revival. In 1919, the Bolsheviks decreed Arkhangelskoe a public museum; a convalescence home was built in the grounds after World War II.

Today, the **palace** is fenced off while restoration work drags on, allowing only glimpses of its inner courtyard, flanked by Ionic-pillared arcades, and shutters prevent even a peek into the rooms, which were fabulously decorated and hung with paintings by Tiepolo, Van Dyck and Boucher; one was filled with portraits of Yusupov's mistresses and lovers.

Two **terraces** topped with Neoclassical busts and urns descend to a formal garden stretching towards the river, with grape arbours running the length of its parterre and derelict pavilions on either side. Whereas the **Rose Pavilion** was meant to be purely decorative, the two-storey **Caprice** was furnished like a miniature palace for garden soirées, and the **Tea House** started out as a library pavilion. Further north stands a small **Temple to Catherine the Great** – who is sculpted in bronze as Themis, goddess of justice – while across the road that has been cut through the estate you'll see the **theatre** built for Yusupov's troupe of serf actors.

At the far end of the parterre looms an enormous Palladian-style **Military Convalescence Home** that's easily mistaken for the palace at first sight. Fans of Stalinist decor will adore its marbled foyers, carpeted in red and hung with inspirational war paintings, but keep a lookout for the *babushka* on duty. No one will mind, however, if you just linger on the terrace outside, with its sweeping **views** of the gardens and the Moskva River, which resembles a lake at this point.

The rest of the park is landscaped in true Italian fashion, with romantic follies. To honour their ancestor, the later Yusupovs had the architect Roman Klein build an imposing rose granite and limestone temple with curved wings, intended to be the family mausoleum but never used as such due to the Revolution. Now signposted as the "**Colonnade**", it is a venue for art exhibitions, plus concerts of classical music some evenings in June, July and August. Further along, the older, Gothic-style **Bridge over the Ravine** is followed by the Corinthian-columned **Holy Gates**, framing the path to the **Church of the Archangel Michael**. A tiny whitewashed edifice with a shingled dome atop a pyramid of *kokoshniki*, the church was built as early as 1667, and subsequently gave its name to the estate. The white stone grave outside is reputedly that of a Yusupov daughter who flung herself off a cliff after being denied permission to marry her beloved.

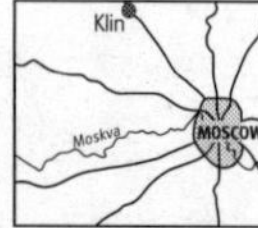

Klin

By the mid-fourteenth century, the Grand Duchy of Muscovy encompassed a ring of towns straddling the rivers that were Russia's chief lines of communication. **KLIN** was founded on the banks of the Sestra (a tributary of the Volga) in 1318, with a Kremlin as its nucleus. As an overland route to Novgorod (and later St Petersburg) grew, Klin became more of a stopover than an *entrepôt*, and eventually found favour with Tchaikovsky, who had spent his summers in the region since 1885, avowing: "I can't imagine myself living anywhere else. I find no words to express how much I feel the charm of the Russian countryside, the Russian landscape and the quiet that I need more than anything else."

Today, he would turn in his grave at the town, with its suburbs of wooden hovels interspersed with the crenellated *kottezhi* of local Mafiosi. There isn't much in the way of sights, but Tchaikovsky lovers can visit his former residence on a Patriarshy Dom excursion ($20) if **getting there** by train from Leningrad Station (1hr 15min), and then a fifteen-minute ride on bus #5 or #14 within Klin, sounds problematic. Travelling by car, Klin is about 80km from Moscow on the Leningradskoe shosse (M10); both the town and the museum are well signposted.

Tchaikovsky's house

A few years before his death in 1893, Tchaikovsky rented a house in the woods below town, telling his brother Modeste, "What a blessing it is to know that no one will come, no one will interrupt neither work, reading nor strolling" – before writing *The Sleeping Beauty*, *The Nutcracker Suite* and his Fifth and Sixth symphonies. At his death, Modeste inherited the house and converted it into a **Tchaikovsky Museum** (Mon, Tues & Fri–Sun 10am–5pm; closed the last Mon of each month; $2), which has been preserved ever since –

surviving the Bolshevik Revolution and World War II (when the Nazis stored fuel and parked motorbikes in the drawing room) – but is slowly succumbing to post-Soviet decline.

Klin

Painted a soft blue-grey with a white trim, the house has a veranda opening onto the back garden, where Tchaikovsky strolled with his dogs. The interior is warm and cosy, with flesh-toned stucco or wood-panelled walls hung with portraits of composers and relatives. On the composer's birthday, May 7, the winners of the international Tchaikovsky Competition have the honour of playing his **grand piano** in the sitting room where he wrote his Sixth Symphony. While the library, with its jigsaw ceiling, verges on baronial grandeur, the bedroom is simple and homely, with his slippers placed beside the bed. In 1964 a concert hall was built in the grounds, where visitors can hear recordings and watch films about the composer.

To check that the Tchaikovsky Museum is open ☎539 816 96.

Peredelkino

Southwest of Moscow the forested countryside harbours numerous *dacha* colonies, including the famous writers' village of **PEREDELKINO**, where Boris Pasternak is buried. In the Brezhnev era a visit to Pasternak's grave on the anniversary of his death (May 30) was a kind of rite of passage for the Muscovite intelligentsia, while foreign journalists found weekend house parties at Peredelkino the best source of gossip about the Kremlin and Moscow's cultural life. Today, Peredelkino signifies less, if only because its best-known living residents have either left or are now regarded as has-beens – except for the Orthodox Patriarch Alexei II, who has a villa here. In 1990, after decades of official hostility towards the writer and his memory, Pasternak's *dacha* was opened as a museum, ensuring his place in the literary firmament.

As with other sites, a Patriarshy Dom excursion ($18) will save you the trouble of **getting there** by Kaluga II line *elektrichka* from Kiev Station (20min), or driving out along the Minskoe shosse (M1) and turning left at the 21km marker. As a sign of how prosperous Peredelkino has become, there is now an Italian **restaurant** and a cosy **hotel** with a sauna, called the *Villa Peredelkino* (☎435 83 45; fax 435 14 78; ③), on 1-ya Chobotovskaya alleya. The surrounding woods are great for nature rambles or cross-country **skiing** – skis can be rented from the hotel.

Pasternak's dacha

Pasternak's dacha (Thurs–Sun 10am–4pm; $1), at ulitsa Pavlenko 3, is hard to locate without asking locals for directions (*Izviníte, pozhálsta, kak praíti k dómu Pasternáka?*). Painted dark brown with a white trim, its main feature is an oblong veranda wing covered by windows that juts into the garden. Built by his artist father Leonid in 1937, the house became Pasternak's refuge after he was forced to decline the Nobel Prize for Literature that he was due to receive for his novel *Doctor Zhivago* in 1953. Vilified by the Soviet media and the Writers' Union, Pasternak spent his final years gardening, writing poetry and entertaining friends at the *dacha*, where he died of lung cancer in 1960 at the age of seventy.

The **dining room** is filled with sketches and portraits by his father, including a large oil painting of Tolstoy, a family friend. It also contains Pasternak's collection of Georgian ceramics and a huge television set that he never watched, preferring to hear news only from visitors. His favourite place was the glassed-in **veranda**, with its wicker furniture and antique samovar. Notice the bucket filled with glass clubs, a "winter bouquet" given as a gift by a crystal factory. Visitors are led upstairs to his **study-bedroom**, covering most of the top floor. His coat and boots are where he last placed them, next to a bookshelf lined with Russian encyclopedias and novels by Virginia Woolf in English. Pasternak knew the language well, having translated Shakespeare into Russian during the Terror years, when translations were a safer way of earning a living than writing poetry or novels.

The village **cemetery** (*kladbische*) where Pasternak is buried can be found by walking up the road from the train station to the church at the top of the hill, and then following the path to the left. **Pasternak's grave** lies beside those of four other members of the family, in a pine grove. His headstone – bearing his signature and a faint portrait – is always laid with flowers by admirers. The bells of the nearby **Church of the Transfiguration** toll at 6pm.

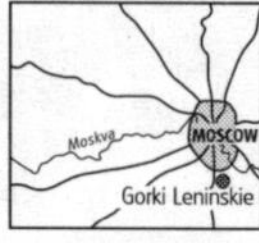

Gorki Leninskie

South of Moscow the country estate of **GORKI LENINSKIE**, where Lenin died, used to be a place of pilgrimage for the faithful, employing two hundred guides to handle the busloads of visitors. Attendances plummeted after the fall of Communism, and the estate-museum's future looked seriously doubtful for some years, but the threat of closure has now receded, leaving it as a fascinating example of the kind of idolatry that was ubiquitous in Soviet times but is almost extinct in Russia today – and as a repository for unwanted Lenin memorabilia from the Kremlin.

Practicalities

As the estate is 32km south of the Kremlin, it's worth taking a Patriarshy Dom excursion ($20) to avoid the hassle of **getting there** by public transport. This involves taking the metro to Domodedovskaya station and then a twenty-minute journey on bus #439, leaving every half hour; ask to be dropped at the Gorki Leninskie stop, right outside the estate. There are buses back to Moscow till about 4pm.

To get there by car, take the Kashirskoe shosse (M4); 15km beyond the Moscow ring road, the turn-off is indicated by a small sign 200m before the bronze statue of Lenin that strides away from the gates of another (locked) entrance to the grounds. Although it's wise to phone (☎548 93 09) to check, the estate should be open from 9am to 4pm, except on Tuesdays and the last Monday of each month.

Gorki Leninskie

There are separate **admission charges** for the museum ($0.30), the mansion ($0.70) and Lenin's quarters in the Kremlin ($0.70).

The museum

In sight of the gates is a monstrously ugly block with a quasi-pharaonic portico, containing the last Lenin Museum opened in the USSR (in 1987), now blandly entitled the **Museum of the Political History of Russia and the Beginning of the Twentieth Century**. Built of black and white marble and furnished with bronze fittings and ruched curtains, its opulence would have appalled Lenin. Visitors are greeted at the top of the stairs by a giant effigy of the leader, seated against a billowing scarlet backdrop in an enclosure paved with cobblestones taken from Moscow's "Red" Presnya district, hallowed for its part in the 1905 and 1917 revolutions.

With its auto-controlled tedious video-montages accompanied by portentous music, the exhibition manages to be dull despite its technical wizardry. As the guide's spiel (in Russian) is of post-glasnost vintage, visitors who ask probing questions are rewarded with the sight of some pages from Lenin's Testament (see below), and told that the attempt to assassinate him in August 1918 may not have been carried out by Fanya Kaplan, the Left SR who was executed for the deed. The attack left Lenin with a bullet lodged in his body and led to his first period of convalescence at Gorki (as it was then called), where he later suffered a series of incapacitating strokes.

The mansion

The real attraction is the elegant yellow-and-white stucco **mansion**, ten minutes' walk through the forest of blue firs. Previously owned by the Borodino hero General Pisarov and Zinaidia Morozova, the widow of Savva Morozov (p.178), the estate was expropriated in 1918 to become a sanatorium for Party leaders. Lenin only agreed to convalesce there because it had a phone line to Moscow – a vital consideration during the Civil War.

Initially Lenin resided with his wife Krupskaya in the small, detached **northern wing**, above his doctors and bodyguards on the floor below. They shared their meals in a dining room with walnut furniture in striped dust covers, where his sister Maria (a *Pravda* journalist) often slept. Their austere separate bedrooms were softened only by wolfskin rugs; the largest room, with a tiled stove, was reserved for guests such

Gorki Leninskie

as Lenin's other siblings, Dmitry and Anna, who lived here after his death. Lenin was moved into the main house after a stroke in May 1922 left him half-paralyzed, temporarily unable to speak, and suicidal. Though he recovered enough to return to work, a second stroke that year enabled Stalin to isolate him from events, and a third left him speechless for the last ten months of his life.

Entering the **main house** via its glassed-in veranda, you'll see a telephone room with three direct lines to the Kremlin, off a hallway where the clock has been stopped at the moment of Lenin's death, and his jacket, boots and hunting gear are preserved in glass cases. The **library** contains four thousand books (Lenin had a working knowledge of nine foreign languages) and a desk set carved with worker and peasant figures, made for the first VDNKh. Next door is a sunny, palmy **conservatory** with a projector for showing silent films and a piano for sing-songs in the evening. Notice the flies embroidered on the curtains, and the special mechanized wheelchair at the foot of the stairs. A gift from factory workers, they never knew that he was paralyzed on his right side and made the wheelchair's controls right-handed, so it was never used.

Upstairs, the dining room displays a large map of Germany, in expectation of the next outbreak of revolution in Europe. While he was still able, Lenin worked in a pretty **study-bedroom**, dictating by phone to a stenographer next door. His secretaries secretly divulged all to Stalin, including Lenin's so-called Testament (written over New Year 1923), which advised dismissing Stalin from the post of General Secretary. After Lenin's death, Stalin brushed it aside as the delusion of "a sick man surrounded by womenfolk", and the postscript was suppressed.

Lenin's funerary train can be seen near Pavelets Station in Moscow (p.252).

Lenin's final hours on January 21, 1924, were spent in a small, gilded room, where he expired shortly before 7pm. His body was laid out in the **salon**, whose mirrors and chandeliers were draped in black according to Russian custom, while the sculptor Merkurov made a death mask and casts of Lenin's hands (the right one clenched into a fist). Next day, his coffin was taken to Moscow by train. Visitors can peer into a shrouded aperture to see a life-sized photo of the body, surrounded by wreaths. In contrast, the last room you enter is richly decorated and crammed with porcelain objects, as it was when inhabited by Morozova.

Following that, you're taken to the garage to view **Lenin's Rolls Royce**. One of two expropriated Rolls Royces used by the Soviet leader, this vehicle was fitted with caterpillar tracks and skis for travelling across country in winter, and converted to run on pure alcohol, which was easier to obtain than petrol during the Civil War. Large enough to seat six bodyguards, it had a top speed of forty kilometres an hour.

To complete the feast of Leninalia, an outbuilding contains a reconstruction of **Lenin's quarters in the Kremlin**, which existed in

Gorki Leninskie

the Senate Palace until Yeltsin had the contents packed off to Gorki Leninskie in 1998. Visitors can feel a frisson at the sight of Lenin's desk with its famous statuette of a monkey pondering a human skull (a gift from Armand Hammer), and wall-maps that place Russia at the centre of the world Revolution. Next door is a mock-up of the simple kitchen where he and Krupskaya ate in their spartan quarters – and guides can point you in the direction of a **statue** of Lenin that formerly sat in the grounds of the Kremlin.

Borodino

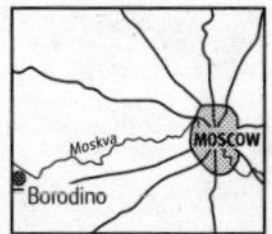

The furthest place of interest within day-trip range of Moscow is **BORODINO**, the site of the bloodiest battle of the Patriotic War. On August 26 (September 7 by today's calendar), 1812, Napoleon's *Grande Armée* of 135,000 men and 600 cannons fought a 121,000-strong Russian host led by Mikhail Kutuzov. In fifteen hours the Russians lost 40,000 men and the French 30,000; Napoleon considered it the "most terrible" of all his battles. Though the Russians withdrew the next day – allowing the French to claim victory and continue advancing – Kutuzov's decision to sacrifice Moscow to preserve his army, and to burn the city to deny the French shelter, was vindicated by events – so Russians see Borodino as a defeat for the French.

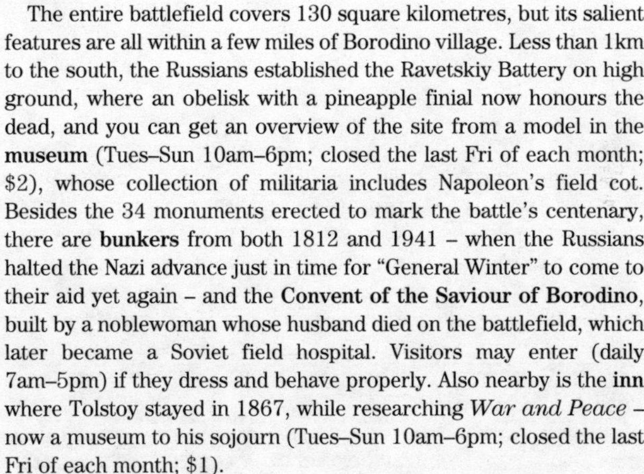

The entire battlefield covers 130 square kilometres, but its salient features are all within a few miles of Borodino village. Less than 1km to the south, the Russians established the Ravetskiy Battery on high ground, where an obelisk with a pineapple finial now honours the dead, and you can get an overview of the site from a model in the **museum** (Tues–Sun 10am–6pm; closed the last Fri of each month; $2), whose collection of militaria includes Napoleon's field cot. Besides the 34 monuments erected to mark the battle's centenary, there are **bunkers** from both 1812 and 1941 – when the Russians halted the Nazi advance just in time for "General Winter" to come to their aid yet again – and the **Convent of the Saviour of Borodino**, built by a noblewoman whose husband died on the battlefield, which later became a Soviet field hospital. Visitors may enter (daily 7am–5pm) if they dress and behave properly. Also nearby is the **inn** where Tolstoy stayed in 1867, while researching *War and Peace* – now a museum to his sojourn (Tues–Sun 10am–6pm; closed the last Fri of each month; $1).

A scaled-down **re-enaction of the battle** occurs every year on the first Sunday of September, starting at noon, when hundreds of military enthusiasts in period costume mount cavalry charges, skirmish with muskets and fire cannons. After two hours the field is obscured by smoke, and solemn music rises from the loudspeakers as a voice intones the names of the Russian regiments, to a chorus of *Vechnaya Slava!* (Immortal Glory!). If you enjoy such spectacles, this is definitely the occasion to visit Borodino. The event kicks off with a religious service by the Ravetskiy Battery.

Borodino is 129km west of Moscow, on the main road (M1) to Minsk; hourly trains from Belarus Station in Moscow take about two hours to get there. Alternatively, you can sign up for Patriarshy Dom's excursion ($38), run on the anniversary day only.

Places

Abramtsevo	Абрамцево
Arkhangelskoe	Архангельское
Borodino	Бородино
Gorki Leninskie	Горки Ленинские
Khotovo	Хотово
Klin	Клин
Peredelkino	Переделкино
Sergiev Posad	Сергиев Посад

Chapter 19

Vladimir and Suzdal

In the heyday of Intourist and the USSR, coach loads of foreign tourists circled the "Golden Ring" of historic towns to the north-east of Moscow, trying to get their tongues around such names as Yaroslavl and Pereslavl-Zalesskiy. Today, relatively few groups venture out beyond Sergiev Posad, and those that do focus almost exclusively on **Vladimir** (pronounced "Vla-*dee*-mir") and **Suzdal** ("Suz-dahl") – two ancient settlements that once surpassed Moscow in importance. Vladimir is an industrial city that doesn't rate a visit on its own, but is an essential staging post for Suzdal – a real gem of a place that's ideal for chilling out after the stress of Moscow.

The two are historically linked as the nexus of a northern Russian polity that arose as the Kievan Rus crumbled due to dissension and invasions, and peasants and boyars abandoned the Dneiper basin for the security of the *zalesskiy* region of the upper Volga, whose fertile soil, abundant timber, stone and waterways provided the essentials for towns and trade to develop – the same conditions that later favoured Moscow as the nucleus of the future Russian state.

Vladimir

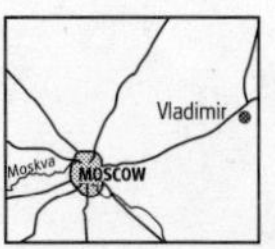

Had it not been for the Mongols who devastated the city in 1238, **VLADIMIR** might be Russia's capital and Moscow a mere provincial town – Vladimir having risen so high and contributed so much to Russian culture within a few generations. Its sublime **cathedrals** are among the few surviving from the time before the Mongol invasion, which inspired Russian architecture and art for centuries to come – and the reason why Vladimir deserves any attention. Although factories and freight yards mar the panorama above the Klyazma River, it is sufficiently grand to make you wonder what Vladimir looked like in its glory days.

Founded in 1108 by Prince Vladimir of Kiev, it became a power base for his son Yuri Dolgoruky (the founder of Moscow), and even more so for Dolgoruky's son, who made Vladimir his capital in 1169. Despite being called "the God-loving", **Andrei Bogolyubsky** (1157–1174) stole a holy icon to enshrine it in Vladimir, warred with Kiev and Novgorod and was so hated that his own wife joined in his murder, which caused universal rejoicing – yet he left his successors a mighty principality and a city whose churches and gates gleamed with gold and silver. Its heyday lasted seven decades, until a 150,000-strong Mongol horde under Genghis Khan's grandson Batu besieged the city and massacred its inhabitants. Although Vladimir rose again, its power inexorably ebbed towards Moscow, the future capital.

The sights

Arriving at the train station, you can see the gilded domes of Vladimir's cathedrals rising from a ridge that was once enclosed by ramparts over four miles long. A steep lane behind the bus terminal leads up to the lower end of Bolshaya Moskovskaya ulitsa – the main street running uphill towards the centre. If you're not pushed for time, it's worth walking around the walls of the old **Monastery of the Nativity** that used to be part of the city's defences and still provides a fine view of the river; otherwise, catch a bus (#20, #52) or trolleybus (#1, #4 or #5) or keep on walking up towards Sobornaya ploshchad, where two magnificent cathedrals stand in a wooded park.

The **Cathedral of the Assumption** (*Uspenskiy sobor*) would be easily recognizable as the model for its namesake in the Kremlin were it not for a colossal belltower erected in the nineteenth century, whose fussy Neo-Medievalism jars with the majestic simplicity of the cathedral. Constructed between 1158 and 1160 by "master craftsmen from all countries" hired by Prince Bogolyubsky, it was damaged by fire and rebuilt in the 1180s, by which time the Russians were skilled enough to dispense with foreign experts and enlarge the cathedral by raising three new outer walls and broadening the altar apse to support a configuration of five domes instead of the original three.

Its **exterior** is notable for its Romanesque appearance, with blind arcades of pilasters that create a "drooping" effect around the apses and drums of the cupolas, echoed by the curves of the windows and gilt-frilled gables. Scholars disagree over the extent to which these forms owed to German, Polish or Byzantine influences or to Russian inventiveness. Symbolically, the cathedral expressed Bogolyubsky's ambition to unify the Russian princedoms, since the Assumption is the name given to the time when the twelve apostles returned from the ends of the earth to gather round the Virgin's death bed – but as fate had it, the wife and children of Vladimir's last prince were burned alive there by the Mongols.

If the cathedral is open, you can see how the original walls were knocked through to create aisles behind the new external walls; in one of the niches are the **sarcophagi** of Bogolyubsky and his successor Vsevolod III, who rebuilt the cathedral. More significantly, there are remains of the **frescoes** painted in 1408 by Andrei Rublev and Daniil Cherniy (the only ones authenticated by contemporary documents as being the work of their artel), the best-preserved being the *Last Judgement* beneath the choir gallery. The 25-metre-high **iconostasis** once contained the revered twelfth-century Byzantine icon *Our Lady of Tenderness*, that Bogolyubsky took from Kiev for his new capital; subsequently called *Our Lady of Vladimir*, it was removed to Moscow in 1395 and is now in the Tretyakov Gallery.

A little way downhill stands the smaller **Cathedral of St Demetrius** (*Dmitrievskiy sobor*), built of the same local limestone in the 1190s by Vsevolod III "Big Nest" – a sobriquet that referred to his many sons. St Demetrius is famous for its **stone carvings**, with rows of saints and mythical creatures on the blind arcades and large compositions beneath the *zakomary*, where Vsevolod and his brood are associated with the biblical David, angels and chimeras, and the ascension to heaven of Alexander the Great. The carvings were originally painted in bright colours, like ancient Greek temples, and it's debated whether their symbolism is pagan or Christian. Its interior boasts a fine *Last Judgement* by artists of the Constantinople school, but, as with the Cathedral of the Assumption, you'll be lucky to find it open.

Beyond Sobornaya ploshchad the avenue widens as it approaches the **Golden Gate** bestriding Vladimir's main square. Completed in 1164, it was once the western entrance to Bogolyubsky's walled city, modelled on the gates of Kiev (themselves copied from Constantinople's), which featured a church above the gateway for divine protection. Vladimir might have withstood the Mongol siege had not the young Prince Yuri lost his nerve and ventured forth carrying gifts, hoping that Batu Khan would spare his life – but "Batu, like a wild beast, ordered that he be slaughtered before him" and launched a final assault on the city – as depicted by a diorama in the **Military History Museum** in one of the bastions at the foot of the gate. Like the gate-church, the bastions date from its reconstruction in the eighteenth century, by which time it no longer had any military function. While nothing remains of the original oaken gates, clad in gilded copper, at Easter you can see a colourful **religious procession** through the gateway.

The Military History Museum is open 10am–5pm, closed Tues & the last Fri of each month; $0.50.

Off to the left is a remnant of the earthen ramparts that enclosed Vladimir in the twelfth century, crowned by a water tower built in 1912, which now contains the **Old Vladimir Museum** – a collection of shop fronts, domestic artefacts and clothing from the 1860s up until the Revolution, whose sobriety is enlivened by figurines of a

The Old Vladimir Museum is open 10am–5pm, Wed & Thurs till 4pm, closed Mon & the last Fri of each month; $0.50.

drunk being reproved by his family, among the porcelain. However, the real attraction is the **panoramic view** of Vladimir from the gallery atop the tower.

One aspect of local history that's omitted is **Vladimir Central Prison** (*Vladimirskiy tsentral*), a Tsarist gaol that the Soviets designated as an "Isolator" for prisoners whom they wished to keep separate from the ordinary camps – lifers with nothing to lose, ex-secret policemen, and foreigners charged with spying, from British engineers working on the Moscow Metro to post-war VIP inmates like Raoul Wallenberg, the "Swedish Schindler", and Gary Powers, the pilot of the American spy plane shot down over the Urals in 1960. As it's still in use for ordinary criminals, it would be tempting fate to snoop around at the end of Bolshaya Nizhgorodskaya ulitsa, where the prison is located.

Practicalities

Vladimir is accessible **from Moscow** by *elektrichka* train from Kursk Station (leaving at around 8am, 1pm & 6pm), or bus from the Central Bus Station (4–5 daily), both of which take about three and a quarter hours – except for the 6pm train, which is an express service taking two and a half hours, but no use to anyone hoping to visit Vladimir and Suzdal as a day-trip; if you want to do that you'll have to sign up for an excursion or hire a car. It's better to spend the night in Suzdal and travel back to Moscow next day, either on the 7.25am fast train (reserve a seat as soon as you arrive in Vladimir) or the ordinary service at 6.20pm.

Should you wish, it's possible to head straight on **to Suzdal** without investigating Vladimir at all. From the bus terminal behind the train station, **buses** run to Suzdal at roughly hourly intervals, or you can save time by hiring a **taxi** ($7), which will get there in 30–40 minutes instead of an hour.

If you *do* spend time in Vladimir, you can **eat** well for not much money at the posh *Stariy Gorod* (Mon–Wed & Sun 11am–midnight, Thurs–Sat 11am–2pm), just uphill from the Monastery of the Nativity, or the folksy *Traktir* (daily 11am–1pm) in a wooden cabin near the Old Vladimir Museum – though the service is slow at both, so they're no good for a quick bite.

In the event that all **accommodation** in Suzdal is taken, you can fall back on the *Hotel Vladimir* (☎0922/323 042; ①), at Bolshaya Moskovskaya ulitsa 74, whose "first category" rooms are comfy and cheerful (the other rooms less so), with a superbly kitsch floor lounge – a better deal than at the *Erlangen Haus* (☎0922/323 795, fax 0922/324 504, *erlan@erlan.elcom.ru*; ②), at Bolshaya Nizhgorodskaya ulitsa 25, whose rooms don't live up to its pleasant exterior and garden.

Use the **ATM** in the *Vladimir*'s lobby if you need cash, as there isn't one in Suzdal.

Suzdal

Unlike Vladimir, **SUZDAL**'s glorious architectural legacy is unmarred by factories and in total harmony with its surroundings, a Russian fairytale vision of onion domes above meadows and woods beside the meandering Kamenka River, spanned by wooden footbridges, and green with reeds and lilies in summertime. It looks gorgeous whatever the season, but especially in winter, blanketed with snow. Most of the houses are of the traditional wood and stone kind, with kitchen gardens; grazing cows and sheep add a pastoral touch, and even tourism doesn't ruffle its tranquillity. The lack of litter or drunks on the streets suggests that the town's self-esteem is still intact, despite its economic woes – perhaps due to its illustrious past.

Suzdal's **history** is entwined with Vladimir's, for it was the princely capital during Dolgoruky's reign – when the court resided at Kideshka, 5km outside Suzdal on the River Nerl – until his successor moved it to Vladimir. Even so, Suzdal became the religious centre of medieval Rus, with monasteries associated with SS Boris and Gleb and Alexander Nevsky, that later princes and tsars lavishly funded in return for using it as a dumping ground for unwanted wives, ensuring that the town prospered during the sixteenth and seventeenth centuries, when a spate of church building saw the emergence of a distinctive Suzdal style. In its heyday, Suzdal had fifty churches, monasteries and cathedrals, forming a unique architectural ensemble – and although the Soviets closed down the religious orders and wantonly destroyed twelve churches and ten monasteries, they preserved others as monuments and declared the whole town a protected museum reserve. It's easy to see why Russian film directors have used it as a location for historical epics – most notably Tarkovsky's masterpiece *Andrei Rublev*.

As the town covers only seven square kilometres you can comfortably explore it on foot, but there's a lot worth seeing, so a couple of hours isn't really enough. The **itinerary** described here can take the best part of a day if you don't hurry. Whether you start or finish with the Convent of the Intercession is likely to depend on whether you're staying at the *GTK* on the edge of town or somewhere more central. A torch will be useful if you go out for a meal in the evening, as the streets are unlit.

The Convent of the Intercession

The Convent of the Intercession is open daily 7am–7pm; free. The museum is open 9.30am–4.45pm, closed Tues, Wed and the last Fri of each month.

Nestled in an oxbow of the river, the white-and-gold **Convent of the Intercession** (*Pokrovskiy monastyr*) is a monument to the length that tsars would go to rid themselves of unwanted spouses. The convent's cathedral was built by Vasily III in the hope of curing his wife Solomonia's infertility; when divine intercession failed to produce an heir, she was browbeaten into taking the veil (but ultimately outlived him, and is said to have secretly borne a child in the convent). The

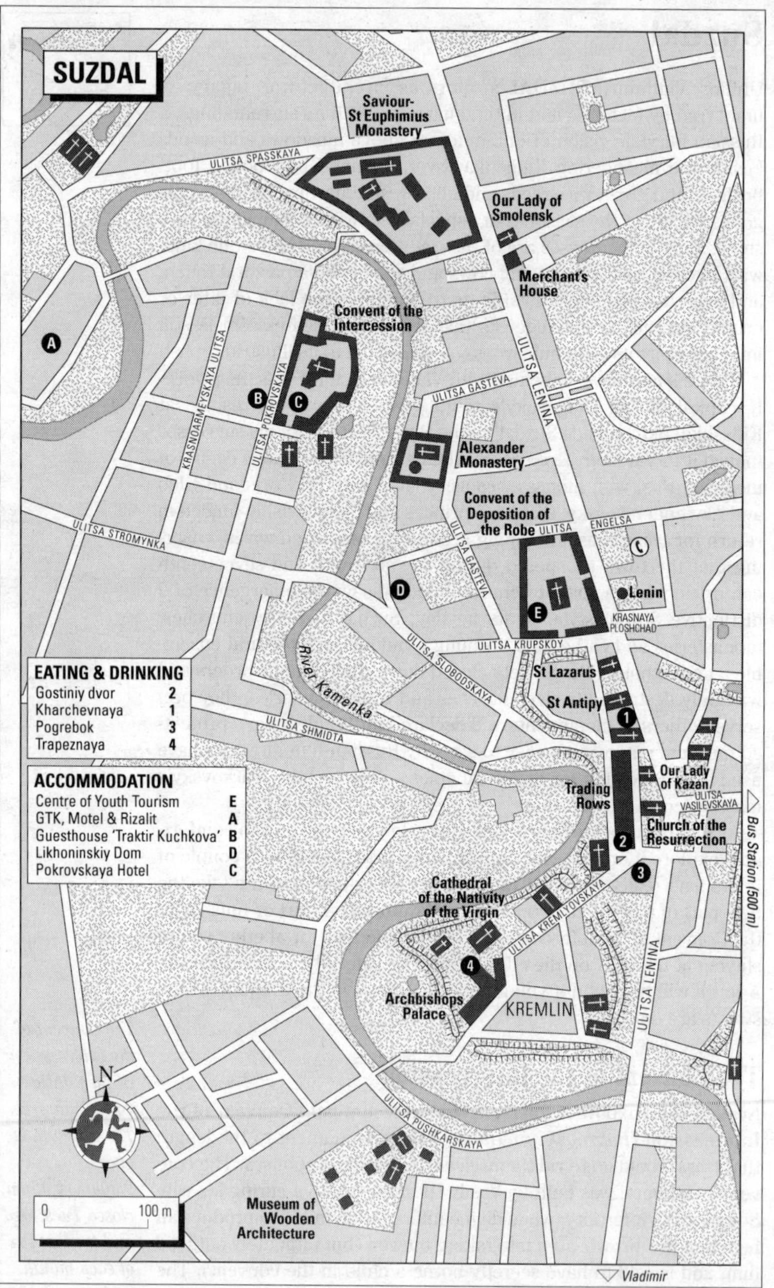
SUZDAL
Saviour-St Euphimius Monastery
ULITSA SPASSKAYA
Our Lady of Smolensk
Merchant's House
Convent of the Intercession
ULITSA LENINA
ULITSA GASTEVA
KRASNOARMEYSKAYA ULITSA
ULITSA POKROVSKAYA
Alexander Monastery
Convent of the Deposition of the Robe
ULITSA ENGELSA
ULITSA STROMYNKA
ULITSA GASTEVA
Lenin
KRASNAYA PLOSHCHAD
ULITSA KRUPSKOY
ULITSA SLOBODSKAYA
River Kamenka
St Lazarus
St Antipy
ULITSA SHMIDTA
Our Lady of Kazan
Trading Rows
ULITSA VASILEVSKAYA
Church of the Resurrection
Bus Station (500 m)
Cathedral of the Nativity of the Virgin
ULITSA KREMLYOVSKAYA
Archbishops Palace
KREMLIN
ULITSA LENINA
ULITSA PUSHKARSKAYA
Museum of Wooden Architecture
N
0
100 m
Vladimir
EATING & DRINKING
Gostiniy dvor 2
Kharchevnaya 1
Pogrebok 3
Trapeznaya 4
ACCOMMODATION
Centre of Youth Tourism E
GTK, Motel & Rizalit A
Guesthouse 'Traktir Kuchkova' B
Likhoninskiy Dom D
Pokrovskaya Hotel C

practice was continued by his son Ivan the Terrible and grandson Ivan (who disposed of two wives this way), while later victims included Boris Godunov's daughter Xenia, and Peter the Great's wife Yevdokiya (who was later exiled to a remoter convent for plotting against Peter and taking a lover).

Today, this grim history is at odds with the convent's manicured beauty; its elegant cathedral, belltower and refectory form a single conjoined entity in a delightful garden created by a new generation of nuns, surrounded by the log cabins of the *Pokrovskaya Hotel*, installed in Soviet times. There's also a small **museum** recreating the *Prikaz* (administration) that controlled the land and serfs owned by the convent until Catherine the Great took them away, whereupon the redundant building was used for storing salt.

To see the rest of Suzdal, cross the river by footbridge and head uphill towards the Saviour-St Euphimius Monastery.

The Saviour-St Euphimius Monastery

The Saviour-St Euphimius Monastery is open Tues–Sun 10am–6pm; closed the last Thurs of each month; $3.

Built atop the steep east bank, enclosed by a fortified wall 1200m in length, the **Saviour-St Euphimius Monastery** (*Spaso-Yevfimiev monastyr*) is easily mistaken for Suzdal's Kremlin, and once doubled as a fortress. Although founded as early as 1352, by abbot Euphimius (after whom it is named), most of what you find today dates from the sixteenth and seventeenth centuries, when the patronage of Vasily III and Prince Pozharsky made it one of the richest monasteries in Russia. To cut it down to size, Catherine the Great established a prison there in 1766, which remained until 1905; during World War II the monastery served as a POW camp for Nazi generals, before being restored in peacetime and turned into a series of museums highlighting different facets of its history.

Try to time your visit to hear the **bells** at 11am: a fifteen-minute symphony performed by one of Suzdal's master bell-ringers, Yuri Yurev or Vladimir Gagarin – whose playing can best be seen from a vantage point on the eastern side of the belltower, which was erected to mark the birth of the future Ivan the Terrible. Beyond rises the **Cathedral of the Transfiguration**, created in 1594 to replace an earlier, single-domed church built over the tomb of St Euphimius, which was turned into a side-chapel. Its interior is decorated with bold, naturalistic frescoes in vivid blues, ochre, turquoise and yellow, and was once the burial place of **Prince Pozharsky**, who led the army that rid Moscow of the Poles and Lithuanians in 1612. He was later reburied beneath a pavilion to the east of the cathedral, where signs direct visitors towards a museum in his memory, in a former church.

Tucked away at the back is the low, linear **Prison Wing** that once held the ringleaders of the Pugachev Revolt, the civil servant Gavril Popov (gaoled for writing "Man is born free" in his diary), and the Decembrist Prince Shakovsky (who died on hunger strike). After 1829 it was used exclusively for clerics, sentenced by the Church authorities – as related in an exhibition that includes a re-creation of a prisoner's cell.

A **Museum of Treasures** in the monastery infirmary contains some fine icons (notably a *Saviour* "with the Wet Beard") and lapis lazuli-inlaid jewellery; while the **Museum of Naïve Art** in the ex-Church of the Annunciation features scenes of village and town life by artists born in the 1920s and 1930s. Finally, there are two exhibitions in the archimandrite's house. **Book Treasures of Six Centuries** displays rare volumes such as Fyodorov's *The Apostle* (1564), the first illustrated *Primer* (1694) and a silver-chased Gospel, presented to the monastery by Prince Pozharsky, that's the largest book in Russia. The other examines the fate of POWs, including the commanders of the German Sixth Army captured at Stalingrad, who were held here in 1943 and suborned into backing the "National Committee for Free Germany".

The Posad

Suzdal's layout is typical of medieval Russian towns, with a Kremlin and monasteries interspersed by a **posad** (trading quarter) and satellite settlements, each with their own parish church built of wood. In the seventeenth century these were replaced by stone ones, often erected in pairs: a high-vaulted church for summer worship, and a lower one where the candles and lamps created an illusion of warmth during winter. Over time their design grew lighter, with facades whose decoratively framed symmetrical windows are visually akin to the embroidered white cloths in peasant households. Architecture buffs can find dozens of examples, but most visitors will be content to see the ones along **ulitsa Lenina**, en route to the Kremlin.

Near the St Euphimius Monastery, the "summer" **Church of Our Lady of Smolensk** has lost its winter counterpart but acquired a tall, freestanding belltower. Across the road is a whitewashed dwelling with a wooden roof, which once belonged to the religious dissenter Nikita Pustosvyat, who was executed on Red Square in 1682. It is now furnished like a **Merchant's House** (10am–6pm; closed Thurs; $1) from the eighteenth century, when its owner was engaged in baking *kalachi* (bagels) and ran a tavern. Vendors outside sell home-brewed mead, a traditional local speciality.

Further down ulitsa Lenina, a gate beside no. 101 opens onto a path to the **Alexander Monastery** (*Aleksandrovskiy monastyr*), high above the river. Founded in 1240 by the warrior-saint Alexander Nevsky, it held the rank of Great *Lavra* until it was usurped by the Alexander Nevsky Monastery in St Petersburg, established by Peter the Great – whose mother, Natalya Naryshkina, had financed the **Cathedral of the Ascension** in Suzdal's monastery twenty years earlier. Today the complex is in a poor state, but worth a detour for the lovely **view** of the Convent of the Intercession across the river.

Back on ulitsa Lenina, the only blot on the landscape is an ugly telephone office and municipal block fronted by an archetypal **Lenin statue** on Krasnaya ploshchad. Lenin appears to be haranguing Suzdal's tallest landmark, a 72-metre-high **belltower** erected by the townsfolk to celebrate Russia's victory in 1812. Its gaping archway is an invitation to enter the **Convent of Deposition of the Veil** (*Rizopolozhenskiy monastyr*), another decrepit walled complex whose origins go back to 1207, that was renowned for the deeds of a nun called Euphrosinia. Its **Cathedral of the Deposition** is unusual for its helmet domes on tall drums, like minarets, and was financed by the boyar who coerced Vasily's wife into a nunnery. The interior is all but gutted, since after the convent was dissolved it was turned into a hostel and workshops, only mentioned in Soviet guidebooks for its chunky sixteenth-century **Holy Gate**.

Further south, **churches** sprout like mushrooms on verges. **St Lazarus**, built in 1667, was one of the first churches where the formerly functional *zakomary* (arched gables) became purely decorative, due to new construction techniques. Its lowly neighbour **St Antipy**, erected eight decades later, has an adjacent belfry painted maroon, cream and white, with an unusual concave tent-roof. While the winter church was invariably built later, the interval varied greatly; only seven years separates the **Church of the Resurrection** from the **Church of Our Lady of Kazan**. The former is a typical Suzdal parish church, shaped like a truncated cube and almost devoid of decoration, bar a frieze of *kokoshniki* beneath the roof. Across the road lie the **Trading Rows**, an early nineteenth-century shopping arcade with another church behind it, and two more on the way to the Kremlin.

The Kremlin

Founded in the twelfth century by Vladimir of Kiev, Suzdal's **Kremlin** has been ravaged and rebuilt many times since – and lost its stone ramparts in the eighteenth century – but its archaic grandeur still captivates. The star-spangled onion domes of its cathedral make it the visual focus of the whole town, which at close quarters becomes a melange of extraordinary buildings, where it's easy to imagine boyars strolling across the yard and livestock grazing between the wooden houses that stood here in medieval times.

The Kremlin grounds are open 24hr; free. The museums are open 10am–6pm, closed Tues & the last Fri of each month; tickets for them all total $2.

The **Cathedral of the Nativity** (*Rozhdestvennskiy sobor*) is a majestic hybrid of early thirteenth- and sixteenth-century architecture. A band of blind arcading delineates the lower half, built of limestone by Prince Yuri Vsevolodovich, from the upper portion, rebuilt with five domes instead of three, as was required by canonical law by the 1530s. While you can admire the carved stonework around its portals, the cathedral is rarely open – which is a real shame, as its frescoes are superb, with ultramarine and orange as the dominant colours and more ancient portions in softer hues – not to mention a chandelier bestowed by the brother of Tsar Vasily Shuysky, and the magnificent Golden Gates (see below).

Happily, there's plenty to see in the **Metropolitan's Palace**, a huge, rambling complex built over the course of two hundred years, completed in the eighteenth century by Metropolitan Hilarion. Having bought a strip of tickets, your first stop is the **Cross Chamber** (*Krestovaya palata*) that he built for official receptions, which is over twice as large as its namesake in Moscow's Kremlin, and likewise unsupported by pillars. Furnished with tiled stoves, a long table covered in red cloth, and portraits of tsars and clerics, it makes a superb setting for performances of Russian church music by the **Blagovest male choir**, coinciding with visits by tour groups.

Afterwards, cross the yard and climb the stairs to the Metropolitan's living quarters, now a **Historical Museum**. Among its prized exhibits is one of the two pairs of **Golden Gates** from the cathedral. These huge bronze doors are the earliest example in Russia of the technique known as fired gilding, producing images in gold on a black background: episodes from the Gospels, and homely scenes such as an angel teaching a man to use a spade. The giant candleholders and urn for dispensing holy water are also memorable, and a model of medieval Suzdal shows how its topography has changed. Don't overlook the sixteenth-century crucifix so finely carved that it needs a magnifying glass to reveal its details, the child's silk tunic, nor the portrait of Vasily's wife, Solomonia Saburova.

Upon exiting you'll find yourself facing the seventeenth-century **Church of St Nicholas**, a simple log edifice whose beetling roof and hanging gallery make it an arresting sight. It was moved here from the village of Glotovo in 1950, as the first of the exhibits in the Museum of Wooden Architecture that was later sited across the river.

The Museum of Wooden Architecture

The Museum of Wooden Architecture is open Mon & Wed 9.30am–3.30pm, Thurs–Sun 9.30am–4.30pm; closed the last Fri of each month; $1. The farmstead interiors can only be visited during summer.

A short walk from the Kremlin via a footbridge, the **Museum of Wooden Architecture** unites diverse buildings that might otherwise have rotted in their native villages. The **Church of the Transfiguration** from Kozlyatevo (1756) has a hexagonal tower, shingled roofs and domes, and a covered porch and galleries; its interior features a folk-Baroque iconostasis, and saints painted on the raw plank ceiling. Nearby are two nineteenth-century **farmsteads** furnished with artefacts and overseen by guides in folk costume; authenticity extends to the visitors' toilet – an earth closet out back. The "winter" **Church of the Resurrection** from Pobshino (1776) and two nineteenth-century **windmills** from Drachevo are more rough-hewn structures; a **waterwheel** and poultry sheds complete the ensemble.

There is also a **shop** in one of the houses selling attractive hand-made quilts and tea-cosies, very cheaply.

Practicalities

Suzdal has **accommodation** for all budgets and tastes, but it's wise to book ahead. The *Pokrovskaya Hotel* (☎09231/208 89; ④) has cosy log cabins with en-suite facilities and a sauna for guests, but its real selling point is its location in the Convent of the Intercession, which has a cachet that the nearby *Guest House Traktir Kuchkov* (☎09231/202 52, fax 09231/215 07; ④) lacks, despite double beds, TV and mini-bar in every room (no singles), and a sauna and pool table on the premises. A better alternative is the *Likhoninskiy Dom* (☎09231/209 37, *aksenova@vsmz.elcom.ru*; ②), a charming nineteenth-century house with folk decor and furnishings, within easy walking distance of all the sights. For the same price, you could stay at the sprawling *GTK* complex (☎09231/209 08, fax 09231/207 66, *gtk@tcsuz.vladimir.ru*; ②) across the river, which is less convenient, but OK; all rooms have bathrooms, and guests may use the swimming pool and sauna at weekends. You can also pay slightly more for a room with superior decor, TV and fridge, in the *Rizalit* wing; or sleep three in the shabbier two-room apartments (②) of the *Motel*, which has private garages. Lastly, there's the *Centre of Youth Tourism* (☎09231/205 53; ①) in the Convent of the Deposition, which has singles with washbasins, doubles with bathrooms and triple rooms with sofas, some newly refurbished and others very dingy – a difference reflected in their prices.

The only decent **restaurant** is the *Trapeznaya* in the Archbishop's Palace in the Kremlin (daily noon–11pm), where guests are seated in a vast whitewashed refectory hall with long trestle tables, once the small room is full. Try *kuritsa pod sloyke*: chicken cooked in an earthenware pot with a mushroom-shaped cap of Yorkshire pudding, that's sliced off to form a bowl from which you eat. As a fallback, the *Kharchevnaya* on ulitsa Lenina (daily 9am–11pm) offers simpler Russian dishes. Don't bother eating at the *Gostiny Dvor* or *Pogrebok*, though one has a nice terrace for **drinking** beer and the other a basement bar serving **honey mead** (*medovukha*). If you enjoy it, buy a bottle in Suzdal, as you won't find it on sale elsewhere. **Nightlife** boils down to a teenagers' disco on Krasnaya ploshchad, and the bar in the *GTK*, with its pool tables and hookers.

Suzdal	Суздаль
Krasnaya ploshchad	Красная площадь
ulitsa Lenina	улица Ленина
Vladimir	Владимир
Bolshaya Moskovskaya ulitsa	Большая Маскавская улица
Nizhgorodskaya ulitsa	Нижгарадская улица
Sobornaya ploshchad	Соборная площадь

Suzdal

When you're ready to leave, bear in mind that the **bus station** is 15–20 minutes' walk from the centre of town; buses run there from Krasnaya ploshchad (#1 & #4) and the *GTK* (#3) at irregular times, and local motorists aren't inclined to act as unofficial taxis. Licensed **taxis** wait outside the *GTK*.

Part 5

The Contexts

A History of Moscow

Moscow's turbulent history can be divided into three distinct phases. The first saw it rise from a minor principality to the capital of a unified Russian state, and the birth of the Romanov dynasty. During the second – from the reign of Peter the Great onwards – Moscow was eclipsed by the new Imperial capital, St Petersburg, and played a secondary role in Russian history until the collapse of Tsarism in 1917. Then, after a year that saw the October Revolution in Petrograd (as St Petersburg was then called), the Bolsheviks returned the seat of government to the Kremlin, and Moscow's modern era began. The city celebrated its 850th birthday in 1997.

Beginnings

Despite evidence of human settlement as early as 500 BC, the first recorded mention of the city was in 1147 AD, when Prince **Yuri Dolgoruky** of Rostov and Suzdal invited Svyatoslav of Novgorod and his boyars (nobles) to feast at Dolgoruky's hunting lodge, on a hill above the rivers Moskva and Neglina. Enlarged over the years and fortified with wooden walls and towers in 1156, this *Kreml* or **Kremlin** was the seed of a township named "Moskva", after the river. Though some claim this is a corruption of the Finnish word for "bear", it is more likely to derive from the Russian *mozgliy*, meaning "marshy". In any event, the town was conveniently located on the River Moskva that linked the great waterways of the Volga and the Okha – a major factor in its eventual rise to power.

Moscow's infancy coincided with two momentous events in Russian history. Early in the twelfth century, the great medieval civilization of the **Kievan Rus** collapsed amid internecine strife and invasions from the east and west. Much of the population fled northwards to the *zalesskiy* (beyond the woods) area of the Okha basin and the upper Volga, where Prince Andrei Bogolyubsky established the new capital, **Vladimir**, in 1169.

Barely fifty years later, the Mongols surged across the Russian steppes, laying waste to villages and towns – including Moscow. The **Mongol invasion** (1237–40) seemed like the end of the world foretold in the Bible, but in fact heralded two centuries of submission to their **Tatar allies**, who demanded tribute in gold, furs and slaves. The princes of Vladimir and other towns were only allowed to rule with the Tatar Khan's *yarlyk* (authority), which was auctioned off to the highest bidder. Their chief concerns were to squeeze as much wealth as possible from their fiefdoms, and to remain in favour with the Khan.

The Moscow princes of the **Rurik dynasty** were no exception to this rule. The town was first recognized as a principality under **Daniil** (1263–1303), the youngest son of Grand Prince Alexander Nevsky of Novgorod, who defeated the Teutonic Knights in a famous battle on Lake Peipus. His grandson, **Ivan "Kalita"** (1325–41), earned his nickname "Moneybags" for his skill at extracting taxes and expanding his influence over other principalities, proving so adept as "the Tatar's hangman, sycophant and slave-in-chief" (as Marx put it) that he got to marry the Khan's daughter and become Great Prince of Vladimir. In recognition of his power, the seat of the **Russian Orthodox Church** was moved from Vladimir to Moscow in 1326. That same year, work began on strengthening the Kremlin with higher oak ramparts, completed in time for the accession of **Simeon the Proud** (1341–53).

The rise of Muscovy

The **rise of Muscovy** (as the principality was named) owed to more than mere servility. An underlying factor was its location in the *mezhdureche* (between the rivers) area at the crossroads of Russia's trade routes, roughly equidistant from the Tatar Khanate on the lower Volga, the Lithuanian-Polish empire to the west, and the powerful city-state of Novgorod to the north. Another was its prestige as the seat of the Russian Orthodox Church, which would assume messianic significance after the fall of Constantinople in the fifteenth century. Moreover, during the 1350s, the Mongol-Tatar Golden Horde was weakened by power struggles within its vast empire, and would later be battered by another force of nomadic invaders, under Timerlane. Meanwhile, the Kremlin was strengthened by the building of limestone walls, from 1367 onwards.

In 1380, Simeon's grandson Dmitry dared to argue over the annual tribute to the Tatars and, when Khan Mamai responded with a punitive invasion, Dmitry led a Russian army to confront the Horde at Kulikovo near the River Don. The **battle of Kulikovo** was the Russians' first victory in nearly a century and a half: a historic event commemorated by the foundation of the Donskoy Monastery on the site where his departing army had prayed for victory, while Dmitry himself assumed the title **Dmitry Donskoy**.

However, the Horde remained a formidable threat, and his successors, Vasily I and Vasily the Dark, paid tribute as normal. It was during this period that Russian **icon painting** and frescoes reached their zenith at the hands of Theophanes the Greek, Andrei Rublev and Daniil Cherniy (all of whom worked in Moscow), and that the Byzantine capital, Constantinople, fell to the Turks, in 1453.

Ivan the Great

The Tatar yoke was finally thrown off in the reign of Ivan III (1462–1505), known as **Ivan the Great** (*Ivan Veliki*). His boldness stemmed from a politically shrewd marriage to **Sofia Paléologue** of Byzantium, and his claim to rule the Eastern and Western Roman Empires was symbolized by the double-headed eagle that he adopted as his emblem. Having gained power over Yaroslavl, Rostov, Tver and Pskov before his marriage, Ivan waited eight years before tearing up the Khan's *yarlyk* in the Cathedral of the Assumption, in 1480. By the end of his reign the Lithuanians had been pushed back to the headwaters of the Dniepr and Dvina, and even proudly independent Novgorod had submitted, giving Muscovy control of a huge area as far north as the White Sea. This fourfold **territorial expansion** earned Ivan the titles "Gatherer of the Russian Lands" and "Autocrat of All the Russias".

Moscow – and the Kremlin in particular – were aggrandized to reflect this. In Sofia's wake came **Italian architects** who supervised the construction of the Kremlin's brick walls and two of its finest stone cathedrals. They also began work on a belltower intended to be the tallest building in Russia, later named after Ivan. The building programme was completed by his successor, who extended it to the Beliy Gorod, where stone parish churches were erected. However, stone buildings were still rare, and Moscow would remain a predominantly wooden city for three centuries, making **fires** a greater threat than Tatar raids. Yet Moscow thrived, its population rising to 100,000 by the mid-sixteenth century, when it was one of the largest cities in Europe.

Ivan the Great's successor, **Vasily III** (1505–33), is mainly remembered for clearing what is now Red Square, and siring the future Ivan the Terrible in 1530 – the moment of birth apparently coincided with a clap of thunder and lightning striking the Kremlin, which was held to signify the child's future greatness. Of equal importance to Moscow's destiny was a **prophecy** by the monk Philotey of Pskov, who told Vasily that "two Romes have already fallen but the third remains standing and a fourth there will not be". This belief that Moscow was the "third Rome" and the heir of Byzantium's sovereignty over Orthodox Christendom would inspire Russia's rulers for generations.

Ivan the Terrible

Despite his infamous deeds, Russians have always had a soft spot for **Ivan the Terrible** (*Ivan Grozny*). In modern times this can partly be attributed to Eisenstein's superb film, which portrays the tsar as a tortured soul driven to cruelty by the imperatives of power – a view that was personally dictated by Stalin, who felt that his own life and Ivan's had much in common. Historians have also pointed out that the title *Grozniy* (usually translated as "Terrible", but really closer to

"Awesome" or "Formidable") was first adopted by his grandfather, Ivan the Great. Nevertheless, his life richly deserves the epithet "Terrible".

Ivan's **childhood** was spent in fear of the boyars, whose struggles for power after Vasily's death (when Ivan was three) worsened after his mother was poisoned five years later. Ivan only survived as the heir to the throne because no one could agree on an alternative figurehead. His chief pleasure was killing birds and dogs; then hunting and reading the Bible. In 1547, aged seventeen, Ivan assumed the Crown of Monomakh and insisted on being proclaimed **Tsar** (Caesar) instead of Grand Duke. However, he left affairs of state to the **Glinskys** until a rival family of boyars, the **Shyuskys**, succeeded in blaming them for a spate of fires in Moscow, inciting a riot. Ivan dismissed the Glinskys and publicly confessed his failings on Red Square, vowing to God to rule better in the future.

Foreign invaders were a major concern – particularly the Tatars, who made frequent incursions into Russia from **Kazan** on the lower Volga. After many attempts, Ivan's army captured Kazan in October 1552 and, to celebrate, St Basil's Cathedral was built. **Astrakhan** on the Caspian Sea fell to the Russians two years later. With the Tatars at bay, Ivan then turned to raid the Grand Duchy of **Livonia** to the west, ignoring protests from Poland and Sweden.

In 1560 his triumphs turned to ashes when his beloved wife **Anastasia** died shortly after a fire in Moscow. This seemed to Ivan a betrayal of his contract with God, and aroused all his latent suspicions of the boyars. As once-favoured courtiers were exiled or met worse fates, others fled abroad, confirming his fear of traitors – until in the winter of 1564 Ivan abruptly quit Moscow, leaving the populace agog. A month later, they received word that he had **abdicated** in protest at the boyars' lack of patriotism. Mobs besieged the Kremlin, demanding that the traitors be identified, until a delegation of clerics went to beg his forgiveness and implore him to rule them again.

The Oprichniki

In return, Ivan demanded that Russia be divided into two spheres: the *oprichnina* – constituting his personal domain – and the *zemshchina*, comprising the rest. The power of the boyars was broken by exiling 12,000 families to distant, inhospitable regions of the *zemshchina*, an act of expropriation carried out by a new militia, handpicked by Ivan and devoted to his orders: the **Oprichniki**. As a symbol of their mission to hunt down and sweep away his enemies, they bore a dog's head and a broom on their saddles. Enjoying total licence to kill, loot, burn and torture, they took their cue from **Malyuta-Skuratov**, the most depraved of Ivan's favourites.

Initially quartered in the Oprichniy dvor (on the site of old Moscow University), they later moved with Ivan to the **Alexandrovskaya Sloboda**, a moated palace north of Vladimir whose interior reflected the different aspects of the tsar's personality. Some rooms were luxurious, others crammed with books, some with a monastic bareness; torture chambers lay beneath them. To demonstrate Ivan's piety, the palace was transformed into a "monastery" where the Oprichniki attended services from 3am until 8pm, when nightly orgies commenced.

Another bizarre story was his **wooing of Queen Elizabeth** of England, which preoccupied Ivan from 1567 to 1569. Besides the prospect of uniting their two nations, Ivan was excited by reports of this Virgin Queen, having tired of his fourth, Circassian, wife. Tactful evasions angered him into placing the English ambassador under house arrest in the Kitay-gorod, but he later forgave the offender. Not so those boyars whom Ivan suspected of treason, who were fed to dogs or raped to death. The atrocious climax was the **massacre of Novgorod** in 1569, when up to 60,000 citizens were tortured to death for supposedly plotting to side with Poland, and 200 more met a similar fate on Red Square.

Ivan's final years

In 1571 the Tatars made a devastating raid on Moscow, burning the city and carrying off thousands of citizens as slaves. Ivan fled to Yaroslavl, only returning once they had left. The last decade of his reign was given over to scheming to gain the throne of **Poland**, which fell vacant in 1572, and again in 1575. To Polish envoys, he confided: "Many people in your country say that I am inhuman; it is true that I am cruel and irascible, but only to those who behave badly towards me. The good ones? Ah, I would not hesitate to give them my gold chain and the coat off my back!" After the Polish Diet had twice rebuffed his overtures, Ivan invaded Livonia, whereupon **Stephen Bathory** led a Polish army into Russia, in conjunction with a Swedish assault further north. Facing defeat, Ivan asked the Vatican to mediate and conceded Livonia to the Poles in 1582.

The previous year the tsar had killed his heir, **Tsarevich Ivan**, by striking him with an iron staff in a fit of rage. Deeply remorseful, he sank into gloom, which even debauchery and sadism could no longer dispel. His dynastic hopes now rested on his eldest son **Fyodor** – an imbecile – and a sickly infant, **Dmitry**. In the last year of his life Ivan compiled a register of all those he had killed, and paid monasteries to recite prayers for their souls. His guts putrefied and his testicles swelled; his only solace was fondling the gems in his treasury. When astrologers foretold the **tsar's death** on March 18, 1584, he swore to have them burned alive if they were wrong. On that day he collapsed over a game of chess and expired on the spot. In accordance with Ivan's wishes, he was buried as a monk.

Boris Godunov and the Time of Troubles

News of Ivan's death was released to the populace only after the details of the succession had been agreed by a Council of Regents. Fyodor reluctantly became tsar, but the power behind the throne was **Boris Godunov**, the brother of Fyodor's wife Irina. During his regency stone walls were built around the Beliy Gorod and the Trinity Monastery of St Sergei. Despised by the other boyars for his Tatar origins, Godunov was later suspected of having arranged the mysterious **death of Dmitry**, at Uglich in 1591 – though all that is certain is that he rewarded one of the Tsarevich's servants afterwards. The official explanation was that Dmitri fatally stabbed himself during an epileptic fit.

Whatever the truth, Godunov deftly staged his own **accession to the throne** after Fyodor died in 1598, bringing the Rurik dynasty to an end. At the instigation of his agents, a crowd of clerics and commoners went to the Novodevichiy Convent to beg Fyodor's widow to bless her brother as the heir. Godunov was waiting there, and with a show of dismay emerged from her quarters to be acclaimed as tsar – a verdict later endorsed by the Assembly of Notables.

However, even his devious statecraft was powerless against a run of **disasters** which occurred after 1601. Famine and plague beggared the towns, and rural areas fell into brigandage, while Godunov was compelled to raise taxes to combat disorder. Under such conditions it was relatively easy for him to be challenged by an impostor claiming descent from the Ruriks – even one who identified himself as Ivan the Terrible's son Dmitry, miraculously saved from his killers at Uglich.

The False Dmitrys

The **first False Dmitry** was a minor official's son named Grigory Otrepiev, who fled to Poland and pressed his claim with the aid of the Jesuits. His small invasion force was helped by Cossacks and robber bands, but above all by Boris Godunov's timely death in April 1605. Though popularly acclaimed as tsar, Dmitry soon alienated Muscovites with his Polish ways and advisers, his unseemly beardlessness and habit of walking in the streets with foreigners, rather than being awesomely remote like a proper ruler. The final straw was his wedding to a Polish bride in May 1606, at which the Poles sat on holy relics and lounged against the iconostasis in the Cathedral of the Ascension, and his betrothed, Marina Mnishekh, kissed an icon of the Virgin on its mouth (not on its hand, as Russians did), arousing indignation among all classes.

A week later the boyar **Vasily Shyusky** led a force of conspirators into the Kremlin while supporters roused the city with cries of "The Poles are killing the tsar." Inside the citadel, Shyusky had a different war cry: "Death to the heretics! Death to the impostor!" As the mob ransacked his palace, Dmitry leapt from the walls to escape and broke his leg. Captured by the Streltsy, he protested his sincerity till he was torn to pieces; his remains were fired from the Tsar Cannon in the direction of Poland. The Shyusky clan took power, but their writ barely extended beyond Moscow.

In 1607 a **second False Dmitry** entered Russia backed by a Polish-Lithuanian army, and ensconced himself at Tushino, outside Moscow, to await the fall of the Shyuskys. However, the "Scoundrel of Tushino" dallied too long, and early in 1610 the Shyuskys drove him out, later bribing his servants to murder him. Soon afterwards, however, Tsar Vasily Shuysky himself was overthrown following the defeat of his army by a Polish force a tenth the size, consisting mainly of Scottish mercenaries. Thereafter, Russia was ravaged by feuding boyars, serf and Cossack revolts, and Swedish and Polish invasions. This **Time of Troubles** (*Smutnoe vreme*) was branded on the national psyche for generations afterwards, with the added humiliation that, in 1610, "Holy Mother" Moscow succumbed to the Poles for the second time.

Then, when all seemed lost, Russia demonstrated the astonishing powers of recovery that would save it at other critical moments in history. Abbot Palitsyn of the Trinity Monastery of St Sergei declared a holy war and vowed to excommunicate anyone who failed to support it. The **liberation of Moscow** was accomplished by a volunteer army under **Prince Pozharsky** of Suzdal and the butcher **Kosma Minin** of Nizhniy Novgorod, who ensured that the latter's merchants did their duty and financed the campaign by holding all their womenfolk hostage till the money was paid. Having recaptured Moscow in 1612, they went on to expel the Poles from Russian soil by the year's end.

The early Romanovs

In the aftermath of the war, dissension arose again among the boyars over who should be elected tsar. Disgruntled that his own candidacy had been rejected, Prince Trubetskoy proposed the four-year-old son of the second False Dmitry, confiding to a friend: "Those sons of bitches won't have me, a Russian Prince and a Cossack Hetman, so I'll slip in their way the son of a thief and a Polish whore. Then let them get out of that mess!" To resolve the impasse, Abbot Palitsyn proposed **Mikhail Romanov**, the brother of Ivan the Terrible's first wife, whose accession in 1613 marked the end of the Time of Troubles and the beginning of the Romanov dynasty.

Moscow made a dramatic recovery, with a spate of new stone churches in the tent-roofed style symbolizing the close co-operation between church and state, which reached its zenith under Mikhail's successor, **Alexei II** (1645–76), known as "The Quiet" for his piety and love of books. It was during his reign that **Patriarch Nikon** precipitated a schism in the Orthodox Church by reforming its rituals, leading to the exile of such prominent "Old Believers" as Bishop Avvakum and the Boyarina Morozova. Another innovation was the establishment of the so-called **German Suburb**, to house foreign soldiers, doctors, engineers, and others with professional skills that Russia lacked, due to its backwardness and conservatism.

In 1669 the tsar's wife Maria Miloslavskaya died during childbirth, leaving two young sons to continue the dynasty: the frail Fyodor and his imbecilic younger brother Ivan. Within a year Tsar Alexei took another wife, Natalya Naryshkina, whose Naryshkin relatives promptly displaced his former wife's kinsfolk at court, and congratulated themselves on their future prospects following the birth of a healthy son named Peter – subsequently known to history as Peter the Great.

Peter the Great

Peter the Great (*Pyotr Veliki*) ranks alongside Ivan the Terrible and Stalin in the pantheon of despots who lashed Russia through a series of fundamental transformations. His greatest monument is St Petersburg, the capital city that he created from nothing – to replace Moscow, which represented all that he detested and reminded him of his traumatic youth. His energy was as extraordinary as his physique: Peter was six feet four inches tall, with a disproportionately small head.

When Peter was three his father's demise made him an unwanted offspring. His sickly half-brother Fyodor became tsar, and the Miloslavsky boyars returned to court, banishing Peter's Naryshkin relatives. Peter continued to live uneventfully at Kolomenskoe until 1682, when the death of Fyodor left him the heir to the throne at the age of ten. The Miloslavskys retaliated by organizing a **Streltsy revolt**, during which several Naryshkins were butchered in front of Peter in the Kremlin. The upshot was that his retarded sibling **Ivan** was recognized as co-tsar, and his scheming half-sister **Sofia** became **Regent**.

While Sofia ruled from the Kremlin, Peter pursued his boyish enthusiasms at Preobrazhenskoe, staging war games with his "toy regiments" and learning how to sail. However, **conflict** was inevitable as he came of age, and in August 1689 Sofia ordered the Streltsy to mobilize, spurring Peter to flee to the Trinity Monastery of St Sergei. Safe within its walls, his party issued appeals for loyalty, and were heartened by the defection of the Patriarch from Sofia's camp. By October her support had collapsed and she was confined to the Novodevichiy Convent.

Initially Peter left affairs of state to his Naryshkin elders, preferring to dally in the German Suburb, imbibing foreign ways with cronies like Lefort and Menshikov. His first serious venture was an attempt to capture the Turkish fort of **Azov**, which failed in 1695, but was pursued the following year until the city fell. It was the first Russian victory since Alexei's reign, and served notice that Russia could no longer be trifled with. Soon afterwards Peter announced plans to colonize Azov and construct a fleet, followed by the astounding news that he intended to tour Europe with a **"Great Embassy"**.

Never before had a tsar travelled abroad; even stranger, Peter chose to go "incognito", to be free to study shipbuilding in Holland and England, where he mastered the skills by working in the dockyards. He also met monarchs and conversed with Isaac Newton and other learned figures of the age. Peter was gripped by it all, and became determined to drag his nation into the modern world. During his homeward journey in 1698 the Streltsy rebelled again, but were crushed by his foreign-officered Guards regiments. Peter later participated in the mass execution of the rebels, on Red Square.

Peter's reforms

The tsar lost no time in assailing everything that Russians held dear. Aided by his court jester, he shaved off the beards of his courtiers, and forced them to smoke tobacco and wear frock coats instead of caftans. The nation's name was changed from Muscovy to Russia, and the Orthodox calendar replaced by the "Popish" Julian version. Foreigners were invited to settle where they liked and worship as they wished. Peter forced the sons of landowners into the military or civil service, and conscripted serfs into the army for 25 years. The Church's power was broken by replacing the self-governing Patriarchate with a Holy Synod, subordinate to the tsar. Even beards were taxed to raise revenue.

To enforce such changes Peter relied on traditional methods of repression, and invented new ones. He introduced the internal passport system, later so beloved of the Communists, and organized forced labour gangs to build his grand projects. Faced with opposition he was ruthless, overseeing the torture and death of his own son, Alexei, whom he suspected of conspiring against him. Many of his reforms were simply intended to improve Russia's strength during the long **Northern War** against **Sweden** (1700–21), which began with their youthful monarch Charles XII putting the Russians to flight at **Narva**. However, Charles failed to press his advantage by marching on Moscow, concentrating on subduing the rebellious Poles instead.

St Petersburg

This lull in the war enabled Peter to strengthen Russia's hold on the Gulf of Finland, and fulfil the **quest for a seaport and a navy** that had long dominated his thinking. According to Pushkin's poetic account of its foundation in 1703, the tsar cut two lengths of turf, laid them crossways, and declaimed: "By nature we are fated here to cut a window through to Europe." As a place to found a city, it was hardly ideal: a fetid marshland prone to flooding, with few natural or human resources.

The **creation of St Petersburg** was accomplished by forced labour, under terrible conditions. Thousands died of starvation, cold, disease and exhaustion. Basic tools were so scarce that earth had to be carried in the workers' clothing. In the summer of 1706, with the city barely on the map, Charles XII invaded from Poland and again came within an ace of victory before making the fateful decision to concentrate his efforts on Ukraine, culminating in his defeat at Poltava in 1709. The Northern War dragged on for another twelve years but, as Peter put it, "Now the final stone has been laid on the foundation of St Petersburg."

In 1710 the Imperial family moved there together with all government offices, and in 1712 St Petersburg was declared the **capital**. To populate the city, landowners and nobles were obliged to resettle there and finance the building of their own houses. The tsar drafted in 40,000 workmen a year from the provinces, and overcame a shortage of stonemasons by prohibiting building in stone elsewhere in Russia. In Moscow church building ceased, and wealthy citizens complained of having to establish new households far from home, at vast expense. Though they hated St Petersburg and returned to Moscow whenever possible, the lure of the court would eventually ensure that the old capital was eclipsed by its new rival. As Pushkin wrote in *The Bronze Horseman*:

Old Moscow's paled before this other
metropolis; it's just the same
as when a widowed Dowager Empress
bows to a young Tsaritsa's claim.

Peter the Great's successors

Having killed his only son, Peter was obliged to issue a decree claiming the right to nominate his successor, but when he died in 1725 he was so ill that he was unable to speak. Initially his wife **Catherine I** was hailed as tsaritsa and ruled in tandem with Menshikov (see p.160), but she died after less than two years. Peter's young grandson **Peter II** became tsar, exiled Menshikov to Siberia and moved the capital back to Moscow in 1728. However, on the eve of his wedding day in 1730 he died of smallpox in the Lefort Palace, leaving the throne vacant and no obvious successor.

In desperation the Supreme Privy Council turned to the widowed Anna Ivanovna, a German-born niece of Peter the Great. **Empress Anna** re-established St Petersburg as the capital and brought with her an entourage of unpopular German courtiers. Her reign (1730–40) was cruel and decadent. Affairs of state were carried out by her German favourite, Ernst-Johann Biron, whose rule of terror, known as the *Bironovshchina*, involved the execution of thousands of alleged opponents.

Anna died childless, leaving the crown to her great-nephew **Ivan VI** (1740–41), who because of his youth was put under the regency of his mother Anna Leopoldovna. However, real power remained in the hands of the hated Biron until a coup, backed by the Preobrazhenskiy Guards and financed with French money, elevated Peter the Great's daughter Elizabeth to the throne.

Empress Elizabeth

Like her father, **Elizabeth** was stubborn, quick-tempered and devoted to Russia but, unlike him, she detested serious occupations and "abandoned herself to every excess of intemperance and lubricity". Elizabeth was almost illiterate, and her court favourite Razumovsky (a Cossack shepherd turned chorister whom she secretly married) couldn't write at all. She liked dancing and hunting, and lived in chaotic apartments, with wardrobes stacked with 15,000 dresses, and the floors littered with unpaid bills. Her continual moving from palace to palace and from hunting party to monastery resulted in a budget deficit of eight million rubles.

Although Elizabeth hated the sight of blood she would order torture at the slightest offence. Yet she abolished the death penalty and was sensible enough to retain as one of her principal advisers the enlightened Count Shuvalov, who encouraged her in the foundation of **Moscow University**, under the direction of **Mikhail Lomonosov** (1711–65), a polymath known as the "Russian Leonardo". In fact, the cultural achievements of Catherine the Great were based more than she liked to admit on the foundations laid in Elizabeth's reign. In foreign affairs Elizabeth displayed a determined hostility towards Prussia, participating in both the War of Austrian Succession (1740–48) and the Seven Years' War (1756–63), during which Russian troops occupied Berlin.

Peter III

On Elizabeth's death in 1761 the new tsar – her nephew, **Peter III** – adopted a strongly pro-Prussian policy, forcing the army into Prussian uniforms and offending the clergy by adhering to the Lutheran faith of his Holstein homeland. The one concession to the nobility during his six-month reign was the abolition of the compulsory 25-year state service. It was a decree of great consequence, for it created a large, privileged leisured class, hitherto unknown in Russia. Childish, moody and impotent, Peter was no match for his intelligent, sophisticated wife, Sophia of Anhalt-Zerbst, who ingratiated herself with her subjects by joining the Orthodox Church, changing her name to Catherine in the process. Their marriage was a sham, and in June 1762 she and her favourite, Grigory Orlov, orchestrated a coup d'état with the backing of the Guards regiments. Peter was imprisoned outside St Petersburg, and later murdered by Orlov.

Catherine the Great

The reign of **Catherine the Great** spanned four decades (1762–96) and saw the emergence of Russia as a truly great European power. Catherine was a woman of considerable culture and learning and a great patron of the arts. Inevitably, however, she is best known for her private life. Her most prominent courtier – and lover – Prince Potemkin, oversaw one of the greatest territorial gains of her reign, the annexation of the Crimea

(1783), which secured the Black Sea coast for Russia.

After consolidating her position as an autocrat – she had no legitimate claim to the throne – Catherine enjoyed a brief honeymoon as a liberal. French became the language of the court, and with it came the ideas of the **Enlightenment**. Catherine herself conducted a lengthy correspondence with Voltaire, while Lomonosov was encouraged to standardize the Russian language. However, the lofty intentions of her reforms were watered down by her advisers to little more than a reassertion of "benevolent" despotism. When it came to the vital question of the emancipation of the serfs, the issue was swept under the carpet. And when writers like **Alexander Radishchev** began to take her at her word and publish critical works she responded by exiling them to Siberia.

Catherine's liberal leanings were given a severe jolt by the **Pugachev revolt**, which broke out east of the River Volga in 1773, under the leadership of a Don Cossack named Pugachev. It was the most serious peasant revolt in the entire 300-year rule of the Romanovs. Encouraged by the hope that, since the nobility had been freed from state service, the serfs would likewise be emancipated, thousands responded to Pugachev's call for freedom from the landowners and division of their estates. For two years Pugachev's forces conducted a guerrilla campaign from Perm in the Urals to Tsaritsyn on the Volga, before being crushed by the army. The French Revolution killed off what was left of Catherine's benevolence, and in her later years she relied ever more heavily on the powers of unbridled despotism.

Paul and Alexander I

On Catherine's death in 1796 her son **Paul** became tsar. Not without good reason Paul detested his mother and everything associated with her, and immediately set about reversing most of her policies: his first act was to give his father Peter III a decent burial. Like his father, Paul was a moody and militarily obsessed man, who worshipped everything Prussian. He offended the army by forcing the Guards regiments back into Prussian uniforms, earned the enmity of the nobility by attempting to curtail some of the privileges they had enjoyed under Catherine, and reintroduced the idea of male hereditary succession abandoned by Peter the Great.

In March 1801 Paul was strangled to death in St Petersburg, in a palace coup that had the tacit approval of his son **Alexander I**. Alexander shared Catherine's penchant for the ideas of the Enlightenment, but also exhibited a strong streak of religious conservatism. His reign (1801–25) was in any case dominated by foreign affairs – the Napoleonic Wars above all. Initially, Alexander sought to contain France by an alliance with Austria and Prussia, but when this failed he signed the Treaty of Tilsit (1807) with Napoleon, in a hut moored on the River Niemen, which separated their domains. Like the pact between Stalin and Hitler 132 years later, this *volte-face* was intended to buy time to prepare for war, which seemed inevitable.

The Patriotic War and the burning of Moscow

In June 1812 **Napoleon** crossed the Niemen and invaded Russia with his *Grande Armée* of 600,000 – twice the size of any force the Russians could muster. The Russians employed "scorched earth" tactics and harassed the French flanks with partisans, but public opinion demanded a stand. Against his wishes, Marshal Kutuzov was obliged to fight a pitched battle, despite being outnumbered. The **Battle of Borodino** (September 7) killed 70,000 on both sides and left Kutuzov's forces so weak that defending Moscow seemed impossible. To save his troops, Kutuzov withdrew northwards, allowing Napoleon to advance on Moscow, which started a frenzied exodus of civilians.

Having waited in vain for a delegation of nobles to offer him the keys to the city, Napoleon entered Moscow on September 14 to find that over 100,000 inhabitants had fled. That same night agents of the Tsarist governor started fires in the Kitay-gorod, which a powerful wind the next day fanned into a conflagration. The following day Napoleon was obliged to flee to a palace outside Moscow, as the Kremlin was engulfed in smoke and cinders, while his troops abandoned fire-fighting in favour of looting. **Moscow burned** for six days, until three-quarters of its buildings were reduced to ashes.

Though the French lived off neighbouring estates and villages as best they could, staying for long was hardly feasible, and Tsar Alexander refused to surrender. With winter approaching and Russian forces mustering to the north,

Napoleon had no choice but to begin the long **retreat** home. Harassed by Cossacks and partisans, and unprepared for the ferocity of the Russian winter, the *Grande Armée* had shrunk to a mere 30,000 men when it finally reached Poland. The Russians didn't stop there but pursued Napoleon all the way back to Paris, which they occupied in 1814. At the Congress of Vienna the following year, Russia was assured of its share in the carve-up of Europe.

The reconstruction of Moscow and the Decembrist revolt

Within months of the fire, a commission for the **reconstruction of Moscow** was formed, and submitted its proposals to Tsar Alexander. The plan involved creating new squares where Moscow's radial avenues met the Beliy and Zemlyanoy Gorod walls, which were levelled and turned into boulevards. Private houses were swiftly rebuilt, and within five years Moscow had almost replaced its residential quarters (chiefly with wooden dwellings, which still accounted for over half the buildings in the city forty years later). The architect Bove was alone responsible for about 500 buildings, many in the Russian Empire style that reflected the widespread mood of patriotic pride.

Another result of the war was that it exposed thousands of Russians to life in other countries. The aristocracy and gentry noted parliaments and constitutional monarchies, while peasant foot soldiers saw how much better their lot could be without serfdom. As the tsar and his ministers were sure that any reforms would endanger autocracy, opposition festered underground. Guards officers and liberal aristocrats formed groups with innocuous names such as the "Southern Society" and the "Northern Society", which disseminated propaganda and even planned to assassinate the tsar.

When Alexander died in November 1825 without leaving a male heir, the plotters sought to take advantage of the dynastic crisis that ensued. The Guards initially swore allegiance to Alexander's brother Constantine, who was next in line for the throne, but who had secretly relinquished the succession. A coup was hurriedly devised, to be staged on the day that troops were to swear a new oath of allegiance to Alexander's younger brother Nicholas. On December 14, in St Petersburg, rebels and loyalist troops faced each other across Senate Square for six hours, both unwilling to shoot, until Nicholas gave the order to attack. Two hours later the revolt was crushed and hundreds of corpses were tipped into the River Neva.

Those of the **Decembrists** who survived were personally interrogated by Nicholas, who sentenced five of the ringleaders to death and exiled more than a hundred to Siberia. Though no mention of this "horrible and extraordinary plot" (as he called it) was allowed in public, the fate of so many aristocrats inevitably resulted in gossip – especially when Countess Volkonskaya followed her husband into exile, inspiring other wives to do likewise. Although the Decembrists themselves failed, their example would be upheld by future generations of Russian revolutionaries.

Nicholas I

The reign of **Nicholas I** (1825–55) was epitomized by the slogan "Orthodoxy, Autocracy, Nationality", as coined by one of his ministers. The status quo was to be maintained at all costs: censorship increased, as did police surveillance, carried out by the infamous **Third Section** of the tsar's personal Chancellery. A uniformed gendarmerie was created and organized along military lines, while an elaborate network of spies and informers kept a close watch on all potential subversives.

As ever, the most intractable problem was **serfdom** – "the powder-magazine under the state", as his police chief put it – which affected eighty percent of the population and gave rise to several rebellions in the late 1820s, though none approached the scale of the Pugachev revolt. It also hampered industrialization in Russia, which was mostly confined to the textiles and sugar-beet industries.

During the 1840s the greatest change occurred in the upper echelons of society, as deferential admiration for Tsarism was gradually replaced by scorn and dissent. The writer Dostoyevsky was among those drawn to the clandestine **Petrashevskiy Circle** of utopian socialists, based in St Petersburg. In 1849 over a hundred of them were arrested as Nicholas clamped down in the wake of revolutions in Poland and Hungary, which his armies put down, earning him the nickname the "Gendarme of Europe".

In early 1854 the **Crimean War** broke out and Russia found itself at war with Britain, France and Turkey. The war highlighted the flaws and inadequacies inherent in the Tsarist Empire: Russian troops defending Sevastopol opposed rifles with muskets; Russian sailing ships had to do battle with enemy steamers; and the lack of railways meant that Russian soldiers were no better supplied than their Allied counterparts, who were thousands of miles from home. The Allied capture of Sevastopol in 1855 almost certainly helped to accelerate the death of the despondent Nicholas, whose last words of advice to his heir were "Hold on to everything!"

The Tsar Liberator: Alexander II

In fact the new Tsar **Alexander II** (1855–81) had little choice but to sue for peace, and for those who hoped for change in Russia the defeats of the Crimean War came as a blessing. The surviving Decembrists and Petrashevskiy exiles were released, police surveillance eased and many of the censorship restrictions lifted.

In 1861 Alexander II signed the historic decree allowing for the **emancipation of the serfs**, earning himself the sobriquet "Tsar Liberator". In reality the Emancipation Act was a fraud, replacing the landowner's legal ownership with a crushing economic dependence in the form of financial compensation, which the freed serfs were forced to pay their landlords over a period of 49 years. However, Alexander did push through other reforms that represented a break with the past, introducing trial by jury and a limited form of local self-government through appointed *zemstva* (assemblies), and reducing military service from 25 years to six.

Populists and assassins

However, Alexander's reforms stopped short of a constitutional shift from autocracy, disappointing those who had hoped for a "revolution from above". The 1860s witnessed an upsurge in peasant unrest and a radicalization of the opposition movement among the educated elite. From their ranks came the amorphous **Populist** (*Narodnik*) movement, which gathered momentum throughout the late 1860s and early 1870s. The Populists' chief ideologue, Nikolai Chernyshevsky, was committed to establishing a socialist society based around the peasant commune. There were, however, widely differing views on the best means of achieving this end. The clandestine organization "Hell" – or "**Nihilists**" as Turgenev dubbed them in his novel *Fathers and Sons* (1862) – led the charge with the first attempt on the tsar's life.

Others believed in taking the Populist message to the people. This campaign reached a climax in the "crazy summer" of 1874, when thousands of students, dressed as simple folk, roamed the countryside attempting to convert the peasantry to their cause. Most of these exhortations fell on deaf ears, for although the peasantry were fed up with their lot they were suspicious of all townspeople, and for the most part remained blindly loyal to the tsar. The authorities were nevertheless sufficiently alarmed to make mass arrests, which culminated in the much publicized trials of "the 50" and "the 193", later held in St Petersburg.

The failure of the campaign led to a return to conspiratorial methods. In 1876 a new revolutionary organization called **Land and Liberty** was founded, rapidly splitting on the one hand into the **Black Partition**, which agitated for seizures of property in the countryside, and on the other into the notorious **People's Will** (*Narodnaya Volya*), whose run of urban terrorist acts culminated in the **assassination of Alexander II** in 1881.

Alexander III and industrialization

However, regicide failed to stir the masses to revolution, and the new Tsar **Alexander III** (1881–94) shelved all constitutional reforms, increased police surveillance and cut back the powers of the *zemstva*. His ultra-reactionary adviser Pobedonostov blamed dissent on the Jews, so that the police stood by during a wave of **pogroms** in 1881–82, which were followed by harsh anti-Semitic laws, under which 20,000 Jews were expelled from Moscow to the "Pale of Settlement".

Industrialization had burgeoned since the Emancipation Act, and foreign investment had nearly doubled, giving Russia a rate of growth outstripping that of other major European powers. In Moscow huge suburban factories and slums sprang up, drawing in thousands of peasants and creating an increasingly large urban working class, whose impact would be felt in the late 1890s. Meanwhile, the nouveau riche **Kuptsy**, whose ancestors had toiled as serfs, displayed their wealth by commissioning architects like Shekhtel to build them fabulous Style Moderne mansions, and sponsored endeavours such as the Tretyakov Gallery and the Moscow Art Theatre.

Nicholas II

When Alexander III died in 1894 the throne passed to his son **Nicholas II** (1894–1917), who signalled his intention to continue his father's policies by denouncing the constitutional reforms proposed by the *zemstvo* of Tver as "senseless dreams". In the same year he married the German-born Princess Alexandra of Hesse, whose autocratic spirit and extreme Orthodoxy exerted an unhealthy influence. Their coronation in Moscow in May 1896 was marred by the **Khodynka Field disaster** (see p.313), widely seen as a bad omen for what would prove to be a doomed reign.

The new opposition

Although Populism had been discredited by the failure of terrorism to ignite a revolution, a new generation of radicals emerged in the late 1890s as the Socialist Revolutionary Party, or **SRs**, publicizing their cause through acts such as the assassination of the tsar's chief minister, Plehve – but they still failed to attract the peasantry to their cause.

Meanwhile, a section of the Russian intelligentsia had begun to shift its ideological stance towards **Marxism**, which pinned its hopes on the urban proletariat as the future agent of revolution. The first Marxist organization, "Emancipation of Labour", was founded in 1883 by a handful of ex-Populist exiles in Switzerland, including the "father of Russian Marxism", **Georgy Plekhanov**. The group was so small that when out boating on Lake Geneva Plekhanov once joked "Be careful: if this boat sinks, it's the end of Russian Marxism."

Plekhanov teamed up with Vladimir Ilyich Ulyanov – later known as **Lenin** – to form the **Russian Social Democratic Labour Party** (RSDLP), which was founded (and immediately suppressed) in 1898. Forced into exile, divisions quickly began to appear: Lenin argued for a conspiratorial, disciplined party, while his chief rival, Martov, wanted a more open, mass membership. In the split that followed, Lenin managed to claim for his supporters the description **Bolsheviks** (meaning "majority" in Russian), while his opponents became known as **Mensheviks** ("minority", with all its connotations of weakness).

Meanwhile, the non-radical liberal bourgeoisie tended to back the Constitutional Democratic Party, or **Kadets**, whose modest demands for freedom of the press, assembly and association were also revolutionary in the context of Tsarist Russia.

The 1905 Revolution

The economic boom of the late 1890s came to an abrupt end in 1900 and was followed by a slump that put many of the urban working class out of work. In January 1904 Russia blundered into a **war with Japan**, which soon exposed the total incompetence of its Naval and Army High Commands. But worse was to follow on the home front, as the Tsarist regime faced its most serious challenge since the Pugachev uprising in the eighteenth century.

In early January 1905 a strike broke out at the giant Putilov engineering works in St Petersburg, which quickly spread to other factories. On January 9, 150,000 strikers and their families set off to hand a petition to the tsar, demanding basic civil rights and labour laws. They marched peacefully, singing hymns and carrying portraits of the tsar – until they met the Imperial Guard, which opened fire to disperse the crowds, killing and wounding several thousand. **Bloody Sunday** marked a fatal breach in the social contract, and for the rest of his reign the tsar would never quite shake off his reputation as "Bloody Nicholas".

When the first wave of strikes petered out, Nicholas hoped that a quick victory in the war against the Japanese would ease his troubles at home, but instead the Russian Fleet was decimated at Tsushima Bay, and a mutiny occurred on the battleship *Potemkin*. Reluctantly, the tsar was obliged to make peace with Japan and forced to agree to the establishment of a consultative assembly – or **Duma** – at home, but this limited concession failed to avert further strikes in St Petersburg or the growing unrest within the army.

Soon Nicholas had little choice but to issue the so-called **October Manifesto**, promising basic civil liberties and the right of the future Duma to veto laws. Meanwhile, the workers seized the initiative and created the **St Petersburg Soviet**, made up of 500-odd delegates, elected by over 200,000 workers. Under the co-chairmanship of **Trotsky** (who had yet to join the Bolsheviks), it pursued a moderate policy, criticizing the proposed Duma, but falling far short of calling for an armed uprising – as the middle classes feared would happen.

By December the regime had recovered its nerve and, emboldened by divisions among the opposition, clamped down in St Petersburg, where the leaders of the Soviet were arrested. In Moscow local Bolsheviks misjudged the situation and led radical workers in a vain attempt to seize power. Having failed to break through into the centre of town, they barricaded themselves into the **Presnya** district. The government used artillery to smash the barricades, and then sent in cavalry and machine-gun units to crush any remaining resistance. In the aftermath hundreds were summarily executed by field tribunals or exiled to Siberia.

The last decade of Tsarism

With the revolutionary tide ebbing (though sporadic unrest persisted until 1907), the main task facing the tsar was how to confront the new Duma, following the first nationwide elections in Russian history. The franchise was broad-based, though a long way from universal suffrage, and the Kadets emerged as the largest grouping. In May 1906 the opening of the **First Duma** in St Petersburg's Tauride Palace was attended by diverse figures, from Grand Dukes to peasants' and workers' deputies in overalls and muddy boots. After ten weeks of debate the issue of land distribution reared its head, prompting the tsar to surround the palace with troops and dissolve the Duma. The succeeding Second Duma suffered a similar fate.

The most positive post-revolutionary repercussions took place within the **arts**. From 1905 to 1914 Moscow and St Petersburg experienced an extraordinary outburst of artistic energy: Diaghilev's *Ballets Russes* dazzled Europe; Chekhov premiered his works at the Moscow Art Theatre; poets and writers held Symbolist seances; while Mayakovsky and other self-proclaimed Futurists toured the country, shocking the general public with their statements on art.

Meanwhile, the Imperial family abandoned the capital for the security of their palaces outside St Petersburg, and fell further under the influence of the charlatan **Rasputin**, upon whom they pinned all their hopes for the survival of the haemophiliac heir, Tsarevich Alexei. The celebrations in honour of the **tercentenary of the Romanov dynasty** in 1913 (during which the Court wore bejewelled caftans in the style of their seventeenth-century forebears) were effectively their swan song.

In the nationalistic fervour that accompanied the outbreak of **World War I** in August 1914 the name of the capital was deemed too Germanic and changed to **Petrograd**. Yet serious deficiencies in the structure of the army and military production were barely acknowledged, let alone tackled. The first Russian offensive ended in defeat at Tannenberg, with 170,000 casualties. From then on there was rarely any good news from the front; in the first year alone, some four million soldiers lost their lives. Hoping to improve matters, the tsar assumed personal command of the armed forces – a post for which he was totally unqualified.

By the end of 1916 even monarchists were voicing reservations. The tsar's German-born wife was openly accused of treason, while Rasputin was assassinated by a group of aristocrats desperate to force a change of policy. Ensconced with his son in the Imperial headquarters at Mogilev, Nicholas refused to be moved. As inflation spiralled and food shortages worsened, strikes began to break out once more in Petrograd. By the beginning of 1917 everyone, from generals to peasants, was talking of an imminent revolution.

The February Revolution

On February 22, there was a lock-out of workers at the Putilov works in Petrograd – the **February Revolution** had begun. The following day (International Women's Day) thousands of women and workers thronged the streets attacking bread shops, singing the *Marseillaise* and calling for the overthrow of the tsar. On February 27 prisons were stormed and the Duma was surrounded by demonstrators and mutinous troops, while Trotsky and the Mensheviks re-established the Soviet. On March 2, en route to the capital, the tsar was persuaded to **abdicate** in favour of his brother, who gave up his own claim the following day, bringing the Romanov dynasty to an end.

Out of the revolutionary ferment a state of "dual power" (*dvoevlastie*) arose. The **Provisional Government** under the liberal Count Lvov attempted to assert itself as the legitimate successor to autocracy by decreeing freedom of speech and an amnesty. There were to be elections for a Constituent Assembly, but no end to the war. This pacified the generals, who might otherwise have tried to suppress the revolution, but eroded the government's popularity. The other power base was the Menshevik-dominated **Petrograd Soviet**, which was prepared to give qualified support to the "bourgeois revolution" until the time was ripe for the establishment of socialism. Their "Order No. 1", calling for the formation of Soviets throughout the army, subverted military discipline.

After ditching some of its right-wing elements the Provisional Government co-operated more closely with the Petrograd Soviet. **Alexander Kerensky** became the Minister of War and toured the front calling for a fresh offensive against the Germans. The attack began well but soon turned into a retreat, while discontent in Petrograd peaked again in a wave of violent protests known as the **July Days**. Lenin, who had returned from exile, felt that the time was not right for a coup and, indeed, loyalist troops soon restored order. Trotsky and others were arrested, Lenin was accused of being a German spy and forced once more into exile, and the Bolsheviks as a whole were branded as traitors.

Kerensky used the opportunity to tighten his grip on the Provisional Government, taking over as leader from Prince Lvov. In late August the army commander-in-chief, General Kornilov, attempted to march on Petrograd and crush Bolshevism once and for all. Whether he had been encouraged by Kerensky remains uncertain, but in the event Kerensky decided to turn on Kornilov, denouncing the coup and calling on the Bolsheviks and workers' militia to defend the capital. Kerensky duly appointed himself commander-in-chief, but it was the Left who were now in the ascendant.

The October Revolution

During September Russia began to slide into chaos: soldiers deserted the front in ever-greater numbers and the countryside was in turmoil, while the "Bolshevization" of the Soviets continued apace. By October Lenin had managed to persuade his colleagues that the time to seize power was nigh. Bolshevik Red Guards were trained and armed under the aegis of the **Military Revolutionary Committee**, based in the former Smolniy Institute for Ladies.

The **October Revolution** began in the early hours of the 25th (November 7 by today's calendar), with the occupation of key points in Petrograd. Posters announcing the overthrow of the Provisional Government appeared on the streets at 10am, though it wasn't until 2am the following morning that the Cabinet was arrested in the Winter Palace. In contrast to the almost bloodless coup in Petrograd, Moscow witnessed a week of fierce battles between Red Guards and loyalist troops holed up in the Kremlin and the *Metropol Hotel*.

The coup had been planned to coincide with the Second All-Russian Congress of Soviets, at which the Bolsheviks' majority was enhanced when the Mensheviks and right-wing SRs walked out in protest. Lenin delivered his famous decrees calling for an end to the war and approving the seizure of land by the peasants. An all-Bolshevik **Council of People's Commissars** was established, and issued a spate of decrees nationalizing banks and financial organizations and instituting an eight-hour working day.

Conditions in Petrograd and Moscow worsened. Food was scarcer than ever, while rumours of anti-Bolshevik plots abounded. In December 1917 Lenin created the "All-Russian Extraordinary Commission for Struggle against Counter-Revolution, Speculation and Sabotage", or **Cheka** for short (meaning "linch-pin" in Russian). Although the Bolsheviks had reluctantly agreed to abolish the death penalty in October, the Cheka, under "Iron" **Felix Dzerzhinsky**, reserved the right to "have recourse to a firing squad when it becomes obvious that there is no other way".

Following elections, the long-awaited **Constituent Assembly** met for the first and only time on January 5, 1918. As the first Russian parliament elected by universal suffrage, this was meant to be "the crowning jewel in Russian democratic life", but Lenin regarded it as "an old fairytale which there is no reason to carry on further". Having received only a quarter of the vote, the Bolsheviks surrounded the premises the next day, preventing many delegates from entering; Red Guards eventually dismissed those inside with the words, "Push off. We want to go home."

The Civil War 1918–20

More pressing than the internecine feuds of the socialist parties was the outcome of the peace negotiations with Germany. In mid-February of 1918, talks broke down and the Germans launched a fresh offensive in Russia, which met little effective resistance. Eventually, on March 3, Trotsky signed the **Treaty of Brest-Litovsk**, which handed over Poland, Finland, Belarus, the Baltics and – most painfully of all – Ukraine, Russia's bread basket. But German artillery remained within range of Petrograd, and renewed hostilities seemed likely, so in March 1918 the Bolshevik government moved to **Moscow**, and proclaimed it the **capital** of the fledgling Soviet state. Lenin stayed at the *National Hotel* before moving into the Kremlin, while the Cheka took over the Rossiya Insurance Company building on Lubyanka Square.

At the Seventh Party Congress, held in the Bolshoy Theatre, the RSDLP was renamed the **Communist Party**, and the Left-SRs quit in protest at the Brest-Litovsk treaty. On July 6–7, the assassination of the German ambassador heralded an **abortive Left-SR coup** in Moscow, during which Dzerzhinsky was held hostage at SR headquarters. In August they struck again, with the murder of the Petrograd Cheka chief, and an unsuccessful attempt on Lenin's life at the Michelson factory in Moscow. The Bolsheviks responded with a wave of repression known as the **Red Terror**. Thousands of hostages were imprisoned and shot. Dzerzhinsky's deputy pronounced that one look at a suspect's hands would suffice to determine his class allegiance.

By this time a **Civil War** was raging across Russia, fuelled by **foreign intervention**. In a vain attempt to force Russia back into the war against Germany, but also from fear of Bolshevism spreading, the Western powers sent troops to fight the Reds. A Czech Legion seized control of the Trans-Siberian Railway; British troops landed in Murmansk and Baku; US, Japanese, French and Italian forces seized Vladivostok; while the Germans controlled the vast tracts of land given to them under the Brest-Litovsk treaty. Fearing that they would be freed from captivity in Yekaterinburg, Lenin and Sverdlov ordered the **execution of the Imperial family**, which was carried out by local Bolsheviks on July 16–17.

The victory of the Soviet regime owed as much to the failings of its enemies as to the tenacity of the Bolsheviks. The anti-Communist forces – or **Whites** – represented every strand of politics from monarchists to SRs, but their bias towards the propertied classes made it impossible for them to accept the land seizures endorsed by the Bolsheviks, thereby alienating the peasantry, whose support was vital. Moreover their forces were dispersed over a vast area, with no centralized command and little co-ordination between them. By contrast, the Reds were united by their ideology and ruthless leaders, with a platform that appealed to peasants and workers. Militarily, they had the advantage of controlling the **railways** emanating from Moscow, which enabled them to switch resources from one battle front to another, while Trotsky solved the infant Red Army's lack of expertise by compelling ex-Tsarist officers to serve under the vigilant eye of Bolshevik commissars, as he ranged across the Russian heartland in his armoured train, shooting commanders who disobeyed orders to hold ground at all costs. However, both sides were evenly matched in numbers, and rivalled each other in ferocity when it came to exacting revenge on collaborators.

Not only did the Civil War cost well over a million lives, but it promoted the militarization of Soviet society, under the rubric of **"War Communism"**. Workers' control in the factories and the nationalization of land had plunged the Soviet economy into chaos just as the Civil War broke out. In an attempt to cope, the Bolsheviks introduced labour discipline of a kind not seen since the pre-trade union days of Tsarism. With money almost worthless, peasants had no incentive to sell their scarce produce in the cities, so Red Guards were sent into the countryside to seize food, and "committees of the poor" set up to stimulate class war against the richer peasantry, or *kulaks*.

The Kronstadt revolt and the NEP

By 1921 Soviet Russia was economically devastated, and the Bolsheviks found themselves confronted with worker unrest at the same time as serious divisions began to appear within the Party. The most outspoken faction was the **Workers' Opposition**, whose main demands were for independent trade unions and fewer wage differentials. In February 1921 sailors at the Kronstadt naval base – who had been among the Bolsheviks' staunchest supporters since 1905 – turned against the Party. The **Kronstadt sailors' revolt** precipitated a general strike in Petrograd when troops once more refused to fire on crowds. Rejecting calls for negotiations, the Bolsheviks accused the sailors of treason and crushed the revolt.

Meanwhile, Lenin was presiding over the **Tenth Party Congress**, at which he declared a virtual end to democratic debate within the Party and banned all factions. From now on, real power was in the hands of the newly emerging Party bureaucracy, or **Secretariat**, whose first General Secretary, appointed towards the end of 1922, was the Georgian Bolshevik **Joseph Stalin**.

At the Congress Lenin unveiled his **New Economic Policy** (NEP), which marked a retreat from War Communism. The state maintained control of the "commanding heights" of the economy, while reintroducing a limited free market for agricultural produce, giving the peasants an incentive to increase productivity. It was a compromise formula that favoured the peasantry (still the majority of the population) over the urban working class, who dubbed NEP the "New Exploitation of the Proletariat".

The rise of Stalin

Following **Lenin's death** on January 24, 1924 an all-out power struggle began. Trotsky, the hero of the Civil War, and Bukharin, the chief exponent of the NEP, were by far the most popular figures in the Party, but it was Stalin, as head of the Secretariat, who held the real power. Stalin organized Lenin's funeral on Red Square and was the chief architect of his deification, which began with the renaming of Petrograd as **Leningrad**. By employing classic divide-and-rule tactics, Stalin picked off his rivals one by one, beginning with the exile of Trotsky in 1925, followed by the neutralization of Bukharin in 1929.

Abandoning the NEP, Stalin embarked on the **forced collectivization** of agriculture, and industrialization on an unprecedented scale, under the **First Five Year Plan** (1928–32). Declaring its aim to be "the elimination of the *kulak* as a class", the Party waged open war on a peasantry that was overwhelmingly hostile to collectivization. The social and economic upheaval wrought on the country has been dubbed the "Third Revolution" – indeed, it transformed society more than any of the previous revolutions. The peasants' passive resistance, the destruction of livestock and the ensuing chaos all contributed to the **famine** of 1932–33, which surpassed even that of 1921–22, resulting in the death of as many as five million people.

The General Plan for Moscow

In Moscow, however, many took pride in the achievements of Soviet power. Workers' families who had lived in shacks before the Revolution were now housed in subdivided apartments once owned by their social superiors, or even brand new flats in the apartment blocks that were rising across town – as in the famous Socialist Realist painting *A New Home on Tomorrow's Street*.

Future developments were laid out in the **General Plan for the Reconstruction of Moscow**, produced by a committee under Stalin and Kaganovich. Its aim was to transform Moscow into the showcase capital of the world's first Socialist state; a city of grand boulevards and public buildings, converging on a ring of skyscrapers and the Palace of Soviets (see p.135). Its most ambitious aspect was the **Metro** (an idea that had been rejected as blasphemous when it was mooted in 1902). The first shaft was sunk in 1931, and the first line (with thirteen stations) opened in May 1935. *Pravda* lauded the efforts of Komsomol volunteers and drew a veil over the forced labourers who also built the metro.

The purges and show trials

It was in this climate that the Seventeenth Party "**Congress of Victors**" met in 1934. Stalin declared that the Party had triumphed over all opposition, and the nation was on the march to a glorious future. "Life has become better, Comrades. Life has become gayer." Of the 2000-odd delegates who applauded, two-thirds would be arrested in the course of the next five years.

The initial pretext for the mass purges was the mysterious assassination of the Leningrad Party boss, **Sergei Kirov**, on December 1, 1934. In Leningrad, 30,000 to 40,000 citizens were arrested during the spring of 1935 alone, while the total number across the Soviet Union over the next three years ran into millions. The **Great Terror** had a profound effect on society, instilling fear and conformity for long afterwards. Many believe that Stalin himself had ordered the murder of Kirov, to remove a potential rival in the Politburo and break any lingering resistance to his dictatorship.

In the summer of 1936 the first of the great **show trials** were held in Moscow's House of Unions, during which the veteran Bolsheviks Bukharin, Kamenev and Zinoviev "confessed" to Kirov's murder and were sentenced to death. In early 1937 similar accusations of spying on behalf of foreign powers were levelled at Yagoda, the head of the secret police, whose dwarfish successor **Nikolai Yezhov** gave his name to the

Great Terror, which Russians call the *Yezhovshchina*. In December 1938 Yezhov was himself replaced by **Lavrenty Beria**, which the long-suffering Soviet people took as a signal that the worst was over, for the moment at least.

Few realized that purges within the **Red Army** had left it gravely weakened. From the defence minister **Marshal Tukhachevsky** downwards, the majority of senior officers had been either shot or sent to labour camps, and their hastily promoted successors were underqualified and afraid to display any initiative. This was known to Hitler (whose secret service fed Stalin's paranoia about spies within the High Command), and figured in his calculations about the European balance of power.

As Anglo-French appeasement allowed Nazi Germany to invade Austria and Czechoslovakia, and to set its sights on Poland, Stalin feared that the USSR would be next on its *Drang nach Osten* (Drive to the East) and authorized Foreign Minister Molotov to negotiate with his Nazi counterpart. The **Molotov–Ribbentrop pact** of August 1939 bound both parties to non-aggression, and the Soviets to the supply of food and raw materials to the Nazis. It also contained secret clauses relating to the division of Poland and the Soviet occupation of the Baltic States, which were put into practice in the first weeks of World War II.

The Great Patriotic War

Despite advance warnings from his agents in Germany and Japan, Stalin refused to believe that Hitler would break the pact, and was stunned by the Nazi invasion on June 22, 1941, which began what Russians call the **Great Patriotic War**. He is thought to have had a nervous breakdown and withdrawn to his *dacha* outside Moscow, while his subordinates attempted to grapple with the crisis. When Stalin returned to the Kremlin he reputedly told them, "Lenin left us a great inheritance, and we, his heirs, have fucked it all up." Not until July 3 did he address the nation by radio, in a speech that began: "Brothers and sisters! I turn to you, my friends . . ."

In the first weeks of the war over 1000 Soviet aircraft were destroyed on the ground; whole armies were encircled and captured; and local officials fled from the advancing *Wehrmacht*. Stalin had four army commanders shot and put two incompetent "cavalry generals" – Voroshilov and Budyonny – in charge of the western front (they were dismissed two months later).

By mid-October the Nazis were almost on the outskirts of **Moscow**; an advance patrol even reached a suburban metro station. Four hundred and fifty thousand Muscovites were mobilized to dig trenches. On October 16, a decree on the evacuation of the government caused **panic**: the streets were choked with refugees and soot from burning archives. But Marshal Zhukov promised that Moscow could be held, so Stalin opted to stay and ordered that the traditional November parade should go ahead. The troops proceeded directly from Red Square to the battle front, which was reinforced by fresh divisions from Siberia, equipped for winter warfare – unlike the Germans, clad in summer uniforms, with guns that jammed when the temperature sank to below –30°C. The front held, and Moscow was saved.

During four years of war, western Russia, Ukraine and Belarus were devastated, and 27 million Soviet citizens were killed. Their sacrifices broke the back of Hitler's forces and brought the Red Army into the heart of Europe, determining the fate of those nations that subsequently formed the Eastern Bloc. On May 9, 1945, cannons and fireworks exploded above the Kremlin, to mark the end of war in Europe, and delirious crowds thronged the streets. At the great **victory parade** on Red Square on June 24 Nazi banners were cast down before the Lenin Mausoleum, and trampled by stallions ridden by Soviet marshals in magnificent uniforms.

The postwar years and Stalin's death

In the immediate postwar years, Moscow was transformed by **huge construction projects**, using POWs and Soviet convicts as slave labour. The widening of the Garden Ring, the Kaluga Gates and the initial stages of Leninskiy and Kutuzovskiy prospekts were all completed at this time, as were several of the famous **Stalin skyscrapers**. Moscow was the mecca of world Communism, whose domain stretched from Berlin to the newly proclaimed People's Republic of China – at least for the years of Sino-Soviet co-operation, symbolized by the *Pekin Hotel*, built to house visiting delegations. In 1949 Stalin's seventieth birthday occasioned a deluge of tributes, and his image was projected onto the clouds above the Kremlin, like a demigod's.

After the enormous sacrifices of the war, Soviet citizens longed for a peaceful, freer life. However, Stalin's advancing years prompted an intensification of the power struggle, which brought with it a fresh wave of arrests and show trials. The most powerful figure among his putative successors was **Andrei Zhdanov**, who had been in charge of Leningrad during the wartime siege. When Zhdanov died of alcoholism (or poison) in 1948, his enemies fabricated the "Leningrad Affair", in which his closest allies were accused of trying to seize power, and executed. Stalin's final show trial was the "**Doctors' Plot**", in which a group of (mostly Jewish) physicians "confessed" to the murder of Zhdanov. Thankfully, two months into the charade, Stalin died, and the charges were later dropped.

The **death of Stalin** on March 5, 1953 (see p.195), occasioned a nationwide outpouring of grief, which was largely genuine. Nobody knows how many mourners were crushed to death outside the House of Unions, where his body lay in state in the Columned Hall where the show trials had been held in the 1930s. After decades of submission to the "Wise Father of all the Peoples", many citizens couldn't imagine how they could continue without him.

Khrushchev and the "Thaw"

Following Stalin's death, the power struggle within the Soviet leadership continued unabated. Beria, the odious secret police chief, was the first to be arrested and executed in July 1953; Malenkov lasted until 1955, before he was forced to resign; while Molotov hung on until 1957. The man who was to emerge as the next Soviet leader was **Nikita Khrushchev** who, in 1956, when his position was by no means unassailable, gave a "**Secret Speech**" to the Twentieth Party Congress, in which Stalin's name was for the first time officially linked with Kirov's murder and the sufferings of millions during the Terror. So traumatic was the revelation that many delegates had heart attacks on the spot. That year scores of thousands were rehabilitated and returned from the camps. Yet for all its outspokenness, Khrushchev's de-Stalinization was limited in scope – after all, he himself had earned the nickname "Butcher of the Ukraine" during the *Yezhovshchina*.

The **cultural thaw** that came in the wake of Khrushchev's speech was equally selective, allowing the publication of Solzhenitsyn's account of the Gulag, *One Day in the Life of Ivan Denisovich*, but rejecting Pasternak's *Doctor Zhivago*. Khrushchev emptied the camps only to fill them again, and added a new twist to the repression, sending many dissidents to psychiatric hospitals. In foreign affairs too, he was not one to shy away from confrontation. Soviet tanks spilled blood on the streets of Budapest in 1956; Khrushchev oversaw the building of the Berlin Wall; and in October 1962 he took the world to the brink of nuclear war during the Cuban Missile Crisis. He also boasted that the Soviet Union would surpass the West in the production of consumer goods within twenty years, and pinned the nation's hopes on developing the "Virgin Lands" of Siberia and Kazakhstan.

By 1964 Khrushchev had managed to alienate all the main interest groups within the Soviet hierarchy. His emphasis on nuclear rather than conventional weapons lost him the support of the military; his de-Stalinization was unpopular with the KGB; while his administrative reforms struck at the heart of the Party apparatus. As the Virgin Lands turned into a dust bowl his economic boasts rang hollow, and the Soviet public was deeply embarrassed by Khrushchev's boorish behaviour at the United Nations, where he interrupted a speech by banging on the table with his shoe. In October 1964 his enemies took advantage of his vacation at the Black Sea to mount a bloodless coup, and on his return to Moscow Khrushchev was presented with his resignation "for reasons of health". It was a sign of the changes since Stalin's death that he was the first disgraced Soviet leader to be allowed to live in obscurity, rather than being shot.

The Brezhnev era

Under Khrushchev's ultimate successor, **Leonid Brezhnev**, many of the more controversial policies were abandoned. Military expenditure was significantly increased, attacks on Stalin ceased and the whole era of the Great Terror was ignored in the official media. The show trial of the writers Sinyavsky and Daniel, which took place in February 1966, marked the official end to the "thaw", and was followed by a clampdown in all the major urban centres. The crushing of the Prague Spring in August 1968 showed that the new Soviet leaders could be just as ruthless as their predecessors, while at home a tiny protest demonstration on Red Square was stamped out within minutes by the KGB.

Thanks to public indifference and press censorship, most Russian citizens knew little of **Alexander Solzhenitsyn** when he was deported to the West in 1974, and even less of **Andrei Sakharov**, the nuclear physicist sentenced to internal exile for his human rights campaigns. Despite the activities of the KGB, the Brezhnev era is now generally remembered in Russia as a rare period of peace and stability. With goods heavily subsidized, citizens could bask in the knowledge that basic foodstuffs like meat and bread cost the same as they had done in 1950 (even if you did have to queue for them), while those with money had recourse to the burgeoning black market. The new-found security of the Party cadres, who were subjected to fewer purges than at any time since the Soviet system began, resulted in unprecedented levels of corruption.

As sclerosis set in across the board, industrial and agricultural output declined. By 1970 the average age of the Politburo was over seventy – embodying the geriatric nature of Soviet politics in what would later be called the **Era of Stagnation** (*zastoy*).

Gorbachev's reforms

Brezhnev died in November 1982 and was succeeded by **Yuri Andropov**, the former KGB boss, who had hardly begun his anti-corruption campaign when he too expired, in February 1984. The Brezhnevite clique took fright at the prospect of yet more change and elected the 73-year-old **Konstantin Chernenko** as General Secretary, but when he also died, in March 1985, it was clear that the post required some new blood.

Mikhail Gorbachev – at 53, the youngest member of the Politburo – was chosen as Chernenko's successor with a brief to "get things moving". The first of his policies to send shock waves through Soviet society – a campaign against alcohol – was probably the most unpopular and unsuccessful of his career. This was followed shortly afterwards by the coining of the two now-famous buzz words of the Gorbachev era: **glasnost** (openness) and **perestroika** (restructuring). The first of these took a battering when, in April 1986, the world's worst nuclear disaster – at **Chernobyl** – was hushed up for a full three days, before the Swedes forced an admission out of the Soviet authorities. Muscovites realized that something was amiss when train-loads of evacuated children began arriving at Kiev Station. Similarly, Gorbachev denied the existence of political prisoners right up until Sakharov's unexpected release from exile in the "closed" city of Gorky. Sakharov returned to Moscow to a hero's welcome, and vowed to fight for the freedom of all.

Equally novel were the investigations into numerous officials who had abused their positions in the Brezhnev years. One of the most energetic campaigners against corruption was the new Moscow Party chief, **Boris Yeltsin**, whose populist antics, such as exposing black market dealings within the *apparat*, infuriated the old guard. In October 1987 Yeltsin openly attacked Gorbachev and the hardline ideologist Yegor Ligachev, and then dramatically resigned from the Politburo; shortly afterwards he was sacked as Moscow Party leader.

Yeltsin's fate was a foretaste of things to come, as Gorbachev abandoned his balancing act between left and right and realigned himself with the hardliners. In the summer of 1988 radicals within the Party formed the **Democratic Union**, the first organized opposition movement to emerge since 1921. Gorbachev promptly banned its meetings and created a new Special-Purpose Militia unit – the **OMON** – to deal with any disturbances. Meanwhile, in the Baltic republics, nationalist **Popular Fronts** emerged, instantly attracting a mass membership. Estonia was the first to make the break, declaring full sovereignty in November 1988 and raising the national flag in place of the hammer and sickle in February of the following year.

1989 and all that

In the **elections** for the Congress of People's Deputies of March 1989, Soviet voters were for the first time in years allowed to choose from more than one candidate, some of whom were even non-Party members. Despite the heavily rigged selection process, radicals, including Yeltsin and Sakharov, managed to get themselves elected. When Sakharov called for an end to one-party rule, his microphone was switched off – a futile gesture, since the sessions were being broadcast live on Russian TV.

Gorbachev's next crisis came with the **miners'**

strike in July, when thousands walked out in protest at shortages, safety standards and low wages. He managed to entice them back to work with promises, but the myth of the Soviet Union as a workers' state had been shattered forever. The events that swept across Eastern Europe throughout 1989, culminating with the **fall of the Berlin Wall** and the Velvet Revolution in Czechoslovakia, were another blow to the old guard, but Gorbachev was more concerned about holding together the Soviet Union itself. That Communism now faced its greatest crisis at home was made humiliatingly plain by unprecedented counter-demonstrations on Red Square during the October Revolution celebrations. One of the banners read: "Workers of the World – we're sorry."

The beginning of the end

1990 proved no better a year for Gorbachev or the Party. On January 19 Soviet tanks rolled into the Azerbaijani capital Baku, to crush the independence movement there – more than a hundred people were killed that night. In February Moscow witnessed the largest **demonstration** since the Revolution of 1917, with scores of thousands converging on Red Square, calling for an end to one-party rule and protesting against rising anti-Semitic violence. Gorbachev attempted to seize the initiative by agreeing to end one-party rule and simultaneously electing himself President, with increased powers to deal with the escalating crisis in the republics.

The voters registered their disgust with the Party at the March **local elections**. In the republics, nationalists swept the board and declarations of independence soon followed, while in Russia itself the new radical alliance, Democratic Platform, gained majorities in the powerful city councils of Leningrad and Moscow. A university professor, **Gavril Popov**, became chairman of the Moscow council, while the equally reformist Anatoly Sobchak was elected to the post in Leningrad. May Day 1990 was another humiliation for Gorbachev, who was jeered by sections of the crowd in Red Square. By the end of the month Yeltsin had secured his election as chairman of the Russian Parliament, and two weeks later, in imitation of the Baltic States, declared **Russian independence** from the Soviet Union (June 12).

In July 1990, the Soviet Communist Party held its last ever congress. Yeltsin tore up his Party card in full view of the cameras – two million had done the same by the end of the year. The economic crisis, spiralling crime and chronic food shortages put Gorbachev under renewed pressure from Party hardliners. The first ominous signs came as winter set in, when a series of leadership reshuffles gave the Interior Ministry and control of the media back to the conservatives. On December 20 the liberal Soviet Foreign Minister Edvard Shevardnadze resigned, warning that "dictatorship is coming".

1991: the Putsch and the collapse of the Soviet Union

The effects of Gorbachev's reshuffle became clear on January 13, 1991, when thirteen Lithuanians were killed by Soviet troops as they defended the national TV centre. Yeltsin immediately flew to the Baltics and signed a joint declaration condemning the violence. A week later, in Latvia, the OMON stormed the Interior Ministry in Riga, killing five people. Hours before this attack Moscow witnessed its largest ever demonstration – 250,000 people came out to protest against the killings. The Russian press had a field day, mocking Gorbachev and backing the Baltics. Gorbachev responded by threatening to suspend the liberal press laws, while adding more hardliners to the Politburo and giving wider powers to the security forces.

In June the citizens of Leningrad narrowly voted in a referendum to rename the city **St Petersburg**, to the fury of Gorbachev. Popular disgust with Party rule was manifest in the overwhelming majority of votes cast for Boris Yeltsin in the **Russian Presidential election** of June 12, despite efforts to block his campaign. As Russia's first ever democratically elected leader he could claim a mandate for bold moves, and within a month had issued a decree calling for the removal of Party "cells" from factories. It was the most serious threat yet to the dominance of the Communist Party in Soviet life, and prompted hardliners to publish a lengthy appeal for action "to lead the country to a dignified and sovereign future".

The August Putsch

On Monday August 19, 1991 the Soviet Union woke up to the soothing sounds of Chopin on the radio and *Swan Lake* on television. A **state of**

emergency had been declared, Gorbachev had "resigned for health reasons" and the country was now ruled by the self-appointed "State Committee for the State of Emergency in the USSR". The main participants included many of Gorbachev's most recently appointed colleagues, under the nominal leadership of Gennady Yenayev. Gorbachev, then on holiday in the Crimea, had been asked to back the coup the previous night, but had refused (to the surprise of the conspirators) and was consequently under house arrest. So began what Russians call the **putsch**.

In Moscow tanks appeared on the streets from mid-morning onwards, stationing themselves at key points, including the Russian Parliament building, known as the **White House**. Here, a small group of protesters gathered, including Yeltsin, who had narrowly escaped arrest that morning. When the first tank approached, he leapt aboard, shook hands with its commander and appealed to the crowd (and accompanying TV crews): "You can erect a throne using bayonets, but you cannot sit on bayonets for long." The Afghan war hero Alexander Rutskoy turned up and started organizing the defence of the building, making it harder for regular troops to contemplate attacking it. Actually, the role of storming the White House had been allocated to the crack KGB Alpha Force, but for reasons unknown they never went into action. News of the standoff – and Yeltsin's appeal to soldiers not to "let yourselves be turned into blind weapons" – was broadcast around the world and beamed back to millions of Russians via the BBC and the Voice of America.

On Tuesday the defenders of the White House were heartened by the news that one of the coup leaders, Pavlov, had resigned due to "high blood pressure" (he had been drinking continuously) and the crowd grew to 100,000 in defiance of a curfew order. Around midnight, three civilians were killed when an advancing armoured column was stopped by barricades on the Garden Ring and firebombed. Next morning it was announced that several tank units had decamped to Yeltsin's side, and on Wednesday afternoon the putsch collapsed as its leaders bolted. One group flew to the Crimea in the hope of obtaining Gorbachev's pardon and was arrested on arrival. Yenayev drank himself into a stupor and several others committed suicide.

The aftermath

Gorbachev flew back to Moscow, not realizing that everything had changed. At his first press conference he pledged continuing support for the Communist Party and Marxist-Leninism, and openly admitted that he had trusted the conspirators as men of "culture and dialogue". He was by now totally estranged from the mood of the country. The same day, jubilant crowds toppled the giant statue of Dzerzhinsky that stood outside the Lubyanka. On Friday Gorbachev appeared before parliament and was publicly humiliated by Yeltsin in front of the television cameras. Yeltsin then decreed the Russian Communist Party an illegal organization, announced the suspension of pro-coup newspapers such as *Pravda*, and had the Central Committee headquarters in Moscow sealed up.

The failure of the putsch spelt the end of Communist rule and the break-up of the Soviet Union. Any possibility of a Slav core remaining united was torpedoed by loose talk of redrawing the border between Russia and Ukraine, and the new-found goodwill between Russia and its former satellites quickly evaporated. In December Ukraine voted overwhelmingly for independence; a week later the leaders of Russia, Belarus and Ukraine formally replaced the USSR with a **Commonwealth of Independent States** (CIS), whose nominal capital would be Minsk; the Central Asian republics declared their intention of joining. On December 25 Gorbachev resigned as President of a state that no longer existed; at midnight the Soviet flag was lowered over the Kremlin and replaced by the Russian tricolour.

The new Russia

On January 2, 1992 Russians faced their New Year hangovers and the harsh reality of massive price rises, following a decree by Yeltsin that lifted controls on a broad range of products. The cost of food rose by up to 500 percent and queues disappeared almost overnight. According to the Western advisers shaping Russia's new economic policy, this would stimulate domestic production and promote the growth of capitalism in the shortest possible time. Initially inflation was limited by keeping a tight rein on state spending, in accordance with the monetarist strategy of Prime Minister **Yegor Gaidar**, but despite Yeltsin's defence of his painful and unpopular measures the policy soon came unstuck after the Central Bank began printing vast amounts of rubles to cover credits issued to state industries on the verge of bankruptcy. Inflation soared.

Stalemate and crisis

By the autumn of 1992 Gaidar's economic policy was in dire straits and pressure grew for his removal. The **Russian Parliament** or Congress of Deputies consisted of numerous factions and parties and a mass of floating delegates known as "the Swamp", but the voting arithmetic favoured the old managerial elite and their ultra-nationalist allies. To ensure his own political survival, Yeltsin was forced to replace Gaidar with the veteran technocrat **Viktor Chernomyrdin**, who surprised parliament by immediately reneging on earlier promises by increasing subsidies to industry and restoring them for vital foodstuffs (including vodka).

For much of 1993 politics was dominated by a "**War of Laws**" between the government and parliament, with each flouting or repealing the other's decrees and budgets, as the Constitutional Court played piggy in the middle. The parliamentary Speaker, **Ruslan Khasbulatov**, exercised such influence over the deputies that articles in the press suggested he had them under some form of hypnosis – although as a leader Khasbulatov suffered the political handicap of being a non-Russian (born in Chechnya), and few believed that his defence of parliamentary privilege was anything but self-serving. Another erstwhile Yeltsin ally who now found himself in opposition was Vice-President **Alexander Rutskoy**, who denounced Gaidar's team as "boys in pink pants", and railed against the government as "scum" and "faggots".

In March 1993 Congress reneged on its earlier promise to hold a referendum on a new Constitution, so Yeltsin appeared on TV to announce the introduction of a special rule suspending the power of Congress, and called for new elections. In the meantime there was a nationwide vote of confidence in the President, plus a referendum on the draft Constitution, and new electoral laws were passed. In response Congress attempted to impeach Yeltsin, but a constitutional crisis was narrowly avoided and a referendum was held. This seemed largely to vindicate Yeltsin and his economic policies but not his calls for early parliamentary elections.

The October "events"

The stalemate lasted until September 21, when Yeltsin brought things to a head by dissolving Congress by a decree of dubious legality. In response, almost 200 **deputies occupied the White House**, voted to strip Yeltsin of his powers and swore in Rutskoy as president, who promptly authorized the execution of officials guilty of "illegal actions". A motley band of supporters erected flimsy barricades: pensioners carrying placards denouncing "Yeltsin the Drunk and his Yid Cabinet", Cossacks and neo-Nazis. The police cordon thrown around the area was so porous that hundreds of firearms were brought into the White House. As the "siege" continued into its second week Rutskoy appealed to the police to switch sides, while the government tried to break parliament's morale by cutting off its electricity, gas and phones, and playing a tape-loop of the song *Happy Nation* day and night. Meanwhile the Federation Council tried to mediate a solution to the crisis, and appeared likely to blame the imbroglio on Yeltsin rather than parliament.

During the third week parliamentary supporters rallied on Smolenskaya ploshchad and set cars ablaze as the Militia stood by, and on October 3 they broke through the cordon round the White House, seizing trucks and riot shields (see p.188). As they rallied in triumph outside the White House, snipers opened fire from nearby buildings, goading Khasbulatov to call for the storming of the Mayoralty, the Ostankino Television Centre and the Kremlin. The Mayoralty was soon captured, and a convoy of trucks headed for Ostankino. Though the **battle for the TV Centre** was televised abroad, Russian viewers simply heard Ostankino warn "We're under attack", and assumed the worst when it went off the air. Actually, Ostankino was held by a unit of commandos which massacred the attackers, but at the time it seemed that Yeltsin had lost control of the TV network and the streets of Moscow.

The ex-Prime Minister Gaidar appealed over local radio for democrats to defend the City Council on Tverskaya ulitsa, which was assumed to be the next target. Hundreds turned up, barricaded Tverskaya with trucks and benches, and spent the night expecting attack. Gun battles flared across the city, as parliamentary supporters attacked the offices of pro-government newspapers. Meanwhile, Yeltsin was in the Defence Ministry, trying to persuade the top brass to obey him and crush the rebellion. They only agreed in the small hours, while the Alpha Force refused until one of their own was shot by a sniper.

The **assault on the White House** began at 7am on October 4. For ten hours tanks shelled the building, watched by crowds of spectators from nearby vantage points, some of whom were killed by stray bullets. Civilians were also slain on the New Arbat, by snipers whose identity has never been established. By nightfall the White House's occupants had been bundled into prison and the rebellion was over. Isolated shoot-outs continued, however, and a curfew was imposed for a fortnight, during which many Caucasians were expelled from Moscow in a racially slanted crackdown on crime that Muscovites welcomed as long overdue.

With his parliamentary foes behind bars Yeltsin turned on his other opponents, the local councils who had supported Congress out of sympathy for their approach or simply as elected representatives. Councils all over Russia were abolished and new elections declared, leaving power concentrated in the hands of local mayors and their bureaucrats. Moscow's Mayor **Yuri Luzhkov** proved as skilful a populist as Yeltsin had been two years earlier, while Yeltsin distanced himself from the party created to represent his government in the forthcoming elections, which bore the presumptuous name of **Russia's Choice** and campaigned as if its triumph was a foregone conclusion.

Zhirinovsky, crime and Chechnya

The result of the December **1993 elections** to the new parliament or Duma was a stunning rebuff for Russia's Choice, which won only fourteen percent of the vote, compared to 23 percent for the so-called Liberal Democratic Party of **Vladimir Zhirinovsky**. An ultra-nationalist with a murky past, he threatened to bomb Germany and Japan and to dump radioactive waste in the Baltic States. His success owed much to a superbly run TV campaign, whose effects lasted just long enough to get the LDP into parliament, beside the "red-brown" alliance of other ultra-nationalists and Communists.

While Russian liberals and world opinion were aghast, evidence later emerged of systematic voting fraud in Zhirinovsky's favour, which could only have been organized at the highest level. For Yeltsin, the crucial point was that Zhirinovsky supported the new **Constitution**, giving unprecedented powers to the president, and backed Yeltsin's government in the Duma, despite his aggressive rhetoric. Even so, it seemed a humiliating rebuff when the Duma promulgated an **amnesty** for the participants in the October "events", and the organizers of the 1991 putsch too.

In the wake of the elections, the government back-pedalled on further economic reforms and tried to improve its nationalist credentials by taking a sterner stand on the rights of Russians in the ex-republics, or "Near Abroad". Resurgent **nationalism** was evident across the board in foreign policy, from warnings against expanding NATO into Eastern Europe or the Baltics, to arguments with Ukraine over Crimea, and increasingly blatant interventions in civil wars in the Caucasus and Central Asia. The Russian Army's new strategic doctrine identified regional wars as the chief threat to national security and defending the old borders of the USSR as a top priority.

At home, cynicism, **crime and corruption** reached new heights in 1994, when car bombs became the favoured means of disposing of business rivals in Moscow, and the finance ministry estimated that $40 billion had been smuggled out of Russia since the fall of Communism. The funeral of the Mafia boss **Otari Kvantrishvili** underscored the extent to which organized crime had meshed with politics and culture, with deputies and pop stars among the mourners. Later that year thousands of Muscovites were ruined by the collapse of the **MMM** investment fund, whose boss then ran for parliament on a pledge to restore their losses, only to scornfully dismiss them once elected. In a further blow to public morale, the murder of a journalist for exposing corruption in the Army was followed early in 1995 by the assassination of the crusading TV presenter **Vladislav Listev**, the director of the national channel ORT, facing a takeover bid by the oligarch Berezovsky.

In December 1994 the Kremlin embarked on a **war in Chechnya** to subdue the breakaway Caucasian republic. The Chechens put up fierce resistance in their capital Grozny, which Defence Minister Grachev had boasted could be taken by a regiment of paratroops in two hours, but in fact only fell after weeks of bombardment, leaving the city in ruins and up to 120,000 dead – including tens of thousands of Russian conscripts. Back home, the debacle was attributed to the so-called "**Party of War**", a shadowy alliance of figures within the military, security and economic ministries, whose geopolitical or personal interests coincided. It was even said that Grachev and other commanders deliberately sacrificed their own troops to write off hundreds of armoured vehicles, to cover up the illicit sale of 1600 tanks from the Soviet Army in East Germany.

Yet despite the war, Russia managed to keep its budget deficit low enough to qualify for a $6.3 billion loan from the International Monetary Fund. Inflation fell as the ruble stabilized, and in Moscow an **economic boom** was led by the new banks and conglomerates such as **Gazprom**, which profited from the huge tax breaks and privatization scams devised by their allies in government.

Yeltsin's second term

As the war dragged on throughout 1995 and Yeltsin's poor health became a national scandal, there was a massive protest vote for the Communists in the December parliamentary elections, which boded ill for Yeltsin's chances in the **Presidential election** of June 1996. Fearing the consequences of a victory by the Communist leader **Gennady Zyuganov**, Russia's financiers and journalists gave unstinting support to Yeltsin, with television, in particular, demonizing Zyuganov and denying the Communists any chance to state their case. Yeltsin's campaign was masterminded by Deputy Prime Minister **Anatoly Chubais**, who banked on the anti-Yeltsin vote being split between Zyuganov and the ex-paratroop general **Alexander Lebed** – as indeed happened. Having gained half the vote, Yeltsin co-opted Lebed by offering him the post of security overlord, and subsequently ordered him to end the war in Chechnya. Lebed duly negotiated the withdrawal of Russian forces – leaving the issue of Chechen independence to be resolved at a future date – only to be sacked from the government soon afterwards, having served his purpose.

With the Communist threat dispelled, the **oligarchs** behind Yeltsin's re-election soon fell out over the remaining spoils. **Vladimir Potanin** acquired thirty percent of the world's nickel reserves for a mere $70 million, and a controlling stake in the telecom giant Svyazinvest due to the intervention of Chubais – enraging **Boris Berezovsky**, whose TV station ORT aired a 29-minute diatribe against Potanin during a news show. Along with the banking and media moguls **Vladimir Gusinsky** and **Mikhail Khodorovsky**, and oil or gas barons such as **Rolan Abramovich**, they became synonymous with a series of scandals – including "book advances" to Chubais and his privatization chief Alfred Kokh, which were patently bribes. After Chubais had to resign as a sop to public opinion (he became boss of the electricity monopoly), Berezovsky's influence in the Kremlin grew even greater, and he was widely seen as the "kingmaker" of Russian politics.

Mayor Luzhkov

Whereas the oligarchs were universally hated, **Mayor Luzhkov** won ninety percent of the vote at the 1996 mayoral elections, reflecting his genuine popularity among Muscovites, who admired his can-do management and staunch defence of local interests. Unlike other cities, Moscow was exempt from rises in housing and heating bills, and retained the Soviet *propiska* system that forbade outsiders to move in without a residency permit – despite this contradicting civil rights enshrined in the new constitution. But as Luzhkov himself said, "It is probably proper to view Moscow as a [separate] state" – and his electorate knew that there were millions who would move to Moscow if it was made easier, since the capital's estimated **population** had already risen by four million people despite a huge drop in the birth rate. Moreover, public services and amenities had visibly improved since their low point in the early 1990s, and the city was rapidly becoming as vibrant as any European capital, with shopping malls and nightclubs vying for big spenders, and confidence in the air. Like autocrats of yore, Luzhkov also gave Moscow some unforgettable **monuments** – the Cathedral of Christ the Saviour, the Resurrection Gate and the Kazan Cathedral, all re-created sixty years after they were destroyed by the Bolsheviks – and mind-bendingly kitsch monuments to Peter the Great and the Great Patriotic War, designed by his favourite artist, Zurab Tsereteli.

Luzhkov's **presidential ambitions** were an open secret. While always careful to assist Yeltsin, he compared Chubais's privatizations to "the way a drunk sells his possessions in the street for nothing", and could rely on favourable media coverage from his long-standing ally Gusinsky. But his strengths were also fatal handicaps, for outside Moscow voters deeply resented the capital where eighty percent of the nation's wealth was concentrated, and his alliance with Gusinsky entailed the enmity of Berezovsky. However, the killer blow was not to fall until after Luzhkov had founded his own party and won pledges of support from regional governors – when a spate of media "exposes" of the Mayor's links to organized crime and the murder of a US businessman (see p.208) undermined his reputation with Muscovites, only months before a new challenger emerged to claim the presidency (see "Yeltsin's endgame", below).

The 1998 crash

In the late 1990s prime ministers and cabinets changed with bewildering frequency, as Yeltsin manoeuvred to build or neutralize coalitions in the Duma and its upper house the Federation Council (dominated by regional governors), and find scapegoats for Russia's economic problems. First he encouraged Russia's creditors by appointing the energetic reformer **Boris Nemtsov** to the cabinet – only to sacrifice him a few months later to placate Chernomyrdin and the Duma, whose featherbedding of the gas, industrial and collective farm lobbies ensured that the state budget went into deficit, obliging it to rely on short-term "hot" loans. By April 1998 Russia's foreign debt stood at $117 billion, workers were owed $9 billion in unpaid wages, and pensioners over $13 billion. With a crisis imminent, Yeltsin stunned the world by dismissing Chernomyrdin's entire cabinet and nominating 35-year-old **Sergei Kirienko** as prime minister. A low-profile technocrat with no power base, his nomination was twice rejected by the Duma, until Yeltsin warned deputies that their Moscow flats and sinecures would be forfeit if they did so a third time.

Unfortunately, Kirienko's rescue plan depended on a "final loan" from the International Monetary Fund, at a time when the collapse of economies across Asia raised fears of a global crash, and pushed down the price of Russia's chief exports, oil and gas. As the IMF loan stalled and hard currency reserves evaporated, the pressure to default or devalue became intolerable, until the Central Bank caved in. In August, the **ruble crashed** and many banks and businesses went into liquidation; the capitalist bubble had burst. Kirienko was promptly sacked and replaced by the veteran diplomat and spymaster **Yevgeny Primakov**, a "safe" candidate accepted across the political spectrum, and also internationally. The US sent 3 million tonnes of emergency food aid, to avert the possibility of food riots during the winter.

Yet the crash had some positive results. With imports so costly, shoppers switched back to domestic products, rewarding firms that survived the crisis with a larger share of the market. It also cut a few of the oligarchs down to size – though others seized the chance to snap up rivals' assets or dump all their own liabilities. By the end of the decade, these changes combined with arms sales and the rising price of gas and oil to produce a modest economic revival, which would contribute to the groundswell of support for Russia's next leader.

Yeltsin's endgame

While his government grappled with governing, Yeltsin was preoccupied with ensuring his own future – if not by running for President again in 2000, then by choosing a successor who would safeguard "**The Family**". By now, the term was widely used to describe his inner circle of advisers and relatives, whose backroom deals with Berezovsky were the source of constant speculation in parts of the media they didn't control. With his health so uncertain that even Prime Minister Primakov expressed doubts that Yeltsin could function as President – for which Primakov was sacked in January 1999 – Yeltsin had no alternative but to find a successor whom he could trust to guarantee The Family's security after they left the Kremlin. There would be no mercy if the Communists won, nor any sympathy from Lebed; Mayor Luzhkov or the recently dismissed Primakov offered little hope either – but any of them could win the next election.

Meanwhile State Prosecutor **Yuri Skuratov** was uncovering the **Mabetex Scandal** (see p.93), which threatened to lay The Family wide open to criminal charges. Skuratov lost his job after state TV broadcast a video of him with two prostitutes (attributed to the KGB's successor, the FSB), but Swiss prosecutors picked up the trail and sought to question a top Kremlin aide, Pavel Borodin, about millions laundered through Kremlin construction deals and Aeroflot ticket sales. Time was running out for The Family.

Yeltsin's chosen successor emerged as suddenly and mysteriously as the apartment-block **bombings** that killed over 300 people in September 1999 – most terrifyingly in Moscow, where 220 died in two massive blasts. Coming only a month after a Chechen warlord seized thousands of hostages in Daghestan, most Russians readily believed that Chechen terrorists were responsible (foreign journalists speculated that the FSB was behind the bombings) and demanded action. The first response was a crackdown on people living in Moscow without a *propiska*, which saw thousands of mostly non-ethnic Russians deported from the city.

Simultaneously, the new acting prime minister, **Vladimir Putin**, made his name by pledging, "We will wipe the terrorists out wherever we find them – even on the toilet." Within weeks Russia launched a **second war in Chechnya**, using overwhelming firepower from the start. By December eighty percent of Grozny was in ruins and the plight of its besieged civilians was an international issue, but in Russia the city's fall was hailed as just revenge for the defeat five years earlier. Berezovsky's media went into overdrive, casting Putin as the resolute, honest leader that Russia needed, while tarring Primakov as old and sick and Luzhkov as hand-in-glove with the Mafia. A new party nicknamed "Bear" materialized overnight to back Putin's candidacy, and was soon riding high in the polls.

The final masterstroke was **Yeltsin's surprise resignation** during his New Year message to the nation on the last night of the old millennium, when Russians would be more inclined to raise a rueful toast than ponder how power had been so deftly passed to Putin. His first decree as acting president was to grant Yeltsin and his family lifelong immunity from arrest, prosecution or seizure of assets, and confer on Yeltsin the title of "First President" in perpetuity.

President Putin

Ensconced as acting president, Putin enjoyed every advantage in the forthcoming election, which most of his opponents tacitly conceded was a foregone conclusion. His **inauguration** on May 5, 2000 was heralded as the first peaceful democratic transfer of power in Russian history, replete with ceremonial trappings harking back to Tsarist times, invented for the occasion. His pledge to restore Russia's greatness was followed by decrees doubling military spending, increasing the powers of the security agencies, and appointing seven "Super Governors" to oversee the regions. The drive to strengthen the state and **centralize authority** after an era of dissolution is one of the leitmotifs of Russian history, exemplified by Ivan the Terrible, Peter the Great, Lenin and Stalin. While stressing his commitment to democracy and the rule of law, Putin's view of Russian history embraced the Soviet, Tsarist and post-Soviet eras as equally worthwhile – symbolized by his decision to restore the Tsarist eagle as the state symbol, and the old Soviet national anthem (with revised words).

For those who feared that totalitarianism was creeping back, an early sign was the **campaign against NTV** and the Media-MOST group, which infuriated the Kremlin by revealing human rights abuses in Chechnya and casualties among Russian troops. Media-MOST's boss, Gusinsky, was arrested and spent several days in Butyurka prison, in what was seen by liberals as a warning to the entire media, but welcomed by most Russians as a blow against the oligarchs. Putin then convened a meeting of the oligarchs that pointedly excluded Gusinsky, Berezovsky and Abramovich, where the invitees reportedly pledged to pay more taxes and quit meddling in state affairs. Gusinsky prudently left Russia, soon to be followed by Berezovsky, who accused Putin of reneging on their deal by authorizing an investigation of the Aeroflot tickets scam. Besides alleging that millions of dollars had been used to finance Putin's election campaign, Berezovsky also implied that he had paid the Chechen warlord to invade Daghestan, to set the stage for a new war in Chechnya and Putin's presidency.

However, Putin's reputation suffered more from the loss of 118 men aboard the submarine *Kursk*, which cast both the Navy and the Kremlin in the role of villains after they rejected offers of foreign help while it was still possible to save some crew. Happening only shortly after a **bomb on Pushkinskaya ploshchad** in the heart of Moscow killed twelve and injured scores, the *Kursk* tragedy was followed by a **fire at Ostankino TV Tower** that blacked out national television for days – creating an impression of disasters spinning out of control.

Nonetheless, Putin's political objectives were broadly accepted by the Duma and the public, foreign heads of state queued up to meet him, and his tour of Asia yielded a promise from North Korea that defused fears of a nuclear arms race in the region and negated the supposed justification for the US "Son of Star Wars" antiballistic missile system. Given US claims that Russia has deployed short-range nuclear missiles in the Baltic enclave of Kaliningrad, and the ascension of George W. Bush to the White House, it seems that arms racing is set to return as a major issue in relations between the two states (not to mention Europe and China).

Books

The number of books available about Russia and the old Soviet Union is vast. We have concentrated on works specifically related to Moscow, and on a general survey of Russian and Soviet history, politics and the arts. Where two publishers are given, they refer to the UK and US publishers respectively. Where books are published in one country only, UK or US follows the publisher's name; where the publisher is the same in the UK and US, only the publisher's name is given; o/p signifies that the book is out of print.

General travel accounts and specific guides

Baedeker's Handbooks (o/p). The 1914 *Baedeker's Handbook to Russia* was a stupendous work that almost bankrupted the company, with dozens of maps and reams of information that were soon rendered irrelevant by the Revolution. A facsimile edition was produced in the 1970s, but nowadays this too is almost as rare as the original, copies of which sell for up to £500 in antiquarian bookshops.

Kathleen Berton, *Moscow: an Architectural History* (I.B. Tauris). Enjoyably erudite study of Moscow's evolution, illuminating scores of buildings and centuries of history, with assured critical appreciations and dozens of photos.

Bruce Chatwin, *What Am I Doing Here* (Picador, UK). Two accounts of the Moscow art world and a lively essay on Russian Futurism are among the gems in this collection of *pensées* and travel pieces.

Peterjon Cresswell & Simon Evans, *European Football – A Fans' Handbook* (Penguin). This *Rough Guide* for footie lovers includes an excellent chapter on Russian soccer, with histories of the main Moscow clubs and all the practical information one needs to see them play.

Vladimir Chernov, *Three Days in Moscow* (Planeta, Moscow). The last in a classic Soviet series of city guides, giving pride of place to Lenin memorial sites and the like; the 1989 edition barely pays lip service to perestroika. Sold by street vendors in Moscow's touristy areas.

Marquis de Custine, *Empire of the Czar* (Doubleday). Classic account of Tsarist Russia by a waspish French diplomat, whose observations on Moscow often ring as true today as when de Custine penned them in the 1830s.

John Freeman & Kathleen Berton, *Moscow Revealed* (Doubleday). Gorgeous photos of Moscow's finest interiors – metro stations, palaces, churches and private homes – in every style from Baroque to Stalin-Gothic. Berton's text provides an essential context and exposes certain aspects of Muscovite life in the early years of perestroika.

Christopher Hope, *Moscow! Moscow!* (Minerva, UK). Rather lacklustre but occasionally penetrating view of Moscow in 1988, when perestroika was in full swing but the old system still hung heavy.

Lawrence Kelly (ed.), *Moscow: A Travellers' Companion* (Constable/Macmillan). Alternately dull and amusing descriptions of court life, eyewitness accounts of historic events and excerpts from books long out of print, which stop short of the Revolution.

Robert Bruce Lockhart, *Memoirs of a British Agent* (o/p). Vivid personal account of Lockhart's efforts to subvert the fledgling Soviet state, which brought him into contact with Trotsky and Dzerzhinsky and resulted in his imprisonment in the Kremlin.

Moscow Traveller's Yellow Pages (InfoServices International, US/Moscow). Annually updated guide to businesses, services and amenities in Moscow, that's useful for residents but not worth buying for a brief visit. If you can understand Cyrillic, the Russian-language version *Lushchee v Moskve* ("Best in Moscow") is widely available on the spot, and contains an index in English. Alternatively, you can dip into the online English version (*www.infoservices.com*).

The Armoury: A Guide (Red Square, Moscow). A profusely illustrated, clearly laid out guide to the treasures of the Kremlin Armoury Museum, that's sold on the premises.

Colin Thubron, *Among the Russians* (Penguin, UK); *In Siberia* (Chatto & Windus, UK). The first includes a chapter on Leningrad, a visit to which formed part of Thubron's angst-ridden journey around the USSR in the early 1980s; the second is as lapidary and insightful and even more gloom-inducing, given such locales as Kolyma and Vorkuta, the worst hells of the Gulag.

Tretyakov Gallery Guidebook (Avant-Garde, Moscow). A well-illustrated room-by-room guide to Moscow's foremost collection of Russian art, from medieval times until the Revolution. A bit large to fit in your pocket, but handy enough to carry round the gallery, where the book is sold in the foyer.

James Young, *Moscow Mule* (Century, UK). A mordantly amusing account of Moscow lowlife in 1993, by the author of *Nico: Songs They Never Play on the Radio.*

History, politics and society

John T. Alexander, *Catherine the Great: Life and Legend* (Oxford University Press). Just what the title says, with rather more credence given to some of the wilder stories than Vincent Cronin's book (see below).

Bruce Clark, *An Empire's New Clothes* (Vintage, UK). A provocative assessment of the *realpolitik* behind the dramas of the 1990s, by a former *Times* correspondent. Clark argues that Yeltsin's "democrats" did more to lay the foundations of a resurgent Russian empire than those who accused them of selling out to the West.

Robert Conquest, *Stalin: Breaker of Nations* (Weidenfeld, UK); *The Great Terror. A Reassessment* (Pimlico). The first is a short, withering biography; the second perhaps the best study of the Terror. In 1990, this was revised on the basis of new evidence suggesting that Conquest's initial tally of the number of victims had been underestimated – he had previously been accused of exaggeration.

Vincent Cronin, *Catherine, Empress of all the Russias* (Collins Harvill/Morrow o/p). Salacious rumours are dispelled in this sympathetic biography of the shy German princess who made it big in Russia.

Isaac Deutscher, *Stalin* (Penguin). This classic political biography has been criticized for being too sympathetic towards its subject.

Harold Elletson, *The General Against the Kremlin* (Little, Brown). An intriguing biography of the maverick soldier-turned-politician Alexander Lebed, up until his dismissal by Yeltsin in 1996, since when his star has waned.

Marc Ferro, *Nicholas II – The Last of the Tsars* (Penguin/OUP). A concise biography of the last of the Tsars, by a French historian who argues that some of the Imperial family escaped execution at Yekaterinburg. Most scholars reckon that the sole survivor was the family spaniel, Joy.

Orlando Figes, *A People's Tragedy: The Russian Revolution 1891–1924* (Pimlico, UK). A vivid history of the fall of Tsarism and the birth of the Soviet state, which includes many little-known facts and colourful vignettes. Highly recommended, but too heavy to pack for a holiday.

Stephen Handleman, *Comrade Criminal: The Theft of the Second Russian Revolution* (Michael Joseph, UK). Fascinating study of how organized crime spread through every level of Russian society and the Communist *apparatchiki* transformed themselves into *bisnesmeni.*

Michel Heller & Aleksandr Nekrich, *Utopia in Power* (Hutchinson/Summit Books). A trenchant *tour de force* by two émigré historians, covering Soviet history from 1917 until the onset of Gorbachev.

Adam Hochschild, *The Unquiet Ghost: Russians Remember Stalin* (Viking Penguin, US). A searching enquiry into the nature of guilt and denial, ranging from the penal camps of Kolyma to the archives of the Lubyanka. Hochschild concludes that the road to hell is paved with good intentions, and most people would behave no better had they lived under the Terror themselves.

John Kampfner, *Inside Yeltsin's Russia* (Cassell, UK). Racy account of Yeltsin's presidency, focusing on political crises, crime and corruption, with vignettes of the highlights and leading characters up to 1994. Best read in conjunction with Clark's book, for a somewhat different view and conclusions.

David King, *The Commissar Vanishes* (Canongate, UK). An intriguing study of the falsification of photographs in Stalin's time, detailing how his victims were erased from history, their final image being a mugshot in the archives of the Lubyanka.

Lionel Kochan & John Keep, *The Making of Modern Russia* (Penguin). A useful pocket-sized history of Russia from the Kievan Rus to Gorby and Yeltsin – though the third edition gives only cursory coverage of events in the 1990s.

Dominic Lieven, *Nicholas II* (John Murray). Another post-Soviet study of the last Tsar, which draws comparisons between both the monarchies of Russia and other states of that period, and the downfall of the Tsarist and Soviet regimes.

Robert Massie, *Peter the Great* (Abacus/Ballantine); *Nicholas and Alexandra* (Gollancz/Atheneum). Both the boldest and the weakest of the Romanov Tsars are minutely scrutinized in these two heavyweight but extremely readable biographies – the one on Peter is especially good.

John Reed, *Ten Days that Shook the World* (Penguin). The classic eyewitness account of the 1917 Bolshevik seizure of power that vividly captures the mood of the time and the hopes pinned on the Revolution.

David Remnick, *Lenin's Tomb* (Penguin; Random House); *Resurrection: The Struggle for a New Russia* (Picador, UK). *Lenin's Tomb* remains the most vivid account of the collapse of the Soviet Union, though some of its judgements seem simplistic with hindsight. *Resurrection* is also riveting, but the jury is still out on Remnick's analysis of the Yeltsin era.

Robert Service, *A History of Twentieth-Century Russia* (Allen Lane, UK). A readable, solid history from the fall of the Romanovs to the '96 elections; the section on Khrushchev is especially good.

Jonathan Steele, *Eternal Russia: Yeltsin, Gorbachev and the Mirage of Democracy* (Faber/Harvard University Press). *The Guardian*'s correspondent provides a thought-provoking, incisive look at the evolution of the new Russia. Like Clark (see previous page), Steele's prognosis makes depressing reading.

Henri Troyat, *Alexander of Russia; Ivan the Terrible* (both New English Library/Dutton). A sympathetic portrayal of the "Tsar Liberator", Alexander II, and a more salacious romp through the misdeeds of Ivan.

Dimitri Volkogonov, *Stalin: Triumph and Tragedy* (Prima Publishing, US). Weighty study of the Soviet dictator, drawing on long-withheld archive material, by Russia's foremost military historian.

The arts

Anna Benn & Rosamund Bartlett, *Literary Russia: A Guide* (Picador/Papermac). Comprehensive guide to Russian writers and places associated with their lives and works, including such Muscovites as Chekhov, Tolstoy, Pasternak and Bulgakov. Highly recommended.

Ronald Bergan, *Eisenstein: A Life in Conflict* (Little, Brown, UK). A new biography of the great Soviet director, which argues that he fared better under Stalinism than in Hollywood, despite his admiration for Walt Disney.

Alan Bird, *A History of Russian Painting* (Phaidon/Macmillan). A comprehensive survey of Russian painting from medieval times to the Brezhnev era, including numerous black-and-white illustrations and potted biographies.

John E. Bowlt (ed), *Russian Art of the Avant-Garde* (Thames & Hudson). An illustrated volume of critical essays on this seminal movement, which anticipated many trends in Western art that have occurred since World War II.

William Craft Brumfield, *A History of Russian Architecture* (Cambridge University Press). The most comprehensive study of the subject, ranging from early Novgorod churches to Olympic sports halls, by way of Naryshkin Baroque monasteries and Style Moderne mansions, illustrated by hundreds of photos and line drawings.

Matthew Cullerne Brown, *Art Under Stalin* (Phaidon/Holmes & Meier); *Contemporary Russian Art* (Phaidon, UK). The former is a fascinating study of totalitarian aesthetics, ranging from ballet to sports stadiums and from films to sculpture; the latter covers art in the Brezhnev and Gorbachev eras.

Leslie Chamberlain, *The Food and Cooking of Russia* (Penguin). Informative and amusing cook book, full of delicious if somewhat vague recipes.

John Drummond (ed.), *Speaking of Diaghilev* (Faber & Faber). What may prove to be the last and definitive work of its kind, given that it consists of interviews with Diaghilev's few remaining contemporaries. Dancers, conductors, choreographers and contemporary observers give their thoughts and memories of the impresario famed for his *Ballets Russes*.

Camilla Gray, *The Russian Experiment in Art 1863–1922* (Thames & Hudson). A concise guide to the multitude of movements that constituted the Russian avant-garde, prior to the imposition of the dead hand of Socialist Realism.

George Heard Hamilton, *The Art and Architecture of Russia* (Penguin in UK and US). An exhaustive rundown of the major trends in painting, sculpture and architecture, from the Kievan Rus to the turn of this century.

Jay Leyda, *Kino* (Allen & Unwin o/p; Princeton University Press). A weighty history of Soviet film up until the early 1980s.

Artemy Troitsky, *Back in the USSR – the True Story of Rock in Russia* (Faber & Faber). First-hand account of 25 years of rock music inside Russia, by the country's former leading rock journalist and critic, who now edits the Russian *Playboy*.

A.N. Wilson, *Tolstoy* (Penguin). Heavyweight but immensely readable biography of the great novelist and appalling family man.

Russian literature

Mikhail Bulgakov, *The Master and Margarita; The Heart of the Dog; The White Guard* (all Harvill/HarperCollins). *The Master and Margarita* is a brilliant satire about Satanic deeds in Moscow, entwined with the story of Pontius Pilate. Unpublished in Bulgakov's lifetime, it became *the* cult novel of the Brezhnev era. *The Heart of the Dog* is an earlier, trenchant allegory on the folly of Bolshevism, while *The White Guard* is a sympathetic portrayal of a monarchist family in Kiev during the Civil War. Stalin so enjoyed the play of the last that Bulgakov was spared during the purges.

Fyodor Dostoyevsky, *Crime and Punishment; Notes from the Underground; Poor Folk and Other Stories; The Brothers Karamazov; The Gambler; The House of the Dead; The Idiot; The Possessed* (all Penguin/Bantam). Pessimistic, brooding tales, often semi-autobiographical (particularly *The Gambler* and *The House of the Dead*). Though few of them are set in Moscow, their atmosphere is evocative of life there in the past.

Boris Pasternak, *Doctor Zhivago* (Collins). A multi-layered story of love and destiny, war and revolution, for which Pasternak was awarded the Nobel Prize for Literature, but forced to decline it. Russians regard him as a poet first and a novelist second. His *dacha* and grave outside Moscow are revered (see p.306).

Victor Pelevin, *A Werewolf Problem in Central Russia and Other Stories; Omon Ra; The Blue Lantern: Stories* (all New Directions, US); *Buddha's Little Finger* (Viking, US); *The Life of Inscets* (Penguin); *The Clay Machine-Gun* (Faber, UK). Digital age fables by the literary voice of Russia's "Generation P", for whom Pepsi, not the Party, set the tone. Essential reading.

Anatoli Rybakov, *Children of the Arbat; Fear; Heavy Sand* (all Arrow, UK). Rybakov's prolix trilogy traces the lives of a dozen Muscovites through the era of the show trials, the Great Terror and the war. Its portrait of Stalin is compelling.

Nina Sadur, *Witch's Tears and Other Stories* (Harbord Publishing, UK). Strikingly original tales of late Soviet times and afterwards, by one of the best writers in Moscow today. Pain and loss are at the heart of them, whether it's the legacy of Chernobyl, emigration to Israel, or Gagarin's mother, talking to her long-dead son.

Alexander Solzhenitsyn, *August 1914* and *Cancer Ward* (Penguin); *First Circle* (Collins Harvill); *The Gulag Archipelago* (Collins Harvill); *One Day in the Life of Ivan Denisovich* (Penguin). The last two books listed here constitute a stunning indictment of the camps and the purges, for which Russia's most famous modern dissident was exiled abroad in 1974; he returned to live in Russia twenty years later.

Lev Tolstoy, *Anna Karenina* and *War and Peace* (Penguin). The latter is the ultimate epic novel, tracing the fortunes of dozens of characters over decades. Its depiction of the Patriotic War of 1812 cast common folk in a heroic mould, while the main, aristocratic characters are flawed – an idealization of the masses that made *War and Peace* politically acceptable in Soviet times.

Venedikt Yerofeev, *Moscow Stations* (Faber & Faber, UK). An underground classic of the Brezhnev era (known to Russians as *Moskva–Petushki*), its 1995 stage adaptation was a hit in London with Tom Courtenay in the role of Venya, whose alcoholic odyssey from Kursk Station to Petushki has the profundity of *Ulysses* and the tragi-comedy of Gogol.

Yevgeny Yevtushenko, *Don't Die Before You're Dead* (Robson Books, UK). Better known as a poet, Yevtushenko's second novel is a melodramatic *roman à clef* of the 1991 putsch, in which Yevtushenko himself makes an appearance, to recite his "very best bad poem" from the balcony of the White House.

Literature by foreign writers

Jeffrey Archer, *The Eleventh Commandment* (HarperCollins). Yeltsin dies and an ultra-nationalist nutter looks set to rule Russia. What can the US President do but have him assassinated? Enjoyable guff by the inimitable Lord Archer.

Rick Bluett, *The Untimely Death of a Nihilist* (Quartet, UK). A bleak satire charting a slob's venture into crime and its grisly consequences. Its picture of Moscow in the early 1990s exudes authenticity and the story never flags, but it's hard to empathize with any of the characters.

Alan Brien, *Lenin – The Novel* (Paladin/Morrow o/p). Brilliant evocation of Lenin's life and character, in the form of a diary by the man himself, every page of which conveys his steely determination and sly irascibility.

Martin Cruz Smith, *Gorky Park; Polar Star; Red Square* (HarperCollins). A trio of atmospheric thrillers featuring the maverick homicide detective Arkady Renko. The first was deservedly acclaimed for its evocation of Moscow in the Era of Stagnation; the second finds Renko in exile aboard an Arctic trawler; while the third returns him to Moscow in time for the putsch of 1991.

John le Carré, *The Russia House* (Coronet). Well-intentioned but over-long attempt to exorcize the ghosts of the Cold War, by the world's best-known spy novelist. Its snapshots of Moscow and Leningrad in the early days of perestroika are less illuminating than the author's own perspective as a former spy.

George Feifer, *Moscow Farewell; The Girl From Petrovka* (both Viking, US). Two bitter-sweet tales of involvement in Moscow lowlife, based on the American author's own experiences as an exchange student. Laced with sex in a very 1970s way.

Robert Littell, *Mother Russia; The Debriefing* (both Faber & Faber). One is a piquant comedy about a manic black-marketeer who moves into a commune in "the last wooden house in central Moscow" and becomes a pawn of the KGB and CIA; the other a more conventional tale of espionage with an equally odd cast of Muscovite characters. Two early works by America's foremost spy novelist.

Emanuel Litvinov, *A Death Out of Season; Blood on the Snow; The Face of Terror* (Penguin). A moving epic trilogy that follows a disparate group of revolutionaries from Edwardian Whitechapel to the cellars of the Lubyanka. The second and third volumes are partly set in Moscow.

Ivy Litvinov, *His Master's Voice* (Virago, UK). A detective story set in Moscow in the 1920s, by the English wife of the then Soviet Foreign Minister, Maxim Litvinov. Though its period authenticity is beyond doubt, the plot stumbles.

Stuart M. Kaminsky, *A Fine Red Rain; A Cold Red Sunrise; The Man Who Walked Like A Bear* (Mandarin, UK). Three Soviet police procedurals starring the weightlifting Inspector Rostnkiov. Self-consciously modelled on Ed McBain's *87th Precinct* series, and just as formulaic.

Fridrikh Neznansky & Edward Topol, *Red Square; Deadly Games; The Fair at Sokolniki* (Bantam). Another trio in the same genre, by two Russian crime writers who missed out on the success now enjoyed in their homeland by Alexandra Marinina and Nikolai Leonov, by emigrating in the Gorbachev years.

Jonathan Treitel, *The Red Cabbage Café* (Paladin, UK). Amusing story of an English idealist working on the Moscow metro in the 1920s, which turns darkly surreal and ends with a savage twist. Good holiday reading.

Language

Russian is a highly complex eastern Slav language and you're unlikely to become very familiar with it during a brief visit to Moscow. English and German are the most common second languages, though few Russians know more than a phrase or two and any attempt to speak Russian will be heartily appreciated. At the very least you should try and learn the Cyrillic alphabet, so that you can read the names of metro stations and the signs around the city. For more detail, check out the *Rough Guide Russian phrasebook*, set out dictionary-style for easy access, with

Cyrillic Characters

Аа	a	Рр	r
Бб	b	Сс	s
Вв	v	Тт	t
Гг	g*	Уу	u
Дд	d	Фф	f
Ее	e*	Хх	kh
Её	e	Цц	ts
Жж	zh	Чч	ch
Зз	z	Шш	sh
Ии	i	Щщ	shch
Ии	y	Ыы	y*
Кк	k	Ээ	e
Лл	l	Яя	ya
Мм	m	Ьь	a silent "soft sign" that softens the preceding consonant
Нн	n		
Оо	o	Ъъ	a silent "hard sign" that keeps the preceding consonant hard*
Пп	p		

*To aid pronunciation and readability, we have also introduced a handful of exceptions to the above transliteration guide:

Гг (g) is written as v when pronounced as such, for example Горкого – Gorkovo.

Ee (e) is written as Ye when at the beginning of a word, for example Ельцин – Yeltsin.

Ыы (y) is written as i, when it appears immediately before и (y), for example Хлебный – Khlebniy.

Note: just to confuse matters further, hand-written Cyrillic is different again from the printed Cyrillic outlined above. The only place you're likely to encounter it is on menus. The most startling differences are:

б which looks similar to a "d"

г which looks similar to a backwards "s"

и which looks like a "u"

т which looks similar to an "m"

English–Russian and Russian–English sections, cultural tips for tricky situations and a menu reader.

The Cyrillic alphabet

Contrary to appearances, the **Cyrillic alphabet** is the least of your problems when trying to learn Russian. There are several different ways of **transliterating** Cyrillic into Latin script (for example "Chajkovskogo" or "Chaykovskovo" for Чайковского). In this book, we've used the Revised English System, with a few minor modifications to help pronunciation (see box). All proper names appear as they are best known, not as they would be transliterated: for example "Tchaikovsky" not "Chaykovskiy".

The list below gives the Cyrillic characters in upper- and lower-case form, followed simply by the Latin equivalent. In order to pronounce the words properly, you'll need to consult the **pronunciation guide** below.

Vowels and word stress

English-speakers find it difficult to pronounce Russian accurately, partly because letters that appear at first to have English equivalents are subtly different. The most important rule to remember, however, is that Russian is a language which relies on **stress**.

The stress in a word can fall on any syllable and there's no way of knowing simply by looking at it – it's something you just have to learn, as you do in English. If a word has only one syllable, you can't get it wrong; where there are two or more, we've placed accents over the stressed syllable, though these do not appear in Russian itself. Once you've located the stressed syllable, you should give it more weight than all the others and far more than you would in English.

Whether a **vowel** is stressed or unstressed sometimes affects the way it's pronounced, most notably with the letter "o" (see below).

а – a – like the *a* in father

я – ya – like the *ya* in yarn, but like the e in evil when it appears before a stressed syllable

э – e – always a short *e* as in get

е – e – like the *ye* in yes

и – i – like the e in evil

й – y – like the *y* in boy

о – o – like the *o* in port when stressed, but like the *a* in plan when unstressed

ё – e – like the *yo* in yonder. Note that in Russia this letter is often printed without the dots.

у – u – like the *u* in June

ю – yu – like the *u* in universe

ы – y – like the *i* in ill, but with the tongue drawn back

Consonants

In Russian **consonants** can be either soft or hard and this difference is an important feature of a "good" accent, but if you're simply trying to get by in the language you needn't worry. The consonants listed below differ significantly from their English equivalents.

б – b – like the *b* in bad; at the end of a word like the *p* in dip

в – v – like the *v* in van but with the upper teeth behind the top of the lower lip; at the end of a word and before certain consonants like *f* in leaf

г – g – like the *g* in goat; at the end of a word like the *k* in lark

д – d – like the *d* in dog but with the tongue pressed against the back of the upper teeth; at the end of a word like the *t* in salt

ж – zh – like the *s* in pleasure; at the end of a word like the *sh* in bush

з – z – like the *z* in zoo; at the end of a word like the *s* in loose

л – l – like the *l* in milk, but with the tongue kept low and touching the back of the upper teeth

н – n – like the *n* in no but with the tongue pressed against the upper teeth

р – r – trilled as the Scots speak it

с – s – always as in soft, never as in sure

т – t – like the *t* in tent, but with the tongue brought up against the upper teeth

х – kh – like the *ch* in the Scottish loch

ц – ts – like the *ts* in boats

ч – ch – like the *ch* in chicken

ш – sh – like the *sh* in shop

щ – shch – like the *sh-ch* in fresh cheese

There are of course exceptions to the above pronunciation rules, but if you remember even the ones mentioned you'll be understood.

A RUSSIAN LANGUAGE GUIDE

Accents over letters indicate the stressed vowel/syllable. For vocabulary relating to food and drink, see p.334.

Basic words and phrases

Yes	*da*	да
No	*net*	нет
Please	*pozháluysta*	пожалуйста
Thank you	*spasíbo*	спасибо
Excuse me	*izvinite*	извините
Sorry	*prostíte*	простите
That's OK/it doesn't matter	*nichevó*	ничего
Hello/goodbye (formal)	*zdrávstvuyte/do svidániya*	здравствуйте/до свидания
Good day	*dóbriy den*	добрый день
Good morning	*dóbroe útro*	доброе утро
Good evening	*dóbriy vécher*	добрый вечер
Good night	*spokóynoy nochi*	спокойнойночи
See you later (informal)	*poká*	пока
Bon voyage	*schastlívovo putí*	счастливого пути
Bon appetit	*priyátnovo appetíta*	приятного аппетита
How are you?	*kak delá*	как дела
Fine/OK	*khoroshó*	хорошо
Go away!	*ostavte menya!*	оставте меня
Help!	*na pómoshch*	на помощь
Today	*sevódnya*	сегодня
Yesterday	*vcherá*	вчера
Tomorrow	*závtra*	завтра
The day after tomorrow	*poslezávtra*	послезавтра
Now	*seychás*	сейчас
Later	*popózzhe*	попозже
This one	*éta*	это
A little	*nemnógo*	немного
Large/small	*bolshóy/málenkiy*	большой/маленький
More/less	*yeshché/ménshe*	ещё/меньше
Good/bad	*khoróshiy/plokhóy*	хороший/плохой
Hot/cold	*goryáchiy/kholódniy*	горячий/холодный
With/without	*s/bez*	с/без

Getting around

Over there	*tam*	там
Round the corner	*za uglóm*	за углом
Left/right	*nalévo/naprávo*	налево/направо
Straight on	*pryámo*	прямо
Where is. . . ?	*gde*	где
How do I get to Peterhof?	*kak mne popást v Petergof*	как мне попасть в Петергоф
Am I going the right way for the Hermitage?	*ya právilno idú k Ermitazhu*	я правилно иду к Эрмитажу
Is it far?	*etó dalekó*	это далеко
By bus	*avtóbusom*	автобусом
By train	*póezdom*	поездом
By car	*na mashine*	на машине

On foot	*peshkóm*	пешком
By taxi	*na taksi*	на такси
Ticket	*bilét*	билет
Return (ticket)	*tudá i obrátno*	туда и обратно
Train station	*vokzál*	вокзал
Bus station	*avtóbusniy vokzal*	автобусный вокзал
Bus stop	*ostanóvka*	остановка
Is this train going to Novgorod?	*étot póezd idét v Nóvgorod*	этот поезд идёт в Новгород
Do I have to change?	*núzhno sdélat peresádku*	нужно сделать пересадку
Small change (money)	*meloch*	мелочь
Questions and answers		
Do you speak English?	*Vy govoríte po-anglíyski*	вы говорите по-английски
I don't speak German	*ya ne govoryú po-nemétski*	я не говорю по-немецки
I don't understand	*ya ne ponimáyu*	я не понимаю
I understand	*ya ponimáy u*	я понимаю
Speak slowly	*govoríte pomédlenee*	говорите помедленее
I don't know	*ya ne znáyu*	я не знаю
How do you say that in Russian?	*kak po-rússki*	как по-русски
Could you write it down?	*zapishíte éto pozháluysta*	запишите это пожалуйста
What . . .	*chto*	что
Where	*gde*	где
When	*kogdá*	когда
Why	*pochemú*	почему
Who	*kto*	кто
How much is it?	*skólko stóit*	сколько стоит
I would like a double room	*ya khochú nómer na dvoíkh*	я хочу номер на двоих
For one night	*tólko sútki*	только сутки
Shower	*dush*	душ
Are these seats free?	*svobódno*	свободно
May I . . . ?	*mózhno*	можно
You can't/it is not allowed	*nelzyá*	нельзя
The bill please	*schet pozháluysta*	счёт пожалуйста
Do you have . . . ?	*u vas yest*	у вас есть
That's all	*eto vsé*	это всё
Some signs		
Entrance	*vkhod*	ВХОД
Exit	*výkhod*	ВЫХОД
Toilet	*stualét*	ТУАЛЕТ
Men's	*múzhi*	МУЖСКОЙ
Women's	*zhény*	ЖЕНСКИЙ
Open	*otkrýto*	ОТКРЫТО
Closed (for repairs)	*zakrýto (na remont)*	ЗАКРЫТО НА РЕМОНТ
Out of order	*ne rabótaet*	НЕ РАБОТАЕТ
No entry	*vkhóda net*	ВХОДА НЕТ
No smoking	*ne kurít*	НЕ КУРИТЬ
Drinking water	*piteváya vodá*	ПИТЬЕВАЯ ВОДА
Information	*správka*	СПРАВКА
Ticket office	*kássa*	КАССА

continues overleaf...

A RUSSIAN LANGUAGE GUIDE contd.

Days of the week

Monday	*ponedélnik*	понедельник	Friday	*pyátnitsa*	пятница
Tuesday	*vtórnik*	вторник	Saturday	*subbóta*	суббота
Wednesday	*sredá*	среда	Sunday	*voskreséne*	воскресенье
Thursday	*chetvérg*	четверг			

Months of the year

January	*yanvár*	январь	July	*iyúl*	июль
February	*fevrál*	февраль	August	*ávgust*	август
March	*mart*	март	September	*sentyábr*	сентябрь
April	*aprél*	апрель	October	*oktyábr*	октябрь
May	*may*	май	November	*noyábr*	ноябрь
June	*iyún*	июнь	December	*dekábr*	декабрь

Numbers

1	*odín*	один	50	*pyatdesyát*	пятьдесят
2	*dva*	два	60	*shestdesyát*	шестьдесят
3	*tri*	три	70	*sémdesyat*	семьдесят
4	*chetýre*	четыре	80	*vósemdesyat*	восемьдесят
5	*pyat*	пять	90	*devyanósto*	девяносто
6	*shest*	шесть	100	*sto*	сто
7	*sem*	семь	200	*dvésti*	двести
8	*vósem*	восемь	300	*trísta*	триста
9	*dévyat*	девять	400	*chetýresta*	четыреста
10	*désyat*	десять	500	*pyatsót*	пятьсот
11	*odínnadtsat*	одиннадцать	600	*shestsót*	шестьсот
12	*dvenádtsat*	двенадцать	700	*semsót*	семьсот
13	*trinádtsat*	тринадцать	800	*vosemsót*	восемьсот
14	*chetýrnadtsat*	четырнадцать	900	*devyatsót*	девятьсот
15	*pyatnádtsat*	пятнадцать	1000	*týsyacha*	тысяча
16	*shestnádtsat*	шестнадцать	2000	*dve týsyachi*	две тысячи
17	*semnádtsat*	семнадцать	3000	*tri týsyachi*	три тысячи
18	*vosemnádtsat*	восемнадцать	4000	*chetýre týsyachi*	четыре тысячи
19	*devyatnádtsat*	девятнадцать			
20	*dvádtsat*	двадцать	5000	*pyat týsyach*	п ять тысяч
21	*dvádtsat odín*	двадцать один	10,000	*désyat týsyach*	десять тысяч
30	*trídtsat*	тридцать	50,000	*pyatdesyát týsyach*	пятьдесят тысяч
40	*sórok*	сорок			

Glossaries

The accents on Russian words below signify which syllable is stressed, but they are not used in the main text of this book.

General Russian terms

bánya bathhouse

báshnya tower

bulvár boulevard

dácha country cottage

dom kultúry communal arts and social centre; literally "house of culture"

dvoréts palace

górod town

kládbishche cemetery

kommunalka communal flat, where several tenants or families share a bathroom, kitchen and corridor

krépost fortress

kréml citadel that formed the nucleus of most Russian towns, including Moscow – from this foreigners coined the name "Kremlin"

lavra the highest rank of monastery in the Orthodox Church

monastyr monastery or convent; the distinction is made by specifying whether it is a *muzhskóy* (men's) or *zhenskiy* (women's) *monastyr*

móst bridge

múzhik before the Revolution it meant a peasant; nowadays it means masculine or macho

náberezhnaya embankment

óstrov island

ózero lake

pámyatnik monument

pereúlok lane

plóshchad square

prospékt avenue

reká river

restorán restaurant

rússkiy/rússkaya Russian

ry´nok market

sad garden/park

shossé highway

sobór cathedral

storoná district

teátr theatre

tsérkov church

úlitsa street

vokzál train station

vy´stavka exhibition

zal room or hall

zámok castle

Art and architectural terms

Art Nouveau French term for the sinuous and stylized form of architecture dating from the turn of the century to World War I; known as Style Moderne in Russia.

Atlantes Supports in the form of carved male figures, used instead of columns to support an entablature.

Baroque Exuberant architectural style of the seventeenth and early eighteenth centuries, which spread to Russia via Ukraine and Belarus. Characterized by ornate decoration, complex spatial arrangement and grand vistas. See "Moscow" and "Naryshkin" Baroque, below.

Caryatids Sculpted female figures used as a column to support an entablature.

Constructivism Soviet version of modernism that pervaded all the arts during the 1920s. In architecture, functionalism and simplicity were the watchwords – though many Constructivist projects were utterly impractical and never got beyond the drawing board.

Deesis row The third tier of an iconostasis (see overleaf), whose central icon depicts Christ in Majesty.

Empire Style Richly decorative version of the Neoclassical style, which prevailed in Russia from 1812 to the 1840s. The French and Russian Empire styles both drew inspiration from Imperial Rome.

Entablature The part of a building supported by a colonnade or column.

Faux marbre Any surface painted to resemble marble.

Fresco Mural painting applied to wet plaster, so that the colours bind chemically with it as they dry.

Futurism Avant-garde art movement glorifying machinery, war, speed and the modern world in general.

Icon Religious image, usually painted on wood and framed upon an iconostasis. See p.219 for more about Russian icons.

Iconostasis A screen that separates the sanctuary from the nave in Orthodox churches, typically consisting of tiers of icons in a gilded frame, with up to three doors that open during services. The central one is known as the Royal Door.

Kokóshniki A purely decorative form of gable that evolved from *zakomary* (see below). Semi-circular or ogee-shaped, they are often massed in a kind of pyramid below the spire or cupola.

Moscow Baroque Distinctly Russian form of Baroque that prevailed from the 1630s to the 1690s. Churches in this style are often wildly colourful and asymmetrical, with a profusion of tent-roofed spires and onion domes, *kokoshniki* and *nalichniki*.

Nalíchniki Mouldings framing a window with pilasters, a scrolled or triangular entablature, and a scalloped or fretted ledge. A leitmotif of Moscow Baroque architecture.

Narthex Vestibule(s) preceding the nave of a church, which are strictly categorized as an esonarthex (if inside the main walls) or an exonarthex (if outside) – many Russian churches had both, to retain warmth. Also see "Refectory", below.

Naryshkin Baroque Late style of Moscow Baroque promoted by the Naryshkin family, characterized by monumental red-brick structures decorated with white stone crenellations and *nalichniki*.

Nave The part of a church where the congregation stands (there are no pews in Orthodox churches). Usually preceded by a narthex.

Neoclassical Late eighteenth- and early nineteenth-century style of architecture and design returning to classical Greek and Roman models as a reaction against Baroque and Rococo excesses.

Neo-Russian (or Pseudo-Russian) Style of architecture and decorative arts that drew inspiration from Russia's medieval and ancient past, its folk arts and myths. This rejection of Western styles was part of a broader Slavophile movement during the late nineteenth century.

Ogee A shape like the cross-section of an onion, widely found in Russian architecture in the form of gables or arches.

Okhlad Chased metal covering for an icon that left uncovered only the figure of the saint (or sometimes just their face and hands). Usually of gold or silver and studded with gems.

Pendant (or Pendule) An elongated boss hanging down from the apex of an arch, often used for decorative effect.

Pilaster A half-column projecting only slightly from the wall; an engaged column stands almost free from the surface.

Podvóre An irregular ensemble of dwellings, stables and outbuildings, enclosing a yard. Medieval Moscow was an agglomeration of thousands of *podvore*, of which only a few – built of stone – have survived.

Portico Covered entrance to a building.

Refectory The narthex of a medieval Russian church was called a Refectory (*Trapeznaya*), as monks and pilgrims were fed there.

Sanctuary (or Naos) The area around the altar, which in Orthodox churches is always screened by an iconostasis.

Stalinist Declamatory style of architecture prevailing from the 1930s to the death of Stalin in 1953, which returned to Neoclassical and Gothic models as a reaction against Constructivism, and reached its "High Stalinist" apogee after World War II. Also dubbed "Stalin-Gothic" or "Soviet Rococo". Moscow's seven Stalin skyscrapers epitomize the genre.

Stucco Plaster used for decorative effects.

Style Moderne Linear, stylized form of architecture and decorative arts, influenced by French Art Nouveau, which took its own direction in Russia, where its greatest exponent was the architect Fyodor Shekhtel.

Tent-roof Form of spire shaped like a wigwam, associated with stone churches in Moscow and wooden ones in northern Russia during the sixteenth and seventeenth centuries. Also added to towers, notably those of the Kremlin. The Russian term is *shatyor* (literally, "tent").

Terem The upper, tower-chambers of the houses of the nobility and the merchant class in medieval Moscow, where womenfolk were secluded.

Trompe l'oeil Painting designed to fool the onlooker into believing that it is actually three-dimensional.

Zakomary Rounded gables that outwardly reflect the vaulting of a church's interior, supporting the cupola. Typical of early churches from Yaroslavl, Novgorod and Pskov, which influenced Muscovite church architecture in the twelfth and thirteenth centuries.

Historical terms and acronyms

Bolshevik Literally "majority"; the name given to the faction that supported Lenin during the internal disputes within the RSDLP during the first decade of this century.

Boyars Medieval Russian nobility, whose feuds and intrigues provoked Ivan the Terrible's wrath and caused the Time of Troubles. To diminish their power Peter the Great instituted a new "service" aristocracy of fourteen ranks, open to anyone who served the state.

Cheka (Extraordinary Commission for Struggle against Counter-Revolution, Speculation and Sabotage), Bolshevik Party secret police 1917–1921.

CIS Commonwealth of Independent States – loose grouping that was formed in December 1991 following the collapse of the USSR. All of the former Soviet republics have since joined, with the exception of the Baltic States.

Civil War 1918–21. Took place between the Bolsheviks and an assortment of opposition forces including Mensheviks, SRs, Cossacks, Tsarists and foreign interventionist armies from the West and Japan (collectively known as the Whites).

Decembrists Those who participated in the abortive coup against the accession of Nicholas I in December 1825.

Duma Parliament (national or municipal).

February Revolution Overthrow of the tsar which took place in February 1917.

Five Year Plan Centralized master plan for every branch of the Soviet economy. The First Five Year Plan was promulgated in 1928.

FSB (Federal Security Service). The name of Russia's secret police since 1994.

Golden Horde (*Zolotaya Orda*) Powerful Tatar state in southern Russia whose threat preoccupied the tsars until the seventeenth century.

Gósplan Soviet State Planning Agency, responsible for devising and overseeing the Five Year Plan. Its goals were set by the Politburo.

GPU (State Political Directorate) Soviet secret police 1921–23.

Gulag (Chief Administration of Corrective Labour Camps) Official title for Siberian hard labour camps set up under Lenin and Stalin.

Hetman Cossack leader.

Kadet Party (Constitutional Democratic Party) Liberal political party 1905–1917.

KGB (Committee of State Security) Soviet secret police 1954–91.

Kuptsy Wealthy merchant class, often of serf ancestry, that rose to prominence in the late nineteenth century.

Menshevik Literally "minority"; the name given to the faction opposing Lenin during the internal disputes within the RSDLP during the first decade of this century.

Metropolitan Senior cleric, ranking between an archbishop and the patriarch of the Russian Orthodox Church.

MVD (Ministry of Internal Affairs) Soviet secret police 1946–54; now runs the regular police (Militia) and the OMON (see below).

Naródnaya Vólya (People's Will) Terrorist group that assassinated Alexander II in 1881.

New Russians Brash nouveaux riches of the Yeltsin era, mocked by countless "New Russian" jokes.

NKVD (People's Commissariat of Internal Affairs) Soviet secret police 1934–46.

October Revolution Bolshevik coup d'état which overthrew the Provisional Government in October 1917.

OGPU (Unified State Political Directorate) Soviet secret police 1923–34.

Okhrána Tsarist secret police.

Old Believers (*Staroobryadtsy*) Russian Orthodox schismatics (see p.264).

Oligarchs Immensely rich and shady financiers and powerbrokers of the post-Soviet era.

OMON Ministry of the Interior Special Forces set up by Gorbachev in 1988. Initially used against the Baltic independence movements, and now for riot control and fighting civil wars within the Russian Federation.

Oprichniki Mounted troops used by Ivan the Terrible to terrorize the population and destroy any real or imaginary threat to his rule.

Patriarch The head of the Russian Orthodox Church.

Petrine Anything dating from the lifetime (1672–1725) or reign (1682–1725) of Peter the Great; Pre-Petrine means before then.

Populist Amorphous political movement of the second half of the nineteenth century that advocated socialism based on the peasant commune.

Purges The name used for the mass arrests of the Stalin era, but also for any systematic removal of unwanted elements from positions of authority.

RSDLP (Russian Social Democratic Labour Party) First Marxist political party in Russia, which rapidly split into Bolshevik and Menshevik factions.

SR Socialist Revolutionary.

Streltsy Riotous musketeers who formed Moscow's army in Pre-Petrine times. Many were beheaded on Red Square in 1682.

Time of Troubles (*Smutnoe vreme*) Anarchic period (1605–12) of civil wars and foreign invasions, following the death of Boris Godunov.

Tsar Emperor. The title was first adopted by Ivan the Terrible.

Tsarevich Crown prince.

Tsarevna Daughter of a tsar and tsaritsa.

Tsaritsa Empress; the foreign misnomer *tsarina* is better known.

USSR Union of Soviet Socialist Republics. Official name of the Soviet Union from 1923 to 1991.

Whites Generic term for Tsarist or Kadet forces during the Civil War, which the Bolsheviks applied to almost anyone who opposed them.

Index

For easy reference see under the headings "Churches and cathedrals", "Kremlin", "Monasteries and convents" and "Museums and galleries".

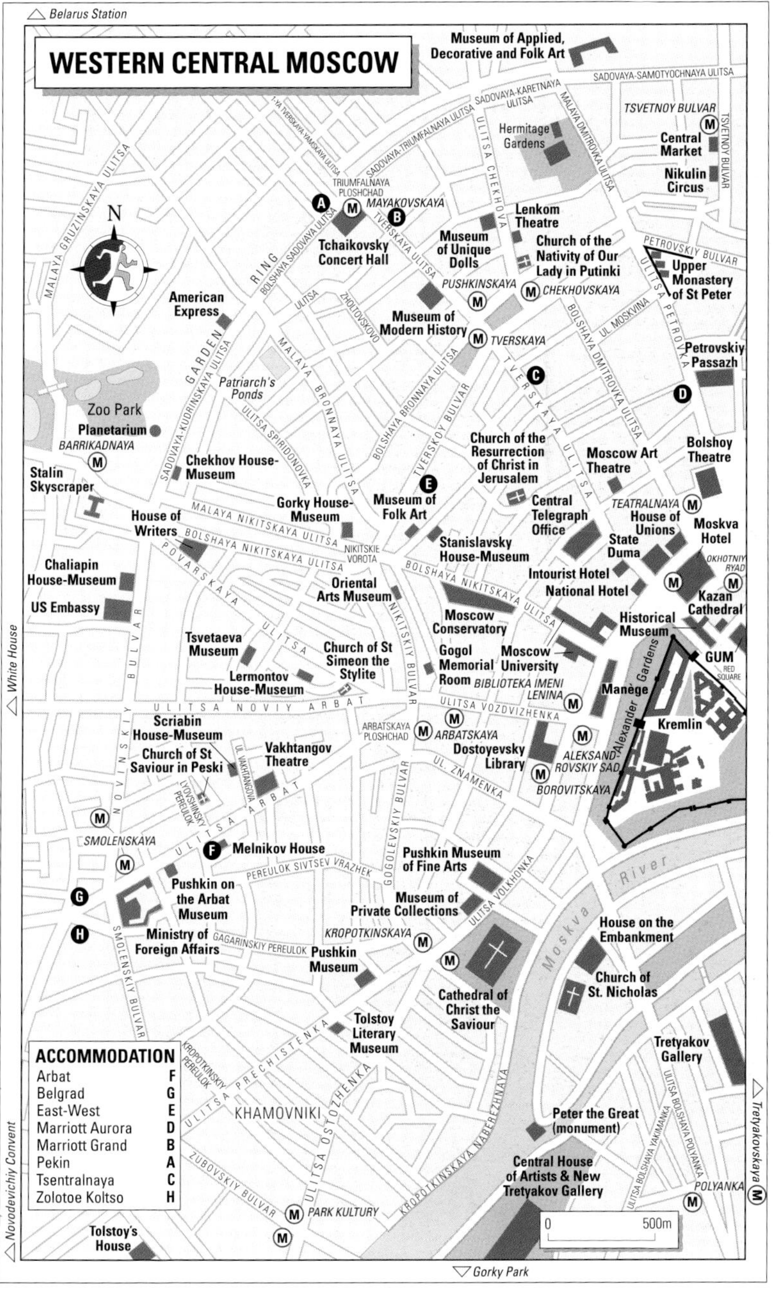
WESTERN CENTRAL MOSCOW
Belarus Station
White House
Novodevichiy Convent
Gorky Park
Tretyakovskaya
N
Museum of Applied, Decorative and Folk Art
SADOVAYA-SAMOTYOCHNAYA ULITSA
SADOVAYA-KARETNAYA ULITSA
SADOVAYA-TRIUMFALNAYA ULITSA
TSVETNOY BULVAR
Hermitage Gardens
Central Market
Nikulin Circus
MALAYA DMITROVKA ULITSA
ULITSA CHEKHOVA
TRIUMFALNAYA PLOSHCHAD
MAYAKOVSKAYA
Lenkom Theatre
Museum of Unique Dolls
Church of the Nativity of Our Lady in Putinki
PETROVSKIY BULVAR
Upper Monastery of St Peter
Tchaikovsky Concert Hall
TVERSKAYA ULITSA
PUSHKINSKAYA
CHEKHOVSKAYA
MALAYA GRUZINSKAYA ULITSA
BOLSHAYA SADOVAYA ULITSA
RING
GARDEN
American Express
ZHOLTOVSKOVO
Museum of Modern History
TVERSKAYA
UL. MOSKVINA
ULITSA PETROVKA
Petrovskiy Passazh
Patriarch's Ponds
MALAYA BRONNAYA ULITSA
BOLSHAYA BRONNAYA ULITSA
TVERSKOY BULVAR
BOLSHAYA DMITROVKA ULITSA
Zoo Park
Planetarium
BARRIKADNAYA
SADOVAYA-KUDRINSKAYA ULITSA
ULITSA SPIRIDONOVKA
Church of the Resurrection of Christ in Jerusalem
Moscow Art Theatre
Bolshoy Theatre
Stalin Skyscraper
Chekhov House-Museum
Museum of Folk Art
Central Telegraph Office
TEATRALNAYA
House of Unions
Moskva Hotel
Gorky House-Museum
House of Writers
MALAYA NIKITSKAYA ULITSA
BOLSHAYA NIKITSKAYA ULITSA
NIKITSKIE VOROTA
Stanislavsky House-Museum
State Duma
OKHOTNIY RYAD
Chaliapin House-Museum
POVARSKAYA ULITSA
Oriental Arts Museum
Intourist Hotel
National Hotel
Kazan Cathedral
US Embassy
Moscow Conservatory
Historical Museum
Tsvetaeva Museum
Church of St Simeon the Stylite
NIKITSKIY BULVAR
Gogol Memorial Room
Moscow University
GUM
RED SQUARE
Lermontov House-Museum
BIBLIOTEKA IMENI LENINA
Alexander Gardens
Manège
ULITSA NOVIY ARBAT
ULITSA VOZDVIZHENKA
Kremlin
Scriabin House-Museum
ARBATSKAYA PLOSHCHAD
ARBATSKAYA
Church of St Saviour in Peski
Vakhtangov Theatre
UL. VAKHTANGOVA
LYOVSHINSKIY PEREULOK
Dostoyevsky Library
ALEKSANDROVSKIY SAD
UL. ZNAMENKA
BOROVITSKAYA
NOVINSKIY BULVAR
SMOLENSKAYA
ULITSA ARBAT
Melnikov House
GOGOLEVSKIY BULVAR
Pushkin Museum of Fine Arts
River
PEREULOK SIVTSEV VRAZHEK
Pushkin on the Arbat Museum
Museum of Private Collections
ULITSA VOLKHONKA
Ministry of Foreign Affairs
GAGARINSKIY PEREULOK
KROPOTKINSKAYA
Pushkin Museum
Moskva
House on the Embankment
Cathedral of Christ the Saviour
Church of St. Nicholas
SMOLENSKIY BULVAR
Tolstoy Literary Museum
Tretyakov Gallery
ULITSA PRECHISTENKA
KROPOTKINSKIY PEREULOK
KHAMOVNIKI
ULITSA OSTOZHENKA
ULITSA BOLSHAYA POLYANKA
ULITSA BOLSHAYA YAKIMANKA
Peter the Great (monument)
ZUBOVSKIY BULVAR
KROPOTKINSKAYA NABEREZHNAYA
Central House of Artists & New Tretyakov Gallery
POLYANKA
PARK KULTURY
Tolstoy's House
0 500m
ACCOMMODATION
Arbat F
Belgrad G
East-West E
Marriott Aurora D
Marriott Grand B
Pekin A
Tsentralnaya C
Zolotoe Koltso H

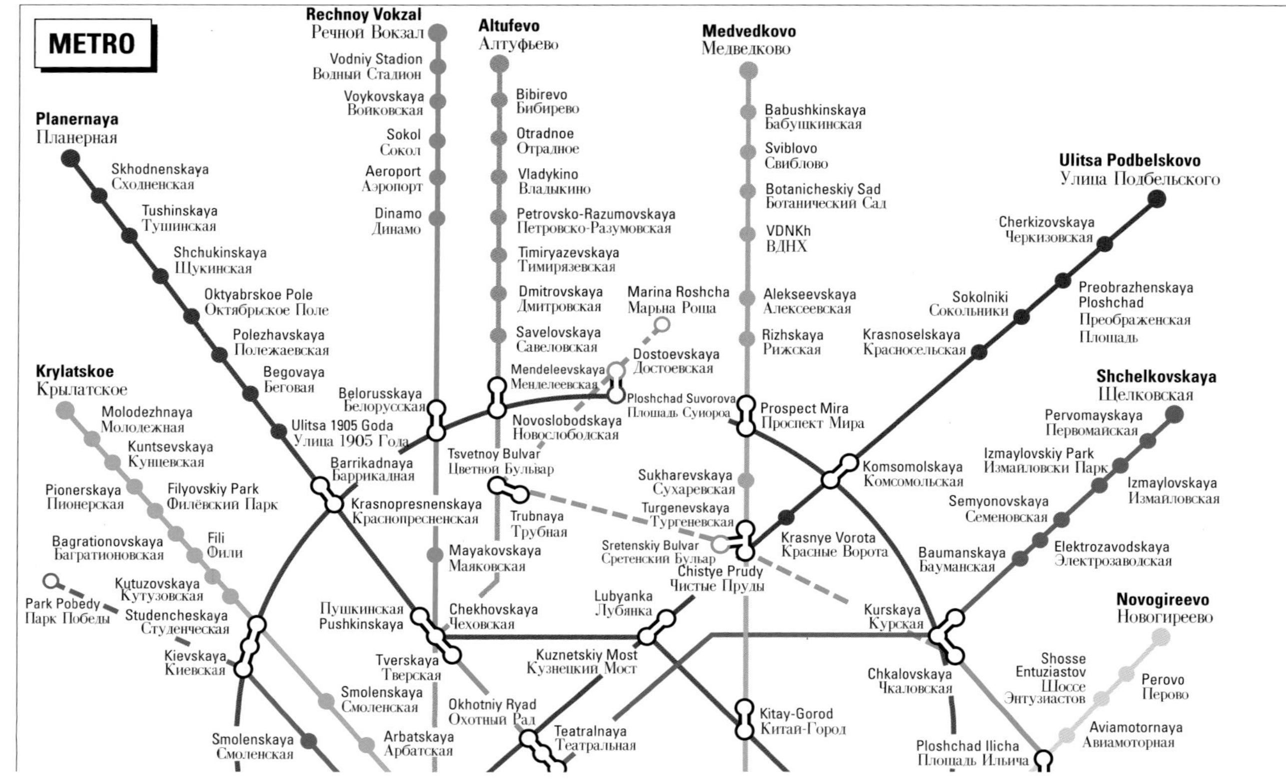

METRO
Planernaya
Планерная
Skhodnenskaya
Сходненская
Tushinskaya
Тушинская
Shchukinskaya
Щукинская
Oktyabrskoe Pole
Октябрьское Поле
Polezhavskaya
Полежаевская
Begovaya
Беговая
Ulitsa 1905 Goda
Улица 1905 Года
Barrikadnaya
Баррикадная
Krasnopresnenskaya
Краснопресненская
Rechnoy Vokzal
Речной Вокзал
Vodniy Stadion
Водный Стадион
Voykovskaya
Войковская
Sokol
Сокол
Aeroport
Аэропорт
Dinamo
Динамо
Belorusskaya
Белорусская
Altufevo
Алтуфьево
Bibirevo
Бибирево
Otradnoe
Отрадное
Vladykino
Владыкино
Petrovsko-Razumovskaya
Петровско-Разумовская
Timiryazevskaya
Тимирязевская
Dmitrovskaya
Дмитровская
Savelovskaya
Савеловская
Mendeleevskaya
Менделеевская
Novoslobodskaya
Новослободская
Tsvetnoy Bulvar
Цветной Бульвар
Trubnaya
Трубная
Mayakovskaya
Маяковская
Marina Roshcha
Марьна Роща
Dostoevskaya
Достоевская
Ploshchad Suvorova
Площадь Суиора
Medvedkovo
Медведково
Babushkinskaya
Бабушкинская
Sviblovo
Свиблово
Botanicheskiy Sad
Ботанический Сад
VDNKh
ВДНХ
Alekseevskaya
Алексеевская
Rizhskaya
Рижская
Prospect Mira
Проспект Мира
Sukharevskaya
Сухаревская
Turgenevskaya
Тургеневская
Sretenskiy Bulvar
Сретенский Бульвар
Chistye Prudy
Чистые Пруды
Krasnye Vorota
Красные Ворота
Ulitsa Podbelskovo
Улица Подбельского
Cherkizovskaya
Черкизовская
Preobrazhenskaya Ploshchad
Преображенская Площадь
Sokolniki
Сокольники
Krasnoselskaya
Красносельская
Komsomolskaya
Комсомольская
Shchelkovskaya
Щелковская
Pervomayskaya
Первомайская
Izmaylovskiy Park
Измайловски Парк
Izmaylovskaya
Измайловская
Semyonovskaya
Семеновская
Elektrozavodskaya
Электрозаводская
Baumanskaya
Бауманская
Kurskaya
Курская
Novogireevo
Новогиреево
Perovo
Перово
Shosse Entuziastov
Шоссе Энтузиастов
Aviamotornaya
Авиамоторная
Chkalovskaya
Чкаловская
Ploshchad Ilicha
Площадь Ильича
Kitay-Gorod
Китай-Город
Lubyanka
Лубянка
Kuznetskiy Most
Кузнецкий Мост
Teatralnaya
Театральная
Okhotniy Ryad
Охотный Рад
Chekhovskaya
Чеховская
Пушкинская
Pushkinskaya
Tverskaya
Тверская
Smolenskaya
Смоленская
Arbatskaya
Арбатская
Krylatskoe
Крылатское
Molodezhnaya
Мололежная
Kuntsevskaya
Кунцевская
Pionerskaya
Пионерская
Filyovskiy Park
Филёвский Парк
Bagrationovskaya
Багратионовская
Fili
Фили
Kutuzovskaya
Кутузовская
Park Pobedy
Парк Победы
Studencheskaya
Студенческая
Kievskaya
Киевская
Smolenskaya
Смоленская

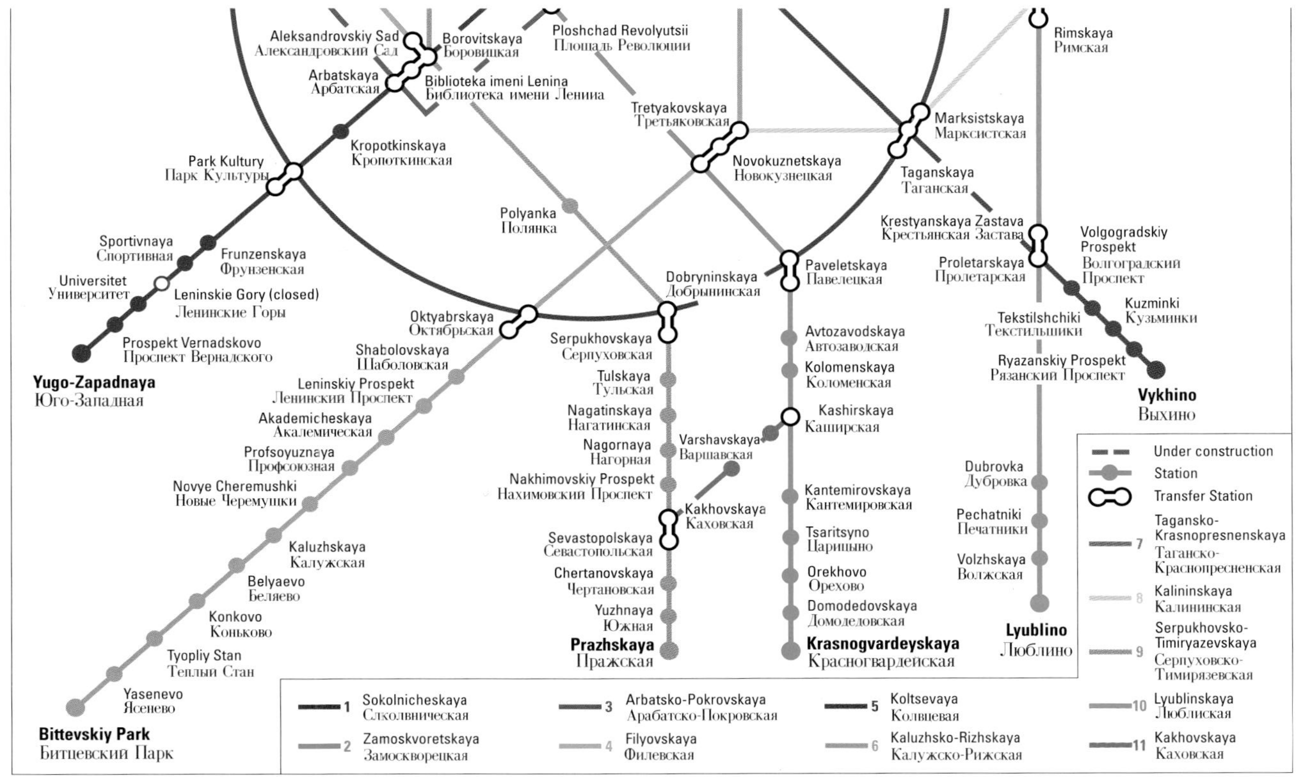

Aleksandrovskiy Sad
Александровский Сад
Borovitskaya
Боровицкая
Ploshchad Revolyutsii
Площадь Революции
Rimskaya
Римская
Arbatskaya
Арбатская
Biblioteka imeni Lenina
Библиотека имени Ленина
Tretyakovskaya
Третьяковская
Marksistskaya
Марксистская
Kropotkinskaya
Кропоткинская
Park Kultury
Парк Культуры
Novokuznetskaya
Новокузнецкая
Taganskaya
Таганская
Polyanka
Полянка
Krestyanskaya Zastava
Крестьянская Застава
Volgogradskiy Prospekt
Волгоградский Проспект
Sportivnaya
Спортивная
Frunzenskaya
Фрунзенская
Proletarskaya
Пролетарская
Paveletskaya
Павелецкая
Dobryninskaya
Добрынинская
Universitet
Университет
Leninskie Gory (closed)
Ленинские Горы
Kuzminki
Кузьминки
Tekstilshchiki
Текстильщики
Oktyabrskaya
Октябрьская
Serpukhovskaya
Серпуховская
Avtozavodskaya
Автозаводская
Prospekt Vernadskovo
Проспект Вернадского
Shabolovskaya
Шаболовская
Kolomenskaya
Коломенская
Ryazanskiy Prospekt
Рязанский Проспект
Yugo-Zapadnaya
Юго-Западная
Leninskiy Prospekt
Ленинский Проспект
Tulskaya
Тульская
Vykhino
Выхино
Akademicheskaya
Академическая
Nagatinskaya
Нагатинская
Kashirskaya
Каширская
Varshavskaya
Варшавская
Nagornaya
Нагорная
Profsoyuznaya
Профсоюзная
Nakhimovskiy Prospekt
Нахимовский Проспект
Dubrovka
Дубровка
Novye Cheremushki
Новые Черемушки
Kantemirovskaya
Кантемировская
Kakhovskaya
Каховская
Pechatniki
Печатники
Sevastopolskaya
Севастопольская
Tsaritsyno
Царицыно
Kaluzhskaya
Калужская
Volzhskaya
Волжская
Chertanovskaya
Чертановская
Orekhovo
Орехово
Belyaevo
Беляево
Yuzhnaya
Южная
Domodedovskaya
Домодедовская
Konkovo
Коньково
Prazhskaya
Пражская
Krasnogvardeyskaya
Красногвардейская
Lyublino
Люблино
Tyopliy Stan
Теплый Стан
Yasenevo
Ясенево
Bittevskiy Park
Битцевский Парк
Under construction
Station
Transfer Station
7 Tagansko-Krasnopresnenskaya
Таганско-Краснопресненская
8 Kalininskaya
Калининская
9 Serpukhovsko-Timiryazevskaya
Серпуховско-Тимирязевская
10 Lyublinskaya
Люблинская
11 Kakhovskaya
Каховская
1 Sokolnicheskaya
Сколвническая
2 Zamoskvoretskaya
Замоскворецкая
3 Arbatsko-Pokrovskaya
Арабатско-Покровская
4 Filyovskaya
Филевская
5 Koltsevaya
Колвцевая
6 Kaluzhsko-Rizhskaya
Калужско-Рижская

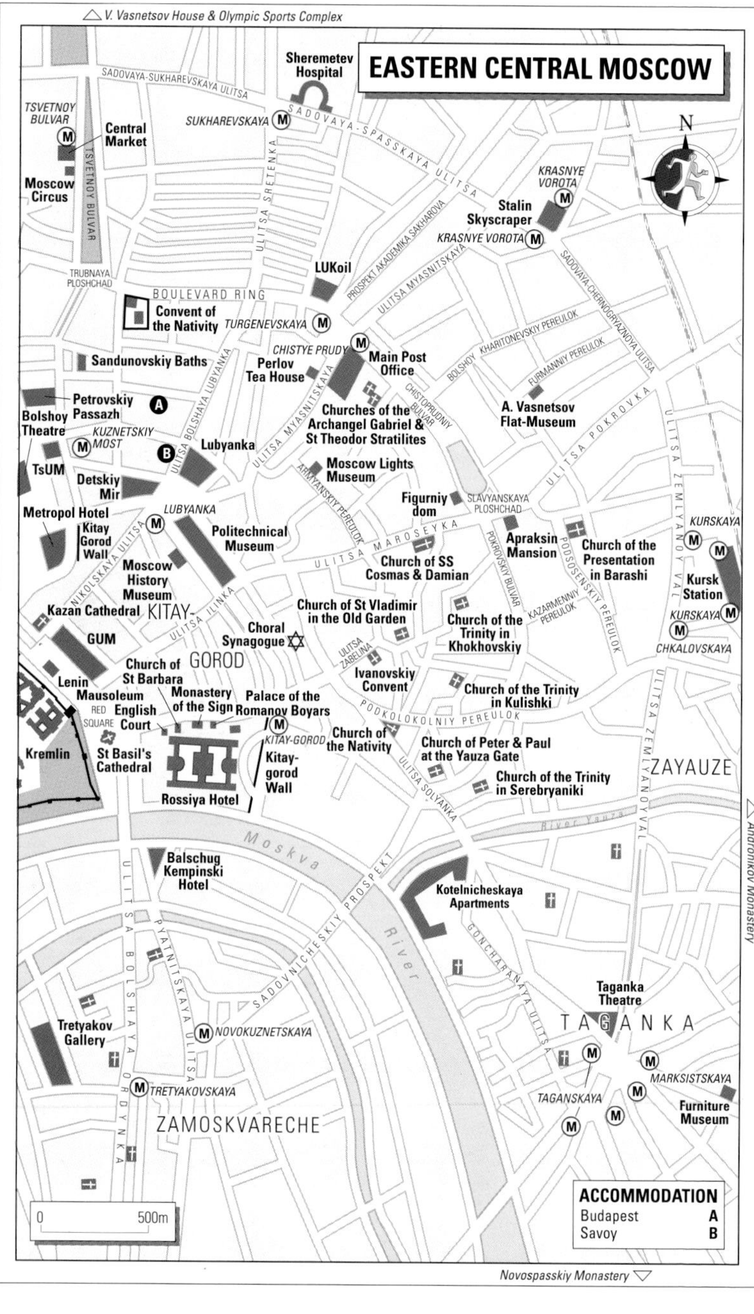
V. Vasnetsov House & Olympic Sports Complex
EASTERN CENTRAL MOSCOW
Sheremetev Hospital
SADOVAYA-SUKHAREVSKAYA ULITSA
SUKHAREVSKAYA
SADOVAYA-SPASSKAYA ULITSA
TSVETNOY BULVAR
Central Market
Moscow Circus
TSVETNOY BULVAR
ULITSA SRETENKA
KRASNYE VOROTA
Stalin Skyscraper
KRASNYE VOROTA
PROSPEKT AKADEMIKA SAKHAROVA
LUKoil
TRUBNAYA PLOSHCHAD
BOULEVARD RING
Convent of the Nativity
TURGENEVSKAYA
ULITSA MYASNITSKAYA
SADOVAYA-CHERNOGRYAZNOVA ULITSA
BOLSHOY KHARITONEVSKIY PEREULOK
FURMANNIY PEREULOK
CHISTYE PRUDY
Main Post Office
Perlov Tea House
Sandunovskiy Baths
BOLSHAYA LUBYANKA
Petrovskiy Passazh
Bolshoy Theatre
KUZNETSKIY MOST
Churches of the Archangel Gabriel & St Theodor Stratilites
CHISTOPRUDNIY BULVAR
A. Vasnetsov Flat-Museum
ULITSA POKROVKA
Lubyanka
ULITSA MYASNITSKAYA
TsUM
Detskiy Mir
Moscow Lights Museum
ARMYANSKIY PEREULOK
Figurniy dom
SLAVYANSKAYA PLOSHCHAD
Metropol Hotel
LUBYANKA
Kitay Gorod Wall
Politechnical Museum
ULITSA MAROSEYKA
Apraksin Mansion
POKROVSKIY BULVAR
PODSOSENSKIY PEREULOK
Church of the Presentation in Barashi
KURSKAYA
Kursk Station
NIKOLSKAYA ULITSA
Moscow History Museum
Church of SS Cosmas & Damian
ULITSA ZEMLYANOY VAL
Kazan Cathedral
KITAY-GOROD
ULITSA ILINKA
Church of St Vladimir in the Old Garden
Church of the Trinity in Khokhovskiy
KAZARMENNIY PEREULOK
KURSKAYA
CHKALOVSKAYA
GUM
Choral Synagogue
ULITSA ZABELINA
Ivanovskiy Convent
Church of St Barbara
Lenin Mausoleum
Monastery of the Sign
Palace of the Romanov Boyars
Church of the Trinity in Kulishki
RED SQUARE
English Court
PODKOLOKOLNIY PEREULOK
KITAY-GOROD
Church of the Nativity
Church of Peter & Paul at the Yauza Gate
ZAYAUZE
St Basil's Cathedral
Kremlin
Kitay-gorod Wall
ULITSA SOLYANKA
Church of the Trinity in Serebryaniki
Rossiya Hotel
River Yauza
Andronikov Monastery
Moskva River
Balschug Kempinski Hotel
SADOVNICHESKIY PROSPEKT
Kotelnicheskaya Apartments
ULITSA BOLSHAYA ORDYNKA
PYATNITSKAYA ULITSA
GONCHARNAYA ULITSA
Taganka Theatre
TAGANKA
Tretyakov Gallery
NOVOKUZNETSKAYA
TAGANSKAYA
MARKSISTSKAYA
TRETYAKOVSKAYA
Furniture Museum
ZAMOSKVARECHE
0
500m
ACCOMMODATION
Budapest A
Savoy B
Novospasskiy Monastery